CICS/ESA Primer

Related Wiley Books

VS COBOL II Highlights and Techniques (Janossy, 1992)

Practical MVS JCL Examples (Janossy, 1993)

Advanced MVS JCL Examples (Janossy, 1994)

Structured COBOL Programming, 7th edition (Stern and Stern, 1994)

Micro Focus Workbench (Jatich and Nowak, 1992)

Getting Started with RM/COBOL-85, 2nd edition (Stern, Stern, and Janossy, 1994)

CICS/ESA Primer

James G. Janossy
DePaul University
and
Steve Samuels
DePaul University

John Wiley & Sons, Inc.
New York • Chichester • Brisbane • Toronto • Singapore

Publisher: Katherine Schowalter
Editor: Theresa Hudson
Managing Editor: Maureen B. Drexel
Text Design & Composition: Publishers' Design and Production Services, Inc.

This text is printed on acid-free paper.

ISBN 0-471-30991-5

Printed in the United States of America
10 9 8 7 6 5 4 3 2

About the Authors

James Janossy is a member of the faculty of the School of Computer Science, Telecommunications, and Information Systems at DePaul University, Chicago. He teaches COBOL, MVS/ESA JCL, systems analysis and design, software testing, project management, relational database, CICS and on-line programming on IBM, VAX, and UNIX systems. Prior to joining DePaul, he worked in the industry for 17 years as programmer, project leader, and manager. Jim earned his B.A. at Northwestern University, his M.S. at California State University, Los Angeles, and is completing a Ph.D. in computer science. Jim has written several books, including *Practical MVS JCL Examples*, *Advanced MVS/ESA JCL Examples*, *VS COBOL II Highlights and Techniques*, *VAX COBOL On-Line*, and others published by John Wiley & Sons.

Steve Samuels has been the director of the Computer Career Program of the School of Computer Science, Telecommunications, and Information Systems at DePaul University, Chicago since its inception in 1982. He teaches COBOL, MVS/ESA JCL, C, systems analysis and design, CICS and DB2, and on-line programming on IBM, VAX, and UNIX systems. He is also a training consultant to several major corporations, and authored *VAX COBOL* for Prentice-Hall, as well as several courses on related technical subjects. Steve received his B.S. at Washington University (St. Louis) and his M.A. at DePaul University.

docendo discimus

Preface

Welcome to the modern world of CICS interactive computing! We have designed this book to give you the smoothest possible learning experience with the Customer Information Control System, by which IBM's largest computer systems (and now, UNIX-based machines) support on-line processing.

We presume you know some COBOL and have written at least a few COBOL programs. For our purposes, it doesn't matter what type of machine you use with COBOL—IBM mainframes, non-IBM minicomputers, or PCs. As long as you know how a COBOL program is coded, and how to read COBOL code, we'll teach you modern CICS, step by step. We'll build on this elementary COBOL background to teach you about CICS screen images, called "maps," and the crucially important technique of pseudoconversational programming that makes CICS so powerful. We'll also show you how to program support for features such as on-line help, file inquiry, indexed file (VSAM) update, and alternate key browse. Our appendixes provide a CICS syntax reference, a tutorial on CECI and the CEDF interactive debugger, a reference to VSAM (with full job control language examples) and a reference to CICS abend codes. We even make the program source code and JCL for all of the examples in the book, and a superb screen painter, available on diskette for uploading, as explained in Appendix F.

The learning progression we have designed in this book reflects our combined experience of over 30 years in teaching programming to professionals, college students, and personnel changing careers. Starting in Chapter 1, we explain where CICS fits into the world of computing, including how CICS relates to client/server and conversational programming. In Chapters 2 and 3, we show you how CICS was developed as part of a comprehensive strategy to support huge numbers of terminals on relatively small equipment.

Beginning in Chapter 4, we take you one step at a time through the process of designing a screen, encoding it, preparing it for use, and how a program "talks" to it. By the time you finish Chapter 6, you will understand how to code and process a small CICS program for execution to simply display the screen we have developed.

In Chapter 7, we show you how pseudoconversational logic works, using the simplest possible example, fully illustrated with a graphic control flow chart and discussion. In Chapter 8, we introduce logic structuring to you, so that you are fully prepared to use CICS for the "real world" programming applications covered in the remainder of the book. Chapter 9 quickly extends your knowledge of communication with CICS by showing you how to intercept program function keys ("PF" keys), while Chapter 10 shows you how to use COPY and CALL.

Chapter 11 demonstrates how you can include on-line help in your CICS programs, while Chapter 12 illustrates the effect on your programs of using a machine-generated description of the data transmission record that carries data between your program and a terminal and vice versa.

Chapters 13, 14, 15, and 16 give you the actual CICS code for the programs making up a small on-line system, beginning with an inquiry function into a VSAM Key Sequenced Data Set (indexed file). Chapter 13 shows you how to program an inquiry function, while Chapter 14 demonstrates how to handle adds, changes and deletions for the VSAM data set. Chapter 15 shows you how to design and code an alternate key browse. Chapter 16 provides guidance and examples to help you create a menu program by which the inquiry, update, browse and other functions can be accessed using the XCTL and LINK commands.

This book is an introduction to modern, highly structured CICS programming, and we have consciously made choices as to what is most productive, today, for a newcomer to CICS to know and use. This is why we cover CICS/ESA 3.3, the most current version of CICS, why we use VS COBOL II, IBM's current and most stable COBOL compiler, and why our JCL examples use MVS/ESA Version 4 features. If you are experienced with CICS, but have not used CICS/ESA Version 3.3 or MVS/ESA Version 4, you'll find this book an interesting exposure to where your world is heading. (Frankly, it's high time for everyone to begin abandoning archaic and troublesome coding practices that earlier versions of CICS made necessary. CICS still has a lot of "kick" to offer, but many of the old coding practices can now be jettisoned!)

In using this book, you are about to experience a new type of guided learning, which shows you concepts with full-length, executable examples. Each example was carefully designed to "let the pictures do the talking." It's possible for us to produce this unique type of book, because we participate in the book production process, creating and annotating all of the illustrations ourselves. Both of us are not only experienced programmers, we are also experienced course developers. To the maximum extent possible, we have made this book behave as if we were guiding you in person, pointing out important things over your shoulder as you work. If you acquire the diskette with all of our examples as described in Appendix F, and/or Gary Weinstein's nominally priced, PC-based GENMAP screen painter, you can fully "animate" your CICS/ESA learning experience as well! CICS can be quick, easy, and fun. Read on and learn how!

If you like the approach you find here covering CICS, you may want to examine three other related books, also published by John Wiley & Sons:

VS COBOL II Highlights and Techniques (Janossy, 1992)

Practical MVS JCL Examples (Janossy, 1993)

Advanced MVS JCL Examples (Janossy, 1994)

These are not prerequisites, but they can help you flesh out your background in traditional mainframe programming subjects. All of these books follow the same friendly, non-stuffy approach to these commercially relevant subjects.

Welcome to modern CICS/ESA, presented in a modern way!

Jim Janossy

Steve Samuels

Contents

1

Interactive Programming: Traditional and Client/Server Approaches

In this opening chapter, we provide you with the background of computer hardware and software you need to build a perspective on modern, interactive computer programming. After reading this chapter, not only will you understand what interactive programming is, but also the different approaches to interactive programming in the modern world. You will also see clearly where Customer Information Control System (CICS) fits into the panorama of programming tools and techniques now available.

1.1 CATEGORIES OF COMPUTERS

We categorize computer hardware according to three classes of machinery, as illustrated in Figure 1.1:

- Mainframes
- Minicomputers
- Microcomputers

Mainframes are the oldest form of computer. These consist of large, expensive, and powerful machines, with designs dating from the 1950s and 1960s. These machines and their modern descendants, such as the IBM ES/9000, are usually shared by a wide diversity of users and can run a dozen or more programs at a time. Their operation is supervised by mature software such as IBM's MVS/ESA (Multiple Virtual Storages) operating system, which communicates with users via job control language (JCL).

Minicomputers such as the Digital Equipment Corporation VAX, Harris Corporation NightHawk, Data General Aviion, IBM AS/400 and others form a second generation of hardware. Think of these machines simply as smaller versions of mainframes, which originated as competitors to the larger IBM, Univac, and Burroughs computers of the 1970s. "Mini" originally referred to their use of 16-bit word sizes, as opposed to 32 bits for the original mainframes. But this distinction was lost as minicomputers benefited from technological progress and now use 32-bit (or larger) words. Minicomputers now support vast amounts of memory and can support hundreds of terminals. Minicomputers usually run either the highly portable UNIX operating system or "closed," proprietary operating system software such as VAX VMS, which is not portable to different machines.

Microcomputers originated in the late 1970s using small, inexpensive memory circuits, as electronics engineers created single integrated circuit "chips" containing multiple logic ele-

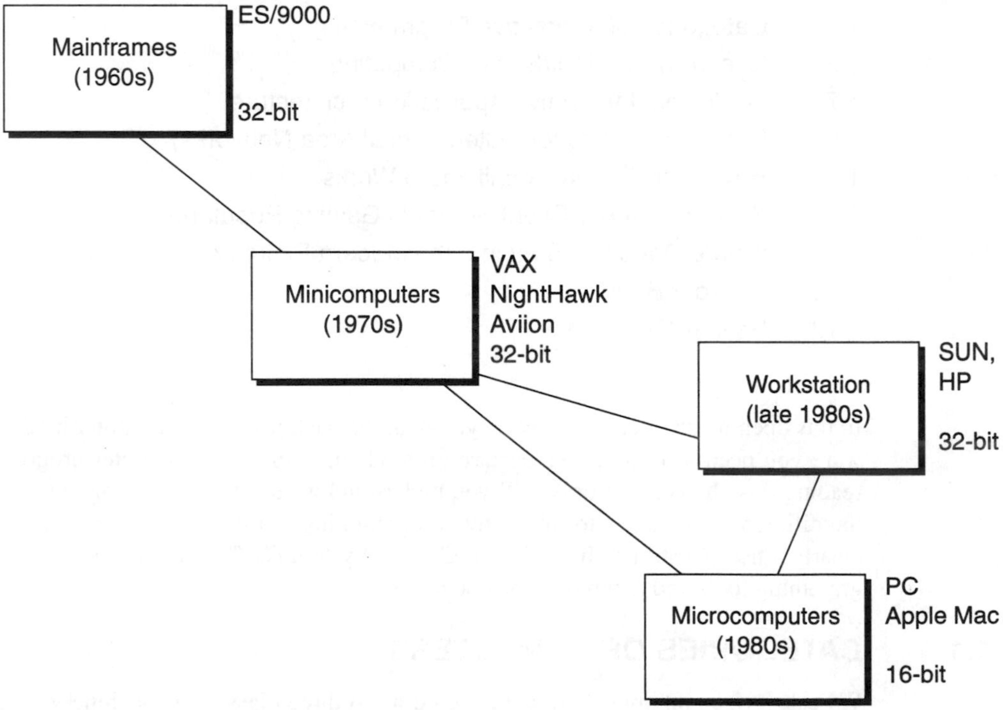

Mainframes
(1960s)
ES/9000
32-bit
Minicomputers
(1970s)
VAX
NightHawk
Aviion
32-bit
Workstation
(late 1980s)
SUN,
HP
32-bit
Microcomputers
(1980s)
PC
Apple Mac
16-bit

Figure 1.1 Three classes of computers.

ments. Microcomputers are miniaturized minicomputers, just as minicomputers were originally smaller versions of mainframes. Microcomputers became standardized into two major camps in the early 1980s: IBM PCs and clones using the MS-DOS or Windows operating system environments form one camp, while Apple Macintosh machinery makes up the other camp. A third form of small computer, a **workstation,** usually runs a dialect of UNIX and is actually more of a minicomputer on a desktop than a microcomputer. Workstations are small computers more powerful than typical microcomputers, popular for computation-intensive tasks such as computer-aided drawing.

1.2 CATEGORIES OF COMPUTER PROGRAMMING

We categorize computer programming according to how people interact with completed programs. As you can see in Figure 1.2, two main categories of interaction exist: batch and interactive.

Batch programs accept information for processing in groups called batches and produce output grouped into sets, such as report pages or records in new files. Think of a batch program like a supermarket coffee grinder, illustrated in Figure 1.3. You put coffee beans into a coffee grinder's hopper, turn on the machine, and it grinds the whole load of beans into granules. Batch programs are useful for tasks such as producing reports from whole files or databases, applying a file of transactions to a master file, or scanning a file to purge it of outdated information. Batch programs do not communicate with anyone as they execute. Once started, their execution is supervised by the computer's operating system. Unless a batch program experiences a problem, it continues to execute "on its own" until its work is finished.

Interactive programs are designed to communicate with people as they run, usually using computer terminal screens. Interactive programs issue messages, called **prompts,** to an

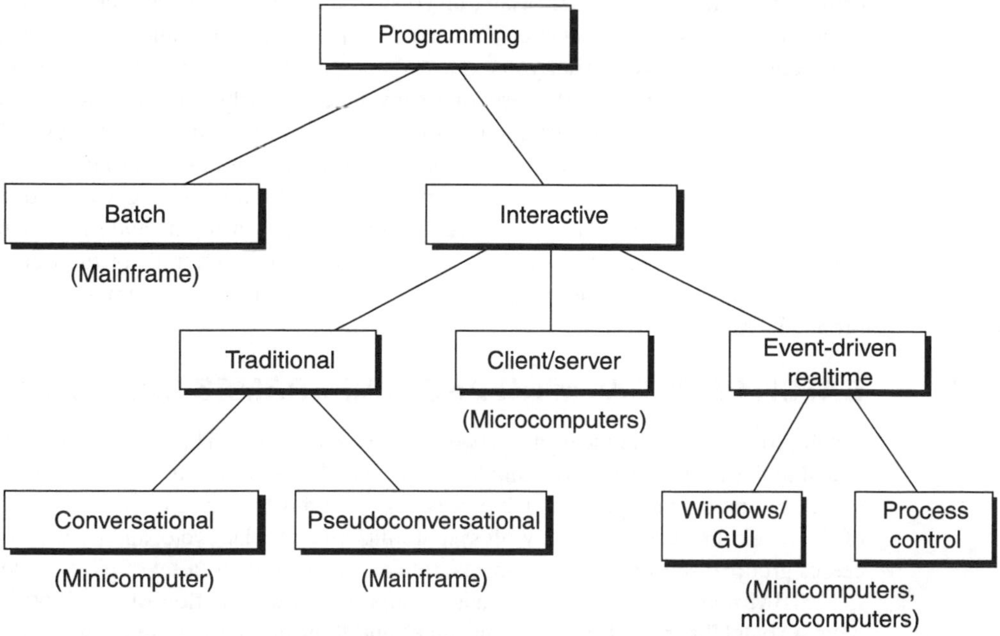
Programming
Batch
(Mainframe)
Interactive
Traditional
Client/server
(Microcomputers)
Event-driven realtime
Conversational
(Minicomputer)
Pseudoconversational
(Mainframe)
Windows/ GUI
Process control
(Minicomputers, microcomputers)

Figure 1.2 Computer programs are either batch or interactive.

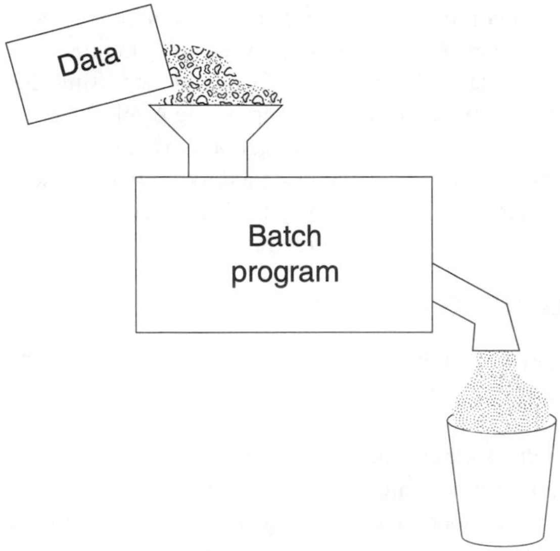
Data
Batch program

Figure 1.3 Batch programs read groups of data and produce grouped output, just like a coffee grinder processes a load of beans into granules.

end user for the entry of information, such as customer id, and retrieve and present related information on the screen.

To continue our supermarket example, think of the operation of an interactive program much like dealing with the clerk at the delicatessen counter, as depicted in Figure 1.4. You browse what the deli counter offers, or you ask the clerk for a product you don't see or for information (such as the price of an item). You place an order, and then you complete your transaction by receiving what you requested and paying for it. All of this requires interaction with the clerk, which takes the form of a conversation in which information is exchanged.

Similarly, interactive programs allow the end user to communicate new information or change existing information, and then put this information into external (disk) storage. You might think about interactive program processing as similar to the way a desk calculator works. You enter information, the calculator processes your inputs and immediately provides you with computed results. You do not pool or "stack up" hundreds or thousands of calculations for your calculator, then run it in batch mode to do all of your computations overnight and produce a report!

1.3 BATCH PROGRAMMING AND MAINFRAMES CAME FIRST

Batch processing is the older of the two forms of processing. The first business activities automated in the 1960s were accounting functions, which operate on regular daily, weekly, monthly, quarterly, and annual cycles. Batch processing was (and continues to be) ideally suited to much of this work. For example, a payroll system runs on a regular cycle, and by its very nature processes grouped sets of data (time sheets) into a grouped output (a set of paychecks).

IBM mainframes were designed to support the automation of the 1960s, and as such have a "batch" personality. These machines and their operating systems were not designed to communicate with end user terminals. In fact, computer terminals were not even a part of the

How much does two pounds of potato salad cost?
We have a special on it right now, three pounds for $9.99.
TAKE A TICKET
SUZIE'S DELI

Figure 1.4 Interactive programs mimic a conversation with a sales clerk.

computing environment when major mainframe design decisions were made in 1962–1963. Even today's mainframe architectures date from this era!

Interactive processing is the newer form of processing and is typical of minicomputers and microcomputers. Mini- and microcomputers are inherently interactive, since they (and their operating systems) were designed with this form of processing in mind. Word processing, spreadsheet analysis, and database information retrieval are all typical mini- and microcomputer applications. These are highly interactive and cannot be handled adequately in a batch mode. Mini- and microcomputers usually support some form of "scripting" language that resembles the job control language of mainframes, so that batch processes, like repetitive file backups, can be arranged and processed on them.

1.4 CICS ADAPTS MAINFRAMES TO INTERACTIVE PROCESSING

IBM mainframes and the MVS/ESA and DOS/VSE operating systems were designed to support batch processing and are adapted to interactive programming with the use of CICS, or **Customer Information Control System**. CICS was developed in 1968 to operate only on IBM mainframes. With its popularity for certain types of interactive processing, versions of CICS and emulators of it have been developed for minicomputers and microcomputers.

CICS makes interactive programming more difficult to arrange, but it provides benefits of efficiency that are important for large-scale applications. CICS implementations for minicomputers are intended for real work, that is, to support end-user applications, just as mainframes do. But CICS implementations for microcomputers, such as MicroFocus Workbench, are intended as development tools. Using microcomputer-based development tools, you can create and test CICS applications, then upload your completed software to a minicomputer or mainframe system for actual "production" use.

Now that you know something about the environment in which CICS functions, let's go further in categorizing interactive software, to complete your perspective on interactive processing.

1.5 CATEGORIES OF INTERACTIVE PROGRAMMING

We classify the world of interactive business computer programming into four categories. Refer again to the lower part of Figure 1.2, and you will see these categories:

- Traditional conversational programming
- Traditional pseudoconversational programming
- Client/server programming
- Event-driven real-time programming

Traditional interactive programming consists of two different approaches to the way the person at a terminal is "talked to" by the software in a shared computer:

Conversational programming carries on a "conversation" with the end user at a terminal using a program that is active all of the time. This form of interactive programming is typical of minicomputers and microcomputers. It is relatively easy to program and provides acceptable support for small numbers of terminals.

Pseudoconversational programming gives the appearance of carrying on a conversation with a terminal user, but gains an efficiency advantage by deactivating the program that the terminal user thinks is communicating with him or her while he or she makes entries on the screen. Pseudoconversational programming logic is much more complicated than conversational logic, but it makes it possible for even a small mainframe or minicomputer to support thousands of computer terminals rather than hundreds.

Conversational and pseudoconversational programming approaches are both represented by the arrangement shown in Figure 1.5. Interactive program logic is housed on a mainframe or minicomputer host that accesses indexed files or a database on disk. End users work at terminals or microcomputers emulating terminals. The number of terminals the host can support is affected by the interactive programming technique used—pseudoconversational techniques let the host support many more terminals than conversational techniques. But ultimately, the arrangement is constrained by the power of the host computer, where all processing actions must be accomplished. Under traditional interactive programming, the workload is not split between the host computer and the desktop device. The desktop device is treated as being entirely dumb.

Client/server interactive programming is a newer form of programming usually involving communication between microcomputers using a local area network (LAN) and different types of software running on different participants in the network. Client/server computing has become a topic of much interest to the industry, because it holds the potential to make interactive programming easier, more accessible, and less expensive. In the remainder of this chapter, we'll focus on client/server computing, to complete your perspective of interactive programming.

Event-driven realtime programming encompasses the internals of graphical user interfaces (GUIs) as well as software that controls machinery. Some aspects of modern business

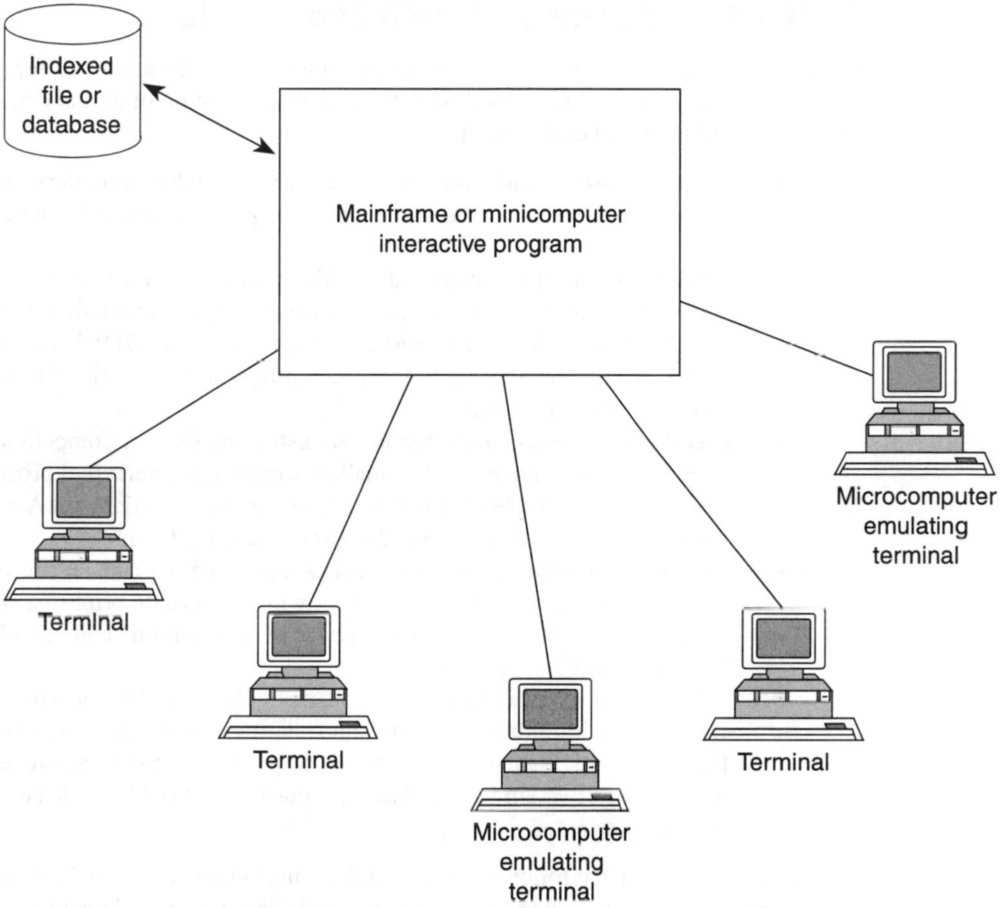

Indexed
file or
database
Mainframe or minicomputer
interactive program
Terminal
Terminal
Microcomputer
emulating
terminal
Terminal
Microcomputer
emulating
terminal

Figure 1.5 Traditional interactive programs execute on a host and do not share processing tasks with terminals.

programming are beginning to involve GUIs as an adjunct to ordinary information acquisition and management. GUI programming is complex; business applications are often confined to making use of GUI features and access provided by modern support software. Tools such as Microsoft Visual Basic and PowerSoft PowerBuilder provide access to the GUI interface of Microsoft Windows, while XWindows provides the same form of access under UNIX. Most client/server tools provide high-level support for the GUI interface, so applications can be simplified and standardized. This means that while GUI is complicated, its internal complexity is hidden.

Process control programming, on the other hand, often involves an intimate knowledge of real-time events and software interfaces to transducers that sense pressure, temperature, location, and speed. Languages such as C and Ada are often used to translate the analog signals generated by transducers in industrial piping, storage tanks, engines, turbines, pumps, lifts, aircraft, and missiles into digital form for interpretation by software and the generation of control signals for related machinery.

1.6 OVERVIEW OF CLIENT/SERVER COMPUTING

The most rational way to consider client/server architecture is to list the different ways that processing tasks have been addressed since the commercialization of digital computers in the 1950s. A useful listing takes this form:

1. **Primitive batch machine:** The earliest vacuum tube computers, which had an operating system so primitive that only one program could be run at a time. An example was the IBM 705 of 1953.
2. **Traditional multiprogrammed architecture:** A mainframe or minicomputer running a capable multiprogramming operating system with **dumb terminals** attached. An example was the IBM System/360 or a VAX/780. Dumb terminals are simply communications devices with no programmable logic of their own—also known as ASCII terminals.
3. **Freestanding microcomputer or workstation:** Only a competitor to a mainframe or minicomputer for the smallest single-user interactive processing tasks. An example is a single PC running a database such as Microsoft Access, FoxPro, Dbase IV, Paradox, Revelation, Dataease, or a spreadsheet.
4. **Networked microcomputers or workstations with print or file server:** Multiple freestanding workstations, each of which can route print to a shared printer and download software or files from a PC or workstation acting as a file server. A Novell network is an example.
5. **Client/server architecture:** Intelligent devices such as PCs or workstations communicating with a database server and sharing processing tasks with the server. This could also be called "cooperative computing," because the processing load is split between two similar or dissimilar machines (the PC/workstation client and the database server).

In the discussion that follows, we'll consider points number 2, 4, and 5 in this list: traditional architecture, networked PCs/workstations, and client/server architecture.

1.7 TRADITIONAL INTERACTIVE APPLICATION ARCHITECTURE

In the traditional interactive system architecture, dumb terminals are connected to a processor such as a mainframe or a minicomputer, as shown in Figure 1.5. In this arrangement, all processing tasks associated with database access and the user interface (such as formatting the terminal screen or accepting and validating user input) are handled by the mainframe or minicomputer.

Although there is no necessary connection between the traditional architecture and the nature of programming tools used to build systems, the chronology of software development has caused some *de facto* associations between architecture and software. Traditional mainframe/minicomputer "production" systems (those strategic applications run on a frequent periodic or continuous basis) tend to be constructed of procedural, third generation languages such as COBOL or PL/I, and are supported by indexed files, hierarchical (IMS), network (IDMS), or relational (DB2) databases. A procedural language forces the user to think through and encode every processing action needed to achieve an end purpose, such as every file access, processing sequence, and action. A nonprocedural language, on the other hand, allows the user to focus on input and output, while the nonprocedural language handles the processing analysis.

Except for DB2/SQL, procedural software suffers from significant inflexibilities. The software development lead times of third generation languages can appear excessive when contrasted with programming time requirements of modern nonprocedural languages on microcomputers.

Traditional architecture is expensive in more ways than its requirements for software development. Processor costs range from millions of dollars for a mainframe to hundreds of thousands of dollars for a minicomputer. With the price of microcomputers, workstations, and Reduced Instruction Set Computer (RISC)-based machine platforms declining while their processing power increases, the difference in cost between mainframes/mini's and these newer levels of equipment is easy to appreciate. Programming in a modern nonprocedural language and sharing processing tasks between a host computer and powerful but inexpensive desktop equipment is a natural direction to explore.

Note that the essential characteristics and expense of traditional interactive system architecture are maintained, even if dumb terminals are replaced with microcomputers emulating terminals. Having a microcomputer emulate a terminal often gains an economy of equipment, as well as slight additional flexibility in capturing, saving, or printing screen images. But terminal emulation does not allocate to the microcomputer any of the processing tasks associated with database access or interaction. The mainframe or minicomputer host is still the workhorse and, for the most part, the bottleneck. You don't necessarily have client/server just because you access a host computer with a PC or Mac!

1.8 NETWORKED MICROCOMPUTERS (LOCAL AREA NETWORKS)

You can visualize a simple network of microcomputers as illustrated in Figure 1.6. In this arrangement, PCs might communicate with a "main" PC acting as a file server, in order to share software located on the server and access an expensive peripheral device such as a laser printer. The network server may provide terminal emulation software and a connection to a host system, so that individual PCs can act as terminals and log on. The file server may be nothing more than a capable PC with a large hard disk.

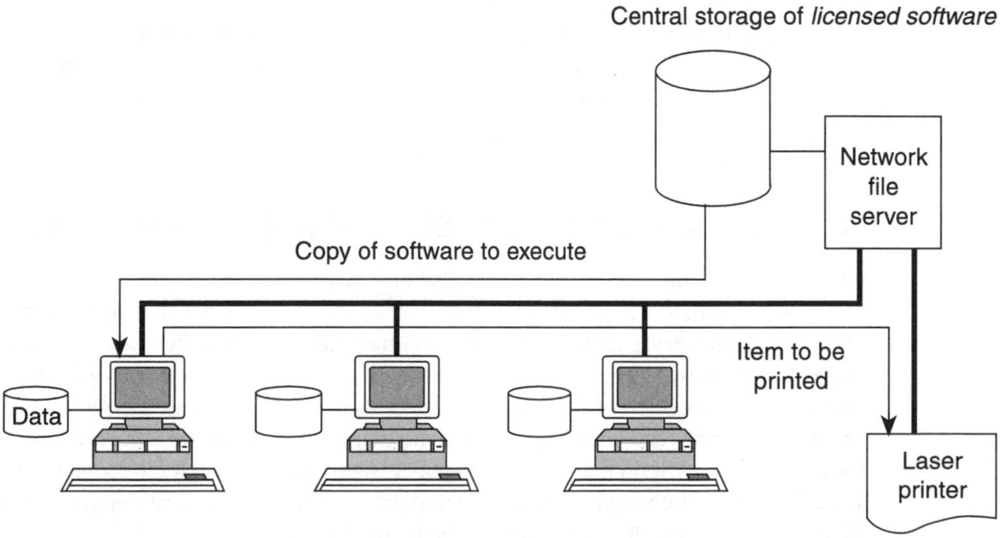
Central storage of *licensed software*
Network file server
Copy of software to execute
Item to be printed
Data
Laser printer

Figure 1.6 Local area networks (LANs) let microcomputers share hardware and software but are not client/server arrangements.

A network of microcomputers, a PC, Mac, or workstation acting as a print or file server is not a client/server arrangement. Networks not only provide conveniences in software licensing and access control, but also greater security than individual microcomputers acting as terminals to a host. In a network, a microcomputer or workstation may receive the software to run an application over the network instead of having the software loaded on its hard disk. But the critical point is that each microcomputer executes software entirely on its own. In other words, the server in the network is simply a central storage location for programs and files. The server performs no real processing on behalf of any application.

1.9 HOW CLIENT/SERVER ARCHITECTURE WORKS

Client/server architecture is a departure from the traditional way in which processing tasks are divided between devices such as computer terminals (or microcomputers acting as terminals) and a host computer. Client/server is also different from a plain local area network. In the client/server arrangement, the server is often a powerful mini- or microcomputer that manages a relational database. The server is capable of processing SQL statements, that is, statements in a standard relational database manipulation language. The server might perform all of the tasks of an ordinary local area network server in addition to acting as an SQL "engine." Figure 1.7 provides an illustration of a simple client/server arrangement.

In client/server architecture, application software resides on the hard disk of every client (microcomputer or workstation), or on the server much as in an ordinary file server network. This software manages the client's user interface, which is often graphic in nature. The end user selects functions via a mouse, pull-down menu selections, fill-in lines, or a combination of these. From these inputs, the application software forms SQL statements unseen by the user and sends these to the database server via the local area network. The server processes the SQL statements and creates a relation (table) containing the results. The server then sends these results back to the client over the network, which stores the data in memory or on its hard disk. The client manipulates the data in any way that the client's user desires, applying the processing horsepower of the client, not the server.

Popular software for the clients in a client/server arrangement includes PowerBuilder from the PowerSoft Corporation, Microsoft Visual Basic, ObjectView from the KnowledgeWare Corporation, and SQLWindows from Gupta Technologies, among many others. Software commonly used for the SQL engine includes Microsoft SQL Server, Sybase, ORACLE, Borland Interbase, and SQLBase from Gupta Technologies.

1.10 WHY AND WHERE CLIENT/SERVER IS GAINING POPULARITY

Client/server architecture is much discussed in the modern environment because it provides effective sharing of workload between clients and the server in a loosely coupled arrangement. The pieces of client/server architecture are very modular, and the differences in operating systems and software between the database server and microcomputers are relatively unimportant. For example, it's possible to mix Windows and DOS-based PCs on the same network, or even PCs and Macintoshes. The only requirements are that each machine be able to communicate on the local area network, and that the SQL statements generated by each microcomputer's client software be standard enough to "talk to" the database server (technical details of communication transmission are handled by the local area network).

The functionality and flexibility of client/server architecture are well suited to small organizations and organizations that automated in the 1980s with freestanding or local area

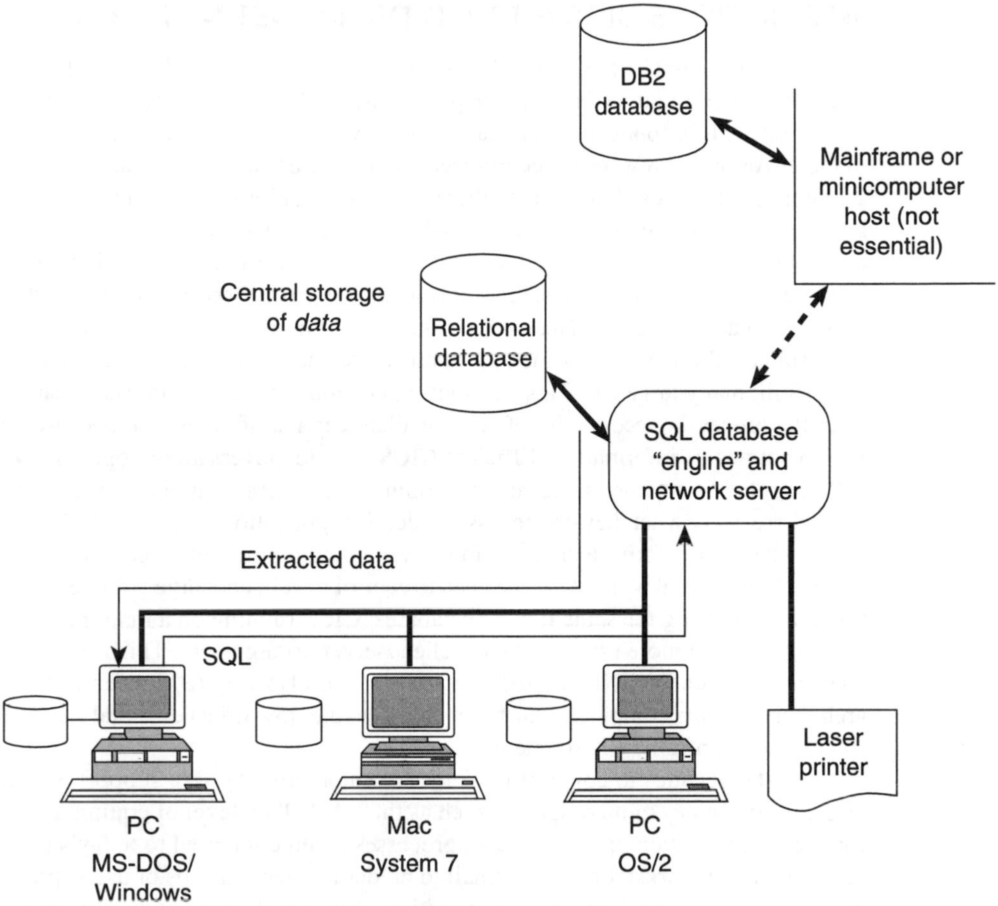
DB2
database
Mainframe or
minicomputer
host (not
essential)
Central storage
of *data*
Relational
database
SQL database
"engine" and
network server
Extracted data
SQL
Laser
printer
PC
MS-DOS/
Windows
Mac
System 7
PC
OS/2

Figure 1.7 A client/server arrangement splits processing tasks between a database server and communicating microcomputer "clients."

networks of microcomputers. In the past, the options of such groups to expand the scope of their automated information processing would have been limited to acquiring a minicomputer or mainframe capable of supporting the required number of terminals. Client/server provides a more evolutionary growth path for such organizations. Client/server also provides an alternative model for larger organizations that want to remove selected applications from a mainframe or minicomputer to downsize their support requirements and use a less expensive machine platform. Mike Ricciuti and Paul Pinella pointed to these examples in an article in *Datamation* as early as 1991:[1]

- The Nature Conservancy supports 80 users (about 20 active at any time) using three 386 database servers running Advanced Revelation; its previous host was a Hewlett Packard 3000 minicomputer.
- In a cost-saving move, TRW, Inc. converted its human resources application, involving 20 billion bytes of data, from traditional mainframe databases to a client/server arrangement on a Compaq 486 PC, running Novell Netware, Microsoft's SQL Server, supporting 20 PCs.

1.11 WHERE DOES CICS FIT INTO THE MODERN PICTURE?

This book is about CICS. Given what we have presented in this chapter, where does CICS fit into the modern picture of interactive processing, and why learn about it now?

Some CICS applications are part of "legacy systems," that is, applications that were built in the 1970s and 1980s for the centralized mainframe environment using third generation programming languages. A portion of these CICS applications—for example, applications with small numbers of users—have been or will be replaced by new systems using microcomputers and database servers. These applications were originally built using CICS and mainframes, because these were the only stable tools available throughout the 1980s (and earlier) when these applications were created. Today, smaller and more flexible mechanisms can economically support these as "departmental" applications rather than centralized systems.

Still, many large CICS applications will continue to remain in use, because they benefit from the processing economies of scale available on mainframes, and because they deal with huge volumes of information. Efficient CICS pseudoconversational operation makes it possible to reliably support thousands of terminal users with a single computer system, and to control precisely what they can access and do. For applications where centralization and stability are vital, CICS forms a crucial part of available programming solutions. When you have a large volume of real work to do, the need to control it well, and large volumes of batch processing to handle using the same files or databases, CICS running on a mainframe or large UNIX platform may be more practical than a client/server arrangement. This is why CICS has been adapted to run under UNIX by IBM and others. It is also why IBM recently opened the CICS architecture to the computer industry at large, leading toward its eventual standardization outside of the mainframe environment.[2]

In the decades to come, it is likely that interactive system support will depend much less on proprietary minicomputers such as the VAX. This level of equipment loses viability for highly computational, single-user processes when compared to today's powerful microcomputers and workstations. For small to moderate-sized groups of users, proprietary minicomputers are now less cost competitive than local area networks and client/server arrangements.

Why learn CICS now? Because CICS is commercially relevant, and will continue to be for several years.

1.12 FOR YOUR REVIEW

Understanding the following terms, introduced in this chapter, will aid your understanding of the next chapter:

- Batch program
- Client/server computing
- Conversational programming
- Customer Information Control System (CICS)
- Database server (SQL engine)
- Dumb terminal
- File server
- Interactive program
- Local area network (LAN)
- Mainframe
- Microcomputer
- Minicomputer
- Nonprocedural language
- Procedural language
- Production system
- Prompt
- Pseudoconversational programming
- SQL database manipulation language
- Terminal emulation software
- Workstation

1.13 REVIEW QUESTIONS

1. Identify and describe the three classes of computer machinery, and briefly describe each.
2. Identify and explain how interactive programs are different from batch programs.
3. Explain how the intended use of mainframe CICS and microcomputer CICS emulators differ.
4. Identify and describe the four categories of interactive business computer programming.
5. Identify and describe how client/server architecture differs from traditional interactive system architecture and simple local area networks.

NOTES

1. Ricciuti, Mike and Pinella, Paul. "A Revelation in Client/Server Tools." *Datamation*, July 15, 1991.
2. "News Shorts: IBM Opens CICS to Industry," *Computerworld,* May 16, 1994.

2

A "Big Picture" Introduction to CICS

In this first chapter devoted to CICS we want to explain to you what, specifically, CICS is, why it is necessary, and how it fits into the mainframe environment. If your background has been entirely in mini- or microcomputer work, you may feel that this chapter covers a lot of unfamiliar ground. Don't worry about details at this stage. We have written this chapter to give you an overview of many topics we will cover in greater depth later.

2.1 MAINFRAME OPERATING SYSTEMS

An **operating system** is software that controls the execution of the entire computer system. The operating system is a program that must be loaded to memory first, so that it can make decisions about how the remainder of memory can be allocated to other programs, how the devices attached to the computer system will be used, and how the attention of the central processing unit (CPU) will be split among different programs. Operating systems provide the infrastructure that application programs need to access disk and tape devices. Without this infrastructure, all programs would have to be much larger and more complicated, since they would have to include voluminous low-level instructions for dealing with input and output devices.

To be practical, any computer system must have an operating system. Microcomputers designed as clones and descendants of IBM's original personal computer most often use the MS-DOS operating system, while Apple Macintoshes use the System/7 or a later operating system. Many minicomputers run the UNIX operating system. IBM mainframes run **MVS/ESA** or **DOS/VSE,** or the Virtual Machine (VM) operating system. MVS/ESA is the premier operating system of IBM mainframes, while DOS/VSE is less capable and was originally designed for small machines in the mainframe family. VM was not intended by IBM as a commercial product, but as a tool for testing operating systems themselves. VM "escaped" from the software lab and is often used as a tool to support the conversion of DOS/VSE systems to MVS/ESA, and to support mainframe office automation system and electronic mail.

Figure 2.1 illustrates how MVS/ESA occupies a part of the memory of an ES/9000 mainframe. We will refer to this figure in the next several sections as we consider other pieces of system software in the mainframe environment.

2.2 THE CICS ENVIRONMENT

IBM mainframes using the MVS/ESA and DOS/VSE operating systems are batch-oriented. This means that they are programmed to accept groups of inputs, perform repeated processing, and create groups of outputs such as files and reports. To do interactive processing on a mainframe, also known as **on-line processing,** you have to use the services of CICS, Customer Information and Control System. CICS is a large program that runs continuously under a batch-operating system such as MVS/ESA or DOS/VSE. On-line programs on a mainframe are not actually "whole" programs, but rather subprograms that run under the direction of CICS. CICS was developed in 1968 to make it practical to use an IBM mainframe for on-line processing.

IBM's original vision of large-scale business data processing did not include smaller computers such as mini- and microcomputers. Instead, IBM saw one or a few mainframes as the center of a given organization's data processing universe. CICS was developed to support pseudoconversational on-line processing. As you will see, pseudoconversational techniques make it possible for even a primitive mainframe (one having as little as a megabyte of memory) to support hundreds or thousands of terminals effectively. But there's no free lunch. To do this, on-line programs written for the CICS environment are much more complex and their logic is much more involved than other forms of on-line programs.

CICS is entirely separate from COBOL, C, PL/I, or any other programming language, and it is separate from the MVS/ESA and DOS/VSE operating systems. In Figure 2.1, you see CICS occupying a large part of the memory of the mainframe. You can also see how on-line programs are given memory within CICS, unlike batch programs, which are given memory by the operating system directly.

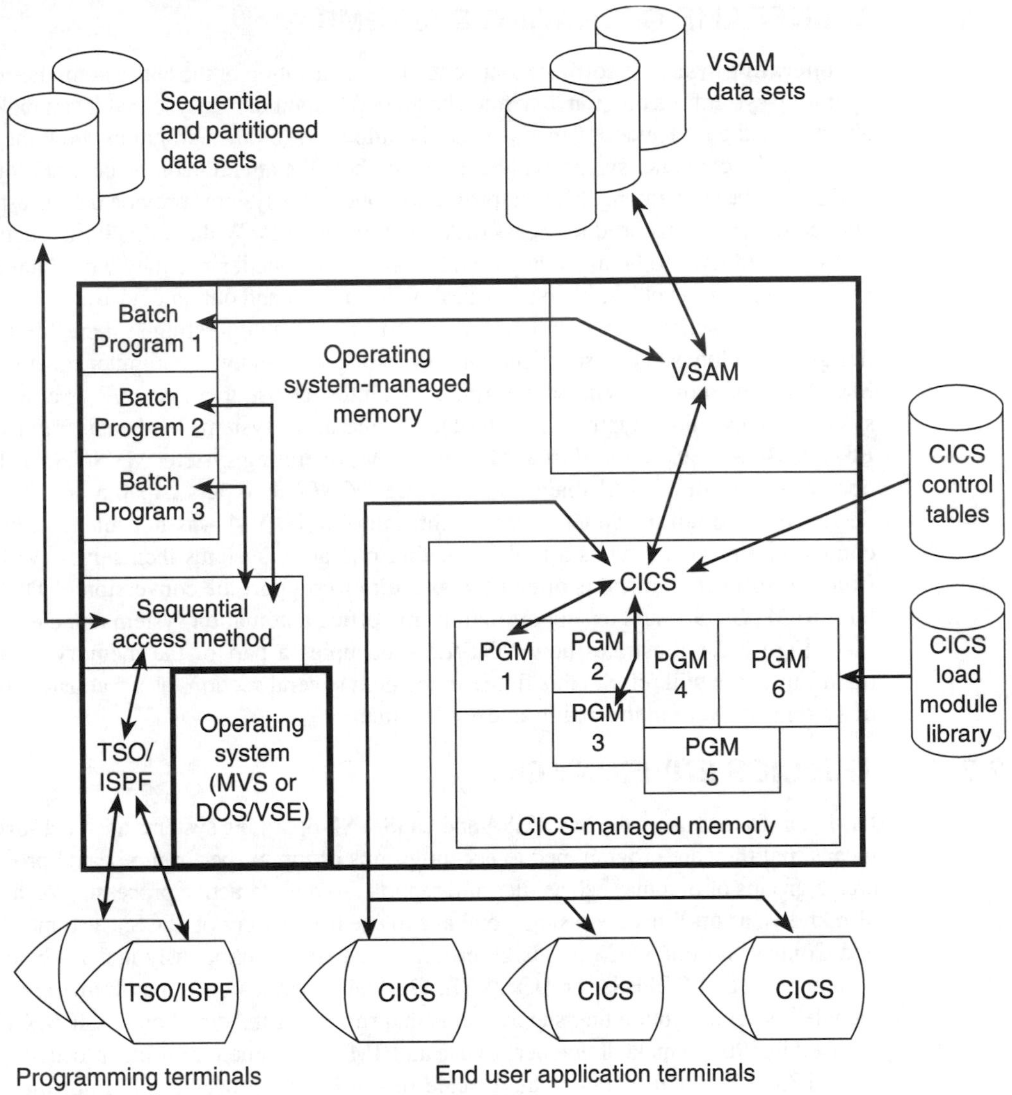

Sequential
and partitioned
data sets
VSAM
data sets
Batch
Program 1
Operating
system-managed
memory
VSAM
Batch
Program 2
Batch
Program 3
CICS
control
tables
CICS
Sequential
access method
PGM
1
PGM
2
PGM
4
PGM
6
CICS
load
module
library
PGM
3
PGM
5
TSO/
ISPF
Operating
system
(MVS or
DOS/VSE)
CICS-managed memory
TSO/ISPF
CICS
CICS
CICS
Programming terminals
End user application terminals

Figure 2.1 How mainframe memory is occupied by the operating system, CICS, and other system software.

2.3 CICS IS A TELEPROCESSING MONITOR

CICS is a **teleprocessing monitor.** It acts as an operating system within an operating system, because it allocates memory and services to on-line programs. CICS is responsible for:

- Dealing with terminals attached to the mainframe for business data processing
- Allocating memory to on-line programs
- Supervising on-line programs to accomplish on-line processing
- Accessing files on behalf of on-line programs

Originally, you could write programs in assembler, PL/I, and COBOL to interact with CICS. The assembler language interface to CICS was known as **macro level,** while the PL/I and COBOL interfaces are known as **command level**. Modern versions of CICS have dropped support for macro level coding. In this book, we focus on programs for CICS that are written using VS COBOL II, IBM's most popular COBOL compiler meeting ANSI 1985 standards.

2.4 HOW THE OPERATING SYSTEM HANDLES BATCH PROGRAMS

At the upper left corner of Figure 2.1, you see several batch programs residing in memory. Batch programs are placed into execution by MVS/ESA by assigning them memory locations and occasionally allocating central processor time to each.

You "run" batch programs by feeding job control language to the operating system requesting that this be done. Since the operating system directly executes batch programs, batch programs access files by issuing requests to the operating system. An MVS/ESA subsystem known as the Queued Sequential Access Method (QSAM) handles sequential files, while another subsystem named Virtual Storage Access Method (VSAM) handles indexed files. If a batch program **abends** (abnormally ends, or "blows up"), the operating system assumes control, "flushes" the program out of execution, and takes rudimentary file closing actions.

2.5 HOW THE OPERATING SYSTEM HANDLES CICS PROGRAMS

Programs that you write for the CICS environment are executed differently than batch programs. The operating system "sees" CICS as a single large program. Like any program, CICS begins running when someone submits job control language telling the operating system to give it memory and run it. This task is typically handled once per day (or less frequently) by the operations personnel of a mainframe installation. From that point on, CICS executes continuously. As far as the operating system is concerned, CICS is just a program that never quits.

CICS manages the memory that the operating system gives it, and activates on-line programs as requested by people at terminals. When a CICS program becomes active, CICS "suballocates" some of its own memory to the program to let it run. Since memory allocation is normally an operating system function, CICS acts like an operating system within the operating system.

It's important to understand that in the mainframe environment you can't just execute an on-line program by requesting that it be run as you do a batch program. This is a major difference between mainframe on-line programming and interactive programming on mini- and microcomputers. The mainframe operating system doesn't handle this form of request; you must ask CICS to execute an on-line program. For this reason, individual on-line programs are not "known" to the mainframe operating system. And, in keeping with this arrangement, mainframe on-line programs can't directly interact with the operating system either; instead, they must request CICS to handle file accesses on their behalf. This means that you can't use several common verbs in on-line programs, as described in section 2.12.

2.6 TSO/ISPF: THE TIME-SHARING OPTION

In order to get the most out of this book, you should be at least familiar with **Time-Sharing Option/Integrated System Programming Facility, TSO/ISPF.** This mouthful of a name identifies the programmer's workbench of the IBM MVS/ESA mainframe environment. TSO/ISPF provides a rich set of formatted screens, labeled "panels," that you use to access files of

```
---------------------- ISPF/PDF PRIMARY OPTION MENU -----------------------
OPTION  ===>
                                                      USERID   - CSCJGJ
   0  ISPF PARMS  - Specify terminal and user parameters    TIME     - 14:00
   1  BROWSE      - Display source data or output listings  TERMINAL - 3278
   2  EDIT        - Create or change source data            PF KEYS  - 24
   3  UTILITIES   - Perform utility functions
   4  FOREGROUND  - Invoke language processors in foreground
   6  COMMAND     - Enter TSO Command, CLIST, or REXX exec
   C  CHANGES     - Display summary of changes for this release
   S  SDSF        - Spool Display and Search Facility
   T  TUTORIAL    - Display information about ISPF/PDF
   X  EXIT        - Terminate ISPF using log and list defaults

Enter END command to terminate ISPF.
```

TSO/ISPF is the programmer's workbench of the MVS/ESA mainframe environment. You access TSO/ISPF through its main menu. The edit function (2) is the workhorse of the TSO/ISPF, and gives you a full screen editor to compose map code, job control language (JCL), and programs. You submit JCL from the edit screen to process map code and program source code into machine language form.

Figure 2.2 TSO/ISPF (Time-Sharing Option/Integrated System Programming Facility) main menu screen.

source code and job control language. TSO/ISPF panels are accessed from the ISPF main menu, shown in Figure 2.2.

You use TSO/ISPF to compose batch programs, on-line programs, and job control language (JCL). You also use TSO/ISPF to submit JCL for processing, and to view batch job output. Both TSO/ISPF and CICS can make terminals "come alive." But TSO/ISPF and CICS have radically different purposes.

As a programmer's workbench, TSO/ISPF is not designed to efficiently support locally written application programs. TSO/ISPF itself is written in a product called **Dialog Manager,** which IBM developed specifically to create TSO/ISPF. You can use Dialog Manager directly to create interactive applications, and program them in the IBM-specific CLIST or REXX languages. Because these languages are interpreted, they are easier to use than CICS in that they require no compilation. But Dialog Manager, CLISTs, and REXX are not efficient enough to support the high-volume applications that CICS is designed to handle. Dialog Manager is sometimes used by systems programmers within an installation to craft extensions to TSO/ISPF as locally customized programming tools. But Dialog Manager is not used to create end user applications in the same way that CICS is used. Neither Dialog Manager nor CICS provide a text editor; each relies on TSO/ISPF for this purpose.

When CICS was developed, punch cards were still widely used to compose program source code and job control language. Even the source code for CICS programs was prepared on a keypunch and submitted for compilation using job control language on punch cards. You now use TSO/ISPF to compose CICS programs rather than punch cards. You compose and submit job control language using TSO/ISPF to process CICS screen definitions and compile on-line program source code. Once these batch jobs execute, you log off from TSO, log on to CICS, and test your on-line program.

2.7 CICS PROVIDES MANY SERVICES TO ON-LINE PROGRAMS

Different models of IBM mainframe terminals have different data transmission and control characteristics. CICS insulates individual programs from the intricacies of terminal hardware. CICS provides standard commands to communicate with terminals on behalf of your on-line programs. You have to learn how to use these commands to be able to write CICS programs. CICS also provides several commands to accomplish input/output actions with files on behalf of your on-line programs. You have to learn what these commands are and how they work to be able to write CICS programs.

If a CICS program abnormally ends (abends), CICS attempts to intercept the event and issues its own form of error code to the terminal involved. You have to become familiar with these error codes in order to debug your CICS programs.

2.8 ALL CICS PROGRAMS ARE RELATED

CICS is a large program. Every on-line program executing on the mainframe is under the control of CICS. Even programs that logically have nothing to do with one another, such as a program handling entry of a customer's order, a program being used to add employees to a payroll system, and a program supporting a personnel department inquiry have in common the fact that they depend on CICS.

CICS cannot catch all logic errors in your on-line programs as it runs them. It's possible for a failed on-line program to cause CICS itself to abend. If this happens, all on-line programs being managed by CICS at that time are affected, and the files being accessed by CICS on behalf of programs may be corrupted! This is very serious and can be disruptive to hundreds or thousands of users. CICS is much more susceptible to upset than separate batch programs being supervised directly by the operating system. For this reason, many installations run one copy of CICS for production processing, and a second copy strictly for new on-line program testing.

IBM has upgraded CICS over the years to improve its stability and provide features that let an installation work more flexibly with it. For instance, in the early days it was necessary to stop CICS execution (and consequently to suspend all on-line activity) in order to make CICS aware of new terminals or programs. The modern release of CICS is CICS/ESA 3.3, for the MVS/ESA environment, and no longer imposes this awkward requirement. In addition, CICS now provides extensive capabilities for recovery from equipment, terminal, and application program failure.

2.9 PROGRAM EXECUTION UNDER CICS

CICS was designed to optimize on-line processing by conserving memory and processing resources. This was especially important in the late 1960s when CICS was developed, because mainframes of that era were constrained to expensive magnetic core memories as limited as 256,000 bytes. Machines are now much larger than in the 1960s, with up to 256 million bytes of memory and more, but the on-line processing workload has also grown and the program management techniques used by CICS remain important. CICS supports multitasking, to handle multiple on-line programs at the same time, and multithreading, to conserve the amount of memory used by each program.

2.10 MULTIPROGRAMMING AND MULTITASKING

A modern operating system supervises the execution of several programs at the same time. This means that several programs are located in machine memory at the same time (in different locations) and each receives a small slice of time to process, one after another. The formal word that describes this is **multiprogramming**.

CICS also manages more than one program at a time in the memory, known as **address space,** that the operating system gives it. This is similar to the way the operating system itself works. The formal term for what CICS does is **multitasking**.

Two more terms come into play in discussing multitasking: multithreading and program reentrancy. Figure 2.3 will help you to understand how multitasking, multithreading, and program reentrancy are related.

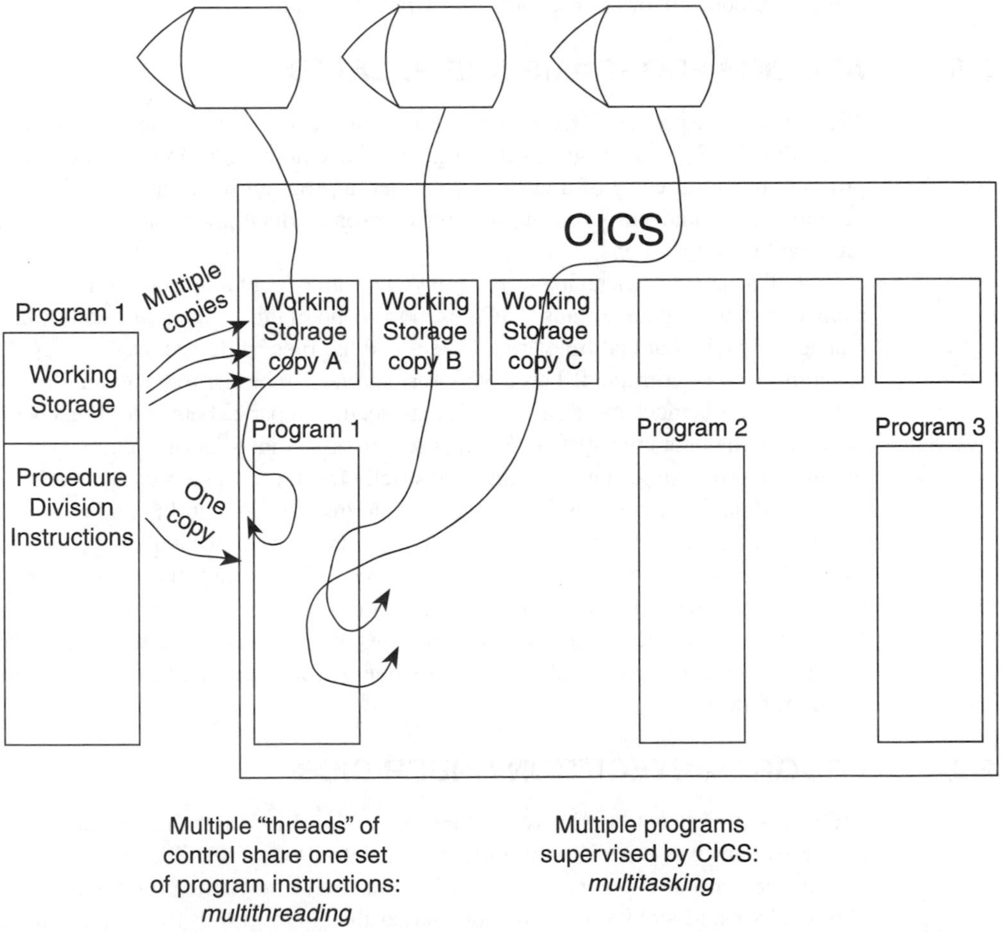
CICS
Program 1
Working Storage
Procedure Division Instructions
Multiple copies
One copy
Working Storage copy A
Working Storage copy B
Working Storage copy C
Program 1
Program 2
Program 3
Multiple "threads" of control share one set of program instructions: *multithreading*
Multiple programs supervised by CICS: *multitasking*

Figure 2.3 CICS supports multithreading by making programs quasi-reentrant, and uses multitasking to run several on-line programs at the same time.

2.11 MULTITHREADING AND PROGRAM REENTRANCY

In the on-line environment, more than one computer terminal may be active, doing the same processing, such as entering insurance claims or adding customer orders to a database. CICS allows more than one computer terminal to execute the same machine language copy of a program's machine language instructions. This is called **multithreading**. Think of this term as if each terminal's use of the same program logic follows its own path (thread) through the maze of machine language instructions.

Because more than one terminal (user) may be following the same program instructions at a time, those instructions must not be changed by any individual user. Two terms exist to describe a program written and handled this way. A program that does not change its own instructions or memory is called a **reentrant program**.

Full reentrancy is not practical because a program that does not store anything in memory can't do much useful work! To make it possible for more than one computer terminal to execute the same program, CICS gives each terminal its own copy of the program's memory fields (WORKING-STORAGE). This takes care of the requirement that an individual terminal's use of a program not change the memory (data) being used by another terminal accessing the program.

You also have to take care to write CICS programs so that they do not modify their own instructions. In COBOL terms, this means that you can't use the ALTER verb, which does change a program's instructions as it executes. But even batch programs now avoid use of ALTER, because self-modifying programs are difficult to debug. This is not really an issue you have to worry much about any more with VS COBOL II.

Because of the fact that CICS gives each terminal using a program its own copy of the program's memory fields, CICS programs can't be called fully reentrant. They are formally called **quasi-reentrant programs**. Programs must be at least quasi-reentrant in order for CICS multiprogramming to be possible.

2.12 IMPACT OF CICS OPERATION ON YOUR PROGRAMS

The way that CICS operates makes it possible for one mainframe to support hundreds or even thousands of terminals at a time. For example, 100 terminals executing a program requiring 80,000 bytes of memory would require 8 million bytes of memory if each terminal required its own copy of the program. Under CICS, each terminal uses the same instructions, and only one copy of the program is retained in memory. And as Figure 2.1 illustrates, more than one on-line program can be active at one time under multitasking. But the way CICS operates does impose restrictions on the way you write programs, and it forces you to recognize some programming conventions that are different from batch programming on IBM mainframes.

A consequence of the quasi-reentrant way that CICS works is that it makes sense to minimize the size of any on-line program's memory requirements. WORKING-STORAGE is replicated for each terminal using the program, but only one copy of the program instructions (PROCEDURE DIVISION) is kept in memory by CICS, no matter how many terminals execute a program. In CICS programs, therefore, it's better to code messages as literal characters in the PROCEDURE DIVISION rather than in WORKING-STORAGE. This is just the reverse of common programming style and organization in batch programs.

CICS programs are not supervised directly by the operating system like batch programs. For this reason you can't use verbs or commands in your CICS programs that directly ask for operating system services. For example, CICS programs can't access files directly using the

READ
WRITE
REWRITE
DELETE
START
ACCEPT
DISPLAY
SORT
INSPECT

Figure 2.4 You can't use verbs that request operating system services in your CICS programs.

READ, WRITE, REWRITE, DELETE, or START verbs, as interactive COBOL programs can use on a computer such as the VAX or a PC. These verbs directly ask the operating system for input/output services. In CICS programs, you ask CICS to access files on your behalf, using commands such as READ DATASET and WRITE DATASET.

In addition, you can't use the SORT verb, Report Writer, or the ACCEPT and DISPLAY verbs in your CICS programs. These verbs make a direct request to the operating system for services. Figure 2.4 simply emphasizes the fact that these verbs are prohibited; if you used them, you would violate the "chain of command" by going around the program's "boss," CICS.

CICS on-line programs differ significantly from on-line programs on mini- and microcomputers in another way. Printed output from an on-line CICS program is difficult and tricky to arrange. It's complicated enough to be considered an advanced CICS programming topic. In fact, it's most common to use batch jobs to print things from files and databases updated by CICS, and to submit those jobs at the end of the business day using job control language.

2.13 CICS SESSIONS, TRANSACTIONS, AND TASKS

When CICS is active, you can use a terminal to log on to it. This involves a procedure in which CICS may verify your identity as a terminal operator. When you successfully log onto CICS, you begin a **session** and CICS becomes able to execute your on-line programs for you.

Each of your CICS programs is associated with a transaction identifier or **trans id,** a four-character code. When you enter the trans id for a program in your CICS session, CICS figures out the name of the corresponding program by looking up the trans id in a table, one of several **control tables** that must be present, as shown at the right of Figure 2.1. Here are some examples of typical trans id's:

```
W001
$001
UP56
```

You can't run an on-line program until CICS "knows" its trans id and program name. You can immediately see that developing an interactive program on a mainframe is not something you do in a vacuum. As a programmer, you can't simply do it alone. You have to have an authorized person first define the trans id you'll use, and the program name. Typically, only one or a few systems programmers can update CICS tables. Programmers almost never have access to CICS control tables.

A **transaction** is defined as one unit of work to the terminal operator. A transaction might consist of bringing a record to the screen to satisfy an inquiry, entering a customer's order into the system, or entering the fields needed for a computation and receiving the result of that computation.

When CICS begins running a program for you, it initiates a **task** to manage the program's execution. A task is the most elementary unit of work to CICS. A task begins when CICS starts doing work for a program, and the task ends when that program gives up control to CICS and "dies."

In pseudoconversational operation most transactions involve many starts and stops of a given on-line program. Typically, each transaction requires multiple CICS tasks. Who figures out where to pick up processing after each task ends? As the author of a CICS program, you do! We'll cover this form of logic, known as pseudoconversational processing, once you have gained some experience defining CICS screens and processing them into usable form.

2.14 CICS CONTROL TABLES

Information about terminal operator identifiers, passwords, trans ids, program names, file names, and other external information is stored in CICS control tables. The CICS tables are accessible to CICS as it executes. A few of the many CICS control tables include:

- **Sign-On Table** (SNT) stores operator identifiers, passwords, and security information about the things a given operator can perform
- **Program Control Table** (PCT) stores trans ids and the program name associated with each
- **Processing Program Table** (PPT) stores names of programs currently being executed and their locations in CICS memory
- **Terminal Control Table** (TCT) stores computer terminal identifiers and their characteristics
- **File Control Table** (FCT) stores eight-character CICS "file names" and equates each to an actual data set name on your computer system

CICS tables are maintained by systems programmers, that is, personnel who maintain operating system software. Personnel such as us, who create application programs, must request that new program names, file names, and transaction identifiers be added to CICS control tables before we can create new on-line programs. From our discussion in this chapter, you can understand why this control is necessary. CICS is centralized support software involved in the work of all users of a computer system. Without a single point of control, various on-line applications could attempt to use the same transaction identifiers or otherwise interfere with each other.

2.15 THE CICS LOAD LIBRARY

In addition to control tables (files), CICS has access to a large partitioned data set (library) that houses machine language, as shown at the right side of Figure 2.1. This library is known as the CICS **load library.** The members of this library include the machine language of your on-line programs. You use job control language to execute the software that turns your COBOL or PL/I programs into machine language and store the machine language in the CICS load library.

Under CICS, the images of the screens that your programs will send to terminals are defined separately from programs themselves. Each screen image is known as a **map**. You code maps using IBM assembler language macro instructions. These maps must, like CICS programs, be turned into machine language that is housed in the CICS load library. Turning map code into machine language is also a process that you accomplish using job control language. As you can see, when you do CICS programming, *you use batch processes to put the things you need for interactive programs into the CICS load library.*

2.16 FOR YOUR REVIEW

Understanding the following terms, introduced in this chapter, will aid your understanding of the next chapter:

Abend
Address space
CICS control tables
Command level CICS
Dialog Manager
DOS/VSE
Load library
Macro level CICS
Map
Multiprogramming
Multitasking
Multithreading
MVS/ESA
On-line
Operating system
Quasi-reentrant program
Reentrant program
Session
Task
Teleprocessing monitor
Transaction identifier (trans id)
Transaction
TSO/ISPF
VM

2.17 REVIEW QUESTIONS

1. Explain what an operating system is and does, and identify the three operating systems provided by IBM for its mainframe equipment, and their intended uses.
2. Explain what a teleprocessing monitor such as CICS is, and identify the four services it provides to programs.
3. Describe what job control language (JCL) is and the role it serves in the mainframe environment.
4. Identify the nature of each of the following software products, and briefly explain what each does or is used for:

a. TSO/ISPF
b. Dialog manager
c. CLIST language
d. REXX language
e. CICS

5. Define each of the following terms related to mainframe CICS programming:
   a. multiprogramming
   b. multitasking
   c. multithreading
   d. reentrant program
   e. quasi-reentrant program
6. Explain the difference between a task and a transaction in the CICS environment.
7. Describe the role played by CICS control tables, and identify who makes changes to them.
8. Describe what the CICS load library is, and identify what it contains.

3

The Mainframe Environment and 3270 Terminals

In this chapter we'll explore the hardware side of the mainframe environment. We will make you aware of features engineered by IBM into the unique line of terminals, named the 3270, to support the mainframe flavor of an interactive system. The material in this chapter will help you see and understand how screen definitions, called maps, tap into the power IBM's engineers put into the 3270 terminal. You will also learn how hardware and software in the mainframe environment was optimized to support reliable and efficient centralized interactive computing.

3.1 IBM'S WORLDVIEW: MAINFRAME AT THE CENTER OF THE UNIVERSE

IBM's large system philosophy was formed in the 1950s and 1960s when there was no such thing as a mini- or microcomputer. Only mainframes existed—large, expensive machines that it seemed would have to handle all of the information processing and computation for an organization. This conception of commercial computing arose in the era of batch machines. It is embodied in MVS/ESA, the descendant of the original operating system for the System/360 of 1964.

Today we still use computers of the von Neumann architecture. This means that in spite of large memory resources, the computer has only one "thinking part," or central processing unit (CPU). All of the instructions actually executed to run programs have to be handled by this CPU. This is a real bottleneck. And in the 1960s the CPU within a mainframe was much less powerful than are today's CPUs!

If your goal is to have a single machine (even a relatively weak 1968 mainframe) at the center of things, supporting thousands of terminals while also running several batch jobs, you have to be smart about what work you require the CPU do. It makes sense to segregate work among different hardware components, to offload as many processing tasks as possible from the main CPU. The main CPU is the only one that can actually execute programs. To the extent possible, IBM offloaded from the CPU the tasks that other slower and cheaper processors could handle. IBM arranged both hardware and software to help do this.

3.2 HOW IBM MINIMIZES THE CPU BOTTLENECK IN HARDWARE

It's possible to shuck off the following kinds of tasks from the main CPU of a computer and have them performed by other smaller dedicated processors either near the mainframe or near the terminal:

- I/O: getting data from disk into memory or writing it from memory
- Communication line management
- Terminal buffering

Look at Figure 3.1 as you read the next three sections. This shows you how dedicated processors called channels surround the mainframe, how the dedicated 3705/3745 communication processor attaches to a channel, and how terminals attach to terminal controllers.

3.3 I/O OFFLOADING: CHANNEL PROCESSORS

Getting data from disk into memory, or writing it from memory to disk, usually involves a lot of CPU effort. In IBM's mainframe architecture, most of the work involved in this is assigned to **channel processors**, which are dedicated minicomputers located within the mainframe's circuitry. A typical mainframe in 1968 might have had six channel processors. A modern mainframe can have 32 or more. Channels communicate with external device controllers at a rate of three or more megabytes per second.

Channel processors are like the nurses surrounding a surgeon in the operating room. They receive directions from the main CPU about the requirements for a data transfer, such as a block of data to be read or written. The CPU shares access to memory with its channel processors. Channel processors execute channel programs, software provided by IBM with the operating system. Transfers of data through channel processors are limited to a maximum size of 32,760 bytes per block. Channel program usage is measured in **EXCPs** (EXecute Channel Programs), each of which transfers one block of data between external storage and memory. The operation of channel programs is invisible to you as an application programmer.

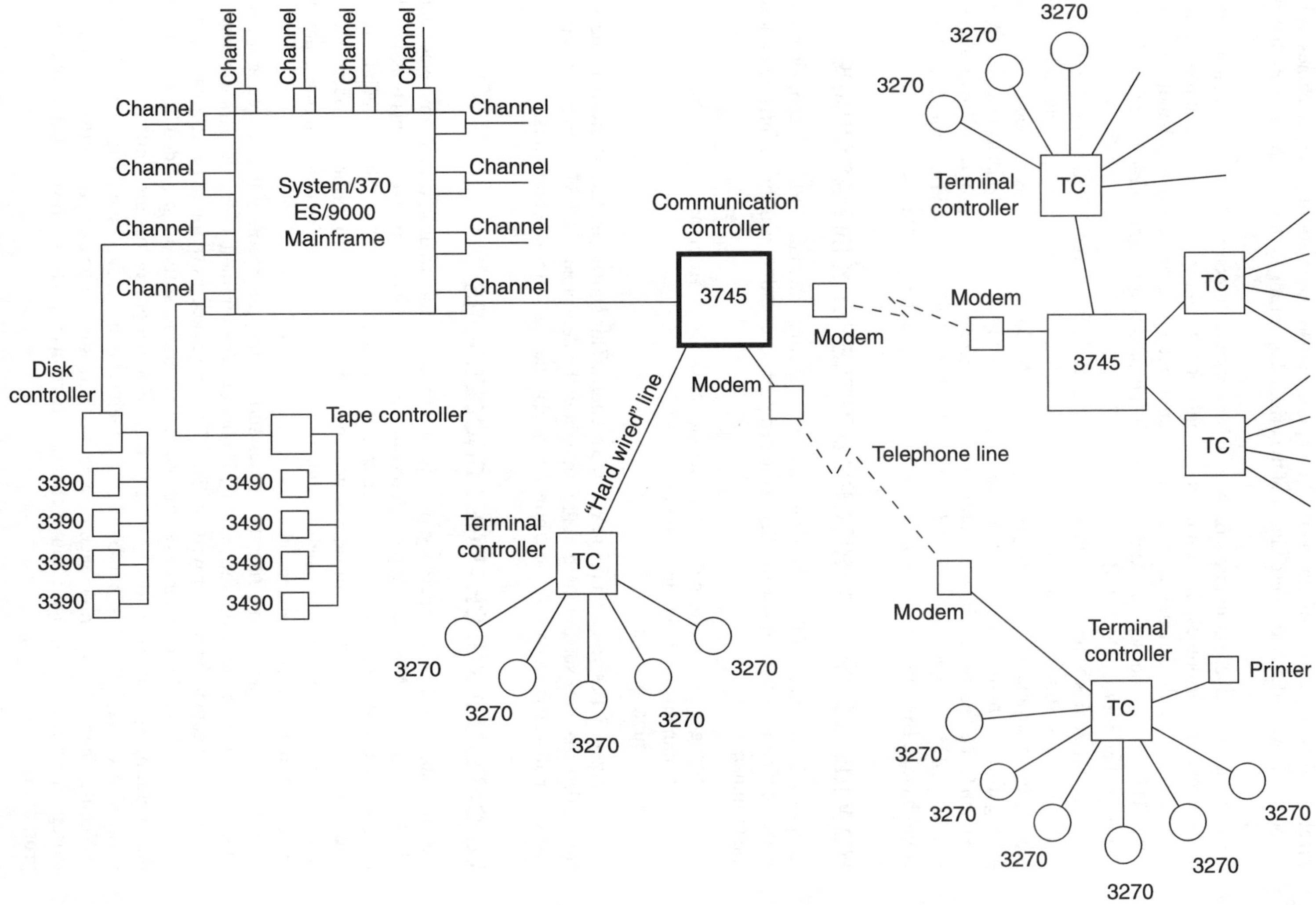
Channel
Channel
Channel
Channel
Channel
Channel
Channel
Channel
Channel
Channel
Channel
Channel
System/370
ES/9000
Mainframe
Disk
controller
3390
3390
3390
3390
Tape controller
3490
3490
3490
3490
Communication
controller
3745
Modem
Modem
"Hard wired" line
Terminal
controller
TC
3270
3270
3270
3270
3270
Telephone line
Modem
3745
TC
TC
Terminal
controller
TC
3270
3270
3270
Modem
Terminal
controller
TC
Printer
3270
3270
3270
3270
3270
3270

Figure 3.1 The IBM mainframe hardware environment was designed to offload as much work as possible from the central processing unit.

3.4 COMMUNICATION LINE MANAGEMENT

Communication line management involves receiving transmission streams from different types of communication devices, translating different communication protocols, breaking apart multiplexed transmissions from several devices, and putting them into a standard format. If the mainframe CPU had to do these tasks, it would be heavily burdened and unable to handle as many interactive terminals as desired.

On the mainframe side, IBM arranged for these communication tasks to be done by a specialized dedicated minicomputer called a communication processor. A **communication processor** is sometimes called a **front end**, because it sits in front of the computer as far as a communication circuit is concerned. IBM's communication processor is identified generically by the model number 3705 (the newer model is the 3745). It runs NCP (Network Control Program), which interacts with VTAM (Virtual Telecommunication Access Method) running in the mainframe. The 3705 or 3745 is maintained by systems programmers to suit the terminal network of the installation.

In certain environments, equipment other than a 3705/3745 is used. A **protocol converter** like the IBM 7171 can handle some of the communication line management tasks, allowing inexpensive ASCII dumb terminals, or microcomputers emulating ASCII terminals (rather than real IBM 3270 terminals), to serve as CICS terminals. Protocol converters, as the name suggests, translate between different signal streams expected by various kinds of equipment. In addition, protocol converters translate the ASCII character set from terminals to EBCDIC encoding, which is used only by IBM mainframes, and EBCDIC from the mainframe back to ASCII for non-IBM terminals. Several vendors, in addition to IBM, manufacture and sell communication front ends.

On the terminal side, the **multiplexing** (combining) of the transmissions from several terminals is handled by the **terminal controller**. 3270s attach to a controller that houses memory and logic circuits. The controller handles your terminal transmission like the post office handles your letter to another person. Your letter is grouped with others in a mail bag, and the bag is transported to the destination. The terminal multiplexes your terminal transmission together with other transmissions, and sends the group of them in a burst of electronic signals. The 3705 demultiplexes the transmissions (separates them) to route each appropriately at the mainframe.

As an applications programmer or end user, nothing is apparent to you about the 3745 and its operation. You are also unaware of the multiplexing being done by your terminal controller or other hardware emulating a terminal controller.

3.5 IBM 3270 TERMINALS: BUFFERING AND ATTRIBUTE BYTES

IBM engineers designed a model of computer terminal, the **3270**, to handle interactive communication with the mainframe. 3270s are considerably smarter than ASCII terminals, which typically have no ability to support local data manipulation.

Terminals in the 3270 family attach to a computer system through a controller, which can handle between eight and 32 terminals. Memory and circuitry in both the terminal and controller allow the terminal to receive a burst of information from the computer, describing an entire screen, and then locally support the manipulation of the screen contents. This supports terminal buffering, which affects the timing and content of data transmissions. Another 3270 terminal feature, the use of attribute bytes, supports minimization of the quantity of data transmission by identifying changed data fields so that only these need to be sent from the terminal to the computer.

3.6 TERMINAL BUFFERING

Terminal buffering involves storing keystrokes to send them in a group rather than key by key. Think of buffering as what happens when you write a letter to someone: You put a lot of characters forming words and sentences onto paper and send the paper in an envelope. You don't send each character of each word in a separate envelope!

With terminal buffering, the keystrokes you make at the keyboard are not sent immediately to the mainframe. Instead, they are stored in memory and displayed on the screen. When you press the Enter key (or a PF key, as we'll explain), all of the entries you have made since the last time you pressed the Enter key are transmitted to the mainframe. This form of terminal buffering in effect gives you screen-by-screen transmission instead of key-by-key transmission.

You can see the economy of terminal buffering. A program in memory awaiting every keystroke is active and consumes memory. Even your rapid keystrokes are separated by small gaps of time. Large gaps of time exist if you have to think about the entries you make on the screen. This "wait time" by the program is wasted. With terminal buffering, all of the time spent between keystrokes is of no consequence to the mainframe. In fact, the mainframe doesn't even know you exist as you work on a screen! Everything you finally leave on the screen (which simply pictures the contents of the terminal's memory for you) after working on it is sent to the mainframe in one chunk when you press the Enter key.

Terminal buffering is done by the 3270 terminal and its controller. These devices were designed to have their own memory, unlike ASCII terminals. This is one reason why 3270s cost over $4,000 in the 1970s, at a time when ASCII terminals cost less than $1,000! Now, we often emulate the buffered operation of 3270 terminals using a protocol converter or local area network server supporting PCs or Macintoshes. With today's inexpensive memory and logic chips, even "real" 3270s are relatively inexpensive.

Terminal buffering has a dramatic impact on the way you design and program mainframe interactive systems. Since communication occurs with a CICS program screen by screen rather than field by field, you cannot plan on checking field entries one at a time as they are entered. You have to plan on reporting field content errors using different techniques than with conversational interactive programs. You also have to understand how pseudoconversational program operation complements terminal buffering.

3.7 MINIMIZING DATA TRANSMISSION

In addition to all of its other hardware features, designed to foster mainframe handling of interactive processing, IBM engineers wanted to reduce data transmission time to a minimum. Since modems were relatively slow and expensive in the late 1960s, economizing on the quantity of data transmitted was a natural way to reduce the data transmission time.

IBM 3270 terminals are designed to keep track of what fields have been entered on the screen since the last data transmission to the mainframe. They are also designed to keep track of the intended treatment of a field, including its display intensity and whether the cursor is allowed to enter the field. All of this information is maintained using actual screen memory in **attribute bytes**.

The byte preceding a field on the screen is appropriated by the terminal to house the attribute byte for the field. This byte will not display anything on the screen, and the cursor cannot change it. In Chapter 4, you'll see how to define attribute bytes when designing a screen image, and we'll show you choices for attribute byte settings. For now, realize that more restrictions apply to your screen designs on the mainframe than on mini- or microcomputers. You have to plan on and design around the screen positions occupied by attribute bytes.

3.8 IBM 3270 KEYBOARD AND PROGRAM FUNCTION (PF) KEYS

A 3270 provides several function and control keys not found on ASCII or microcomputer keyboards. CICS is designed to "talk" to real 3270s. To work with CICS you have to know about function and control keys and how a real 3270 uses them. You also have to know how ASCII terminals and microcomputers emulate these keys.

Figure 3.2 depicts the keyboard of the original IBM 3270 display station. PF keys 1 through 12 were at the top of the "typewriter" keys. You activated them by pressing Alt and the number key. The newer 3191 provides 24 entirely separate function keys at the top of the keyboard. You need to know how other 3270 keys operate.

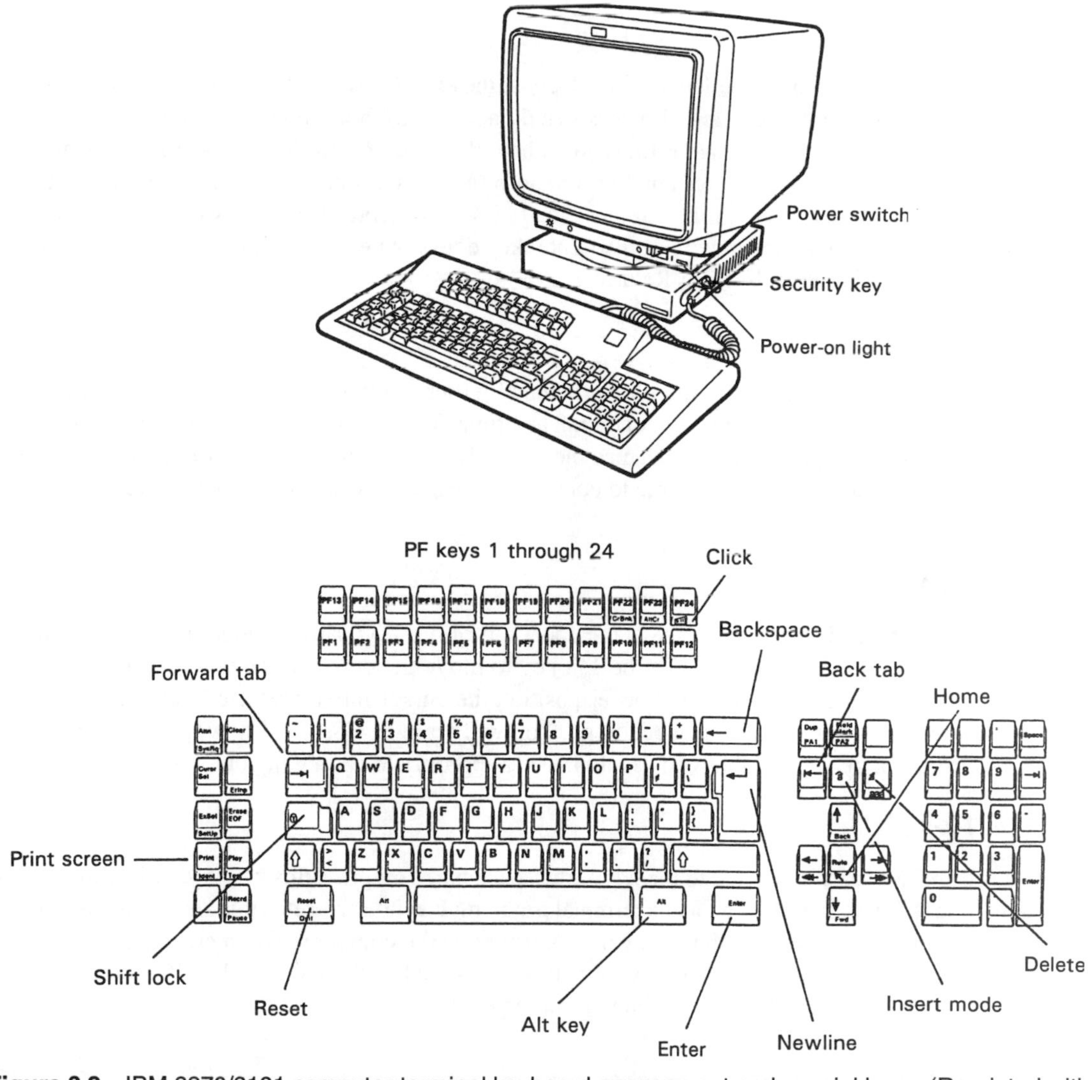
Power switch
Security key
Power-on light
PF keys 1 through 24
Click
Backspace
Forward tab
Back tab
Home
Print screen
Shift lock
Reset
Alt key
Enter
Newline
Insert mode
Delete

Figure 3.2 IBM 3270/3191 computer terminal keyboard arrangement and special keys. (Reprinted with annotations by permission from *IBM 3191 Display Station User's Guide*, Copyright 1987 by International Business Machines Corporation.)

Return or Newline

The Return key is at the right of the letter keys and corresponds to an ASCII terminal "carriage return" key. Return is often labeled with a downward left arrow and can be called the Newline key. It is simply a tab key that moves the cursor down a line and to the left, like an ASCII terminal Linefeed key. Pressing Return on a real 3270 does not signal the mainframe. To the mainframe, the terminal appears completely inactive until you press the Enter key or one of the PF or PA (program attention) keys. On ASCII lab terminals and on PCs emulating terminals there is no handy key to use as the Return key. You might find a Linefeed key, or you can use the Tab key. The Return key on your ASCII terminal or microcomputer keyboard acts like Enter on a 3270 terminal.

Enter

On a real 3270 the Enter key is a small key at the extreme right of the space bar. You don't use Enter to position the cursor. Enter is strictly a signal to the terminal controller and computer that the user of the terminal is finished with work on the screen. In other words, pressing Enter "enters" the data in the terminal into mainframe consideration. On ASCII terminals and on microcomputers emulating terminals, you press the Carriage Return key to generate the Enter signal. Note that the numeric keypad Enter key does not necessarily produce the same result as the typewriter keys Enter or Return!

Arrows

Cursor positioning capabilities are provided by four arrow keys. You can move the cursor up, down, left, and right one row or column at a time. You can intrude on "protected" fields using these keys. If you attempt to change the contents of protected fields, however, your keyboard will lock up (you won't be able to continue entries until you reset the keyboard as described below).

Tab

The Tab key is usually located at the upper left of the keyboard. It moves the cursor from one enterable field to another. Use the Tab key to move the cursor when you use the mainframe. Unlike the arrow keys, it will never position the cursor into a protected field, that is, a field where the cursor is not intended to go. You will learn in Chapter 4 how to make some fields protected on screens that you develop, using appropriate coding in your mapsets.

Reset

The Reset key is located to the left of the space bar. You press this key if your keyboard locks due to invalid entry of data or a terminal problem. Keyboard reset is this key's only use; it does not affect operation of the terminal's controller or the computer. On microcomputers emulating a 3270, the Reset function is sometimes assigned to the Esc key. In CICS programming, you also have a software method to reset the keyboard.

Alt

The Alt key is to the right of the space bar on real 3270 terminals. It operates like the Shift key, except that you use it only in combination with keys on the top row and sides of the keyboard (not with letter keys). Alt makes the top row of keys (number keys) into function keys on a traditional 3270. For example, pressing number 1 while holding Alt down sends a PF1, which is "program function 1." Newer models of the 3270 family have dedicated PF keys, but still carry Alt keys to change the meaning of a few other keys.

PF Keys (F keys)

On modern IBM terminals you'll find either 12 or 24 special function keys called PF or F keys. These keys are like Enter in that they cause the transmission of your accumulated keystrokes. If they all act like Enter, why are they present? Because the mainframe can detect which one you pressed.

Software such as TSO or CICS can recognize the program function key you pressed and take some action based on that. This makes it possible for software to assign functional meanings to PF keys. The TSO/ISPF editor assigns meanings to these keys. Those meanings have no relevance to CICS programs; in CICS, you assign whatever meanings (or no meanings) to PF keys. Program attention (PA) keys are like PF keys, except that while they signal the mainframe, they don't cause any accumulated keystrokes to be transmitted.

The whole set of keys that gain the attention of the host computer are called **Attention Identifier Keys**, or **AID keys**. The Enter, PF, Clear, and PA keys do this. However, only Enter and the PF keys also cause data to be transmitted; Clear and PA keys signal the host computer but do not cause the terminal to transmit data.

Insert and Delete

The insert and delete keys are usually above the arrow keys on a 3270 keyboard. On real 3270s Insert is sometimes marked with an upward pointing caret, the proofreader's "insert" notation. Delete is usually marked with a curly squiggle, a proofreader's pictograph for this action. Insert puts the 3270 terminal into "insert" or "pushright" mode. Delete eliminates a character to the right, with the cursor remaining in the same position. To emulate the Insert key on lab terminals through the IBM 7171 protocol converter, press the decimal point on the numeric keypad. This does not work on microcomputer keyboards. To emulate Insert on a PC emulating a terminal, you may need to press Esc then capital O then lowercase n, that is, Esc On, or the Ins key.

Clear

The Clear key combines important hardware and software functions. As a hardware function it completely clears the screen of any image being displayed and establishes an unformatted screen with no attribute bytes. As a software key, Clear is the universal "I want to end what I'm doing" key in CICS. It signals the mainframe but does not transmit any data. Clear has already cleared the screen by the time CICS detects it. On an ASCII terminal working through the IBM 7171 protocol converter, you press the Enter key on the numeric keypad to signal Clear. On a microcomputer emulating a terminal, you may have to press Esc then capital O then capital M, that is, Esc OM to generate the Clear signal.

Erase EOF

This key causes the rightward contents of the field in which the cursor is positioned to be "erased" and replaced with nulls (low-values). Nulls are not transmitted by the 3270 or CICS.

The cursor position is not changed by Erase EOF. This key provides a convenient way on 3270s to clear out the end of a field in which you want to make an insert. Erase EOF is not conveniently emulated on many PCs and ASCII terminals. Inserts handled through the IBM 7171 protocol converter do not require this field clearing out process.

3.9 PSEUDOCONVERSATION: MINIMIZING THE CPU BOTTLENECK IN SOFTWARE

Much hardware engineering went into the IBM mainframe to enable it to offload work from the CPU and minimize the bottleneck it presents to large-scale interactive processing. The hardware features were developed to facilitate pseudoconversational program operation, which complements the hardware measures. This interactive software technique also has the goal of offloading work from the CPU.

In a fully **conversational interactive program**, the program seeking input from a terminal remains in memory and awaits operator entry. Such a program on a mini- or microcomputer typically uses the ACCEPT verb to receive information from the keyboard. The program is active and executing the ACCEPT verb as the terminal operator enters keystrokes. When you press the Return key, the operating system hands the field over to the program.

In a **pseudoconversational program**, the program seeking input from the terminal is quite dead as the entries are made, and likely not even in memory. The entries made at the terminal are stored up by the terminal and the controller to which it is attached. Only when all entries have been made on the screen and you press Enter or a PF key do the entries go to the mainframe, and only at that time is the appropriate program loaded to memory by CICS and given processing attention.

Pseudoconversation makes program logic much more complex. It is used because of the efficiencies it allows in allocating memory and processing time. Pseudoconversation eliminates almost all use of memory and CPU power during the time that the terminal operator is making entries on the screen. We'll get into the details of pseudoconversational logic structure in Chapter 6, once you have had some hands-on experience with screen image definition and the JCL required to put screen images into the CICS load library.

3.10 FOR YOUR REVIEW

Understanding the following terms, introduced in this chapter, will aid your understanding of the next chapter:

Attention Identifier Keys (AID keys)
3270 terminal
Attribute byte
Channel processor
Clear key
Communication line management
Communication processor
Conversational program
Enter key
EXCP
Front end
Multiplexing
Network Control Program (NCP)
PF program function keys
Protocol converter
Pseudoconversational program
Tab key
Terminal buffering
Terminal controller
Virtual Telecommunications Access Method (VTAM)

3.11 REVIEW QUESTIONS

1. Identify and describe the three ways that IBM electronics engineers minimized the processing bottleneck associated with interactive programming from a hardware perspective.
2. Describe how IBM electronics engineers minimized data transmission requirements of interactive processing, to make this processing as responsive as possible.
3. Discuss why IBM's 3270 terminals provide both a Carriage Return key and an Enter key, while ASCII terminals provide only a Carriage Return key.
4. Identify and describe the role of the Clear key on IBM's 3270 terminals, in connection with CICS programming.
5. Briefly describe the software technique of pseudoconversation, and how IBM's software engineers used it to minimize the processing demands of interactive programming.

4

Coding Screens Using Basic Mapping Support (BMS)

Under CICS, the code defining the appearance of a screen is called a **map**, and is separate from the logic of the program using the screen. In this chapter we'll show you how to create screen maps using the facilities of the CICS Basic Mapping Support (BMS) subsystem. We'll also review how to use TSO/ISPF to code the screen image. Finally, we'll demonstrate a PC-based product named GENMAP, which is an inexpensive yet capable screen painter that you can use to build CICS screens much more rapidly than by hand coding them.

4.1 BASIC MAPPING SUPPORT SUBSYSTEM

CICS provides a subsystem known as **Basic Mapping Support**, or **BMS**. BMS deals with computer terminals and "packages" the data transmissions to and from a terminal as shown in Figure 4.1. In a nutshell, your CICS program actually "sees" only a record, called the **data transmission record**, when it "talks" to a terminal. BMS handles the details of terminal communication, freeing your program from most terminal-specific concerns. To send something to a terminal, your program puts the information into the data transmission record, and asks CICS to send it to the terminal. To receive data from a terminal, your program asks CICS to receive a transmission from it, and BMS packages the received data into a data transmission record, which it hands over to your program.

BMS makes it possible for you to define the screen appearance apart from program logic. Because of this, a CICS program "knows" only about the contents of screen fields, not their locations on the screen. As Figure 4.1 illustrates, BMS combines these stored screen definitions and your data when you send information to a terminal screen.

The best way to learn how Basic Mapping Support works is to actually try out a simple screen and program. We'll help you do precisely that. The screen you create here will be used in a program named CALC1, which we'll present in Chapter 6.

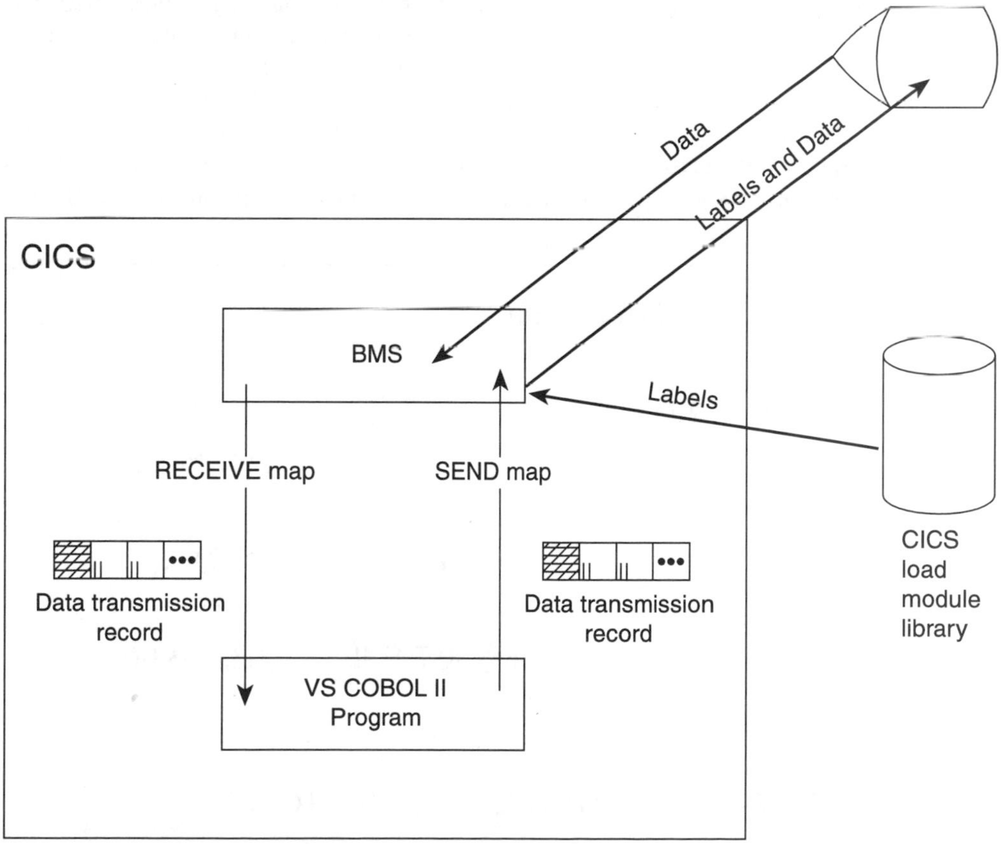

Data
Labels and Data
CICS
BMS
Labels
RECEIVE map
SEND map
Data transmission record
Data transmission record
VS COBOL II Program
CICS load module library

Figure 4.1 The CICS Basic Mapping support subsystem handles communication between CICS programs and terminals.

4.2 A SIMPLE CICS PROGRAMMING REQUIREMENT

Figure 4.2 shows a sketch for a screen to be used by a simple CICS program named CALC1. This program prompts the terminal user to enter two values, representing the quantity of an item purchased, and the unit price (price each) for this item. When this data has been entered, the program multiplies the two values to compute the total (extended) price, computes 8% sales tax on the total, and then computes the grand total price as the sum of the total and sales tax.

In Figure 4.2 we have distinguished **screen labels** from data fields. You can also see a special line at the bottom of the screen called the **prompt**. Screen labels simply inform the terminal user of the item of data in each screen field, while the prompt line is used by the program to tell the terminal user what action to take next or to point out errors in entered data.

Let's proceed to formalize the design for the CALC1 screen, which also determines the format of the data transmission record used to communicate with it. In Chapter 6 we'll develop the program logic to drive this screen.

4.3 DESIGNING A CICS SCREEN

When you develop screens for use by CICS programs, you must first decide where to place fields on the screen, just as you do on reporting documents. The standard 3270 computer terminal screen size is 24 rows, each with 80 columns. This gives 1,920 screen positions. (Microcomputers have 25 lines per screen, but when a microcomputer is used to emulate a terminal, the extra line at the bottom is not used by CICS.)

Designing a screen usually involves trying out different locations for fields and field labels, working toward a visually pleasing and readable screen appearance. Figure 4.3 shows how we did this for the CALC1 screen. We have included a label at the top of the screen so that you can put your own name into the screen as you develop your first CICS screen.

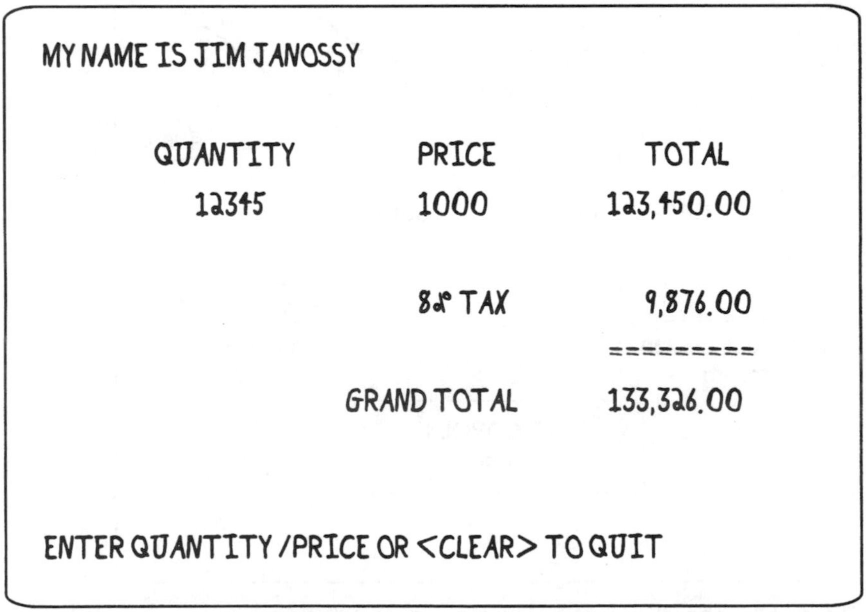
MY NAME IS JIM JANOSSY
QUANTITY
PRICE
TOTAL
12345
1000
123,450.00
8% TAX
9,876.00
=========
GRAND TOTAL
133,326.00
ENTER QUANTITY/PRICE OR <CLEAR> TO QUIT

Figure 4.2 Sketch of the screen to be used by the CALC1 program.

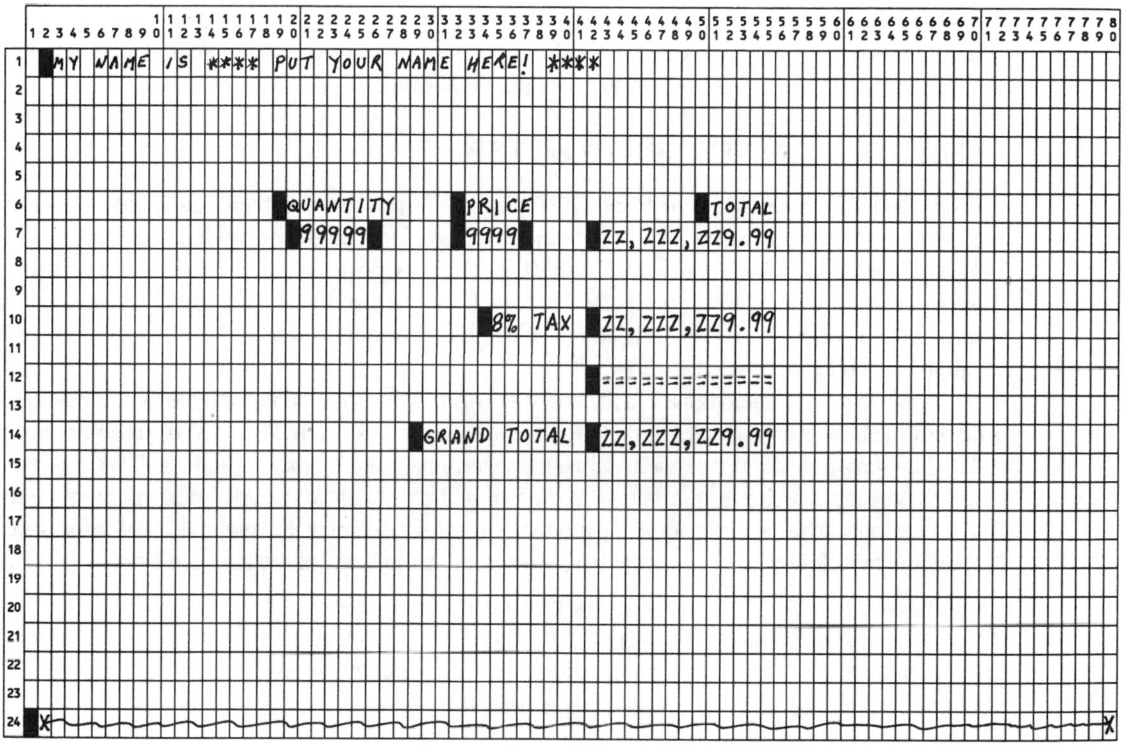
MY NAME IS **** PUT YOUR NAME HERE! ****
QUANTITY
PRICE
TOTAL
99999
9999
ZZ,ZZZ,ZZ9.99
8% TAX
ZZ,ZZZ,ZZ9.99
GRAND TOTAL
ZZ,ZZZ,ZZ9.99
X
X

Figure 4.3 Sketch of the screen to be used by the CALC1 program.

In designing CICS screens, you should follow some of the same rules that guide good technical writing:

- Always use the same word or abbreviation to mean the same thing; for example, don't create synonyms and refer to a customer number as CUST NUMBER in one place and as CUST NUM in another place.
- Don't use the same word or abbreviation to mean more than one thing. For example, don't refer to the extended price as TOTAL and the cost including sales tax as TOTAL.

In addition, minimize or eliminate the use of periods at the end of abbreviations on screens, and don't use colons at the end of field labels to imply "put something here." Periods and colons at the end of screen labels usually clutter a screen and consume screen positions that may be needed for other data fields. As with accounting documents, align decimal points in columns of numbers so that values can quickly be seen in correct proportion to one another.

You'll notice that each of the fields to be presented on the CALC1 screen in Figure 4.3 has, in front of it, a shaded box. Each of the shaded boxes is an **attribute byte**. Every field on a CICS screen must be prefaced by an attribute byte, which houses information about the intensity and permitted access to the field that follows. Fields in which the terminal user will make an entry also end with specially coded attribute bytes. Your design for each CICS screen has to take the positions of the necessary attribute bytes into account.

You can use a paper grid form or a word processor to design CICS screens, or a screen painter such as GENMAP, which is described at the end of this chapter. Once you have designed a screen using a paper grid form or word processor, you have to code the appropriate statements to define the screen to CICS. You process this coding to generate machine language that is stored in the CICS load library as a **physical map**.

4.4 THE ROLE OF ATTRIBUTE BYTES

When IBM engineers designed the 3270 terminal family, one of their major goals was the minimization of data transmission. To achieve this goal, the engineers included circuitry in the 3270 to make dual use of every one of the 1,920 display positions on the screen. Each display position can either be used to display data, or it can be used to control the treatment of the screen field following it. When used to control the treatment of the field following, a byte is called an **attribute byte**.

When a screen field is used in the ordinary way (to display data) its attribute byte can be set to display the field at normal intensity (NORM) or at bright intensity (BRT). It is also possible to house data in a screen field but make it invisible to the terminal user, by making it dark (DRK). When a screen position is used as an attribute byte, the terminal always makes it dark. You can't see anything in an attribute byte, but it is not available for data entry or display. Several pieces of information about the field following an attribute byte are housed in the 8 bits of the attribute byte:

Field intensity	NORM, BRT, or DRK
Field protection	UNPROT or PROT
Field "shift"	unstated (alphanumeric) or NUMeric
Modified data tag	unstated or set (FSET)

The **modified data tag** (**MDT**) is simply a one-bit switch. It assumes one value when data is sent by the program to the screen, but it is changed to a different value if the terminal user moves the cursor to the screen field and changes anything. When the terminal transmits data to the program, it sends only those fields in which the attribute byte's modified data tag is set to indicate "changed." This allows the terminal to prevent transmission of fields that have not been changed by the terminal user. Coding FSET in the ATTRB specification, as we discuss in section 4.8, forces the modified data tag to be set on continuously, so that the field is always transmitted from the terminal to the program. (We'll discuss the modified data tag and FSET usage much more in Chapter 7.)

Some newer 3270 terminals with color screens provide additional circuitry and store more information in attribute bytes about colors and special features such as underlining, reverse video, and blinking. For our purposes we will consider only the most basic attribute byte coding, which works on all 3270 terminals and microcomputers emulating 3270 terminals.

4.5 BMS MAP SOURCE CODE

Figure 4.4 shows you the complete BMS map for our CALC1 screen. The language represented here is actually IBM assembler, which is very fussy language indeed. This language was designed for use with punch cards, and is therefore highly column dependent rather than free-form. We have included a column ruler at the top of this coding so that you can readily see where each item of coding starts.

Here are seven general rules for BMS map coding:

1. An asterisk in column 1 makes a line into a comment.
2. A coded action or command begins in column 10.

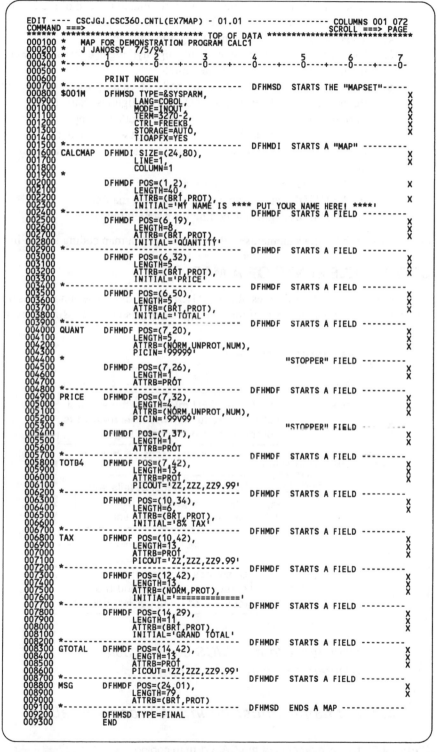

```
EDIT ---- CSCJGJ.CSC360.CNTL(EX7MAP) - 01.01 ---------------- COLUMNS 001 072
COMMAND ===>                                                  SCROLL ===> PAGE
****** ****************************** TOP OF DATA ******************************
*     MAP FOR DEMONSTRATION PROGRAM CALC1
*     J JANOSSY  7/5/94
*         1         2         3         4         5         6         7
*---+----0----+----0----+----0----+----0----+----0----+----0----+----0-
*
         PRINT NOGEN
*------------------------------------ DFHMSD  STARTS THE "MAPSET"-----
$001M    DFHMSD TYPE=&SYSPARM,                                         X
               LANG=COBOL,                                             X
               MODE=INOUT,                                             X
               TERM=3270-2,                                            X
               CTRL=FREEKB,                                            X
               STORAGE=AUTO,                                           X
               TIOAPFX=YES
*------------------------------------ DFHMDI  STARTS A "MAP" ---------
CALCMAP  DFHMDI SIZE=(24,80),                                          X
               LINE=1,                                                 X
               COLUMN=1
*
         DFHMDF POS=(1,2),                                             X
               LENGTH=40,                                              X
               ATTRB=(BRT,PROT),
               INITIAL='MY NAME IS **** PUT YOUR NAME HERE! ****'
*------------------------------------ DFHMDF  STARTS A FIELD ---------
         DFHMDF POS=(6,19),                                            X
               LENGTH=8,                                               X
               ATTRB=(BRT,PROT),                                       X
               INITIAL='QUANTITY'
*------------------------------------ DFHMDF  STARTS A FIELD ---------
         DFHMDF POS=(6,32),                                            X
               LENGTH=5,                                               X
               ATTRB=(BRT,PROT),                                       X
               INITIAL='PRICE'
*------------------------------------ DFHMDF  STARTS A FIELD ---------
         DFHMDF POS=(6,50),                                            X
               LENGTH=5,                                               X
               ATTRB=(BRT,PROT),                                       X
               INITIAL='TOTAL'
*------------------------------------ DFHMDF  STARTS A FIELD ---------
QUANT    DFHMDF POS=(7,20),                                            X
               LENGTH=5,                                               X
               ATTRB=(NORM,UNPROT,NUM),                                X
               PICIN='99999'
*                                             "STOPPER" FIELD ---------
         DFHMDF POS=(7,26),                                            X
               LENGTH=1,                                               X
               ATTRB=PROT
*------------------------------------ DFHMDF  STARTS A FIELD ---------
PRICE    DFHMDF POS=(7,32),                                            X
               LENGTH=4,                                               X
               ATTRB=(NORM,UNPROT,NUM),                                X
               PICIN='99V99'
*                                             "STOPPER" FIELD ---------
         DFHMDF POS=(7,37),                                            X
               LENGTH=1,                                               X
               ATTRB=PROT
*------------------------------------ DFHMDF  STARTS A FIELD ---------
TOTB4    DFHMDF POS=(7,42),                                            X
               LENGTH=13,                                              X
               ATTRB=PROT,                                             X
               PICOUT='ZZ,ZZZ,ZZ9.99'
*------------------------------------ DFHMDF  STARTS A FIELD ---------
         DFHMDF POS=(10,34),                                           X
               LENGTH=6,                                               X
               ATTRB=(BRT,PROT),
               INITIAL='8% TAX'
*------------------------------------ DFHMDF  STARTS A FIELD ---------
TAX      DFHMDF POS=(10,42),                                           X
               LENGTH=13,                                              X
               ATTRB=PROT,                                             X
               PICOUT='ZZ,ZZZ,ZZ9.99'
*------------------------------------ DFHMDF  STARTS A FIELD ---------
         DFHMDF POS=(12,42),                                           X
               LENGTH=13,                                              X
               ATTRB=(NORM,PROT),                                      X
               INITIAL='============='
*------------------------------------ DFHMDF  STARTS A FIELD ---------
         DFHMDF POS=(14,29),                                           X
               LENGTH=11,                                              X
               ATTRB=(BRT,PROT),                                       X
               INITIAL='GRAND TOTAL'
*------------------------------------ DFHMDF  STARTS A FIELD ---------
GTOTAL   DFHMDF POS=(14,42),                                           X
               LENGTH=13,                                              X
               ATTRB=PROT,                                             X
               PICOUT='ZZ,ZZZ,ZZ9.99'
*------------------------------------ DFHMDF  STARTS A FIELD ---------
MSG      DFHMDF POS=(24,01),                                           X
               LENGTH=79,                                              X
               ATTRB=(BRT,PROT)
*------------------------------------ DFHMSD  ENDS A MAP ------------
         DFHMSD TYPE=FINAL
         END
```

Figure 4.4 Complete BMS map coding for the CALC1 screen.

3. Lines that are continued must have a comma at the end of the coding, *and* a non-blank character in position 72.
4. The continuation of a line must begin in column 16.
5. Even a comment line must avoid having anything in column 72 besides a space, or it will be regarded as a continued line!
6. You can't code spaces within the body of coding; for example, you must code things such as ATTRB=(BRT,PROT) as contiguous characters.
7. Various parts of BMS map coding rely on rather strange looking words that you can regard as "commands." These words start with the letters DFH and are actually macro instructions to the software that processes a map. These macro instructions are:
   a. **DFHMSD** begins and ends mapset coding
   b. **DFHMDI** begins map coding within the mapset
   c. **DFHMDF** begins the coding for a screen field

Let's consider the various elements of the CALC1 screen map coding shown in Figure 4.4.

4.6 GLOBAL ELEMENTS OF A MAP

Figure 4.5 depicts the first 18 lines of our CALC1 map coding. The annotations on this illustration describe what this first part of map coding accomplishes. These first lines of map coding

```
*    MAP FOR DEMONSTRATION PROGRAM CALC1
*    J JANOSSY  7/5/94
*           1         2         3         4         5         6         7
*---+----0----+----0----+----0----+----0----+----0----+----0----+----0-
*
          PRINT NOGEN
*
*
*
*
*------------------------------------ DFHMSD  STARTS THE "MAPSET"-----
$001M     DFHMSD TYPE=&SYSPARM,                                        X
               LANG=COBOL,                                             X
               MODE=INOUT,                                             X
               TERM=3270-2,                                            X
               CTRL=FREEKB,                                            X
               STORAGE=AUTO,                                           X
               TIOAPFX=YES
*
*------------------------------------ DFHMDI  STARTS A "MAP" ---------
*
CALCMAP   DFHMDI SIZE=(24,80),                                         X
               LINE=1,                                                 X
               COLUMN=1
```

PRINT NOGEN minimizes the amount of print produced when the mapset is processed into machine language

Describes global details such as the language of the programs using this screen

Describes the size of the screen coded here, and the location of its upper left corner

***Map name** (not in CICS control table; programmer can make it up)*

***Mapset name** (must be in CICS control table)*

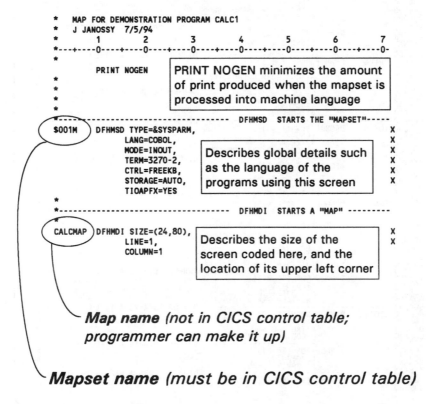

Figure 4.5 Global elements of the CALC1 map coding

are almost always identical in all maps in a given installation. We show here the coding relevant to CICS programming in VS COBOL II.

You see two names associated with the map in Figure 4.5. The first of these, $001, is referred to as the **mapset name**. The second of these, coded here as CALCMAP, is the **map name**. Why are two names necessary for map coding?

IBM's original scheme for map coding allows you to house more than one screen definition in a set of coding. Our $001M mapset could, for example, house more than just the CALCMAP screen. Modern practice, however, is to code just one screen image in each mapset. Therefore, it appears here that the dual names are redundant, simply because we now make no use of the multiple-maps-in-one-mapset feature.

More importantly, you need to understand that the mapset name is the name that CICS must be able to find in its control tables. In order for our map to be accessible to CICS, its mapset name $001M must be entered into the CICS control tables. Once this is done, the one (or more) maps coded within the mapset are accessible by their individual map names, such as CALCMAP. Map names, like CALCMAP, are not defined in CICS control tables. But you must use both names in the CICS command that accesses this map.

4.7 THE BMS MAP FIELD CODING PATTERN

If you examine lines 002000 and beyond in the CALC1 screen map in Figure 4.4, you will see what appears to be a complex collection of dozens of lines of coding. It helps for you to understand the pattern of these lines of coding. In any screen map, there are basically four types of screen field coding, all of which begin with the DFHMDF "field definition" macro instruction:

- Coding for a literal field, called **screen labels**
- Coding for enterable numeric fields
- Coding for enterable alphanumeric fields
- Coding for screen fields that contain only program-supplied data, which the cursor is not allowed to enter

Screen fields must be coded in a map in a top-to-bottom, left-to-right sequence. That is, we have to start at the top of a screen design such as that shown in Figure 4.3, and code each field appearing on the screen in ascending sequence of line number and column. Every field definition begins with DFHMDF, which is the name of an IBM assembler macro instruction. Every screen field definition is a separate block of coding, in which lines are continued until the definition is complete.

4.8 MAP CODING FOR A LITERAL (SCREEN LABEL) FIELD

Figure 4.6 is a portion of coding from the CALC1 map that we have extracted and annotated. This coding defines the screen label for the word QUANTITY that appears on line 6 of the CALC1 screen. Read the annotations on this illustration for important information about screen label coding.

The most distinctive thing about a screen label is that it will not change during the use of the screen by a program. As a convention, we encode screen labels as ATTRB=(BRT,PROT) for "bright, protected" in the CALC1 program. **BRT** will make the label appear at higher intensity than normal. **PROT** makes the field protected, preventing the terminal user from putting the cursor into the screen label field and changing it.

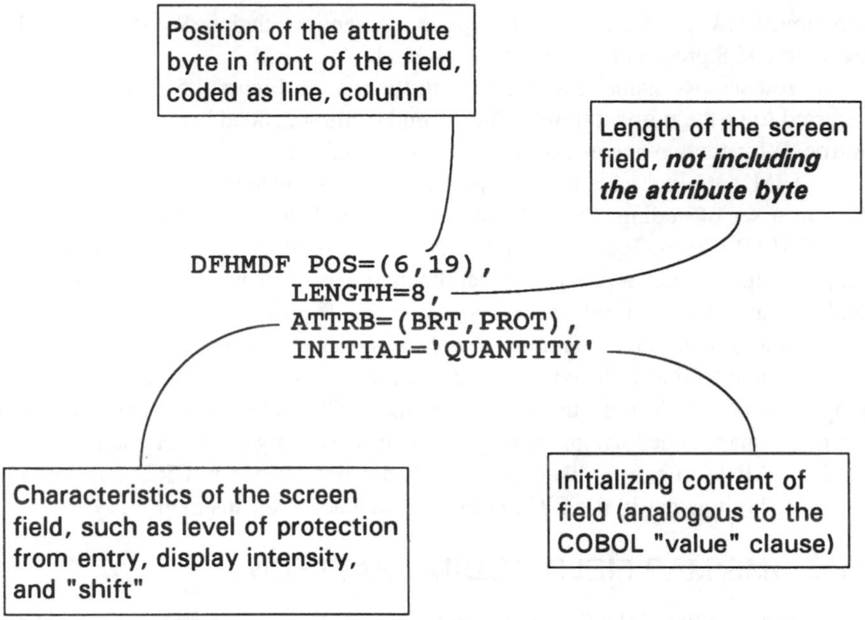
Position of the attribute byte in front of the field, coded as line, column
Length of the screen field, *not including the attribute byte*
DFHMDF POS=(6,19),
LENGTH=8,
ATTRB=(BRT,PROT),
INITIAL='QUANTITY'
Characteristics of the screen field, such as level of protection from entry, display intensity, and "shift"
Initializing content of field (analogous to the COBOL "value" clause)

Figure 4.6 Map coding for a screen label.

4.9 SCREEN FIELD ATTRIBUTES

You can see from Figure 4.6 that a significant part of your coding for screen fields within a BMS map deals with expressing your choice for the display **intensity** and treatment of the field, using the **ATTRB** (attribute) specification. Figure 4.7 provides a reference for the various choices you have for ATTRB coding.

While Figure 4.7 may give you the impression that a wide variety of combinations of ATTRB coding are possible, only a few combinations are actually useful. Here is a list of these combinations:

ATTRB=(BRT,PROT)	screen labels
ATTRB=(NORM,UNPROT,NUM)	enterable numeric fields
ATTRB=(NORM,UNPROT)	enterable alphanumeric fields
ATTRB=(DRK,PROT)	stopper fields

Stopper fields can also be coded as ATTRB=PROT since they will be dark on the screen in any case.

4.10 MAP CODING FOR AN ENTERABLE NUMERIC FIELD

An **enterable numeric field** is a field in which you intend the terminal user to be able to put the cursor and enter the symbols 0, 1, 2, 3, 4, 5, 6, 7, 8, or 9. Unlike a screen label, an enterable field must be accessible to the program using the screen. For this reason, you must code a name on the map coding definition of an enterable field. *But do not code names on screen field definitions just for "documentation" or information. Coding a name on a field makes it a part of the data transmission record.*

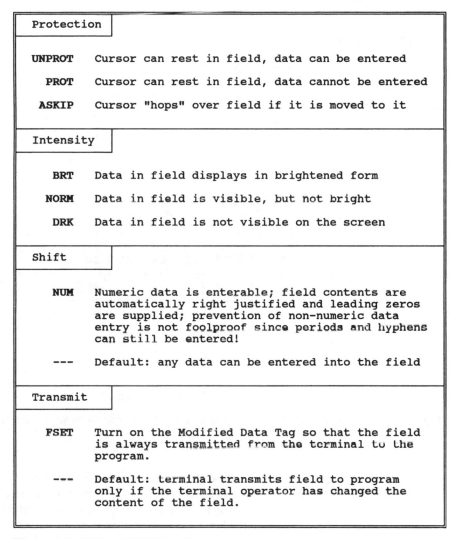

Protection	
UNPROT	Cursor can rest in field, data can be entered
PROT	Cursor can rest in field, data cannot be entered
ASKIP	Cursor "hops" over field if it is moved to it
Intensity	
BRT	Data in field displays in brightened form
NORM	Data in field is visible, but not bright
DRK	Data in field is not visible on the screen
Shift	
NUM	Numeric data is enterable; field contents are automatically right justified and leading zeros are supplied; prevention of non-numeric data entry is not foolproof since periods and hyphens can still be entered!
---	Default: any data can be entered into the field
Transmit	
FSET	Turn on the Modified Data Tag so that the field is always transmitted from the terminal to the program.
---	Default: terminal transmits field to program only if the terminal operator has changed the content of the field.

Figure 4.7 Table of ATTRB coding choices for screen fields.

Line 004000 of the BMS map coding for the CALC1 screen shown in Figure 4.4 begins the coding for the quantity field, which is intended for terminal user entry of a five-digit number. Figure 4.8 breaks out the coding at lines 004000 through 004700 so that we can examine them more closely. You can see that we have begun this field definition with the name QUANT.

Examine the lower part of Figure 4.8 and you will see a portion of the screen design for line 7, with column positions indicated. Note that the POS (position) coding for the quantity field is coded as 7,20 for line 7, column 20. This is the position of the attribute byte before the field, not the first displayed or enterable part of the field. The length of the field is coded as 5, since a five-digit number will be housed here. The length is not coded as 6, because the length does not include the attribute byte.

Notice also in Figure 4.8 that a second field, the **stopper field**, is defined immediately

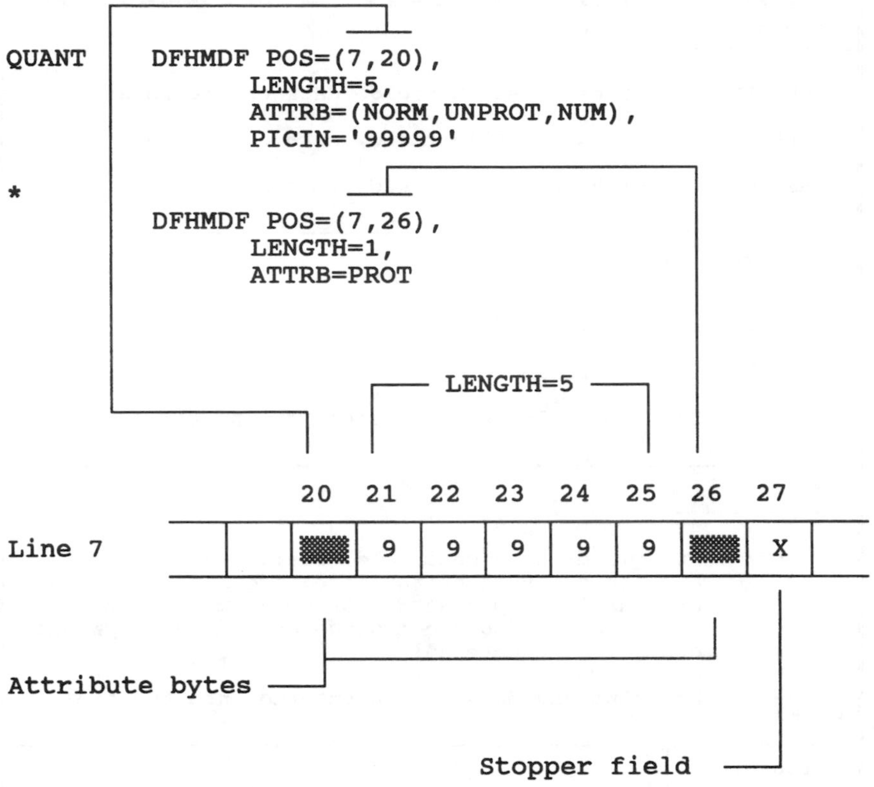
QUANT
DFHMDF POS=(7,20),
LENGTH=5,
ATTRB=(NORM,UNPROT,NUM),
PICIN='99999'
*
DFHMDF POS=(7,26),
LENGTH=1,
ATTRB=PROT
LENGTH=5
20 21 22 23 24 25 26 27
Line 7
9 9 9 9 9 X
Attribute bytes
Stopper field

Figure 4.8 How map coding for an enterable numeric field relates to the screen design.

after the quantity field. As the annotations on Figure 4.9 indicate, this stopper field arrests the cursor in position 7,27 if the terminal user completely fills the quantity field and continues to enter keystrokes. A stopper field is actually nothing more than a single-byte, PROT or ASKIP screen field, coded after an enterable field. At the cost of two screen positions, it forms a barrier that either prevents the cursor from moving beyond the end of an enterable field or skips it to the next enterable field. *You define stopper fields only after enterable fields, to prevent the terminal user from fouling up the screen with undesirable cursor movement and entries.*

4.11 MAP CODING FOR AN ENTERABLE ALPHANUMERIC FIELD

Our CALC1 screen design does not contain any **enterable alphanumeric field**, but Figure 4.10 illustrates how to handle such a field. We have named this field CNAME, for "customer name." In most respects, the coding for this enterable alphanumeric field is the same as for an enterable numeric field, except that the specification NUM is not used as a part of ATTRB attribute coding. When you don't specify NUM, the default—no numeric input filtering and processing—takes effect.

You will also notice in Figure 4.10 that the **PICIN** specification accurately depicts the intended PIC for field in COBOL terms. The PICIN for the quantity field was coded as PICIN='9(5)', while here it is coded PICIN='X(28)'. As we will describe in Chapter 5, PICIN

This attribute coding makes the screen field appear at normal intensity (**NORM**), and allows the cursor to enter the field (**UNPROT**) to change field contents. **NUM** requests the terminal to disallow entry of most nonnumeric symbols in the field, and causes BMS to right justify the field and supply leading zeros when it is given to the program in the data transmission record.

Putting a name onto a field in the map causes it to be made a part of the data transmission record. Names can be up to seven characters long, and can be composed of letters and numbers. The first position must be a letter.

```
QUANT    DFHMDF POS=(7,20),
               LENGTH=5,
               ATTRB=(NORM,UNPROT,NUM),
               PICIN='99999'
*
         DFHMDF POS=(7,26),
               LENGTH=1,
               ATTRB=PROT
```

You need to code a stopper field immediately after any enterable screen field. A **PROT** stopper field prevents the cursor from going beyond the end of the enterable field by causing it to get "stuck" in a one-byte protected field. If you code the stopper as **ATTRB = ASKIP** the cursor will automatically skip to the next enterable field when it enters the stopper field. Every stopper field requires a minimum of two bytes on the screen (one byte for the attribute, and one byte for the actual stopper field).

Figure 4.9 Map coding for an enterable numeric field.

(and PICOUT) coding does not really affect the screen at all, but is used by the screen processing software to produce a description of the field in the data transmission record. If you choose to code your own COBOL description of the data transmission record, you can omit PICIN and PICOUT coding from your map field definitions.

4.12 MAP CODING FOR AN OUTPUT SCREEN FIELD

The only remaining category of screen field that you have to consider is properly termed an **output screen field**. There are four such fields on the CALC1 screen. If you refer back

The coding for an enterable alphanumeric field is similar to the coding for an enterable numeric field, except that you omit NUM in the ATTRB specification.

PICIN and **PICOUT** specifications are required only if you plan on using a machine-generated symbolic map (description of the data transmission record). PICIN and PICOUT cause no harm even if you use a manually coded symbolic map.

```
CNAME     DFHMDF POS=(14,31),
                 LENGTH=28,
                 ATTRB=(NORM,UNPROT),
                 PICIN='X(28)'
*
                 DFHMDF POS=(14,59),
                 LENGTH=1,
                 ATTRB=PROT
```

?

If you don't code PICIN or PICOUT specifications, PIC X for the length of the field is assumed in a machine-generated symbolic map.

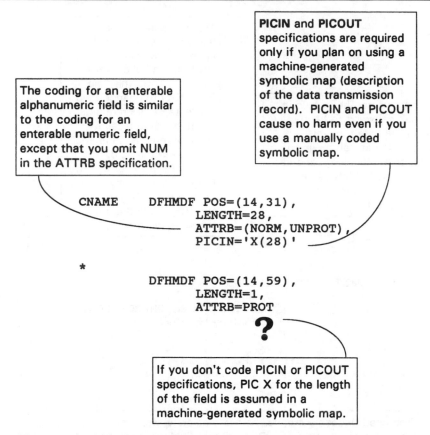

Figure 4.10 Map coding for an enterable alphanumeric field.

to Figure 4.3, you can see that these fields are the ones computed or filled in by the program itself:

```
Total
8% tax
Grand total
Prompt
```

The terminal user has no business putting the cursor into these fields, but the program must be able to put values and information here. If you examine Figure 4.11, you'll see that we meet these requirements by making output screen fields accessible to the program by giving each a name, but we prevent terminal user access by coding these fields as protected (PROT). PROT only prevents terminal user cursor access; it does not limit program access to the field.

PICOUT provides a picture that the program can use in putting data into an output screen field. Figure 4.11 shows PICOUT='ZZ,ZZZ,ZZ9.99' so that this PIC will be used in a machine-generated description of the data transmission record. If you choose to code your own description of the data transmission record, you can omit coding PICOUT for output fields.

Coding a name on a screen field makes it a part of the data transmission record, so the program can access it.

The screen field coded here is intended for output, that is, the program using this screen will put data here. The terminal user, however, will *not* be allowed to put the cursor here and change the field value. **ATTRB=PROT** prevents the terminal user from accessing the field, *but allows the program to access it.*

```
TOTB4       DFHMDF POS=(7,42),
                   LENGTH=13,
                   ATTRB=PROT,
                   PICOUT='ZZ,ZZZ,ZZ9.99'
```

The **PICOUT** coded here will put this numeric formatted PIC into the machine-generated symbolic map, so that it appears in the description of the data transmission record. If you code your own description of this record you can omit coding PICOUT here.

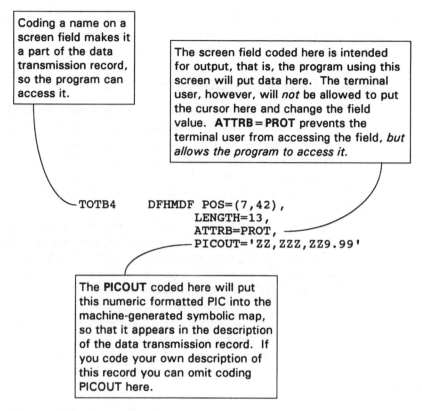

Figure 4.11 Map coding for an output screen field.

4.13 USING TSO/ISPF TO CREATE A SCREEN MAP

Once you have designed the placement of fields on a screen, as shown in our design for the CALC1 screen in Figure 4.3, you must compose the actual BMS map in machine-readable form. Most programmers accomplish this using TSO/ISPF, the programmer's workbench and text editor of the MVS/ESA mainframe environment.

To begin the process of map encoding, create a member within your job control language (CNTL) library, or within a library that you have created specifically to house map code. Since map code begins in column 1, you cannot conveniently use a COBOL library to house maps (TSO/ISPF automatically inserts six-digit line numbers in columns 1 through 6 of members in a COBOL library). The TSO/ISPF main menu selection 2 provides access to the text editor that you can use to compose BMS map code.

You will find that it is much more productive to begin a new map by copying the map code for an existing screen and modifying it, rather than trying to enter each new map "fresh." When you copy and modify, you gain from the indentation pattern already established. In addition, you can continue to use the comments in an existing map to delimit the start of fields, and the old code serves as a guide.

In order to make your acclimation to CICS and MAP coding quicker and smoother, we have provided machine-readable source code for all of the maps and programs in this book on an optional diskette. Appendix F describes how you can obtain a copy of the diskette at nominal cost. You can upload the items on that diskette to your mainframe and use the CALC1 map as a basis for coding your own maps, to gain a head start.

4.14 JCL FOR CHECKING MAP CODING SYNTAX

Figure 4.12 illustrates the MVS/ESA job control language to invoke the IBM assembler, IEV90, to read and syntax check your BMS map code. The assembler is controlled by an external parameter named SYSPARM, which is set by the coding at line 20 in this job control language. When SYSPARM is given the value MAP, the assembler regards the input as a BMS map and attempts to process it into an object file. The assembler's reporting output conveys a listing of the BMS map code it has processed, and includes messages documenting any syntax errors it has located.

You can key enter the job control language shown in Figure 4.12 and adjust it to serve your purposes in checking your BMS map coding. To do this, you have to modify the JOB statement to suit your local job naming conventions. You might also have to adjust the data set names at various places in the JCL to conform to your local naming conventions. The JCL in Figure 4.12 makes use of an MVS/ESA Version 4 feature (the SET statement). If your installation still uses an earlier version of MVS/ESA, you have to eliminate the symbolic parameters for library and member name at line 23, and perhaps hard code these values in your JCL.

Alternatively, you can use an existing cataloged procedure in your installation to process your BMS map code. A common cataloged procedure for map processing is named DFHMAPS. This IBM-standard proc, or a locally customized version of it, is usually found in any installation using CICS.

4.15 RESULT OF A BMS MAP SYNTAX CHECKING RUN

Figure 4.13 provides a complete listing produced by our submission of the job control language shown in Figure 4.12, the CHECKMAP job stream. You can see by examining the second page of this illustration that the assembler has issued a COND CODE of 0008 for the map processed. To make this run, we intentionally introduced an error into the EX7MAP coding shown in Figure 4.3: We eliminated the closing parenthesis at the ATTRB specification on line 002700. Page 3 of this figure shows how the assembler reports this error. The error is also noted at the end of the listing, which indicates that one statement was flagged in the assembly.

As a learning technique, consider taking a correct BMS map and make various types of errors in it to see how the assembler reports them. The error messages are, in some cases, not very friendly. You will benefit from seeing how controlled errors are reported before trying to deal with "real" errors which are all too easy to introduce in BMS map coding!

4.16 INTRODUCING THE GENMAP SCREEN PAINTER

GENMAP is a PC-based screen painter that allows you to place fields on a screen, indicate the attributes you desire them to have, and automatically build BMS map code and a COBOL description for the data transmission record matching the screen. GENMAP was developed by Gary Weinstein of DePaul University and is available on diskette for a one-time nominal charge as described in Appendix F. We demonstrate GENMAP here since it is typical of CICS

```
EDIT ---- CSCJGJ.CSC360.CNTL(CHECKMAP) - 01.02 --------------- COLUMNS 001 072
COMMAND ===>                                                  SCROLL ===> PAGE
****** ******************************* TOP OF DATA ******************************
//CSCJGJA    JOB 1,                     ACCOUNTING INFORMATION
//   'BIN 7--JANOSSY',                  PROGRAMMER NAME AND DELIVERY BIN
//   CLASS=A,                           INPUT QUEUE CLASS
//   MSGLEVEL=(1,1),                    HOW MUCH MVS SYSTEM PRINT DESIRED
//   MSGCLASS=X,                        PRINT DESTINATION X A L N OR O
//   TIME=(0,6),                        SAFETY LIMIT: RUN TIME UP TO 6 SECS
//   REGION=2M,                         ALLOW UP TO 2 MEGS VIRTUAL MEMORY
//*  TYPRUN=SCAN,                       UNCOMMENT THIS LINE TO DO SCAN ONLY
//   NOTIFY=CSCJGJ                      WHO TO TELL WHEN JOB IS DONE
//*-----------------------------------------------------------------
//*   CHECK YOUR BMS MAP CODING FOR SYNTAX ERRORS
//*   THIS JCL IS STORED AT CSCJGJ.CSC360.CNTL(CHECKMAP)
//*-----------------------------------------------------------------
//*
//   SET  LIBRARY='CSCJGJ.CSC360.CNTL',   LIBRARY HOUSING MAP CODE
//        MEMBER='EX7MAPX'                MEMBER NAME OF MAP CODE
//*
//STEP010  EXEC  PGM=IEV90,
//   REGION=2M,
//   PARM=('SYSPARM(MAP)',               PRODUCE A PHYSICAL MAP
//         'DECK',
//         'NOLOAD')
//SYSIN      DD  DSN=&LIBRARY(&MEMBER),          MAP SOURCE CODE IN
//   DISP=SHR
//SYSLIB     DD  DSN=CICS330.SDFHMAC,DISP=SHR    SYSTEM LIBRARY
//           DD  DSN=SYS1.MACLIB,DISP=SHR        SYSTEM LIBRARY
//SYSUT1     DD  UNIT=VIO,SPACE=(CYL,(5,5))      WORK FILE
//SYSUT2     DD  UNIT=VIO,SPACE=(CYL,(5,5))      WORK FILE
//SYSUT3     DD  UNIT=VIO,SPACE=(CYL,(5,5))      WORK FILE
//SYSPRINT   DD  SYSOUT=*                        SOURCE CODE LISTING
//SYSPUNCH   DD  DUMMY                           OBJECT FILE OUT
//
```

This job stream executes the IBM assembler, a program named IEV90, and gives it the appropriate parameter (PARM) value, MAP, to cause it to process BMS map coding defining a screen for a CICS program. The BMS map code enters the assembler at the ddname //SYSIN. The listing of the map code, carrying error messages if the map code is flawed, is produced at //SYSPRINT. Other job streams we'll show you later in this book use JCL similar to this but actually send the machine-readable output produced at //SYSPUNCH into further processing to turn it into a physical map stored in the CICS load library. Your installation provides a cataloged procedure, which may be named DFHMAPS, to accomplish this process. The library names coded at //SYSLIB may be installation-specific.

Figure 4.12 The CHECKMAP job stream, which invokes the IBM assembler to perform a syntax check on your BMS map coding.

screen painters in general, and is so reasonably priced that it is available to all. Figure 4.14 depicts GENMAP's introductory screen. Documentation provided with GENMAP provides step-by-step explanation of its use, and help screens are built into it.

Figure 4.15 is a snapshot of the GENMAP editing screen. Here we have begun the process of laying out the CALC1 screen, and are only partly finished. As with most screen painters, you can move the cursor to desired locations and physically "paint" the screen to appear as you wish. Unlike some screen painting software, however, with GENMAP, you are not constrained to record all of the field-specific information on the screen you are designing. As

```
                    J E S 2  J O B  L O G  --  S Y S T E M  I B M 1  --  N O D E  N 1

10.11.34 JOB01104  IRR010I  USERID CSCJGJ   IS ASSIGNED TO THIS JOB.
10.11.34 JOB01104  ICH70001I CSCJGJ   LAST ACCESS AT 10:10:51 ON FRIDAY, JULY 8, 1994
10.11.34 JOB01104  $HASP373 CSCJGJA  STARTED - INIT  1 - CLASS A - SYS IBM1
10.11.39 JOB01104  $HASP395 CSCJGJA  ENDED

------ JES2 JOB STATISTICS ------
    08 JUL 94 JOB EXECUTION DATE
           31 CARDS READ
          224 SYSOUT PRINT RECORDS
            0 SYSOUT PUNCH RECORDS
           21 SYSOUT SPOOL KBYTES
         0.07 MINUTES EXECUTION TIME

        1 //CSCJGJA   JOB 1,                   ACCOUNTING INFORMATION              JOB01104
          //   'BIN 7--JANOSSY',               PROGRAMMER NAME AND DELIVERY BIN    00020000
          //   CLASS=A,                        INPUT QUEUE CLASS                   00030000
          //   MSGLEVEL=(1,1),                 HOW MUCH MVS SYSTEM PRINT DESIRED   00040000
          //   MSGCLASS=X,                     PRINT DESTINATION X A L N OR O      00050000
          //   TIME=(0,6),                     SAFETY LIMIT: RUN TIME UP TO 6 SECS 00060000
          //   REGION=2M,                      ALLOW UP TO 2 MEGS VIRTUAL MEMORY   00070000
          //*  TYPRUN=SCAN,                    UNCOMMENT THIS LINE TO DO SCAN ONLY 00080000
          //   NOTIFY=CSCJGJ                   WHO TO TELL WHEN JOB IS DONE        00090000
          //*-----------------------------------------------------------------    00100000
          //*  CHECK YOUR BMS MAP CODING FOR SYNTAX ERRORS                         00110000
          //*  THIS JCL IS STORED AT CSCJGJ.CSC360.CNTL(CHECKMAP)                  00120000
          //*-----------------------------------------------------------------    00100000
          //*                                                                    00120000
        2 //   SET  LIBRARY='CSCJGJ.CSC360.CNTL',     LIBRARY HOUSING MAP CODE     00130000
          //        MEMBER='EX7MAPX'                  MEMBER NAME OF MAP CODE
          //*
        3 //STEP010  EXEC  PGM=IEV90,
          //   REGION=2M,
          //   PARM=('SYSPARM(MAP)',            PRODUCE A PHYSICAL MAP
          //         'DECK',
          //         'NOLOAD')
        4 //SYSIN       DD  DSN=&LIBRARY(&MEMBER),          MAP SOURCE CODE IN
          //   DISP=SHR
          IEFC653I SUBSTITUTION JCL - DSN=CSCJGJ.CSC360.CNTL(EX7MAPX),DISP=SHR
        5 //SYSLIB      DD  DSN=CICS330.SDFHMAC,DISP=SHR    SYSTEM LIBRARY
        6 //            DD  DSN=SYS1.MACLIB,DISP=SHR        SYSTEM LIBRARY
        7 //SYSUT1      DD  UNIT=VIO,SPACE=(CYL,(5,5))      WORK FILE
        8 //SYSUT2      DD  UNIT=VIO,SPACE=(CYL,(5,5))      WORK FILE
        9 //SYSUT3      DD  UNIT=VIO,SPACE=(CYL,(5,5))      WORK FILE
       10 //SYSPRINT    DD  SYSOUT=*                        SOURCE CODE LISTING
       11 //SYSPUNCH    DD  DUMMY                           OBJECT FILE OUT

ICH70001I CSCJGJ   LAST ACCESS AT 10:10:51 ON FRIDAY, JULY 8, 1994

IEF236I ALLOC. FOR CSCJGJA STEP010
```

This is the MVS/ESA system output from a run of the CHECKMAP job stream. This job stream executes the IBM assembler, a program named IEV90, feeding in the BMS map code. The output of this is normally a machine-readable file containing "object" code, which is partly on its way to becoming machine language, which emerges at the ddname //SYSPUNCH. In the CHECKMAP job stream //SYSPUNCH is dummied out, meaning that it is cast aside. The printlines emerging at //SYSPRINT are the only desired output here. This output provides a listing of your BMS map code, with any errors detected by the assembler flagged and explained with error messages. The //SYSPRINT output is listed in this printout after MVS/ESA system reporting.

Figure 4.13 MVS/ESA system output and assembler output from BMS map processing.

```
IEF237I 111  ALLOCATED TO SYSIN
IEF237I 114  ALLOCATED TO SYSLIB
IEF237I 110  ALLOCATED TO
IEF237I VIO  ALLOCATED TO SYSUT1
IEF237I VIO  ALLOCATED TO SYSUT2
IEF237I VIO  ALLOCATED TO SYSUT3
IEF237I JES2 ALLOCATED TO SYSPRINT
IEF237I DMY  ALLOCATED TO SYSPUNCH
IEF142I CSCJGJA STEP010 - STEP WAS EXECUTED - COND CODE 0008
IEF285I   CSCJGJ.CSC360.CNTL                       KEPT
IEF285I   VOL SER NOS= USER00.
IEF285I   CICS330.SDFHMAC                          KEPT
IEF285I   VOL SER NOS= ACSAPP.
IEF285I   SYS1.MACLIB                              KEPT
IEF285I   VOL SER NOS= ACSRES.
IEF285I   SYS94189.T101135.RA000.CSCJGJA.R0430022  DELETED
IEF285I   SYS94189.T101135.RA000.CSCJGJA.R0430023  DELETED
IEF285I   SYS94189.T101135.RA000.CSCJGJA.R0430024  DELETED
IEF285I   CSCJGJ.CSCJGJA.JOB01104.D0000101.?       SYSOUT
IEF373I STEP /STEP010 / START 94189.1011
IEF374I STEP /STEP010 / STOP  94189.1011 CPU    0MIN 01.57SEC SRB    0MIN 00.07SEC VIRT  2048K SYS   416K EXT      4K SYS    9112K
IEF375I  JOB /CSCJGJA / START 94189.1011
IEF376I  JOB /CSCJGJA / STOP  94189.1011 CPU    0MIN 01.57SEC SRB    0MIN 00.07SEC
```

A COND CODE of 0000 or 0004 from the assembler indicates that your BMS map code is syntactically correct. A value of 0008 or greater indicates that one or more syntax errors exist in map coding.

```
                              EXTERNAL SYMBOL DICTIONARY                                   PAGE    1

SYMBOL    TYPE  ID   ADDR   LENGTH  LD ID FLAGS                              ASM H V 02 10.11 07/08/94
           PC 0001 000000 000129          00
```

```
                                                                                           PAGE    2

  LOC  OBJECT CODE    ADDR1 ADDR2  STMT   SOURCE STATEMENT                   ASM H V 02 10.11 07/08/94

                                      1 *   MAP FOR DEMONSTRATION PROGRAM CALC1                00010000
                                      2 *   J JANOSSY  7/5/94                                  00020000
                                      3 *        1         2         3         4         5         6         7  00030000
                                      4 *---+----0----+----0----+----0----+----0----+----0----+----0----+----0- 00040000
                                      5 *                                                       00050000
                                      6          PRINT NOGEN                                    00060000
                                      7 *------------------------------------ DFHMSD  STARTS THE "MAPSET"----- 00070000
                                      8 $001M    DFHMSD TYPE=&SYSPARM,                         X00080000
```

Your BMS map code is listed here, line numbered by the assembler.

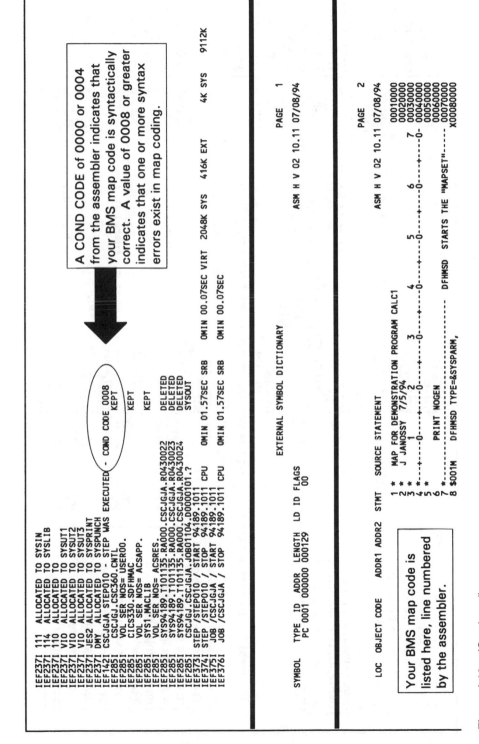

Figure 4.13 *(Continued)*

Gaps exist in line numbers because PRINT NOGEN at line 000600 suppresses printing of the macro instruction code generated by the DFHMSD, DFHMDI, and DFHMDF instructions.

```
                          LANG=COBOL,                                              X00090000
                          MODE=INOUT,                                              X00100000
                          TERM=3270-2,                                             X00110000
                          CTRL=FREEKB,                                             X00120000
                          STORAGE=AUTO,                                            X00130000
                          TIOAPFX=YES                                               00140000
 10+               PRINT OFF                                                 @PAA 02-DFHSY
 93 *-----------------------------------  DFHMDI   STARTS A "MAP" ---------  00150000
 94 CALCMAP   DFHMDI SIZE=(24,80),                                             X00160000
                          LINE=1,                                              X00170000
                          COLUMN=1                                              00180000
 96+               PRINT OFF                                                 @PAA 02-DFHSY
213 *-----------------------------------  DFHMDF   STARTS A FIELD ---------  00190000
214                DFHMDF POS=(1,2),                                           X00200000
                          LENGTH=40,                                           X00210000
                          ATTRB=(BRT,PROT),                                    X00220000
                          INITIAL='MY NAME IS ** [illegible] UT YOUR NAME HERE! ****'    00230000
216+               PRINT OFF                                                 @PAA 02-DFHSY
301 *-----------------------------------  DFHMDF   STARTS A FIELD ---------  00240000
302                DFHMDF POS=(6,19),                                          X00250000
                          LENGTH=8,                                            X00260000
                          ATTRB=(BRT,PROT,                                     X00270000
                          INITIAL='QUANTITY'                                    00280000

     IEV088  *** ERROR ***  UNBALANCED PARENTHESES IN MACRO CALL OPERAND  --  OPENC/(BRT,PROT,

304+               PRINT OFF                                                 @PAA 02-DFHSY
388 *-----------------------------------  DFHMDF   STARTS A FIELD ---------  00290000
389                DFHMDF POS=(6,32),                                          X00300000
                          LENGTH=5,                                            X00310000
                          ATTRB=(BRT,PROT),                                    X00320000
                          INITIAL='PRICE'                                       00330000
391+               PRINT OFF                                                 @PAA 02-DFHSY
476 *-----------------------------------  DFHMDF   STARTS A FIELD ---------  00340000
477                DFHMDF POS=(6,50),                                          X00350000
                          LENGTH=5,                                            X00360000
                          ATTRB=(BRT,PROT),                                    X00370000
                          INITIAL='TOTAL'                                       00380000
479+               PRINT OFF                                                 @PAA 02-DFHSY
564 *-----------------------------------  DFHMDF   STARTS A FIELD ---------  00390000
565 QUANT          DFHMDF POS=(7,20),                                          X00400000
                          LENGTH=5,                                            X00410000
                          ATTRB=(NORM,UNPROT,NUM),                             X00420000
                          PICIN='99999'                                         00430000
567+               PRINT OFF                                                 @PAA 02-DFHSY
651 *                                       "STOPPER" FIELD ---------  00440000
652                DFHMDF POS=(7,26),                                          X00450000
                          LENGTH=1,                                            X00460000
                          ATTRB=PROT                                            00470000
```

The assembler issues error messages such as this when it detects incorrect BMS map coding. We intentionally caused the error here for example purposes by removing the closing parenthesis after the ATTRB coding for the QUANTITY screen label field.

We use standard line numbers on BMS map code. These numbers are applied by TSO/ISPF in columns 73-80. These numbers, which you can get by putting RENUM STD on the command line while you are editing, help you see that the X's for continued lines are actually in column 72.

Figure 4.13 *(Continued)*

```
                                                                                                    PAGE    3
LOC  OBJECT CODE    ADDR1 ADDR2  STMT   SOURCE STATEMENT                              ASM H V 02 10.11 07/08/94
                                 654+          PRINT OFF                                           @PAA 02-DFHSY
                                 738 *-------------------------------------- DFHMDF  STARTS A FIELD --------- 00480000
                                 739 PRICE     DFHMDF POS=(7,32),                                        X00490000
                                                     LENGTH=4,                                           X00500000
                                                     ATTRB=(NORM,UNPROT,NUM),                            X00510000
                                                     PICIN='99V99'                                        00520000
                                 741+          PRINT OFF                                           @PAA 02-DFHSY
                                 825 *                                       "STOPPER" FIELD --------- 00530000
                                 826           DFHMDF POS=(7,37),                                        X00540000
                                                     LENGTH=1,                                           X00550000
                                                     ATTRB=PROT                                           00560000
                                 828+          PRINT OFF                                           @PAA 02-DFHSY
                                 912 *-------------------------------------- DFHMDF  STARTS A FIELD --------- 00570000
                                 913 TOTB4     DFHMDF POS=(7,42),                                        X00580000
                                                     LENGTH=13,                                          X00590000
                                                     ATTRB=PROT,                                         X00600000
                                                     PICOUT='ZZ,ZZZ,ZZ9.99'                               00610000
                                 915+          PRINT OFF                                           @PAA 02-DFHSY
                                 999 *-------------------------------------- DFHMDF  STARTS A FIELD --------- 00620000
                                1000           DFHMDF POS=(10,34),                                       X00630000
                                                     LENGTH=6,                                           X00640000
                                                     ATTRB=(BRT,PROT),                                   X00650000
                                                     INITIAL='8% TAX'                                     00660000
                                1002+          PRINT OFF                                           @PAA 02-DFHSY
                                1087 *-------------------------------------- DFHMDF  STARTS A FIELD --------- 00670000
                                1088 TAX       DFHMDF POS=(10,42),                                       X00680000
                                                     LENGTH=13,                                          X00690000
                                                     ATTRB=PROT,                                         X00700000
                                                     PICOUT='ZZ,ZZZ,ZZ9.99'                               00710000
                                1090+          PRINT OFF                                           @PAA 02-DFHSY
                                1174 *-------------------------------------- DFHMDF  STARTS A FIELD --------- 00720000
                                1175           DFHMDF POS=(12,42),                                       X00730000
                                                     LENGTH=13,                                          X00740000
                                                     ATTRB=(NORM,PROT),                                  X00750000
                                                     INITIAL='============='                              00760000
                                1177+          PRINT OFF                                           @PAA 02-DFHSY
                                1262 *-------------------------------------- DFHMDF  STARTS A FIELD --------- 00770000
                                1263           DFHMDF POS=(14,29),                                       X00780000
                                                     LENGTH=11,                                          X00790000
                                                     ATTRB=(BRT,PROT),                                   X00800000
                                                     INITIAL='GRAND TOTAL'                                00810000
                                1265+          PRINT OFF                                           @PAA 02-DFHSY
                                1350 *-------------------------------------- DFHMDF  STARTS A FIELD --------- 00820000
                                1351 GTOTAL    DFHMDF POS=(14,42),                                       X00830000
                                                     LENGTH=13,                                          X00840000
                                                     ATTRB=PROT,                                         X00850000
                                                     PICOUT='ZZ,ZZZ,ZZ9.99'                               00860000
```

No errors were detected on this page.

Figure 4.13 *(Continued)*

```
1353+          PRINT OFF                                                        @PAA 02-DFHSY
1437 *-----------------------------------  DFHMDF  STARTS A FIELD ---------  00870000
1438 MSG       DFHMDF POS=(24,01),                                                 X00880000
                     LENGTH=79,                                                    X00890000
                     ATTRB=(BRT,PROT)                                               00900000
1440+          PRINT OFF                                                        @PAA 02-DFHSY
1524 *-----------------------------------  DFHMSD  ENDS A MAP ------------  00910000
1525           DFHMSD TYPE=FINAL                                                    00920000
```

```
                                                                                PAGE    4
  LOC  OBJECT CODE    ADDR1 ADDR2  STMT   SOURCE STATEMENT           ASM H V 02 10.11 07/08/94
                                   1527+         PRINT OFF                         @PAA 02-DFHSY
                                   1603+         PRINT OFF                         @PAA 03-DFHSY
                                   1691          END                                    00930000
```

```
                                   CROSS REFERENCE                              PAGE    5
SYMBOL    LEN      VALUE  DEFN  REFERENCES                   ASM H V 02 10.11 07/08/94
CALCMAP   00001    00000C 0172
DFHBK101  00001  0000004F 0210  0174
DFHBL101  00001  0000000C 0173  0210 1686
DFHBM101  00001  00000119 1686  0179
DFHBM201  00001  00000098 1680  0181
DFHBM301  00001  00000146 1681  0182
DFHBM401  00001  00000000 1682  0185
DFHBM501  00001  00000125 1685  1686
DFHBM601  00001  00000096 1679  0180
DFHBM701  00001  00000010 1683  0191
DFHBM801  00001  00000000 1687  0088
GTOTAL    00001    000113 1429
MSD0001   00008    000000 0086
MSG       00001    00011B 1516
PRICE     00001    0000BD 0817
QUANT     00001    0000AD 0643
TAX       00001    0000E3 1166
TOTB4     00001    0000CD 0991
```

This cross reference is alphabetical, not according to the order of the fields on the screen. It lists screen fields and fields used internally by CICS, and shows line numbers under the DEFN column that the PRINT OFF specification hides. It's not very useful, except to confirm that you have coded a name for each screen field that you intend to use for input and/or output.

Figure 4.13 *(Continued)*

```
                         DIAGNOSTIC CROSS REFERENCE AND ASSEMBLER SUMMARY                        PAGE    6
                                                                                  ASM H V 02 10.11 07/08/94
THE FOLLOWING STATEMENTS WERE FLAGGED
   000302
      1 STATEMENT  FLAGGED IN THIS ASSEMBLY        8 WAS HIGHEST SEVERITY CODE

   OVERRIDING PARAMETERS-  SYSPARM(MAP),DECK,NOLOAD
   OPTIONS FOR THIS ASSEMBLY
    DECK, NOOBJECT, LIST, XREF(FULL), NORENT, NOTEST, NOBATCH, ALIGN, ESD, RLD, NOTERM, NODBCS,
    LINECOUNT(55), FLAG(0), SYSPARM(MAP)
   NO OVERRIDING DD NAMES

      93 CARDS FROM SYSIN     6341 CARDS FROM SYSLIB
     158 LINES OUTPUT            8 CARDS OUTPUT
```

The line number of any statement with erroneous coding is listed, such as 000302 here. You have to look back at the BMS map source code listing (above) to see the line with the mistake, and the error message associated with it.

Figure 4.13 *(Continued)*

```
                          GENMAP - A BMS Map Generator
                                       by
                                 Gary Weinstein

    This disk should contain at least the following files:

             GENMAP.EXE - The program itself
             GENMAP.HLP - The program's help file
             GENMAP.DOC - The documentation file
             T.EXE      - A simple substitute for the DOS TYPE command
             README.1ST - This file
             READ.BAT   - A simple batch file to type this file and then
                          optionally run T.EXE to allow you to read the
                          documentation file
             GETYN.COM  - A simple program to ask a question and return a
                          Yes/No answer. Used by READ.BAT

    Though GENMAP is quite simple to use, I strongly urge you to read the
    documentation file. The answers to most of the questions you may have are
    there. I have made this as easy for you as I could. Just type READ and
    press Enter. (If you aren't doing that now.)

Do you want to read the documentation file now? (Y/N)
```

Figure 4.14 GENMAP screen painter introductory screen.

```
 MY NAME IS JIM JANOSSY



               QUANTITY     PRICE
                99999       9999




















 F1=Help F2=Save F3=Load ◄┘=Edit Insert Delete ^F1=Quick help Alt-X=Exit  6:34
```

Figure 4.15 Beginning the CALC1 screen design using the GENMAP screen painter.

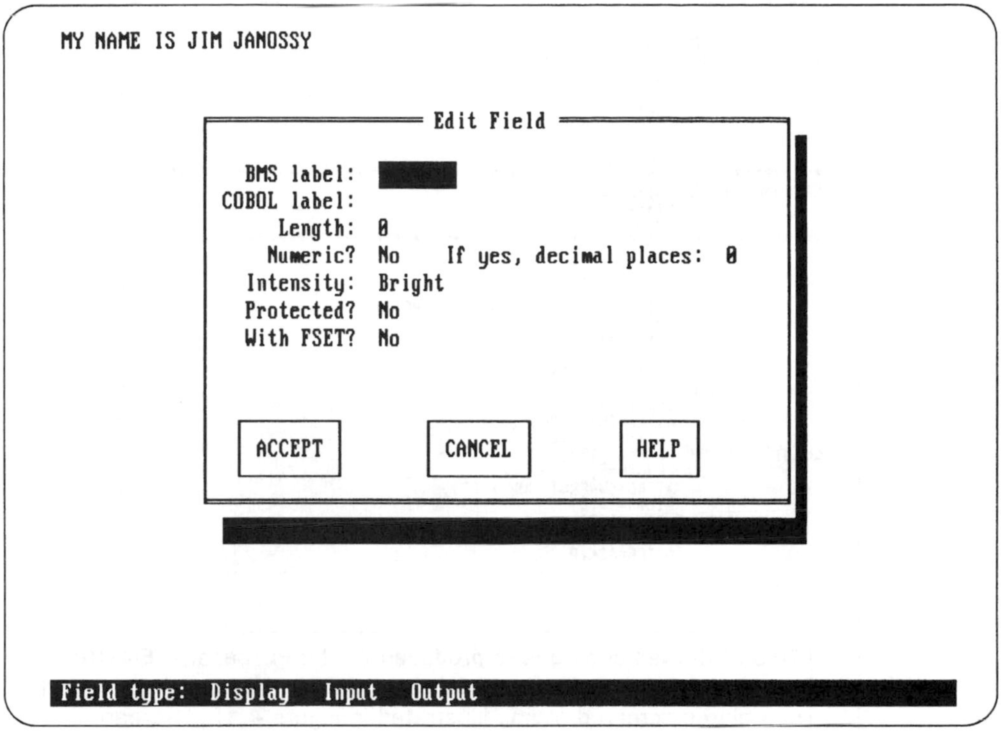
MY NAME IS JIM JANOSSY
Edit Field
BMS label:
COBOL label:
Length: 0
Numeric? No If yes, decimal places: 0
Intensity: Bright
Protected? No
With FSET? No
ACCEPT
CANCEL
HELP
Field type: Display Input Output

Figure 4.16 The GENMAP screen painter uses pop-up windows to capture information about the screen fields as you design a screen.

Figure 4.16 illustrates, pop-up screens appear to give you adequate room to indicate information about each field, which is retained in a file and used to construct the BMS map code and the related data transmission record description (symbolic map).

Figure 4.17 shows you the format of BMS map code generated by the GENMAP screen painter. What you see here is the plain ASCII file created by GENMAP, ready for uploading to a mainframe for processing.

As you can see from these samples, GENMAP, like most screen painters, saves you the bother of hand coding all of the fussy assembler statements needed to define a screen. As with "clean" hand-coded BMS map code, you could take this GENMAP-produced code and process it into physical and symbolic maps, as we describe in Chapter 5.

4.17 AN ASSIGNMENT TO TEST YOUR SKILL

The best way to learn CICS screen design and BMS map coding is to try it out. Design a screen that meets the following requirements, then code a BMS map to define it.

1. The top of the screen will have the literal characters

   ```
   HERE IS MY FIRST CICS SCREEN (your name)
   ```

   centered on the first line. The value "(your name)" will be your actual name. These literals will display at bright intensity.

```
         PRINT NOGEN
A001     DFHMSD TYPE=&SYSPARM,                                               X
               LANG=COBOL,                                                   X
               MODE=INOUT,                                                   X
               TERM=3270-2,                                                  X
               CTRL=FREEKB,                                                  X
               STORAGE=AUTO,                                                 X
               TIOAPFX=YES
***********************************************************************
CALCMAP  DFHMDI SIZE=(24,80),                                                X
               LINE=1,                                                       X
               COLUMN=1
***********************************************************************
         DFHMDF POS=(1,1),                                                   X
               LENGTH=22,                                                    X
               ATTRB=(BRT,PROT),                                             X
               INITIAL='MY NAME IS JIM JANOSSY'
         DFHMDF POS=(5,14),                                                  X
               LENGTH=12,                                                    X
               ATTRB=(BRT,PROT),                                             X
               INITIAL='QUANTITY    '
         DFHMDF POS=(5,29),                                                  X
               LENGTH=5,                                                     X
               ATTRB=(BRT,PROT),                                             X
               INITIAL='PRICE'
QUANT    DFHMDF POS=(6,15),                                                  X
               LENGTH=5,                                                     X
               ATTRB=(UNPROT,NUM,FSET),                                      X
               PICIN='9(5)'
         DFHMDF POS=(6,21),                                                  X
               LENGTH=1,                                                     X
               ATTRB=ASKIP
   -
   -
   -
```

This BMS map coding was produced by the PC-based GENMAP screen painter in a fraction of a second from the partially completed screen drawing illustrated in Figure 4.15. Screen painters such as GENMAP give you a tremendous productivity advantage in designing and coding screens for CICS programs. GENMAP also produces the symbolic map matching the BMS coding, as we'll demonstrate in Chapter 5. Appendix F provides information on obtaining the GENMAP screen painter as well as the programs in this book, on diskette.

Figure 4.17 BMS map code generated automatically by the GENMAP screen painter from a screen design.

2. The screen will have seven screen labels, to be displayed with bright intensity:

```
FIRST NAME
MIDDLE INITIAL
LAST NAME
RATE OF PAY
HOURS WORKED

AMOUNT OF PAY
PAY TO NAME
```

Position these fields in any way you like, *except* listed vertically single-spaced as shown here.

3. There will be five enterable fields, one each immediately after the first five screen labels. The "name" fields will each be alphanumeric of suitable length, while the rate of pay will be a numeric integer, and the rate of pay will be a dollars and cents value (you decide how large). The entry fields will be displayed at normal intensity. (Don't forget the stopper fields at the end of each enterable field.)
4. The "amount of pay" and "pay to" fields will be output screen fields. Their contents will be created by a program we'll discuss later. The amount of pay field is two bytes longer than the rate of pay field, and the "pay to" field is fifty bytes long.
5. The prompt line will be on the twenty-fourth line of the screen, and will be 79 bytes long (the maximum field length, since the first position of the line will house the attribute byte). The prompt will display at bright intensity.

When you have entered the BMS map code into a member of a library using TSO/ISPF, use JCL similar to the CHECKMAP job stream to identify syntax errors in your work, and clean up the map to make it entirely free of errors. You'll see more about this assignment in the next several chapters, as you learn how to process BMS map code into machine language, build the description of the data transmission record a screen generates, and learn how to write a CICS program that accesses the screen.

4.18 FOR YOUR REVIEW

Understanding these terms introduced in this chapter will aid your understanding of the next chapter:

ASKIP	Mapset name
ATTRB	Modified data tag (MDT)
Attribute byte	NUM
Basic Mapping Support (BMS)	Output screen field
Data transmission record	Physical map
DFHMSD, DFHMDI, DFHMDF macros	PICIN
Display intensity	PICOUT
Enterable alphanumeric field	Prompt
Enterable numeric field	PROT
FSET	Screen labels
Map	Screen painter
Map name	Stopper field

4.19 REVIEW QUESTIONS

1. Explain what the data transmission record is, and how it is related to a CICS program.
2. Identify what an attribute byte is, and discuss the role attribute bytes play in CICS screen design and programming.
3. Describe what the modified data tag is, and explain how it affects the transmission of data between a terminal and a CICS program.
4. Explain why two names, mapset name and map name, are associated with the same coded definition of a CICS screen.
5. Code the appropriate ATTRB portion of attribute byte coding for each of the fol-

lowing fields:
- **a.** an enterable alphanumeric field
- **b.** an enterable numeric field
- **c.** a screen label
- **d.** a stopper field

6. Identify and describe the difference in cursor movement when a stopper field is coded ATTRB=(DRK,PROT) and ATTRB=(DRK,ASKIP).

7. Identify the role played by PICIN and PICOUT in BMS map source code, and identify the condition under which can you omit PICIN and PICOUT coding from your BMS map source code.

8. Identify the services provided by NUM when you code it with an enterable numeric field on a screen, and discuss whether or not any nonnumeric characters can be entered into a field coded this way (try periods and hyphens!).

9. Examine Figure 4.3 and explain why attribute bytes are shown after the QUANTITY and PRICE fields, but not after the TOTAL, 8% TAX, and GRAND TOTAL fields.

10. Identify the actual programming language in which BMS map source code is created, and cite at least five specific syntax requirements of this language.

5

Physical and Symbolic Maps

In Chapter 4 you learned how screen images are defined as maps using Basic Mapping Support (BMS), a subsystem of CICS. You also saw how the IBM assembler, a regular item of software in the mainframe environment, can process your coded BMS screen map to check its syntax. In this chapter, we proceed further with the processing of your coded map, converting it into two forms, a physical map and a symbolic map. After you complete this chapter you will be able to prepare both of these forms of finished maps, and you will understand how each is used by CICS. Once you know that, you'll be ready to develop a CICS program to access your map.

5.1 THREE KINDS OF MAPS

It's essential for you to have a clear understanding of the terminology and nature of three types of maps that exist in the CICS environment. For this reason, we start here with formal definitions of these types of maps, building on what you have already learned in Chapter 4. We'll then discuss how you create physical and symbolic maps.

BMS Map Source Code

BMS map source code is the coding you create using IBM assembler language macro instructions, defining the image of a screen in terms of label placement, input fields, and output fields. Map source code looks like Figure 4.4. As you saw in Chapter 4, you can manually code this from a screen design using TSO/ISPF, or you can use a screen painter such as GENMAP to produce this coding and upload it to a mainframe. Map source code consists of 80-byte punch card-image records. You store it in a library such as your CNTL (job control language) library or in a separate library you create for this purpose.

Physical Map

A **physical map** is produced by processing BMS map source code through the IBM assembler using the SYSPARM(MAP) option, as shown in the CHECKMAP job control language in Figure 4.12. *The physical map is machine language,* and it makes no sense to attempt to look at it directly. The physical map is put into the CICS load library by the job control language that you submit to create it. You can think of the physical map as the image of the screen that actually "programs" the 3270 terminal screen to appear as you wish. The physical map contains the coded attribute bytes that control the way the fields on the terminal appear. The physical map also contains coded information used by BMS to create the data transmission record that conveys data from the screen to a CICS program and vice versa.

Symbolic Map

A **symbolic map** is produced by processing BMS map source code through the IBM assembler a second time, using the SYSPARM(DSECT) option. *The symbolic map is a COBOL description of the data transmission record.* The symbolic map can be produced from the BMS map source code, because the map source code is what dictates the format of the data transmission record. The format of this record is easy to understand and work with, since it is, like all mainframe COBOL source code, 80-byte punch card-image records. You can print the symbolic map, or capture it in a library so that the COBOL compiler can copy it into any program that needs to use it.

You can, if you wish, decline to use or even produce an assembler-created symbolic map, and instead code your own description of the data transmission record using a coding style that better suits your programming conventions. Like most screen painters, the GENMAP screen painter also creates a symbolic map at the same it creates BMS map source code from a screen design. A GENMAP-produced symbolic map is of higher quality than the IBM machine-produced symbolic map, and is easier to use.

5.2 CREATING THE PHYSICAL MAP

Figure 5.1 provides you with an overview of physical and symbolic map processing, as well as CICS program processing. We'll use the same underlying flowchart to discuss all three types of processing. In Figure 5.1, you'll notice that physical map processing is shaded to focus your attention on it.

Turning your BMS map source code into a physical map is done in two steps, as shown in the shaded part of Figure 5.1. The first step involves running the IBM assembler with the SYSPARM(MAP) option, having the assembler read your BMS map source code as input at its

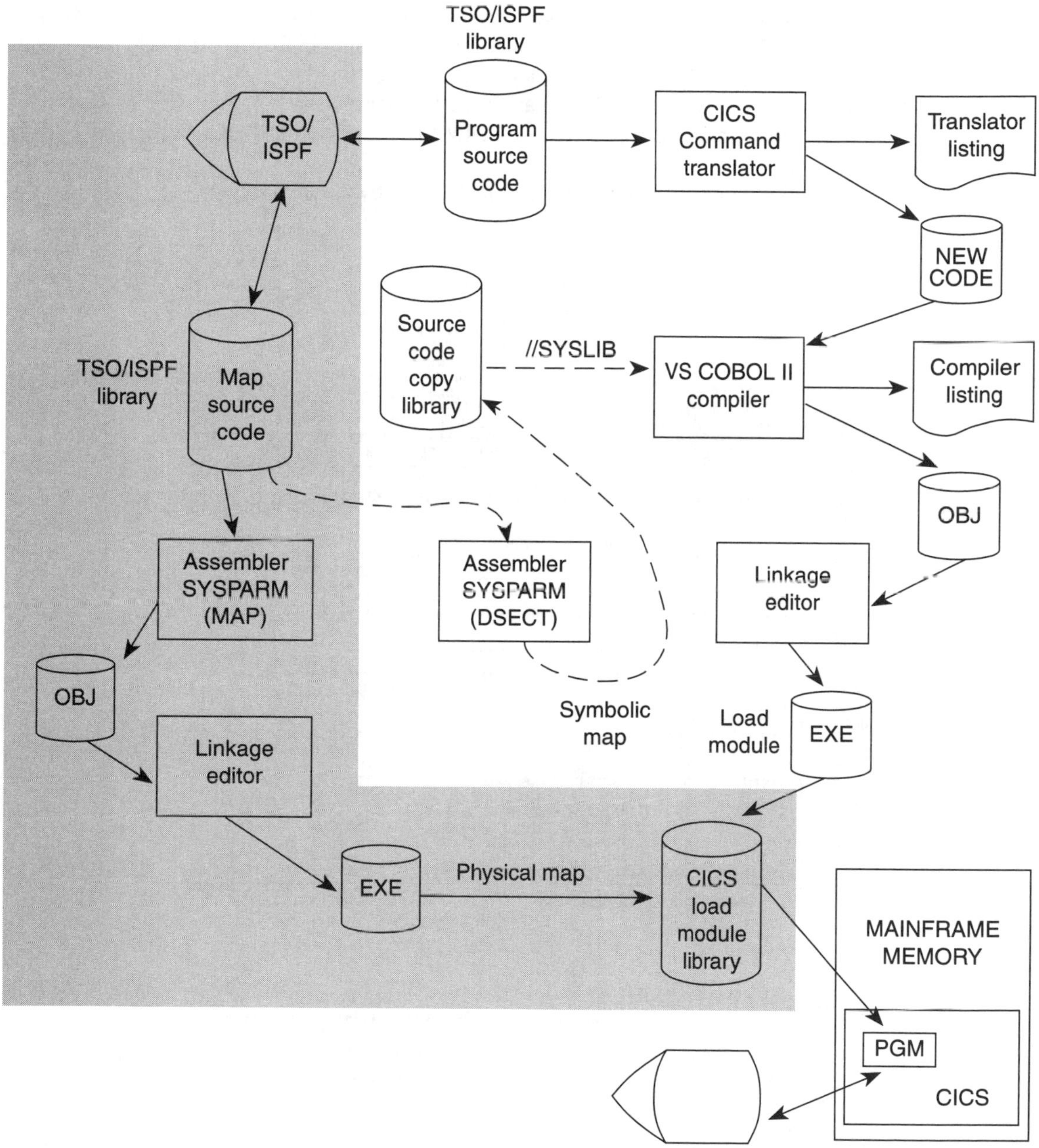
TSO/ISPF
library
TSO/
ISPF
Program
source
code
CICS
Command
translator
Translator
listing
NEW
CODE
Source
code
copy
library
//SYSLIB
VS COBOL II
compiler
Compiler
listing
TSO/ISPF
library
Map
source
code
OBJ
Assembler
SYSPARM
(MAP)
Assembler
SYSPARM
(DSECT)
Linkage
editor
OBJ
Symbolic
map
Load
module
EXE
Linkage
editor
EXE
Physical map
CICS
load
module
library
MAINFRAME
MEMORY
PGM
CICS

Figure 5.1 Overview of map and CICS program processing, with physical map processing shaded for emphasis.

//SYSIN DD statement. The assembler creates an object file as 80-byte punch card-image records at its //SYSPUNCH output (we discarded this output in the CHECKMAP job stream, but now we'll use it). The object file must then be link edited to create machine language, a process performed by the standard mainframe **linkage editor** program, IEWL. Figure 5.2 shows you a job stream named MAKEPMAP (MAKE Physical MAP) that accomplishes these two executions.

You will notice four value assignments handled by the SET statement in lines 15-18 of

```
EDIT ---- CSCJGJ.CSC360.CNTL(MAKEPMAP) - 01.03 --------------- COLUMNS 001 072
COMMAND ===>                                                  SCROLL ===> PAGE
****** ****************************** TOP OF DATA ******************************
000001 //CSCJGJA   JOB 1,                    ACCOUNTING INFORMATION
000002 //  'BIN 7--JANOSSY',                 PROGRAMMER NAME AND DELIVERY BIN
000003 //  CLASS=A,                          INPUT QUEUE CLASS
000004 //  MSGLEVEL=(1,1),                   HOW MUCH MVS SYSTEM PRINT DESIRED
000005 //  MSGCLASS=X,                       PRINT DESTINATION X A L N OR O
000006 //  TIME=(0,6),                       SAFETY LIMIT: RUN TIME UP TO 6 SECS
000007 //  REGION=2M,                        ALLOW UP TO 2 MEGS VIRTUAL MEMORY
000008 //* TYPRUN=SCAN,                      UNCOMMENT THIS LINE TO DO SCAN ONLY
000009 //  NOTIFY=CSCJGJ                     WHO TO TELL WHEN JOB IS DONE
000010 //*-----------------------------------------------------------------
000011 //*  PREPARE A PHYSICAL MAP FROM BMS MAP CODE
000012 //*  THIS JCL IS STORED AT CSCJGJ.CSC360.CNTL(MAKEPMAP)
000013 //*-----------------------------------------------------------------
000014 //*
000015 //  SET  SORCLIB='CSCJGJ.CSC360.CNTL',     SOURCE LIBRARY FOR MAP CODE
000016 //         BNAME='EX7MAP',                BMS MAP CODE MEMBER NAME
000017 //       LOADLIB='CCP.LOADLIB',           CICS LOAD LIBRARY
000018 //         PNAME='$001M'                  PHYSICAL MAP MEMBER NAME
000019 //*
000020 //*******************************************************************
000021 //*
000022 //*  ASSEMBLE THE BMS MAP SOURCE CODE, CREATING OBJECT FILE
000023 //*
000024 //*******************************************************************
000025 //*
000026 //STEP010  EXEC  PGM=IEV90,
000027 //  REGION=2M,
000028 //  PARM=('SYSPARM(MAP)',                             MAKE PMAP OBJECT FILE
000029 //         'DECK',
000030 //         'NOLOAD')
000031 //SYSIN      DD  DSN=&SORCLIB(&BNAME),                 BMS MAP CODE IN
000032 //  DISP=SHR
000033 //SYSLIB     DD  DSN=CICS330.SDFHMAC,DISP=SHR          SYSTEM LIBRARY
000034 //           DD  DSN=SYS1.MACLIB,DISP=SHR              SYSTEM LIBRARY
000035 //SYSUT1     DD  UNIT=VIO,SPACE=(CYL,(5,5))            WORK FILE
000036 //SYSUT2     DD  UNIT=VIO,SPACE=(CYL,(5,5))            WORK FILE
000037 //SYSUT3     DD  UNIT=VIO,SPACE=(CYL,(5,5))            WORK FILE
000038 //SYSPRINT   DD  SYSOUT=*                              SOURCE CODE LISTING
000039 //SYSPUNCH   DD  DSN=&&OBJECT,                         OBJECT FILE OUT
000040 //  DISP=(NEW,PASS),
000041 //  UNIT=VIO,
000042 //  RECFM=FB,
000043 //  LRECL=80,
000044 //  BLKSIZE=3120,
000045 //  SPACE=(CYL,(1,1))
000046 //*
000047 //*******************************************************************
000048 //*
000049 //*  IF CODE OK, LINK EDIT THE OBJECT TO PRODUCE THE PHYSICAL MAP
000050 //*
000051 //*******************************************************************
000052 //*
000053 //    IF ( STEP010.RC <= 4 ) THEN
000054 //STEP020  EXEC  PGM=IEWL,
000055 //  PARM=('LIST',
000056 //        'LET',
000057 //        'XREF',                                       CROSS REFERENCE
000058 //        'RMODE(24)')                                  PHY MAP RES. MODE
000059 //SYSLIN     DD  DSN=&&OBJECT,DISP=(OLD,DELETE)         OBJECT FILE IN
000060 //SYSPRINT   DD  SYSOUT=*                               LINKAGE EDIT RPT
000061 //SYSUT1     DD  UNIT=VIO,SPACE=(CYL,(1,1))             WORK FILE
000062 //SYSLMOD    DD  DSN=&LOADLIB(&PNAME),DISP=SHR          PHYSICAL MAP OUT
000063 //    ENDIF
000064 //
```

Figure 5.2 The MAKEMAP job stream executes the assembler and the linkage editor to create a physical map from BMS map code.

the MAKEPMAP job stream in Figure 5.2. SET is a feature of MVS/ESA Version 4 job control language. We use SET to give actual values to symbolic parameters in a job stream. The symbolic parameters in the MAKEPMAP job stream are:

SORCLIB	the "source" library name where the BMS map source code is housed
BNAME	the BMS map code member name
LOADLIB	the name of the CICS load library that houses machine language (physical) maps and the machine language of CICS programs
PNAME	the physical map member name (note that this should be the same as the map set name you coded in the BMS map code)

If your mainframe does not yet run Version 4 of the MVS/ESA operating system, you will be forced to use a job stream such as MAKEPMAP as a cataloged or instream procedure. In that case, you would give actual values to the four symbolic parameters using an EXEC statement, and the body of the JCL (line 19 onward) would be housed separately.

We developed the MAKEPMAP job stream specifically for this book and class use. You will probably encounter locally developed JCL or a locally customized proc of a different name for your own use, since every mainframe installation is responsible for creating its own naming convention for libraries, maps, and CICS programs. DFHMAPS is a cataloged procedure commonly used to do what our MAKEPMAP job stream does.

The end of the output of the MAKEPMAP job stream is shown in Figure 5.3, as you would view it on a TSO/ISFP screen. You might recognize that the end of the assembler's

```
 SDSF OUTPUT DISPLAY CSCJGJA  JOB06532  DSID   101 LINE 142      COLUMNS 02- 81
 COMMAND INPUT ===>                                              SCROLL ===> PAGE
QUANT     00001    0000B5 0644
TAX       00001    0000EB 1167
TOTB4     00001    0000D5 0992
                                       DIAGNOSTIC CROSS REFERENCE AND ASSEMBLER SUMMA

     NO STATEMENTS FLAGGED IN THIS ASSEMBLY
   OVERRIDING PARAMETERS-  SYSPARM(MAP),DECK,NOLOAD
   OPTIONS FOR THIS ASSEMBLY
     DECK, NOOBJECT, LIST, XREF(FULL), NORENT, NOTEST, NOBATCH, ALIGN, ESD, RLD,
     LINECOUNT(55), FLAG(0), SYSPARM(MAP)
   NO OVERRIDING DD NAMES
      93 CARDS FROM SYSIN     6341 CARDS FROM SYSLIB
     155 LINES OUTPUT            8 CARDS OUTPUT

 MVS/DFP VERSION 3 RELEASE 3 LINKAGE EDITOR     13:06:26  THU  JUL 14, 1994
 JOB CSCJGJA     STEP STEP020
 INVOCATION PARAMETERS - LIST,LET,XREF,RMODE(24)
 ACTUAL SIZE=(317440,86016)
 OUTPUT DATA SET CCP.LOADLIB IS ON VOLUME ACSRES
                                                  CROSS REFERENCE TABLE

  CONTROL SECTION                           ENTRY
     NAME    ORIGIN  LENGTH                   NAME    LOCATION     NAME    LOCATION
 $PRIVATE        00     131

 ENTRY ADDRESS        00
 TOTAL LENGTH        138
 ** $001M     REPLACED AND HAS AMODE 24
 ** LOAD MODULE HAS RMODE 24
 ** AUTHORIZATION CODE IS            0.
```

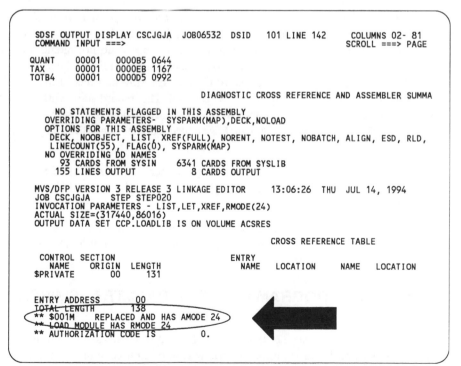

Figure 5.3 Last lines of output from the MAKEPMAP job stream, indicating that a physical map named $001 has been created or replaced.

listing is on the top of this screen, followed by messages from the linkage editor. If the assembler had detected errors in your BMS map code, the MAKEPMAP job stream would have not run the link edit step. In this case, you would find only messages from the assembler in Figure 5.3, calling your attention to syntax errors in your BMS map coding.

5.3 OVERVIEW OF THE DATA TRANSMISSION RECORD

A CICS program communicates with the terminal screen using a record containing only the contents of the attribute byte fields and the data fields of the screen. We call this record the **data transmission record** for a screen. As the designer and encoder of a screen, you actually determine the content of the data transmission record by the way you code the BMS map.

Figure 5.4 provides a second copy of the BMS map code for the CALC1 screen. You saw this in Figure 4.4, but in Figure 5.4 we have circled the names coded on the fields that we want included in the data transmission record. We want to be able to receive or send information to these fields, so we have coded **field names** on their definitions:

QUANT	Quantity entered by terminal user
PRICE	Price entered by terminal user
TOTB4	Total before taxes to be computed by program
TAX	Sales tax to be computed by program
GTOTAL	Grand total to be computed by program
MSG	Prompt line to be issued by program

You code field names only for fields you want to have present in the data transmission record. We have not coded any other field names in Figure 5.4, because no other fields are relevant to manipulation by the program. For example, we do not intend that the program access or change any field labels, so we do not code names on field labels.

Figure 5.5 shows you the format of the data transmission record that BMS constructs when it processes the BMS map code of Figure 5.4. This record starts with 12 bytes of CICS overhead information, which we indicated as FILLER. Then BMS provides three fields of information for every map field on which we coded a name in the BMS map. Here is what the three fields for each named screen field contain:

Entry length	16-bit signed binary number	PIC S9(4) BINARY
Attribute byte	one character byte	PIC X
Field data	data entered or sent	PIC . . .

The length of the data transmission record depends entirely on the sizes of the fields you code in the BMS map. You dictate the content of the data transmission record by your coding of the BMS map source code.

5.4 HOW A CICS PROGRAM USES THE DATA TRANSMISSION RECORD

A CICS program has to have a definition of the data transmission record in its WORKING-STORAGE section, because this record is how your program communicates with the terminal. To send data to a terminal screen, your program puts the data into the appropriate data transmission record field and issues the CICS SEND MAP command. To receive data, your pro-

```
EDIT ---- CSCJGJ.CSC360.CNTL(EX7MAP) - 01.01 ----------------- COLUMNS 001 072
COMMAND ===>                                                   SCROLL ===> PAGE
****** ***************************** TOP OF DATA ******************************
*    MAP FOR DEMONSTRATION PROGRAM CALC1
*    J JANOSSY  7/5/94
*          1         2         3         4         5         6         7
*---+----0----+----0----+----0----+----0----+----0----+----0----+----0-
*
         PRINT NOGEN
*-------------------------------- DFHMSD  STARTS THE "MAPSET"-----
$001M    DFHMSD TYPE=&SYSPARM,                                         X
               LANG=COBOL,                                             X
               MODE=INOUT,                                             X
               TERM=3270-2,                                            X
               CTRL=FREEKB,                                            X
               STORAGE=AUTO,                                           X
               TIOAPFX=YES
*-------------------------------- DFHMDI  STARTS A "MAP" ---------
CALCMAP  DFHMDI SIZE=(24,80),                                          X
               LINE=1,                                                 X
               COLUMN=1
*-------------------------------- DFHMDF  STARTS A FIELD ---------
         DFHMDF POS=(1,2),                                             X
               LENGTH=40,                                              X
               ATTRB=(BRT,PROT),
               INITIAL='MY NAME IS **** PUT YOUR NAME HERE! ****'
*-------------------------------- DFHMDF  STARTS A FIELD ---------
         DFHMDF POS=(6,19),                                            X
               LENGTH=8,                                               X
               ATTRB=(BRT,PROT),                                       X
               INITIAL='QUANTITY'
*-------------------------------- DFHMDF  STARTS A FIELD ---------
         DFHMDF POS=(6,32),                                            X
               LENGTH=5,                                               X
               ATTRB=(BRT,PROT),                                       X
               INITIAL='PRICE'
*-------------------------------- DFHMDF  STARTS A FIELD ---------
         DFHMDF POS=(6,50),                                            X
               LENGTH=5,                                               X
               ATTRB=(BRT,PROT),                                       X
               INITIAL='TOTAL'
*-------------------------------- DFHMDF  STARTS A FIELD ---------
QUANT    DFHMDF POS=(7,20),                                            X
               LENGTH=5,                                               X
               ATTRB=(NORM,UNPROT,NUM),                                X
               PICIN='99999'
*
         DFHMDF POS=(7,26),                                            X
               LENGTH=1,                                               X
               ATTRB=PROT
*-------------------------------- DFHMDF  STARTS A FIELD ---------
PRICE    DFHMDF POS=(7,32),                                            X
               LENGTH=4,                                               X
               ATTRB=(NORM,UNPROT,NUM),                                X
               PICIN='99V99'
*                                 "STOPPER" FIELD ---------
         DFHMDF POS=(7,37),                                            X
               LENGTH=1,                                               X
               ATTRB=PROT
*-------------------------------- DFHMDF  STARTS A FIELD ---------
TOTB4    DFHMDF POS=(7,42),                                            X
               LENGTH=13,                                              X
               ATTRB=PROT,                                             X
               PICOUT='ZZ,ZZZ,ZZ9.99'
*-------------------------------- DFHMDF  STARTS A FIELD ---------
         DFHMDF POS=(10,34),                                           X
               LENGTH=6,                                               X
               ATTRB=(BRT,PROT),
               INITIAL='8% TAX'
*-------------------------------- DFHMDF  STARTS A FIELD ---------
TAX      DFHMDF POS=(10,42),                                           X
               LENGTH=13,                                              X
               ATTRB=PROT,                                             X
               PICOUT='ZZ,ZZZ,ZZ9.99'
*-------------------------------- DFHMDF  STARTS A FIELD ---------
         DFHMDF POS=(12,42),                                           X
               LENGTH=13,                                              X
               ATTRB=(NORM,PROT),                                      X
               INITIAL='============='
*-------------------------------- DFHMDF  STARTS A FIELD ---------
         DFHMDF POS=(14,29),                                           X
               LENGTH=11,                                              X
               ATTRB=(BRT,PROT),                                       X
               INITIAL='GRAND TOTAL'
*-------------------------------- DFHMDF  STARTS A FIELD ---------
GTOTAL   DFHMDF POS=(14,42),                                           X
               LENGTH=13,                                              X
               ATTRB=PROT,                                             X
               PICOUT='ZZ,ZZZ,ZZ9.99'
*-------------------------------- DFHMDF  STARTS A FIELD ---------
MSG      DFHMDF POS=(24,01),                                           X
               LENGTH=79,                                              X
               ATTRB=(BRT,PROT)
*-------------------------------- DFHMSD  ENDS A MAP ------------
         DFHMSD TYPE=FINAL
         END
```

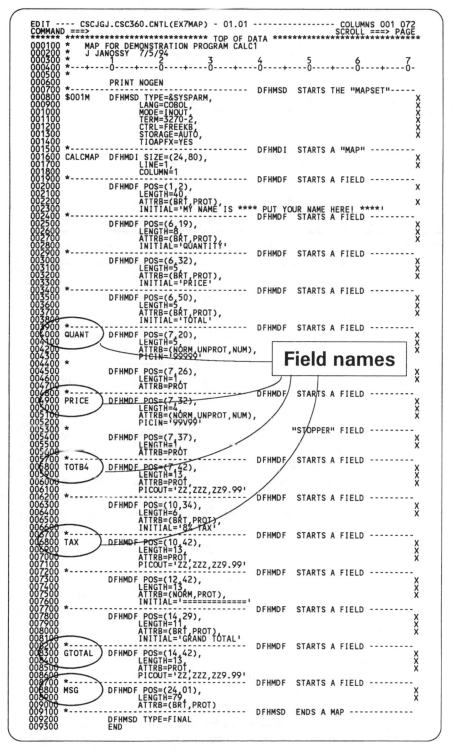

Field names

Figure 5.4 Field names on the BMS code for the CALC1 screen (the design for this screen was presented in Figure 4.3).

	QUANT			PRICE		
Filler x(12)	length S9(4) comp	attrib byte x(1)	data 9(5) x(5)	length S9(4) comp	attrib byte x(1)	data 99V99 x(4)
1 12	13 14	15	16 20	21 22	23	24 27

TOTB4			TAX		
length S9(4) comp	attrib byte x(1)	data ZZ, ZZZ, ZZ9.99 x(13)	length S9(4) comp	attrib byte x(1)	data 22, 222, 2229.99 x(13)
28 29	30	31 43	44 45	46	47 59

GTOTAL			MSG		
length S9(4) comp	attrib byte x(1)	data ZZ, ZZZ, ZZ9.99 x(13)	length S9(4) comp	attrib byte x(1)	data x(79)
60 61	62	63 75	76 77	78	79 157

Figure 5.5 Graphic record layout showing format of the data transmission record for the CALC1 screen.

gram issues the CICS RECEIVE MAP command and then looks into the data transmission record to access the data.

The PIC S9(4) BINARY (BINARY is the 1985 COBOL way to say COMP) length value associated with each field serves no purpose when your program sends data to a terminal. When your program receives data from a terminal, CICS automatically puts a value into each length field. For each field, this value indicates how many keystrokes the terminal operator put into the field before its transmission to the program. A value of zero here when the data transmission record is received means that the operator did not make or change an entry in the field on the screen.

The PIC X(1) attribute byte field associated with each field in the data transmission record allows a program to change the attribute byte of the field on the screen when it sends data to the terminal. When your program sends data to a terminal, this value will replace the value in the screen's attribute byte for the field.

You can use each field's attribute byte in the data transmission record to make the field that is currently displayed at normal intensity become bright, or vice versa, or "hide" a field that is on the screen by making it dark (DRK). This field also lets you "protect" a field after the operator has entered something into it, or make a protected field unprotected, to allow cursor access to it. We'll show you how to use the attribute byte fields in the data transmission record within a program when we consider the logic of the CALC1 program in Chapter 7. The attribute byte fields in the data transmission record serve no purpose when your program receives data from a terminal.

5.5 SYMBOLIC MAP: DESCRIBING THE DATA TRANSMISSION RECORD

The symbolic map is simply a COBOL description of the data transmission record. You can have the assembler produce this COBOL record description coding for you by feeding it your BMS map code at its //SYSIN input and specifying SYSPARM(DSECT) when you execute the assembler. Figure 5.6 shows how this process fits into the overall picture of

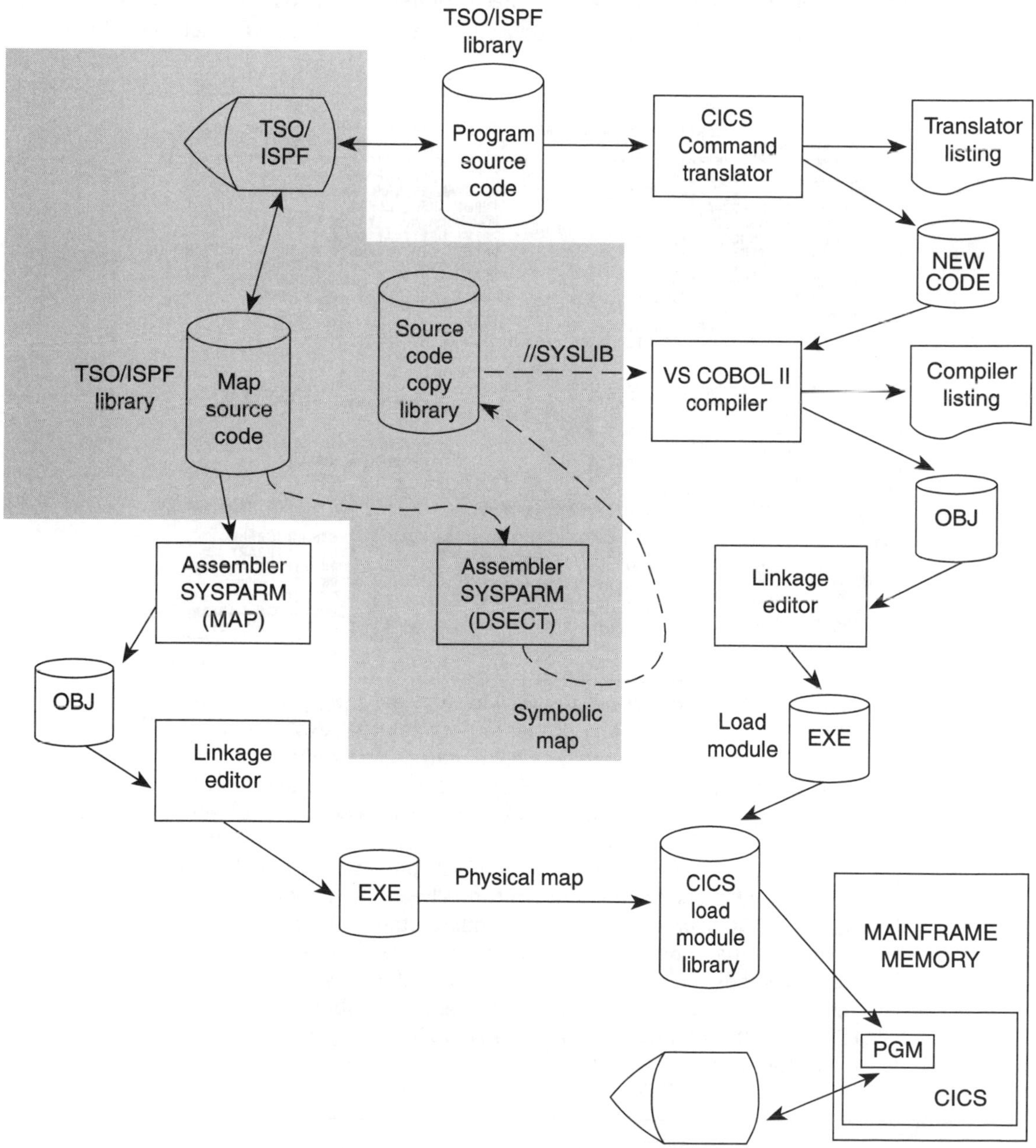
TSO/ISPF
library
TSO/
ISPF
Program
source
code
CICS
Command
translator
Translator
listing
NEW
CODE
Source
code
copy
library
//SYSLIB
VS COBOL II
compiler
Compiler
listing
TSO/ISPF
library
Map
source
code
OBJ
Assembler
SYSPARM
(MAP)
Assembler
SYSPARM
(DSECT)
Linkage
editor
OBJ
Symbolic
map
Load
module
EXE
Linkage
editor
EXE
Physical map
CICS
load
module
library
MAINFRAME
MEMORY
PGM
CICS

Figure 5.6 You can have the IBM assembler read your BMS map code and use it to produce a symbolic map.

CICS programming. The shaded part of Figure 5.6 shows the symbolic mapping being produced by the assembler and being housed, as 80-byte punch card-image records, in a source code copy library.

Figure 5.7 shows you a job stream named MAKESMAP (MAKE Symbolic MAP) that represents a part of the symbolic map processing shown in Figure 5.6. Here, the assembler reads BMS map source code, but instead of capturing the symbolic map output at //SYSPUNCH for future use, we have directed it to paper so you can see it. In this JCL, you code the name of the library housing your BMS map code at the SET statement in lines 15-16

```
EDIT ---- CSCJGJ.CSC360.CNTL(MAKESMAP) - 01.00 --------------- COLUMNS 001 072
COMMAND ===>                                                   SCROLL ===> PAGE
****** ****************************** TOP OF DATA ******************************
000001 //CSCJGJA   JOB 1,                        ACCOUNTING INFORMATION
000002 //   'BIN 7--JANOSSY',                    PROGRAMMER NAME AND DELIVERY BIN
000003 //   CLASS=A,                             INPUT QUEUE CLASS
000004 //   MSGLEVEL=(1,1),                      HOW MUCH MVS SYSTEM PRINT DESIRED
000005 //   MSGCLASS=X,                          PRINT DESTINATION X A L N OR O
000006 //   TIME=(0,6),                          SAFETY LIMIT: RUN TIME UP TO 6 SECS
000007 //   REGION=2M,                           ALLOW UP TO 2 MEGS VIRTUAL MEMORY
000008 //*  TYPRUN=SCAN,                         UNCOMMENT THIS LINE TO DO SCAN ONLY
000009 //   NOTIFY=CSCJGJ                        WHO TO TELL WHEN JOB IS DONE
000010 //*-----------------------------------------------------------------------
000011 //*  PREPARE A MACHINE-GENERATED SYMBOLIC MAP FROM MAP CODE
000012 //*  THIS JCL IS STORED AT CSCJGJ.CSC360.CNTL(MAKESMAP)
000013 //*-----------------------------------------------------------------------
000014 //*
000015 //   SET  SORCLIB='CSCJGJ.CSC360.CNTL',         LIBRARY HOUSING MAP CODE
000016 //        BNAME='EX7MAP'                        MEMBER NAME OF MAP CODE
000017 //*
000018 //STEP010  EXEC  PGM=IEV90,
000019 //   REGION=2M,
000020 //   PARM=('SYSPARM(DSECT)',                    PRODUCE A SYMBOLIC MAP
000021 //         'DECK',
000022 //         'NOLOAD')
000023 //SYSIN        DD  DSN=&SORCLIB(&BNAME),                MAP SOURCE CODE IN
000024 //   DISP=SHR
000025 //SYSLIB       DD  DSN=CICS330.SDFHMAC,DISP=SHR         SYSTEM LIBRARY
000026 //             DD  DSN=SYS1.MACLIB,DISP=SHR             SYSTEM LIBRARY
000027 //SYSUT1       DD  UNIT=VIO,SPACE=(CYL,(5,5))           WORK FILE
000028 //SYSUT2       DD  UNIT=VIO,SPACE=(CYL,(5,5))           WORK FILE
000029 //SYSUT3       DD  UNIT=VIO,SPACE=(CYL,(5,5))           WORK FILE
000030 //SYSPRINT     DD  SYSOUT=*                             SOURCE CODE LISTING
000031 //SYSPUNCH     DD  SYSOUT=*                             SYMBOLIC MAP OUT
000032 //
```

This job stream executes the IBM assembler, a program named IEV90, and gives it the appropriate parameter (PARM) value, **DSECT**, to cause it to process BMS map coding defining a screen into a COBOL description of the data transmission record matching the screen. The **data transmission record** is the record formed by BMS when it "packages" the transmission from the terminal into a form that a COBOL/CICS program can deal with. The record description is known formally as the **symbolic map**. It is COBOL source code (of, by modern standards, poor legibility) that emerges at the ddname //SYSPUNCH. This JCL simply sends the symbolic map to the printer so you see it. Other JCL, such as MAPJOB, captures the symbolic map in a file so that it can be copied into any COBOL program dealing with this screen.

Figure 5.7 Job stream MAKESMAP, executing the IBM assembler to have it process BMS map code into a symbolic map.

at the symbolic parameter SORCLIB, and you code the name of the member housing the BMS map code at BNAME.

Figure 5.8 shows you the symbolic map as the last part of the output of a run of the MAKESMAP job stream, as you would view this output using TSO/ISPF. By changing the

```
SDSF OUTPUT DISPLAY CSCJGJA  JOB01105  DSID   101 LINE 112      COLUMNS 02- 81
COMMAND INPUT ===>                                              SCROLL ===> PAGE

                                   1285+         PRINT OFF
                                   1365 *-----------------------------------
                                   1366          DFHMSD TYPE=FINAL
                                   1368+         PRINT OFF
                                   1444+         PRINT OFF
                                   1533          END

                                DIAGNOSTIC CROSS REFERENCE AND ASSEMBLER SUMMA

   NO STATEMENTS FLAGGED IN THIS ASSEMBLY
  OVERRIDING PARAMETERS-  SYSPARM(DSECT),DECK,NOLOAD
  OPTIONS FOR THIS ASSEMBLY
   DECK, NOOBJECT, LIST, XREF(FULL), NORENT, NOTEST, NOBATCH, ALIGN, ESD, RLD,
   LINECOUNT(55), FLAG(0), SYSPARM(DSECT)
  NO OVERRIDING DD NAMES
     93 CARDS FROM SYSIN     6341 CARDS FROM SYSLIB
    130 LINES OUTPUT           46 CARDS OUTPUT

       01  CALCMAPI.
           02  FILLER PIC X(12).

           02  QUANTL      COMP  PIC  S9(4).
           02  QUANTF      PICTURE X.
           02  FILLER REDEFINES QUANTF.
             03 QUANTA       PICTURE X.
           02  QUANTI  PIC 99999.

           02  PRICEL      COMP  PIC  S9(4).
           02  PRICEF      PICTURE X.
           02  FILLER REDEFINES PRICEF.
             03 PRICEA       PICTURE X.
           02  PRICEI  PIC 99V99.

           02  TOTB4L      COMP  PIC  S9(4).
           02  TOTB4F      PICTURE X.
           02  FILLER REDEFINES TOTB4F.
             03 TOTB4A       PICTURE X.
           02  TOTB4I  PIC X(13).

           02  TAXL      COMP  PIC  S9(4).
           02  TAXF      PICTURE X.
           02  FILLER REDEFINES TAXF.
             03 TAXA       PICTURE X.
           02  TAXI  PIC X(13).

           02  GTOTALL      COMP  PIC  S9(4).
           02  GTOTALF      PICTURE X.
           02  FILLER REDEFINES GTOTALF.
             03 GTOTALA       PICTURE X.
           02  GTOTALI  PIC X(13).

           02  MSGL      COMP  PIC  S9(4).
           02  MSGF      PICTURE X.
           02  FILLER REDEFINES MSGF.
             03 MSGA       PICTURE X.
           02  MSGI  PIC X(79).

       01  CALCMAPO REDEFINES CALCMAPI.
           02  FILLER PIC X(12).
           02  FILLER PICTURE X(3).
           02  QUANTO  PIC X(5).
           02  FILLER PICTURE X(3).
           02  PRICEO  PIC X(4).
           02  FILLER PICTURE X(3).
           02  TOTB4O PIC ZZ,ZZZ,ZZ9.99.
           02  FILLER PICTURE X(3).
           02  TAXO PIC ZZ,ZZZ,ZZ9.99.
           02  FILLER PICTURE X(3).
           02  GTOTALO PIC ZZ,ZZZ,ZZ9.99.
           02  FILLER PICTURE X(3).
           02  MSGO  PIC X(79).
```

End of assembler's listing of BMS map code

PICIN coding

PICOUT coding

An assembler-produced **symbolic map**, output at the //SYSPUNCH DD statement in response to SYSPARM(DSECT). This is a COBOL description of the **data transmission record**. The assembler forms the field names here using the field names you coded in the BMS map, appending the suffix L, F, A, I, or O. The assembler-produced symbolic map is awkward, since it contains redundant names and the names are much shorter and cryptic than you would expect for modern COBOL programs. The first 01 level, named CALC1I here, provides PICIN coding from your BMS map coding. The redefinition of CALC1I, named CALC1O, provides PICOUT coding from your BMS map.

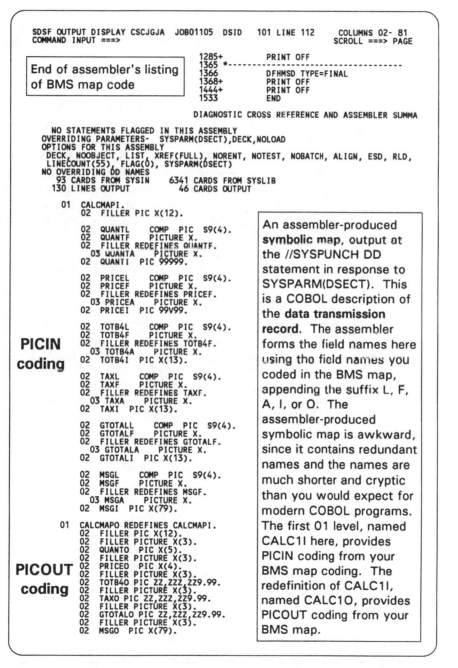

Figure 5.8 Symbolic map for the CALC1 screen, as produced by the IBM assembler.

coding at //SYSPUNCH we could capture this COBOL source code in a file for use in a program, as we do in the MAPJOB job stream discussed later in this chapter.

5.6 MANUALLY CODING THE SYMBOLIC MAP

The **machine-generated symbolic map** shown in Figure 5.8 will always exactly match the actual data transmission record for a screen, because it is generated from the same BMS map source code. Some installations actually use this version of the symbolic map. But this record description is hard to work with because it uses short, cryptic field names built from the field names coded in the BMS map. The assembler simply adds one letter to the field names. The machine-generated map is also hard to work with because it uses unusual indentation and level numbering, and it uses a REDEFINES to call the same memory fields by different names.

You can, if you wish, develop your own coded description of the data transmission record. We have done this for the CALC1 screen, naming the manually coded symbolic map SCALC1. We have listed our coded description in Figure 5.9. Our **manually coded symbolic map** is much clearer because it uses a modern naming convention to assign descriptive names to each data transmission field. This record description does exactly the same job as the machine-generated symbolic map in Figure 5.7, and makes program logic easier to follow. Since it's manually coded, however, it is possible to make a mistake, creating an inaccurate description of the data transmission record.

In this book, we begin CICS program examples in Chapter 6, using the manually coded symbolic map shown in Figure 5.9. For variety, in later chapters we use the assembler-generated

```
EDIT ---- CSCJGJ.CSC360.COBOL(SCALC1) - 01.00 --------------- COLUMNS 007 078
COMMAND ===>                                                SCROLL ===> PAGE
****** ****************************** TOP OF DATA ******************************
       *---------------------------------------------------------------
       *
       *  MANUALLY-CODED SYMBOLIC MAP FOR CALC1 PROGRAM     JIM JANOSSY
       *
       *---------------------------------------------------------------
        01  CALC1-SYMBOLIC-MAP.
            05 FILLER                         PIC X(12).

            05 CSM-L-QUANTITY                 PIC S9(4)  BINARY.
            05 CSM-A-QUANTITY                 PIC X(1).
            05 CSM-D-QUANTITY                 PIC 9(5).

            05 CSM-L-PRICE                    PIC S9(4)  BINARY.
            05 CSM-A-PRICE                    PIC X(1).
            05 CSM-D-PRICE                    PIC 99V99.

            05 CSM-L-TOTAL-BEFORE-TAX         PIC S9(4)  BINARY.
            05 CSM-A-TOTAL-BEFORE-TAX         PIC X(1).
            05 CSM-D-TOTAL-BEFORE-TAX         PIC ZZ,ZZZ,ZZ9.99.

            05 CSM-L-TAX                      PIC S9(4)  BINARY.
            05 CSM-A-TAX                      PIC X(1).
            05 CSM-D-TAX                      PIC ZZ,ZZZ,ZZ9.99.

            05 CSM-L-GRAND-TOTAL              PIC S9(4)  BINARY.
            05 CSM-A-GRAND-TOTAL              PIC X(1).
            05 CSM-D-GRAND-TOTAL              PIC ZZ,ZZZ,ZZ9.99.

            05 CSM-L-MESSAGE                  PIC S9(4)  BINARY.
            05 CSM-A-MESSAGE                  PIC X(1).
            05 CSM-D-MESSAGE                  PIC X(79).
```

Figure 5.9 This manually coded symbolic map for the CALC1 program describes the data transmission record depicted in Figure 5.5.

symbolic map for other screens, so you can see the effect of its short data names on program legibility.

5.7 ELIMINATING PICIN AND PICOUT CODING FROM BMS MAPS

PICIN and **PICOUT** BMS map code specifications exist only to support the generation of the symbolic map by the assembler. PICIN and PICOUT have no effect on the physical map. If you will be using manually coded symbolic maps, or symbolic maps generated by a screen painter such as GENMAP, you can omit PICIN and PICOUT coding from your BMS map code. Retaining PICIN and PICOUT causes no harm, even if you do not use machine-generated symbolic maps, and you might regard PICIN and PICOUT as documentation.

5.8 SYMBOLIC MAP PRODUCED BY A SCREEN PAINTER

Screen painting software can generate a symbolic map for your use just as it generates BMS map coding. If you use the PC-based GENMAP screen painter as described in Chapter 4, you will automatically receive a well-formed symbolic map matching each BMS map. This symbolic map will follow a format similar to our manually coded symbolic map in Figure 5.9. The GENMAP "COBOL label" field shown in Figure 4.16 is the place where you enter the descriptive part of each COBOL field name for use in the symbolic map.

5.9 ROLE OF A SOURCE CODE COPY LIBRARY

A CICS program requires that a symbolic map for a screen be present in its WORKING-STORAGE section, so that fields in the data transmission record can be accessed. It does not matter to the CICS program whether you use a symbolic map created by the assembler, a manually coded symbolic map, or a symbolic map created by a screen painter. Simply put, COBOL source code is COBOL source code, no matter who (or what) creates it.

Similarly, it does not matter to a CICS program *how* the symbolic map comes to be present in the program source code. You can hard code the symbolic map in the source code of a program, or you can use the **COPY compiler directive** to bring the symbolic map in from a source code copy library. We illustrate both forms of symbolic map treatment in this book, providing you with examples of each method.

If you refer to Figure 5.6, you will see that the symbolic map output of the assembler is directed into a library as a member. This is the most common handling of symbolic maps. The library you use to house symbolic maps can be your own COBOL library, a separate copy library you establish for this purpose, or a centralized symbolic map library established and maintained by your installation. A library to house symbolic maps must be defined with record length 80. The block size can be as large as your installation permits, but a block size of 3,120 bytes is typical for a library such as this.

You can house symbolic maps created by a screen painter such as GENMAP in the same library that houses symbolic maps created by the IBM assembler. If you generate symbolic maps on a PC, as GENMAP does, just upload them as ASCII files to your symbolic map library.

5.10 CREATING PHYSICAL AND SYMBOLIC MAPS USING MAPJOB

If you will be using manually coded or screen-painter-generated symbolic maps, you need only be concerned with the processing accomplished by the MAKEPMAP job stream illus-

```
EDIT ---- CSCJGJ.CSC360.CNTL(MAPJOB) - 01.01 ----------------- COLUMNS 001 072
COMMAND ===>                                                   SCROLL ===> PAGE
****** ***************************** TOP OF DATA ******************************
//CSCJGJA   JOB 1,                  ACCOUNTING INFORMATION
//  'BIN 7--JANOSSY',               PROGRAMMER NAME AND DELIVERY BIN
//  CLASS=A,                        INPUT QUEUE CLASS
//  MSGLEVEL=(1,1),                 HOW MUCH MVS SYSTEM PRINT DESIRED
//  MSGCLASS=X,                     PRINT DESTINATION X A L N OR O
//  TIME=(0,6),                     SAFETY LIMIT: RUN TIME UP TO 6 SECS
//  REGION=2M,                      ALLOW UP TO 2 MEGS VIRTUAL MEMORY
//* TYPRUN=SCAN,                    UNCOMMENT THIS LINE TO DO SCAN ONLY
//  NOTIFY=CSCJGJ                   WHO TO TELL WHEN JOB IS DONE
//*
//*-----------------------------------------------------------------
//*  PREPARE PHYSICAL AND SYMBOLIC MAPS FROM BMS MAP CODE
//*  THIS JCL IS STORED AT CSCJGJ.CSC360.CNTL(MAPJOB)
//*-----------------------------------------------------------------
//*
//  SET  SORCLIB='CSCJGJ.CSC360.CNTL',    SOURCE LIBRARY FOR MAP CODE
//         BNAME='BCALC1',                BMS MAP CODE MEMBER NAME
//*
//       LOADLIB='CCP.LOADLIB',           CICS LOAD LIBRARY
//         PNAME='$001M',                 PHYSICAL MAP MEMBER NAME
//*
//       COPYLIB='CSCJGJ.CSC360.COBOL',   COBOL LIBRARY FOR SYM MAPS
//         SNAME='ACALC1'                 SYMBOLIC MAP MEMBER NAME
//*
//*****************************************************************
//*
//*  ASSEMBLE THE BMS MAP SOURCE CODE, CREATING OBJECT FILE
//*
//*****************************************************************
//*
//STEP010  EXEC  PGM=IEV90,
//  REGION=2M,
//  PARM=('SYSPARM(MAP)',                            MAKE PMAP OBJ FILE
//        'DECK',
//        'NOLOAD')
//SYSIN      DD  DSN=&SORCLIB(&BNAME),               BMS MAP CODE IN
//  DISP=SHR
//SYSLIB     DD  DSN=CICS330.SDFHMAC,DISP=SHR        SYSTEM LIBRARY
//           DD  DSN=SYS1.MACLIB,DISP=SHR            SYSTEM LIBRARY
//SYSUT1     DD  UNIT=VIO,SPACE=(CYL,(5,5))          WORK FILE
//SYSUT2     DD  UNIT=VIO,SPACE=(CYL,(5,5))          WORK FILE
//SYSUT3     DD  UNIT=VIO,SPACE=(CYL,(5,5))          WORK FILE
//SYSPRINT   DD  SYSOUT=*                            SOURCE CODE LISTING
//SYSPUNCH   DD  DSN=&&OBJECT,                       OBJECT FILE OUT
//  DISP=(NEW,PASS),
//  UNIT=VIO,
//  RECFM=FB,
//  LRECL=80,
//  BLKSIZE=3120,
//  SPACE=(CYL,(1,1))
//*
//*****************************************************************
//*
//*  IF CODE OK, LINK EDIT THE OBJECT TO CREATE THE PHYSICAL MAP
//*
//*****************************************************************
//    IF ( STEP010.RC <= 4 ) THEN
//STEP020  EXEC  PGM=IEWL,
//  PARM=('LIST',
//        'LET',
//        'XREF',                                    CROSS REFERENCE
//        'RMODE(24)')                               PHY MAP RES. MODE
//SYSLIN     DD  DSN=&&OBJECT,DISP=(OLD,DELETE)      OBJECT FILE IN
//SYSPRINT   DD  SYSOUT=*                            LINKAGE EDIT RPT
//SYSUT1     DD  UNIT=VIO,SPACE=(CYL,(1,1))          WORK FILE
//SYSLMOD    DD  DSN=&LOADLIB(&PNAME),DISP=SHR       PHYSICAL MAP OUT
//*
//*****************************************************************
//*
//*  IF CODE OK, PREPARE A SYMBOLIC MAP FROM THE BMS MAP CODE
//*
//*****************************************************************
//*
//STEP030  EXEC  PGM=IEV90,
//  REGION=2M,
//  PARM=('SYSPARM(DSECT)',                          PRODUCE SYMBOLIC MAP
//        'DECK',
//        'NOLOAD')
//SYSIN      DD  DSN=&SORCLIB(&BNAME),               MAP SOURCE CODE IN
//  DISP=SHR
//SYSLIB     DD  DSN=CICS330.SDFHMAC,DISP=SHR        SYSTEM LIBRARY
//           DD  DSN=SYS1.MACLIB,DISP=SHR            SYSTEM LIBRARY
//SYSUT1     DD  UNIT=VIO,SPACE=(CYL,(5,5))          WORK FILE
//SYSUT2     DD  UNIT=VIO,SPACE=(CYL,(5,5))          WORK FILE
//SYSUT3     DD  UNIT=VIO,SPACE=(CYL,(5,5))          WORK FILE
//SYSPRINT   DD  SYSOUT=*                            SOURCE CODE LISTING
//SYSPUNCH   DD  DSN=&COPYLIB(&SNAME),DISP=SHR       SYMBOLIC MAP OUT
//    ENDIF
//
```

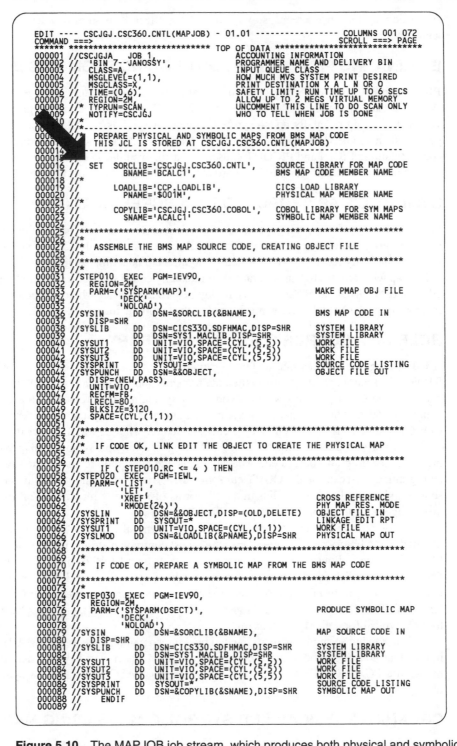

Figure 5.10 The MAPJOB job stream, which produces both physical and symbolic maps from your BMS map code in one job submission.

trated in Figure 5.2. If, however, you will be using machine-generated symbolic maps, you will find it inconvenient to run MAKEPMAP to create a physical map, and then submit a separate run such as MAKESMAP to create the corresponding symbolic map.

We provide the MAPJOB job stream, listed in Figure 5.10, to make it easy for you to process your BMS map code into both physical and symbolic maps in one job submission. To provide necessary flexibility, we provide six symbolic parameters in this job stream:

SORCLIB	the "source" library name where the BMS map source code is housed
BNAME	the BMS map code member name
LOADLIB	the name of the CICS load library that houses machine language (physical) maps and the machine language of CICS programs
PNAME	the physical map member name
COPYLIB	the name of the COBOL source code library in which you want to store the symbolic map
SNAME	the symbolic map member name

You assign actual data set and member names to these symbolic parameters at the SET statement in lines 16 through 23 of the MAPJOB job stream in Figure 5.10. If you wish, you can house this job stream as a cataloged procedure and assign the symbolic parameter values using the EXEC statement in traditional pre-MVS/ESA Version 4 JCL style.

You might also have access to an existing IBM proc named DFHMAPS, which is common for physical and symbolic map processing. For more information about DFHMAPS and its enhancement and customization, see Chapter 6 in *Advanced MVS/ESA JCL Examples,* by James Janossy, published in 1994 by John Wiley & Sons, Inc.

5.11 FOR YOUR REVIEW

Understanding these terms, introduced in this chapter, will aid your understanding of the next chapter:

BMS map field names
BMS map source code
COPY compiler directive
Data transmission record
Linkage editor program
Machine-generated symbolic map
Manually coded symbolic map
Physical map
PICIN
PICOUT
Symbolic map

5.12 REVIEW QUESTIONS

1. Identify the three kinds of maps used with CICS programming, and describe the contents and role of each.
2. What software do you execute to process your BMS map code?
3. How do you control what fields are present in the data transmission record?
4. Describe clearly the pattern for the format of fields in the data transmission record.
5. Explain how a CICS program uses a data transmission record.
6. When you receive a transmission from a terminal and are examining the contents of the data transmission record, how do you tell if the terminal operator entered any data in a field?

7. Can you change the value of the attribute byte for a field on the computer screen when your CICS program transmits data to the screen? If so, explain how.
8. Explain what the symbolic map is, and identify and describe three ways that you can get the coding for it.
9. Explain what PICIN and PICOUT in your BMS map code do.
10. Where within a CICS program does the description of the data transmission record reside, and what two methods exist for you to arrange for it to be there?

5.13 HANDS-ON EXERCISES

If you have completed the assignment described in section 4.17, you can move ahead to accomplish the tasks listed here to gain additional hands-on experience with CICS.

A. Process the BMS map source code you developed in section 4.17 for your FIRST CICS SCREEN using the MAKESMAP job control language shown in Figure 5.7, or using similar JCL provided locally. MAKESMAP prints the machine-generated symbolic map resulting from by your BMS map source code. Examine the symbolic map produced, and use it to prepare a graphic record layout similar in format to Figure 5.5. Label each of the fields in your graphic record layout in an appropriate way, including field name, starting position, ending position, length in bytes, and PIC.

B. Make a copy of your BMS map source code, and eliminate PICIN and PICOUT in the copy. Process the modified BMS map source code again using the MAKESMAP JCL. Compare the machine-generated symbolic map from your first run and this run. Be ready to explain the effect of removing PICIN and PICOUT from your coding.

C. Using the graphic record layout you developed in task A, and the machine-generated symbolic map, develop a manually coded symbolic map for your screen, similar in format to the symbolic map shown in Figure 5.9.

D. Process the BMS map source code you developed in section 4.17 for your FIRST CICS SCREEN using the MAPJOB JCL shown in Figure 5.10, or using similar JCL provided locally. Examine the MVS/ESA system reporting from this job. By examining the COND CODEs for each of the three steps in the job, confirm that the job has successfully created both the physical and symbolic maps for your screen. Note: Since MAPJOB creates two new files housing the physical and symbolic maps, you will have to code locally appropriate data set names at the SET statement to house these files.

6

Introduction to CICS Programming

You have now seen and learned how to express the image of a screen in terms of Basic Mapping Support coding, and how your coding determines the format of the data transmission record by which a program communicates with the screen. In this chapter, we explore a simple CICS program that sends a map to a computer terminal. You'll see the steps necessary to process this program into executable form using job control language. We'll also show you how to activate this program under CICS to execute it, and how to make CICS aware of a new copy of the program when you revise and replace it.

6.1 OVERVIEW OF A SIMPLE CICS PROGRAM

Figure 6.1 lists the VS COBOL II source code for a simple program named SHOWMAP. We'll use this program to show you some of the most important elements of CICS programming and program processing. Let's begin with a general description of this short program.

A COBOL program normally contains four divisions: IDENTIFICATION, ENVIRON-

```
EDIT ---- CSCJGJ.CSC360.COBOL(SHOWMAP) - 01.04 --------------- COLUMNS 007 078
COMMAND ===>                                                   SCROLL ===> PAGE
****** ****************************** TOP OF DATA ******************************
       ID DIVISION.
       PROGRAM-ID. SHOWMAP.

      *-----------------------------------------------------------------
      *  THIS SIMPLE CICS PROGRAM JUST PRESENTS A MAP AND THEN ENDS
      *  EXECUTION.  CODING, COMPILING, AND ARRANGING TO EXECUTE IT
      *  WILL GIVE YOU EXPERIENCE WITH THE MECHANICS OF CICS.
      *-----------------------------------------------------------------

       DATA DIVISION.
       WORKING-STORAGE SECTION.
      *-----------------------------------------------------------------
      *
      *  MANUALLY-CODED SYMBOLIC MAP FOR CALC1 PROGRAM    JIM JANOSSY
      *
      *-----------------------------------------------------------------
       01  CALC1-SYMBOLIC-MAP.
           05 FILLER                          PIC X(12).

           05 CSM-L-QUANTITY                  PIC S9(4)  COMP.
           05 CSM-A-QUANTITY                  PIC X(1).
           05 CSM-D-QUANTITY                  PIC 9(5).

           05 CSM-L-PRICE                     PIC S9(4)  COMP.
           05 CSM-A-PRICE                     PIC X(1).
           05 CSM-D-PRICE                     PIC 99V99.

           05 CSM-L-TOTAL-BEFORE-TAX          PIC S9(4)  COMP.
           05 CSM-A-TOTAL-BEFORE-TAX          PIC X(1).
           05 CSM-D-TOTAL-BEFORE-TAX          PIC ZZ,ZZZ,ZZ9.99.

           05 CSM-L-TAX                       PIC S9(4)  COMP.
           05 CSM-A-TAX                       PIC X(1).
           05 CSM-D-TAX                       PIC ZZ,ZZZ,ZZ9.99.

           05 CSM-L-GRAND-TOTAL               PIC S9(4)  COMP.
           05 CSM-A-GRAND-TOTAL               PIC X(1).
           05 CSM-D-GRAND-TOTAL               PIC ZZ,ZZZ,ZZ9.99.

           05 CSM-L-MESSAGE                   PIC S9(4)  COMP.
           05 CSM-A-MESSAGE                   PIC X(1).
           05 CSM-D-MESSAGE                   PIC X(79).

       LINKAGE SECTION.
       01  DFHCOMMAREA                        PIC X(1).

       PROCEDURE DIVISION.
       1000-MAIN.

           MOVE LOW-VALUES TO CALC1-SYMBOLIC-MAP.
           MOVE -1 TO CSM-L-QUANTITY.
           MOVE 'HERE IS MY CALC1 MAP!  JIM JANOSSY' TO CSM-D-MESSAGE.

           EXEC CICS
               SEND MAP     ('CALCMAP')
                    MAPSET  ('$001M')
                    FROM    (CALC1-SYMBOLIC-MAP)
                    ERASE
                    CURSOR
           END-EXEC.

           EXEC CICS
                    RETURN
           END-EXEC.
```

I hardcoded the symbolic map in this program, but I could have use COPY to bring it in. Here I used COMP instead of BINARY to illustrate older COBOL syntax for a binary field.

This is a CICS command

Figure 6.1 Source code of the SHOWMAP CICS program.

MENT, DATA, and PROCEDURE. But the SHOWMAP program in Figure 6.1 lacks an ENVIRONMENT division. VS COBOL II permits you to omit coding any unnecessary divisions. SHOWMAP, and all other CICS programs, have no need for an ENVIRONMENT division, since CICS programs cannot deal directly with files. (You could, if you prefer, code an ENVIRONMENT division heading but leave this division empty.)

In Figure 6.1 you see our manually coded symbolic map for the CALC1 screen in the WORKING-STORAGE section. **WORKING-STORAGE** represents memory "owned" by the program. CICS will place information into this memory when we receive a transmission from the CALC1 screen. When we want to transmit information from the program to the CALC1 screen on a terminal, we put that information into the symbolic map and send the map to the terminal.

The SHOWMAP program contains a **LINKAGE section** at lines 4400 and 4500. We have coded this in a minimal form, indicating only a one-byte field named **DFHCOMMAREA**. This entry will become important as we demonstrate actual CICS program logic. For now, think of this entry as simply a "landmark" that our program processing will find and use as a reference point to automatically add statements into the LINKAGE section of the program.

The PROCEDURE division of the SHOWMAP program consists of three MOVE statements and two special CICS commands. The MOVE statements are all straightforward and put things into the symbolic map prior to its transmission to a terminal:

```
MOVE LOW-VALUES TO CALC1-SYMBOLIC-MAP.
MOVE -1 TO CSM-L-QUANTITY.
MOVE 'HERE IS MY CALC1 MAP! JIM JANOSSY' TO CSM-D-MESSAGE.
```

The first of the two CICS commands in the SHOWMAP program actually transmits the physical map and the data in the symbolic map to the terminal through the Basic Mapping Support (BMS) subsystem:

```
EXEC CICS
   SEND MAP    ('CALCMAP')
        MAPSET ('$001M')
        FROM   (CALC1-SYMBOLIC-MAP)
        ERASE
        CURSOR
END-EXEC.
```

The last of the CICS commands in the SHOWMAP program, **RETURN**, gives control back to CICS. This command ends execution of the CICS program:

```
EXEC CICS
        RETURN
END-EXEC.
```

What is missing in SHOWMAP? Do you see any STOP RUN statement? STOP RUN is the COBOL command to end execution of a program and give control back to the operating system. *You do not code STOP RUN in CICS programs.* A CICS program never gives control back to the operating system. A CICS program is executed by CICS; when a CICS program finishes it gives control back to CICS.

Let's examine each element of the SHOWMAP program's PROCEDURE division in greater detail. We'll then consider how we can turn SHOWMAP source code into machine language to make it executable.

6.2 PROGRAM ACTIONS TO MAKE A MAP READY TO SEND

The **SEND MAP** command is the heart of the SHOWMAP program. The MOVEs to the symbolic map that precede SEND MAP prepare the symbolic map for transmission. We do this

MOVE to fill the symbolic map with LOW-VALUES:

```
MOVE LOW-VALUES TO CALC1-SYMBOLIC-MAP.
```

LOW-VALUES is a COBOL figurative constant that stands for "all bits off" in every byte. LOW-VALUES is represented by 0000 0000 in binary form, which is known as X'00' in hexadecimal. This bit pattern is unique among all bit patterns in IBM communication arrangements in that is it *never transmitted* to a computer terminal. By making this MOVE, we fill every byte of the symbolic map with LOW-VALUES, so no part of it will be transmitted. We then selectively MOVE desired values to the fields that we *do* want to have transmitted:

```
MOVE -1 TO CSM-L-QUANTITY.
```

Putting a negative 1 into the "length" value of a data field in the symbolic map demands more explanation. Recall that the length value for each field in the data transmission record is actually intended to convey a number indicating the quantity of keystrokes made in a data field by the terminal operator when a map is *received* by a program. The length field can also serve another purpose. You can make the terminal put the cursor into a particular enterable field by making its length value negative, and specifying the CURSOR option of the SEND MAP command. If you do not give instructions for positioning the cursor in this way, it will be placed at the upper left corner of the screen by default. In that case the terminal operator will have to press the Tab key to get the cursor into the first enterable field.

The last MOVE in SHOWMAP, at line 5200, puts the initial prompting message into the symbolic map for transmission. We could have coded this initial message in the BMS map source code itself, at the bottom of Figure 4.4, using the INITIAL option, but we use this MOVE instead:

```
MOVE 'HERE IS MY CALC1 MAP! JIM JANOSSY' TO CSM-D-MESSAGE.
```

Coding this MOVE in the program lets the program customize the first presentation of the screen with a unique message.

6.3 THE SEND COMMAND

You send information from a CICS program to the terminal screen by issuing the SEND command:

```
EXEC CICS
   SEND MAP     ('CALCMAP')
        MAPSET  ('$001M')
        FROM    (CALC1-SYMBOLIC-MAP)
        ERASE
        CURSOR
END-EXEC.
```

It's important to realize that by issuing this command, you cause non–LOW-VALUES data from the symbolic map and screen labels from the physical map to be combined by CICS for transmission. This SEND command is typical of the first-time transmission from a CICS program to a terminal. Here is what each part of the SEND command means:

MAP The map name as coded in the BMS map shown in Figure 4.4. This name is from one to seven characters long and is *not* predefined in any CICS table.

MAPSET The map name as coded in the BMS map in Figure 4.4. This name *must* be predefined to CICS as an entry in the Program Control Table (PCT).

FROM Specifies the name of the symbolic map to be transmitted.

ERASE Indicates that we want the terminal screen to be completely blanked out before the new transmission reaches it.

CURSOR Tells CICS to put the cursor into the first enterable (unprotected) field it encounters that contains a negative value in its "length" indicator. By specifying this option, we activate the placement of the cursor intended by MOVE -1 TO CSM-L-QUANTITY.

A few other options also exist with SEND. You can specify these options to cause different processing to occur:

MAPONLY Causes only the physical map to be transmitted; that is, only screen labels to be transmitted. If you specify this, it makes no sense to code FROM, since the symbolic map is not sent.

DATAONLY Causes only non–LOW-VALUES data in the symbolic map to be transmitted, and the physical map is not accessed. You can't specify both MAPONLY and DATAONLY in the same SEND command.

ERASEAUP Tells CICS to erase "all unprotected fields" rather than the entire screen, before the transmission is received. This is handy for a "clean the input fields" function that we'll show you how to program in Chapter 7.

CURSOR(nn) Puts the cursor at a specific location on the screen. You code nn as a number from 0 through 1919. 0 is the same as map coding of POS=(1,1), 80 is the same as POS=(2,1), and 1919 is the same as POS=(24,80).

Here are some examples of various SEND codings:

```
EXEC CICS
   SEND MAP     ('CALCMAP')
        MAPSET ('$001M')
        MAPONLY
        ERASE
        CURSOR
END-EXEC.
```

Sends the physical map (screen labels) only, no program-supplied data

```
EXEC CICS
   SEND MAP     ('CALCMAP')
        MAPSET ('$001M')
        FROM   (CALC1-SYMBOLIC-MAP)
        DATAONLY
        ERASE
        CURSOR
END-EXEC.
```

Sends the symbolic map only, no screen labels

Why worry about sending DATAONLY after the first time? This minimizes the amount of data transmission. Since the labels are already on the screen, they do not need to be transmitted again. Note that you still specify the map and mapset even if you send DATAONLY, because CICS needs to determine the field locations from the physical map.

6.4 OVERVIEW OF CICS TRANSLATE, COMPILE, AND LINK

The SHOWMAP program in Figure 6.1 is a complete CICS program, albeit a very simple one. But even though it's simple, it still requires the same multiple steps of processing in order to become machine language capable of execution. The shaded part of the flowchart in Figure 6.2 shows you the processing necessary to accomplish this. Once you understand how this sequence of processing is accomplished for SHOWMAP, you will understand how to do it for any CICS program.

A CICS program like SHOWMAP contains non-COBOL elements in the form of its CICS commands. EXEC CICS and END-EXEC, as well as CICS commands such as SEND and RETURN, are not a part of the COBOL language. These must be "translated" into valid COBOL syntax elements before the VS COBOL II compiler can successfully process a CICS program. The **CICS translator** rewrites any CICS program it processes, and does these five things:

1. Adds field definitions to WORKING-STORAGE for its own use.
2. Adds field definitions to the LINKAGE section so that CICS can pass information to you.
3. Creates a new PROCEDURE division heading to make activation by CICS possible (this makes your CICS program into a subprogram of CICS).
4. Makes comments out of CICS commands, by putting * in column 7 of these statements.
5. Adds a CALL statement following each of your CICS commands, forming the arguments for the CALL from the specifications in your CICS commands and the WORKING-STORAGE fields it has inserted into your program.

As you can see in the shaded part of Figure 6.2, the input to the translator is 80-byte punch card-image records containing your CICS program source code. The output of the translator is 80-byte punch card-image records consisting of rewritten COBOL source code. The translator also produces a listing of your program, and error messages relating to problems it detects in your coding of CICS commands.

After translation, your rewritten CICS program is ready for compilation and link editing, the same as any ordinary non-CICS program. The **VS COBOL II compiler** accepts the rewritten COBOL source code, and compiles it into an intermediate form known as an "object file." This intermediate form is only partly machine language, and partly a series of references to standard machine language service routines. The **linkage editor** completes the process of turning the object file into machine language. The machine language is output to the CICS load library as a member. The program machine language is stored in the same partitioned data set library in which your physical maps reside.

6.5 JCL FOR CICS TRANSLATE, COMPILE, AND LINK

The three-step CICS translate, compile, and link process shown in the shaded part of Figure 6.2 must be orchestrated using job control language (JCL). We illustrate a JCL job stream that

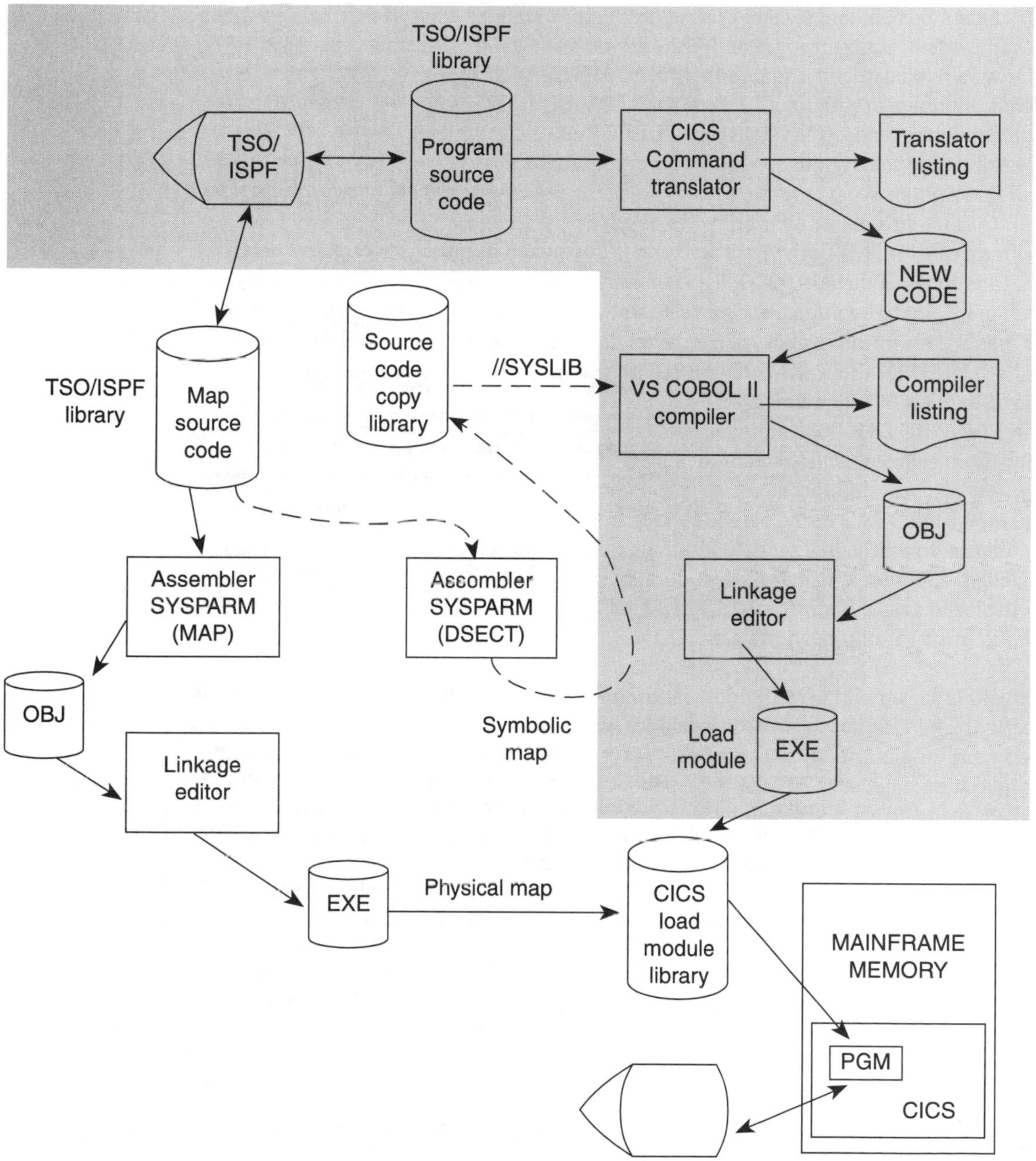
TSO/ISPF library
TSO/ ISPF
Program source code
CICS Command translator
Translator listing
NEW CODE
TSO/ISPF library
Map source code
Source code copy library
//SYSLIB
VS COBOL II compiler
Compiler listing
OBJ
Assembler SYSPARM (MAP)
Assembler SYSPARM (DSECT)
Linkage editor
OBJ
Linkage editor
Symbolic map
Load module
EXE
EXE
Physical map
CICS load module library
MAINFRAME MEMORY
PGM
CICS

Figure 6.2 Overview of CICS program processing, with CICS translator, VS COBOL II compiler, and link edit steps shaded for emphasis.

```
EDIT ---- CSCJGJ.CSC360.CNTL(PGMJOB) - 01.00 ---------------- COLUMNS 001 072
COMMAND ===>                                                 SCROLL ===> PAGE
****** ****************************** TOP OF DATA ******************************
//CSCJGJA   JOB 1,                        ACCOUNTING INFORMATION
//  'BIN 7--JANOSSY',                     PROGRAMMER NAME AND DELIVERY BIN
//  CLASS=A,                              INPUT QUEUE CLASS
//  MSGLEVEL=(1,1),                       HOW MUCH MVS SYSTEM PRINT DESIRED
//  MSGCLASS=X,                           PRINT DESTINATION X A L N OR O
//  TIME=(0,6),                           SAFETY LIMIT: RUN TIME UP TO 6 SECS
//  REGION=2M,                            ALLOW UP TO 2 MEGS VIRTUAL MEMORY
//* TYPRUN=SCAN,                          UNCOMMENT THIS LINE TO DO SCAN ONLY
//  NOTIFY=CSCJGJ                         WHO TO TELL WHEN JOB IS DONE
//*-----------------------------------------------------------------------
//*  TRANSLATE, COMPILE, AND LINK A CICS PROGRAM
//*  THIS IS A LOCALLY CUSTOMIZED VERSION OF STANDARD PROC DFHEITVL
//*  THIS JCL IS STORED AT CSCJGJ.CSC360.CNTL(PGMJOB)
//*-----------------------------------------------------------------------
//*
//  SET  SORCLIB='CSCJGJ.CSC360.COBOL',   SOURCE LIB WITH PROGRAM CODE
//       SORNAME='SHOWMAP',               SOURCE PROGRAM MEMBER NAME
//       COPYLIB='CSCJGJ.CSC360.COBOL',   YOUR COBOL COPY LIBRARY
//*
//       LOADLIB='CCP.LOADLIB',           CICS LOAD LIBRARY
//       LOADNAM='C360A001'               LOAD MODULE MEMBER NAME
//*
//*************************************************************************
//*
//*  TRANSLATE THE PROGRAM, REPLACING "EXEC CICS" WITH CALLS
//*
//*************************************************************************
//*
//STEP010  EXEC  PGM=DFHECP1$,                        TRANSLATOR
//  PARM='COBOL2',
//  REGION=2048K
//STEPLIB     DD  DSN=CICS330.SDFHLOAD,DISP=SHR       CICS 3.3 LIBRARY
//SYSIN       DD  DSN=&SORCLIB(&SORNAME),DISP=SHR     SOURCE CODE IN
//SYSPRINT    DD  SYSOUT=*                            SOURCE CODE LIST
//SYSPUNCH    DD  DSN=&&TEMP1,                        TRANSLATED CODE
//  DISP=(NEW,PASS,DELETE),
//  UNIT=VIO,
//  RECFM=FB,
//  LRECL=80,
//  BLKSIZE=3120,
//  SPACE=(CYL,(1,1),RLSE)
```

(JCL continues on next page...)

You can use job control language such as PGMJOB (the start of which you see here) to process a CICS program into machine language. This is a *three-step process* that begins with the CICS translator, a program named DFHECP1$. The translator reads your source code and creates a new file of source code. In the new program code created by the translator, your CICS commands are made into comments, and new lines are inserted forming a CALL to CICS software to accomplish what you indicated you wanted to do. The translator also inserts necessary field definitions into the WORKING-STORAGE and LINKAGE SECTIONs to make its CALLs possible.

Figure 6.3 PGMJOB, a job stream that processes a COBOL CICS program into machine language

does this, named PGMJOB, in Figure 6.3. We built PGMJOB from IBM's standard proc DFHEITVL, and optimized it for execution using MVS/ESA Version 4.

As with our MAPJOB JCL for processing BMS source code (Figure 5.10), our PGMJOB JCL localizes at its top the things that you have to change from one run to another,

```
//*
//***********************************************************************
//*
//*  COMPILE THE TRANSLATED PROGRAM WITH VS COBOL II
//*
//***********************************************************************
//*
//     IF ( RC <= 4 ) THEN
//STEP020  EXEC  PGM=IGYCRCTL,
//  REGION=2048K,
//  PARM=('NOADV',                 PGM RESERVES CC BYTE COL 1
//         'NOCMPR2',              DON'T EMULATE RELEASE 2
//         'NUMPROC(PFD)',         PREFERRED SIGN HANDLING
//         'FLAG(I,E)',            ALL MSGS; IMBED ERROR MSGS
//         'NODYN',                DON'T USE DYNAMIC LOADING
//         'LANGUAGE(UE)',         HEADING/MSGS UPPERCASE
//         'APOST',                USE APOSTROPHE AS QUOTE
//         'FDUMP',                GIVE FORMATTED ABEND DUMP
//         'LIB',                  COPY LIBRARY OK
//         'NOMAP',                NO IMBEDDED CELL REFS
//         'OBJ',                  PRODUCE OBJECT CODE
//         'RES',                  MAKE CODE RESIDENT
//         'NOOPT',                NOOPT GIVES LINE# ON FDUMP
//         'XREF')                 PROVIDE IMBEDDED CROSS REF
//STEPLIB     DD  DSN=SYS1.COB2COMP,DISP=SHR           VS COBOL II LIB
//SYSIN       DD  DSN=&&TEMP1,DISP=(OLD,DELETE)        TRANSLATED PGM IN
//SYSLIB      DD  DSN=CICS330.SDFHCOB,DISP=SHR         STD CICS COPY LIB
//            DD  DSN=CICS330.SDFHMAC,DISP=SHR         STD CICS COPY LIB
//            DD  DSN=&COPYLIB,DISP=SHR                YOUR COPY LIB
//SYSPRINT    DD  SYSOUT=*                             COMPILER LISTING
//SYSLIN      DD  DSN=&&OBJECT,                        OBJECT FILE
//  UNIT=VIO,
//  DISP=(NEW,PASS,DELETE),
//  RECFM=FB,
//  LRECL=80,
//  BLKSIZE=3120,
//  SPACE=(CYL,(1,1),RLSE)
//SYSUT1      DD  UNIT=VIO,SPACE=(CYL,(1,1))           COMPILER WORK FILE
//SYSUT2      DD  UNIT=VIO,SPACE=(CYL,(1,1))           COMPILER WORK FILE
//SYSUT3      DD  UNIT=VIO,SPACE=(CYL,(1,1))           COMPILER WORK FILE
//SYSUT4      DD  UNIT=VIO,SPACE=(CYL,(1,1))           COMPILER WORK FILE
//SYSUT5      DD  UNIT=VIO,SPACE=(CYL,(1,1))           COMPILER WORK FILE
//SYSUT6      DD  UNIT=VIO,SPACE=(CYL,(1,1))           COMPILER WORK FILE
//SYSUT7      DD  UNIT=VIO,SPACE=(CYL,(1,1))           COMPILER WORK FILE
//     ENDIF
//*
//***********************************************************************
//*
//*  LINK EDIT THE COMPILED PROGRAM
//*
//***********************************************************************
//*
//     IF ( RC <= 4 ) THEN
//STEP030  EXEC  PGM=IEWL,                             LINKAGE EDITOR PGM
//  REGION=2048K,
//  PARM='LIST,XREF'
//SYSLIN      DD  DSN=CICS330.SDFHCOB(DFHEILIC),DISP=SHR
//            DD  DSN=&&OBJECT,DISP=(OLD,DELETE)       OBJECT MODULE IN
//SYSLIB      DD  DSN=CICS330.SDFHLOAD,DISP=SHR        CICS 3.3 LIB
//            DD  DSN=SYS1.COB2CICS,DISP=SHR           COB2/CICS LIB
//            DD  DSN=SYS1.COB2LIB,DISP=SHR            VS COBOL II LIB
//            DD  DSN=&LOADLIB,DISP=SHR                CICS LOAD LIB
//SYSLMOD     DD  DSN=&LOADLIB(&LOADNAM),DISP=SHR      NEW CICS PGM OUT
//SYSPRINT    DD  SYSOUT=*                             LINK EDIT REPORT
//SYSUT1      DD  UNIT=VIO,                            WORK FILE
//  DCB=BLKSIZE=1024,
//  SPACE=(CYL,(1,1))
//     ENDIF
//
```

Figure 6.3 *(Continued)*

using the SET statement. We have highlighted these items with a large oval and arrow on Figure 6.3. If you run PGMJOB exactly as illustrated, the items coded at this SET statement are automatically substituted into the appropriate points of the JCL. If your installation uses PGMJOB as a cataloged procedure, you specify these "changeable" items on an EXEC statement that invokes the proc.

6.6 PROGRAM NAMES AND TRANS-IDS

You'll note in the top part of Figure 6.3 that we specify a particular name for the LOADNAM (load module name) of the machine language load module we produce for the SHOWMAP program. In fact, although we have stored the program source code as member SHOWMAP in source code library CSCJGJ.CSC360.COBOL, and named it SHOWMAP in its PROGRAM-ID, we create the load module as C360A001. Why is this?

For CICS to recognize a program name, the name must be entered into the Program Control Table (PCT) by a system programmer or CICS administrator. In other words, **program names** must be assigned to you; you can't make them up yourself. At the time a program name is made known to CICS, an entry is also made to establish a corresponding **transaction identifier**, or **trans-id**. Trans-ids are four characters long. For example, at DePaul University, program name C360A001 is associated with trans-id $001.

The trans-id of program C360A001 (our SHOWMAP program) does not appear anywhere in the PGMJOB job control language. But when we want to execute the program under CICS, we have to use its trans-id. As you start to do hands-on CICS programming, your instructor or installation will make you aware of the program names you must use, and the corresponding trans-ids established in your local CICS control tables.

6.7 OUTPUT OF CICS TRANSLATION, COMPILE, AND LINK

Figure 6.4 lists the complete MVS/ESA system reporting, translator output, VS COBOL II compiler output, and linkage editor output from our submission of the PGMJOB job stream to process the SHOWMAP program. We have annotated this output to completely illustrate its important points. We suggest that you carefully examine Figure 6.4, since its annotations tell their own story. In particular, make sure that you examine and learn from these important parts of the output in Figure 6.4:

- The COND CODEs issued by the translator, compiler, and linkage editor (see also section 6.8)
- The messages from the CICS translator, which indicate whether or not it could successfully translate your CICS commands into CALL statements
- The data fields that the translator inserts into the WORKING-STORAGE and LINKAGE sections
- The way that the CICS translator comments out CICS commands and replaces them with CALLs that accomplish the intended processing actions
- The final messages from the linkage editor indicating that the program load module was produced

If you can successfully locate and recognize these important parts of the PGMJOB job stream output reporting for the SHOWMAP program, you are on the road to becoming a CICS programmer.

6.8 DID YOUR CICS TRANSLATE, COMPILE, AND LINK WORK?

The most important question you need to ask after attempting a CICS translate, compile, and link is "Did it work?" Both the translator and compiler produce many messages, but each also leaves behind a four-digit numeric value labeled the **COND CODE** in MVS/ESA system re-

```
                  J E S 2  J O B  L O G  --  S Y S T E M  I B M 1  --  N O D E  N 1

13.09.15 JOB07737  IRR010I  USERID CSCJGJ   IS ASSIGNED TO THIS JOB.
13.09.16 JOB07737  ICH70001I CSCJGJ   LAST ACCESS AT 13:07:43 ON FRIDAY, JULY 15, 1994
13.09.16 JOB07737  $HASP373 CSCJGJA  STARTED - INIT  1 - CLASS A - SYS IBM1
13.09.20 JOB07737  $HASP395 CSCJGJA  ENDED

------ JES2 JOB STATISTICS ------
   15 JUL 94 JOB EXECUTION DATE
         109 CARDS READ
         662 SYSOUT PRINT RECORDS
           0 SYSOUT PUNCH RECORDS
          36 SYSOUT SPOOL KBYTES
        0.07 MINUTES EXECUTION TIME

        1 //CSCJGJA   JOB 1,                  ACCOUNTING INFORMATION                  JOB07737
          //  'BIN 7--JANOSSY',               PROGRAMMER NAME AND DELIVERY BIN
          //  CLASS=A,                        INPUT QUEUE CLASS
          //  MSGLEVEL=(1,1),                 HOW MUCH MVS SYSTEM PRINT DESIRED
          //  MSGCLASS=X,                     PRINT DESTINATION X A L N OR O
          //  TIME=(0,6),                     SAFETY LIMIT: RUN TIME UP TO 6 SECS
          //  REGION=2M,                      ALLOW UP TO 2 MEGS VIRTUAL MEMORY
          //* TYPRUN=SCAN,                    UNCOMMENT THIS LINE TO DO SCAN ONLY
          //  NOTIFY=CSCJGJ                   WHO TO TELL WHEN JOB IS DONE
          //*-------------------------------------------------------------------
          //*  TRANSLATE, COMPILE, AND LINK A CICS PROGRAM
          //*  THIS IS A LOCALLY CUSTOMIZED VERSION OF STANDARD PROC DFHEITVL
          //*  THIS JCL IS STORED AT CSCJGJ.CSC360.CNTL(PGMJOB)
          //*-------------------------------------------------------------------
          //*
        2 //  SET  SORCLIB='CSCJGJ.CSC360.COBOL',   SOURCE LIB WITH PROGRAM CODE
          //       SORNAME='SHOWMAP',               SOURCE PROGRAM MEMBER NAME
          //       COPYLIB='CSCJGJ.CSC360.COBOL',   YOUR COBOL COPY LIBRARY
          //*
          //       LOADLIB='CCP.LOADLIB',           CICS LOAD LIBRARY
          //       LOADNAM='C360A001'               LOAD MODULE MEMBER NAME
          //*
          //********************************************************************
          //*
          //*  TRANSLATE THE PROGRAM, REPLACING "EXEC CICS" WITH CALLS
          //*
          //********************************************************************
          //*
```

Figure 6.4 Complete reporting from a run of the PGMJOB job stream.

CICS Translate, Compile, and Link Output

The listing that starts here shows you the complete MVS/ESA Version 4 system output, CICS translator output, VS COBOL II compiler output, and linkage editor output when our PGMJOB job stream is used to process a CICS program into machine language. ***Read our concise annotations on this listing to gain firsthand knowledge of CICS program processing.***

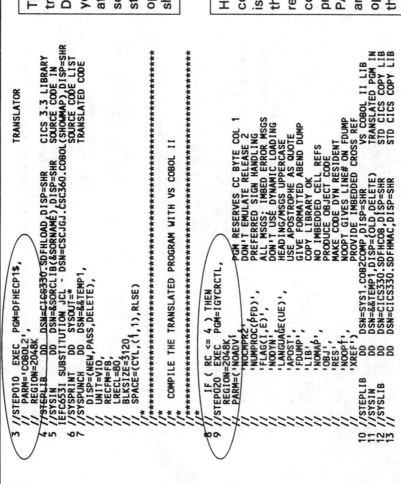

```
 3 //STEP010   EXEC  PGM=DFHECP1$,                       TRANSLATOR
   //  PARM='COBOL2',
   //  REGION=2048K
 4 //STEPLIB     DD  DSN=CICS330.SDFHLOAD,DISP=SHR      CICS 3.3 LIBRARY
 5 //SYSIN       DD  DSN=&SORCLIB(&SORNAME),DISP=SHR    SOURCE CODE IN
   IEFC653I SUBSTITUTION JCL - DSN=CSCJGJ.CSC360.COBOL(SHOWMAP),DISP=SHR
 6 //SYSPRINT    DD  SYSOUT=*                           SOURCE CODE LIST
 7 //SYSPUNCH    DD  DSN=&&TEMP1,                       TRANSLATED CODE
   //  DISP=(NEW,PASS,DELETE),
   //  UNIT=VIO,
   //  RECFM=FB,
   //  LRECL=80,
   //  BLKSIZE=3120,
   //  SPACE=(CYL,(1,1),RLSE)
   //*
   //*****************************************************************
   //*
   //*  COMPILE THE TRANSLATED PROGRAM WITH VS COBOL II
   //*
   //*****************************************************************
   //*
 8 //     IF ( RC <= 4 ) THEN
 9 //STEP020  EXEC  PGM=IGYCRCTL,
   //  REGION=2048K,
   //  PARM=('NOADV',               PGM RESERVES CC BYTE COL 1
   //        'NOCMPR2',             DON'T EMULATE RELEASE 2
   //        'NUMPROC(PFD)',        PREFERRED SIGN HANDLING
   //        'FLAG(I,E)',           ALL MSGS; IMBED ERROR MSGS
   //        'NODYN',               DON'T USE DYNAMIC LOADING
   //        'LANGUAGE(UE)',        HEADING/MSGS UPPERCASE
   //        'APOST',               USE APOSTROPHE AS QUOTE
   //        'FDUMP',               GIVE FORMATTED ABEND DUMP
   //        'LIB',                 COPY LIBRARY OK
   //        'NOMAP',               NO IMBEDDED CELL REFS
   //        'OBJ',                 PRODUCE OBJECT CODE
   //        'RES',                 MAKE CODE DYN RESIDENT
   //        'NOOPT',               NOOPT GIVES LINE# ON FDUMP
   //        'XREF')                PROVIDE IMBEDDED CROSS REF
10 //STEPLIB    DD  DSN=SYS1.COB2COMP,DISP=SHR        VS COBOL II LIB
11 //SYSIN      DD  DSN=&&TEMP1,DISP=(OLD,DELETE)     TRANSLATED PGM IN
12 //SYSLIB     DD  DSN=CICS330.SDFHCOB,DISP=SHR      STD CICS COPY LIB
13 //           DD  DSN=CICS330.SDFHMAC,DISP=SHR      STD CICS COPY LIB
```

This step executes the CICS program translator, a program named DFHECP1$. Its input at //SYSIN is your program source code. Its output at //SYSPUNCH is newly rewritten source code. PARM on the EXEC statement lets you set the translator's options, the settings for which are shown on page 6 of this listing.

Here we execute the VS COBOL II compiler only if the COND CODE (RC) issued by the CICS translator is less than or equal to 4. The newly rewritten CICS program enters the compiler at //SYSIN. The object file is produced at //SYSLIN (next page). PARM on this EXEC allows you to set any of the more than 40 compiler options, shown on pages 8 and 9 of this listing.

Figure 6.4 *(Continued)*

```
14 //            DD  DSN=&COPYLIB,DISP=SHR                YOUR COPY LIB
   IEFC653I SUBSTITUTION JCL - DSN=CSCJGJ.CSC360.COBOL,DISP=SHR
15 //SYSPRINT   DD  SYSOUT=*                             COMPILER LISTING
16 //SYSLIN     DD  DSN=&&OBJECT,                        OBJECT FILE
   //  UNIT=VIO,
   //  DISP=(NEW,PASS,DELETE),
   //  RECFM=FB,
   //  LRECL=80,
   //  BLKSIZE=3120,
   //  SPACE=(CYL,(1,1),RLSE)
17 //SYSUT1     DD  UNIT=VIO,SPACE=(CYL,(1,1))           COMPILER WORK FILE
18 //SYSUT2     DD  UNIT=VIO,SPACE=(CYL,(1,1))           COMPILER WORK FILE
19 //SYSUT3     DD  UNIT=VIO,SPACE=(CYL,(1,1))           COMPILER WORK FILE
20 //SYSUT4     DD  UNIT=VIO,SPACE=(CYL,(1,1))           COMPILER WORK FILE
21 //SYSUT5     DD  UNIT=VIO,SPACE=(CYL,(1,1))           COMPILER WORK FILE
22 //SYSUT6     DD  UNIT=VIO,SPACE=(CYL,(1,1))           COMPILER WORK FILE
23 //SYSUT7     DD  UNIT=VIO,SPACE=(CYL,(1,1))           COMPILER WORK FILE
24 //    ENDIF
   //*
   //*****************************************************************
   //*
   //*  LINK EDIT THE COMPILED PROGRAM
   //*
   //*****************************************************************
   //*
25 //    IF ( RC <= 4 ) THEN
26 //STEP030  EXEC  PGM=IEWL,                             LINKAGE EDITOR PGM
   //  REGION=2048K,
   //  PARM='LIST,XREF'
27 //SYSLIN     DD  DSN=CICS330.SDFHCOB(DFHEILIC),DISP=SHR
28 //           DD  DSN=&&OBJECT,DISP=(OLD,DELETE)       OBJECT MODULE IN
29 //SYSLIB     DD  DSN=CICS330.SDFHLOAD,DISP=SHR        CICS 3.3 LIB
30 //           DD  DSN=SYS1.COB2CICS,DISP=SHR           COB2/CICS LIB
31 //           DD  DSN=SYS1.COB2LIB,DISP=SHR            VS COBOL II LIB
32 //SYSLMOD    DD  DSN=&LOADLIB(&LOADNAM),DISP=SHR      NEW CICS PGM OUT
   IEFC653I SUBSTITUTION JCL - DSN=CCP.LOADLIB(C360A001),DISP=SHR
33 //SYSPRINT   DD  SYSOUT=*                             LINK EDIT REPORT
34 //SYSUT1     DD  UNIT=VIO,                            WORK FILE
   //  DCB=BLKSIZE=1024,
   //  SPACE=(CYL,(1,1))
35 //    ENDIF
```

Here the linkage editor is executed only if the COND CODE (RC) issued by the CICS translator and the COND CODE issued by the VS COBOL II compiler are less than or equal to 4. The object file enters the linkage editor at //SYSLIN, concatenated after an item named CICS330.SDFHCOB(DFHEILIC). CICS program machine language (the load module) is produced by the linkage editor at its //SYSLMOD output.

Figure 6.4 *(Continued)*

```
ICH70001I CSCJGJ   LAST ACCESS AT 13:07:43 ON FRIDAY, JULY 15, 1994

IEF236I ALLOC. FOR CSCJGJA STEP010
IEF237I 114  ALLOCATED TO STEPLIB
IEF237I 111  ALLOCATED TO SYSIN
IEF237I JES2 ALLOCATED TO SYSPRINT
IEF237I VIO  ALLOCATED TO SYSPUNCH
IEF142I CSCJGJA STEP010 - STEP WAS EXECUTED - COND CODE 0000
IEF285I   CICS330.SDFHLOAD                             KEPT
IEF285I   VOL SER NOS= ACSAPP.
IEF285I   CSCJGJ.CSC360.COBOL                          KEPT
IEF285I   VOL SER NOS= USER00.
IEF285I   CSCJGJ.CSCJGJA.JOB07737.D0000101.?           SYSOUT
IEF285I   SYS94196.T130916.RA000.CSCJGJA.TEMP1         PASSED
IEF373I STEP /STEP010 / START 94196.1309
IEF374I STEP /STEP010 / STOP  94196.1309 CPU    0MIN 00.27SEC SRB    0MIN 00.01SEC VIRT  2048K SYS   412K EXT       4K SYS    9104K

IEF236I ALLOC. FOR CSCJGJA STEP020
IEF237I 110  ALLOCATED TO STEPLIB
IEF237I VIO  ALLOCATED TO SYSIN
IEF237I 114  ALLOCATED TO SYSLIB
IEF237I 114  ALLOCATED TO
IEF237I 111  ALLOCATED TO
IEF237I JES2 ALLOCATED TO SYSPRINT
IEF237I VIO  ALLOCATED TO SYSLIN
IEF237I VIO  ALLOCATED TO SYSUT1
IEF237I VIO  ALLOCATED TO SYSUT2
IEF237I VIO  ALLOCATED TO SYSUT3
IEF237I VIO  ALLOCATED TO SYSUT4
IEF237I VIO  ALLOCATED TO SYSUT5
IEF237I VIO  ALLOCATED TO SYSUT6
IEF237I VIO  ALLOCATED TO SYSUT7
IEF142I CSCJGJA STEP020 - STEP WAS EXECUTED - COND CODE 0000
IEF285I   SYS1.COB2COMP                                KEPT
IEF285I   VOL SER NOS= ACSRES.
IEF285I   SYS94196.T130916.RA000.CSCJGJA.TEMP1         DELETED
IEF285I   CICS330.SDFHCOB                              KEPT
IEF285I   VOL SER NOS= ACSAPP.
IEF285I   CICS330.SDFHMAC                              KEPT
IEF285I   VOL SER NOS= ACSAPP.
IEF285I   CSCJGJ.CSC360.COBOL                          KEPT
IEF285I   VOL SER NOS= USER00.
IEF285I   CSCJGJ.CSCJGJA.JOB07737.D0000102.?           SYSOUT
```

STEP010 of the PGMJOB job stream executes the CICS translator. COND CODE 0000 or 0004 indicates successful translation of your program.

STEP020 of the PGMJOB job stream executes the VS COBOL II compiler. COND CODE 0000 or 0004 indicates successful compilation into an object file.

Figure 6.4 *(Continued)*

```
IEF285I   SYS94196.T130916.RA000.CSCJGJA.OBJECT        PASSED
IEF285I   SYS94196.T130916.RA000.CSCJGJA.R0458610      DELETED
IEF285I   SYS94196.T130916.RA000.CSCJGJA.R0458611      DELETED
IEF285I   SYS94196.T130916.RA000.CSCJGJA.R0458612      DELETED
IEF285I   SYS94196.T130916.RA000.CSCJGJA.R0458613      DELETED
IEF285I   SYS94196.T130916.RA000.CSCJGJA.R0458614      DELETED
IEF285I   SYS94196.T130916.RA000.CSCJGJA.R0458615      DELETED
IEF285I   SYS94196.T130916.RA000.CSCJGJA.R0458616      DELETED
IEF373I STEP /STEP020 / START 94196.1309
IEF374I STEP /STEP020 / STOP  94196.1309 CPU    0MIN 00.72SEC SRB    0MIN 00.01SEC VIRT  2048K SYS   380K EXT   32740K SYS    9544K

IEF236I ALLOC. FOR CSCJGJA STEP030
IEF237I 114  ALLOCATED TO SYSLIN
IEF237I VIO  ALLOCATED TO
IEF237I 114  ALLOCATED TO SYSLIB
IEF237I 110  ALLOCATED TO
IEF237I 110  ALLOCATED TO
IEF237I 110  ALLOCATED TO SYSLMOD
IEF237I JES2 ALLOCATED TO SYSPRINT
IEF237I VIO  ALLOCATED TO SYSUT1
IEF142I CSCJGJA STEP030 - STEP WAS EXECUTED - COND CODE 0000
IEF285I   CICS330.SDFHCOB                              KEPT
IEF285I   VOL SER NOS= ACSAPP.
IEF285I   SYS94196.T130916.RA000.CSCJGJA.OBJECT        DELETED
IEF285I   CICS330.SDFHLOAD                             KEPT
IEF285I   VOL SER NOS= ACSAPP.
IEF285I   SYS1.COB2CICS                                KEPT
IEF285I   VOL SER NOS= ACSRES.
IEF285I   SYS1.COB2LIB                                 KEPT
IEF285I   VOL SER NOS= ACSRES.
IEF285I   CCP.LOADLIB                                  KEPT
IEF285I   VOL SER NOS= ACSRES.
IEF285I   CSCJGJ.CSCJGJA.JOB07737.D0000103.?           SYSOUT
IEF285I   SYS94196.T130916.RA000.CSCJGJA.R0458617      DELETED
IEF373I STEP /STEP030 / START 94196.1309
IEF374I STEP /STEP030 / STOP  94196.1309 CPU    0MIN 00.31SEC SRB    0MIN 00.02SEC VIRT   396K SYS   424K EXT      4K SYS    9108K
IEF375I  JOB /CSCJGJA / START 94196.1309
IEF376I  JOB /CSCJGJA / STOP  94196.1309 CPU    0MIN 01.30SEC SRB    0MIN 00.04SEC
```

STEP030 of the PGMJOB job stream executes the linkage editor, which completes conversion of the program to machine language by editing the object file produced by the compiler together with service routines from system and CICS libraries. COND CODE 0000 or 0004 indicates successful link editing of your program.

Figure 6.4 *(Continued)*

```
CICS/ESA COMMAND LANGUAGE TRANSLATOR VERSION 3.3                TIME 13.09 DATE 15 JULY 94  PAGE 1

OPTIONS SPECIFIED:-COBOL2

*OPTIONS IN EFFECT*

  CICS
  DEBUG
NOFE
  SPIE
  EDF
  LINECOUNT(60)
  TABLE(DFHEITAB)
  NATLANG(EN)
  SOURCE
NOVBREF
  OPTIONS
  FLAG(W)
  SEQ
  APOST
NONUM
  OPT
  SPACE(1)
  LANGLVL(2)
  COBOL2
NOSYSEIB
NOFEPI
```

> This begins the output from the CICS translator. The options you can specify to tailor its operation are listed here. "NO" in front of an option means that it is turned off, while the lack of "NO" in front of the option indicates that it is active. We explicitly activated the COBOL2 option since we are using the VS COBOL II compiler. We accepted the default settings for the other translator options.

```
            LINE          SOURCE LISTING

00001     000100 ID DIVISION.
00002     000200 PROGRAM-ID. SHOWMAP.
00003     000300
00004     000400*------------------------------------------------------------
00005     000500*  THIS SIMPLE CICS PROGRAM JUST PRESENTS A MAP AND THEN ENDS
00006     000600*  EXECUTION.  CODING, COMPILING, AND ARRANGING TO EXECUTE IT
00007     000700*  WILL GIVE YOU EXPERIENCE WITH THE MECHANICS OF CICS.
00008     000800*------------------------------------------------------------
```

Figure 6.4 *(Continued)*

```
000900
001000 DATA DIVISION.
001100 WORKING-STORAGE SECTION.
001200*-----------------------------------------------------------------
001300*
001400*  MANUALLY-CODED SYMBOLIC MAP FOR CALC1 PROGRAM    JIM JANOSSY
001500*
001600*-----------------------------------------------------------------
001700 01  CALC1-SYMBOLIC-MAP.
001800     05 FILLER                        PIC X(12).
001900
002000     05 CSM-L-QUANTITY                PIC S9(4)  COMP.
002100     05 CSM-A-QUANTITY                PIC X(1).
002200     05 CSM-D-QUANTITY                PIC 9(5).
002300
002400     05 CSM-L-PRICE                   PIC S9(4)  COMP.
002500     05 CSM-A-PRICE                   PIC X(1).
002600     05 CSM-D-PRICE                   PIC 99V99.
002700
002800     05 CSM-L-TOTAL-BEFORE-TAX        PIC S9(4)  COMP.
002900     05 CSM-A-TOTAL-BEFORE-TAX        PIC X(1).
003000     05 CSM-D-TOTAL-BEFORE-TAX        PIC ZZ,ZZZ,ZZ9.99.
003100
003200     05 CSM-L-TAX                     PIC S9(4)  COMP.
003300     05 CSM-A-TAX                     PIC X(1).
003400     05 CSM-D-TAX                     PIC ZZ,ZZZ,ZZ9.99.
003500
003600     05 CSM-L-GRAND-TOTAL             PIC S9(4)  COMP.
003700     05 CSM-A-GRAND-TOTAL             PIC X(1).
003800     05 CSM-D-GRAND-TOTAL             PIC ZZ,ZZZ,ZZ9.99.
003900
004000     05 CSM-L-MESSAGE                 PIC S9(4)  COMP.
004100     05 CSM-A-MESSAGE                 PIC X(1).
004200     05 CSM-D-MESSAGE                 PIC X(79).
004300
004400 LINKAGE SECTION.
004500 01  DFHCOMMAREA                      PIC X(1).
004600
004700 PROCEDURE DIVISION.
004800 1000-MAIN.
004900
005000     MOVE LOW-VALUES TO CALC1-SYMBOLIC-MAP.
005100     MOVE -1 TO CSM-L-QUANTITY.
```

The CICS translator lists your CICS program source code unchanged. You will not see any of the items inserted into the program in the translator's listing. Unfortunately, unlike the VS COBOL II compiler, the translator also does not embed error messages within the source code listing. The SHOWMAP program translated here has no source code CICS command errors, but the version shown in Figure 6.5 does contain an error so that you can see how the translator reports problems.

Figure 6.4 *(Continued)*

```
00052     005200     MOVE 'HERE IS MY CALC1 MAP!  JIM JANOSSY' TO CSM-D-MESSAGE.
00053     005300
00054     005400     EXEC CICS
00055     005500         SEND MAP    ('CALCMAP')
00056     005600              MAPSET ('$001M')
00057     005700              FROM   (CALC1-SYMBOLIC-MAP)
00058     005800              ERASE
00059     005900              CURSOR
00060     006000     END-EXEC.
00061     006100
00062     006200     EXEC CICS
00063     006300              RETURN
00064     006400     END-EXEC.

NO MESSAGES PRODUCED BY TRANSLATOR.
TRANSLATION TIME:-    0.00 MINS.
```

No CICS command errors were detected by the translator in this program.

```
          PP 5668-958 IBM VS COBOL II RELEASE 3.2 09/05/90                    DATE 07/15/94  TIME 13:09:18   PAGE     1
INVOCATION PARAMETERS:
NOADV,NOCMPR2,NUMPROC(PFD),FLAG(I,E),DYN,LANGUAGE(UE),APOST,FDUMP,LIB,NOMAP,OBJ,RES,NOOPT,XREF

PROCESS(CBL) STATEMENTS:
      CBL RENT,RES,NODYNAM,LIB

OPTIONS IN EFFECT:
    NOADV
      APOST
    NOAWO
      BUFSIZE(4096)
    NOCMPR2
    NOCOMPILE(S)
      DATA(31)
    NODBCS
    NODECK
    NODUMP
    NODYNAM
    NOEXIT
```

This begins the output from the VS COBOL II compiler. You can tailor its operation with over 40 different compiler options. "NO" in front of an option means that it is turned off, while the lack of "NO" in front of an option means that it is active. Invocation parameters are those specified in the JCL. PROCESS(CBL) statements are compiler option settings supplied with a PROCESS statement in the source code, supplied in this case by the translator. OPTIONS IN EFFECT is the complete summary of the options as they were set for the compile, and reflects the combined effect of invocation parameters,

Figure 6.4 *(Continued)*

```
NOFASTSRT
  FDUMP
  FLAG(I,E)
NOFLAGMIG
NOFLAGSAA
NOFLAGSTD
  LANGUAGE(UE)
  LIB
  LINECOUNT(60)
NOLIST
NOMAP
NONAME
NONUMBER
  NUMPROC(PFD)
  OBJECT
NOOFFSET
NOOPTIMIZE
  OUTDD(SYSOUT)
  RENT
  RESIDENT
  SEQUENCE
  SIZE(MAX)
  SOURCE
  SPACE(1)
NOSSRANGE
NOTERM
NOTEST
  TRUNC(STD)
NOVBREF
NOWORD
  XREF(FULL)
  ZWB
```

This is the continuation and conclusion of the VS COBOL II compiler parameter option settings list. Since both the RENT (reentrant) and RESIDENT options are active, the program load module will be produced with AMODE=31 to support 31-bit addressing (the program can access data above the 16-megabyte line), and RMODE=ANY to allow the program itself to be housed above or below the 16-megabyte line.

Figure 6.4 *(Continued)*

```
PP 5668-958 IBM VS COBOL II RELEASE 3.2 09/05/90            SHOWMAP   DATE 07/15/94  TIME 13:09:18   PAGE     2
  LINEID  PL SL  ----+-*A-1-B--+----2----+----3----+----4----+----5----+----6----+----7-|--+----8  MAP AND CROSS REFERENCE

  000001          000100 ID DIVISION.
  000002          000200 PROGRAM-ID. SHOWMAP.
  000003          000300
  000004          000400*-----------------------------------------------------------------
  000005          000500*  THIS SIMPLE CICS PROGRAM JUST PRESENTS A MAP AND THEN ENDS
  000006          000600*  EXECUTION.  CODING, COMPILING, AND ARRANGING TO EXECUTE IT
  000007          000700*  WILL GIVE YOU EXPERIENCE WITH THE MECHANICS OF CICS.
  000008          000800*-----------------------------------------------------------------
  000009          000900
  000010          001000 DATA DIVISION.
  000011          001100 WORKING-STORAGE SECTION.
  000012          001200*-----------------------------------------------------------------
  000013          001300*
  000014          001400*  MANUALLY-CODED SYMBOLIC MAP FOR CALC1 PROGRAM     JIM JANOSSY
  000015          001500*
  000016          001600*-----------------------------------------------------------------
  000017          001700 01  CALC1-SYMBOLIC-MAP.
  000018          001800     05 FILLER                        PIC X(12).
  000019          001900
  000020          002000     05 CSM-L-QUANTITY                PIC S9(4)  COMP.
  000021          002100     05 CSM-A-QUANTITY                PIC X(1).
  000022          002200     05 CSM-D-QUANTITY                PIC 9(5).
  000023          002300
  000024          002400     05 CSM-L-PRICE                   PIC S9(4)  COMP.
  000025          002500     05 CSM-A-PRICE                   PIC X(1).
  000026          002600     05 CSM-D-PRICE                   PIC 99V99.
  000027          002700
  000028          002800     05 CSM-L-TOTAL-BEFORE-TAX        PIC S9(4)  COMP.
  000029          002900     05 CSM-A-TOTAL-BEFORE-TAX        PIC X(1).
  000030          003000     05 CSM-D-TOTAL-BEFORE-TAX        PIC ZZ,ZZZ,ZZ9.99.
  000031          003100
  000032          003200     05 CSM-L-TAX                     PIC S9(4)  COMP.
  000033          003300     05 CSM-A-TAX                     PIC X(1).
  000034          003400     05 CSM-D-TAX                     PIC ZZ,ZZZ,ZZ9.99.
  000035          003500
  000036          003600     05 CSM-L-GRAND-TOTAL             PIC S9(4)  COMP.
  000037          003700     05 CSM-A-GRAND-TOTAL             PIC X(1).
  000038          003800     05 CSM-D-GRAND-TOTAL             PIC ZZ,ZZZ,ZZ9.99.
  000039          003900
  000040          004000     05 CSM-L-MESSAGE                 PIC S9(4)  COMP.
```

Here you see the beginning of the VS COBOL II compiler's listing of the rewritten program source code that it received from the CICS translator. Note that there is no ENVIRONMENT DIVISION in a CICS program, since it cannot deal directly with files, but must request file access services from CICS. While we hardcoded our symbolic map for the CALC1 screen in WORKING-STORAGE, it is more common to use the COPY compiler directive and acquire this as a copy book from a copy library.

Figure 6.4 *(Continued)*

```
004100     05 CSM-A-MESSAGE                 PIC X(1).
004200     05 CSM-D-MESSAGE                 PIC X(79).
004300
       01  DFHLDVER PIC X(22) VALUE 'LD TABLE DFHEITAB 330.'.
       01  DFHEIDO PICTURE S9(7) COMPUTATIONAL-3 VALUE ZERO.              IMP
       01  DFHEIBO PICTURE S9(4) COMPUTATIONAL VALUE ZERO.                IMP
       01  DFHEICB  PICTURE X(8) VALUE IS '        '.

       01   DFHB0040  COMP PIC S9(8).
       01   DFHB0041  COMP PIC S9(8).
       01   DFHB0042  COMP PIC S9(8).
       01   DFHB0043  COMP PIC S9(8).
       01   DFHB0044  COMP PIC S9(8).
       01   DFHB0020  COMP PIC S9(4).
       01   DFHB0021  COMP PIC S9(4).
       01   DFHB0022  COMP PIC S9(4).
       01   DFHB0023  COMP PIC S9(4).
       01   DFHB0024  COMP PIC S9(4).
       01   DFHB0025  COMP PIC S9(4).
       01   DFHC0040  PIC X(4).
       01   DFHC0041  PIC X(4).
       01   DFHC0042  PIC X(4).
       01   DFHC0043  PIC X(4).
       01   DFHC0044  PIC X(4).
       01   DFHC0080  PIC X(8).
       01   DFHC0081  PIC X(8).
       01   DFHC0082  PIC X(8).
       01   DFHC0083  PIC X(8).
       01   DFHC0084  PIC X(8).
       01   DFHC0085  PIC X(8).
       01   DFHC0020  PIC X(2).
       01   DFHC0021  PIC X(2).
       01   DFHC0022  PIC X(2).
       01   DFHC0023  PIC X(2).
       01   DFHD0040  PIC S9(7) COMP-3.
       01   DFHC0010  PIC X(1).
       01   DFHC0011  PIC X(1).
       01   DFHC0060  PIC X(6).
       01   DFHC0120  PIC X(12).
       01   DFHC2460  PIC X(246).
       01   DFHC0070  PIC X(7).
       01   DFHC0071  PIC X(7).
       01   DFHC0650  PIC X(65).
```

The CICS translator inserted these fields into WORKING-STORAGE to support the CALLs it generates as it translates CICS commands into ordinary COBOL statements. You do not reference any of these fields in your program. While the CALLs generated by the translator use these fields, you can ignore them.

Figure 6.4 *(Continued)*

```
000084           01   DFHDUMMY COMP PIC S9(4) VALUE ZERO.                              IMP
000085           01   DFHEIVO  PICTURE X(69).
000086    004400 LINKAGE SECTION.
000087           01  DFHEIBLK.
000088           02    EIBTIME  PIC S9(7) COMP-3.
000089           02    EIBDATE  PIC S9(7) COMP-3.
000090           02    EIBTRNID PIC X(4).
000091           02    EIBTASKN PIC S9(7) COMP-3.
000092           02    EIBTRMID PIC X(4).
000093           02    DFHEIGDI COMP PIC S9(4).
000094           02    EIBCPOSN COMP PIC S9(4).
000095           02    EIBCALEN COMP PIC S9(4).
000096           02    EIBAID   PIC X(1).
000097           02    EIBFN    PIC X(2).
000098           02    EIBRCODE PIC X(6).
000099           02    EIBDS    PIC X(8).
000100           02    EIBREQID PIC X(8).
000101           02    EIBRSRCE PIC X(8).
000102           02    EIBSYNC  PIC X(1).
000103           02    EIBFREE  PIC X(1).
000104           02    EIBRECV  PIC X(1).
000105           02    EIBFIL01 PIC X(1).
000106           02    EIBATT   PIC X(1).
000107           02    EIBEOC   PIC X(1).
000108           02    EIBFMH   PIC X(1).
000109           02    EIBCOMPL PIC X(1).
000110           02    EIBSIG   PIC X(1).
000111           02    EIBCONF  PIC X(1).
000112           02    EIBERR   PIC X(1).
000113           02    EIBERRCD PIC X(4).
000114           02    EIBSYNRB PIC X(1).
000115           02    EIBNODAT PIC X(1).
000116           02    EIBRESP  COMP PIC S9(8).
000117           02    EIBRESP2 COMP PIC S9(8).
000118           02    EIBRLDBK PIC X(1).
000119    004500 01  DFHCOMMAREA                   PIC X(1).
000120    004600
000121    004700 PROCEDURE DIVISION USING DFHEIBLK DFHCOMMAREA.
000122    004800 1000-MAIN.
000123    004900
000124    005000     MOVE LOW-VALUES TO CALC1-SYMBOLIC-MAP.
000125    005100     MOVE -1 TO CSM-L-QUANTITY.
000126    005200     MOVE 'HERE IS MY CALC1 MAP!  JIM JANOSSY' TO CSM-D-MESSAGE.
```

The CICS translator inserted these fields into the program. As we coded the LINKAGE SECTION, it contained only the DFHCOMMAREA shown at line 000119. The DFHEIBLK group that starts at line 000087 is ***very important*** to you, because *it contains information that CICS shares with your program when the program is given control, and after the execution of any CICS command.* We'll discuss the contents of these fields in Chapter 7. The SHOWMAP program makes use only of EIBCALEN, which indicates the number of bytes of memory passed by the program to itself, in the DFHCOMMAREA, from one activation to another. The first time a terminal executes a program, EIBCALEN is 0. This is how we detect the "first time" execution of a program by CICS.

Procedure Division heading rewritten by translator; program has become a subprogram.

Figure 6.4 *(Continued)*

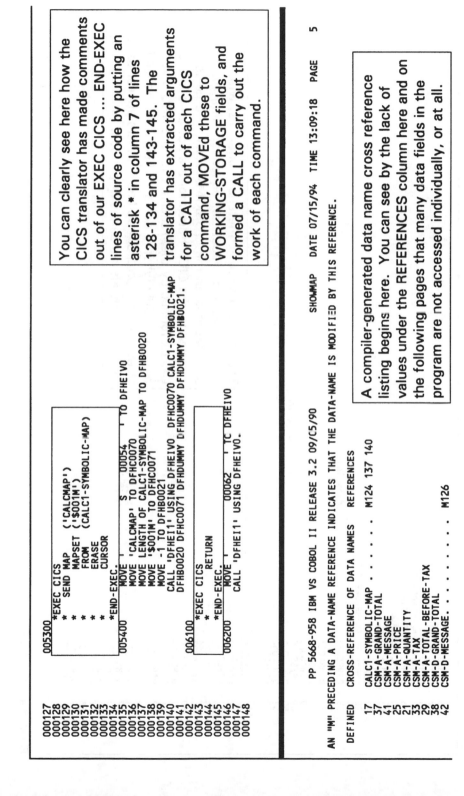

```
000127         005300
000128                *EXEC CICS
000129                *   SEND MAP    ('CALCMAP')
000130                *        MAPSET ('$001M')
000131                *        FROM   (CALC1-SYMBOLIC-MAP)
000132                *        ERASE
000133                *        CURSOR
000134                *END-EXEC.
000135         005400      MOVE '         S    00054     ' TO DFHEIVO
000136                     MOVE 'CALCMAP' TO DFHC0070
000137                     MOVE LENGTH OF CALC1-SYMBOLIC-MAP TO DFHB0020
000138                     MOVE '$001M' TO DFHC0071
000139                     MOVE -1 TO DFHB0021
000140                    CALL 'DFHEI1' USING DFHEIVO  DFHC0070 CALC1-SYMBOLIC-MAP
000141                    DFHB0020 DFHC0071 DFHDUMMY DFHDUMMY DFHDUMMY DFHB0021.
000142         006100
000143                *EXEC CICS
000144                *        RETURN
000145                *END-EXEC.
000146         006200      MOVE '         00062     ' TO DFHEIVO
000147                    CALL 'DFHEI1' USING DFHEIVO.
000148
```

You can clearly see here how the CICS translator has made comments out of our EXEC CICS ... END-EXEC lines of source code by putting an asterisk * in column 7 of lines 128-134 and 143-145. The translator has extracted arguments for a CALL out of each CICS command, MOVEd these to WORKING-STORAGE fields, and formed a CALL to carry out the work of each command.

```
      PP 5668-958 IBM VS COBOL II RELEASE 3.2 09/05/90            SHOWMAP   DATE 07/15/94  TIME 13:09:18   PAGE     5

AN "M" PRECEDING A DATA-NAME REFERENCE INDICATES THAT THE DATA-NAME IS MODIFIED BY THIS REFERENCE.

 DEFINED    CROSS-REFERENCE OF DATA NAMES    REFERENCES

      17    CALC1-SYMBOLIC-MAP . . . . . .   M124 137 140
      37    CSM-A-GRAND-TOTAL
      41    CSM-A-MESSAGE
      25    CSM-A-PRICE
      21    CSM-A-QUANTITY
      33    CSM-A-TAX
      29    CSM-A-TOTAL-BEFORE-TAX
      38    CSM-D-GRAND-TOTAL
      42    CSM-D-MESSAGE. . . . . . . . .   M126
```

A compiler-generated data name cross reference listing begins here. You can see by the lack of values under the REFERENCES column here and on the following pages that many data fields in the program are not accessed individually, or at all.

Figure 6.4 *(Continued)*

```
 26   CSM-D-PRICE
 22   CSM-D-QUANTITY
 34   CSM-D-TAX
 30   CSM-D-TOTAL-BEFORE-TAX
 36   CSM-L-GRAND-TOTAL
 40   CSM-L-MESSAGE
 24   CSM-L-PRICE
 20   CSM-L-QUANTITY . . . . . . . . .  M125
 32   CSM-L-TAX
 28   CSM-L-TOTAL-BEFORE-TAX
 54   DFHB0020 . . . . . . . . . . . .  M137 141
 55   DFHB0021 . . . . . . . . . . . .  M139 141
 56   DFHB0022
 57   DFHB0023
 58   DFHB0024
 59   DFHB0025
 49   DFHB0040
 50   DFHB0041
 51   DFHB0042
 52   DFHB0043
 53   DFHB0044
119   DFHCOMMAREA. . . . . . . . . . .  121
 76   DFHC0010
 77   DFHC0011
 71   DFHC0020
 72   DFHC0021
 73   DFHC0022
 74   DFHC0023
 60   DFHC0040
 61   DFHC0041
 62   DFHC0042
 63   DFHC0043
 64   DFHC0044
 78   DFHC0060
 81   DFHC0070 . . . . . . . . . . . .  M136 140
 82   DFHC0071 . . . . . . . . . . . .  M138 141
 65   DFHC0080
 66   DFHC0081
 67   DFHC0082
 68   DFHC0083
 69   DFHC0084
 70   DFHC0085
 79   DFHC0120
```

The data name cross reference continues, with data names in alphabetical sequence. Here you can see that most of the WORKING-STORAGE fields inserted by the CICS translator are not used in the CALLs formed by the translator for the SHOWMAP program. Only when a declared field is referenced elsewhere in a program do line numbers appear to the right of it, after a series of periods.

Figure 6.4 *(Continued)*

```
 83   DFHC0650
 80   DFHC2460
 84   DFHDUMMY . . . . . . . . . . .  141 141 141
 75   DFHD0040
 87   DFHEIBLK . . . . . . . . . . .  121
 46   DFHEIB0
 47   DFHEICB
 45   DFHEID0
 93   DFHEIGDI
 85   DFHEIV0. . . . . . . . . . . .  M135 140 M146 147
 44   DFHLDVER
 96   EIBAID
106   EIBATT
 95   EIBCALEN
109   EIBCOMPL
111   EIBCONF
 94   EIBCPOSN
 89   EIBDATE
 99   EIBDS
107   EIBEOC
112   EIBERR
113   EIBERRCD
105   EIBFIL01
108   EIBFMH
 97   EIBFN
103   EIBFREE
115   EIBNODAT
 98   EIBRCODE
104   EIBRECV
100   EIBREQID
116   EIBRESP
117   EIBRESP2
118   EIBRLDBK
101   EIBRSRCE
110   EIBSIG
102   EIBSYNC
114   EIBSYNRB
 91   EIBTASKN
 88   EIBTIME
 92   EIBTRMID
 90   EIBTRNID
```

The data name cross reference continues, with data names in alphabetical sequence. Here you can see that most of the WORKING-STORAGE fields inserted by the CICS translator are not used in the CALLs formed by the translator for the SHOWMAP program. Only when a declared field is referenced elsewhere in a program do line numbers appear to the right of it, after a series of periods.

Figure 6.4 *(Continued)*

```
* STATISTICS FOR COBOL PROGRAM SHOWMAP:
*     SOURCE RECORDS = 148
*     DATA DIVISION STATEMENTS = 93
*     PROCEDURE DIVISION STATEMENTS = 11

END OF COMPILATION 1,  PROGRAM SHOWMAP,  NO STATEMENTS FLAGGED.
RETURN CODE 0
```

The VS COBOL II compiler reports no problems with the translated source code.

```
          MVS/DFP VERSION 3 RELEASE 3 LINKAGE EDITOR     13:09:19  FRI  JUL 15, 1994
 JOB CSCJGJA     STEP STEP030
 INVOCATION PARAMETERS - LIST,XREF
 ACTUAL SIZE=(317440,86016)
 OUTPUT DATA SET CCP.LOADLIB IS ON VOLUME ACSRES
IEW0000       INCLUDE SYSLIB(DFHECI)                                              50000000
                                                 CROSS REFERENCE TABLE

  CONTROL SECTION                      ENTRY
    NAME    ORIGIN  LENGTH               NAME    LOCATION     NAME   LOCATION     NAME   LOCATION     NAME   LOCATION
  DFHELII     00        26
                                       DFHEPIN        00    DFHEXEC         8   DFHEI1          8   DFHEI2          8
                                       DFHEI3          8    DFHEI4          8   DFHEI5          8   DFHEI6          8
                                       DFHEI7          8    DFHEI8          8   DFHEI9          8   DFHEI10         8
                                       DFHEI11         8    DFHEI12         8   DFHEI13         8   DFHEI14         8
                                       DFHEI15         8    DFHEI16         8   DFHEI17         8   DFHEI18         8
                                       DFHEI01         8    DLZEI01         8   DLZEI02         8   DLZEI03         8
                                       DLZEI04         8
  SHOWMAP     28      3796
  IGZEBST *  37C0      1A8

  LOCATION  REFERS TO SYMBOL  IN CONTROL SECTION          LOCATION  REFERS TO SYMBOL  IN CONTROL SECTION
     94          IGZEBST          IGZEBST                        B8        DFHEI1          DFHELII
   3958          IGZETUN        $UNRESOLVED(W)                 395C        IGZEOPT       $UNRESOLVED(W)
 ENTRY ADDRESS      28

 TOTAL LENGTH     3968

 ** C360A001 DID NOT PREVIOUSLY EXIST BUT WAS ADDED AND HAS AMODE 31
 ** LOAD MODULE HAS RMODE ANY
 ** AUTHORIZATION CODE IS          0.
```

The linkage editor reports success in producing the machine language load module for the program.

Figure 6.4 *(Continued)*

porting. The COND CODEs for the translate, compile, and link steps in Figure 6.4 appear on pages 4 and 5 of the figure.

Typical of IBM system and utility software, the CICS translator, VS COBOL II compiler, and the linkage editor will leave behind a COND CODE of 0000 if no errors are detected. If noncritical warning messages only are triggered by some condition, this software will leave behind a COND CODE of 0004. More serious problems cause the translator, compiler, and the linkage editor to generate COND CODE 0008 or higher. You can therefore examine the COND CODEs returned by PGMJOB to quickly determine if a CICS translate, compile, and link was successful.

Figure 6.5 shows you how the CICS translator "complains" if it detects a syntax error in your CICS program source code. To create this illustration we introduced an intentional error in the SEND command, by omitting the closing parenthesis on line 57, at the FROM specification. We extracted the COND CODE lines from the MVS/ESA system reporting so that you could better see the COND CODE 0008 issued by the translator. You can see from the first page of Figure 6.5 that the "IF" coding in our PGMJOB job stream shuts off the compile and link steps if the translator indicates one or more problems in your source code. In such a case there is no reason to attempt to compile or link. The last part of the output lists the error messages produced by the CICS translator.

6.9 EXECUTING THE SHOWMAP PROGRAM

Once you have achieved a "clean" (no error message) translate, compile, and link of a CICS program, you can execute it under CICS. Take these steps to execute a program such as SHOWMAP (C360A001):

1. Log off of TSO/ISPF by entering =X on the command line. You may also need to issue the command LOGOFF at the TSO READY prompt if that prompt appears as you log off.
2. Log in to CICS. The login processing is installation-specific, but can be as simple as entering CICS at a beginning screen. At login to CICS, you will see a screen similar to that shown in Figure 6.6. Press the Clear key to clear this screen. (On computer systems using the IBM 7171 protocol converter and ASCII terminals instead of real 3270 terminals, you can generate the Clear key by pressing Escape, then capital "O" then capital "M". If you use a microcomputer as a terminal, consult your documentation about Clear key emulation.)
3. Enter the transaction identifier (trans-id) associated with the program name at the upper left corner of the screen. The SHOWMAP program, for example, is associated with trans-id $001 at our installation, so we entered this at the upper left corner of a clear screen:

   ```
   $001
   ```

   This produced the screen shown in Figure 6.7.
4. Execute the program. Since SHOWMAP does not really do anything with a screen other than transmit it to a terminal, it has already ended execution by the time the screen in Figure 6.7 becomes visible. Pressing the Enter key again at the screen in

```
                         J E S 2  J O B  L O G  --  S Y S T E M  I B M 1  --  N O D E  N 1

13.26.18 JOB07764  IRR010I  USERID CSCJGJ   IS ASSIGNED TO THIS JOB.
13.26.19 JOB07764  ICH70001I CSCJGJ   LAST ACCESS AT 13:18:58 ON FRIDAY, JULY 15, 1994
13.26.19 JOB07764  $HASP373 CSCJGJA  STARTED - INIT  1 - CLASS A - SYS IBM1
13.26.20 JOB07764  $HASP395 CSCJGJA  ENDED
 -
 -
IEF142I CSCJGJA STEP010 - STEP WAS EXECUTED - COND CODE 0008
 -
 -
IEF206I CSCJGJA STEP020 - STEP WAS NOT RUN BECAUSE OF CONDITIONAL EXPRESSION ON STATEMENT 8
 -
 -
IEF206I CSCJGJA STEP030 - STEP WAS NOT RUN BECAUSE OF CONDITIONAL EXPRESSION ON STATEMENT 25
 -
 -
```

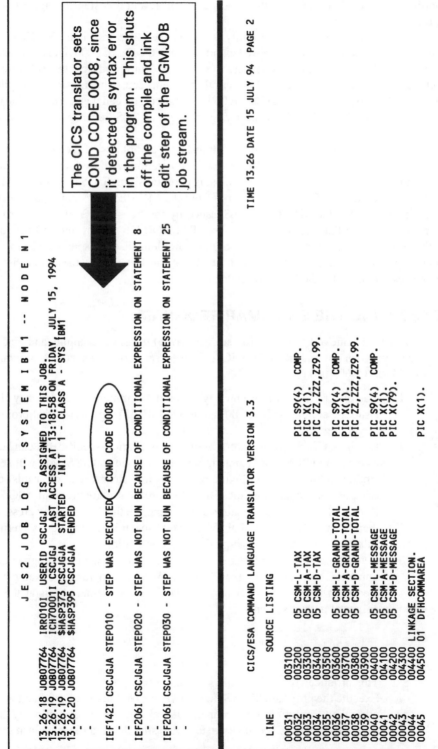

The CICS translator sets COND CODE 0008, since it detected a syntax error in the program. This shuts off the compile and link edit step of the PGMJOB job stream.

```
         CICS/ESA COMMAND LANGUAGE TRANSLATOR VERSION 3.3                        TIME 13.26 DATE 15 JULY 94  PAGE 2

 LINE         SOURCE LISTING

00031      003100
00032      003200      05 CSM-L-TAX                   PIC S9(4)  COMP.
00033      003300      05 CSM-A-TAX                   PIC X(1).
00034      003400      05 CSM-D-TAX                   PIC ZZ,ZZZ,ZZ9.99.
00035      003500
00036      003600      05 CSM-L-GRAND-TOTAL           PIC S9(4)  COMP.
00037      003700      05 CSM-A-GRAND-TOTAL           PIC X(1).
00038      003800      05 CSM-D-GRAND-TOTAL           PIC ZZ,ZZZ,ZZ9.99.
00039      003900
00040      004000      05 CSM-L-MESSAGE               PIC S9(4)  COMP.
00041      004100      05 CSM-A-MESSAGE               PIC X(1).
00042      004200      05 CSM-D-MESSAGE               PIC X(79).
00043      004300
00044      004400 LINKAGE SECTION.
00045      004500 01  DFHCOMMAREA                     PIC X(1).
```

Figure 6.5 How the CICS translator reports CICS command syntax errors.

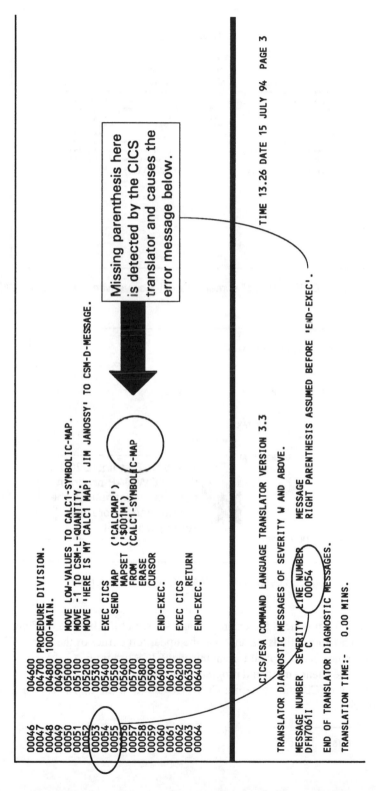

```
00046      004600
00047      004700 PROCEDURE DIVISION.
00048      004800 1000-MAIN.
00049      004900
00050      005000     MOVE LOW-VALUES TO CALC1-SYMBOLIC-MAP.
00051      005100     MOVE -1 TO CSM-L-QUANTITY.
00052      005200     MOVE 'HERE IS MY CALC1 MAP!  JIM JANOSSY' TO CSM-D-MESSAGE.
00053      005300
00054      005400     EXEC CICS
00055      005500        SEND MAP    ('CALCMAP')
00056      005600             MAPSET ('$001M')
00057      005700             FROM   (CALC1-SYMBOLIC-MAP
00058      005800             ERASE
00059      005900             CURSOR
00060      006000     END-EXEC.
00061      006100
00062      006200     EXEC CICS
00063      006300             RETURN
00064      006400     END-EXEC.
```

Missing parenthesis here is detected by the CICS translator and causes the error message below.

```
            CICS/ESA COMMAND LANGUAGE TRANSLATOR VERSION 3.3                    TIME 13.26 DATE 15 JULY 94  PAGE 3

TRANSLATOR DIAGNOSTIC MESSAGES OF SEVERITY W AND ABOVE.

MESSAGE NUMBER  SEVERITY  LINE NUMBER     MESSAGE
DFH7061I           C        00054         RIGHT PARENTHESIS ASSUMED BEFORE 'END-EXEC'.

END OF TRANSLATOR DIAGNOSTIC MESSAGES.

TRANSLATION TIME:-   0.00 MINS.
```

Figure 6.5 *(Continued)*

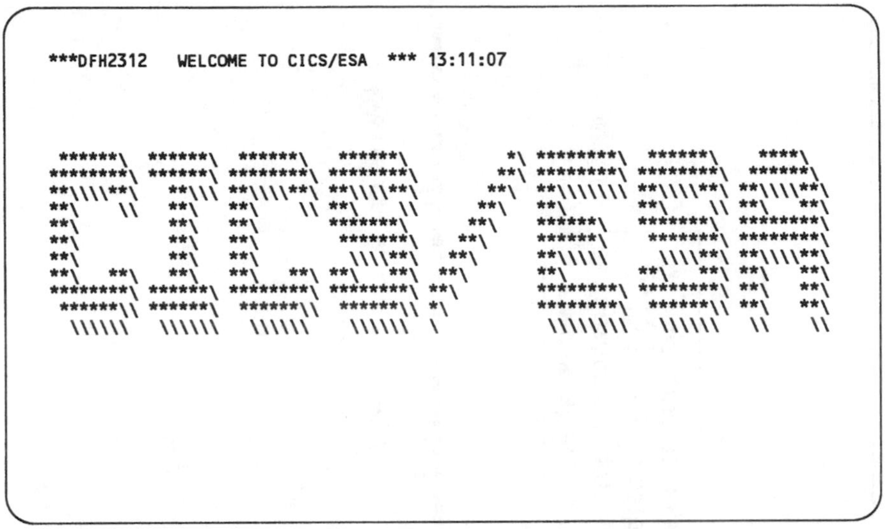
***DFH2312 WELCOME TO CICS/ESA *** 13:11:07

Figure 6.6 This is the CICS "Startup" screen you will receive when you log into CICS.

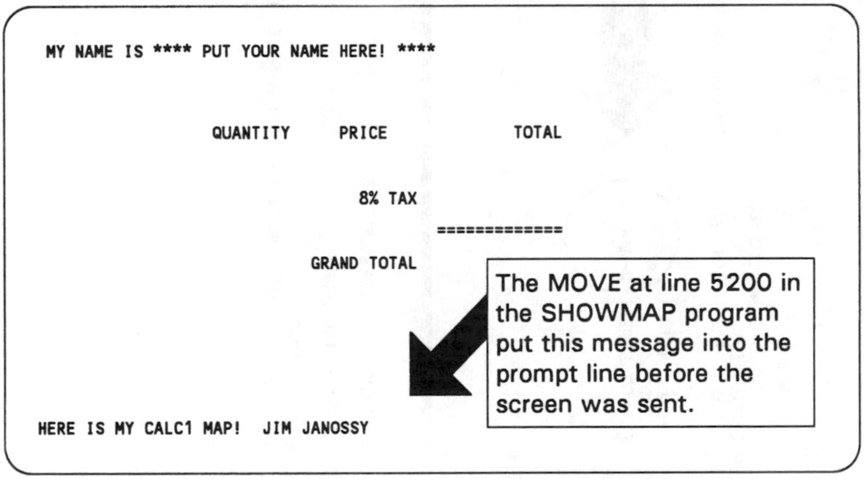
MY NAME IS **** PUT YOUR NAME HERE! ****
QUANTITY
PRICE
TOTAL
8% TAX
=============
GRAND TOTAL
The MOVE at line 5200 in the SHOWMAP program put this message into the prompt line before the screen was sent.
HERE IS MY CALC1 MAP! JIM JANOSSY

Figure 6.7 Screen produced by the SHOWMAP (C360A001) program.

Figure 6.7 produces the error message shown at the bottom of Figure 6.8, since CICS no longer finds a trans-id at the upper left corner of the screen. This type of occurrence is not typical for a nontrivial CICS program.

5. Press the Clear key to end program execution.
6. Log out of CICS by entering CESF LOGOFF at the upper left corner of a clear screen:

```
cesf logoff
```

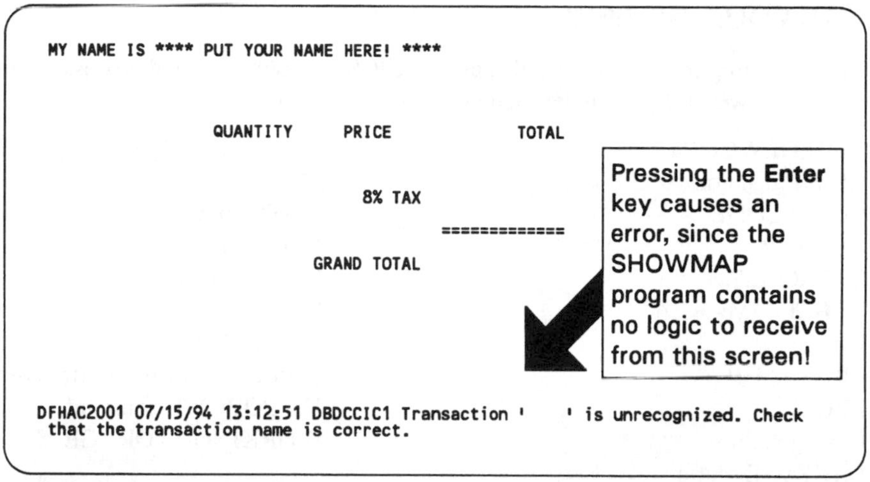
MY NAME IS **** PUT YOUR NAME HERE! ****
QUANTITY
PRICE
TOTAL
8% TAX
=============
GRAND TOTAL
DFHAC2001 07/15/94 13:12:51 DBDCCIC1 Transaction ' ' is unrecognized. Check that the transaction name is correct.
Pressing the Enter key causes an error, since the SHOWMAP program contains no logic to receive from this screen!

Figure 6.8 CICS error message produced by pressing Enter a second time when executing the SHOWMAP program (SHOWMAP ends execution after just sending a screen).

CESF is a special CICS service transaction. When you execute it with its LOGOFF function, CICS returns control to the operating system. All CICS special service transactions begin with the letter "C" and an installation cannot name its own trans-ids beginning with "C."

You can follow these steps to execute any CICS program directly with its trans-id. If your CICS system includes security provisions, you may be required to identify yourself during your CICS logon process, and you may be prevented from executing certain restricted transactions.

6.10 CECI NEWCOPY: REPLACING A PROGRAM LOAD MODULE

When you first process a CICS program, such as SHOWMAP, into machine language, you need not make CICS aware of it in any special way in order to execute it. (This presumes, of course, that you have been issued a valid program name and have been told of the trans-id that CICS associates with the program name.) But if you make a change in the CICS program source code, and retranslate, recompile, and re-link edit it to create replacement machine language, *you must inform CICS about the replacement*!

Since it's likely that you will want to experiment with programs such as SHOWMAP and others, and will replace machine language with revised and corrected programs, you need to know the details of the replacement process. You can use job control language such as PGMJOB to create replacement machine language. But you will need to read Appendix B, dealing with the **NEWCOPY** function of the special service transaction **CECI**, in order to execute a replacement of a program. *Read or at least browse Appendix B now to become familiar with **CECI NEWCOPY**.*

6.11 FOR YOUR REVIEW

Understanding these terms and elements of CICS programming and processing, introduced in Chapter 6, will aid your understanding of the next chapter:

CECI NEWCOPY
CICS translator
COND CODE
CURSOR
DATAONLY
DFHCOMMAREA
ERASE
ERASEAUP
FROM
Linkage editor
LINKAGE section
LOW-VALUES
MAP
MAPONLY
MAPSET
Program name
RETURN
SEND MAP
Transaction identifier (trans-id)
VS COBOL II compiler
WORKING-STORAGE

6.12 REVIEW QUESTIONS

1. Why can you omit coding an ENVIRONMENT division in a CICS program? If you do code it, what do you put into it?
2. What purpose does your coding of a LINKAGE section serve in your CICS programs?
3. Why would coding STOP RUN serve no useful purpose in a CICS program?
4. What is the purpose of the MOVEs prior to the SEND MAP command in the SHOWMAP program? Could these be done with BMS map coding instead?
5. Describe LOW-VALUES and its special significance in CICS programming and mainframe data communication.
6. Explain what processing occurs involving the symbolic map and the physical map with the SEND MAP command as coded in the SHOWMAP program.
7. What purpose is served by the statement

```
MOVE -1 TO CSM-L-QUANTITY
```

   in the SEND MAP command of the SHOWMAP program?
8. Explain how you must code the SEND MAP command to arrange to position the cursor at the beginning of a specific enterable field when you transmit the map for the screen to the computer terminal.
9. Explain what roles the MAPONLY and DATAONLY options of the SEND MAP command play, and why they are provided by CICS.
10. Explain why it is necessary to translate a CICS program before compiling it, and describe the five things that the CICS translator does to your program source code.
11. How can you determine if a translate, compile, and link of a CICS program actually succeeded before attempting to execute the program under CICS?
12. Describe the difference between program name and transaction identifier (trans-id), and explain how these are established.
13. Describe what action you take to end the execution of a CICS program.
14. Explain the steps you must take to log off from CICS.

15. Why must you learn to use the NEWCOPY function of the special CICS service transaction CECI, as described in Appendix B?

6.13 HANDS-ON EXERCISES

Do these exercises in sequence to gain the most from the information in this chapter:

A. Design a screen that has these fields:

- Your name and the title "CICS AVERAGE CALCULATOR"
- Labeled entry fields for five 4-digit integers
- A protected, labeled 5-digit field for computed total
- A protected, PIC 9(5)V99 field for computed average
- A prompt line

Develop BMS map code for this screen, either by manual coding or by using a screen painter such as GENMAP, described in Chapter 4 and Appendix F. Prepare physical and symbolic maps for this screen using the MAPJOB JCL shown in Chapter 5, or similar JCL. Then prepare a program similar to SHOWMAP to present your new screen on a terminal. Use SHOWMAP as a guide, and use the PGMJOB JCL, or similar JCL, to prepare the machine language program load module for your SHOWMAP program. Execute your SHOWMAP program under CICS to confirm that it works.

B. Change the SHOWMAP program you developed in Exercise A so that its initial prompt uses different wording. Prepare a load module for your revised program. Log into CICS and execute the program again. Does the original version of the revised version of the initial prompt appear on the screen? Read Appendix B, then explain why you got the results you received.

C. Use the CECI NEWCOPY command as illustrated in Appendix B to inform CICS about the your revised SHOWMAP program load module. Then execute your SHOWMAP program. Does the original version or the revised version of the prompt appear on the screen? Explain why you got these results.

D. Save the BMS map code, physical map, and symbolic map you prepared in exercise A above, since an exercise at the end of Chapter 7 will build on it.

7

Introducing Pseudoconversational Logic

Our previous chapters have laid the groundwork for you to understand the role that CICS plays in the interactive mainframe environment and the goals its designers had in mind when they created it. In Chapters 4 and 5 you learned how to design and code screen images (maps) and how to use job control language (JCL) to process them into executable form. In Chapter 6 you learned how to code a trivial CICS program and how to use JCL to turn the program into executable form. But how do you actually code a CICS program that does significant work? This involves pseudoconversational logic, a form of logic far different from the logic in non-CICS programs. In this chapter, we begin to explore this real-life aspect of CICS, building on what you have already learned about maps, CICS, and JCL.

7.1 THE CALC1 PROGRAM: WHAT DOES IT DO?

In Figures 4.2 and 4.3, we designed a screen (map) that produces the terminal image shown in Figure 7.1. You have already seen this screen image as transmitted to a computer terminal by the SHOWMAP program (Figure 6.7). Now, we'll use a program named CALC1 to put necessary processing logic behind this screen, so that you can actually use it. We'll refer to this screen as the CALC1 screen.

```
MY NAME IS **** PUT YOUR NAME HERE! ****


                QUANTITY      PRICE              TOTAL
                 25           1250

                                 8% TAX

                                             =============

                           GRAND TOTAL




ENTER VALUES, PRESS <ENTER>, <CLEAR> TO QUIT
```

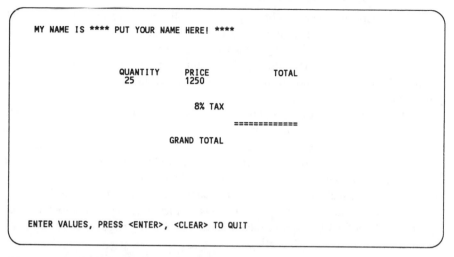

Figure 7.1 CALC1 screen after entry of QUANTITY and PRICE, before the terminal operator has pressed the Enter key.

As you can see from Figure 7.1, the CALC1 screen lets a terminal operator enter two numbers, labeled QUANTITY and PRICE. For the entries shown, 25 has been entered into the quantity field, and a value of $12.50 has been entered into the price field. (Since our first simple CICS program does not provide for very fancy numeric entry deediting, we have entered $12.50 as 1250.) The quantity and price fields are the only user-enterable (unprotected) fields on the CALC1 screen. After entering these two fields, the terminal operator presses the Enter key.

Figure 7.2 shows you what the CALC1 program responds with when it processes valid

```
MY NAME IS **** PUT YOUR NAME HERE! ****


                QUANTITY      PRICE              TOTAL
                 00025        1250              312.50

                                 8% TAX          25.00

                                             =============

                           GRAND TOTAL          337.50




RESULTS COMPUTED, ENTER MORE DATA OR <CLEAR> TO QUIT
```

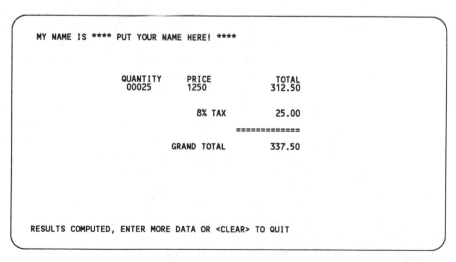

Figure 7.2 CALC1 screen showing program-computed results after the terminal operator has pressed the Enter key.

entries for quantity and price. The program multiplies quantity 25 and price $12.50, and computes a total of $312.50. It then computes 8 percent sales tax on this amount, which comes to $25.00. Finally, the CALC1 program adds 312.50 and 25.00 and calculates a grand total purchase price of $337.50. After putting these values onto the screen, as well as an appropriate prompt, the program stands ready to receive new quantity and price values, and repeat its processing actions.

How does the CALC1 program accomplish its required processing? If CALC1 were to be written conversationally on a minicomputer or a PC, it would take the forms already documented in other Wiley books. You can look in *VAX COBOL On-Line,* by James Janossy, published by John Wiley & Sons, Inc. (1992) to see how CALC1 is implemented conversationally in COBOL on the VAX minicomputer. You can look in *Getting Started with RM/COBOL-85* by Nancy Stern, Robert Stern, and James Janossy, published by John Wiley & Sons, Inc. (1994) to see several ways that CALC1 can be implemented conversationally in COBOL on a PC. To see how CALC1 is constructed under CICS using pseudoconversational techniques, just read on.

7.2 WHAT IS PSEUDOCONVERSATION?

The prefix "pseudo" is pronounced "soodoh" and means "false." In biology, an amoeba—a microscopic single-celled creature—is called a pseudopod. As it moves, it changes its shape to give an appearance that it has a foot on which it moves. But the appearance is an illusion. An amoeba is really like a shapeless mass of jello, which deforms in shape as it moves. Since "pseudo" means false and "pod" means foot, we really call the amoeba a "false-footed" animal.

Pseudoconversation is "false conversation." It gives the appearance of a conversation between a human terminal operator and a program executing in a computer system. Pseudoconversation appears to be a conversation, because the human receives appropriate information from the computer system in response to entries at a computer terminal, and then enters more information and again receives responses, and so on. But in pseudoconversation, one of the essential elements of true conversation is missing. When you have a conversation with a person, you take it for granted that the other person is alive and hearing you as you speak. But in CICS pseudoconversation, the thing you are "talking to," a program, is never alive (executing) when you are talking. The program is always dead when you "talk." And quite unlike a human participant in a conversation, the program is resurrected and wakes up again to respond each time you finish what you have to say.

Pseudoconversation saves machine memory and processing power at the expense of introducing complexity into programs. It saves memory because the program you are using is out of memory while you make entries on a terminal screen. It saves processing power for the same reason—a program that is not in memory demands no computer processing attention. But pseudoconversation introduces complexity in program logic because you, the programmer, must arrange logic so as to be able to resume processing (resume the conversation) at the correct point each time the program must be reactivated.

CICS fosters your use of pseudoconversational programming techniques, there are several patterns or models you can follow to arrange your pseudoconversational logic. In this chapter, we'll explore the simplest of these patterns, called "in-line logic." In-line logic most readily lets you see exactly what happens in pseudoconversation. Then, in Chapter 8, we'll show you how the same logic is better arranged in structured form, which sacrifices a bit of legibility for the sake of flexibility and expandability.

7.3 PSEUDOCONVERSATIONAL LOGIC FLOW

Figure 7.3 is a simple diagram showing the pseudoconversational cycle of operation. This cycle of operation presumes that you have already logged onto CICS, as described in Chapter 6. Once logged on, you enter the trans-id of a CICS program on a blank screen. This causes CICS to locate the load module (the machine language) of the program associated with the trans-id, suballocate some of CICS memory to the program and load it to that memory, and give the program control (execute it). Figure 7.3 shows you what possible processing actions the program might take. Let's talk about each of these actions. Then, we'll look at actual program code that implements the logic shown on this chart.

The possible pseudoconversational program processing actions illustrated in Figure 7.3 are:

1. When a CICS program receives control, it must determine what to do to start or continue a pseudoconversation. The first decision it must make is whether this is the first time the terminal is executing it. Is this a new pseudoconversation at this specific terminal? You can of course understand why this is important. The first time the program responds to a terminal—and only the first time—it must send the map image with labels and attribute bytes to properly format the terminal screen. After this transmission, the program does not and should not send the labels, because they will already be present on the screen. If the program determines that this is the first time it has been invoked from the terminal, it sends the map and then returns control to CICS (dies), asking CICS to wake it up again when the terminal operator next presses an **attention identifier (AID) key** such as Enter, a PF key, or Clear.
2. If this invocation of the program is not the first time for a given terminal, the program must receive the transmission from the terminal—that is, receive the map sent by the terminal. The terminal operator will have pressed an attention identifier (AID) key, such as Enter, or a PF key to initiate this transmission, or, possibly, the Clear key to quit using this program.
3. If the terminal operator pressed the Clear key, it's time for this program to return control to CICS (die), *not* asking to be awoken when the terminal operator presses an AID key. In this case, the program has ended for good, or until the terminal operator again enters its trans-id on the screen to invoke it "fresh."
4. If the program determines that the terminal operator did not press Clear to wake it up, did the operator actually send any data? That is, did the operator make any entries into the data fields intended for entry purposes? If the answer to this question is "no," the program needs to tell the operator that no data was sent for processing, then return control to CICS (die), asking to be awakened again when the terminal operator presses an AID key. If data was sent, the program must determine if it is valid or not.
5. The program takes data validation actions on the data entered by the terminal operator. If one or more fields is invalid, the program must issue a meaningful message telling the terminal operator what to correct, and then return control to CICS (die), asking to be awakened when the operator presses an AID key. If the data entered by the terminal operator is entirely valid, the program can process it, then return control to CICS (die), and ask to be awakened when the operator presses an AID key.

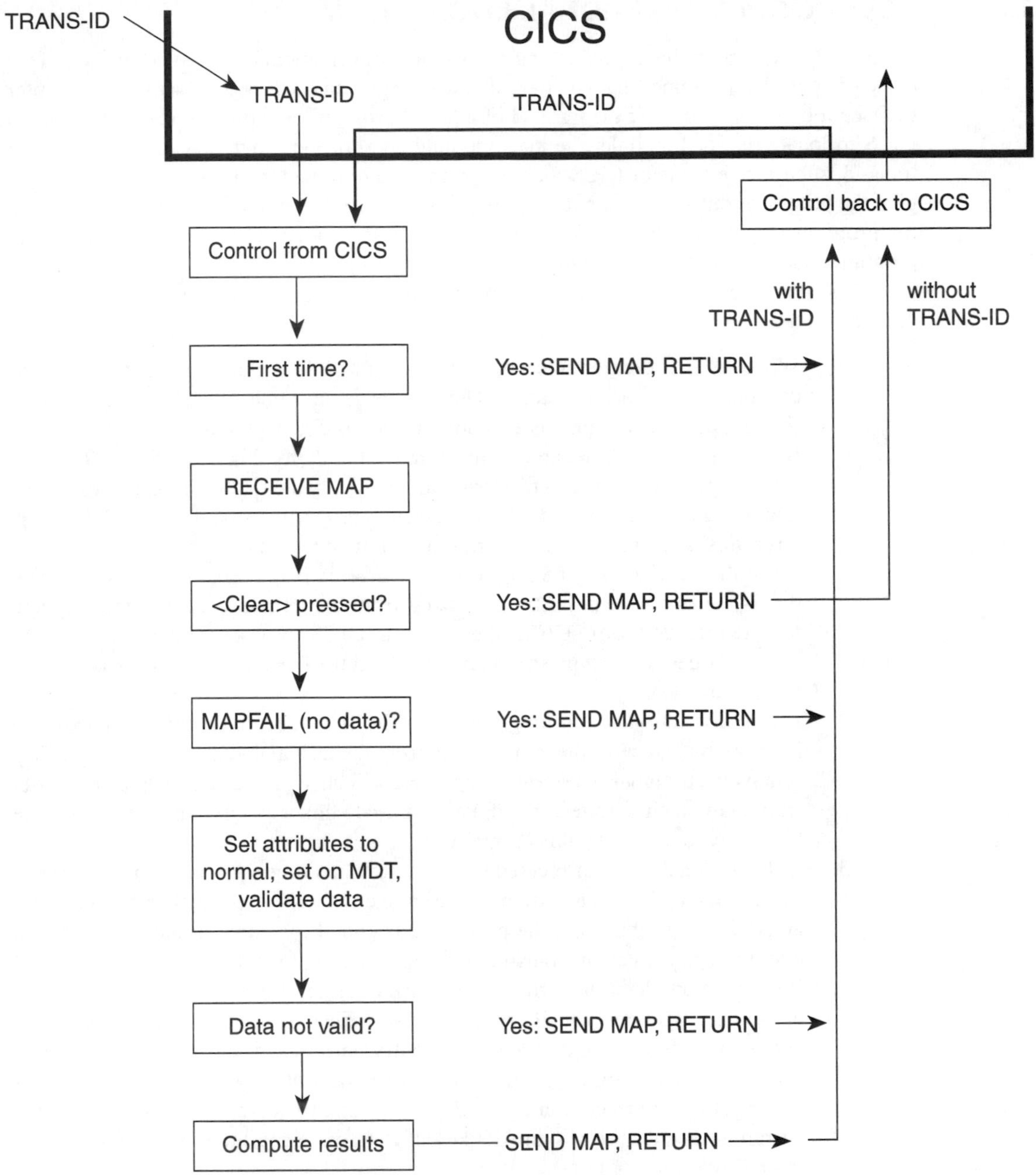
TRANS-ID
CICS
TRANS-ID
TRANS-ID
Control back to CICS
Control from CICS
with
TRANS-ID
without
TRANS-ID
First time?
Yes: SEND MAP, RETURN
RECEIVE MAP
<Clear> pressed?
Yes: SEND MAP, RETURN
MAPFAIL (no data)?
Yes: SEND MAP, RETURN
Set attributes to
normal, set on MDT,
validate data
Data not valid?
Yes: SEND MAP, RETURN
Compute results
SEND MAP, RETURN

Figure 7.3 Logic flow of the CALC1 pseudoconversational CICS program.

As you can see, a pseudoconversational program receives control from CICS only when a terminal operator needs its services. It is crucial for a pseudoconversational program to give control back to CICS, to release the memory and resources it is using, when the program has responded to the operator's input. The program must be able to return control to CICS in two ways:

- **end pseudoconversationally**, when the program must be resurrected later to continue servicing the terminal
- **end unconditionally**, when it is time to quit execution for good.

As you'll see in the CALC1 program source code itself, these returns of control from the program back to CICS are done with the RETURN command, with the TRANSID option or without it.

7.4 CALC1: A SIMPLE PSEUDOCONVERSATIONAL PROGRAM

Figure 7.4 lists the source code of the simplest practical pseudoconversational program we can consider. As you examine the 289 lines of this program, compare it closely to the cycle of operation depicted in Figure 7.3. You will see that the procedure division of CALC1, starting at its line 10900, follows exactly the processing actions shown in the flowchart of Figure 7.3. This represents **in-line logic**. In this logic scheme, the program quits execution by returning control to CICS at whatever point is required, just as the flowchart indicates. The flow of control begins at the start of the Procedure Division and proceeds downward until branching back to CICS. There are no PERFORMs in in-line logic.

Let's consider the various parts of the CALC1 program in detail. The letter annotations on the program listing correspond to the description that follows:

a. WS-TRANS-ID, WS-MAPSET-NAME, and WS-MAP-NAME are coded as literal values so that each of these items needs to be coded only once in the program. Various CICS commands will access these fields throughout the program. Coding these values as named literals eliminates potential problems of inconsistency in the program.

b. WS-RESPONSE-CODE is a field used by CICS to give a "status" value to the program after each CICS command. WS-GOOD-BAD-FLAG is a value we'll use to keep track of the outcome of each data validation. WS-SALES-TAX-RATE, like the literals above at (a), is a named literal value, which makes it easier to change the sales tax than if sales tax were coded as a literal in the logic of the program. WS-COMMUNICATION-AREA is a field we will ask CICS to store for us between pseudoconverses. A **pseudoconverse** is one activation of a program, and lasts until the program again gives control back to CICS. We'll give WS-COMMUNICATION-AREA to CICS when we do a RETURN with TRANSID. CICS will give us back this value in the DFHCOMMAREA field in the LINKAGE SECTION each time the program "wakes up."

c. WS-END-MESSAGE is a brief message displayed on the terminal when the program ends execution normally.

d. WS-ERROR-MESSAGES represent message lines that we'll use only if a CICS failure has been detected. You'll see these mentioned in logic following a CICS command.

e. CALC1-SYMBOLIC-MAP describes the data transmission record by which the program deals with the screen. We discussed the coding for this in Chapter 5.

f. DEFINITIONS-FOR-EIBAID-FIELDS provides data names associated with the values we'll receive from CICS in the **EIBAID** field of the **execute interface block** in the LINKAGE SECTION. Refer back to Figure 6.4, at lines 87 through 118, to see this shared memory area into which CICS inserts values. (Since the execute interface block, labeled DFHEIBLK, is inserted into the program by the CICS translator, you won't see this field in the source code shown in Figure 7.4. The execute interface block is also documented in Appendix A of this book.) The definitions at DEFINITIONS-FOR-EIBAID-FIELDS make it possible for us to detect whether the Enter key or a PF key was pressed by the terminal operator to reawaken the program. To detect the key pressed, we simply compare EIBAID to ENTER-KEY, CLEAR-KEY, and so forth, seeking which field is equal to EIBAID. (We document a standard definition provided by IBM as a copybook item, named DFHAID, in Appendix A. DFHAID provides values and field names for all 24 PF keys, program attention keys, and the Enter and Clear keys.

g. ATTRIBUTE-VALUES-TO-SET are named data fields that carry the bit patterns required to make screen fields become bright or normal intensity, and to turn on the modified data tag (MDT) in a field. We'll use these fields in the data validation sequence by putting the appropriate value into the attribute byte of each screen field in the data transmission record, prior to sending the data transmission record to the terminal screen.

h. **DFHCOMMAREA** in the LINKAGE SECTION is where CICS gives us back any value that we ask it to store for us between pseudoconverses. (We get the field named WS-COMMUNICATION-AREA back in DFHCOMMAREA as a result of the way we code the RETURN command with TRANSID.)

i. **EIBCALEN** is another field in the execute interface block, as you can see in line 95 of Figure 6.4. EIBCALEN has a value of 0 when no data is returned to the program at the start of a pseudoconverse; otherwise, EIBCALEN carries a value equal to the number of characters passed by the program, through CICS storage, back to itself. We arrange our RETURNs to CICS to always pass at least one byte of data back to our program. Therefore, the only time that EIBCALEN will be zero is the first time a program is invoked from a terminal. This is what happens when you put the trans-id of the program on a blank screen and press Enter to begin executing a program.

j. Executing CICS **RETURN with TRANSID** and COMMAREA is the way to return control to CICS and ask for the program to be awakened again when the operator presses an AID key. WS-TRANS-ID is the named data field that carries the program's own trans-id (see line 1300). The content of WS-COMMUNICATION-AREA is, for purposes of this program, not important. Simply the fact that we pass a byte of data back to ourselves between pseudoconverses by using the COMMAREA option means that EIBCALEN will not be zero the next time the program receives control.

k. The RECEIVE MAP command causes CICS to decode the transmission from the terminal and build the data transmission record for us in the INTO field, which we named as CALC1-SYMBOLIC-MAP. The RESP option puts the CICS **response code**, which is a number value representing the outcome of the processing action,

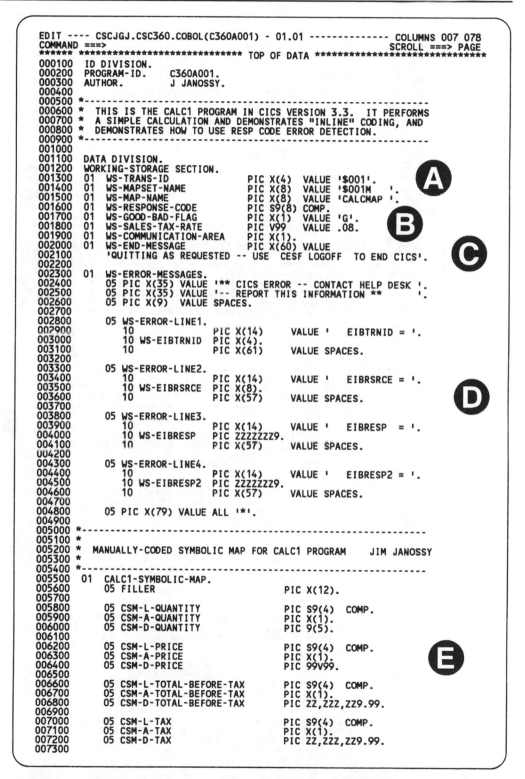

```
EDIT ---- CSCJGJ.CSC360.COBOL(C360A001) - 01.01 -------------- COLUMNS 007 078
COMMAND ===>                                                   SCROLL ===> PAGE
****** ***************************** TOP OF DATA ******************************
 ID DIVISION.
 PROGRAM-ID.    C360A001.
 AUTHOR.        J JANOSSY.

*-----------------------------------------------------------------
*  THIS IS THE CALC1 PROGRAM IN CICS VERSION 3.3.  IT PERFORMS
*  A SIMPLE CALCULATION AND DEMONSTRATES "INLINE" CODING, AND
*  DEMONSTRATES HOW TO USE RESP CODE ERROR DETECTION.
*-----------------------------------------------------------------

 DATA DIVISION.
 WORKING-STORAGE SECTION.
 01  WS-TRANS-ID                   PIC X(4)  VALUE '$001'.
 01  WS-MAPSET-NAME                PIC X(8)  VALUE '$001M   '.
 01  WS-MAP-NAME                   PIC X(8)  VALUE 'CALCMAP '.
 01  WS-RESPONSE-CODE              PIC S9(8) COMP.
 01  WS-GOOD-BAD-FLAG              PIC X(1)  VALUE 'G'.
 01  WS-SALES-TAX-RATE             PIC V99   VALUE .08.
 01  WS-COMMUNICATION-AREA         PIC X(1).
 01  WS-END-MESSAGE                PIC X(60) VALUE
     'QUITTING AS REQUESTED -- USE  CESF LOGOFF  TO END CICS'.

 01  WS-ERROR-MESSAGES.
     05 PIC X(35) VALUE '** CICS ERROR -- CONTACT HELP DESK '.
     05 PIC X(35) VALUE '-- REPORT THIS INFORMATION **      '.
     05 PIC X(9)  VALUE SPACES.

     05 WS-ERROR-LINE1.
        10                 PIC X(14)     VALUE '    EIBTRNID = '.
        10 WS-EIBTRNID     PIC X(4).
        10                 PIC X(61)     VALUE SPACES.

     05 WS-ERROR-LINE2.
        10                 PIC X(14)     VALUE '    EIBRSRCE = '.
        10 WS-EIBRSRCE     PIC X(8).
        10                 PIC X(57)     VALUE SPACES.

     05 WS-ERROR-LINE3.
        10                 PIC X(14)     VALUE '    EIBRESP  = '.
        10 WS-EIBRESP      PIC ZZZZZZZ9.
        10                 PIC X(57)     VALUE SPACES.

     05 WS-ERROR-LINE4.
        10                 PIC X(14)     VALUE '    EIBRESP2 = '.
        10 WS-EIBRESP2     PIC ZZZZZZZ9.
        10                 PIC X(57)     VALUE SPACES.

     05 PIC X(79) VALUE ALL '*'.

*-----------------------------------------------------------------
*
*  MANUALLY-CODED SYMBOLIC MAP FOR CALC1 PROGRAM    JIM JANOSSY
*
*-----------------------------------------------------------------
 01  CALC1-SYMBOLIC-MAP.
     05 FILLER                              PIC X(12).

     05 CSM-L-QUANTITY                      PIC S9(4)  COMP.
     05 CSM-A-QUANTITY                      PIC X(1).
     05 CSM-D-QUANTITY                      PIC 9(5).

     05 CSM-L-PRICE                         PIC S9(4)  COMP.
     05 CSM-A-PRICE                         PIC X(1).
     05 CSM-D-PRICE                         PIC 99V99.

     05 CSM-L-TOTAL-BEFORE-TAX              PIC S9(4)  COMP.
     05 CSM-A-TOTAL-BEFORE-TAX              PIC X(1).
     05 CSM-D-TOTAL-BEFORE-TAX              PIC ZZ,ZZZ,ZZ9.99.

     05 CSM-L-TAX                           PIC S9(4)  COMP.
     05 CSM-A-TAX                           PIC X(1).
     05 CSM-D-TAX                           PIC ZZ,ZZZ,ZZ9.99.
```

Figure 7.4 Source code of the pseudoconversational CALC1 program.

```
           05 CSM-L-GRAND-TOTAL                PIC S9(4)  COMP.
           05 CSM-A-GRAND-TOTAL                PIC X(1).
           05 CSM-D-GRAND-TOTAL                PIC ZZ,ZZZ,ZZ9.99.

           05 CSM-L-MESSAGE                    PIC S9(4)  COMP.
           05 CSM-A-MESSAGE                    PIC X(1).
           05 CSM-D-MESSAGE                    PIC X(79).

      *-----------------------------------------------------------
      *
      *  VALUE MEANINGS FOR EIBAID FIELD OF DFHEIBLK
      *
      *-----------------------------------------------------------
       01  DEFINITIONS-OF-EIBAID-FIELD.
           05 ENTER-KEY                        PIC X  VALUE ''''.
           05 CLEAR-KEY                        PIC X  VALUE '_'.
           05 PF1-KEY                          PIC X  VALUE 'T'.
           05 PF2-KEY                          PIC X  VALUE '2'.
           05 PF3-KEY                          PIC X  VALUE '3'.

      *-----------------------------------------------------------
      *
      *  VALUE MEANINGS FOR SYMBOLIC MAP ATTRIBUTE BYTE FIELDS
      *
      *-----------------------------------------------------------
       01  ATTRIBUTE-VALUES-TO-SET.
           05 ATT-UNPROT-CHAR-MDT              PIC X  VALUE 'A'.
           05 ATT-UNPROT-CHAR-MDT-BRIGHT       PIC X  VALUE 'I'.
           05 ATT-UNPROT-NUM-MDT               PIC X  VALUE 'J'.
           05 ATT-UNPROT-NUM-MDT-BRIGHT        PIC X  VALUE 'R'.

       LINKAGE SECTION.
       01  DFHCOMMAREA                         PIC X(1).

       PROCEDURE DIVISION.
      *====================================== FIRST TIME? =========
      *  IF FIRST TIME THIS TERMINAL ACTIVATES THE PROGRAM, EIBCALEN
      *  WILL BE ZERO, SO SEND THE SCREEN LABELS AND EXIT BUT HAVE
      *  CICS "REMEMBER" THE TRANS-ID OF THIS PROGRAM TO RESTART IT.
      *-----------------------------------------------------------
           IF EIBCALEN = 0

                MOVE LOW-VALUES TO CALC1-SYMBOLIC-MAP
                MOVE 'ENTER VALUES, PRESS <ENTER>, <CLEAR> TO QUIT'
                   TO CSM-D-MESSAGE
                MOVE -1 TO CSM-L-QUANTITY
                EXEC CICS
                     SEND MAPSET     (WS-MAPSET-NAME)
                          MAP        (WS-MAP-NAME)
                          FROM       (CALC1-SYMBOLIC-MAP)
                          ERASE
                          CURSOR
                END-EXEC

                EXEC CICS
                   RETURN TRANSID    (WS-TRANS-ID)
                          COMMAREA   (WS-COMMUNICATION-AREA)
                END-EXEC

           END-IF.

      *====================================== RECEIVE SCREEN ======
      *  IT'S NOT THE FIRST TIME THE TERMINAL ACTIVATED THIS PROGRAM;
      *  USER HAS SENT BACK DATA OR PRESSED CLEAR TO EXIT
      *-----------------------------------------------------------
           EXEC CICS
                RECEIVE MAP        (WS-MAP-NAME)
                        MAPSET     (WS-MAPSET-NAME)
                        INTO       (CALC1-SYMBOLIC-MAP)
                        RESP       (WS-RESPONSE-CODE)
           END-EXEC.

      *==================================== WAS <CLEAR> PRESSED?===
      *  IF PROGRAM WAS ACTIVATED BECAUSE THE TERMINAL USER PRESSED
      *  THE CLEAR KEY, IT'S TIME TO QUIT THIS PROGRAM COMPLETELY
      *-----------------------------------------------------------
```

Figure 7.4 *(Continued)*

```
      IF EIBAID = CLEAR-KEY

           EXEC CICS
                SEND TEXT FROM (WS-END-MESSAGE)
                     ERASE
                     FREEKB
           END-EXEC

           EXEC CICS
                RETURN
           END-EXEC

      END-IF.

*========================================= WAS DATA SENT? ===
*  WE MUST CHECK THE OUTCOME OF EVERY RECEIVE MAP COMMAND.
*  IF NORMAL, WE GOT DATA.  IF TERMINAL OPERATOR PRESSED ENTER
*  BUT HAD NOT ENTERED ANY DATA, CICS WILL SEE A "MAP FAIL"
*  ERROR; WE MUST HANDLE IT.  IF OUTCOME WAS NOT NORMAL AND NOT
*  MAP FAIL, OUTCOME IS A CICS ERROR AND WE MUST MAKE INFO
*  VISIBLE FOR PROBLEM DIAGNOSIS, THEN ABORT EXECUTION.
*-----------------------------------------------------------

      EVALUATE  WS-RESPONSE-CODE
*=========
        WHEN  DFHRESP(NORMAL)
           CONTINUE
*=========
        WHEN  DFHRESP(MAPFAIL)

           MOVE -1 TO CSM-L-QUANTITY
           MOVE 'NO DATA ENTERED; ENTER DATA OR <CLEAR> TO QUIT'
              TO CSM-D-MESSAGE

           EXEC CICS
                SEND MAP        (WS-MAP-NAME)
                     MAPSET     (WS-MAPSET-NAME)
                     FROM       (CALC1-SYMBOLIC-MAP)
                     DATAONLY
                     CURSOR
           END-EXEC

           EXEC CICS
              RETURN TRANSID    (WS-TRANS-ID)
                     COMMAREA   (WS-COMMUNICATION-AREA)
           END-EXEC
*=========
        WHEN  OTHER

           MOVE EIBTRNID    TO  WS-EIBTRNID
           MOVE EIBRSRCE    TO  WS-EIBRSRCE
           MOVE EIBRESP     TO  WS-EIBRESP
           MOVE EIBRESP2    TO  WS-EIBRESP2

           EXEC CICS
              SEND TEXT FROM (WS-ERROR-MESSAGES)
                   ERASE
                   ALARM
                   FREEKB
           END-EXEC

           EXEC CICS
                RETURN
           END-EXEC
*=========
      END-EVALUATE.

*====================== WE GOT DATA, SO WE MUST VALIDATE IT===
*  BEGIN BY RESETTING ALL INPUT FIELD ATTRIBUTE BYTES TO NORMAL
*  INTENSITY AND SETTING THE MODIFIED DATA TAG ON FOR ALL INPUT
*  FIELDS SO ALL FIELDS ARE TRANSMITTED BACK TO THE PROGRAM THE
*  NEXT TIME THE TERMINAL OPERATOR PRESSES ENTER.  THEN CHECK
*  EACH INPUT FIELD; IF BAD, MAKE ITS ATTRIBUTE BYTE THE ONE FOR
*  "BRIGHT" INTENSITY AND PUT THE CURSOR INTO THE FIELD.  CHECK
*  FIELDS IN REVERSE SEQUENCE TO LEAVE ERROR MESSAGE FOR FIRST
*  ERROR FIELD FROM TOP IN PROMPT LINE.
```

Figure 7.4 *(Continued)*

```
      *----------------------------------------------------------------
           MOVE ATT-UNPROT-NUM-MDT TO  CSM-A-QUANTITY
                                       CSM-A-PRICE.

           IF CSM-D-PRICE NOT NUMERIC
              MOVE 'B' TO WS-GOOD-BAD-FLAG
              MOVE ATT-UNPROT-NUM-MDT-BRIGHT TO CSM-A-PRICE
              MOVE -1 TO CSM-L-PRICE
              MOVE 'PRICE MUST BE NUMERIC; CORRECT, PRESS <ENTER>'
                 TO CSM-D-MESSAGE
           END-IF.

           IF CSM-D-QUANTITY NOT NUMERIC
              MOVE 'B' TO WS-GOOD-BAD-FLAG
              MOVE ATT-UNPROT-NUM-MDT-BRIGHT TO CSM-A-QUANTITY
              MOVE -1 TO CSM-L-QUANTITY
              MOVE 'QUANTITY MUST BE NUMERIC; CORRECT, PRESS <ENTER>'
                 TO CSM-D-MESSAGE
           END-IF.

           IF WS-GOOD-BAD-FLAG = 'B'

              EXEC CICS
                   SEND MAP        (WS-MAP-NAME)
                        MAPSET     (WS-MAPSET-NAME)
                        FROM       (CALC1-SYMBOLIC-MAP)
                        DATAONLY
                        CURSOR
              END-EXEC

              EXEC CICS
                 RETURN TRANSID    (WS-TRANS-ID)
                        COMMAREA   (WS-COMMUNICATION-AREA)
              END-EXEC

           END-IF.
      *============================== DATA OK, COMPUTE, PRESENT ===
      *  IF CONTROL REACHES THIS POINT THE INPUT DATA IS KNOWN TO
      *  BE GOOD.  GO AHEAD AND COMPUTE WITH IT AND SET THE PROMPT
      *  TO BE READY FOR THE NEXT TRANSACTION
      *----------------------------------------------------------------
           COMPUTE CSM-D-TOTAL-BEFORE-TAX =
              CSM-D-QUANTITY * CSM-D-PRICE.
           COMPUTE CSM-D-TAX =
              CSM-D-QUANTITY * CSM-D-PRICE * WS-SALES-TAX-RATE.
           COMPUTE CSM-D-GRAND-TOTAL =
              CSM-D-QUANTITY * CSM-D-PRICE * WS-SALES-TAX-RATE +
              CSM-D-QUANTITY * CSM-D-PRICE.
           MOVE 'RESULTS COMPUTED, ENTER MORE DATA OR <CLEAR> TO QUIT'
              TO CSM-D-MESSAGE.
           MOVE -1 TO CSM-L-QUANTITY.

           EXEC CICS
                SEND MAP        (WS-MAP-NAME)
                     MAPSET     (WS-MAPSET-NAME)
                     FROM       (CALC1-SYMBOLIC-MAP)
                     DATAONLY
                     CURSOR
           END-EXEC.

           EXEC CICS
              RETURN TRANSID    (WS-TRANS-ID)
                     COMMAREA   (WS-COMMUNICATION-AREA)
           END-EXEC.
```

Figure 7.4 *(Continued)*

into the WS-RESPONSE-CODE field. This makes it possible to evaluate the CICS response code, as you see starting at line 17300.

l. We check to see if the terminal operator pressed the Clear key by comparing the value in the EIBAID field of the execute interface block with the literal value CLEAR-KEY (defined at line 8900).

m. If the Clear key was pressed, we return control unconditionally to CICS, and this program dies with no hope of resuscitation. Executing CICS **RETURN without TRANSID** is how to return control to CICS with no hope of reviving the pseudoconversation.

n. We test the **response code** from CICS for the RECEIVE MAP command. If the response was NORMAL, we can proceed (CONTINUE sends control to the point after the END-EVALUATE at line 21500). If the CICS response code indicated a MAPFAIL condition—meaning no data was entered by the terminal operator before Enter was pressed—we send back a message stating so. If any OTHER response code was conveyed by CICS for the RECEIVE MAP command, we move various diagnostic values, provided by CICS in the execute interface block, to message lines that will be sent to the terminal screen, send those lines to the screen, and end unconditionally. This last potential outcome represents a "disaster" situation that ends execution of the program, since it requires manual problem solving.

o. If control gets to this point, it means we received data from the terminal. We initialize the attribute bytes of the data fields to normal intensity with modified data tag on, as a prelude to data validation actions. Subsequent data validations may reset any attribute byte to a "bright" condition if invalid data is detected in a field. Here is a review question: Why do we take no action to give WS-GOOD-BAD-FLAG a value of "good" before starting the data validation sequence, as we would in a batch program? The answer? Recall that each CICS programs gets a fresh copy of WORKING-STORAGE when it begins execution. WS-GOOD-BAD-FLAG is always "G" when the CALC1 program receives control, due to the VALUE clause at its declaration in line 1700.

p. We validate the contents of enterable fields starting with the last (the physically lowest, rightmost field). If invalid data is detected, we put an appropriate prompt in the data transmission record prompt field, and move a negative value to the screen field's "length" value in the data transmission record. By checking fields from the bottom of the screen to the top, the cursor will stop at the first field, left to right and top to bottom, that has an error, and the prompt will be the appropriate one for this field, no matter how many screen fields there are, and how many fields contain invalid data. (We'll discuss data validation logic in CICS programs in detail in Section 7.5 below.)

q. The final contents of WS-GOOD-BAD-FLAG determines whether or not we send the screen back to the terminal operator now, or proceed to use the data received.

r. If control reaches this point, we know that the data received from the terminal operator is acceptable for computation. We compute the "result" values and put them into the appropriate fields in the data transmission record, and give the prompt field the "results computed . . . " message.

s. We send the completed screen to the terminal.

```
MY NAME IS **** PUT YOUR NAME HERE! ****


                    QUANTITY      PRICE            TOTAL
                     -.7..        --.3

                                  8% TAX

                                                ==============

                              GRAND TOTAL





QUANTITY MUST BE NUMERIC; CORRECT, PRESS <ENTER>
```

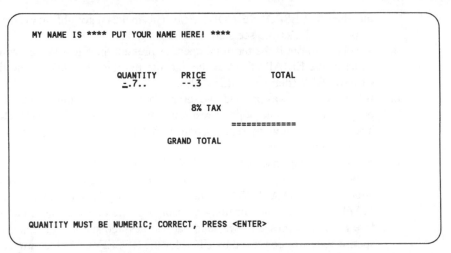

Figure 7.5 CALC1 screen with invalid data entered into the QUANTITY and PRICE fields; cursor and message for QUANTITY field error.

t. We end execution with RETURN with TRANSID and COMMAREA, to make entry of another transaction possible.

7.5 THE STANDARD DATA VALIDATION SEQUENCE

Lines 22700 through 26100 of the CALC1 program contain the **standard data validation sequence** by which we check the contents of the data fields received from the terminal. In CALC1, this sequence is very short, since only two fields, both numeric, are received from the terminal. Yet if you see and understand the pattern here, you can "scale up" the pattern to any quantity of fields on a screen. Simply put, we check the contents of fields in a bottom-to-top, right-to-left order. Each validation includes, if the field contents are judged to be invalid, actions to move -1 to the field's length field in the data transmission record, actions to brighten the intensity of the field on the screen, and actions to put an appropriate error message in the prompt line.

It is in the area of data validation that **pseudoconversational processing** differs significantly, in terms of user interface, from **conversational processing**. In pseudoconversational processing the program does not receive field contents one at a time, but rather gets the content of all fields at one time, when an AID key is pressed. Many fields might contain invalid contents. Yet the screen has only one, or at most two, prompt lines. As a compromise to deal with these factors, we want the processing actions shown in Figures 7.5, 7.6, and 7.7 to occur.

In Figure 7.5, you see the entry of invalid data in both the QUANTITY and PRICE fields of the CALC1 screen. While we have defined these fields as numeric using the NUM attribute, the screening provided by NUM is not entirely comprehensive. NUM still lets us enter periods (decimal points) and hyphens (negative signs), though it does screen out the entry of letters and other punctuation. But hyphens and periods are not numeric, so our logic detects them as field content errors. Notice that in Figure 7.5, due to the data validation sequence we used, the cursor is positioned at the first field with a content error, QUANTITY, and the message at the bottom of the screen refers to this field.

```
MY NAME IS **** PUT YOUR NAME HERE! ****


                QUANTITY     PRICE              TOTAL
                 00117       --.3

                                8% TAX

                                            =============

                            GRAND TOTAL




PRICE MUST BE NUMERIC; CORRECT, PRESS <ENTER>
```

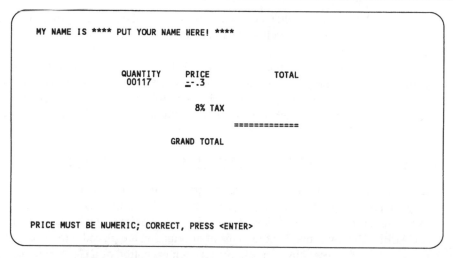

Figure 7.6 CALC1 screen with invalid data in QUANTITY field corrected; cursor and message for PRICE field error.

Figure 7.6 shows you what happens when we correct the contents of the QUANTITY field, and press Enter. NUM "packages" the now-valid quantity right justified with leading zeros. The cursor now shifts to the PRICE field, where a data content error still exists, and the error message in the prompt line refers, appropriately, to this field. This message was put into the prompt line during the first validation sequence, but the data content error detected in the QUANTITY field preempted it. With the QUANTITY field error corrected, the PRICE field error becomes the "first" one from top to bottom and left to right, so it is the one shown on the screen.

Figure 7.7 shows you the result when we correct the PRICE field error and press Enter.

```
MY NAME IS **** PUT YOUR NAME HERE! ****


                QUANTITY     PRICE              TOTAL
                 00117       0003               3.51

                                8% TAX          0.28

                                            =============

                            GRAND TOTAL         3.79




RESULTS COMPUTED, ENTER MORE DATA OR <CLEAR> TO QUIT
```

Computation now proceeds and results are shown.

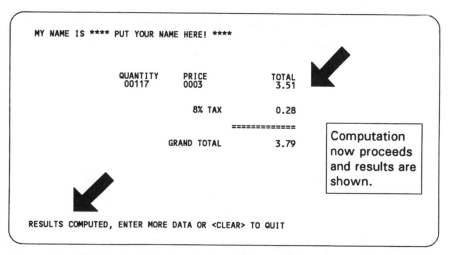

Figure 7.7 CALC1 screen with all invalid data corrected; results computed and prompt indicates another transaction is possible.

Since no invalid enterable field contents are now present, the program proceeds to use the data for computations after the standard data validation sequence, and the computed results are shown.

If a screen had 25 enterable fields, you could follow the same data validation sequence as shown in CALC1. If invalid data was present in all 25 fields, the terminal operator could work through the errors, one by one, in exactly the same way as demonstrated by the CALC1 program. That is what we mean when we say that the standard data validation sequence technique "scales up" well!

7.6 MORE ABOUT THE EXECUTE INTERFACE BLOCK

The execute interface block is contained in a group item named DFHEIBLK, which is inserted into your program's LINKAGE SECTION by the CICS translator. The CALC1 program makes use of only a few fields in the execute interface block, such as EIBAID and EIBCALEN. However, many more items of information are placed into the execute interface block by CICS for access by a program after each execution of a CICS command, including the date, time, terminal id, transaction id, and cursor position. While you can see the contents of the execute interface block in Figure 6.4, lines 87 through 118, we have also included reference information about the execute interface block in Appendix A of this book.

7.7 HOW CALC1 ENDS EXECUTION

When the terminal operator presses the Clear key, two things happen. Clear causes the image on the terminal screen to be cleared away, purely as a local terminal function. The mainframe is not involved in this clearing action. But as an AID key, Clear does signal the mainframe, yet transmits no data from the screen. We detect the Clear key at line 15000 in the CALC1 program, send a brief confirming message to the terminal screen, then return control unconditionally to CICS. Figure 7.8 shows you what the terminal screen looks like when the CALC1 program ends.

```
QUITTING AS REQUESTED -- USE  CESF LOGOFF  TO END CICS
```

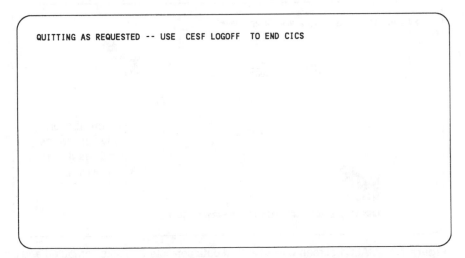

Figure 7.8 CALC1 screen when the CALC1 program ends execution normally.

7.8 FOR YOUR REVIEW

Understanding these terms and elements of CICS programming and processing, introduced in Chapter 7, will aid your understanding of the next chapter:

AID key
Conversational processing
DFHCOMMAREA
EIBAID field
EIBCALEN field
Execute interface block (DFHEIBLK)
In-line logic
Pseudoconversational ending
Pseudoconversational processing
Pseudoconverse
Response code
RETURN with TRANSID and COMMAREA
RETURN without TRANSID
Standard data validation sequence
Unconditional ending

7.9 REVIEW QUESTIONS

1. Explain the basis for the word "pseudoconversation" by explaining what the two parts of this word actually mean.
2. Identify the tradeoff underlying the use of pseudoconversational processing. That is, what do we gain from using it, and what do we sacrifice?
3. Why does a pseudoconversational CICS program have to check, every time it is invoked, if it is the first time that a given terminal is invoking it?
4. Explain how a pseudoconversational CICS program checks if it is the first time that a given terminal is invoking it.
5. Explain what a MAPFAIL condition is, and how it is caused.
6. Identify the two ways that a pseudoconversational program must be able to end (give control back to CICS), and give an example of the coding syntax to do this.
7. Explain why it is advantageous to declare data names such as WS-TRANS-ID, WS-MAPSET-NAME, WS-MAP-NAME in WORKING-STORAGE, and give them the values appropriate to the program they are declared in.
8. Identify and describe the role of the field named WS-RESPONSE-CODE in a CICS program, and explain what purpose is served by coding it.
9. Explain how program logic can be arranged to determine which attention identifier (AID) key was pressed to resume a pseudoconversation, and give an example of this coding.
10. Explain how program logic can be arranged to make a field on a screen change from normal intensity to bright intensity, and give an example of this coding.
11. Explain in detail how a program can preserve data values from one pseudoconverse to another, that is, between the time that the program gives control back to CICS and the time it is reawakened by the terminal operator pressing an AID key.
12. Identify and describe the two things that the Clear key does when it is pressed.
13. Explain why we do not have to reinitialize the WS-GOOD-BAD-FLAG field in the CALC1 program with "G" before beginning the validation sequence for the entered data fields, as would be customary in a batch data validation program.
14. Describe what the standard data validation sequence is in a pseudoconversational CICS program, and explain how and why it provides a beneficial effect.

7.10 HANDS-ON EXERCISES

Do these exercises in the sequence listed here to gain the most from the information in this chapter:

A. Review the hands-on exercises at the end of Chapter 6, in which you designed a screen entitled the CICS AVERAGE CALCULATOR. If you haven't already done so, prepare the BMS map code for this screen, and prepare physical and symbolic maps as directed at the end of Chapter 6. Make sure you use a valid, installation-specific map id.

B. Follow the pattern of logic and the standard data validation sequence shown in the CALC1 program, and develop in-line program logic for your CICS AVERAGE CALCULATOR screen. Use the PGMJOB job control language shown in Figure 6.3, or comparable JCL provided by your installation, to prepare a machine language load module for your program, using a valid, installation-specific program name and trans-id.

C. Test your CICS AVERAGE CALCULATOR in the same way that you executed the SHOWMAP program at the end of Chapter 6.

Here is a more challenging exercise:

D. Refer to section 4.17, in which you developed a screen carrying the title MY FIRST CICS SCREEN, which included your name in the title. You may already have prepared BMS map code for this screen while studying Chapter 4, and you may have already prepared physical and symbolic maps for this screen in accomplishing an exercise at the end of Chapter 5. Prepare a CICS program, using in-line logic to process this screen, which contains these enterable fields:

FIRST NAME	Must not be blank, and must be alphabetic
MIDDLE INITIAL	Must be alphabetic
LAST NAME	Must not be blank, and must be alphabetic
RATE OF PAY	Must be numeric, greater then $4.50
HOURS WORKED	Must be numeric, greater than zero

For your information only, the appropriate data validations are as listed to the right of each enterable data item above.

The following computed fields are also shown on the screen and are produced by program logic when all data field entries above are judged to be valid:

AMOUNT OF PAY

Hours worked up to and including 40 are paid at straight time, which is the pay rate × hours. Hours worked beyond 40 and up to and including 60 are paid at time and one-half, which is rate × 1.5 × hours. Hours worked beyond 60 are paid at double time, which is rate × 2.0 × hours. For example, the amount of pay for a person who worked 35 hours at $5.00 an hour would be:

35 ×	5	=	175
0	5 × 1.5	=	0
0	5 × 2.0	=	0
35 hours			$ 175

but the pay for a person who worked 63 hours at the same rate of pay ($5) would be:

40	× 5	=	200
20	5 × 1.5	=	150
3	5 × 2.0	=	30
63 hours			$ 380

PAY TO NAME

The first name, middle initial, and last name fields are to be concatenated so that the parts of the name appear in customary sequence with no excess spaces between them. For example, these entries may be made on your screen:

```
FIRST NAME      alice
MIDDLE INITIAL  b
LAST NAME       toklas
```

But the PAY TO NAME field should appear as below as output by the program, with appropriate punctuation after the middle initial (a period) if the middle initial field is other than a space:

```
PAY TO NAME     ALICE B. TOKLAS
```

If the middle initial field is a space, such as in this case:

```
FIRST NAME      john
MIDDLE INITIAL
LAST NAME       smith
```

the PAY TO NAME field should be formatted like this:

```
PAY TO NAME     JOHN SMITH
```

Consider using the STRING verb to concatenate the fields into the appropriate sequence. The PAY TO NAME field should be long enough to accommodate the concatenation of completely filled separate parts of the name, with one space between each part. (Do not forget that STRING, unlike MOVE, requires that you clear out the target character field by moving SPACES to it before your execute STRING, or you may wind up with remnants of concatenating long fields when you subsequently concatenate short fields.)

8

Structured Pseudoconversational Logic

Pseudoconversational processing is the primary strength of the CICS environment. It makes it possible for one computer to support thousands of terminals, a feat that is impossible to accomplish in a conversational mode. But as you saw in Chapter 7, pseudoconversational processing introduces a whole new way of thinking into program logic. We initially demonstrated the simple CALC1 program with logic arranged in an "in-line" style, which closely follows the actual cycle of pseudoconversational operation, because this makes it easiest for you to see and understand that cycle. But in actual practice, in-line logic presents limitations and does not "scale up" well to more complicated programs. In this chapter we explore why in-line logic is not used for "real" CICS programs, and how structure is introduced into CICS programs. You'll see CALC1 again in this chapter, but now in a form that is well structured and readily susceptible to functional enhancement.

8.1 WHAT'S WRONG WITH IN-LINE CICS PROGRAM CODING?

The CALC1 program of Chapter 7 certainly works fine, and you may have used it as a model to complete one or both of the exercises at the end of that chapter. In-line logic directly follows the pseudoconversational processing cycle, which made this a popular coding style in the early days. But the predominant industry experience with in-line style caused this style of logic to be abandoned by most organizations. Why?

The fact is, in-line coding style, while acceptable and workable for small programs, leads to major headaches and bowl-of-spaghetti coding when attempted in larger, more complex programs. If you examine the original CALC1 program in Chapter 7, you will note that much code redundancy exists in the repeated codings of the RETURN commands. If you try to eliminate those redundancies by housing one RETURN in a paragraph, but you use GO TO to change the flow of control to proceed to that paragraph, it's almost inevitable that some code will have to branch backward. The more backward branching you have, the more difficult code is to follow and debug. In-line coding style becomes less and less amenable to reliable maintenance and enhancement as the size and logical complexity of programs increase.

An important criterion of modern programming is to reduce or eliminate dependence on the physical placement of logic, and instead rely on controlled, orchestrated execution of **functional modules** of code. This form of code structuring, or **structured coding**, has been demonstrated to lead to more rapidly constructed, reliable, and readily maintained programs. This style of coding relies on the use of functional paragraphs of code that are PERFORMed under the direction of a "mainline" at the beginning of the procedure division.

Code structuring took longer to work its way into the CICS environment than it did into batch programming, partly because of syntax limitations in the original CICS commands of the early 1970s. Early CICS command syntax, for example, lacked a response code in the execute interface block, and used a form of coding involving HANDLE AID and HANDLE CONDITION commands. These commands inherently caused logic branching as if GO TOs had been coded, and were patterned on the operation of IBM assembler, a very branch-oriented language. With 1985 COBOL—that is, VS COBOL II—and modern versions of CICS, such as version 3.3, code structuring is now much easier to achieve. Most organizations take advantage of structured coding, and insist that new CICS programs be built in this way rather than with in-line coding techniques.

8.2 HOW DO YOU STRUCTURE CICS CODE?

Figure 8.1 depicts a common form of diagram that describes the structure of a modern CICS program, as applied to a structured version of the CALC1 program. In this chart, each paragraph is a box. This **structure chart** is very similar to an organization chart for a business. The placement of the boxes indicates which paragraphs "work for" which other paragraphs—in other words, which paragraphs are PERFORMed by which others. The box at the top represents the first paragraph in the procedure division, the mainline.

You read the chart in Figure 8.1 from top to bottom, left to right. For example, 0000-MAINLINE receives control first. The first thing 0000-MAINLINE invokes is the 3333-ALWAYS-TEST box (paragraph). The first thing the 0500-NORMAL-PROCESSING paragraph invokes is the 1000-RECEIVE-MAP paragraph, then next the 5000-VALIDATE-FIELDS paragraph.

The symbols on the chart in Figure 8.1 require a small amount of explanation. The shaded corner of a box indicates that the paragraph represented by the box has been "reused." That is, a box with a shaded upper right corner is a copy of a box that exists elsewhere, most likely at a lower level. For example, box 8000-RETURN "works for" 1000-RECEIVE-MAP,

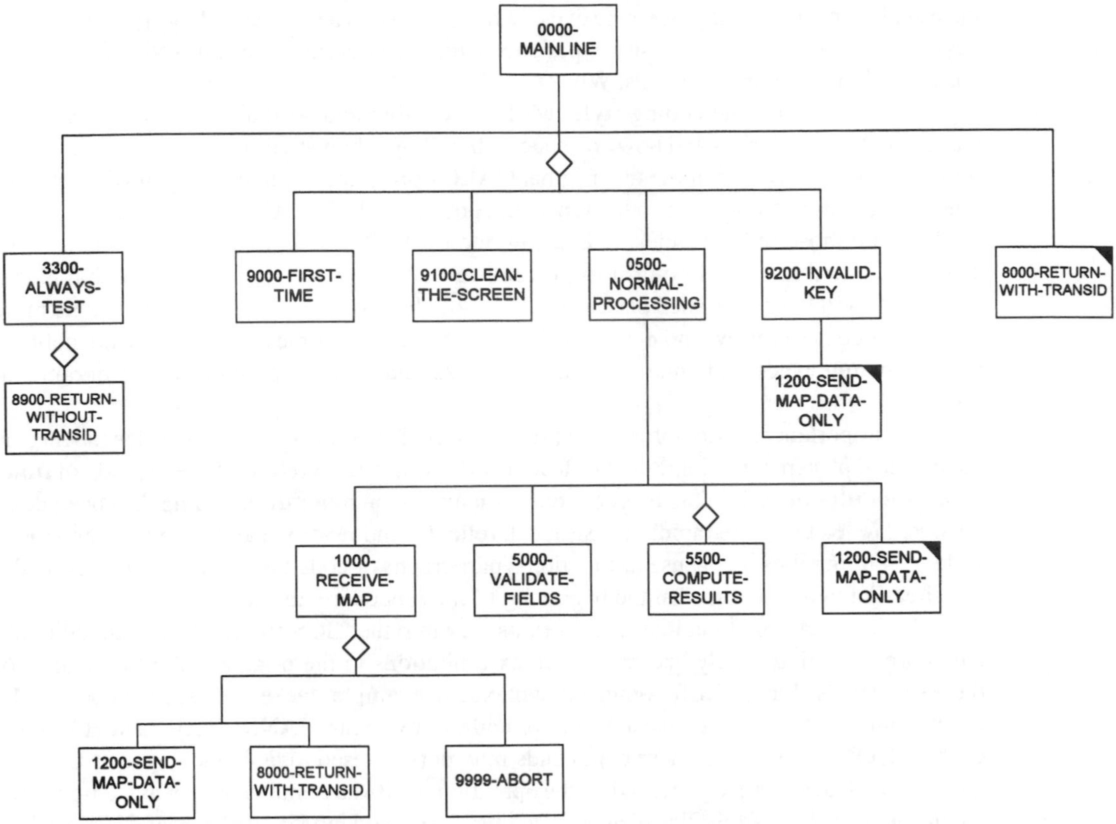

0000-MAINLINE
3300-ALWAYS-TEST
9000-FIRST-TIME
9100-CLEAN-THE-SCREEN
0500-NORMAL-PROCESSING
9200-INVALID-KEY
8000-RETURN-WITH-TRANSID
8900-RETURN-WITHOUT-TRANSID
1200-SEND-MAP-DATA-ONLY
1000-RECEIVE-MAP
5000-VALIDATE-FIELDS
5500-COMPUTE-RESULTS
1200-SEND-MAP-DATA-ONLY
1200-SEND-MAP-DATA-ONLY
8000-RETURN-WITH-TRANSID
9999-ABORT

Figure 8.1 Structure chart for the revised CALC1 program, showing the functional grouping of logic into paragraphs.

but is also invoked from the mainline. There is really only one 8000-RETURN paragraph, represented by the box with the name that has no shaded corner.

The small diamond symbol, shown between the 0000-MAINLINE and the 9000, 9100, 0500, and 9200 boxes, indicates "selection"—the fact that one of the four paragraphs is chosen for execution, not all of them. Similarly, the diamond above the 5500-COMPUTE-RESULTS box indicates that it may or may not be selected for execution.

While the form of structure chart shown in Figure 8.1 does leave out some processing detail, its strength is that it gives you a broad picture of the parts of a structured program and how they are interrelated. While some people actually called this form of diagram a "structure chart," others refer to this as a **visual table of contents** or **VTOC**. Either name is appropriate and indicates the purpose of the chart. The chart overcomes the weakness of a purely linear listing of source code paragraphs, which does not reveal how the paragraphs are interrelated in execution.

8.3 THE STRUCTURED CALC1 PROGRAM

Figure 8.2 lists the source code of the CALC1 program, now in a modern structured form. Since we wanted to bring this program code up to 1985 COBOL standards in terms of logic arrangement, we also revised some unrelated coding elements, and have included comments at the top of the program to document all of the changes. You'll note, for instance, that we have replaced the word **COMP** (COMPUTATIONAL) with the more understandable word **BINARY** for fields such as WS-RESPONSE-CODE at line 3300 and in the symbolic map (letters "a" and "b"). We also eliminated the word FILLER since this has become optional with 1985 COBOL, and omitting it makes the program more readable, with greater white space. Aside from these changes, the first two pages of the source code listing, through the WORKING-STORAGE and LINKAGE sections, are not affected by the code structuring.

Beginning with the procedure division, you'll note that the revised CALC1 program is entirely different from the earlier version in Chapter 7. The 0000-MAINLINE paragraph, at letter "c", does indeed orchestrate the execution of lower-level code modules as depicted in the structure chart. 3333-ALWAYS-TEST, located at letter "e", is always performed. Then a choice is made to execute the 9000-FIRST-TIME ("g"), 9100-CLEAN-THE-SCREEN ("h"), 0500-NORMAL-PROCESSING ("d"), or 9200-INVALID-KEY paragraphs ("i"). Finally, regardless of which of these four paragraphs was chosen for execution, 8000-RETURN-WITH-TRANS-ID is invoked. There is no STOP RUN at the end of the mainline, because the 8000 paragraph, at letter "f", returns control to CICS and ends program execution.

While you could pore over the functional module code of the revised CALC1 program in its linear listing form in Figure 8.2, a better way to examine this code is in the form of an action diagram. An **action diagram** is simply a graphic form of code, in which paragraphs that are PERFORMed are placed to the right of where they are PERFORMed from. We have physically cut up a copy of the procedure division coding for CALC1, and arranged it in the form of an action diagram in Figure 8.3.

Examine Figure 8.3 and you will readily understand how the functional parts of the structured CALC1 program operate. As you can tell, the actual processing actions of the lowest level code, including CICS commands themselves, are the same as in the original in-line version of CALC1. The same actions are being taken in regard to CICS. The change in moving from in-line to structured coding is in the way that the program parts are controlled and their execution orchestrated.

8.4 THE ROLE OF THE 3333-ALWAYS-TEST MODULE

You will notice that the first paragraph PERFORMed in the structured CALC1 program is 3333-ALWAYS-TEST. This is a good technique to use in any CICS program, because it makes certain that you almost always have a way to break out of a program—that is, to stop the execution of a program—containing a logic error. As a general rule, you should always perform logic to immediately detect pressing of the clear key when a CICS program receives control, to provide this safeguard.

The 3333-ALWAYS-TEST paragraph puts the EIBAID field from the execute interface block into a field named EIBAID-TEST-FIELD, so that 88-level condition names such as ENTER-KEY, CLEAR-KEY, and so forth can be used in the mainline EVALUATE. **EVALUATE** is a modern form of a "case type" IF/ELSE structure, in which different specific cases are tested for, and one outcome is given control. EVALUATE improves the legibility and reliability of program logic, and makes it easy to handle additional PF keys (as you will see in Chapter 9, where we enhance CALC1 further). By putting the EIBCALEN value into a similar field, named WS-FIRST-TIME-FLAG, we gain the ability to make all mainline EVALUATE conditions on 88-level names.

```
EDIT ---- CSCJGJ.CSC360.COBOL(C360A00S) - 01.01 -------------- COLUMNS 007 078
COMMAND ===>                                                  SCROLL ===> PAGE
****** ***************************** TOP OF DATA ******************************
        ID DIVISION.
        PROGRAM-ID.     C360A001.
        AUTHOR.         J JANOSSY.

       *-----------------------------------------------------------------
       *  VERSION C360A00S
       *  THIS IS THE REVISED CALC1 PROGRAM IN CICS VERSION 3.3.  IT
       *  PERFORMS A SIMPLE CALCULATION AND DEMONSTRATES:
       *
       *    1. STRUCTURED CODING (INSTEAD OF "IN-LINE" CODING)
       *    2. LOGIC TO HELP CATCH AND BREAK OUT OF RUNAWAY PROGRAMS
       *    3. A "CLEAN THE SCREEN FIELDS" FUNCTION
       *    4. WHY MANUALLY CODED SYMBOLIC MAPS GET HARDER TO CODE
       *    5. "EXPANDABLE" MAINLINE LOGIC USING EVALUATE
       *    6. 88-LEVEL BASED FUNCTION KEY IDENTIFICATION
       *    7. USE OF "BINARY" INSTEAD OF "COMP" FOR CLARITY
       *    8. ELIMINATION OF THE WORD "FILLER" FOR CLARITY
       *
       *-----------------------------------------------------------------

        DATA DIVISION.
        WORKING-STORAGE SECTION.
        01  WS-TRANS-ID                   PIC X(4)  VALUE '$001'.
        01  WS-MAPSET-NAME                PIC X(8)  VALUE '$001M   '.
        01  WS-MAP-NAME                   PIC X(8)  VALUE 'CALCMAP '.

        01  WS-FIRST-TIME-FLAG            PIC S9(4) BINARY.
            88 FIRST-TIME                           VALUE 0.

        01  WS-GOOD-BAD-FLAG              PIC X(1)  VALUE 'G'.
            88 DATA-GOOD                            VALUE 'G'.

        01  WS-RESPONSE-CODE              PIC S9(8) BINARY.
        01  WS-SALES-TAX-RATE             PIC V99   VALUE .08.
        01  WS-COMMUNICATION-AREA         PIC X(1).
        01  WS-END-MESSAGE                PIC X(60) VALUE
            'QUITTING AS REQUESTED -- USE  CESF LOGOFF  TO END CICS'.

        01  WS-ERROR-MESSAGES.
            05 PIC X(35) VALUE '** CICS ERROR -- CONTACT HELP DESK '.
            05 PIC X(35) VALUE '-- REPORT THIS INFORMATION **      '.
            05 PIC X(9)  VALUE SPACES.

            05 WS-ERROR-LINE1.
               10               PIC X(14)     VALUE '    EIBTRNID = '.
               10 WS-EIBTRNID   PIC X(4).
               10               PIC X(61)     VALUE SPACES.

            05 WS-ERROR-LINE2.
               10               PIC X(14)     VALUE '    EIBRSRCE = '.
               10 WS-EIBRSRCE   PIC X(8).
               10               PIC X(57)     VALUE SPACES.

            05 WS-ERROR-LINE3.
               10               PIC X(14)     VALUE '    EIBRESP  = '.
               10 WS-EIBRESP    PIC ZZZZZZZ9.
               10               PIC X(57)     VALUE SPACES.

            05 WS-ERROR-LINE4.
               10               PIC X(14)     VALUE '    EIBRESP2 = '.
               10 WS-EIBRESP2   PIC ZZZZZZZ9.
               10               PIC X(57)     VALUE SPACES.

            05 PIC X(79) VALUE ALL '*'.
```

Figure 8.2 Source code for the revised CALC1 program, which has been recoded in modern structured format.

```

*-----------------------------------------------------------------
*
*  MANUALLY CODED SYMBOLIC MAP FOR CALC1 PROGRAM    JIM JANOSSY
*  REDEFINES ALLOW SCREEN CLEANING WITH SPACES
*
*-----------------------------------------------------------------
 01  CALC1-SYMBOLIC-MAP.
     05                               PIC X(12).

     05 CSM-L-QUANTITY                PIC S9(4)  BINARY.
     05 CSM-A-QUANTITY                PIC X(1).
     05 CSM-D-QUANTITY                PIC 9(5).

     05 CSM-L-PRICE                   PIC S9(4)  BINARY.
     05 CSM-A-PRICE                   PIC X(1).
     05 CSM-D-PRICE                   PIC 99V99.

     05 CSM-L-TOTAL-BEFORE-TAX        PIC S9(4)  BINARY.
     05 CSM-A-TOTAL-BEFORE-TAX        PIC X(1).
     05 CSM-D-TOTAL-BEFORE-TAX        PIC ZZ,ZZZ,ZZ9.99.
     05 CSM-D-TOTAL-BEFORE-TAX-X   REDEFINES
        CSM-D-TOTAL-BEFORE-TAX        PIC X(13).

     05 CSM-L-TAX                     PIC S9(4)  BINARY.
     05 CSM-A-TAX                     PIC X(1).
     05 CSM-D-TAX                     PIC ZZ,ZZZ,ZZ9.99.
     05 CSM-D-TAX-X  REDEFINES
        CSM-D-TAX                     PIC X(13).

     05 CSM-L-GRAND-TOTAL             PIC S9(4)  BINARY.
     05 CSM-A-GRAND-TOTAL             PIC X(1).
     05 CSM-D-GRAND-TOTAL             PIC ZZ,ZZZ,ZZ9.99.
     05 CSM-D-GRAND-TOTAL-X  REDEFINES
        CSM-D-GRAND-TOTAL             PIC X(13).

     05 CSM-L-MESSAGE                 PIC S9(4)  BINARY.
     05 CSM-A-MESSAGE                 PIC X(1).
     05 CSM-D-MESSAGE                 PIC X(79).

*-----------------------------------------------------------------
*
*  VALUE MEANINGS FOR EIBAID FIELD OF DFHEIBLK
*  88-LEVELS ARE CODED TO MINIMIZE MEMORY USE AND IMPROVE
*  THE CLARITY OF LOGIC TO IDENTIFY FUNCTION KEY USAGE
*
*-----------------------------------------------------------------
 01  EIBAID-TEST-FIELD                PIC X(1).
     88 ENTER-KEY                               VALUE ''''.
     88 CLEAR-KEY                               VALUE '_'.
     88 PF1-KEY                                 VALUE 'T'.
     88 PF2-KEY                                 VALUE '2'.
     88 PF3-KEY                                 VALUE '3'.

*-----------------------------------------------------------------
*
*  VALUE MEANINGS FOR SYMBOLIC MAP ATTRIBUTE BYTE FIELDS
*
*-----------------------------------------------------------------
 01  ATTRIBUTE-VALUES-TO-SET.
     05 ATT-UNPROT-CHAR-MDT           PIC X  VALUE 'A'.
     05 ATT-UNPROT-CHAR-MDT-BRIGHT    PIC X  VALUE 'I'.
     05 ATT-UNPROT-NUM-MDT            PIC X  VALUE 'J'.
     05 ATT-UNPROT-NUM-MDT-BRIGHT     PIC X  VALUE 'R'.

 LINKAGE SECTION.
 01  DFHCOMMAREA                      PIC X(1).

```

B

Figure 8.2 *(Continued)*

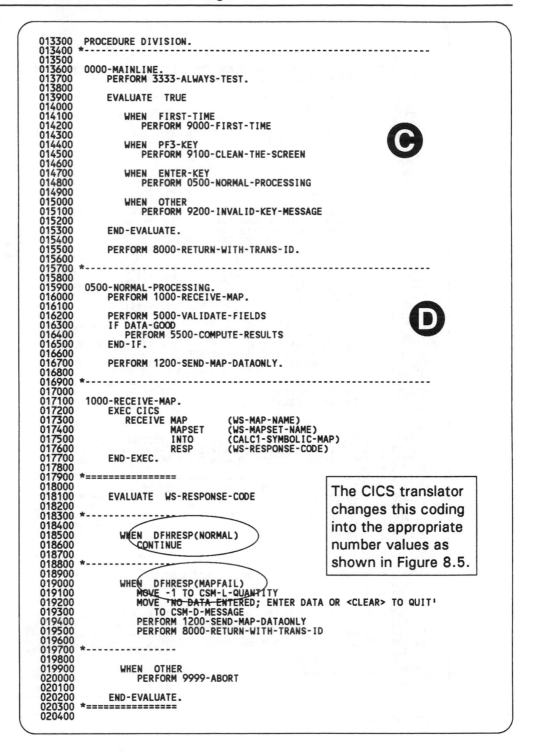

```
 PROCEDURE DIVISION.
*-----------------------------------------------------------------

 0000-MAINLINE.
     PERFORM 3333-ALWAYS-TEST.

     EVALUATE  TRUE

        WHEN  FIRST-TIME
           PERFORM 9000-FIRST-TIME

        WHEN  PF3-KEY
           PERFORM 9100-CLEAN-THE-SCREEN

        WHEN  ENTER-KEY
           PERFORM 0500-NORMAL-PROCESSING

        WHEN  OTHER
           PERFORM 9200-INVALID-KEY-MESSAGE

     END-EVALUATE.

     PERFORM 8000-RETURN-WITH-TRANS-ID.

*-----------------------------------------------------------------

 0500-NORMAL-PROCESSING.
     PERFORM 1000-RECEIVE-MAP.

     PERFORM 5000-VALIDATE-FIELDS
     IF DATA-GOOD
        PERFORM 5500-COMPUTE-RESULTS
     END-IF.

     PERFORM 1200-SEND-MAP-DATAONLY.
*-----------------------------------------------------------------

 1000-RECEIVE-MAP.
     EXEC CICS
        RECEIVE MAP        (WS-MAP-NAME)
                MAPSET     (WS-MAPSET-NAME)
                INTO       (CALC1-SYMBOLIC-MAP)
                RESP       (WS-RESPONSE-CODE)
     END-EXEC.

*===============

     EVALUATE  WS-RESPONSE-CODE

*---------------

       WHEN  DFHRESP(NORMAL)
          CONTINUE

*---------------

       WHEN  DFHRESP(MAPFAIL)
          MOVE -1 TO CSM-L-QUANTITY
          MOVE 'NO DATA ENTERED; ENTER DATA OR <CLEAR> TO QUIT'
             TO CSM-D-MESSAGE
          PERFORM 1200-SEND-MAP-DATAONLY
          PERFORM 8000-RETURN-WITH-TRANS-ID

*---------------

       WHEN  OTHER
          PERFORM 9999-ABORT

     END-EVALUATE.
*===============

```

C

D

The CICS translator changes this coding into the appropriate number values as shown in Figure 8.5.

Figure 8.2 *(Continued)*

```
*-----------------------------------------------------------------

 1200-SEND-MAP-DATAONLY.
     EXEC CICS
          SEND MAP        (WS-MAP-NAME)
                MAPSET    (WS-MAPSET-NAME)
                FROM      (CALC1-SYMBOLIC-MAP)
                DATAONLY
                CURSOR
     END-EXEC.

*-----------------------------------------------------------------

 3333-ALWAYS-TEST.
     MOVE EIBAID    TO  EIBAID-TEST-FIELD.
     IF CLEAR-KEY
        PERFORM 8900-QUIT.
     MOVE EIBCALEN  TO  WS-FIRST-TIME-FLAG.

*-----------------------------------------------------------------

 5000-VALIDATE-FIELDS.

     MOVE ATT-UNPROT-NUM-MDT TO  CSM-A-QUANTITY
                                 CSM-A-PRICE.

     IF CSM-D-PRICE NOT NUMERIC
        MOVE 'B' TO WS-GOOD-BAD-FLAG
        MOVE ATT-UNPROT-NUM-MDT-BRIGHT TO CSM-A-PRICE
        MOVE -1 TO CSM-L-PRICE
        MOVE 'PRICE MUST BE NUMERIC; CORRECT, PRESS <ENTER>'
           TO CSM-D-MESSAGE
     END-IF.

     IF CSM-D-QUANTITY NOT NUMERIC
        MOVE 'B' TO WS-GOOD-BAD-FLAG
        MOVE ATT-UNPROT-NUM-MDT-BRIGHT TO CSM-A-QUANTITY
        MOVE -1 TO CSM-L-QUANTITY
        MOVE 'QUANTITY MUST BE NUMERIC; CORRECT, PRESS <ENTER>'
           TO CSM-D-MESSAGE
     END-IF.

*-----------------------------------------------------------------

 5500-COMPUTE-RESULTS.
     COMPUTE CSM-D-TOTAL-BEFORE-TAX =
        CSM-D-QUANTITY * CSM-D-PRICE.
     COMPUTE CSM-D-TAX =
        CSM-D-QUANTITY * CSM-D-PRICE * WS-SALES-TAX-RATE.
     COMPUTE CSM-D-GRAND-TOTAL =
        CSM-D-QUANTITY * CSM-D-PRICE * WS-SALES-TAX-RATE +
        CSM-D-QUANTITY * CSM-D-PRICE.
     MOVE 'RESULTS COMPUTED, ENTER MORE DATA OR <CLEAR> TO QUIT'
        TO CSM-D-MESSAGE.
     MOVE -1 TO CSM-L-QUANTITY.

*-----------------------------------------------------------------

 8000-RETURN-WITH-TRANS-ID.
     EXEC CICS
        RETURN TRANSID   (WS-TRANS-ID)
               COMMAREA  (WS-COMMUNICATION-AREA)
     END-EXEC.

*-----------------------------------------------------------------

 8900-QUIT.
     EXEC CICS
          SEND TEXT FROM (WS-END-MESSAGE)
               ERASE
               FREEKB
     END-EXEC.

     EXEC CICS
          RETURN
     END-EXEC.
```

Figure 8.2 *(Continued)*

```
      *-----------------------------------------------------------
```

G

```
       9000-FIRST-TIME.
           MOVE LOW-VALUES TO CALC1-SYMBOLIC-MAP.
           MOVE 'ENTER VALUES, PRESS <ENTER>, <CLEAR> TO QUIT'
              TO CSM-D-MESSAGE.
           MOVE -1 TO CSM-L-QUANTITY.

           EXEC CICS
               SEND MAPSET    (WS-MAPSET-NAME)
                    MAP       (WS-MAP-NAME)
                    FROM      (CALC1-SYMBOLIC-MAP)
                    ERASE
                    CURSOR
           END-EXEC.

      *-----------------------------------------------------------
```

H

```
       9100-CLEAN-THE-SCREEN.
           MOVE LOW-VALUES TO CALC1-SYMBOLIC-MAP.
           MOVE SPACES TO  CSM-D-TOTAL-BEFORE-TAX-X
                           CSM-D-TAX-X
                           CSM-D-GRAND-TOTAL-X.

           MOVE 'ENTER VALUES, PRESS <ENTER>, <CLEAR> TO QUIT'
              TO CSM-D-MESSAGE.
           MOVE -1 TO CSM-L-QUANTITY.

           EXEC CICS
               SEND MAP       (WS-MAP-NAME)
                    MAPSET    (WS-MAPSET-NAME)
                    FROM      (CALC1-SYMBOLIC-MAP)
                    DATAONLY
                    ERASEAUP
                    CURSOR
           END-EXEC.

      *-----------------------------------------------------------
```

I

```
       9200-INVALID-KEY-MESSAGE.
           MOVE LOW-VALUES TO CALC1-SYMBOLIC-MAP.
           MOVE 'YOU PRESSED WRONG KEY! PRESS <ENTER>, <CLEAR> TO QUIT'
              TO CSM-D-MESSAGE.
           MOVE -1 TO CSM-L-QUANTITY.
           PERFORM 1200-SEND-MAP-DATAONLY.

      *-----------------------------------------------------------

       9999-ABORT.
           MOVE EIBTRNID    TO  WS-EIBTRNID.
           MOVE EIBRSRCE    TO  WS-EIBRSRCE.
           MOVE EIBRESP     TO  WS-EIBRESP.
           MOVE EIBRESP2    TO  WS-EIBRESP2.

           EXEC CICS
              SEND TEXT FROM (WS-ERROR-MESSAGES)
                   ERASE
                   ALARM
                   FREEKB
           END-EXEC.

           EXEC CICS
                RETURN
           END-EXEC.
```

Figure 8.2 *(Continued)*

8.5 INCREASED FUNCTIONALITY OF THE STRUCTURED CALC1

By structuring logic, we gain the capability to increase the functionality of a program by extending the pattern inherent in its modularization. Whoa! What's that mouthful mean? This is just a fancy, formal way of saying that a structured program is easy to change and enhance. Take a look at the message at the bottom of Figure 8.4 and you'll notice one enhancement we get almost for nothing just because we used a mainline to decide what to do when CALC1 receives control. Here, we detect and reject the use of an AID key other than Enter or PF3.

The EVALUATE statement in the mainline of the revised CALC1 decides what action to take based on whether it's the first time CALC1 has been invoked at a terminal, if the PF3 clean-the-screen function key has been pressed, or if the Enter key has been pressed to dictate normal processing. This EVALUATE gives us the chance to consider an OTHER case, that is, the fact that some other AID key has been pressed (except Clear) to awaken the program. You'll see in Chapter 9 how readily we can extend the functionality of the program even more with this "structured infrastructure" in place.

8.6 HOW THE CICS TRANSLATOR HANDLES DFHRESP(condition)

The **DFHRESP(condition)** feature of modern CICS helps structure program error condition handling. This coding feature makes it possible to list words describing the potential outcomes of CICS command execution, without having to know the specific values of response codes that CICS returns. We used DFHRESP(condition) in the earlier version of CALC1, but we explain it here since you see it used in lines 18100 through 20200 of the structured version of CALC1 in Figure 8.2.

You code DFHRESP(condition) in combination with the numeric field in which you direct CICS to place the response code for CICS command execution. We coded the RECEIVE MAP command in this way:

```
EXEC CICS
   RECEIVE MAP    (WS-MAP-NAME)
           MAPSET (WS-MAPSET-NAME)
           INTO   (CALC1-SYMBOLIC-MAP)
           RESP   ( WS-RESPONSE-CODE )
END-EXEC.
```

We then code the following response code checking in this form:

```
EVALUATE WS-RESPONSE-CODE

   WHEN DFHRESP(NORMAL)
      CONTINUE

   WHEN DFHRESP(MAPFAIL)
      MOVE -1 TO CSM-L-QUANTITY
      MOVE 'NO DATA ENTERED; ENTER DATA OR CLEAR TO QUIT'
         TO CSM-D-MESSAGE
      PERFORM 1200-SEND-MAP-DATAONLY
      PERFORM 8000-RETURN-WITH-TRANS-ID
```

```
0000-MAINLINE.
  PERFORM 3333-ALWAYS-TEST.

  EVALUATE TRUE

   WHEN FIRST-TIME
    PERFORM 9000-FIRST-TIME

   WHEN PF3-KEY
    PERFORM 9100-CLEAN-THE-SCREEN

   WHEN ENTER-KEY
    PERFORM 0500-NORMAL-PROCESSING

   WHEN OTHER
    PERFORM 9200-INVALID-KEY-MESSAGE

  END-EVALUATE.

  PERFORM 8000-RETURN-WITH-TRANS-ID.
```

```
3333-ALWAYS-TEST.
  MOVE EIBAID  TO EIBAID-TEST-FIELD.
  IF CLEAR-KEY
    PERFORM 8900-QUILT
  MOVE EIBCALEN  TO  WS-FIRST-TIME-FLAG.
```

```
9000-FIRST-TIME.
  MOVE LOW-VALUES TO CALC1-SYMBOLIC-MAP.
  MOVE 'ENTER VALUES, PRESS <ENTER>, <CLEAR> TO QUIT'
   TO CSM-D-MESSAGE.
  MOVE -1 TO CSM-L-QUANTITY.

  EXEC CICS
    SEND MAPSET  (WS-MAPSET-NAME)
      MAP    (WS-MAP-NAME)
      FROM    (CALC1-SYMBOLIC-MAP)
      ERASE
      CURSOR
  END-EXEC.
```

```
9100-CLEAN-THE SCREEN.
  MOVE LOW-VALUES TO CALC1-SYMBOLIC-MAP.
  MOVE SPACES TO CSM-D-TOTAL-BEFORE-TAX-X
         CSM-D-TAX-X
         CSM-D-GRAND-TOTAL-X.

  MOVE 'ENTER VALUES, PRESS <ENTER>, <CLEAR> TO QUIT'
   TO CSM-D-MESSAGE.
  MOVE -1 TO CSM-L-QUANTITY.

  EXEC CICS
    SEND MAP     (WS-MAP-NAME)
      MAPSET   (WS-MAPSET-NAME)
      FROM     (CALC1-SYMBOLIC-MAP)
      DATAONLY
      ERASEAUP
      CURSOR
  END-EXEC.
```

```
0500-NORMAL-PROCESSING.
  PERFORM 1000-RECEIVE-MAP.

  PERFORM 5000-VALIDATE-FIELDS
  IF DATA-GOOD
    PERFORM 5500-COMPUTE-RESULTS
  END-IF.

  PERFORM 1200-SEND-MAP-DATAONLY.
```

```
9200-INVALID-KEY-MESSAGE.
  MOVE LOW-VALUES TO CALC1-SYMBOLIC-MAP.
  MOVE 'YOU PRESSED WRONG KEY! PRESS <ENTER>, <CLEAR> TO QUIT'
   TO CSM-D-MESSAGE.
  MOVE -1 TO CSM-L-QUANTITY.
  PERFORM 1200-SEND-MAP-DATAONLY.
```

```
8000-RETURN-WITH-TRANS-ID.
  EXEC CICS
   RETURN TRANSID  (WS-TRANS-ID)
      COMMAREA (WS-COMMUNICATION-AREA)
```

Figure 8.3 Source code for the revised CALC1 program arranged in the form of an action diagram.

```
8900-QUIT.
  EXEC CICS
    SEND TEXT FROM (WS-END-MESSAGE)
      ERASE
      FREEKB
  END-EXEC.

  EXEC CICS
    RETURN
  END-EXEC.
```

```
1000-RECEIVE-MAP.
  EXEC CICS
   RECEIVE MAP   (WS-MAP-NAME)
      MAPSET   (WS-MAPSET-NAME)
      INTO   (CALC1-SYMBOLIC-MAP)
      RESP    (WS-RESPONSE-CODE)
  END-EXEC.


  EVALUATE WS-RESPONSE-CODE
*______

   WHEN DFHRESP(NORMAL)
    CONTINUE


   WHEN DFHRESP(MAPFAIL)
    MOVE -1 TO CSM-L-QUANTITY
    MOVE 'NO DATA ENTERED; ENTER DATA OR <CLEAR> TO QUIT'
     TO CSM-D-MESSAGE
    PERFORM 1200-SEND-MAP-DATAONLY
    PERFROM 8000-RETURN-WITH-TRANS-ID


   WHEN OTHER
    PERFORM 9999-ABORT

  END-EVALUATE.
```

```
5000-VALIDATE-FIELDS.

  MOVE ATT UNPROT-NUM-MDT TO CSM-A-QUANTITY
            CSM-A-PRICE.

  IF CSM-D-PRICE NOT NUMERIC
    MOVE 'B' TO WS-GOOD-BAD-FLAG
    MOVE ATT-UNPROT-NUM-MDT-BRIGHT TO CSM-A-PRICE
    MOVE-1 TO CSM-L-PRICE
    MOVE 'PRICE MUST BE NUMBERIC; CORRECT, PRESS <ENTER>'
     TO CSM-D-MESSAGE
  END-IF.

  IF CSM-D-QUANTITY NOT NUMERIC
    MOVE 'B' TO WS-GOOD-BAD-FLAG
    MOVE ATT-UNPROT-NUM-MDT-BRIGHT TO CSM-A-QUANTITY
    MOVE -1 TO CSM-L-QUANTITY
    MOVE 'QUANTITY MUST BE NUMERIC;CORRECT, PRESS <ENTER>'
     TO CSM-D-MESSAGE
  END-IF.
```

```
5500-COMPUTE-RESULTS.
  COMPUTE CSM-D-TOTAL-BEFORE-TAX =
   CSM-D-QUANTITY * CSM-D-PRICE
  COMPUTE CSM-D-TAX =
   CSM-D-QUANTITY * CSM-D-PRICE * WS-SALES-TAX-RATE.
  COMPUTE CSM-D-GRAND-TOTAL =
   CSM-D-QUANTITY * CSM-D-PRICE * WS-SALES-TAX-RATE +
   CSM-D-QUANTITY * CSM-D-PRICE.
  MOVE 'RESULTS COMPUTED, ENTER MORE DATA OR <CLEAR> TO QUIT'
   TO CSM-D-MESSAGE.
```

```
1200-SEND-MAP-DATAONLY.
  EXEC CICS
   SEND MAP      (WS-MAP-NAME)
     MAPSET     (WS-MAPSET-NAME)
     FROM      (CALC1-SYMBOLIC-MAP)
     DATAONLY
     CURSOR
  END-EXEC.
```

```
9999-ABORT.
  MOVE EIBTRNID  TO WS-EIBTRNID.
  MOVE EIBRSRCE   TO WS-EIBRSRCE.
  MOVE EIBRESP   TO WS-EIBRESP.
  MOVE EIBRESP2   TO WS-EIBRESP2.

  EXEC CICS
   SEND TEXT FROM (WS-ERROR-MESSAGES)
     ERASE
     ALARM
     FREEKB
  END-EXEC.

  EXEC CICS
    RETURN
  END-EXEC.
```

Figure 8.3 *(Continued)*

```
WHEN OTHER
   PERFORM 9999-ABORT.
```

DFHRESP(condition) provides a convenience to you. It makes it unnecessary for you to know the numeric value of the response code that stands for each CICS error condition you must anticipate. The potential normal and error conditions you code within parentheses after the word DFHRESP are listed in Appendix E. Figure 8.5 illustrates a small part of the translated CALC1 program. You can see how the CICS translator automatically replaces DFHRESP(condition) coding with the correct response code number value for each condition, without your having to know what the number values are.

8.7 ROLE OF AN ABORT MODULE

DFHRESP(condition) provides a convenience to you in detecting error conditions. Convenience aside, you must realize that it is still your responsibility to correctly anticipate potential failures that can accrue in executing specific CICS commands. In response to a RECEIVE MAP command, for example, it is reasonable to anticipate either a normal response (map was received with data) or a map failure (no data was transmitted).

In addition, you must take into account that CICS may encounter an abnormal condition and issue a response code not indicating NORMAL or MAPFAIL conditions. If neither NORMAL nor MAPFAIL conditions are experienced, you need to make the CICS response code visible for diagnostic purposes. A special paragraph for this purpose is often called an "abort module." An abort module can be invoked from anywhere within a program to provide a standard display containing CICS-supplied values, such as **EIBRESP**, which are useful for error diagnosis purposes. EIBRESP, and other diagnostic values, are housed in the fields of the execute interface block in the LINKAGE SECTION, inserted into a program by the CICS translator.

We handle abort processing in CALC1 by invoking the logic of the 9999-ABORT module. Figure 8.6 illustrates the terminal screen display that results from invocation of the 9999-

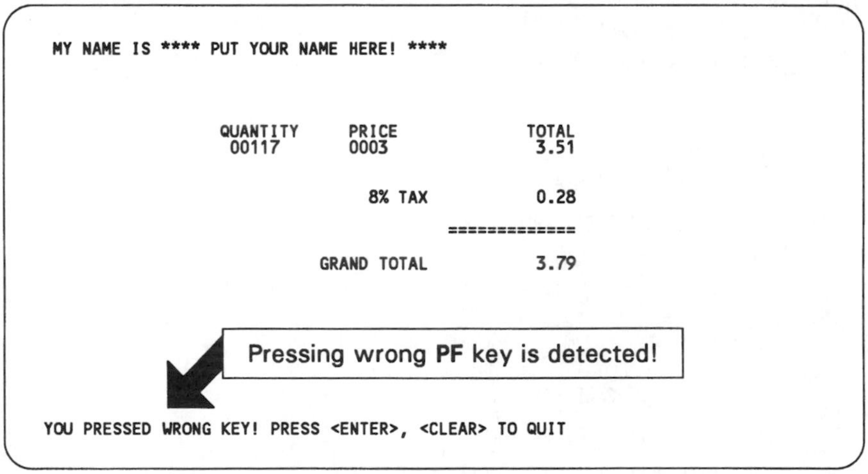
MY NAME IS **** PUT YOUR NAME HERE! ****
QUANTITY
00117
PRICE
0003
TOTAL
3.51
8% TAX
0.28
=============
GRAND TOTAL
3.79
Pressing wrong PF key is detected!
YOU PRESSED WRONG KEY! PRESS <ENTER>, <CLEAR> TO QUIT

Figure 8.4 The structured CALC1 program detects the use of an AID key other than Enter or PF3 and issues this error message.

ABORT module for a CICS failure. You identify the basis for such a failure by looking up the EIBRESP value in Appendix E of this book.

8.8 ROLE OF A CLEAN-THE-SCREEN MODULE

We included logic in the mainline of our structured CALC1 program to detect when the program had been reawakened by the terminal operator pressing the PF3 key, as you will note at line 14400 in the program in Figure 8.2. We'll talk much more about function keys and how to intercept them, but you see here a preview of what is involved in it.

What happens when the terminal operator presses PF3 and we detect it? You can answer this question yourself by examining the 9100-CLEAN-THE-SCREEN paragraph at lines 30000 through 31700. We reinitialize the symbolic map by moving LOW-VALUES to it, which are not transmitted when the map is sent. We then move SPACES to the "X" version PICtures of all output screen fields. These are the fields that program logic puts values into, but which are protected from terminal operator access. We then set the prompt to its initial value, position the cursor at the first enterable field on the screen, and send the symbolic map with the ERASEAUP option. ERASEAUP (Erase All UnProtected fields) removes the contents of fields that the terminal operator can put data into. The combination of these actions "cleans the screen" of any prior transaction data.

The terminal operator does not have to clean the screen using PF3; it's optional to use it. If the next transaction will contain some of the same data as the existing transaction, the operator can leave data on the screen and have it carry over to the next transaction. Some operators prefer to begin entirely new transactions on clean screens; having this function in place provides a convenience for these personnel.

We suggest you consider including a clean-the-screen function in your programs, based on the model shown here and in our subsequent programs.

8.9 FOR YOUR REVIEW

Understanding these terms and elements of CICS programming and processing, introduced in Chapter 8, will aid your understanding of the next chapter:

Action diagram
BINARY
COMP
DFHRESP(condition)
EIBRESP
ERASEAUP option
EVALUATE
Functional modules
Structure chart
Structured coding
Visual table of contents
VTOC

8.10 REVIEW QUESTIONS

1. Compare in-line CICS coding style with structured coding, describing how the two styles differ.
2. Identify and describe some of the limitations of in-line CICS coding style.
3. Cite one of the important criteria of modern programming, which is achieved by the use of functional modules of source code.
4. Explain why structured coding often leads to more rapidly constructed and more readily modified coding.

```
SDSF OUTPUT DISPLAY CSCJGJA  JOB09640  DSID   102 LINE 319      COLUMNS 17- 96
COMMAND INPUT ===>                                              SCROLL ===> PAGE
      *================

           EVALUATE  WS-RESPONSE-CODE

      *----------------

             WHEN           0
                CONTINUE

      *----------------

             WHEN           36
                MOVE -1 TO CSM-L-QUANTITY
                MOVE 'NO DATA ENTERED; ENTER DATA OR <CLEAR> TO QUIT'
                   TO CSM-D-MESSAGE
                PERFORM 1200-SEND-MAP-DATAONLY
                PERFORM 8000-RETURN-WITH-TRANS-ID

      *----------------

             WHEN  OTHER
                PERFORM 9999-ABORT
```

This is the code produced by the CICS translator. Compare this to the original coding in Figure 8.2.

Figure 8.5 The CICS translator replaces DFHRESP(condition) coding with the specific response code value tnat applies to each condition.

5. Discuss why structured coding took longer to become popular in CICS coding than in batch programming.
6. Describe and explain the meaning of the symbols used on a structure chart, and discuss how the chart represents program structure.
7. Describe how an action diagram shows the relationships between the paragraphs of logic in a CICS program.
8. Explain how you can create an action diagram of an existing CICS program from its source code, as an aid in understanding the structure and logic of the program.
9. Describe the difference in effect of coding BINARY instead of COMP for integer fields in WORKING-STORAGE and symbolic maps.

```
** CICS ERROR -- CONTACT HELP DESK -- REPORT THIS INFORMATION **
   EIBTRNID = $001
   EIBRSRCE =  ALCMAP
   EIBRESP  =        2
   EIBRESP2 =        0
*****************************************************************************
```

Standard coding in your CICS programs, such as the 9999-ABORT paragraph, can make these execute interface block fields visible for diagnostic purposes if an unusual situation arises.

Figure 8.6 The 9999-ABORT routine clears the screen and makes the EIBRESP response code field and other values visible for diagnostic purposes.

10. Explain why it is a good idea to include a module such as 3333-ALWAYS-TEST in a CICS program, and to PERFORM it as the first action in the procedure division.
11. Explain why a structured program is easier to enhance (increase in functionality) than a program coded with an in-line coding style.
12. Describe the DFHRESP(condition) coding feature of modern CICS, and explain how it is handled by the CICS translator.
13. Discuss the role of an abort module in a CICS program, identifying what it does and when it does it.
14. Identify the possible outcomes of executing the RECEIVE MAP command, describing the outcomes you can detect and handle and the outcome you can anticipate but not resolve by program action.
15. Explain how you can diagnose a problem using an EIBRESP code value issued after execution of a CICS command.

8.11 HANDS-ON EXERCISES

Do these exercises in the sequence listed here to gain the most from the information in this chapter.

A. If you have completed Exercises A through C at the end of Chapter 7, you have constructed and tested a working CICS AVERAGE CALCULATOR program using an in-line style. Using the example of the revised CALC1 program discussed in Chapter 8, prepare a structure chart for a revised CICS AVERAGE CALCULATOR program that will use a structured coding style. Develop the structure chart by analyzing the code of your in-line program and factoring out the functional elements of the code, grouping these into functional modules.

B. Using the structure chart you developed in Exercise A, convert your CICS AVERAGE CALCULATOR program to a structured coding style. Include logic to test for Clear key entry similar to the 3333-ALWAYS-TEST module in the CALC1 program. Test your revised program and compare its operation with that of your in-line version.

C. If you have completed Exercise D at the end of Chapter 7, you have constructed and tested a working program using the screen labeled MY FIRST CICS SCREEN and an in-line style. Using the example of the revised CALC1 program discussed in Chapter 8, prepare a structure chart for a revised program that will use a structured coding style. Develop the structure chart by analyzing the code of your in-line program and factoring out the functional elements of the code, grouping these into functional modules.

D. Using the structure chart you developed in Exercise C, convert your program driving the "FIRST" screen to a structured coding style. Include logic to test for Clear key entry similar to the 3333-ALWAYS-TEST module in the CALC1 program. Test your revised program and compare its operation with that of your in-line version.

9

Programming Your Function Keys

Program function keys, referred to as PF keys, are attention identifier (AID) keys just as Enter and Clear. Pressing a PF key causes transmission to the host computer of data you entered on the screen. This, course, causes the appropriate CICS program to be reawakened, beginning a new pseudoconversational response from the program. Since the program invoked can identify the PF you pressed, it can take actions that your logic associates with the key. In this chapter, we demonstrate how to intercept PF keys using the EIBAID field of the execute interface block. We also show you how to predefine screen messages using the DRK attribute, then selectively make them visible by **attribute byte manipulation**. We then apply these techniques to a revision of the CALC1 program, enhancing it to use selected functions keys for a specific purpose.

9.1 REVIEW OF ATTENTION IDENTIFIER KEYS

Ordinary ASCII terminals used with minicomputers communicate with their host computer in a character-by-character mode. Every time you press a key on the keyboard of a minicomputer or microcomputer, the signal for a byte (eight bits) is emitted by the keyboard (and the embedded software driving it), travels to the central processing unit (CPU) of the computer, and is echoed back to the terminal screen, where its character representation is displayed. This form of operation requires the CPU to spend some of its time servicing the display of information for each keystroke. It is one of the factors limiting the number of simultaneously active terminals a single minicomputer can support.

The mainframe hardware environment and CICS were designed to offload tasks from the CPU, to let it support a maximum number of terminals. Terminal-to-host communication in the mainframe environment is therefore handled much differently than in the minicomputer environment. A 3270-type mainframe terminal and its controller (or a PC and protocol converter emulating 3270 operation) stores almost all of your keystrokes locally, in the terminal and controller, and displays entered information directly on the terminal screen. Only when you press an **attention identifier key** (AID key) is a transmission made to the host computer. AID keys include Enter, PF keys, PA keys, and the Clear key. Each of these keys provides "evidence," in the form of a value in the **EIBAID field** of the execute interface block, indicating the key's identity. Your program can therefore detect which AID key was pressed to reawaken it.

While all AID keys signal CICS, three categories of AID keys act differently in what else they cause to happen:

- **Enter and PF keys:** Signal CICS and cause newly entered information on the screen to be transmitted. Specifically, these keys cause fields that have the modified data tag (MDT) in their attribute byte to be transmitted. The MDT is set on by terminal circuitry when you make a change in the value of an unprotected field on the screen. You can set the MDT on permanently for a screen field by coding the FSET attribute in the BMS map source code for the field, or by moving the appropriate bit pattern to the field's attribute byte before sending the map to the terminal.
- **PA1, PA2, and PA3 (Program Attention) keys:** Cause a signal to be transmitted to CICS to reawaken a program to begin another pseudoconverse, but do not transmit any data. That is, fields you have changed on the screen are not transmitted. PA keys enjoy limited use.
- **Clear:** Signals CICS but does not transmit any screen field contents; also electronically clears the terminal screen as a locally handled hardware function.

In the program examples in this book, we use Enter, PF keys, and the Clear key. Let's consider a demonstration program that does something interesting with them and the terminal screen.

9.2 HOW THE PF KEY DEMONSTRATION PROGRAM WORKS

Figure 9.1 shows you the demonstration screen produced by a simple program named C360B003. This screen provides a title line, four other lines each indicating a PF key number, and a prompt line. Not visible in Figure 9.1, however, is the fact that a message is actually on the screen to the right of each PF key label. You can't see any of those message lines, because the attribute byte of each is set to DRK, for "dark." In each case the message is there, but invisible.

```
*** JIM'S PROGRAM TO DEMO PF KEY USAGE ***
PF1
PF2
PF3
PF4





PRESS PF1, PF2, PF3, PF4, OR <CLEAR> TO QUIT
```

Figure 9.1 Screen for a PF key demonstration program as program execution begins.

Figure 9.2 illustrates how the PF key demonstration screen looks when you press the PF3 key. The label "PF3" is brightened, and the "you pressed" arrow and message appear. Figure 9.3 illustrates how the screen changes if you next press the PF1 key. It may seem to you that the "you pressed" arrow and label have moved. What really happened? The label next to "PF3" was again made invisible (darkened) and the label next to "PF1" made visible. We made this happen by sending the correct value to the attribute byte for each of these fields, not by sending blanking-out spaces and a new copy of the arrow and message.

Figure 9.4 shows you what is really on the demonstration screen. Here you see the actual contents of the screen, which includes arrows and labels next to all of the "PF" labels. All of these message lines are protected and, initially, dark. You can't enter data into this screen at all. But by pressing the appropriate PF keys, you can make the message associated with the corresponding PF key become visible, and shut off any other message line.

```
*** JIM'S PROGRAM TO DEMO PF KEY USAGE ***
PF1
PF2
PF3  <=== YOU PRESSED
PF4





PRESS PF1, PF2, PF3, PF4, OR <CLEAR> TO QUIT
```

Figure 9.2 Appearance of the PF key demonstration screen when PF3 is pressed.

```
*** JIM'S PROGRAM TO DEMO PF KEY USAGE ***
PF1  <=== YOU PRESSED
PF2
PF3
PF4










PRESS PF1, PF2, PF3, PF4, OR <CLEAR> TO QUIT
```

Figure 9.3 Appearance of the PF key demonstration screen when PF1 is pressed.

```
*** JIM'S PROGRAM TO DEMO PF KEY USAGE ***
PF1  <=== YOU PRESSED
PF2  <=== YOU PRESSED
PF3  <=== YOU PRESSED
PF4  <=== YOU PRESSED










PRESS PF1, PF2, PF3, PF4, OR <CLEAR> TO QUIT
```

Figure 9.4 Actual content of the PF key demonstration screen showing all of the message fields that are normally dark (DRK).

9.3 BMS MAP CODE FOR THE PF KEY DEMONSTRATION PROGRAM

Figure 9.5 lists the BMS map source code for our PF key demonstration program. The actual mapset name for this screen is #003M, while the map name is DEMOPF. The form of this BMS map code is similar to that for the CALC1 screen shown in Figure 4.4. Here, you see the label and message fields for each of the four PF keys that will be programmed for recognition with the screen. The **(DRK,PROT)** attribute coded on each message line initially makes each message invisible. All messages are sent with the first transmission of the screen to a terminal, which is accomplished with the initial SEND MAP command of a program. *Even though the*

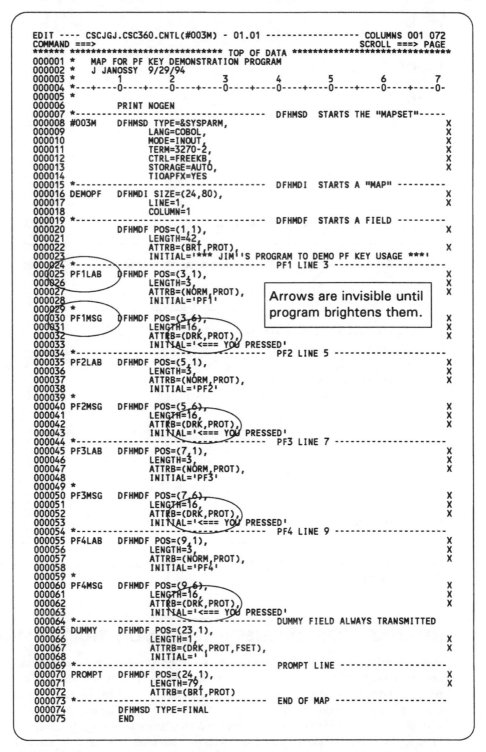

```
EDIT ---- CSCJGJ.CSC360.CNTL(#003M) - 01.01 ------------------ COLUMNS 001 072
COMMAND ===>                                                   SCROLL ===> PAGE
****** ****************************** TOP OF DATA ******************************
*    MAP FOR PF KEY DEMONSTRATION PROGRAM
*    J JANOSSY  9/29/94
*         1         2         3         4         5         6         7
*---+----0----+----0----+----0----+----0----+----0----+----0----+----0-
*
         PRINT NOGEN
*------------------------------------ DFHMSD  STARTS THE "MAPSET"-----
#003M    DFHMSD TYPE=&SYSPARM,                                         X
               LANG=COBOL,                                             X
               MODE=INOUT,                                             X
               TERM=3270-2,                                            X
               CTRL=FREEKB,                                            X
               STORAGE=AUTO,                                           X
               TIOAPFX=YES
*------------------------------------ DFHMDI  STARTS A "MAP" ---------
DEMOPF   DFHMDI SIZE=(24,80),                                          X
               LINE=1,                                                 X
               COLUMN=1
*------------------------------------ DFHMDF  STARTS A FIELD ---------
         DFHMDF POS=(1,1),                                             X
               LENGTH=42,                                              X
               ATTRB=(BRT,PROT),                                       X
               INITIAL='*** JIM''S PROGRAM TO DEMO PF KEY USAGE ***'
*------------------------------------ PF1 LINE 3 ---------------------
PF1LAB   DFHMDF POS=(3,1),                                             X
               LENGTH=3,                                               X
               ATTRB=(NORM,PROT),                                      X
               INITIAL='PF1'
*
PF1MSG   DFHMDF POS=(3,6),                                             X
               LENGTH=16,                                              X
               ATTRB=(DRK,PROT),                                       X
               INITIAL='<=== YOU PRESSED'
*------------------------------------ PF2 LINE 5 ---------------------
PF2LAB   DFHMDF POS=(5,1),                                             X
               LENGTH=3,                                               X
               ATTRB=(NORM,PROT),                                      X
               INITIAL='PF2'
*
PF2MSG   DFHMDF POS=(5,6),                                             X
               LENGTH=16,                                              X
               ATTRB=(DRK,PROT),                                       X
               INITIAL='<=== YOU PRESSED'
*------------------------------------ PF3 LINE 7 ---------------------
PF3LAB   DFHMDF POS=(7,1),                                             X
               LENGTH=3,                                               X
               ATTRB=(NORM,PROT),                                      X
               INITIAL='PF3'
*
PF3MSG   DFHMDF POS=(7,6),                                             X
               LENGTH=16,                                              X
               ATTRB=(DRK,PROT),                                       X
               INITIAL='<=== YOU PRESSED'
*------------------------------------ PF4 LINE 9 ---------------------
PF4LAB   DFHMDF POS=(9,1),                                             X
               LENGTH=3,                                               X
               ATTRB=(NORM,PROT),                                      X
               INITIAL='PF4'
*
PF4MSG   DFHMDF POS=(9,6),                                             X
               LENGTH=16,                                              X
               ATTRB=(DRK,PROT),                                       X
               INITIAL='<=== YOU PRESSED'
*------------------------------------ DUMMY FIELD ALWAYS TRANSMITTED
DUMMY    DFHMDF POS=(23,1),                                            X
               LENGTH=1,                                               X
               ATTRB=(DRK,PROT,FSET),                                  X
               INITIAL=' '
*------------------------------------ PROMPT LINE ---------------------
PROMPT   DFHMDF POS=(24,1),                                            X
               LENGTH=79,                                              X
               ATTRB=(BRT,PROT)
*------------------------------------ END OF MAP ----------------------
         DFHMSD TYPE=FINAL
         END
```

Arrows are invisible until program brightens them.

Figure 9.5 Basic mapping support (BM) map source code for the PF key demonstration screen.

program makes the messages selectively appear and disappear, each message remains on the screen and is not transmitted again during the time the screen is used.

You may find it strange that we have defined field names for screen labels, especially the "PFxLAB" names for the screen labels "PF1," "PF2," and so forth. By putting field names on these in the BMS map, we make these fields a part of the data transmission record (and consequently, a necessary part of the symbolic map). Why do this? *You must make label fields like "PFx" and the arrow messages here a part of the data transmission record, if you will be manipulating their attribute bytes to make the fields visible, bright, or again dark during use of the screen.*

9.4 FSET A DUMMY FIELD TO AVOID MAPFAIL

The BMS map source code in Figure 9.5 reveals a gimmick useful in simplifying CICS program logic. We coded a one-byte field named DUMMY at the first position of line 23 of the screen, and set it with ATTRB=(DRK,PROT,**FSET**). This field hardly detracts from the data capacity of the screen, and is not visible on the screen. But it makes it unnecessary to test for **MAPFAIL**, or the lack of data transmission, from the terminal.

When you **FSET** a field, you cause the bit representing its modified data tag (MDT) in its attribute byte to be permanently set on. This means that the field will always be transmitted when the Enter or a PF key is pressed. Thus, at least this onc byte will always be transmitted from the screen to the program, and CICS will never experience a "no data transmitted" MAPFAIL condition when you execute a RECEIVE MAP command.

We did not make use of the DUMMY field technique in CALC1, because you need to realize what MAPFAIL is. In addition, you need to see DFHRESP syntax and how it is used; MAPFAIL is a convenient condition to demonstrate DFHRESP coding. We'll apply the DUMMY/FSET technique in other BMS maps and programs in this book, so that you can see how it simplifies program logic. The location of the single-byte dummy field is not important. In programs you see in the rest of this book, we will place it in the last screen position (line 24, column 80), which is where the GENMAP screen painter puts it.

9.5 VS COBOL II SOURCE CODE FOR PF KEY DEMONSTRATION

Figure 9.6 shows you the source code for our program C360B003, which drives the PF key demonstration screen. We built this in an in-line style to best illustrate the simple logic elements you need to intercept PF keys pressed at a terminal. Here is what the parts of this program do (the following discussion relates to the annotation letters on the figure itself):

- **a.** The **symbolic map** for the PF key demonstration screen includes definitions for each PF label and "<=== YOU PRESSED" message. You may find this strange, especially in the case of the PF labels, since we don't ordinarily transmit screen labels. We need to define fields in the symbolic map, because their definitions in the BMS map carried field names, to make them a part of the data transmission record. Even though we won't send the content of the label, we need access to the field's attribute byte, to be able to transmit new values to it. Notice that we used the newer, more meaningful coding **BINARY** in place of **COMP**, as allowed by VS COBOL II. Both mean "binary value."
- **b.** The definitions of the EIBAID field shown here are sufficient to recognize the AID fields we're interested in. A full definition, named KEYDEFS, covering all AID

```
EDIT ---- CSCJGJ.CSC360.COBOL(C360B003) - 01.04 -------------- COLUMNS 007 078
COMMAND ===>                                                   SCROLL ===> PAGE
****** ****************************** TOP OF DATA ******************************
       IDENTIFICATION DIVISION.
       PROGRAM-ID.    C360B003.
       AUTHOR.        J JANOSSY.
       INSTALLATION.  DEPAUL UNIVERSITY.
      *
      *  THIS IS A DEMONSTRATION PROGRAM ONLY.  IT SHOWS YOU HOW
      *  YOU CAN USE THE EIBAID FIELD TO DETECT WHAT AID KEY WAS
      *  PRESSED.  USE THIS PROGRAM TO LEARN:
      *
      *     1. HOW TO DETECT PF KEYS.
      *     2. HOW TO USE FSET TO TRANSMIT A DUMMY FIELD AND
      *          AVOID ANY MAPFAIL ERRORS.
      *     3. HOW TO HIDE FIELDS ALREADY ON SCREEN USING
      *        "DRK" ATTRIBUTE, MAKE THEM APPEAR BY CHANGING
      *        THE ATTRIBUTE.
      *
       ENVIRONMENT DIVISION.
      *
       DATA DIVISION.
       WORKING-STORAGE SECTION.
       01  WS-TRANS-ID                 PIC X(4)  VALUE '#003'.
       01  WS-MAPSET-NAME              PIC X(8)  VALUE '#003M   '.
       01  WS-MAP-NAME                 PIC X(8)  VALUE 'DEMOPF  '.
       01  WS-RESPONSE-CODE            PIC S9(8) BINARY.
       01  WS-COMMUNICATION-AREA       PIC X(1).
       01  WS-END-MESSAGE              PIC X(60) VALUE
           'PF KEY DEMO ENDED, USE    CESF LOGOFF  TO END CICS'.
      *
      ****************************************************************
      *  MANUALLY CODED SYMBOLIC MAP FOR PFDEMO PROGRAM    JGJ       *
      ****************************************************************
       01  DEMOPF-SYMBOLIC-MAP.
           05 FILLER                           PIC X(12).
      *
           05 DSM-L-PF1LAB                     PIC S9(4)  BINARY.
           05 DSM-A-PF1LAB                     PIC X(1).
           05 DSM-D-PF1LAB                     PIC X(3).
      *
           05 DSM-L-PF1MSG                     PIC S9(4)  BINARY.
           05 DSM-A-PF1MSG                     PIC X(1).
           05 DSM-D-PF1MSG                     PIC X(16).
      *---------------------------------------------------------------
           05 DSM-L-PF2LAB                     PIC S9(4)  BINARY.
           05 DSM-A-PF2LAB                     PIC X(1).
           05 DSM-D-PF2LAB                     PIC X(3).
      *
           05 DSM-L-PF2MSG                     PIC S9(4)  BINARY.
           05 DSM-A-PF2MSG                     PIC X(1).
           05 DSM-D-PF2MSG                     PIC X(16).
      *---------------------------------------------------------------
           05 DSM-L-PF3LAB                     PIC S9(4)  BINARY.
           05 DSM-A-PF3LAB                     PIC X(1).
           05 DSM-D-PF3LAB                     PIC X(3).
      *
           05 DSM-L-PF3MSG                     PIC S9(4)  BINARY.
           05 DSM-A-PF3MSG                     PIC X(1).
           05 DSM-D-PF3MSG                     PIC X(16).
```

A

Figure 9.6 VS COBOL II source code for the program driving the PF key demonstration screen.

keys with 88-level names, is available for copying in to your program, as shown in Chapter 10. (The IBM definition for this purpose is named DFHAID and is shown in Appendix A.) We'll demonstrate the use of KEYDEFS in Chapter 10.

c. The definitions of attribute byte values shown here to produce various screen effects are sufficient for the purposes of this program. A full set of definitions, cov-

```
005800 *-----------------------------------------------------------------
005900      05 DSM-L-PF4LAB                        PIC S9(4)  BINARY.
006000      05 DSM-A-PF4LAB                        PIC X(1).
006100      05 DSM-D-PF4LAB                        PIC X(3).
006200 *
006300      05 DSM-L-PF4MSG                        PIC S9(4)  BINARY.
006400      05 DSM-A-PF4MSG                        PIC X(1).
006500      05 DSM-D-PF4MSG                        PIC X(16).
006600 *-----------------------------------------------------------------
006700      05 DSM-L-DUMMY                         PIC S9(4)  BINARY.
006800      05 DSM-A-DUMMY                         PIC X(1).
006900      05 DSM-D-DUMMY                         PIC X(1).
007000 *-----------------------------------------------------------------
007100      05 DSM-L-PROMPT                        PIC S9(4)  BINARY.
007200      05 DSM-A-PROMPT                        PIC X(1).
007300      05 DSM-D-PROMPT                        PIC X(79).
007400 *
007500 *****************************************************************
007600 *  VALUE MEANINGS FOR THE EIBAID FIELD OF THE E. I. BLOCK *
007700 *****************************************************************
007800  01  DFH-DEFINITIONS-OF-EIBAID.
007900      05 DFHCLEAR                            PIC X  VALUE ' '.
008000      05 DFHPF1                              PIC X  VALUE '1'.
008100      05 DFHPF2                              PIC X  VALUE '2'.
008200      05 DFHPF3                              PIC X  VALUE '3'.
008300      05 DFHPF4                              PIC X  VALUE '4'.
008400 *
008500 *****************************************************************
008600 *  VALUE MEANINGS FOR THE ATTRIBUTE BYTE FIELD                  *
008700 *****************************************************************
008800  01  ATTRIBUTE-BYTE-VALUES.
008900      05 ABV-PROT-BRIGHT                     PIC X  VALUE 'Y'.
009000      05 ABV-PROT-NORM                       PIC X  VALUE '-'.
009100      05 ABV-PROT-DARK                       PIC X  VALUE '%'.
009200 *
009300  LINKAGE SECTION.
009400  01  DFHCOMMAREA                            PIC X(1).
009500 *
009600  PROCEDURE DIVISION.
009700 *======================================== FIRST TIME? =========
009800 *  IF FIRST TIME THIS TERMINAL ACTIVATES THE PROGRAM, EIBCALEN
009900 *  WILL BE ZERO, SO SEND THE SCREEN LABELS AND EXIT BUT HAVE
010000 *  CICS "REMEMBER" THE TRANS-ID OF THIS PROGRAM TO RESTART IT.
010100 *-----------------------------------------------------------------
010200      IF EIBCALEN = 0
010300         MOVE LOW-VALUES TO DEMOPF-SYMBOLIC-MAP
010400         MOVE 'PRESS PF1, PF2, PF3, PF4, OR <CLEAR> TO QUIT'
010500            TO DSM-D-PROMPT
010600         EXEC CICS
010700              SEND MAPSET     (WS-MAPSET-NAME)
010800                   MAP        (WS-MAP-NAME)
010900                   FROM       (DEMOPF-SYMBOLIC-MAP)
011000                   ERASE
011100                   END-EXEC
011200         EXEC CICS
011300            RETURN TRANSID    (WS-TRANS-ID)
011400                   COMMAREA   (WS-COMMUNICATION-AREA)
011500                   END-EXEC.
```

B

C

D

Figure 9.6 *(Continued)*

ering all combinations of field protection, visibility, and NUM is available for copying into your program, as shown in Chapter 10. We'll demonstrate the use of it later in this book.

d. Refer back to our initial discussion of pseudoconversational logic in Chapter 6 as you consider the first part of the Procedure Division, lines 10200 through 14200.

```
*======================================= RECEIVE SCREEN ======
*  IT'S NOT THE FIRST TIME THE TERMINAL ACTIVATED THIS PROGRAM
*------------------------------------------------------------
     EXEC CICS
          RECEIVE MAP         (WS-MAP-NAME)
                  MAPSET      (WS-MAPSET-NAME)
                  INTO        (DEMOPF-SYMBOLIC-MAP)
                  RESP        (WS-RESPONSE-CODE)
                  END-EXEC.
*=================================== WAS <CLEAR> PRESSED?===
*  IF PROGRAM WAS ACTIVATED BECAUSE THE TERMINAL USER PRESSED
*  THE <CLEAR> KEY, IT'S TIME TO QUIT THIS PROGRAM COMPLETELY
*------------------------------------------------------------
     IF EIBAID = DFHCLEAR
        EXEC CICS
             SEND TEXT FROM (WS-END-MESSAGE)
                  ERASE
                  FREEKB
                  END-EXEC
        EXEC CICS
             RETURN
                  END-EXEC.
*=========================================== WE GOT A PF KEY
*  RETURN ALL OF THE PF LABELS TO NORMAL INTENSITY AND HIDE ALL
*  OF THE "<=== YOU PRESSED" MESSAGES USING DRK, THEN CHECK TO
*  SEE WHAT AID KEY WAS PRESSED:
*------------------------------------------------------------
     MOVE ABV-PROT-NORM  TO  DSM-A-PF1LAB
                             DSM-A-PF2LAB
                             DSM-A-PF3LAB
                             DSM-A-PF4LAB.
*
     MOVE ABV-PROT-DARK  TO  DSM-A-PF1MSG
                             DSM-A-PF2MSG
                             DSM-A-PF3MSG
                             DSM-A-PF4MSG.
*
     MOVE 'PRESS PF1, PF2, PF3, PF4, OR <CLEAR> TO QUIT'
        TO DSM-D-PROMPT.
*
     IF EIBAID = DFHPF1
        MOVE ABV-PROT-BRIGHT TO  DSM-A-PF1LAB  DSM-A-PF1MSG
      ELSE
     IF EIBAID = DFHPF2
        MOVE ABV-PROT-BRIGHT TO  DSM-A-PF2LAB  DSM-A-PF2MSG
      ELSE
     IF EIBAID = DFHPF3
        MOVE ABV-PROT-BRIGHT TO  DSM-A-PF3LAB  DSM-A-PF3MSG
      ELSE
     IF EIBAID = DFHPF4
        MOVE ABV-PROT-BRIGHT TO  DSM-A-PF4LAB  DSM-A-PF4MSG
      ELSE
        MOVE 'YOU DID NOT PRESS PF1, PF2, PF3, PF4, OR <CLEAR>'
           TO DSM-D-PROMPT.
*
     EXEC CICS
         SEND MAP             (WS-MAP-NAME)
              MAPSET          (WS-MAPSET-NAME)
              FROM            (DEMOPF-SYMBOLIC-MAP)
              DATAONLY
              END-EXEC
     EXEC CICS
       RETURN TRANSID         (WS-TRANS-ID)
              COMMAREA        (WS-COMMUNICATION-AREA)
              END-EXEC.
```

Figure 9.6 *(Continued)*

e. To start the AID key interception and screen field highlighting process in the program, we move the attribute value for normal intensity to the attribute bytes for the "PFx" screen labels, and the attribute value for "dark" to the "<=== YOU PRESSED" screen messages. This reinitializes any message that was highlighted and made visible. Taking this action does not immediately change the condition of the field on the screen. The symbolic map must be transmitted to the terminal to make the new attribute values take effect.

f. Detecting which AID key was pressed to awaken the program involves comparing the value in the EIBAID field of the execute interface block (inserted by the CICS translator) to the "known" values in our DFH-DEFINITIONS-OF-EIBAID fields. Here we used IF/ELSE logic to do this, providing for the "otherwise" case at the bottom, which becomes effective if the terminal operator has pressed a key other than PF1, PF2, PF3, PF4, or Clear. (In our other programs we also show you how to use the newer **EVALUATE** statement to make tests such as this.) When we recognize a PF key with this logic, we move the attribute value that brightens a protected field to the appropriate "PF" and arrow message screen fields.

g. The program concludes a pseudoconverse by sending the symbolic map to the terminal, then returning control to CICS with the TRANSID option, to continue pseudoconversational operation.

9.6 PF KEY DETECTION IN A REVISED CALC1 PROGRAM

Now that you have seen how you can arrange logic to detect which AID key was pressed to reawaken a program, we want to show you a typical use that real CICS programs make of this capability. Figure 9.7 shows you a revised version of the CALC1 screen. We have put a large typeset arrow onto this screen, pointing to the sales tax rate field. Notice that this field is labeled TAX AT RATE but no rate appears. We have also added a line near the bottom of the

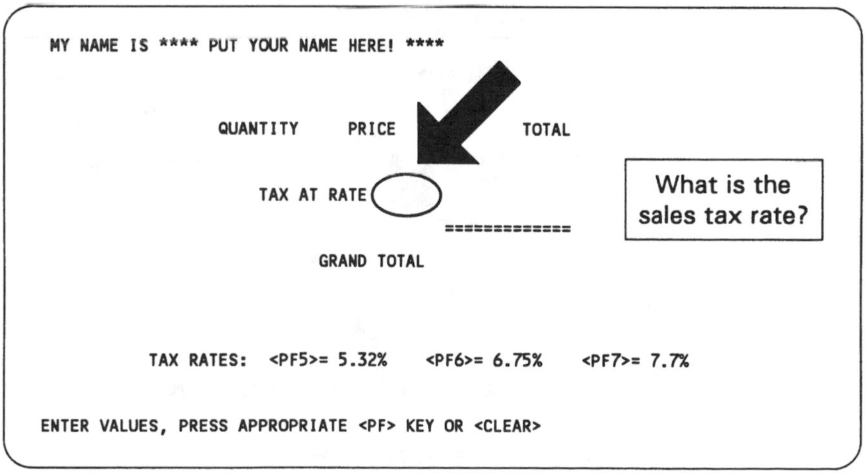
MY NAME IS **** PUT YOUR NAME HERE! ****
QUANTITY
PRICE
TOTAL
TAX AT RATE
=============
GRAND TOTAL
What is the sales tax rate?
TAX RATES: <PF5>= 5.32% <PF6>= 6.75% <PF7>= 7.7%
ENTER VALUES, PRESS APPROPRIATE <PF> KEY OR <CLEAR>

Figure 9.7 Revised CALC1 screen showing the new "dynamic" sales tax field, which receives its value when you press PF5, PF6, or PF7.

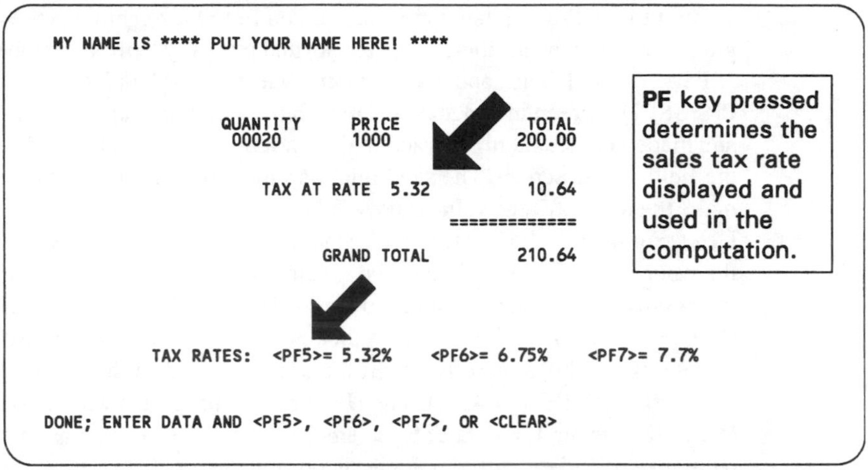
MY NAME IS **** PUT YOUR NAME HERE! ****
PF key pressed determines the sales tax rate displayed and used in the computation.
QUANTITY 00020
PRICE 1000
TOTAL 200.00
TAX AT RATE 5.32 10.64
=============
GRAND TOTAL 210.64
TAX RATES: <PF5>= 5.32% <PF6>= 6.75% <PF7>= 7.7%
DONE; ENTER DATA AND <PF5>, <PF6>, <PF7>, OR <CLEAR>

Figure 9.8 Revised CALC1 screen after pressing PF5, to select a tax rate of 5.32%.

screen that informs the terminal operator of three different sales tax rates, selectable by pressing PF5, PF6, or PF7.

Figure 9.8 illustrates what happens on the revised CALC1 screen when we enter the value 20 for QUANTITY, and 1000 (ten dollars) for PRICE, and then press PF5. Program logic assigns the rate 5.32% to sales tax, then completes the transaction to calculate total (200.00), 5.32% sales tax on this total (10.64) and finally the grand total including sales tax, 210.64. If we immediately press PF6, we see the screen in Figure 9.9 appear, repeating the transaction with the sales tax rate 6.75%. Figure 9.10 shows you what happens if we press PF7; a sales tax rate of 7.7% applies. Figure 9.11 shows what happens if a PF key other than PF5, PF6, or PF7 is pressed.

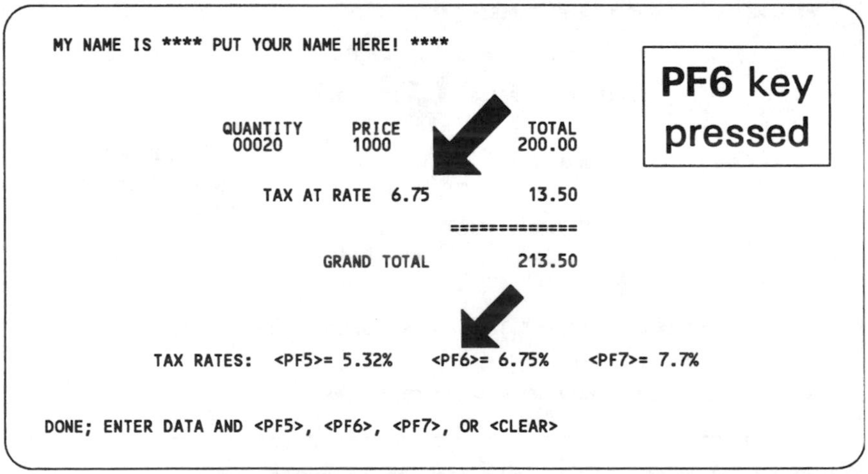
MY NAME IS **** PUT YOUR NAME HERE! ****
PF6 key pressed
QUANTITY 00020
PRICE 1000
TOTAL 200.00
TAX AT RATE 6.75 13.50
=============
GRAND TOTAL 213.50
TAX RATES: <PF5>= 5.32% <PF6>= 6.75% <PF7>= 7.7%
DONE; ENTER DATA AND <PF5>, <PF6>, <PF7>, OR <CLEAR>

Figure 9.9 Revised CALC1 screen after pressing PF6, to select a tax rate of 6.75%.

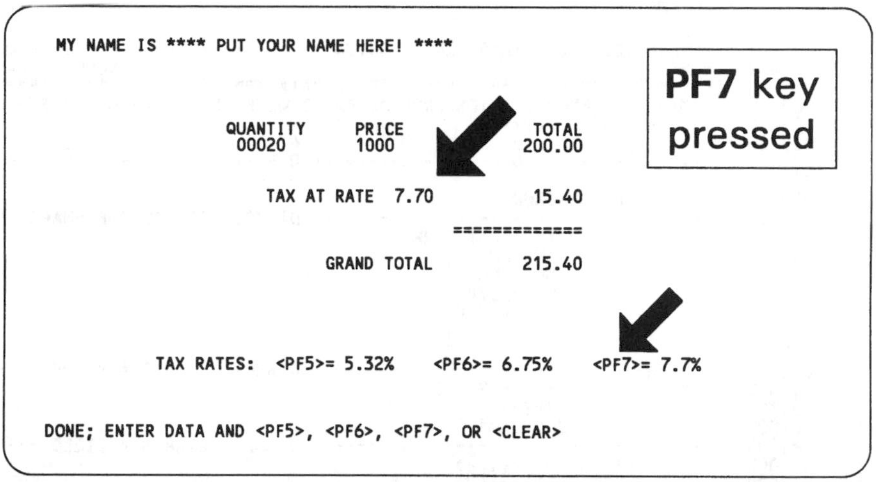
MY NAME IS **** PUT YOUR NAME HERE! ****
PF7 key pressed
QUANTITY
00020
PRICE
1000
TOTAL
200.00
TAX AT RATE 7.70
15.40
=============
GRAND TOTAL
215.40
TAX RATES: <PF5>= 5.32% <PF6>= 6.75% <PF7>= 7.7%
DONE; ENTER DATA AND <PF5>, <PF6>, <PF7>, OR <CLEAR>

Figure 9.10 Revised CALC1 screen after pressing PF7, to select a tax rate of 7.7%.

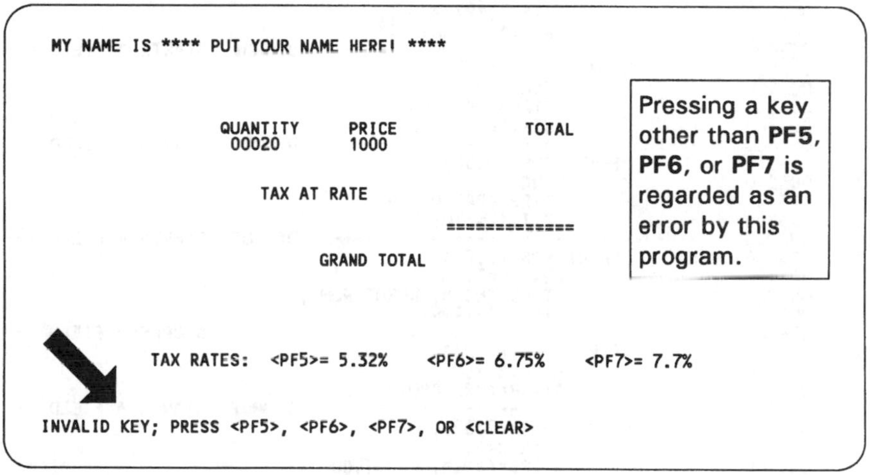
MY NAME IS **** PUT YOUR NAME HERE! ****
Pressing a key other than PF5, PF6, or PF7 is regarded as an error by this program.
QUANTITY
00020
PRICE
1000
TOTAL
TAX AT RATE
=============
GRAND TOTAL
TAX RATES: <PF5>= 5.32% <PF6>= 6.75% <PF7>= 7.7%
INVALID KEY; PRESS <PF5>, <PF6>, <PF7>, OR <CLEAR>

Figure 9.11 Revised CALC1 screen after pressing a PF key other than PF5, PF6, or PF7.

9.7 BMS MAP FOR THE REVISED CALC1 PROGRAM

Figure 9.12 shows you the BMS map source code for the revised CALC1 screen with dynamic sales tax value selection. We have highlighted the two parts of the map coding that are most relevant to this added feature.

You see a new field named TAXRATE in the BMS map for the CALC1 screen at line 6800, for the tax rate. This protected field is not directly changeable by the terminal operator. The value inserted here by the program is assigned by the operator's choice of PF key. You also see the coding for the unlabeled literal line at the bottom of the screen that tells the operator the PF choices to complete a transaction.

```
EDIT ---- CSCJGJ.CSC360.CNTL(#002M) - 01.04 ----------------- COLUMNS 001 072
COMMAND ===>                                                   SCROLL ===> PAGE
****** ****************************** TOP OF DATA *******************************
*   MAP FOR DEMONSTRATION PROGRAM CALC1 WITH <PF5>, <PF6>, <PF7> KEYS
*   J JANOSSY  9/29/94
*        1         2         3         4         5         6         7
*---+----0----+----0----+----0----+----0----+----0----+----0----+----0-
*
         PRINT NOGEN
*------------------------------------ DFHMSD  STARTS THE "MAPSET"-----
#002M    DFHMSD TYPE=&SYSPARM,                                        X
               LANG=COBOL,                                            X
               MODE=INOUT,                                            X
               TERM=3270-2,                                           X
               CTRL=FREEKB,                                           X
               STORAGE=AUTO,                                          X
               TIOAPFX=YES
*------------------------------------ DFHMDI  STARTS A "MAP" ---------
MAPFKEY  DFHMDI SIZE=(24,80),                                         X
               LINE=1,                                                X
               COLUMN=1
*------------------------------------ DFHMDF  STARTS A FIELD ---------
         DFHMDF POS=(1,2),                                            X
               LENGTH=40,
               ATTRB=(BRT,PROT),                                      X
               INITIAL='MY NAME IS **** PUT YOUR NAME HERE! ****'
*------------------------------------ DFHMDF  STARTS A FIELD ---------
         DFHMDF POS=(6,19),                                           X
               LENGTH=8,                                              X
               ATTRB=(BRT,PROT),                                      X
               INITIAL='QUANTITY'
*------------------------------------ DFHMDF  STARTS A FIELD ---------
         DFHMDF POS=(6,32),                                           X
               LENGTH=5,                                              X
               ATTRB=(BRT,PROT),                                      X
               INITIAL='PRICE'
*------------------------------------ DFHMDF  STARTS A FIELD ---------
         DFHMDF POS=(6,50),                                           X
               LENGTH=5,                                              X
               ATTRB=(BRT,PROT),                                      X
               INITIAL='TOTAL'
*------------------------------------ DFHMDF  STARTS A FIELD ---------
QUANT    DFHMDF POS=(7,20),                                           X
               LENGTH=5,                                              X
               ATTRB=(NORM,UNPROT,NUM),                               X
               PICIN='99999'
*                                             "STOPPER" FIELD ---------
         DFHMDF POS=(7,26),                                           X
               LENGTH=1,                                              X
               ATTRB=(DRK,PROT)
*------------------------------------ DFHMDF  STARTS A FIELD ---------
PRICE    DFHMDF POS=(7,32),                                           X
               LENGTH=4,                                              X
               ATTRB=(NORM,UNPROT,NUM),                               X
               PICIN='99V99'
*                                             "STOPPER" FIELD ---------
         DFHMDF POS=(7,37),                                           X
               LENGTH=1,                                              X
               ATTRB=(DRK,PROT)
*------------------------------------ DFHMDF  STARTS A FIELD ---------
```

Figure 9.12 BMS map code for the revised CALC1 screen, showing dynamic sales tax display field and explanatory screen literal line.

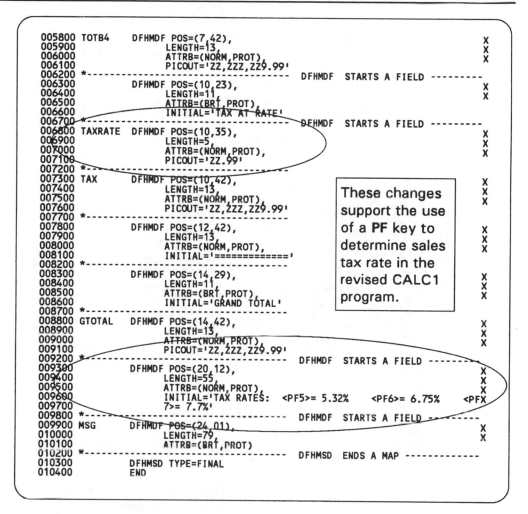

```
005800 TOTB4    DFHMDF POS=(7,42),                                     X
005900                 LENGTH=13,                                      X
006000                 ATTRB=(NORM,PROT),                              X
006100                 PICOUT='ZZ,ZZZ,ZZ9.99'
006200 *-------------------------------- DFHMDF  STARTS A FIELD ---------
006300          DFHMDF POS=(10,23),                                    X
006400                 LENGTH=11,                                      X
006500                 ATTRB=(BRT,PROT),
006600                 INITIAL='TAX AT RATE'
006700 *-------------------------------- DFHMDF  STARTS A FIELD ---------
006800 TAXRATE  DFHMDF POS=(10,35),                                    X
006900                 LENGTH=5,                                       X
007000                 ATTRB=(NORM,PROT),                              X
007100                 PICOUT='ZZ.99'
007200 *--------------------------------
007300 TAX      DFHMDF POS=(10,42),                                    X
007400                 LENGTH=13,                                      X
007500                 ATTRB=(NORM,PROT),                              X
007600                 PICOUT='ZZ,ZZZ,ZZ9.99'
007700 *--------------------------------
007800          DFHMDF POS=(12,42),                                    X
007900                 LENGTH=13,                                      X
008000                 ATTRB=(NORM,PROT),                              X
008100                 INITIAL='============='
008200 *--------------------------------
008300          DFHMDF POS=(14,29),                                    X
008400                 LENGTH=11,                                      X
008500                 ATTRB=(BRT,PROT),                               X
008600                 INITIAL='GRAND TOTAL'
008700 *--------------------------------
008800 GTOTAL   DFHMDF POS=(14,42),                                    X
008900                 LENGTH=13,                                      X
009000                 ATTRB=(NORM,PROT),                              X
009100                 PICOUT='ZZ,ZZZ,ZZ9.99'
009200 *-------------------------------- DFHMDF  STARTS A FIELD ---------
009300          DFHMDF POS=(20,12),                                    X
009400                 LENGTH=55,                                      X
009500                 ATTRB=(NORM,PROT),                              X
009600                 INITIAL='TAX RATES:  <PF5>= 5.32%    <PF6>= 6.75%    <PFX
009700                 7>= 7.7%'
009800 *-------------------------------- DFHMDF  STARTS A FIELD ---------
009900 MSG      DFHMDF POS=(24,01),                                    X
010000                 LENGTH=79,                                      X
010100                 ATTRB=(BRT,PROT)
010200 *-------------------------------- DFHMSD  ENDS A MAP -------------
010300          DFHMSD TYPE=FINAL
010400          END
```

These changes support the use of a **PF** key to determine sales tax rate in the revised CALC1 program.

Figure 9.12 *(Continued)*

9.8 VS COBOL II SOURCE CODE FOR THE REVISED CALC1 PROGRAM

We enhanced our original CALC1 program to give it the dynamically assigned sales tax value illustrated in Figures 9.8 through 9.10. Unlike the PF key demonstration program we showed you earlier in the chapter, which was based on in-line coding style, we used the structured version of CALC1 introduced in Chapter 8 at Figure 8.2. You can also compare the two coding styles in this chapter. We feel you'll agree that our **structured coding model** "scales up" to greater functionality very easily.

Here are the highlights of program C360B002, illustrated in full in Figure 9.13 (as in earlier examples, this discussion is tied to the letter annotations on the program source code):

a. The beginning of the program has not changed from the code shown in Figure 8.2.

b. A tax rate field is now defined in the symbolic map at lines 8100-8500, matching

```
EDIT ---- CSCJGJ.CSC360.COBOL(C360B002) - 01.03 ------------- COLUMNS 007 078
COMMAND ===>                                                  SCROLL ===> PAGE
****** ***************************** TOP OF DATA ******************************
 ID DIVISION.
 PROGRAM-ID.      C360B002.
 AUTHOR.          J JANOSSY.

*-----------------------------------------------------------------
*  VERSION C360B002 -- SALES TAX RATE SELECTED BY FUNCTION KEY
*
*  THIS IS A VERSION OF THE STRUCTURED CALC1 PROGRAM THAT
*  INCLUDES LOGIC TO INTERCEPT PROGRAM FUNCTION KEYS <PF5>,
*  <PF6> AND <PF7> TO USE DIFFERENT SALES TAX RATES
*-----------------------------------------------------------------

 DATA DIVISION.
 WORKING-STORAGE SECTION.
 01  WS-TRANS-ID                 PIC X(4)  VALUE '#002'.
 01  WS-MAPSET-NAME              PIC X(8)  VALUE '#002M   '.
 01  WS-MAP-NAME                 PIC X(8)  VALUE 'MAPFKEY '.

 01  WS-FIRST-TIME-FLAG          PIC S9(4) BINARY.
     88 FIRST-TIME                         VALUE 0.

 01  WS-GOOD-BAD-FLAG            PIC X(1)  VALUE 'G'.
     88 DATA-GOOD                          VALUE 'G'.

 01  WS-RESPONSE-CODE            PIC S9(8) BINARY.
 01  WS-SALES-TAX-RATE           PIC V9999.
 01  WS-COMMUNICATION-AREA       PIC X(1).
 01  WS-END-MESSAGE              PIC X(60) VALUE
     'QUITTING AS REQUESTED -- USE  CESF LOGOFF  TO END CICS'.

 01  WS-ERROR-MESSAGES.
     05 PIC X(35) VALUE '** CICS ERROR -- CONTACT HELP DESK '.
     05 PIC X(35) VALUE '-- REPORT THIS INFORMATION **      '.
     05 PIC X(9)  VALUE SPACES.

     05 WS-ERROR-LINE1.
        10              PIC X(14)     VALUE '   EIBTRNID = '.
        10 WS-EIBTRNID  PIC X(4).
        10              PIC X(61)     VALUE SPACES.

     05 WS-ERROR-LINE2.
        10              PIC X(14)     VALUE '   EIBRSRCE = '.
        10 WS-EIBRSRCE  PIC X(8).
        10              PIC X(57)     VALUE SPACES.

     05 WS-ERROR-LINE3.
        10              PIC X(14)     VALUE '   EIBRESP  = '.
        10 WS-EIBRESP   PIC ZZZZZZZ9.
        10              PIC X(57)     VALUE SPACES.

     05 WS-ERROR-LINE4.
        10              PIC X(14)     VALUE '   EIBRESP2 = '.
        10 WS-EIBRESP2  PIC ZZZZZZZ9.
        10              PIC X(57)     VALUE SPACES.

     05 PIC X(79) VALUE ALL '*'.

```

A

Figure 9.13 VS COBOL II source code for the revised CALC1 program, incorporating dynamic sales tax rate selection by PF key.

```
      *--------------------------------------------------------------
      *
      *  MANUALLY CODED SYMBOLIC MAP FOR CALC1 PROGRAM    JIM JANOSSY
      *  REDEFINES ALLOW SCREEN CLEANING WITH SPACES
      *
      *--------------------------------------------------------------
       01  CALC1-SYMBOLIC-MAP.
           05                               PIC X(12).

           05 CSM-L-QUANTITY                PIC S9(4)  BINARY.
           05 CSM-A-QUANTITY                PIC X(1).
           05 CSM-D-QUANTITY                PIC 9(5).

           05 CSM-L-PRICE                   PIC S9(4)  BINARY.
           05 CSM-A-PRICE                   PIC X(1).
           05 CSM-D-PRICE                   PIC 99V99.

           05 CSM-L-TOTAL-BEFORE-TAX        PIC S9(4)  BINARY.
           05 CSM-A-TOTAL-BEFORE-TAX        PIC X(1).
           05 CSM-D-TOTAL-BEFORE-TAX        PIC ZZ,ZZZ,ZZ9.99.
           05 CSM-D-TOTAL-BEFORE-TAX-X  REDEFINES
              CSM-D-TOTAL-BEFORE-TAX        PIC X(13).

           05 CSM-L-TAXRATE                 PIC S9(4)  BINARY.
           05 CSM-A-TAXRATE                 PIC X(1).
           05 CSM-D-TAXRATE                 PIC ZZ.99.
           05 CSM-D-TAXRATE-X  REDEFINES
              CSM-D-TAXRATE                 PIC X(5).

           05 CSM-L-TAX                     PIC S9(4)  BINARY.
           05 CSM-A-TAX                     PIC X(1).
           05 CSM-D-TAX                     PIC ZZ,ZZZ,ZZ9.99.
           05 CSM-D-TAX-X  REDEFINES
              CSM-D-TAX                     PIC X(13).

           05 CSM-L-GRAND-TOTAL             PIC S9(4)  BINARY.
           05 CSM-A-GRAND-TOTAL             PIC X(1).
           05 CSM-D-GRAND-TOTAL             PIC ZZ,ZZZ,ZZ9.99.
           05 CSM-D-GRAND-TOTAL-X  REDEFINES
              CSM-D-GRAND-TOTAL             PIC X(13).

           05 CSM-L-MESSAGE                 PIC S9(4)  BINARY.
           05 CSM-A-MESSAGE                 PIC X(1).
           05 CSM-D-MESSAGE                 PIC X(79).

      *--------------------------------------------------------------
      *
      *  VALUE MEANINGS FOR EIBAID FIELD OF DFHEIBLK
      *  88-LEVELS ARE CODED TO MINIMIZE MEMORY USE AND IMPROVE
      *  THE CLARITY OF LOGIC TO IDENTIFY FUNCTION KEY USAGE
      *
      *--------------------------------------------------------------
       01  EIBAID-TEST-FIELD                PIC X(1).
           88 ENTER-KEY                               VALUE ''''.
           88 CLEAR-KEY                               VALUE ' '.
           88 PF1-KEY                                 VALUE '1'.
           88 PF2-KEY                                 VALUE '2'.
           88 PF3-KEY                                 VALUE '3'.
           88 PF4-KEY                                 VALUE '4'.
           88 PF5-KEY                                 VALUE '5'.
           88 PF6-KEY                                 VALUE '6'.
           88 PF7-KEY                                 VALUE '7'.

      *--------------------------------------------------------------
      *
      *  VALUE MEANINGS FOR SYMBOLIC MAP ATTRIBUTE BYTE FIELDS
      *
      *--------------------------------------------------------------
       01  ATTRIBUTE-VALUES-TO-SET.
           05 ATT-UNPROT-CHAR-MDT          PIC X  VALUE 'A'.
           05 ATT-UNPROT-CHAR-MDT-BRIGHT   PIC X  VALUE 'I'.
           05 ATT-UNPROT-NUM-MDT           PIC X  VALUE 'J'.
           05 ATT-UNPROT-NUM-MDT-BRIGHT    PIC X  VALUE 'R'.
```

B **C** **D**

Figure 9.13 *(Continued)*

```
 LINKAGE SECTION.
 01  DFHCOMMAREA                         PIC X(1).
 PROCEDURE DIVISION.
*-----------------------------------------------------------------
 0000-MAINLINE.
     PERFORM 3333-ALWAYS-TEST.
     EVALUATE  TRUE
        WHEN  FIRST-TIME
           PERFORM 9000-FIRST-TIME
        WHEN  PF3-KEY
           PERFORM 9100-CLEAN-THE-SCREEN
        WHEN  PF5-KEY
           MOVE  .0532 TO WS-SALES-TAX-RATE
           PERFORM 0500-NORMAL-PROCESSING
        WHEN  PF6-KEY
           MOVE  .0675 TO WS-SALES-TAX-RATE
           PERFORM 0500-NORMAL-PROCESSING
        WHEN  PF7-KEY
           MOVE  .077  TO WS-SALES-TAX-RATE
           PERFORM 0500-NORMAL-PROCESSING
        WHEN  OTHER
           PERFORM 9200-INVALID-KEY-MESSAGE
     END-EVALUATE.
     PERFORM 8000-RETURN-WITH-TRANS-ID.
*-----------------------------------------------------------------
 0500-NORMAL-PROCESSING.
     PERFORM 1000-RECEIVE-MAP.
     COMPUTE CSM-D-TAXRATE = WS-SALES-TAX-RATE * 100.
     PERFORM 5000-VALIDATE-FIELDS
     IF DATA-GOOD
        PERFORM 5500-COMPUTE-RESULTS
     END-IF.
     PERFORM 1200-SEND-MAP-DATAONLY.
*-----------------------------------------------------------------
 1000-RECEIVE-MAP.
     EXEC CICS
        RECEIVE MAP        (WS-MAP-NAME)
                MAPSET     (WS-MAPSET-NAME)
                INTO       (CALC1-SYMBOLIC-MAP)
                RESP       (WS-RESPONSE-CODE)
     END-EXEC.
*================
     EVALUATE  WS-RESPONSE-CODE
*----------------
        WHEN  DFHRESP(NORMAL)
           CONTINUE
*----------------
        WHEN  DFHRESP(MAPFAIL)
           MOVE -1 TO CSM-L-QUANTITY
           MOVE 'NO DATA ENTERED; ENTER DATA OR <CLEAR> TO QUIT'
              TO CSM-D-MESSAGE
           PERFORM 1200-SEND-MAP-DATAONLY
           PERFORM 8000-RETURN-WITH-TRANS-ID
```

Figure 9.13 *(Continued)*

```

      *----------------

               WHEN  OTHER
                  PERFORM 9999-ABORT

           END-EVALUATE.
      *================

      *-----------------------------------------------------------

       1200-SEND-MAP-DATAONLY.
           EXEC CICS
               SEND MAP       (WS-MAP-NAME)
                    MAPSET    (WS-MAPSET-NAME)
                    FROM      (CALC1-SYMBOLIC-MAP)
                    DATAONLY
                    CURSOR
           END-EXEC.

      *-----------------------------------------------------------

       3333-ALWAYS-TEST.
           MOVE EIBAID    TO  EIBAID-TEST-FIELD.
           IF CLEAR-KEY
              PERFORM 8900-QUIT.
           MOVE EIBCALEN  TO  WS-FIRST-TIME-FLAG.

      *-----------------------------------------------------------

       5000-VALIDATE-FIELDS.

           MOVE ATT-UNPROT-NUM-MDT TO  CSM-A-QUANTITY
                                       CSM-A-PRICE.

           IF CSM-D-PRICE NOT NUMERIC
              MOVE 'B' TO WS-GOOD-BAD-FLAG
              MOVE ATT-UNPROT-NUM-MDT-BRIGHT TO CSM-A-PRICE
              MOVE -1 TO CSM-L-PRICE
              MOVE 'PRICE MUST BE NUMERIC; CORRECT, PRESS <PF> KEY'
                 TO CSM-D-MESSAGE
           END-IF.

           IF CSM-D-QUANTITY NOT NUMERIC
              MOVE 'B' TO WS-GOOD-BAD-FLAG
              MOVE ATT-UNPROT-NUM-MDT-BRIGHT TO CSM-A-QUANTITY
              MOVE -1 TO CSM-L-QUANTITY
              MOVE 'QUANTITY MUST BE NUMERIC; CORRECT, PRESS <PF> KEY'
                 TO CSM-D-MESSAGE
           END-IF.

      *-----------------------------------------------------------

       5500-COMPUTE-RESULTS.
           COMPUTE CSM-D-TOTAL-BEFORE-TAX =
              CSM-D-QUANTITY * CSM-D-PRICE.
           COMPUTE CSM-D-TAX =
              CSM-D-QUANTITY * CSM-D-PRICE * WS-SALES-TAX-RATE.
           COMPUTE CSM-D-GRAND-TOTAL =
              CSM-D-QUANTITY * CSM-D-PRICE * WS-SALES-TAX-RATE +
              CSM-D-QUANTITY * CSM-D-PRICE.
           MOVE 'DONE; ENTER DATA AND <PF5>, <PF6>, <PF7>, OR <CLEAR>'
              TO CSM-D-MESSAGE.
           MOVE -1 TO CSM-L-QUANTITY.

      *-----------------------------------------------------------

       8000-RETURN-WITH-TRANS-ID.
           EXEC CICS
              RETURN TRANSID   (WS-TRANS-ID)
                     COMMAREA  (WS-COMMUNICATION-AREA)
           END-EXEC.

      *-----------------------------------------------------------

```

Figure 9.13 *(Continued)*

```
 8900-QUIT.
     EXEC CICS
          SEND TEXT FROM (WS-END-MESSAGE)
                    ERASE
                    FREEKB
     END-EXEC.

     EXEC CICS
          RETURN
     END-EXEC.

*-------------------------------------------------------------

 9000-FIRST-TIME.
     MOVE LOW-VALUES TO CALC1-SYMBOLIC-MAP.
     MOVE 'ENTER VALUES, PRESS APPROPRIATE <PF> KEY OR <CLEAR>'
        TO CSM-D-MESSAGE.
     MOVE -1 TO CSM-L-QUANTITY.

     EXEC CICS
         SEND MAPSET    (WS-MAPSET-NAME)
              MAP       (WS-MAP-NAME)
              FROM      (CALC1-SYMBOLIC-MAP)
              ERASE
              CURSOR
     END-EXEC.

*-------------------------------------------------------------

 9100-CLEAN-THE-SCREEN.
     MOVE LOW-VALUES TO CALC1-SYMBOLIC-MAP.
     MOVE SPACES TO  CSM-D-TOTAL-BEFORE-TAX-X
                     CSM-D-TAXRATE-X
                     CSM-D-TAX-X
                     CSM-D-GRAND-TOTAL-X.

     MOVE 'ENTER VALUES, PRESS APPROPRIATE <PF> KEY OR <CLEAR>'
        TO CSM-D-MESSAGE.
     MOVE -1 TO CSM-L-QUANTITY.

     EXEC CICS
         SEND MAP       (WS-MAP-NAME)
              MAPSET    (WS-MAPSET-NAME)
              FROM      (CALC1-SYMBOLIC-MAP)
              DATAONLY
              ERASEAUP
              CURSOR
     END-EXEC.

*-------------------------------------------------------------

 9200-INVALID-KEY-MESSAGE.
     MOVE LOW-VALUES TO CALC1-SYMBOLIC-MAP.
     MOVE 'INVALID KEY; PRESS <PF5>, <PF6>, <PF7>, OR <CLEAR>'
        TO CSM-D-MESSAGE.
     MOVE -1 TO CSM-L-QUANTITY.
     PERFORM 1200-SEND-MAP-DATAONLY.

*-------------------------------------------------------------

 9999-ABORT.
     MOVE EIBTRNID   TO  WS-EIBTRNID.
     MOVE EIBRSRCE   TO  WS-EIBRSRCE.
     MOVE EIBRESP    TO  WS-EIBRESP.
     MOVE EIBRESP2   TO  WS-EIBRESP2.

     EXEC CICS
        SEND TEXT FROM (WS-ERROR-MESSAGES)
              ERASE
              ALARM
              FREEKB
     END-EXEC.

     EXEC CICS
          RETURN
     END-EXEC.
```

Figure 9.13 *(Continued)*

the tax rate field in the BMS map code. Note that we have redefined this output field so that we can "see" it as both PIC ZZ.99 and PIC X(5). This makes it possible to move an actual numeric value to it and receive appropriate editing (numeric formatting actions) there, but we can also move spaces there in the clean the screen function activated by the PF3 key.

c. We have expanded the definitions of the EIBAID field, and also changed the description to a single PIC X(1) field with 88 levels. Our 3333-ALWAYS-TEST logic moves the EIBAID field to EIBAID-TEST-FIELD so that we can use the 88-level names to identify the AID key that awakened or reawakened the program for each pseudoconverse.

d. Here we coded attribute byte values appropriate to the program. At this point, we could alternatively have copied in the standard attribute definitions shown in Appendix A.

e. Here in the mainline you see how our major enhancement of the CALC1 program fits in so readily with structured coding style. In order to accommodate the use of additional PF keys we simply added cases to the existing EVALUATE statement. We readily identify if the PF5, PF6, or PF7 was pressed to reawaken the program, and insert the appropriate sales tax value in each case.

f. In the revised CALC1 program, it was necessary to slightly modify our existing "normal processing" module for CALC1. It must now compute the percentage value of the sales tax and place it into the symbolic map field that will convey it to the terminal.

g. Compare the logic from line 18300 onward in Figure 9.13 with the original logic of the CALC1 program in Figure 8.2. You will see that the logic of this program is identical from this line onward. The **logic modularization** of the structured approach lets you increase program functionality by focusing attention only on the parts of the program that need to change. Since we originally used WORKING-STORAGE fields for all variables, including WS-SALES-TAX, the "standard program logic parts" from line 18200 onward do not need to change.

As you consider the use of PF keys in programs of your own design, we strongly suggest that you elaborate on the structured coding style shown in Figure 9.13.

9.9 PRE-SENT ERROR MESSAGES AND ATTRIBUTE BYTE MANIPULATION

In our PF key demonstration program you saw how you can arrange program logic to detect PF keys and use this information to affect program logic. You also saw the technique of including **pre-sent messages** on a screen, and turning them on and off. Our revised CALC1 program made use of *PF key detection,* but not message visibility manipulation. The technique of pre-sending messages, then turning the messages on or off by sending an attribute byte, is also used in real CICS programs. It can be put to good effect in minimizing data transmission and speeding the responsivity and user friendliness of screens. We show you how to do that in a full-length example in Chapter 10, as we demonstrate how to implement modern software modularization practices in CICS programs using subprograms and CALL.

9.10 FOR YOUR REVIEW

The following terms were introduced or reviewed in this chapter. If you understand this chapter, you should be comfortable with defining each of these terms in relationship to CICS:

Attention identifier (AID) keys
Attribute byte manipulation
BINARY
BMS map source code
COMP
(DRK,PROT)
EIBAID field
EVALUATE
FSET
MAPFAIL
Modified data tag (MDT)
Modularization of logic
PF key detection
Pre-sent error messages
Program attention (PA) keys
Program function (PF) keys
Pseudoconverse
Structured coding model
Symbolic map

9.11 REVIEW QUESTIONS

1. Identify the three categories of AID keys, give an example of each, and explain the general nature of each category.
2. Explain how the DRK attribute can be used in combination with message fields that remain continuously on a screen.
3. Explain how you brighten or hide the contents of a screen field by program action.
4. We wish to be able to manipulate the attribute byte of a field on the screen. Must we give the field a name in BMS map source code? Explain why or why not, and describe what coding treatment the field requires in the symbolic map.
5. Describe what FSET attribute byte coding does, and why you might consider coding it.
6. Explain what a MAPFAIL condition is, and describe a simple technique for eliminating its potential in CICS programs.
7. Describe generally what is found in the EIBAID field of the execute interface block after each invocation (reawakening) of a CICS program, and give three specific examples.
8. Identify what you have to code in the WORKING-STORAGE of a CICS program in order to be able to detect what PF key was pressed to reawaken the program.
9. Describe two types of decisionmaking logic a program can use to detect what AID key was pressed to reawaken it to begin another pseudoconverse.
10. Identify what it is convenient to code in the WORKING-STORAGE of a CICS program in order to be able to manipulate the intensity of a screen field through program logic.

9.12 HANDS-ON EXERCISES

A. Develop the BMS source code for a simple screen that allows the entry of two five-digit numbers, and the presentation of a computed result with PIC Z,ZZZ,ZZ9.9(5). Arrange a title at the top of this screen that indicates MATH CALCULATOR BY XXXXXXXXXXXXXXXXXXXX, including your name at the X's. Put labels on this screen in normal intensity that state:

```
Enter two numbers and press:
    PF1 to add
    PF2 to subtract second from first
    PF3 to multiply
    PF4 to divide first by second
```

Create a structured VS COBOL II program to drive this screen, including logic that detects which PF was pressed and performs the proper calculation based on that. Present the computed answer in the result field. The program should also highlight the message line that corresponds to the PF key pressed; for example, the entire line:

```
PF2 to subtract second from first
```

should become brightened when the terminal operator presses PF2, and all other messages lines should revert to normal intensity. Use appropriate prompts to guide the terminal operator's actions. If the terminal operator presses a PF key other than PF1, PF2, PF3, or PF4, or the operator presses the Enter key, provide a prompt that indicates that an invalid key was pressed. Thoroughly test and debug your program.

B. Develop the BMS source code for a screen that allows the entry of three 20-byte character fields labeled A, B, and C and provides a single output field of 62 bytes length. Arrange a title at the top of this screen that indicates STRING CONCATENATOR BY XXXXXXXXXXXXXXXXXXXX including your name at the X's. Put labels on this screen in normal intensity that state:

```
Enter three words at A, B, and C and press:
    PF1 to concatenate in order A + B + C
    PF2 to concatenate in order B + C + A
    PF3 to concatenate in order C + A + B
    PF4 to concatenate in order A + C + B
    PF5 to concatenate in order C + B + A
    PF6 to concatenate in order B + A + C
```

Create a structured VS COBOL II program to drive this screen, including logic that detects which PF was pressed and performs the proper concatenation based on that. Include a single space between each concatenated field. Use the STRING verb for this concatenation processing. Don't forget to clear out the receiving field before each STRING action, as in this example of the STRING verb for the concatenation A + B + C:

```
MOVE SPACE TO RESULT-FIELD.
STRING FIELD-A  DELIMITED BY SPACE
       SPACE    DELIMITED BY SIZE
       FIELD-B  DELIMITED BY SPACE
       SPACE    DELIMITED BY SIZE
       FIELD-C  DELIMITED BY SPACE
  INTO RESULT-FIELD.
```

Present the appropriate concatenation in the result field. The program should also highlight the message line that corresponds to the PF key pressed; for example, the line:

```
PF4 to concatenate in order A + C + B
```

should become brightened when the terminal operator presses PF4, and all other messages lines should revert to normal intensity. Use appropriate prompts to guide the terminal operator's actions. If the terminal operator presses a PF key other than PF1, PF2, PF3, PF4, PF5, or PF6, or the operator presses the Enter key, provide a prompt that indicates that an invalid key was pressed. Thoroughly test and debug your program.

10

Using COPY and CALL in CICS Programs

In this chapter we show you how to use COPY and CALL in your CICS programs. COPY and CALL are two powerful mechanisms that foster program modularization and reliability. We show you these features using a major program example that also lets us demonstrate a modern pattern for input data field validation using pre-sent error messages, and several 1985 COBOL (VS COBOL II) language features.

"Real" CICS programs benefit from the use of COPY to acquire standard elements of WORKING-STORAGE, such as the symbolic map, EIBAID definitions for PF key recognition, and attribute byte definitions. In this chapter, we'll show you several standard items of CICS program code, and we will begin using COPY to acquire them in the compilation process.

Until CICS/ESA and VS COBOL II, CICS programs were prohibited from using the CALL verb. CALL is now fully supported for your CICS programs. **CALL** is the standard COBOL mechanism to invoke a separately compiled **subprogram**, and functions as an "external PERFORM." Like PERFORM, CALL is a great aid in modularizing program logic. It allows you to **reuse** logic for standard functions, such as date validation, abbreviation lookups, and numeric field de-editing, and to **separately test** algorithms before invoking them from larger programs.

10.1 MARKO'S CREDIT CARD APPLICATION

Figure 10.1 shows you a screen intended to capture data about an applicant for a credit card at Marko's Department Store. As you can see in Figure 10.1, several items of information are to be entered when a customer applies for credit. We have designed this screen with a short error message next to each field. Figure 10.2 shows you what is really "on" each screen. The messages to the right of each input field are, like the messages shown in our PF key demonstration program in Chapter 9, Figures 9.1 through 9.6, part of the BMS map source code for the credit card application screen, but are made invisible with the DRK intensity attribute. (You can get all messages to appear, as we did, simply by making no data entries and pressing the Enter key; as we programmed the transaction, we also included logic activated by the PF3 key to clear all entry and message fields.)

Figure 10.3 shows you how Marko's credit card application screen appears when data for a credit card application has been entered, but the Enter key has not yet been pressed. You might recognize that some fields contain invalid entries. The DATE OF BIRTH field, for example,

```
              APPLICATION FOR MARKO'S DEPARTMENT STORE CREDIT CARD

             TITLE
        FIRST NAME
    MIDDLE INITIAL
         LAST NAME
               SSN
     DATE OF BIRTH
     CITY OF BIRTH
    STATE OF BIRTH

   CURRENT ADDRESS INFORMATION:

  HOUSE NUM/STREET
         APARTMENT
              CITY
             STATE
               ZIP

     ANNUAL INCOME

 ENTER DATA, PRESS <ENTER>, <PF3>, OR <CLEAR> TO QUIT
```

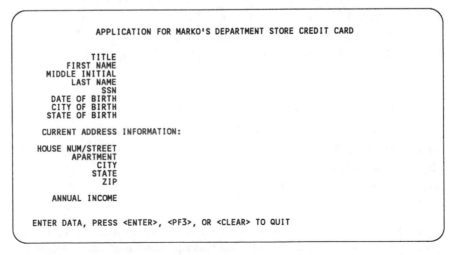

Figure 10.1 How the CICS screen for entry of data for a credit card application appears when sent to a terminal.

```
              APPLICATION FOR MARKO'S DEPARTMENT STORE CREDIT CARD

          TITLE                        <=== REQUIRED, MS MR MRS OR MISS
     FIRST NAME                        <=== REQUIRED, LETTERS ONLY
 MIDDLE INITIAL
      LAST NAME                        <=== REQUIRED, LETTERS ONLY
            SSN                        <=== REQUIRED, NUMBERS/HYPHENS ONLY
  DATE OF BIRTH                        <=== INVALID
  CITY OF BIRTH                        <=== REQUIRED
 STATE OF BIRTH                        <=== INVALID; USE XX IF NOT U.S.A.

CURRENT ADDRESS INFORMATION:

HOUSE NUM/STREET                            <=== REQUIRED, NO PUNCTUATION
       APARTMENT
            CITY                            <=== REQUIRED
           STATE                            <=== REQUIRED, USE STD ABBREV
             ZIP                            <=== REQUIRED, U.S., 5 DIGITS

   ANNUAL INCOME                            <=== REQUIRED, DOLLARS / CENTS

ERROR(S) EXIST, CORRECT AND PRESS <ENTER> TO PROCEED OR <CLEAR> TO QUIT
ENTER DATA, PRESS <ENTER>, <PF3>, OR <CLEAR> TO QUIT
```

Figure 10.2 The screen for credit card application data actually includes the field error messages at the right side, which are ordinarily hidden with DRK attribute coding.

contains 019970, and clearly, no month has a day number 99. Similarly, STATE OF BIRTH has been entered as "lx" whereas "la", for Louisiana, was intended. In addition, the state for the current address information is incorrect, and no data was entered for postal zip code.

Figure 10.4 is a picture of the credit card application screen after we pressed the Enter key to transmit our entries. Wow! You may now grasp the power of the same-line, hidden error messages programmed on the credit card application screen. Pre-sent error messages make it possible to provide explicit, field-specific information about multiple errors to the terminal operator all at once. Our program has validated all of the data fields we entered and transmitted. Having detected incorrect data in five fields, program logic has simply "turned on" the

```
              APPLICATION FOR MARKO'S DEPARTMENT STORE CREDIT CARD

          TITLE  ms
     FIRST NAME  alice
 MIDDLE INITIAL  n
      LAST NAME  wonderland
            SSN  123-45-6789
  DATE OF BIRTH  019970
  CITY OF BIRTH  new orleans
 STATE OF BIRTH  lx

CURRENT ADDRESS INFORMATION:

HOUSE NUM/STREET  123 n. hoople st.
       APARTMENT
            CITY  chicago
           STATE  uk
             ZIP

   ANNUAL INCOME  $22,500

ENTER DATA, PRESS <ENTER>, <PF3>, OR <CLEAR> TO QUIT
```

More than one entered field has invalid content. To be most productive, we need to see multiple error messages all at once.

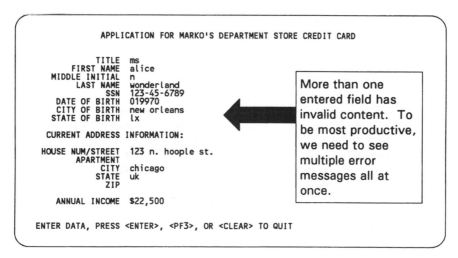

Figure 10.3 Credit card application data after entry of data but before we press the Enter key.

```
                APPLICATION FOR MARKO'S DEPARTMENT STORE CREDIT CARD

             TITLE  MS
        FIRST NAME  ALICE
    MIDDLE INITIAL  N
         LAST NAME  WONDERLAND
               SSN  123-45-6789
     DATE OF BIRTH  019970                  <=== INVALID
     CITY OF BIRTH  NEW ORLEANS
    STATE OF BIRTH  LX                      <=== INVALID; USE XX IF NOT U.S.A.

  CURRENT ADDRESS INFORMATION:

  HOUSE NUM/STREET  123 N. HOOPLE ST.       <=== REQUIRED, NO PUNCTUATION
         APARTMENT
              CITY  CHICAGO
             STATE  UK                      <=== REQUIRED, USE STD ABBREV
               ZIP                          <=== REQUIRED, U.S., 5 DIGITS

     ANNUAL INCOME  $    225.00

  ERROR(S) EXIST, CORRECT AND PRESS <ENTER> TO PROCEED OR <CLEAR> TO QUIT
  ENTER DATA, PRESS <ENTER>, <PF3>, OR <CLEAR> TO QUIT
```

Multiple error messages

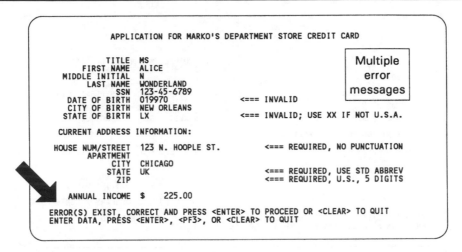

Figure 10.4 Appropriate field error messages are made visible on the credit card application screen when we press the Enter key.

appropriate error messages by setting their attribute bytes to make them visible. In addition to the five field error messages, program logic has also turned on the first of the two prompt lines, which indicates that one or more field errors exist.

You might notice in Figure 10.4 that two errors we had not expected are apparent. Apparently, punctuation such as periods is not permitted in the HOUSE NUM/STREET field. In addition, logic has de-edited the ANNUAL INCOME field, but has interpreted our entry of $22,500 as $ 225.00. In the next sections we'll show you how and why these results were produced. Figure 10.5 shows you what the credit card application screen looks like after all field errors have been corrected and we press the Enter key.

```
                APPLICATION FOR MARKO'S DEPARTMENT STORE CREDIT CARD

             TITLE  MS
        FIRST NAME  ALICE
    MIDDLE INITIAL  N
         LAST NAME  WONDERLAND
               SSN  123-45-6789
     DATE OF BIRTH  011970
     CITY OF BIRTH  NEW ORLEANS
    STATE OF BIRTH  LA

  CURRENT ADDRESS INFORMATION:

  HOUSE NUM/STREET  123 N HOOPLE ST
         APARTMENT
              CITY  CHICAGO
             STATE  IL
               ZIP  60678

     ANNUAL INCOME  $ 22,500.00

  DONE; ENTER MORE, <PF3>, OR <CLEAR> TO QUIT
```

All error messages return to invisible (DRK) when invalid field contents are corrected.

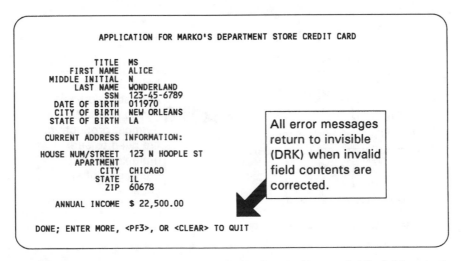

Figure 10.5 Credit card application screen after we correct all data field content errors and press Enter.

10.2 BMS MAP SOURCE CODE FOR CREDIT CARD APPLICATION SCREEN

Before considering the actual program code for Marko's credit card application, let's take a quick look at the BMS map code for the screen in Figures 10.1 through 10.5, which is shown in Figure 10.6. You'll notice that we coded this in a more compact form than earlier examples.

While the text of the BMS map code in Figure 10.6 might appear complicated, it is actually easy to read because we used two-digit numbers for column throughout it. This makes it possible to align the LENGTH and ATTRIB fields on all coding lines. In addition, we included comment lines full of hyphens to visually group the screen label, entry field, stopper field, and error message coding for each enterable field. Yes, the BMS map coding is still "dense" and tedious, but it is manageable, especially using a screen painter such as GENMAP, which we introduced in Chapter 4. (We actually used GENMAP to design and prepare Marko's credit card screen, then edited the ASCII file it output as the BMS map code, to produce the coding shown in Figure 10.6.)

You can see that for enterable fields, such as FIRST NAME, we use this pattern in the BMS map code for the credit card screen:

Field label	(BRT,PROT)
Enterable field	(NORM,UNPROT,FSET)
Enterable field stopper field	(DRK,PROT)
Pre-sent error message field	(DRK,PROT)

To improve clarity, we coded the attribute bytes in a consistent format, not taking the default NORM for some fields, so that our choices are clearly apparent. Notice that the pre-sent (hidden) error message fields carry field names, such as EFIRSTN for the FIRSTN field, so that they become part of the data transmission record and we have access to their attribute bytes in the symbolic map. We'll explain in the next sections why we chose to FSET each enterable field, forcing it to be transmitted back to the terminal, even if its contents have not changed.

10.3 SYMBOLIC MAP FOR THE CREDIT CARD APPLICATION SCREEN

Figure 10.7 lists the symbolic map matching the BMS map code of Figure 10.6. You'll recall that correspondence between the BMS map and the symbolic map is essential; the BMS map code determines what the data transmission record will contain, and the symbolic map is a COBOL description of the data transmission record. Our symbolic map code is separate from the source code for the C360B001 program. We housed it in a member named CREDSCR1, and placed it into a library named CSCJGJ.CSC360.COPYLIB. We'll use COPY to get the symbolic map into the program at compile time.

Our symbolic map contains entries for all of the pre-sent error messages, simply to gain access to their attribute bytes. Since we have no intention of changing the content of the hidden error messages, we could have coded FILLER for the "-D" field names instead of using actual COBOL data names, or we could have left out any name entirely, since "FILLER" is no longer a necessary word for a filler field. We could not, however, omit the PIC coding for the content of the error message fields, because these fields actually are in the data transmission record.

We have coded REDEFINES at two fields in the symbolic map, for different reasons. REDEFINES at the DATE OF BIRTH field at line 5100 lets us move spaces to this numeric field when we want to clear the screen using PF3. (Having the numeric PIC 9(6) as well as the

```
EDIT ---- CSCJGJ.CSC360.CNTL(CREDSCR1) - 01.03 --------------- COLUMNS 001 072
COMMAND ===>                                                  SCROLL ===> PAGE
****** ******************************** TOP OF DATA ***************************
              PRINT NOGEN
#001M         DFHMSD TYPE=&SYSPARM,                                           X
                     LANG=COBOL,                                              X
                     MODE=INOUT,                                              X
                     TERM=3270-2,                                             X
                     CTRL=FREEKB,                                             X
                     STORAGE=AUTO,                                            X
                     TIOAPFX=YES
*-----------------------------------------------------------------------
CRED1         DFHMDI SIZE=(24,80),LINE=01,COLUMN=01
*-----------------------------------------------------------------------
              DFHMDF POS=(1,14),LENGTH=52,ATTRB=(BRT,PROT),                   X
                     INITIAL='APPLICATION FOR MARKO''S DEPARTMENT STORE CREDIX
                     T CARD'
*-----------------------------------------------------------------------
              DFHMDF POS=(4,13),LENGTH=05,ATTRB=(BRT,PROT),                   X
                     INITIAL='TITLE'
TITLE         DFHMDF POS=(4,20),LENGTH=04,ATTRB=(NORM,UNPROT,FSET)
              DFHMDF POS=(4,25),LENGTH=01,ATTRB=(DRK,PROT)
ETITLE        DFHMDF POS=(4,41),LENGTH=32,ATTRB=(DRK,PROT),                   X
                     INITIAL='<=== REQUIRED, MS MR MRS OR MISS'
*-----------------------------------------------------------------------
              DFHMDF POS=(5,08),LENGTH=10,ATTRB=(BRT,PROT),                   X
                     INITIAL='FIRST NAME'
FIRSTN        DFHMDF POS=(5,20),LENGTH=12,ATTRB=(NORM,UNPROT,FSET)
              DFHMDF POS=(5,33),LENGTH=01,ATTRB=(DRK,PROT)
EFIRSTN       DFHMDF POS=(5,41),LENGTH=28,ATTRB=(DRK,PROT),                   X
                     INITIAL='<=== REQUIRED, LETTERS ONLY '
*-----------------------------------------------------------------------
              DFHMDF POS=(6,04),LENGTH=15,ATTRB=(BRT,PROT),                   X
                     INITIAL='MIDDLE INITIAL '
MIDINIT       DFHMDF POS=(6,20),LENGTH=01,ATTRB=(NORM,UNPROT,FSET)
              DFHMDF POS=(6,22),LENGTH=01,ATTRB=(DRK,PROT)
EMIDINI       DFHMDF POS=(6,41),LENGTH=28,ATTRB=(DRK,PROT),                   X
                     INITIAL='<=== MUST BE SPACE OR LETTER'
*-----------------------------------------------------------------------
              DFHMDF POS=(7,09),LENGTH=09,ATTRB=(BRT,PROT),                   X
                     INITIAL='LAST NAME'
LASTNA        DFHMDF POS=(7,20),LENGTH=20,ATTRB=(NORM,UNPROT,FSET)
ELASTNA       DFHMDF POS=(7,41),LENGTH=27,ATTRB=(DRK,PROT),                   X
                     INITIAL='<=== REQUIRED, LETTERS ONLY'
*-----------------------------------------------------------------------
              DFHMDF POS=(8,15),LENGTH=03,ATTRB=(BRT,PROT),
                     INITIAL='SSN'
SSN           DFHMDF POS=(8,20),LENGTH=11,ATTRB=(NORM,UNPROT,FSET)
              DFHMDF POS=(8,32),LENGTH=01,ATTRB=(DRK,PROT)
ESSN          DFHMDF POS=(8,41),LENGTH=35,ATTRB=(DRK,PROT),                   X
                     INITIAL='<=== REQUIRED, NUMBERS/HYPHENS ONLY'
*-----------------------------------------------------------------------
              DFHMDF POS=(9,05),LENGTH=13,ATTRB=(BRT,PROT),                   X
                     INITIAL='DATE OF BIRTH'
DATEB         DFHMDF POS=(9,20),LENGTH=06,ATTRB=(NORM,UNPROT,FSET)
              DFHMDF POS=(9,27),LENGTH=01,ATTRB=(DRK,PROT)
EDATEB        DFHMDF POS=(9,41),LENGTH=12,ATTRB=(DRK,PROT),                   X
                     INITIAL='<=== INVALID'
*-----------------------------------------------------------------------
              DFHMDF POS=(10,05),LENGTH=13,ATTRB=(BRT,PROT),                  X
                     INITIAL='CITY OF BIRTH'
BCITY         DFHMDF POS=(10,20),LENGTH=16,ATTRB=(NORM,UNPROT,FSET)
              DFHMDF POS=(10,37),LENGTH=01,ATTRB=(DRK,PROT)
EBCITY        DFHMDF POS=(10,41),LENGTH=13,ATTRB=(DRK,PROT),                  X
                     INITIAL='<=== REQUIRED'
*-----------------------------------------------------------------------
```

Figure 10.6 BMS map source code for the credit card application screen.

```
         DFHMDF POS=(11,04),LENGTH=14,ATTRB=(BRT,PROT),                X
               INITIAL='STATE OF BIRTH'
STATE    DFHMDF POS=(11,20),LENGTH=02,ATTRB=(NORM,UNPROT,FSET)
         DFHMDF POS=(11,23),LENGTH=01,ATTRB=(DRK,PROT)
ESTATE   DFHMDF POS=(11,41),LENGTH=34,ATTRB=(DRK,PROT),                X
               INITIAL='<=== INVALID; USE XX IF NOT U.S.A.'
*----------------------------------------------------------------------
         DFHMDF POS=(13,03),LENGTH=28,ATTRB=(BRT,PROT),                X
               INITIAL='CURRENT ADDRESS INFORMATION:'
*----------------------------------------------------------------------
         DFHMDF POS=(15,02),LENGTH=16,ATTRB=(BRT,PROT),                X
               INITIAL='HOUSE NUM/STREET'
HNUMST   DFHMDF POS=(15,20),LENGTH=22,ATTRB=(NORM,UNPROT,FSET)
         DFHMDF POS=(15,43),LENGTH=01,ATTRB=(DRK,PROT)
EHNUMST  DFHMDF POS=(15,46),LENGTH=29,ATTRB=(DRK,PROT),                X
               INITIAL='<=== REQUIRED, NO PUNCTUATION'
*----------------------------------------------------------------------
         DFHMDF POS=(16,09),LENGTH=09,ATTRB=(BRT,PROT),                X
               INITIAL='APARTMENT'
APART    DFHMDF POS=(16,20),LENGTH=06,ATTRB=(NORM,UNPROT,FSET)
         DFHMDF POS=(16,27),LENGTH=01,ATTRB=(DRK,PROT)
*----------------------------------------------------------------------
         DFHMDF POS=(17,14),LENGTH=04,ATTRB=(BRT,PROT),                X
               INITIAL='CITY'
RCITY    DFHMDF POS=(17,20),LENGTH=15,ATTRB=(NORM,UNPROT,FSET)
         DFHMDF POS=(17,36),LENGTH=01,ATTRB=(DRK,PROT)
ERCITY   DFHMDF POS=(17,46),LENGTH=13,ATTRB=(DRK,PROT),                X
               INITIAL='<=== REQUIRED'
*----------------------------------------------------------------------
         DFHMDF POS=(18,13),LENGTH=05,ATTRB=(BRT,PROT),                X
               INITIAL='STATE'
RSTATE   DFHMDF POS=(18,20),LENGTH=02,ATTRB=(NORM,UNPROT,FSET)
         DFHMDF POS=(18,23),LENGTH=01,ATTRB=(DRK,PROT)
ERSTATE  DFHMDF POS=(18,46),LENGTH=29,ATTRB=(DRK,PROT),                X
               INITIAL='<=== REQUIRED, USE STD ABBREV'
*----------------------------------------------------------------------
         DFHMDF POS=(19,15),LENGTH=03,ATTRB=(BRT,PROT),                X
               INITIAL='ZIP'
RZIP     DFHMDF POS=(19,20),LENGTH=05,ATTRB=(NORM,UNPROT,FSET)
         DFHMDF POS=(19,26),LENGTH=01,ATTRB=(DRK,PROT)
ERZIP    DFHMDF POS=(19,46),LENGTH=29,ATTRB=(DRK,PROT),                X
               INITIAL='<=== REQUIRED, U.S., 5 DIGITS'
*----------------------------------------------------------------------
         DFHMDF POS=(21,05),LENGTH=13,ATTRB=(BRT,PROT),                X
               INITIAL='ANNUAL INCOME'
INCOME   DFHMDF POS=(21,20),LENGTH=11,ATTRB=(NORM,UNPROT,FSET)
         DFHMDF POS=(21,32),LENGTH=01,ATTRB=(DRK,PROT)
EINCOME  DFHMDF POS=(21,46),LENGTH=30,ATTRB=(DRK,PROT),                X
               INITIAL='<=== REQUIRED, DOLLARS / CENTS'
*----------------------------------------------------------------------
ERMSG    DFHMDF POS=(23,01),LENGTH=71,ATTRB=(DRK,PROT),                X
               INITIAL='ERROR(S) EXIST, CORRECT AND PRESS <ENTER> TO PRX
               OCEED OR <CLEAR> TO QUIT'
*----------------------------------------------------------------------
PROMPT   DFHMDF POS=(24,01),LENGTH=77,ATTRB=(NORM,PROT)
DUMMY    DFHMDF POS=(24,79),LENGTH=01,ATTRB=(DRK,PROT,FSET),INITIAL=' '
         DFHMSD TYPE=FINAL
         END
```

Figure 10.6 *(Continued)*

```
EDIT ---- CSCJGJ.CSC360.COPYLIB(CREDSCR1) - 01.03 ----------- COLUMNS 001 072
COMMAND ===>                                                  SCROLL ===> PAGE
****** ***************************** TOP OF DATA ******************************
       *-----------------------------------------------------------------
       *  CREDSCR1
       *  SYMBOLIC MAP FOR MARKO'S CREDIT APPLICATION SCREEN #1
       *-----------------------------------------------------------------
        01  SYMBOLIC-MAP.
            05  FILLER                                PIC X(12).
       *-----------------------------------------------------------------
            05  CRE-TITLE-L                           PIC S9(4)   COMP.
            05  CRE-TITLE-A                           PIC X.
            05  CRE-TITLE-D                           PIC X(4).

            05  CRE-ETITLE-L                          PIC S9(4)   COMP.
            05  CRE-ETITLE-A                          PIC X.
            05  CRE-ETITLE-D                          PIC X(32).
       *-----------------------------------------------------------------
            05  CRE-FIRST-NAME-L                      PIC S9(4)   COMP.
            05  CRE-FIRST-NAME-A                      PIC X.
            05  CRE-FIRST-NAME-D                      PIC X(12).

            05  CRE-EFIRST-NAME-L                     PIC S9(4)   COMP.
            05  CRE-EFIRST-NAME-A                     PIC X.
            05  CRE-EFIRST-NAME-D                     PIC X(28).
       *-----------------------------------------------------------------
            05  CRE-MIDDLE-INITIAL-L                  PIC S9(4)   COMP.
            05  CRE-MIDDLE-INITIAL-A                  PIC X.
            05  CRE-MIDDLE-INITIAL-D                  PIC X(1).

            05  CRE-EMIDDLE-INITIAL-L                 PIC S9(4)   COMP.
            05  CRE-EMIDDLE-INITIAL-A                 PIC X.
            05  CRE-EMIDDLE-INITIAL-D                 PIC X(28).
       *-----------------------------------------------------------------
            05  CRE-LAST-NAME-L                       PIC S9(4)   COMP.
            05  CRE-LAST-NAME-A                       PIC X.
            05  CRE-LAST-NAME-D                       PIC X(20).

            05  CRE-ELAST-NAME-L                      PIC S9(4)   COMP.
            05  CRE-ELAST-NAME-A                      PIC X.
            05  CRE-ELAST-NAME-D                      PIC X(27).
       *-----------------------------------------------------------------
            05  CRE-SOC-SEC-NUMBER-L                  PIC S9(4)   COMP.
            05  CRE-SOC-SEC-NUMBER-A                  PIC X.
            05  CRE-SOC-SEC-NUMBER-D                  PIC X(11).

            05  CRE-ESOC-SEC-NUMBER-L                 PIC S9(4)   COMP.
            05  CRE-ESOC-SEC-NUMBER-A                 PIC X.
            05  CRE-ESOC-SEC-NUMBER-D                 PIC X(35).
       *-----------------------------------------------------------------
            05  CRE-DATE-OF-BIRTH-L                   PIC S9(4)   COMP.
            05  CRE-DATE-OF-BIRTH-A                   PIC X.
            05  CRE-DATE-OF-BIRTH-D                   PIC 9(6).
            05  CRE-DATE-OF-BIRTH-DX  REDEFINES
                CRE-DATE-OF-BIRTH-D                   PIC X(6).

            05  CRE-EDATE-OF-BIRTH-L                  PIC S9(4)   COMP.
            05  CRE-EDATE-OF-BIRTH-A                  PIC X.
            05  CRE-EDATE-OF-BIRTH-D                  PIC X(12).
       *-----------------------------------------------------------------
```

Figure 10.7 Symbolic map for the credit card application screen.

```
              05  CRE-CITY-OF-BIRTH-L                   PIC S9(4)    COMP.
              05  CRE-CITY-OF-BIRTH-A                   PIC X.
              05  CRE-CITY-OF-BIRTH-D                   PIC X(16).
              05  CRE-ECITY-OF-BIRTH-L                  PIC S9(4)    COMP.
              05  CRE-ECITY-OF-BIRTH-A                  PIC X.
              05  CRE-ECITY-OF-BIRTH-D                  PIC X(13).
      *-----------------------------------------------------------------
              05  CRE-STATE-OF-BIRTH-L                  PIC S9(4)    COMP.
              05  CRE-STATE-OF-BIRTH-A                  PIC X.
              05  CRE-STATE-OF-BIRTH-D                  PIC X(2).
              05  CRE-ESTATE-OF-BIRTH-L                 PIC S9(4)    COMP.
              05  CRE-ESTATE-OF-BIRTH-A                 PIC X.
              05  CRE-ESTATE-OF-BIRTH-D                 PIC X(34).
      *-----------------------------------------------------------------
              05  CRE-HOUSE-NUM-STREET-L                PIC S9(4)    COMP.
              05  CRE-HOUSE-NUM-STREET-A                PIC X.
              05  CRE-HOUSE-NUM-STREET-D                PIC X(22).
              05  CRE-EHOUSE-NUM-STREET-L               PIC S9(4)    COMP.
              05  CRE-EHOUSE-NUM-STREET-A               PIC X.
              05  CRE-EHOUSE-NUM-STREET-D               PIC X(29).
      *-----------------------------------------------------------------
              05  CRE-APARTMENT-NUM-L                   PIC S9(4)    COMP.
              05  CRE-APARTMENT-NUM-A                   PIC X.
              05  CRE-APARTMENT-NUM-D                   PIC X(6).
      *-----------------------------------------------------------------
              05  CRE-RCITY-L                           PIC S9(4)    COMP.
              05  CRE-RCITY-A                           PIC X.
              05  CRE-RCITY-D                           PIC X(15).
              05  CRE-ERCITY-L                          PIC S9(4)    COMP.
              05  CRE-ERCITY-A                          PIC X.
              05  CRE-ERCITY-D                          PIC X(13).
      *-----------------------------------------------------------------
              05  CRE-RSTATE-L                          PIC S9(4)    COMP.
              05  CRE-RSTATE-A                          PIC X.
              05  CRE-RSTATE-D                          PIC X(2).
              05  CRE-ERSTATE-L                         PIC S9(4)    COMP.
              05  CRE-ERSTATE-A                         PIC X.
              05  CRE-ERSTATE-D                         PIC X(29).
      *-----------------------------------------------------------------
              05  CRE-ZIP-L                             PIC S9(4)    COMP.
              05  CRE-ZIP-A                             PIC X.
              05  CRE-ZIP-D                             PIC X(5).
              05  CRE-EZIP-L                            PIC S9(4)    COMP.
              05  CRE-EZIP-A                            PIC X.
              05  CRE-EZIP-D                            PIC X(29).
      *-----------------------------------------------------------------
              05  CRE-ANNUAL-INCOME-L                   PIC S9(4)    COMP.
              05  CRE-ANNUAL-INCOME-A                   PIC X.
              05  CRE-ANNUAL-INCOME-D                   PIC X(11).
              05  CRE-ANNUAL-INCOME-DX  REDEFINES
                  CRE-ANNUAL-INCOME-D                   PIC $ZZZ,ZZZ.99.
              05  CRE-EANNUAL-INCOME-L                  PIC S9(4)    COMP.
              05  CRE-EANNUAL-INCOME-A                  PIC X.
              05  CRE-EANNUAL-INCOME-D                  PIC X(30).
      *-----------------------------------------------------------------
              05  CRE-ERRMSG-L                          PIC S9(4)    COMP.
              05  CRE-ERRMSG-A                          PIC X.
              05  CRE-ERRMSG-D                          PIC X(71).
      *-----------------------------------------------------------------
              05  CRE-PROMPT-L                          PIC S9(4)    COMP.
              05  CRE-PROMPT-A                          PIC X.
              05  CRE-PROMPT-D                          PIC X(77).
      *-----------------------------------------------------------------
              05  DUMMY-L                               PIC S9(4)    COMP.
              05  DUMMY-A                               PIC X.
              05  DUMMY-D                               PIC X.
```

Figure 10.7 *(Continued)*

PIC X(6) field is handy here, since it would allow us to code NUM on the BMS map code for this field, which we have chosen not to do.)

We also coded a REDEFINES on the ANNUAL INCOME field at line 11300, but here we use it to associate a second, numeric edited PIC with a field defined originally as PIC X(11). Why not use NUM for this dollars and cents field in our BMS map source code, and code this field with a PIC such as PIC 9(9)V99? Quite simply, we have not used NUM and a numeric PIC here, because we want to allow the terminal operator to enter a dollars and cents value in a user-friendly format with dollar sign, commas, and decimal point. Coding NUM would not allow this. The program will receive the annual income as a character string value and de-edit it with a subprogram of our own design, an operation typical of "real" CICS programs and systems.

Why do we FSET each enterable field in the BMS map for the credit card screen? Recall that **FSET** turns on the modified data tag (MDT) for a field. When the modified data tag is on for a field, it is transmitted from the terminal to the program. We FSET all enterable fields here because we will not be manipulating the attribute bytes of the enterable fields by program logic as we did in CALC1. Since we will not take the opportunity in the program to turn these MDTs on, we set them on in the BMS map code. We need the fields transmitted from the terminal each time, even if their content has not changed, because we don't store the fields in the program between pseudoconverses. Remember: when you execute CICS RETURN, all WORKING-STORAGE used by the program is lost as the program dies.

10.4 SOURCE CODE FOR THE C360B001 PROGRAM

The C360B001 program drives Marko's credit card application screen, and is listed in Figure 10.8. We'll use this program to show you how COPY and CALL are used in modern CICS programs. We'll also show you features new to the CICS environment, compliments of VS COBOL II, such as user-defined data classes and SET with 88-level condition names. You will see how these coding elements make data validation much easier than it used to be. Just to make sure you don't miss the emphasis on this point, let's be forthright about it: What we show you here is new and modern. Folks who learned CICS even a few years ago probably are not aware of many of the techniques we demonstrate here, because they became available only with VS COBOL II.

Program C360B001 captures data from the credit card application screen, and shows you how to go about validating the entered data and reporting on errors. But it does not actually deal with a file to store any entered data. We have developed this program to serve as a capstone for our discussion of CICS coding practices and logic arrangement. We'll consider file access in later chapters, and you'll see how to go about adding logic to handle files to this program.

At this point, examine the source code in Figure 10.8 to get a general idea of the logic of C360B001. You will see several coding features here that were not in CALC1 and earlier programs, and we'll explain each in detail. Our discussion of source code details for C360B001 is, as in earlier chapters, tied to letter annotations on the source code listing.

10.5 USER-DEFINED DATA CLASSES

The word **COPY** at letter "a" in Figure 10.8 (line 2300) brings in a special definition within a CONFIGURATION SECTION into program C360B001. We'll discuss COPY in Section 10.7, since it is also used to bring in several other standard items of coding, but we'll explain user-defined data classes now, since you encounter them first in the C360B001 program.

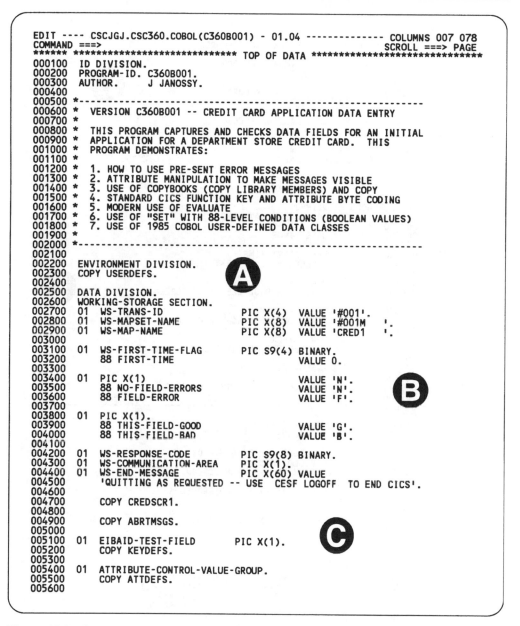

```
EDIT ---- CSCJGJ.CSC360.COBOL(C360B001) - 01.04 -------------- COLUMNS 007 078
COMMAND ===>                                                   SCROLL ===> PAGE
****** ***************************** TOP OF DATA ******************************
 ID DIVISION.
 PROGRAM-ID. C360B001.
 AUTHOR.     J JANOSSY.

*-----------------------------------------------------------------
*   VERSION C360B001 -- CREDIT CARD APPLICATION DATA ENTRY
*
*   THIS PROGRAM CAPTURES AND CHECKS DATA FIELDS FOR AN INITIAL
*   APPLICATION FOR A DEPARTMENT STORE CREDIT CARD.  THIS
*   PROGRAM DEMONSTRATES:
*
*   1. HOW TO USE PRE-SENT ERROR MESSAGES
*   2. ATTRIBUTE MANIPULATION TO MAKE MESSAGES VISIBLE
*   3. USE OF COPYBOOKS (COPY LIBRARY MEMBERS) AND COPY
*   4. STANDARD CICS FUNCTION KEY AND ATTRIBUTE BYTE CODING
*   5. MODERN USE OF EVALUATE
*   6. USE OF "SET" WITH 88-LEVEL CONDITIONS (BOOLEAN VALUES)
*   7. USE OF 1985 COBOL USER-DEFINED DATA CLASSES
*
*-----------------------------------------------------------------

 ENVIRONMENT DIVISION.
 COPY USERDEFS.                                    (A)

 DATA DIVISION.
 WORKING-STORAGE SECTION.
 01  WS-TRANS-ID                PIC X(4)  VALUE '#001'.
 01  WS-MAPSET-NAME             PIC X(8)  VALUE '#001M   '.
 01  WS-MAP-NAME                PIC X(8)  VALUE 'CRED1   '.

 01  WS-FIRST-TIME-FLAG         PIC S9(4) BINARY.
     88 FIRST-TIME                        VALUE 0.

 01  PIC X(1)                             VALUE 'N'.
     88 NO-FIELD-ERRORS                   VALUE 'N'.        (B)
     88 FIELD-ERROR                       VALUE 'F'.

 01  PIC X(1).
     88 THIS-FIELD-GOOD                   VALUE 'G'.
     88 THIS-FIELD-BAD                    VALUE 'B'.

 01  WS-RESPONSE-CODE           PIC S9(8) BINARY.
 01  WS-COMMUNICATION-AREA      PIC X(1).
 01  WS-END-MESSAGE             PIC X(60) VALUE
     'QUITTING AS REQUESTED -- USE  CESF LOGOFF  TO END CICS'.

     COPY CREDSCR1.

     COPY ABRTMSGS.

 01  EIBAID-TEST-FIELD         PIC X(1).           (C)
     COPY KEYDEFS.

 01  ATTRIBUTE-CONTROL-VALUE-GROUP.
     COPY ATTDEFS.
```

Figure 10.8 Source code for the C360B001 program that drives the credit card application screen.

```
*--------------------------------
*  CALLED MODULE LINKAGE RECORDS:
*--------------------------------
  01 DATECHEK-LINKAGE-RECORD.
     COPY DATELINK.
                                                      D
  01 NUMCHEK-LINKAGE-RECORD.
     COPY NUMLINK.

  01 PLACCHEK-LINKAGE-RECORD.
     COPY PLACLINK.

 LINKAGE SECTION.
 01  DFHCOMMAREA                         PIC X(1).

 PROCEDURE DIVISION.
*--------------------------------------------------------------

 0000-MAINLINE.
     PERFORM 3333-ALWAYS-TEST.

     EVALUATE  TRUE

        WHEN  FIRST-TIME
           PERFORM 9000-FIRST-TIME

        WHEN  PF3-KEY                                          E
           PERFORM 9100-CLEAN-THE-SCREEN

        WHEN  ENTER-KEY
           PERFORM 0500-NORMAL-PROCESSING

        WHEN  OTHER
           PERFORM 9200-INVALID-KEY-MESSAGE

     END-EVALUATE.

     PERFORM 8000-RETURN-WITH-TRANS-ID.

*--------------------------------------------------------------

 0500-NORMAL-PROCESSING.
     PERFORM 1000-RECEIVE-MAP.

     PERFORM 5000-VALIDATE-FIELDS
     IF NO-FIELD-ERRORS
        PERFORM 5500-FINISH-SCREEN
      ELSE
        MOVE PROT-BRT TO CRE-ERRMSG-A
     END-IF.

     PERFORM 1200-SEND-MAP-DATAONLY.

*--------------------------------------------------------------

 1000-RECEIVE-MAP.
     EXEC CICS
        RECEIVE MAP        (WS-MAP-NAME)
                MAPSET     (WS-MAPSET-NAME)
                INTO       (SYMBOLIC-MAP)
                RESP       (WS-RESPONSE-CODE)
     END-EXEC.

```

Figure 10.8 *(Continued)*

```
     EVALUATE  WS-RESPONSE-CODE
       WHEN  DFHRESP(NORMAL)
          CONTINUE
       WHEN  DFHRESP(MAPFAIL)
          MOVE -1 TO CRE-TITLE-L
          MOVE 'NO DATA ENTERED; ENTER DATA OR <CLEAR> TO QUIT'
             TO CRE-PROMPT-D
          PERFORM 1200-SEND-MAP-DATAONLY
          PERFORM 8000-RETURN-WITH-TRANS-ID
       WHEN  OTHER
          PERFORM 9999-ABORT
     END-EVALUATE.
*---------------------------------------------------------------
 1200-SEND-MAP-DATAONLY.
     EXEC CICS
         SEND MAP       (WS-MAP-NAME)
              MAPSET    (WS-MAPSET-NAME)
              FROM      (SYMBOLIC-MAP)
              DATAONLY
              CURSOR
     END-EXEC.
*---------------------------------------------------------------
 3333-ALWAYS-TEST.
     MOVE EIBAID     TO  EIBAID-TEST-FIELD.
     IF CLEAR-KEY
        PERFORM 8900-QUIT.
     MOVE EIBCALEN  TO  WS-FIRST-TIME-FLAG.
*---------------------------------------------------------------
 5000-VALIDATE-FIELDS.
     MOVE PROT-DARK TO  CRE-ETITLE-A
                        CRE-EFIRST-NAME-A
                        CRE-EMIDDLE-INITIAL-A          F
                        CRE-ELAST-NAME-A
                        CRE-ESOC-SEC-NUMBER-A
                        CRE-EDATE-OF-BIRTH-A
                        CRE-ECITY-OF-BIRTH-A
                        CRE-ESTATE-OF-BIRTH-A
                        CRE-EHOUSE-NUM-STREET-A
                        CRE-ERCITY-A
                        CRE-ERSTATE-A
                        CRE-EZIP-A
                        CRE-EANNUAL-INCOME-A
                        CRE-ERRMSG-A.
*
* CHECK FIELDS IN REVERSE SEQUENCE (LOWEST, RIGHTMOST FIRST,
* THEN PROCEEDING UPWARDS) SO THAT CURSOR IS LEFT IN FIRST
* FIELD ON SCREEN FROM TOP WITH ERROR.
*
*---------------------------------------------------------------
     MOVE CRE-ANNUAL-INCOME-D TO NUM-INPUT.
     MOVE 2 TO NUM-RIGHT-OF-DECIMAL.
     CALL 'NUMCHEK' USING DFHEIBLK                        G
                          DFHCOMMAREA
                          NUMCHEK-LINKAGE-RECORD.
     IF NUM-CONVERSION-OK
        MOVE NUM-OUTPUT TO CRE-ANNUAL-INCOME-DX
      ELSE
        MOVE PROT-BRT TO CRE-EANNUAL-INCOME-A
        MOVE -1 TO CRE-ANNUAL-INCOME-L
        SET FIELD-ERROR TO TRUE.
*---------------------------------------------------------------
```

Figure 10.8 *(Continued)*

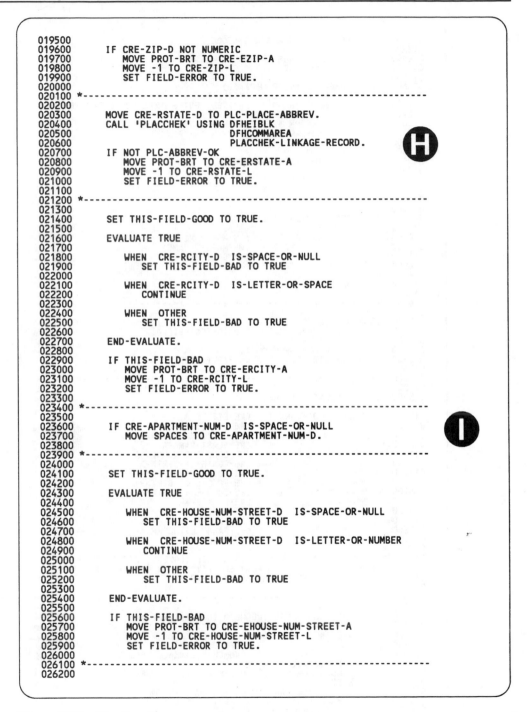

```
     IF CRE-ZIP-D NOT NUMERIC
        MOVE PROT-BRT TO CRE-EZIP-A
        MOVE -1 TO CRE-ZIP-L
        SET FIELD-ERROR TO TRUE.

*--------------------------------------------------------------

     MOVE CRE-RSTATE-D TO PLC-PLACE-ABBREV.
     CALL 'PLACCHEK' USING DFHEIBLK
                           DFHCOMMAREA
                           PLACCHEK-LINKAGE-RECORD.            H
     IF NOT PLC-ABBREV-OK
        MOVE PROT-BRT TO CRE-ERSTATE-A
        MOVE -1 TO CRE-RSTATE-L
        SET FIELD-ERROR TO TRUE.

*--------------------------------------------------------------

     SET THIS-FIELD-GOOD TO TRUE.

     EVALUATE TRUE

        WHEN  CRE-RCITY-D  IS-SPACE-OR-NULL
           SET THIS-FIELD-BAD TO TRUE

        WHEN  CRE-RCITY-D  IS-LETTER-OR-SPACE
           CONTINUE

        WHEN  OTHER
           SET THIS-FIELD-BAD TO TRUE

     END-EVALUATE.

     IF THIS-FIELD-BAD
        MOVE PROT-BRT TO CRE-ERCITY-A
        MOVE -1 TO CRE-RCITY-L
        SET FIELD-ERROR TO TRUE.

*--------------------------------------------------------------

     IF CRE-APARTMENT-NUM-D IS-SPACE-OR-NULL                       I
        MOVE SPACES TO CRE-APARTMENT-NUM-D.

*--------------------------------------------------------------

     SET THIS-FIELD-GOOD TO TRUE.

     EVALUATE TRUE

        WHEN  CRE-HOUSE-NUM-STREET-D  IS-SPACE-OR-NULL
           SET THIS-FIELD-BAD TO TRUE

        WHEN  CRE-HOUSE-NUM-STREET-D  IS-LETTER-OR-NUMBER
           CONTINUE

        WHEN  OTHER
           SET THIS-FIELD-BAD TO TRUE

     END-EVALUATE.

     IF THIS-FIELD-BAD
        MOVE PROT-BRT TO CRE-EHOUSE-NUM-STREET-A
        MOVE -1 TO CRE-HOUSE-NUM-STREET-L
        SET FIELD-ERROR TO TRUE.

*--------------------------------------------------------------
```

Figure 10.8 *(Continued)*

```
           SET THIS-FIELD-GOOD TO TRUE.

           EVALUATE CRE-STATE-OF-BIRTH-D

              WHEN 'XX'
                 CONTINUE

              WHEN OTHER
                 MOVE CRE-STATE-OF-BIRTH-D TO PLC-PLACE-ABBREV
                 CALL 'PLACCHEK' USING DFHEIBLK                      J
                                      DFHCOMMAREA
                                      PLACCHEK-LINKAGE-RECORD
                 END-CALL
                 IF NOT PLC-ABBREV-OK
                    SET THIS-FIELD-BAD TO TRUE
                 END-IF

           END-EVALUATE.

           IF THIS-FIELD-BAD
              MOVE PROT-BRT TO CRE-ESTATE-OF-BIRTH-A
              MOVE -1 TO CRE-STATE-OF-BIRTH-L
              SET FIELD-ERROR TO TRUE.

      *-------------------------------------------------------------

           SET THIS-FIELD-GOOD TO TRUE.

           EVALUATE TRUE

              WHEN  CRE-CITY-OF-BIRTH-D  IS-SPACE-OR-NULL
                 SET THIS-FIELD-BAD TO TRUE

              WHEN  CRE-CITY-OF-BIRTH-D  IS-LETTER-OR-SPACE
                 CONTINUE

              WHEN  OTHER
                 SET THIS-FIELD-BAD TO TRUE

           END-EVALUATE.

           IF THIS-FIELD-BAD
              MOVE PROT-BRT TO CRE-ECITY-OF-BIRTH-A
              MOVE -1 TO CRE-CITY-OF-BIRTH-L
              SET FIELD-ERROR TO TRUE.

      *-------------------------------------------------------------

           MOVE CRE-DATE-OF-BIRTH-D TO DATE-INPUT.
           CALL 'DATECHEK' USING DFHEIBLK
                                 DFHCOMMAREA
                                 DATECHEK-LINKAGE-RECORD.
           IF DATE-OK                                                K
              NEXT SENTENCE
            ELSE
              MOVE PROT-BRT TO CRE-EDATE-OF-BIRTH-A
              MOVE -1 TO CRE-DATE-OF-BIRTH-L
              SET FIELD-ERROR TO TRUE.

      *-------------------------------------------------------------

           SET THIS-FIELD-GOOD TO TRUE.

           EVALUATE TRUE

              WHEN  CRE-SOC-SEC-NUMBER-D  IS-NUMBER-OR-HYPHEN
                 CONTINUE

              WHEN  OTHER
                 SET THIS-FIELD-BAD TO TRUE

           END-EVALUATE.

```

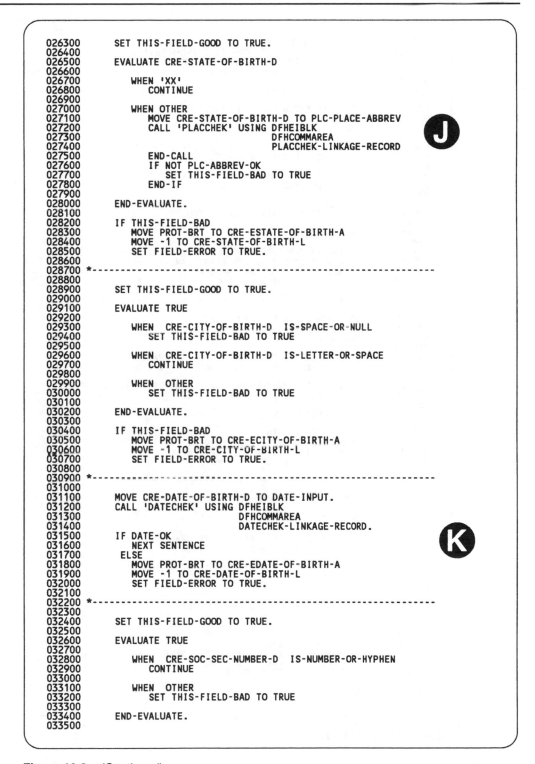

Figure 10.8 *(Continued)*

```
           IF THIS-FIELD-BAD
              MOVE PROT-BRT TO CRE-ESOC-SEC-NUMBER-A
              MOVE -1 TO CRE-SOC-SEC-NUMBER-L
              SET FIELD-ERROR TO TRUE.

      *-------------------------------------------------------------

           SET THIS-FIELD-GOOD TO TRUE.

           EVALUATE TRUE

              WHEN  CRE-LAST-NAME-D  IS-SPACE-OR-NULL
                 SET THIS-FIELD-BAD TO TRUE

              WHEN  CRE-LAST-NAME-D  IS-LETTER-OR-SPACE
                 CONTINUE

              WHEN  OTHER
                 SET THIS-FIELD-BAD TO TRUE

           END-EVALUATE.

           IF THIS-FIELD-BAD
              MOVE PROT-BRT TO CRE-ELAST-NAME-A
              MOVE -1 TO CRE-LAST-NAME-L
              SET FIELD-ERROR TO TRUE.

      *-------------------------------------------------------------

           SET THIS-FIELD-GOOD TO TRUE.

           EVALUATE TRUE

              WHEN  CRE-MIDDLE-INITIAL-D  IS-SPACE-OR-NULL
                 MOVE SPACE TO CRE-MIDDLE-INITIAL-D

              WHEN  CRE-MIDDLE-INITIAL-D  NOT IS-LETTER-OR-SPACE
                 SET THIS-FIELD-BAD TO TRUE

           END-EVALUATE.

           IF THIS-FIELD-BAD
              MOVE PROT-BRT TO CRE-EMIDDLE-INITIAL-A
              MOVE -1 TO CRE-MIDDLE-INITIAL-L
              SET FIELD-ERROR TO TRUE.

      *-------------------------------------------------------------

           SET THIS-FIELD-GOOD TO TRUE.

           EVALUATE TRUE

              WHEN  CRE-FIRST-NAME-D  IS-SPACE-OR-NULL
                 SET THIS-FIELD-BAD TO TRUE

              WHEN  CRE-FIRST-NAME-D  IS-LETTER-OR-SPACE
                 CONTINUE

              WHEN  OTHER
                 SET THIS-FIELD-BAD TO TRUE

           END-EVALUATE.

           IF THIS-FIELD-BAD
              MOVE PROT-BRT TO CRE-EFIRST-NAME-A
              MOVE -1 TO CRE-FIRST-NAME-L
              SET FIELD-ERROR TO TRUE.

      *-------------------------------------------------------------
```

Figure 10.8 *(Continued)*

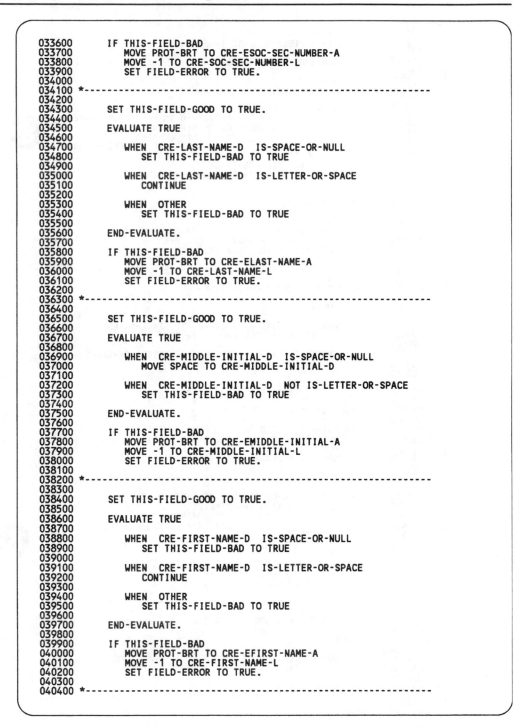

```

           SET THIS-FIELD-GOOD TO TRUE.

           EVALUATE CRE-TITLE-D
              WHEN  'MS  '  CONTINUE
              WHEN  'MRS '  CONTINUE
              WHEN  'MR  '  CONTINUE
              WHEN  'MISS'  CONTINUE
              WHEN OTHER    SET THIS-FIELD-BAD TO TRUE
           END-EVALUATE.

           IF THIS-FIELD-BAD
              MOVE PROT-BRT TO CRE-ETITLE-A
              MOVE -1 TO CRE-TITLE-L
              SET FIELD-ERROR TO TRUE.

      *-------------------------------------------------------------

       5500-FINISH-SCREEN.
      *
      * IF UPDATE WAS UNDERWAY, STATEMENTS HERE WOULD WRITE OR
      * REWRITE INFORMATION TO A FILE OR DABATASE AT THIS POINT; IN
      * THIS DEMONSTRATION PROGRAM, WE WILL NOT STORE THE ENTERED
      * DATA.
      *
           MOVE 'DONE; ENTER MORE, <PF3>, OR <CLEAR> TO QUIT'
              TO CRE-PROMPT-D.
           MOVE PROT-NORM TO CRE-PROMPT-A.
           MOVE -1 TO CRE-TITLE-L.

      *-------------------------------------------------------------

       8000-RETURN-WITH-TRANS-ID.
           EXEC CICS
              RETURN TRANSID   (WS-TRANS-ID)
                     COMMAREA  (WS-COMMUNICATION-AREA)
           END-EXEC.

      *-------------------------------------------------------------

       8900-QUIT.
           EXEC CICS
               SEND TEXT FROM (WS-END-MESSAGE)
                    ERASE
                    FREEKB
           END-EXEC.

           EXEC CICS
               RETURN
           END-EXEC.

      *-------------------------------------------------------------

       9000-FIRST-TIME.
           MOVE LOW-VALUES TO SYMBOLIC-MAP.
           MOVE 'ENTER DATA, PRESS <ENTER>, <PF3>, OR <CLEAR> TO QUIT'
              TO CRE-PROMPT-D.
           MOVE -1 TO CRE-TITLE-L.

           EXEC CICS
               SEND MAPSET    (WS-MAPSET-NAME)
                    MAP       (WS-MAP-NAME)
                    FROM      (SYMBOLIC-MAP)
                    ERASE
                    CURSOR
           END-EXEC.

      *-------------------------------------------------------------

```

Figure 10.8 *(Continued)*

```
 9100-CLEAN-THE-SCREEN.
     MOVE LOW-VALUES TO SYMBOLIC-MAP.

*   NOTE: NO NEED TO MOVE SPACES HERE EXCEPT TO COMPUTED FIELDS
*   SINCE ERASEAUP (ERASE ALL UNPROTECTED FIELDS) WILL ERASE
*   ALL INPUT FIELDS.  UNLIKE CALC1, CREDSCR1 HAS NO PROTECTED
*   PROGRAM-COMPUTED FIELDS.

     MOVE PROT-DARK TO  CRE-ETITLE-A
                        CRE-EFIRST-NAME-A
                        CRE-EMIDDLE-INITIAL-A
                        CRE-ELAST-NAME-A
                        CRE-ESOC-SEC-NUMBER-A
                        CRE-EDATE-OF-BIRTH-A
                        CRE-ECITY-OF-BIRTH-A
                        CRE-ESTATE-OF-BIRTH-A
                        CRE-EHOUSE-NUM-STREET-A
                        CRE-ERCITY-A
                        CRE-ERSTATE-A
                        CRE-EZIP-A
                        CRE-EANNUAL-INCOME-A
                        CRE-ERRMSG-A.

     MOVE 'ENTER DATA, PRESS <ENTER>, <PF3>, OR <CLEAR> TO QUIT'
         TO CRE-PROMPT-D.
     MOVE -1 TO CRE-TITLE-L.

     EXEC CICS
          SEND MAP       (WS-MAP-NAME)
                MAPSET    (WS-MAPSET-NAME)
                FROM      (SYMBOLIC-MAP)
                DATAONLY
                ERASEAUP
                CURSOR
     END-EXEC.

*-----------------------------------------------------------------

 9200-INVALID-KEY-MESSAGE.
     MOVE LOW-VALUES TO SYMBOLIC-MAP.
     MOVE 'YOU PRESSED WRONG KEY! PRESS <ENTER>, <CLEAR> TO QUIT'
         TO CRE-PROMPT-D.
     MOVE -1 TO CRE-TITLE-L.
     PERFORM 1200-SEND-MAP-DATAONLY.

*-----------------------------------------------------------------

 9999-ABORT.
     MOVE EIBTRNID    TO  WS-EIBTRNID.
     MOVE EIBRSRCE    TO  WS-EIBRSRCE.
     MOVE EIBRESP     TO  WS-EIBRESP.
     MOVE EIBRESP2    TO  WS-EIBRESP2.

     EXEC CICS
         SEND TEXT FROM (WS-ERROR-MESSAGES)
              ERASE
              ALARM
              FREEKB
     END-EXEC.

     EXEC CICS
          RETURN
     END-EXEC.
```

Figure 10.8 *(Continued)*

```
EDIT ---- CSCJGJ.CSC360.COPYLIB(USERDEFS) - 01.03 ----------- COLUMNS 001 072
COMMAND ===>                                                  SCROLL ===> PAGE
****** ***************************** TOP OF DATA ******************************
       CONFIGURATION SECTION.
       SPECIAL-NAMES.
           CLASS  IS-SPACE-OR-NULL        SPACE            X'00'
           CLASS  IS-NUMBER-OR-HYPHEN     '0' THRU '9'     '-'
           CLASS  IS-LETTER-OR-SPACE      'A' THRU 'Z'     SPACE
           CLASS  IS-LETTER-ONLY          'A' THRU 'Z'
           CLASS  IS-LETTER-OR-NUMBER     'A' THRU 'Z'
                                          SPACE
                                          '0' THRU '9'.
```

Code only *one* period, after the last CLASS definition.

Figure 10.9 Copybook member USERDEFS, containing several user-defined data classes used in the C360B001 program.

Figure 10.9 shows you what comes into the program from member USERDEFS. It is similar to this coding, which represents a subset of it:

```
CONFIGURATION SECTION.
SPECIAL-NAMES.
    CLASS IS-SPACE-OR-NULL       SPACE            X'00'
    CLASS IS-LETTER-OR-NUMBER    'A' THRU 'Z'
                                 SPACE
                                 '0' THRU '9'.
```

Each **user-defined data class** creates a logical name that tests as "true" if the field it is applied to contains only the characters in the data class. Let's see how these two data classes make it easy to validate the contents of the house number and street field.

Our client's instructions are that the house number and street field must contain only numbers, letters, and spaces—no punctuation. In addition, the field can't be *all* spaces, that is, blank. We use the two data classes shown above to test the CRE-HOUSE-NUM-STREET-D field. The combination of tests shown here, extracted from lines 24100 through 25600 of the C360B001 program, identifies the house number and street field to be invalid if it is missing or contains any type of punctuation:

```
SET THIS-FIELD-GOOD TO TRUE.
EVALUATE TRUE
   WHEN  CRE-HOUSE-NUM-STREET-D IS-SPACE-OR-NULL
      SET THIS-FIELD-BAD TO TRUE
   WHEN  CRE-HOUSE-NUM-STREET-D IS-LETTER-OR-NUMBER
      CONTINUE
   WHEN OTHER
      SET THIS-FIELD-BAD TO TRUE
END-EVALUATE.

IF THIS-FIELD-BAD
   (actions here to brighten error message for field) . . .
```

The data class IS-SPACE-OR-NULL contains the two characters SPACE and LOW-VALUES. When we code the following WHEN clause, COBOL automatically compares each character in CRE-HOUSE-NUM-STREET-D to SPACE and LOW-VALUES:

```
WHEN  CRE-HOUSE-NUM-STREET-D  IS-SPACE-OR-NULL
```

If *every* character in CRE-HOUSE-NUM-STREET is space or low-values, the WHEN clause is satisfied—the condition is true. This means that the field fails our validation; it is "blank." We set the Boolean flag value THIS-FIELD-BAD to logical "true," indicating that the field has an error, and control passes to the sentence after the **explicit scope delimiter** END-EVALUATE. If this WHEN is not satisfied, the EVALUATE continues with the next WHEN test. (We'll explain more about Boolean flags in Section 10.6.) **END-EVALUATE**, as an explicit scope delimiter, has the potential to end the range of the EVALUATE verb even without a period after it. It is one of several features added to COBOL by VS COBOL II.

The second WHEN in the coding here employs the data class IS-LETTER-OR-NUMBER to validate this house number and street field. Here, each byte of the field is compared to the set of upper case letters and numerals 0 through 9, and space. We only reach this test if the field is not entirely blank. If this WHEN is satisfied (the data class name test returns "true"), the CONTINUE sends control to the sentence after the scope delimiter **END-EVALUATE**. In this case, the Boolean value THIS-FIELD-GOOD remains true (and its opposite, THIS-FIELD-BAD, remains false) so the field is judged to contain valid data.

You can create whatever user-defined data classes you need to meet your client's specific **data validation** requirements. If you name your custom-created user-defined data classes with the pattern shown here, involving the word "IS-," each data validation reads almost as a plain sentence.

Each user-defined data class can contain a collection of single characters only. You make up your own user-defined data classes to suit requirements, to supplement predefined data classes such as NUMERIC and ALPHABETIC. We suggest coding your user-defined data classes externally, as we did here, and adding to them as new data validation requirements become known. Every program can receive the benefit of a standard set of user-defined data classes, if you document the existence and content of a standard copybook member like USERDEFS.

Review Figure 10.9 carefully to save yourself a potential problem with data class coding, however. Notice that all class definitions are part of *one sentence*, and you code a period only after the last definition. While the word CLASS is repeated for each class, you *cannot* put a period at the end of each class definition.

You can find detailed information and executable program examples showing more about user-defined data classes, the EVALUATE verb, SET for 88-level condition names, and the many other features of VS COBOL II in *VS COBOL II Highlights and Techniques* by James Janossy, published in 1992 by John Wiley & Sons, Inc.

10.6 BOOLEAN FLAG FIELDS

At letter "b" in Figure 10.8, you see two **Boolean true/false fields** defined as permitted by 1985 COBOL. We have omitted coding a data name for each of these fields, since we can now logically **SET** the true/false value of each without referring to a field name.

NO-FIELD-ERRORS is true if the one-byte field defined at line 3400 contains 'N'. This value is false, and FIELD-ERROR is true, if the field contains 'F'. We could have used any other values here, so long as we initialized the field to have NO-FIELD-ERRORS be true.

THIS-FIELD-GOOD is true if THIS-FIELD-BAD is false, and vice versa, so long as the values 'G' and 'B' are properly SET into the field defined at line 3800. We did not bother to code an initial value setting this flag one way or the other, since each field validation must reinitialize this flag anyway.

You might have seen 88-level condition names used in older COBOL programs, since 88-levels have been a part of COBOL for many years. The **SET** capability, however, is new with VS COBOL II and frees us from having to actually MOVE some specific value to a field to make a given 88-level name "true." Look at line 19200 of the C360B001 program, and you will see the SET verb used like this:

```
SET FIELD-ERROR TO TRUE.
```

SET automatically figures out what value is needed in the field coded above FIELD-ERROR to make FIELD-ERROR true, and moves that value to the field for us. We make great use of this reliability-boosting feature in the modern CICS programs in this book.

10.7 USING COPY FOR STANDARD CODE ELEMENTS

At letter "c" in Figure 10.8, you see several COPY statements, each naming a different item. COPY is a compiler directive, not a COBOL language verb. It directs the VS COBOL II compiler to access the item mentioned, obtaining it from the library named at the compiler's //SYSLIB DD statement, and to bring that item into the source code. The compiler does this prior to beginning compilation of the program.

We have used COPY at letter "c" to bring in these four items:

CREDSCR1	The symbolic map
ABRTMSGS	Standard abort messages used by the 9999-ABORT paragraph
KEYDEFS	Standard 88-level names for each of the AID key values that the EIBAID field might assume (This provides more convenient coding than IBM's member DFHAID, listed in Appendix A)
ATTDEFS	Standard fields carrying attribute byte values to be used in making screen fields dark or visible (This provides more convenient coding than IBM's member DFHBMSCA, listed in Appendix A)

You see a variation in 01 level coding with these items. CREDSCR1 and ABRTMSGS are self-contained in that each has an 01 level coded within it. KEYDEFS is a list of 88-level names only, and so requires an 01 level to be provided above it. ATTDEFS is a collection of fields that require an 01 level to be provided above them. COPY accommodates these variations in coding, and brings in whole lines of whatever code you put into each copy item. (Don't, however, put CICS commands into copy members, because copy members don't come into your program until *after* it has been processed by the CICS translator.)

You have already seen the coded symbolic map in Figure 10.7. A symbolic map is usually specific to one or a few programs. We placed our symbolic map for the credit card screen into a member named CREDSCR1 in CSCJGJ.CSC360.COPYLIB. The other items copied in at lines 4900, 5200, and 5500 apply to most CICS programs you will write. Figures 10.10, 10.11, and 10.12 list the code contained in the ABRTMSGS, KEYDEFS, and ATTDEFS mem-

```
EDIT ---- CSCJGJ.CSC360.COPYLIB(ABRTMSGS) - 01.01 ----------- COLUMNS 001 072
COMMAND ===>                                                  SCROLL ===> PAGE
****** ***************************** TOP OF DATA ******************************
       *-----------------------------------------------------------------
       *  ERRMSGS
       *  STANDARD CICS ERROR MESSAGES
       *  MATCHES ABRTCODE COPYBOOK MEMBER
       *-----------------------------------------------------------------
        01  WS-ERROR-MESSAGES.

            05 PIC X(35) VALUE '** CICS ERROR -- CONTACT HELP DESK '.
            05 PIC X(35) VALUE '-- REPORT THIS INFORMATION **      '.
            05 PIC X(9)  VALUE SPACES.

            05 WS-ERROR-LINE1.
               10              PIC X(14)     VALUE '    EIBTRNID = '.
               10 WS-EIBTRNID  PIC X(4).
               10              PIC X(61)     VALUE SPACES.

            05 WS-ERROR-LINE2.
               10              PIC X(14)     VALUE '    EIBRSRCE = '.
               10 WS-EIBRSRCE  PIC X(8).
               10              PIC X(57)     VALUE SPACES.

            05 WS-ERROR-LINE3.
               10              PIC X(14)     VALUE '    EIBRESP  = '.
               10 WS-EIBRESP   PIC ZZZZZZZ9.
               10              PIC X(57)     VALUE SPACES.

            05 WS-ERROR-LINE4.
               10              PIC X(14)     VALUE '    EIBRESP2 = '.
               10 WS-EIBRESP2  PIC ZZZZZZZ9.
               10              PIC X(57)     VALUE SPACES.

            05 WS-ERROR-LINE5  PIC X(79)     VALUE SPACES.

            05 PIC X(79) VALUE ALL '*'.
```

Figure 10.10 Copybook member ABRTMSGS, messages used by the 9999-ABORT paragraph.

bers. The general term for items of code such as this is **copybook** or **copy library member**. Figure 10.13 shows you the member list (directory) of the copy library we established to house these and other copybook members.

10.8 LINKAGE RECORDS FOR SUBPROGRAM USAGE

Letter "d" calls your attention to three additional COPY statements in the C360B001 program, at which these items are brought into the source code:

DATELINK	Fields used to communicate with the DATECHEK **date validation** subprogram
NUMLINK	Fields used to communicate with the NUMCHEK **numeric field de-editing** subprogram
PLACLINK	Fields used to communicate with the PLACCHEK subprogram, which looks up a two-character state abbreviation to see if it is valid

The actual code for these copybook members is listed in Figures 10.14, 10.15, and 10.16. We house these linkage records as freestanding descriptions, because the subprograms they communicate with are general-purpose modules that are of use in a variety of situations. By placing

```
EDIT ---- CSCJGJ.CSC360.COPYLIB(KEYDEFS) - 01.01 ------------ COLUMNS 001 072
COMMAND ===>                                                  SCROLL ===> PAGE
****** ***************************** TOP OF DATA ******************************
       *------------------------------------------------------------------
       *  KEYDEFS
       *  88-LEVEL CONDITION NAMES FOR AID KEYS
       *  NOTE: X'00' IS LOW-VALUES AND X'7D' IS AN APOSTROPHE
       *  AS CODED IN VS COBOL II USING HEXADECIMAL LITERALS
       *------------------------------------------------------------------
            88 NULL-BYTE          VALUE X'00'.
            88 ENTER-KEY          VALUE X'7D'.
            88 CLEAR-KEY          VALUE '_'.
            88 CLRP-KEY           VALUE '¦'.
            88 PEN-KEY            VALUE '='.
            88 OPID-KEY           VALUE 'W'.
            88 MSRE-KEY           VALUE 'X'.
            88 STRF-KEY           VALUE 'h'.
            88 TRIG-KEY           VALUE '"'.
            88 PA1-KEY            VALUE '%'.
            88 PA2-KEY            VALUE '>'.
            88 PA3-KEY            VALUE ','.
            88 PF1-KEY            VALUE '1'.
            88 PF2-KEY            VALUE '2'.
            88 PF3-KEY            VALUE '3'.
            88 PF4-KEY            VALUE '4'.
            88 PF5-KEY            VALUE '5'.
            88 PF6-KEY            VALUE '6'.
            88 PF7-KEY            VALUE '7'.
            88 PF8-KEY            VALUE '8'.
            88 PF9-KEY            VALUE '9'.
            88 PF10-KEY           VALUE ':'.
            88 PF11-KEY           VALUE '#'.
            88 PF12-KEY           VALUE '@'.
            88 PF13-KEY           VALUE 'A'.
            88 PF14-KEY           VALUE 'B'.
            88 PF15-KEY           VALUE 'C'.
            88 PF16-KEY           VALUE 'D'.
            88 PF17-KEY           VALUE 'E'.
            88 PF18-KEY           VALUE 'F'.
            88 PF19-KEY           VALUE 'G'.
            88 PF20-KEY           VALUE 'H'.
            88 PF21-KEY           VALUE 'I'.
            88 PF22-KEY           VALUE '\'.
            88 PF23-KEY           VALUE '.'.
            88 PF24-KEY           VALUE '<'.
```

Figure 10.11 Copybook member KEYDEFS, 88-level condition names you can use to identify the PF key indicated by the EIBAID field.

these linkage records outside of any specific program, both the subprograms and any program using them can access the identical descriptions of the memory to be shared for communication purposes. You'll see how these shared memory areas are used to pass data to subprograms in the 5000-VALIDATE-FIELDS paragraph.

10.9 PROGRAM LOGIC AND FIELD VALIDATIONS

Beginning at the Procedure Division of the C360B001 program, marked by the letter "e" at line 7200 in Figure 10.8, you see standard structured logic for a pseudoconversational program. The mainline is identical to that in our structured CALC1 program of Chapter 8, Figure 8.2, and so is much of the remainder of the program.

The key to understanding how C360B001 works lies in understanding how the 5000-VALIDATE-FIELDS paragraph operates. It is in this paragraph that field contents are checked,

```
EDIT ---- CSCJGJ.CSC360.COPYLIB(ATTDEFS) - 01.01 ------------ COLUMNS 001 072
COMMAND ===>                                                  SCROLL ===> PAGE
****** ***************************** TOP OF DATA ******************************
       *-----------------------------------------------------------------
       *  ATTDEFS
       *  ATTRIBUTE CONTROL VALUES TO MOVE TO SYMBOLIC MAP -A FIELD
       *-----------------------------------------------------------------
            05 UNPROT-NORM               PIC X(1)  VALUE SPACE.
            05 UNPROT-NORM-MDT           PIC X(1)  VALUE 'A'.
            05 UNPROT-BRT                PIC X(1)  VALUE 'H'.
            05 UNPROT-BRT-MDT            PIC X(1)  VALUE 'I'.
            05 UNPROT-DARK               PIC X(1)  VALUE '<'.
            05 UNPROT-DARK-MDT           PIC X(1)  VALUE '('.
            05 UNPROT-NUM                PIC X(1)  VALUE '&'.
            05 UNPROT-NUM-MDT            PIC X(1)  VALUE 'J'.
            05 UNPROT-NUM-BRT            PIC X(1)  VALUE 'Q'.
            05 UNPROT-NUM-BRT-MDT        PIC X(1)  VALUE 'R'.
            05 UNPROT-NUM-DARK           PIC X(1)  VALUE '*'.
            05 UNPROT-NUM-DARK-MDT       PIC X(1)  VALUE ')'.
            05 PROT-NORM                 PIC X(1)  VALUE '-'.
            05 PROT-NORM-MDT             PIC X(1)  VALUE '/'.
            05 PROT-BRT                  PIC X(1)  VALUE 'Y'.
            05 PROT-BRT-MDT              PIC X(1)  VALUE 'Z'.
            05 PROT-DARK                 PIC X(1)  VALUE '%'.
            05 PROT-DARK-MDT             PIC X(1)  VALUE '.'.
            05 PROT-SKIP-NORM            PIC X(1)  VALUE '0'.
            05 PROT-SKIP-NORM-MDT        PIC X(1)  VALUE '1'.
            05 PROT-SKIP-BRT             PIC X(1)  VALUE '8'.
            05 PROT-SKIP-BRT-MDT         PIC X(1)  VALUE '9'.
            05 PROT-SKIP-DARK            PIC X(1)  VALUE '@'.
            05 PROT-SKIP-DARK-MDT        PIC X(1)  VALUE QUOTE.
```

Figure 10.12 Copybook member ATTDEFS, data fields containing the control values to control attribute bytes.

```
EDIT --- CSCJGJ.CSC360.COPYLIB ---------------------------- ROW 00001 OF 00011
COMMAND ===>                                                   SCROLL ===> PAGE
   NAME              VV.MM  CREATED      CHANGED          SIZE  INIT   MOD   ID
  B001S
  B002S
  ABRTCODE           01.00 94/09/30 94/09/30 19:58         20    20      0 CSCJGJ
  ABRTMSGS           01.01 94/09/30 94/09/30 23:15         32    32      0 CSCJGJ
  ATTDEFS            01.01 94/09/30 94/09/30 23:16         28    28      1 CSCJGJ
  CREDSCR1           01.03 94/09/30 94/10/01 10:36        130   126      7 CSCJGJ
  DATELINK           01.01 94/09/30 94/09/30 23:13         15    15      1 CSCJGJ
  KEYDEFS            01.01 94/09/30 94/09/30 23:15         42    42      0 CSCJGJ
  NUMLINK            01.00 94/09/30 94/09/30 20:15         12    12      0 CSCJGJ
  PLACLINK           01.01 94/09/30 94/09/30 23:13         10    10      1 CSCJGJ
  USERDEFS           01.03 94/09/30 94/10/01 17:24          9     9      9 CSCJGJ
  **END**
```

Figure 10.13 Typical member list for a library housing copybook members.

```
EDIT ---- CSCJGJ.CSC360.COPYLIB(NUMLINK) - 01.00 ------------ COLUMNS 001 072
COMMAND ===>                                                  SCROLL ===> PAGE
****** ***************************** TOP OF DATA ******************************
       *------------------------------------------------------------------
       *  NUMLINK
       *  LINKAGE RECORD FOR NUMCHEK DE-EDITING SUBPROGRAM
       *------------------------------------------------------------------
           05 NUM-INPUT                   PIC X(22).
           05 NUM-RIGHT-OF-DECIMAL        PIC 9(1).
           05 NUM-STATUS-FLAG             PIC X(1).
              88 NUM-CONVERSION-OK                    VALUE '0'.
              88 NUM-RIGHT-OF-DECIMAL-NOT-0-6         VALUE '1'.
              88 NUM-HAS-EXTRA-ALPHA-SYMBOLS          VALUE '2'.
              88 NUM-DECIMAL-PT-OUT-OF-PLACE          VALUE '3'.
           05 NUM-OUTPUT                  PIC 9(11)V9(6).
```

Figure 10.14 Copybook member NUMLINK, describing the memory to be shared by a program and the NUMCHEK field de-editing subprogram.

```
EDIT ---- CSCJGJ.CSC360.COPYLIB(PLACLINK) - 01.01 ----------- COLUMNS 001 072
COMMAND ===>                                                  SCROLL ===> PAGE
****** ***************************** TOP OF DATA ******************************
       *------------------------------------------------------------------
       *  PLACLINK
       *  LINKAGE RECORD FOR PLACE NAME SUBPROGRAM
       *------------------------------------------------------------------
           05 PLC-PLACE-ABBREV            PIC X(2).
           05 PLC-COUNTRY                 PIC X(3).
           05 PLC-PLACE-NAME              PIC X(20).
           05 PLC-STATUS-FLAG             PIC X(1).
              88 PLC-ABBREV-OK                        VALUE '0'.
              88 PLC-ABBREV-INVALID                   VALUE '1'.
```

Figure 10.15 Copybook member PLACLINK, describing the memory to be shared by a program and the PLACCHEK subprogram.

```
EDIT ---- CSCJGJ.CSC360.COPYLIB(DATELINK) - 01.01 ----------- COLUMNS 001 072
COMMAND ===>                                                  SCROLL ===> PAGE
****** ***************************** TOP OF DATA ******************************
       *------------------------------------------------------------------
       *  DATELINK
       *  LINKAGE RECORD FOR DATECHEK VALIDATION/FORMATTER
       *------------------------------------------------------------------
           05 DATE-INPUT.
              10 DATE-INPUT-MO            PIC X(2).
              10 DATE-INPUT-DA            PIC X(2).
              10 DATE-INPUT-YR            PIC X(2).
           05 DATE-STATUS-FLAG            PIC X(1).
              88 DATE-OK                              VALUE '0'.
              88 DATE-NOT-NUMERIC                     VALUE '1'.
              88 DATE-MO-NOT-1-THRU-12                VALUE '2'.
              88 DATE-DA-TOO-BIG-FOR-MO               VALUE '3'.
           05 DATE-IN-JULIAN              PIC 9(5).
           05 DATE-AND-DAY-IN-WORDS       PIC X(29).
```

Figure 10.16 Copybook member DATELINK, describing the memory to be shared by a program and the DATECHEK subprogram.

field by field, beginning with the last field on the screen and moving upward. Move ahead to letter "f" in the program listing in Figure 10.8 to see what this paragraph does.

10.10 THE VALIDATION SEQUENCE

The validation sequence accomplished in the 5000-VALIDATE-FIELDS begins by reinitializing the attribute bytes of all of the error messages fields to hide the messages. We'll assume that all entry fields now have valid contents. Each field content test has the potential to turn its corresponding error message back on, and to set the FIELD-ERRORS Boolean value "true."

Review the CALC1 program, at lines 23300 and 24100 in Figure 8.2. Compare that coding to the logic in C360B001 for a validation, such as lines 19000 through 19200. You will see that in C360B001 we don't ever change the settings of the attribute bytes for the input fields. In CALC1, we made a field that contained invalid data brighten by moving an appropriate value to the attribute byte of that entry field. But here, in C360B001, we use the method of making a specific error message for a field visible, if a content error is detected in the field. This means that we don't have to reset the intensity of the entry fields to "normal" before beginning the validation sequence.

We validate data fields one by one, starting with the last field on the screen, ANNUAL INCOME. Strictly speaking, this order is not really necessary when using separately placed, pre-sent error messages to communicate errors to the terminal operator. We use it here since it is standard in validating fields when only one error message at a time can be presented using a prompt line. In such a case, this order leaves the error message for the topmost field error in the prompt line, since the topmost field in error is where we position the cursor. When each field has its own error message, the order of field validation is not of concern.

Many field validations in program C360B001 involve the use of EVALUATE or IF, and one or more user defined data classes. Some of the validations, however, involve the use of a CALL to a subprogram to accomplish a particular involved check of field contents, or, as in the case of the ANNUAL INCOME field, numeric de-editing. We'll discuss each subprogram validation in detail. After reading the discussion of user-defined data classes earlier in this chapter, the non-subprogram data validations in the 5000-VALIDATE-FIELDS paragraph should be understandable to you.

The validation actions we take at letter "i" may need a bit of explanation:

```
IF CRE-APARTMENT-NUM-D  IS-SPACE-OR-NULL
  MOVE SPACES TO CRE-APARTMENT-NUM-D.
```

Why move spaces to a field that already has spaces or **null (LOW-VALUES)** in it? We take this action simply to make sure we have a space, rather than a null character, in this field. The test could have been coded without the use of a data class, as:

```
IF CRE-APARTMENT-NUM-D = LOW-VALUES
  MOVE SPACES TO CRE-APARTMENT-NUM-D.
```

Nulls would remain in this field if the user did not enter anything into it. If the field is intended to be a space, we would prefer to have a space there, representing a blank, rather than LOW-VALUES.

The conclusion of the validation sequence occurs back in the 0500-NORMAL-PROCESSING paragraph, immediately after it invokes 5000-VALIDATE-FIELDS. Lines 10200 through 10600 either perform a finish-the-screen action or brighten the special error message prompt, based on whether or not any field errors exist. For either outcome, the next action taken is to send the screen back to the terminal, and end the pseudoconverse.

10.11 HOW THE NUMCHEK DE-EDITING SUBPROGRAM WORKS

The NUMCHEK de-editing subprogram is invoked at letter "g" in C360B001. Its complete source code is listed in Figure 10.17. As with each of the other subprograms used in our data validation sequence, using NUMCHEK requires three distinct actions:

```
EDIT ---- CSCJGJ.CSC360.COBOL(NUMCHEK) - 01.03 -------------- COLUMNS 007 078
COMMAND ===>                                                 SCROLL ===> PAGE
****** ****************************** TOP OF DATA ******************************
 ID DIVISION.
 PROGRAM-ID. NUMCHEK.
 AUTHOR.      J JANOSSY.
*-------------------------------------------------------------------
*     THIS SUBPROGRAM ACCEPTS A PIC X(22) FIELD NAMED NUM-INPUT
*     AND A VALUE FOR THE INTENDED NUMBER OF DIGITS RIGHT OF A
*     DECIMAL POINT. IT ACCEPTS ANY CUSTOMARY RENDITION OF THE
*     INPUT AS A CHARACTER STRING AND PROVIDES THE NUMERIC FORM
*     OF THE INPUT IN A PIC 9(11)V9(6) FIELD NAMED NUM-OUTPUT.
*     THE FOLLOWING CODES RESULT AT NUM-STATUS-FLAG:
*
*          0     INPUT VALID, TRANSFORMED TO PIC 9(11)V9(6)
*          1     CALLING PROGRAM DID NOT SPECIFY
*                   NUM-RIGHT-OF-DECIMAL IN THE RANGE 0 - 6
*          2     INPUT CONTAINED ALPHANUMERIC SYMBOLS OTHER
*                   THAN ONE $, COMMAS, ONE PERIOD SERVING
*                   AS A DECIMAL POINT
*          3     INPUT VALUE HAS FEWER OR MORE DIGITS RIGHT
*                   OF THE EXPLICIT DECIMAL POINT THAN THE
*                   CALLING PROGRAM STATED IN NUM-RIGHT-OF-
*                   DECIMAL.  INPUT NEED NOT CARRY AN EXPLICIT
*                   DECIMAL POINT BUT IF IT DOES IT MUST
*                   AGREE IN POSITIONING WITH THE VALUE IN
*                   NUM-RIGHT-OF-DECIMAL.
*-------------------------------------------------------------------

 DATA DIVISION.
 WORKING-STORAGE SECTION.
 01  W1-AREA.
     05 W1-BYTE   OCCURS 22 TIMES   PIC X(1).

 01  W2-AREA.
     05 W2-BYTE   OCCURS 22 TIMES   PIC X(1).

 01  W1-SUB                         PIC S9(4) BINARY.
 01  W2-SUB                         PIC S9(4) BINARY.
 01  W3-SUB                         PIC S9(4) BINARY.
 01  WS-DOLLAR-SIGNS-COUNTED        PIC S9(4) BINARY.
 01  WS-DEC-POINTS-COUNTED          PIC S9(4) BINARY.
 01  WS-COMPUTED-DEC-PLACES         PIC S9(4) BINARY.

 01  WS-ALMOST-DONE-X               PIC X(17)  JUSTIFIED RIGHT.
 01  WS-ALMOST-DONE-9  REDEFINES
     WS-ALMOST-DONE-X               PIC 9(17).

 LINKAGE SECTION.
 01  NUMCHEK-LINKAGE-RECORD.  COPY NUMLINK.
```

Figure 10.17 Source code for the NUMCHEK subprogram.

```

 PROCEDURE DIVISION USING NUMCHEK-LINKAGE-RECORD.
 0000-MAINLINE.
     MOVE 'X'         TO NUM-STATUS-FLAG.
     MOVE ZEROS       TO NUM-OUTPUT.
     MOVE NUM-INPUT   TO W1-AREA.

     EVALUATE TRUE
        WHEN NUM-RIGHT-OF-DECIMAL  NOT NUMERIC
           MOVE '1' TO NUM-STATUS-FLAG
        WHEN NUM-RIGHT-OF-DECIMAL >= 0 AND <= 6
           PERFORM 1000-PROCESS
        WHEN OTHER
           MOVE '1' TO NUM-STATUS-FLAG
     END-EVALUATE.

     GOBACK.

*----------------------------------------------------------------
*  REPLACE FIRST $ WITH A SPACE, ALL COMMAS WITH SPACES:
*----------------------------------------------------------------
 1000-PROCESS.
     MOVE +0 TO WS-DOLLAR-SIGNS-COUNTED.
     PERFORM 2100-DOLLAR-SIGN-DELETE
        VARYING W1-SUB FROM +1 BY +1
           UNTIL W1-SUB > +22
              OR WS-DOLLAR-SIGNS-COUNTED = +1.

     PERFORM 2200-COMMA-REPLACE
        VARYING W1-SUB FROM +1 BY +1
           UNTIL W1-SUB > +22.

*----------------------------------------------------------------
*  MOVE W1-AREA TO W2-AREA BYTE-BY-BYTE FROM RIGHT TO LEFT,
*  ELIMINATING IMBEDDED SPACES AND PROVIDING LEADING ZEROS:
*----------------------------------------------------------------
     MOVE +23       TO W2-SUB.
     MOVE ZEROS     TO W2-AREA.
     PERFORM 2300-SQUISH-RIGHT
        VARYING W1-SUB FROM +22 BY -1
           UNTIL W1-SUB < +1.

*----------------------------------------------------------------
*  FIND EXPLICIT DECIMAL POINT(S) IF PRESENT, MAKE W3-SUB
*  HOLD THE POSITION FROM RIGHT OF THE FIRST DECIMAL POINT:
*----------------------------------------------------------------
     MOVE +0 TO WS-DEC-POINTS-COUNTED.
     PERFORM 2400-DEC-POINT-SCAN-FROM-RT
        VARYING W2-SUB FROM +22 BY -1
           UNTIL W2-SUB < +1.

     IF WS-DEC-POINTS-COUNTED = +0
        PERFORM 1120-CONCLUSION
      ELSE
     IF WS-DEC-POINTS-COUNTED = +1
        PERFORM 1100-EXPLICIT-DECIMAL-WORK
      ELSE
        MOVE '2' TO NUM-STATUS-FLAG.
```

Figure 10.17 *(Continued)*

1. Putting values it needs for operation into the linkage record to be shared with it. The COBOL description of the NUMCHEK-LINKAGE-RECORD is shown in Figure 10.14.
2. Passing control to the subprogram by CALLing it appropriately, sharing the linkage record with it.
3. Determining what the subprogram indicates about the validity of the field contents it was given to check.

```
      *---------------------------------------------------------------
       1100-EXPLICIT-DECIMAL-WORK.
           COMPUTE WS-COMPUTED-DEC-PLACES = 22 - W3-SUB.
           IF WS-COMPUTED-DEC-PLACES = NUM-RIGHT-OF-DECIMAL
              PERFORM 1110-ELIMINATE-DECIMAL
              PERFORM 1120-CONCLUSION
            ELSE
              MOVE '3'  TO NUM-STATUS-FLAG.

       1110-ELIMINATE-DECIMAL.
           MOVE ' '        TO W2-BYTE(W3-SUB).
           MOVE W2-AREA   TO W1-AREA.
           MOVE ZEROS     TO W2-AREA.
           MOVE +23 TO W2-SUB.
           PERFORM 2300-SQUISH-RIGHT
              VARYING W1-SUB FROM +22 BY -1
                 UNTIL W1-SUB < +1.

       1120-CONCLUSION.
           IF W2-AREA IS NUMERIC
              PERFORM 1130-FINAL-MOVE
              MOVE '0' TO NUM-STATUS-FLAG
            ELSE
              MOVE '2' TO NUM-STATUS-FLAG.

       1130-FINAL-MOVE.
           MOVE W2-AREA TO WS-ALMOST-DONE-X.
           IF NUM-RIGHT-OF-DECIMAL = 0
              MOVE WS-ALMOST-DONE-9 TO NUM-OUTPUT
            ELSE
              COMPUTE NUM-OUTPUT =
                 WS-ALMOST-DONE-9 / ( 10.000 ** NUM-RIGHT-OF-DECIMAL ).

      *---------------------------------------------------------------
      *  PERFORMED CHARACTER STRING ROUTINES (USED INSTEAD OF THE
      *  INSPECT VERB SO THIS ROUTINE ALSO WORKS WITH OLDER CICS):
      *---------------------------------------------------------------
       2100-DOLLAR-SIGN-DELETE.
           IF W1-BYTE(W1-SUB) = '$'
              MOVE ' ' TO W1-BYTE(W1-SUB)
              ADD +1 TO WS-DOLLAR-SIGNS-COUNTED.

       2200-COMMA-REPLACE.
           IF W1-BYTE(W1-SUB) = ','
              MOVE ' ' TO W1-BYTE(W1-SUB).

       2300-SQUISH-RIGHT.
           IF W1-BYTE(W1-SUB) NOT = ' '
              SUBTRACT +1 FROM W2-SUB
              MOVE W1-BYTE(W1-SUB) TO W2-BYTE(W2-SUB).

       2400-DEC-POINT-SCAN-FROM-RT.
           IF W2-BYTE(W2-SUB) = '.'
              ADD +1 TO WS-DEC-POINTS-COUNTED
              IF WS-DEC-POINTS-COUNTED = +1
                 MOVE W2-SUB TO W3-SUB.
```

Figure 10.17 *(Continued)*

NUMCHEK requires two inputs to do its work. The field to be de-edited and validated is given to it as NUM-INPUT in the NUMCHEK-LINKAGE-RECORD. (As a general term, **linkage record** means a group of fields collected into a record to ease coding of a CALL to a subprogram. In older IBM terminology you might refer to this as a "control block.") But we also must tell NUMCHEK how many digits are intended to the right of a decimal point in the number to be output. For NUMCHEK, this can be as little as 0 or as great as 6. NUMCHEK uses this value, named NUM-RIGHT-OF-DECIMAL, in this way:

- If the entered value contains an explicit decimal point (period), NUMCHEK sees the number as invalid if there are not NUM-RIGHT-OF-DECIMAL digits to the right of it. That is, if NUM-RIGHT-OF-DECIMAL is 2, the entry $1,234.56 is valid, but the entry $1,234.5 would not be. If the explicit decimal point is in the intended position, the number finally developed is aligned in the numeric output field, NUM-OUTPUT, with this position at the implied decimal point.
- If the entered value does not contain an explicit decimal point, such as $22,500, NUMCHEK will put a decimal point into the output value at the location specified by NUM-RIGHT-OF-DECIMAL. That is, $22,500 is aligned in the NUM-OUT with an implied decimal between the 5 and 0, producing an interpreted value of 225.00. This is why the ANNUAL INCOME in Figure 10.4 is interpreted as shown.

NUMCHEK is actually a de-editing routine that accepts a character string of up to 22 bytes in length, and weeds out symbols such as spaces, dollar signs, commas, and a period (decimal point). It judges whether the input given to it can be turned into a numeric value based on rules about how many of these symbols it found in the string. If the string can be interpreted as a number, NUMCHEK provides the value in a numeric field named NUM-OUT. If NUMCHEK cannot interpret the input and form a number in NUM-OUT, it leaves zeros in the NUM-OUT field. NUM-OUT has a PIC 9(11)V9(6), which is adequate in terms of capacity and precision for its purposes. When the number returned in NUM-OUT is MOVEd to a field of lesser size on either side of the decimal point, excess digits are dropped.

NUMCHEK is easy to use for numeric input validation because, as any subprogram should do, it also provides a convenient **status flag** indicating the outcome of the CALL. NUM-STATUS-FLAG will contain '0' if NUMCHEK was able to interpret the field given to it and form a number from it. NUM-STATUS-FLAG will contain a non-zero value if NUMCHEK could not interpret its input as a number. As you can see in Figure 10.14, the linkage record description contains 88-level condition names on the NUM-STATUS-FLAG field. The condition names document the meaning of the non-zero flag values that indicate *why* an input was judged invalid.

You say you don't care for the way NUMCHEK works? That's fine. You're perfectly free to "roll your own" numeric de-editing subprogram! In fact, creating or acquiring a numeric de-editing routine such as NUMCHEK is something each installation has to do on its own, because CICS is not endowed with any capable de-editing routine. On the other hand, if you find NUMCHEK satisfactory, you now have a de-editing routine you can put to good use.

10.12 HOW THE PLACCHEK SUBPROGRAM WORKS

The PLACCHEK subprogram is invoked at letter "h" in C360B001, at lines 20400 through 21000. You can see the linkage record used to provide its input and receive its output in Figure 10.15, and the complete source code for the subprogram in Figure 10.18.

As you can see in Figure 10.18, most of PLACCHEK coding is a table of U.S. state and Canadian province postal abbreviations. Its procedural logic consists of a binary search of this table. While PLACCHEK returns the identity of the country (USA or CAN) and the spelled-out place name matching an abbreviation, such as "BRITISH COLUMBIA," we make no use of that information in C360B001. We simply check the PLC-STATUS-FLAG to see if it re-

```
EDIT ---- CSCJGJ.CSC360.COBOL(PLACCHEK) - 01.01 ------------- COLUMNS 007 078
COMMAND ===>                                                  SCROLL ===> PAGE
****** ****************************** TOP OF DATA ******************************
ID DIVISION.
PROGRAM-ID. PLACCHEK.
AUTHOR.     J JANOSSY.

*------------------------------------------------------------------
*    IF YOU CALL THIS SUBPROGRAM WITH A PIC X(2) FIELD IT LOOKS
*    UP THE CONTENTS AND RETURNS THE COUNTY AS PIC X(3), STATE
*    OR PROVINCE NAME AS PIC X(20), AND PLC-STATUS-FLAG AS '0'
*    FOR VALID CODE OR '1' FOR INVALID CODE.
*------------------------------------------------------------------

DATA DIVISION.
WORKING-STORAGE SECTION.
01  PLACE-TABLE-SETUP.
    05 PIC X(27)  VALUE 'AB CAN ALBERTA             '.
    05 PIC X(27)  VALUE 'AK USA ALASKA              '.
    05 PIC X(27)  VALUE 'AL USA ALABAMA             '.
    05 PIC X(27)  VALUE 'AR USA ARKANSAS            '.
    05 PIC X(27)  VALUE 'AZ USA ARIZONA             '.
    05 PIC X(27)  VALUE 'BC CAN BRITISH COLUMBIA    '.
    05 PIC X(27)  VALUE 'CA USA CALIFORNIA          '.
    05 PIC X(27)  VALUE 'CN USA CONNECTICUT         '.
    05 PIC X(27)  VALUE 'CO USA COLORADO            '.
    05 PIC X(27)  VALUE 'DC USA DISTRICT OF COLUMBIA'.
    05 PIC X(27)  VALUE 'DE USA DELAWARE            '.
    05 PIC X(27)  VALUE 'FL USA FLORIDA             '.
    05 PIC X(27)  VALUE 'GA USA GEORGIA             '.
    05 PIC X(27)  VALUE 'HI USA HAWAII              '.
    05 PIC X(27)  VALUE 'IA USA IOWA                '.
    05 PIC X(27)  VALUE 'ID USA IDAHO               '.
    05 PIC X(27)  VALUE 'IL USA ILLINOIS            '.
    05 PIC X(27)  VALUE 'IN USA INDIANA             '.
    05 PIC X(27)  VALUE 'KS USA KANSAS              '.
    05 PIC X(27)  VALUE 'KY USA KENTUCKY            '.
    05 PIC X(27)  VALUE 'LA USA LOUISIANA           '.
    05 PIC X(27)  VALUE 'MA USA MASSACHUSETTS       '.
    05 PIC X(27)  VALUE 'MB CAN MANITOBA            '.
    05 PIC X(27)  VALUE 'MD USA MARYLAND            '.
    05 PIC X(27)  VALUE 'ME USA MAINE               '.
    05 PIC X(27)  VALUE 'MI USA MICHIGAN            '.
    05 PIC X(27)  VALUE 'MN USA MINNESOTA           '.
    05 PIC X(27)  VALUE 'MO USA MISSOURI            '.
    05 PIC X(27)  VALUE 'MS USA MISSISSIPPI         '.
    05 PIC X(27)  VALUE 'MT USA MONTANA             '.
    05 PIC X(27)  VALUE 'NB CAN NEW BRUNSWICK       '.
    05 PIC X(27)  VALUE 'NC USA NORTH CAROLINA      '.
    05 PIC X(27)  VALUE 'ND USA NORTH DAKOTA        '.
    05 PIC X(27)  VALUE 'NE USA NEBRASKA            '.
    05 PIC X(27)  VALUE 'NF CAN NEWFOUNDLAND        '.
    05 PIC X(27)  VALUE 'NH USA NEW HAMPSHIRE       '.
    05 PIC X(27)  VALUE 'NJ USA NEW JERSEY          '.
    05 PIC X(27)  VALUE 'NM USA NEW MEXICO          '.
    05 PIC X(27)  VALUE 'NS CAN NOVA SCOTIA         '.
    05 PIC X(27)  VALUE 'NT CAN NORTH WEST TERR.    '.
```

Figure 10.18 Source code for the PLACCHEK subprogram.

turns as "0", using the 88-level condition name PLC-ABBREV-OK. This tells us if the state abbreviation entered by the terminal operator for state of residence is valid.

We also CALL PLACCHEK at letter "j" in program C360B001, at lines 27200 through 27800. Here, PLACCHEK validates the entry made by the terminal operator for the state of birth field.

```
        05 PIC X(27)  VALUE 'NV USA NEVADA                '.
        05 PIC X(27)  VALUE 'NY USA NEW YORK              '.
        05 PIC X(27)  VALUE 'OH USA OHIO                  '.
        05 PIC X(27)  VALUE 'OK USA OKLAHOMA              '.
        05 PIC X(27)  VALUE 'ON CAN ONTARIO               '.
        05 PIC X(27)  VALUE 'OR USA OREGON                '.
        05 PIC X(27)  VALUE 'PA USA PENNSYLVANIA          '.
        05 PIC X(27)  VALUE 'PE CAN PRINCE EDWARD ISLAND'.
        05 PIC X(27)  VALUE 'PQ CAN QUEBEC                '.
        05 PIC X(27)  VALUE 'PR USA PUERTO RICO           '.
        05 PIC X(27)  VALUE 'RI USA RHODE ISLAND          '.
        05 PIC X(27)  VALUE 'SC USA SOUTH CAROLINA        '.
        05 PIC X(27)  VALUE 'SD USA SOUTH DAKOTA          '.
        05 PIC X(27)  VALUE 'SK CAN SASKATCHEWAN          '.
        05 PIC X(27)  VALUE 'TN USA TENNESSEE             '.
        05 PIC X(27)  VALUE 'TX USA TEXAS                 '.
        05 PIC X(27)  VALUE 'UT USA UTAH                  '.
        05 PIC X(27)  VALUE 'VA USA VIRGINIA              '.
        05 PIC X(27)  VALUE 'VT USA VERMONT               '.
        05 PIC X(27)  VALUE 'WA USA WASHINGTON            '.
        05 PIC X(27)  VALUE 'WI USA WISCONSIN             '.
        05 PIC X(27)  VALUE 'WV USA WEST VIRGINIA         '.
        05 PIC X(27)  VALUE 'WY USA WYOMING               '.
        05 PIC X(27)  VALUE 'YU CAN YUKON                 '.

    01  PLACE-TABLE REDEFINES PLACE-TABLE-SETUP.
        05 PLACE-TABLE-ELEMENT  OCCURS 64 TIMES
                                ASCENDING KEY IS PT-ABBREV
                                INDEXED BY PT-INDEX.
           10 PT-ABBREV                   PIC X(2).
           10                             PIC X(1).
           10 PT-COUNTRY                  PIC X(3).
           10                             PIC X(1).
           10 PT-NAME                     PIC X(20).

    LINKAGE SECTION.
    01  LS-LINKAGE-RECORD.  COPY PLACLINK.

    PROCEDURE DIVISION USING LS-LINKAGE-RECORD.
    0000-MAINLINE.
        SEARCH ALL PLACE-TABLE-ELEMENT
           AT END
              MOVE '1'                        TO  PLC-STATUS-FLAG
              MOVE ALL '*'                    TO  PLC-COUNTRY
                                                  PLC-PLACE-NAME
           WHEN PT-ABBREV(PT-INDEX) = PLC-PLACE-ABBREV
              MOVE '0'                        TO  PLC-STATUS-FLAG
              MOVE PT-COUNTRY(PT-INDEX)       TO  PLC-COUNTRY
              MOVE PT-NAME(PT-INDEX)          TO  PLC-PLACE-NAME.
        GOBACK.
```

Figure 10.18 *(Continued)*

10.13 HOW THE DATECHEK SUBPROGRAM WORKS

The DATECHEK subprogram is invoked at letter "k" in program C360B001, at lines 31200 through 32000. You can see the linkage record used to provide its input and receive its output in Figure 10.16, and the complete source code for the subprogram in Figure 10.19. DATECHEK performs sophisticated *date validation*, that is, testing to see if the date indicated by a value entered by the terminal operator did or could exist.

Our use of DATECHEK is very similar to the use we make of NUMCHEK and PLACCHEK. We provide DATECHEK with the Gregorian date entered by the operator in the DATE OF BIRTH field, and DATECHEK determines if it is valid. **Gregorian dates** take the

```
EDIT ---- CSCJGJ.CSC360.COBOL(DATECHEK) - 01.00 ------------- COLUMNS 007 078
COMMAND ===>                                                  SCROLL ===> PAGE
****** ***************************** TOP OF DATA ******************************
 ID DIVISION.
 PROGRAM-ID. DATECHEK.
 AUTHOR.     J JANOSSY.
*-----------------------------------------------------------------
*   SUBROUTINE FOR GREGORIAN (MMDDYY) DATE VALIDATION AND
*   CONVERSION TO JULIAN AND SPELLED-OUT FORM.
*
*   CENTURY '19' IS ASSUMED BUT THE ALGORITHM USED WILL
*   PROPERLY COMPUTE THE DAY OF WEEK FOR DATES FROM 1500 A.D.
*   ONWARD.  FOR VALID DATES A 29-CHARACTER FANCY DATE IS
*   PRODUCED WITH DAY OF WEEK AND MONTH SPELLED OUT:
*
*         WEDNESDAY  NOVEMBER 23, 1994
*
*   A STATUS CODE IS PASSED BACK TO THE CALLING PROGRAM
*   INDICATING THE OUTCOME OF THE CALL:
*
*         0   GREGORIAN DATE IS VALID
*         1   DATE IS NOT NUMERIC
*         2   MONTH IS NOT IN RANGE 1 THROUGH 12
*         3   DAY INVALID (00 OR NOT VALID WITHIN MONTH)
*
*-----------------------------------------------------------------

 DATA DIVISION.
 WORKING-STORAGE SECTION.
 01  WORK-FIELDS.
     05 WS-CENTURY                       PIC 9(2).
     05 WS-LEAPYR-FLAG                   PIC X(1).
     05 WS-VALUE                         PIC S9(5).
     05 WS-REMAINDER                     PIC S99.
     05 WS-COMPUTED-DAY                  PIC S9.
     05 WS-INTERMED-1                    PIC S999.
     05 WS-INTERMED-2                    PIC S999.
     05 WS-INTERMED-3                    PIC S999.

 01  MONTH-TABLE-SETUP.
     05 PIC X(21)  VALUE '   JANUARY 031 000 000'.
     05 PIC X(21)  VALUE '  FEBRUARY 029 031 031'.
     05 PIC X(21)  VALUE '     MARCH 031 059 060'.
     05 PIC X(21)  VALUE '     APRIL 030 090 091'.
     05 PIC X(21)  VALUE '       MAY 031 120 121'.
     05 PIC X(21)  VALUE '      JUNE 030 151 152'.
     05 PIC X(21)  VALUE '      JULY 031 181 182'.
     05 PIC X(21)  VALUE '    AUGUST 031 212 213'.
     05 PIC X(21)  VALUE 'SEPTEMBER 030 243 244'.
     05 PIC X(21)  VALUE '   OCTOBER 031 273 274'.
     05 PIC X(21)  VALUE '  NOVEMBER 030 304 305'.
     05 PIC X(21)  VALUE '  DECEMBER 031 334 335'.
 01  MONTH-TABLE  REDEFINES  MONTH-TABLE-SETUP.
     05 MONTH-ELEMENT   OCCURS 05 TIMES
                        INDEXED BY MONTH-INDEX.
        10 MONTH-NAME                    PIC X(10).
        10 MONTH-MAX-DAYS                PIC 9(3).
        10                               PIC X.
        10 MONTH-DAYS-BEFORE-NO-LEAP     PIC 9(3).
        10                               PIC X.
        10 MONTH-DAYS-BEFORE-LEAP        PIC 9(3).
```

This table provides month name, data to validate day, and values used to compute Julian date.

Figure 10.19 Source code for the DATECHECK subprogram.

```
01  DAY-TABLE-SETUP.
    05 PIC X(10)  VALUE 'SUNDAY    '.
    05 PIC X(10)  VALUE 'MONDAY    '.
    05 PIC X(10)  VALUE 'TUESDAY   '.
    05 PIC X(10)  VALUE 'WEDNESDAY '.
    05 PIC X(10)  VALUE 'THURSDAY  '.
    05 PIC X(10)  VALUE 'FRIDAY    '.
    05 PIC X(10)  VALUE 'SATURDAY  '.
01  DAY-TABLE  REDEFINES  DAY-TABLE-SETUP.
    05 DAY-NAME  OCCURS 7 TIMES       PIC X(10).
01  WS-DATE-X.
    05 WS-MO-X                        PIC X(2).
    05 WS-DA-X.
       10 WS-DA-X-HIGH-ORDER          PIC X(1).
       10 WS-DA-X-LOW-ORDER           PIC X(1).
    05 WS-YR-X                        PIC X(2).
01  WS-DATE-9  REDEFINES  WS-DATE-X.
    05 WS-MO-9                        PIC 9(2).
    05 WS-DA-9                        PIC 9(2).
    05 WS-YR-9                        PIC 9(2).
01  WS-SIGNED-DATE.
    05 WS-SIGNED-MO                   PIC S99.
    05 WS-SIGNED-DA                   PIC S99.
    05 WS-SIGNED-YR                   PIC S99.
    05 WS-SIGNED-CENTURY              PIC S99.
01  WS-JULIAN-DATE                    PIC 9(5).
01  WS-JULIAN-DATE-X  REDEFINES  WS-JULIAN-DATE.
    05 WS-JULIAN-YR                   PIC 9(2).
    05 WS-JULIAN-DA                   PIC 9(3).
01  WS-FANCY-DATE.
    05 WS-FD-DATE-FRONT.
       10 WS-FD-DAY-NAME              PIC X(10).
       10                             PIC X(1)   VALUE SPACE.
       10 WS-FD-MONTH-NAME            PIC X(10).
       10 WS-FD-DA.
          18 WS-FD-DA-HIGH-ORDER      PIC X(1).
          18 WS-FD-DA-LOW-ORDER       PIC X(1).
    05 WS-FD-DATE-END.
       10                             PIC X(2)   VALUE ', '.
       10 WS-FD-CENTURY               PIC X(2).
       10 WS-FD-YR                    PIC X(2).
LINKAGE SECTION.
01  DATECHEK-LINKAGE-RECORD.  COPY DATELINK.
PROCEDURE DIVISION  USING  DATECHEK-LINKAGE-RECORD.
0000-MAINLINE.
    MOVE 'N'          TO WS-LEAPYR-FLAG.
    MOVE 19           TO WS-CENTURY.
    MOVE DATE-INPUT   TO WS-DATE-X.
    MOVE ZERO         TO DATE-STATUS-FLAG.
    MOVE 99999        TO DATE-IN-JULIAN.
    MOVE ALL '*'      TO DATE-AND-DAY-IN-WORDS.
```

This table provides day name for the spelled-out date character string.

Figure 10.19 *(Continued)*

```

           IF DATE-INPUT NOT NUMERIC
              MOVE '1' TO DATE-STATUS-FLAG
            ELSE
           IF WS-MO-9 < 1 OR > 12
              MOVE '2' TO DATE-STATUS-FLAG
            ELSE
           IF WS-DA-9 < 1 OR > 31
              MOVE '3' TO DATE-STATUS-FLAG.

           IF DATE-STATUS-FLAG = '0'
              SET MONTH-INDEX TO WS-MO-9
              PERFORM 1000-DATE-VALIDATION.

           IF DATE-STATUS-FLAG = '0'
              PERFORM 1100-COMPUTE-JULIAN-DATE
              PERFORM 1200-COMPUTE-DAY-IN-WEEK
              PERFORM 1300-BUILD-FANCY-DATE.
           GOBACK.

      *-----------------------------------------------------------------
       1000-DATE-VALIDATION.

      * TEST FOR LEAP YEAR; LEAP YEARS ARE EVENLY DIVISIBLE BY 4
      * BUT FOR CENTURY YEARS SUCH AS 2000 THE CENTURY MUST ALSO
      * BE EVENLY DIVISIBLE BY 4

           DIVIDE 4 INTO WS-YR-9
              GIVING WS-VALUE  REMAINDER WS-REMAINDER.
           IF WS-YR-9 NOT = 0 AND WS-REMAINDER = 0
              MOVE 'Y' TO WS-LEAPYR-FLAG.
           DIVIDE 4 INTO WS-CENTURY
              GIVING WS-VALUE  REMAINDER WS-REMAINDER.
           IF WS-YR-9 = 0 AND WS-REMAINDER = 0
              MOVE 'Y' TO WS-LEAPYR-FLAG.

           IF WS-DA-9 > MONTH-MAX-DAYS(MONTH-INDEX)
              MOVE '3' TO DATE-STATUS-FLAG.

           IF WS-LEAPYR-FLAG = 'N'
              AND WS-MO-9 = 2
              AND WS-DA-9 = 29
              MOVE '3' TO DATE-STATUS-FLAG.

      *-----------------------------------------------------------------
       1100-COMPUTE-JULIAN-DATE.
           MOVE WS-YR-9 TO WS-JULIAN-YR.
           IF WS-LEAPYR-FLAG = 'N'
              COMPUTE WS-JULIAN-DA =
                 MONTH-DAYS-BEFORE-NO-LEAP(MONTH-INDEX) + WS-DA-9
              ELSE
              COMPUTE WS-JULIAN-DA =
                 MONTH-DAYS-BEFORE-LEAP(MONTH-INDEX) + WS-DA-9.
           MOVE WS-JULIAN-DATE TO DATE-IN-JULIAN.

      *-----------------------------------------------------------------
       1200-COMPUTE-DAY-IN-WEEK.
           MOVE WS-DA-9      TO WS-SIGNED-DA.
           MOVE WS-MO-9      TO WS-SIGNED-MO.
           MOVE WS-YR-9      TO WS-SIGNED-YR.
           MOVE WS-CENTURY   TO WS-SIGNED-CENTURY.
```

Figure 10.19 *(Continued)*

```
*
* SET THE DATE BACK BY TWO MONTHS, ADJUSTING THE YEAR AND
* CENTURY IF NECESSARY:
*
      IF WS-SIGNED-MO > +2
         SUBTRACT +2 FROM WS-SIGNED-MO
       ELSE
         ADD +10 TO WS-SIGNED-MO
         IF WS-SIGNED-YR > +0
            SUBTRACT +1 FROM WS-SIGNED-YR
          ELSE
            MOVE +99 TO WS-SIGNED-YR
            SUBTRACT +1 FROM WS-SIGNED-CENTURY.
*
*   USE ZELLER'S CONGRUENCE TO COMPUTE THE DAY OF THE WEEK:
*
      COMPUTE WS-INTERMED-1 = WS-SIGNED-YR / 4.
      COMPUTE WS-INTERMED-2 = WS-SIGNED-CENTURY / 4.
      COMPUTE WS-INTERMED-3 = (2.6 * WS-SIGNED-MO) - .2.
      COMPUTE WS-VALUE =
         WS-INTERMED-1 +
            WS-INTERMED-2 +
               WS-INTERMED-3 +
                  WS-SIGNED-DA +
                     WS-SIGNED-YR -
                        (2.00 * WS-SIGNED-CENTURY).

      DIVIDE 7 INTO WS-VALUE
         GIVING WS-VALUE  REMAINDER WS-REMAINDER.
      COMPUTE WS-COMPUTED-DAY = WS-REMAINDER + 1.
      IF WS-COMPUTED-DAY < +1
         ADD +7 TO WS-COMPUTED-DAY.

*-----------------------------------------------------------------
 1300-BUILD-FANCY-DATE.
      MOVE SPACES TO DATE-AND-DAY-IN-WORDS.
      MOVE DAY-NAME(WS-COMPUTED-DAY)  TO WS-FD-DAY-NAME.
      MOVE MONTH-NAME(MONTH-INDEX)    TO WS-FD-MONTH-NAME.

      IF WS-DA-X-HIGH-ORDER = '0'
         MOVE WS-DA-X-LOW-ORDER TO WS-FD-DA-HIGH-ORDER
         MOVE '/' TO WS-FD-DA-LOW-ORDER
       ELSE
         MOVE WS-DA-X TO WS-FD-DA.

      MOVE WS-CENTURY                 TO WS-FD-CENTURY.
      MOVE WS-YR-X                    TO WS-FD-YR.

      STRING WS-FD-DATE-FRONT    DELIMITED BY '/'
             WS-FD-DATE-END      DELIMITED BY SIZE
         INTO DATE-AND-DAY-IN-WORDS.
```

Figure 10.19 *(Continued)*

form MMDDYY, where MM is month, DD is day of the month, and YY is the year. For example, November 6, 1994 is 110694 in Gregorian form. If the Gregorian date is valid, DATECHEK returns '0' in DATE-STATUS-FLAG, which makes the DATE-OK condition name associated with this field "true."

Like PLACCHEK, DATECHEK returns more than just an indication of whether the input date is valid. For valid dates, DATECHEK gives us the corresponding date in Julian form. A **Julian date** is of the form YYDDD, where DDD is the number of the day within the year YY. For example, the date 020194, February 1, 1994, was the thirty-second day of 1994. In Julian form, this date is 94032. The last day of non-leap year 1995 will be Julian 95365.

In addition, DATECHEK uses a clever algorithm named Zeller's Congruence to determine the day of the week for the input date, if that date is valid. It does this without the use of any "anchor date" such as January 1, 1900, a more common (and much more limited) method for handling date conversions. After determining the day of the week, DATECHEK "packages" a 29-byte character string with the spelled-out name of the day of the week and month, century and year, which you can use for labeling purposes. Date validation is sufficient for our purposes in C360B001, and here we ignore the other information DATECHEK provides.

10.14 CALL IS SUPPORTED IN VS COBOL II CICS PROGRAMS!

Now that you understand how program C360B001 benefits from the use of CALLs, you need a little background on CALLs and CICS. Under older versions of COBOL (before VS COBOL II), your use of the CALL verb was prohibited in CICS programs. But in the modern environment, CALL is fully supported and provides the same excellent way to gain the benefits of functional modularization in your CICS programs as it does in your batch programs. You can use any CICS commands in the VS COBOL II subprogram that are permitted in a VS COBOL II CALLing (main) program including READ/WRITE DATASET. You can use the CALL statement in a VS COBOL II CICS program to call a subprogram written in VS COBOL II or assembler. But a VS COBOL program cannot CALL a VS COBOL II subprogram, or vice versa. (For VS COBOL/VS COBOL II program mixtures you must continue to use the CICS LINK command, which we discuss in Chapter 16.)

Why is the "legalization" of CALL in CICS programs so important? Unlike the case with the CICS LINK command, which approximates a CALL (see Chapter 16), the name of the program you are passing control to *does not* have to be established in the Program Control Table (PCT) by a systems programmer. Therefore, you need make no special arrangements to use a CALL. This provides real flexibility to you, since you can evolve subprograms as the need for the **separate testing** they provide becomes apparent in designing and coding a program.

You can now, for example, as I did, decide that a module such as DATECHEK is required, and can build it and thoroughly test it separate from any CICS program, using a testing driver. You can then CALL it from a CICS program and have a very high degree of trust in it when you eventually access it from your CICS program. In fact, I separately tested DATECHEK, PLACCHEK, and NUMCHEK extensively before using them, and worked out many errors of commission and omission before they were ever associated with C360B001. That bit of software engineering practice has finally become attainable and practical with CALL in CICS programs!

Starting with CICS Release 2.1, subprograms that you CALL can be either static (**hard linked**) or dynamically accessed. Static CALLs execute much more efficiently than the CICS LINK command. We'll review the issue of static and dynamic CALLs in discussing how to compile the subprograms you will CALL from your CICS programs.

10.15 COMPILING SUBPROGRAMS FOR CICS CALLs

You should compile subprograms that you will call with your CICS programs using the same job control language that you use to compile CICS programs themselves, even if your subprograms do not use CICS commands. Using the CICS compile and link proc for these subprograms will insure that you use consistently appropriate compiler and linkage editor options. To show you the impact of this practice on a subprogram and the CALL to it, we have listed the compile listing for our NUMCHEK subprogram in Figure 10.20, which we'll refer to in this discussion.

You share data with a subprogram by coding a LINKAGE SECTION within it. As with any CICS program you code the first item in the LINKAGE SECTION as your DFHCOMMAREA. (If you do not code DFHCOMMAREA, the translator inserts it anyway.) As you can see in Figure 10.20, the translator will automatically insert code for DFHEIBLK (the execution interface block) in the LINKAGE SECTION of the subprogram in front of DFHCOMMAREA.

When you compile the subprogram with the CICS proc, you code its Procedure Division heading with USING and just the ordinary data fields you intend pass to it. As you can see in Figure 10.20, the translator will automatically recode the subprogram Procedure Division heading to cite DFHEIBLK and DFHCOMMAREA first after USING, then the data you are sharing with the subprogram. To match this you need to state DFHEIBLK and DFHCOMMAREA first in any CALL to the subprogram:

```
CALL 'NUMCHEK' USING   DFHEIBLK
                       DFHCOMMAREA
                       (other shared fields).
```

This passes the addresses of the execution interface block and your common area to the subprogram as its PROCEDURE DIVISION heading expects. *If you forget to CALL using DFHEIBLK and DFHCOMMAREA before citing your shared data fields, expect a raft of problems as your subprogram misinterprets what you are sharing with it.* If you examine lines 18400-18600 of the C360B001 program (and the other locations in it where we have made CALLs), you'll see that we have CALLed subprograms passing DFHEIBLK and DFHCOMMAREA, then the intended shared data fields, precisely as prescribed.

10.16 UNDERSTANDING STATIC AND DYNAMIC CALLs

Static and dynamic refer to the point at which **binding**, or connection, occurs between a main program that CALLs a subprogram, and the subprogram itself. At what points can the process of binding between these separate sets of code occur?

With a **static CALL**, binding occurs during the finalization of the machine language for the load module. The linkage editor accepts as input the **object file** from your compiled main program, and resolves references made in the program to all CALLed subprograms, in what is known as a **hard link**. For this to be possible, the linkage editor must have access to either the object files produced by compiling each subprogram, or access to the machine language resulting from compiling and linking the subprogram. Static CALLs produce faster response time, at the expense of larger load modules, because the system does not have to access a library for the first instance of a CALL, to bring the load module of the subprogram into memory. With static CALLs, the machine language for every subprogram is already present in the load module of the main program.

With a **dynamic CALL**, binding between the main program and the subprogram is deferred until execution time. The machine language for each subprogram is separate from the machine language of any main program that CALLs them. When a CALL is processed in the main program, the system must seek and retrieve the machine language for the subprogram from a library and load it to memory to continue execution. This can slow down response time, since it involves disk input/output actions and a search of the directory of the load module library.

With dynamic CALLs, you lose on-line responsivity, but gain flexibility. You can change a subprogram without relinking any main programs. With static CALLs, you gain on-line

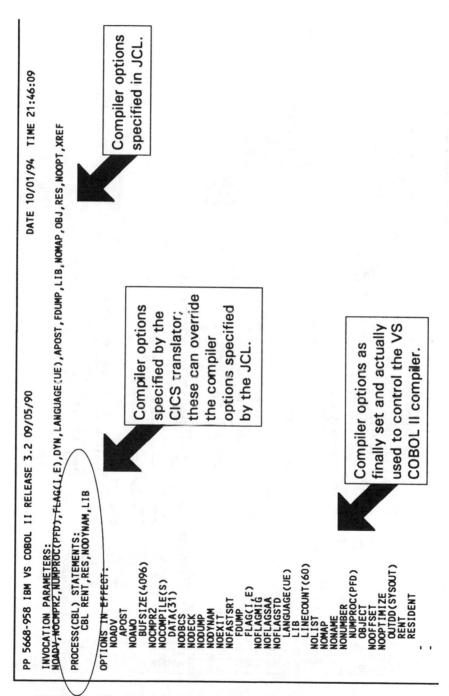

```
PP 5668-958 IBM VS COBOL II RELEASE 3.2 09/05/90                    DATE 10/01/94  TIME 21:46:09

INVOCATION PARAMETERS:
NOADV,NOCMPR2,NUMPROC(PFD),FLAG(I,E),DYN,LANGUAGE(UE),APOST,FDUMP,LIB,NOMAP,OBJ,RES,NOOPT,XREF

PROCESS(CBL) STATEMENTS:
       CBL RENT,RES,NODYNAM,LIB

OPTIONS IN EFFECT:
    NOADV
      APOST
    NOAWO
      BUFSIZE(4096)
    NOCMPR2
    NOCOMPILE(S)
      DATA(31)
    NODBCS
    NODECK
    NODUMP
    NODYNAM
    NOEXIT
    NOFASTSRT
      FDUMP
      FLAG(I,E)
    NOFLAGMIG
    NOFLAGSAA
    NOFLAGSTD
      LANGUAGE(UE)
      LIB
      LINECOUNT(60)
    NOLIST
    NOMAP
    NONAME
    NONUMBER
      NUMPROC(PFD)
      OBJECT
    NOOFFSET
    NOOPTIMIZE
      OUTDD(SYSOUT)
      RENT
      RESIDENT
    -
    -
```

Compiler options specified in JCL.

Compiler options specified by the CICS translator; these can override the compiler options specified by the JCL.

Compiler options as finally set and actually used to control the VS COBOL II compiler.

Figure 10.20 Compile listing of the NUMCHEK subprogram, showing changes made by the CICS translator that affect CALLs to it.

```
000111              02    EIBCOMPL PIC X(1).
000112              02    EIBSIG   PIC X(1).
000113              02    EIBCONF  PIC X(1).
000114              02    EIBERR   PIC X(1).
000115              02    EIBERRCD PIC X(4).
000116              02    EIBSYNRB PIC X(1).
000117              02    EIBNODAT PIC X(1).
000118              02    EIBRESP  COMP PIC S9(8).
000119              02    EIBRESP2 COMP PIC S9(8).
000120              02    EIBRLDBK PIC X(1).
000121              01  DFHCOMMAREA PICTURE X(1).
000122       004700 01  NUMCHEK-LINKAGE-RECORD.
000123                                    COPY NUMLINK.
000124C            *-----------------------------------------------------------     00010000
000125C            *  NUMLINK                                                        00020000
000126C            *  LINKAGE RECORD FOR NUMCHEK DE-EDITING SUBPROGRAM               0003000
000127C            *-----------------------------------------------------------     00040
000128C                 05 NUM-INPUT                PIC X(22).                       000
000129C                 05 NUM-RIGHT-OF-DECIMAL     PIC 9(1).                        000
000130C                 05 NUM-STATUS-FLAG          PIC X(1).                        0000
000131C                    88 NUM-CONVERSION-OK              VALUE '0'.              80000
000132C                    88 NUM-RIGHT-OF-DECIMAL-NOT-0-6   VALUE '1'.              0090000
000133C                    88 NUM-HAS-EXTRA-ALPHA-SYMBOLS    VALUE '2'.              00100000
000134C                    88 NUM-DECIMAL-PT-OUT-OF-PLACE    VALUE '3'.              00110000
000135C                 05 NUM-OUTPUT               PIC 9(11)V9(6).                  00120000
000136       004800
000137       004900 PROCEDURE DIVISION USING  DFHEIBLK  DFHCOMMAREA                       89 121
000138                  NUMCHEK-LINKAGE-RECORD.                                           122
000139       005000 0000-MAINLINE.
000140       005100     MOVE 'X'          TO NUM-STATUS-FLAG.                             130
000141       005200     MOVE ZEROS        TO NUM-OUTPUT.                                  IMP 135
000142       005300     MOVE NUM-INPUT    TO W1-AREA.                                     128 29
000143       005400
000144       005500     EVALUATE TRUE
000145       005600        WHEN NUM-RIGHT-OF-DECIMAL  NOT NUMERIC                         129
000146     1 005700           MOVE '1' TO NUM-STATUS-FLAG                                 130
000147       005800        WHEN NUM-RIGHT-OF-DECIMAL >= 0 AND <= 6                        129
000148     1 005900           PERFORM 1000-PROCESS                                        158
000149       006000        WHEN OTHER
000150     1 006100           MOVE '1' TO NUM-STATUS-FLAG                                 130
-
-
-
```

Copied-in linkage record description is listed by compiler.

Compare this rewritten Procedure Division heading to line 49 in Figure 10.17.

Figure 10.20 *(Continued)*

responsivity, but lose flexibility, since you have to recompile all main programs that use a subprogram if you change that subprogram. As a general recommendation, use dynamic CALLs for batch programs, and static CALLs for on-line programs.

Your CICS translator is most likely set to insert a compiler option-controlling CBL statement at the beginning of your translated COBOL programs, the effect of which you see at the beginning of the compiler output shown in Figure 10.20. This insures that the compile is done with the RENT, RES, and NODYNAM options. These compiler settings create a load module that does not expect to use dynamic calling conventions. Our job stream named PGMJOB (listed in full in Chapter 6, Figure 6.3) includes your machine language load module library in the concatenated //SYSLIB input to the linkage editor at line 10200, and uses the appropriate options. So long as you compile your subprograms first, then the main (CALLing) program, the PGMJOB job stream will cause the linkage editor to hard link your main and subprograms into one load module, so that you gain the efficiency of a static CALL.

10.17 SEPARATE BATCH TESTING OF ON-LINE SUBPROGRAMS

Many programmers were taught that you should consider housing logic in a subprogram only if there was some possibility of reusing the logic. That is, general purpose logic such as a date validation routine, which could be useful to a number of programs, would be housed as a subprogram. But the notion of reusability, while important, misses a major point. You should think about housing logic in a separately compiled subprogram even when there is little potential for reuse, if the logic really is functionally separate from other logic. *This facilitates testing the logic.* A freestanding subprogram can readily be tested in isolation from a large main program by using a testing driver program.

A subprogram testing driver is nothing more than a very small main program that acquires test data, makes it visible, sends it to the subprogram being tested, and makes the result of the CALL visible. Figure 10.21 shows you the compiled listing of a testing driver named NUMTEST. We used this to test the NUMCHEK de-editing routine before invoking NUMCHEK in the C360B001 program.

NUMTEST was developed on a PC using a PC-based COBOL compiler, as was NUMCHEK. A number of capable PC-based COBOL compilers exist, including MicroFocus COBOL, RM/COBOL-85, and CA-Realia COBOL. Since one of the authors (Jim Janossy) collaborated with Nancy and Robert Stern on the second edition of *Getting Started with RM/COBOL-85*, published in 1994 by John Wiley & Sons, Inc., we used RM/COBOL-85 for this work. PC-based CICS subprogram development and testing is rapid and productive, and you don't need a CICS emulator to do it. We included SELECT statements for both PC and IBM mainframe environments in the NUMTEST driver program, commenting out one or the other SELECT as appropriate to the environment. The compile listing you see in Figure 10.21 was actually produced by RM/COBOL-85.

Figure 10.22 shows you the output of a preliminary test of the NUMCHEK de-editing subprogram, demonstrating the output of the testing driver using only a small (not sufficient!) quantity of test data. A discrepancy is highlighted between the predicted output of one test case and the actual output of the subprogram. "Real" software testing means making a prediction of the output, then evaluating the actual output by comparing it to the prediction. A testing driver makes it as easy as possible to arrange this for real subprogram testing.

Consider housing complex algorithms used in CICS programs in subprograms. Separately test those subprograms using a test driver such as NUMTEST. There is nothing holding

```
ID DIVISION.
PROGRAM-ID. NUMTEST.
*-----------------------------------------------------------------
*  DRIVER PROGRAM TO SEPARATELY TEST THE NUMCHEK SUBPROGRAM
*  COPYRIGHT 1994 JAMES JANOSSY  ALL RIGHTS RESERVED
*-----------------------------------------------------------------

ENVIRONMENT DIVISION.
INPUT-OUTPUT SECTION.
FILE-CONTROL.
*-----------------------------------------------------------------
* FOR IBM MAINFRAMES:
*    SELECT TEST-FILE   ASSIGN TO NUMIN.
*-----------------------------------------------------------------
* FOR A PC-BASED COMPILER:
     SELECT TEST-FILE   ASSIGN TO DISK 'NUMIN.DAT'
         ORGANIZATION IS LINE SEQUENTIAL.
*-----------------------------------------------------------------

DATA DIVISION.
FILE SECTION.
FD  TEST-FILE
     BLOCK CONTAINS 0 RECORDS
     RECORD CONTAINS 80 CHARACTERS.
01   TEST-RECORD                    PIC X(80).

WORKING-STORAGE SECTION.
01   NUM-LINK.  COPY NUMLINK.
+1+       *-----------------------------------------------------------------
+1+       *  NUMLINK
+1+       *  LINKAGE RECORD FOR NUMCHEK DE-EDITING SUBPROGRAM
+1+       *-----------------------------------------------------------------
+1+            05 NUM-INPUT                PIC X(22).
+1+            05 NUM-RIGHT-OF-DECIMAL     PIC 9(1).
+1+            05 NUM-STATUS-FLAG          PIC X(1).
+1+               88 NUM-CONVERSION-OK               VALUE '0'.
+1+               88 NUM-RIGHT-OF-DECIMAL-NOT-0-6    VALUE '1'.
+1+               88 NUM-HAS-EXTRA-ALPHA-SYMBOLS     VALUE '2'.
+1+               88 NUM-DECIMAL-PT-OUT-OF-PLACE     VALUE '3'.
+1+            05 NUM-OUTPUT               PIC 9(11)V9(6).
```

This program reads test data and displays it, then feeds it to the NUMCHEK subprogram and displays the result returned by the subprogram. You can use a batch driver program such as this to thoroughly test a batch module or a module that will be CALLed by a CICS program.

Copied-in linkage record description is listed by compiler.

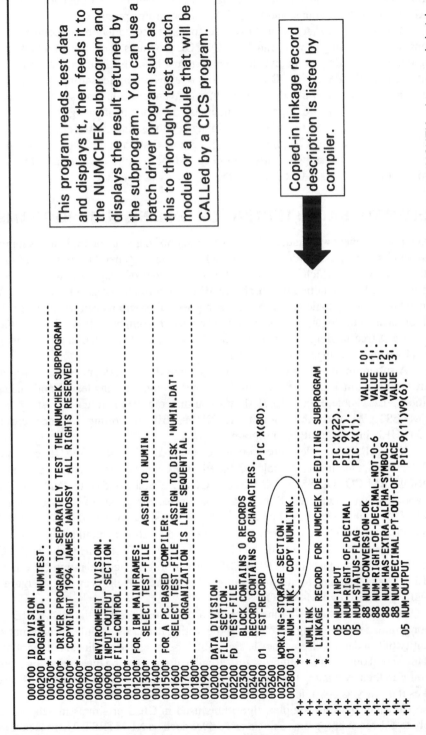

Figure 10.21 Compile listing of source code of the NUMTEST driver program, to be used to test the NUMCHEK subprogram in batch mode.

```
01  WS-RECORD-COUNT                PIC 9(5)   VALUE 0.
01  WS-EOF-FLAG                    PIC X(1)   VALUE 'M'.
01  LINE-OF-HYPHENS                PIC X(70) VALUE ALL '-'.

PROCEDURE DIVISION.
0000-MAINLINE.
    PERFORM 1000-BOJ.
    PERFORM 2000-PROCESS UNTIL WS-EOF-FLAG = 'E'.
    PERFORM 3000-EOJ.
    STOP RUN.

1000-BOJ.
    DISPLAY 'DRIVER PROGRAM NUMTEST STARTING'.
    DISPLAY LINE-OF-HYPHENS.
    OPEN INPUT TEST-FILE.
    PERFORM 2700-READ.

2000-PROCESS.
    DISPLAY                      TEST-RECORD.
    MOVE TEST-RECORD(1:22)   TO  NUM-INPUT.
    MOVE TEST-RECORD(23:1)   TO  NUM-RIGHT-OF-DECIMAL.
    CALL 'NUMCHEK' USING         NUM-LINK.
    DISPLAY  NUM-LINK(1:22),
             NUM-LINK(23:1), ' ',
             NUM-LINK(24:1), ' ',
             NUM-LINK(25:).
    DISPLAY LINE-OF-HYPHENS.
    PERFORM 2700-READ.

2700-READ.
    MOVE SPACES TO TEST-RECORD.
    READ TEST-FILE
       AT END
          MOVE 'E' TO WS-EOF-FLAG
       NOT AT END
          ADD 1 TO WS-RECORD-COUNT.

3000-EOJ.
    CLOSE TEST-FILE.
    DISPLAY 'RECORDS READ = ', WS-RECORD-COUNT.
    DISPLAY 'END OF TEST'.
```

Coding such as NUM-LINK(23:1) is called *reference modification* and amounts to a substring capability in 1985 COBOL. The first number is the **position** within a string to begin access, and the second number is the **quantity of bytes** to be accessed beginning with the starting position.

Figure 10.21 *(Continued)*

```
DRIVER PROGRAM NUMTEST STARTING
-------------------------------------------------------------------
$123.45              2   prediction: status flag 0
$123.45              2 0 00000000123450000
-------------------------------------------------------------------
$123                 0   prediction: status flag 0
$123                 0 0 00000000123000000
-------------------------------------------------------------------
1234.5               2   prediction: status flag 3  num right of dec wrong
1234.5               2 3 00000000000000000
-------------------------------------------------------------------
1234.5               1   prediction: status flag 0
1234.5               1 0 00000001234500000
-------------------------------------------------------------------
123,456,789.14       2   prediction: status flag 0
123,456,789.14       2 0 00123456789140000
-------------------------------------------------------------------
$$987,654.32         2   prediction: status flag 2  extra $$ invalid
$$987,654.32         2 2 00000000000000000
-------------------------------------------------------------------
123,4567,,89         3   prediction: status flag 2  extra commas invalid
123,4567,,89         3 0 00000123456789000
-------------------------------------------------------------------
123x567y             0   prediction: status flag 2  alphanumeric in number
123x567y             0 2 00000000000000000
-------------------------------------------------------------------
5678.33              7   prediction: status flag 1  7 too big right of dec
5678.33              7 1 00000000000000000
-------------------------------------------------------------------
RECORDS READ = 00009
END OF TEST
```

By definition, software testing is an organized process aimed at detecting defects (it's not a process of "proving" that software works). In this output from the NUMTEST driver program, we see the input to the computation done by the NUMCHEK module, including a prediction of the valid output to be generated for each test case. A potential flaw is identified by a discrepancy between the predicted and actual outputs. Here we expect the NUMCHEK module to identify an input that is invalid due to two commas within it, but NUMCHEK fails to detect the error. In this case NUMCHEK has not done something it is supposed to do.

Figure 10.22 Output from a preliminary batch test of the NUMCHEK subprogram with the NUMTEST driver, showing input test cases with predicted output, and output Actually produced by the subprogram.

you back from applying sound software engineering practices in your CICS program development, and you have every reason in the world to do so.

10.18 CHANGES IN THE CLEAN-THE-SCREEN FUNCTION

We included a feature in our earlier programs to allow the terminal operator to clear the screen of all entries and program-generated outputs. That function also exists in the C360B001 program. Since we are using the pre-sent error message technique, however, and do not have any program-generated output fields, the clear the screen function now must do things a little differently.

You can see by examining lines 47400 through line 50800 of program C360B001 in Figure 10.8 that the 9100-CLEAN-THE-SCREEN paragraph must set all message fields to PROT-DARK to hide them. After positioning the cursor to the first enterable field by putting -1 in its length field in the symbolic map, the SEND MAP command is used as before. As in the programs we have shown you earlier in this book, we use the **ERASEAUP** option of the SEND command to blank out the contents of enterable fields for the clean-the-screen function.

10.19 FOR YOUR REVIEW

The following terms were introduced or reviewed in this chapter. If you understand this chapter, you should be comfortable with defining each of these terms in relationship to CICS:

Binding
Boolean "true/false" field
CALL
COPY
Copy library member
Copybook member
Data validation
Date validation
Dynamic CALL
END-EVALUATE
ERASEAUP
EVALUATE
Explicit scope delimiter
FSET
Gregorian date
Hard linked
Julian date
Linkage record
Logic reuse
LOW-VALUES
Null
Numeric field de-editing
Object file
Separate testing
SET condition name
Static CALL
Status flag
Subprogram
User-defined data classes

10.20 REVIEW QUESTIONS

1. Describe some of the kinds of items that we often use COPY to bring into a CICS program, citing at least three specific examples.
2. How are COPY and CALL related? That is, how is COPY often used to support CALLs?
3. In a program such as C360B001, which drives Marko's Department Store Credit Card Application screen, discuss how you can quickly see most or all of the pre-sent error messages when executing the program.
4. Identify two important benefits of using pre-sent error messages on a CICS screen, as demonstrated by the C360B001 program and Marko's Credit Card Application screen.

5. Describe what program actions have to be taken to make a pre-sent (hidden) error message visible on the terminal screen.
6. Explain why the coding provided by the ATTDEFS copybook member is an important part of almost all CICS programs.
7. Explain why we need to code names on the BMS map coding for pre-sent error messages, when we do not intend to make any changes in the content of those messages using program logic.
8. Briefly explain how user-defined data classes work, using as an example a data class that can be used to validate the "direction" part of a street address, which must be N, E, W, S (North, East, West, South) or space.
9. Explain what the attribute byte coding FSET accomplishes when it is coded on an enterable (unprotected) screen field.
10. Identify the main reason for developing and using a de-editing routine such as the NUMCHEK subprogram demonstrated in this chapter.
11. Identify and describe two reasons why it is sometimes necessary to use REDEFINES in symbolic map coding for numeric fields.
12. Explain what capability the SET verb gives you in connection with 88-level condition names, and how you can use this capability to create Boolean true/false flags.
13. Describe why a copybook member like KEYDEFS, locally developed in an installation, can be more convenient to use to identify which PF key was pressed than IBM's older copybook member DFHAID.
14. Describe why a copybook member like ATTDEFS, locally developed in an installation, can be more convenient to use to set attribute bytes than IBM's old copybook member DFHBMSCA.
15. Explain what a linkage record is, and what it contains.
16. Identify and describe an important advantage CALL has over the CICS LINK command, which can also invoke another program in a way similar to CALL.
17. Describe the role a field such as NUM-STATUS-FLAG in Figure 10.14 plays in a linkage record.
18. Explain why, in program C360B001, we checked the contents of enterable fields in reverse sequence, starting with the bottom field on the screen and working upward.
19. Explain the significance of LOW-VALUES to CICS programming, and why we initialize the symbolic map with this value at the start of processing in a CICS program.
20. Describe the steps you need to follow so that you can test your coding of a complex computational algorithm, to be used in a CICS program, apart from the program itself.
21. Why should you compile a subprogram to be CALLed by CICS programs with the same procedure used with CICS programs, involving the CICS translator, even if the subprogram itself contains no CICS commands?
22. Give an example of how you code the CALL to a subprogram in a CICS program, when the subprogram has been compiled as indicated in question 21 (use a hypothetical subprogram and linkage record name).
23. Explain the difference between static and dynamic CALLs in terms of the concept of "binding."

24. Identify and describe the tradeoffs in using dynamic as opposed to static CALLs.
25. Identify and briefly describe the operation of a subprogram testing driver, explaining what a driver is and generally does.

10.21 HANDS-ON EXERCISES

A. Design a BMS map for the entry of information about your own personal checks. Put a title on the top of the screen that says CHECKBOOK DATA ENTRY BY XXXXXXXXXXXXXXXXXXXXXXX, and put your name in place of the X's. Include an appropriately sized prompt line. Develop appropriate screen labels and data entry fields for these items of information:

```
CHECK NUMBER
CHECK DATE
CLEARED?
PAYABLE TO NAME
EXPENDITURE CODE
CHECK AMOUNT
```

Document reasonable data validation requirements for each of these fields. Here are some suggestions:

- CHECK NUMBER should be numeric, but 0000 should be rejected as invalid
- CHECK DATE should be a valid Gregorian date
- CLEARED? should be space or "X" only; "X" indicates that the cancelled check has been returned by the bank, indicating it was paid
- PAYABLE TO NAME should not be omitted, but can consist of spaces, letters, numbers, and punctuation
- EXPENDITURE CODE should be one of these letters only, with the meaning shown for each:

  A Appliances (television, stereo, refrigerator, stove, washer, dryer, and so forth)
  C Clothing
  F Food
  H Housing (mortgage, rent, home insurance, taxes)
  L Loan repayments
  R Recreation (hobbies, movies, records, vacations/trips, and so forth)
  S School supplies, books, tuition
  T Transportation (car, gasoline, car insurance)
  Z Miscellaneous expenditures (no other category applies)
- CHECK AMOUNT should be numeric, greater than zero.

To these suggestions, add whatever data validation criteria appear appropriate to your circumstances, such as a value range for check number or check amount.

Include in your screen design a pre-sent error message suited to the data validation criteria for each field. After designing this screen, prepare the BMS source code to implement it, and process your BMS code into a physical map. Test the screen using CECI as described in Appendix B. Consider and describe what your next step can be to determine if your pre-sent error messages are correct.

B. After completing exercise A, design and develop a structured program to drive your Check Data Entry screen for data validation. Base your program on the C360B001 program illustrated in this chapter, including the use of:

- User-defined data classes appropriate to the data validation requirements suggested above, as amended by your own circumstances, including a user-defined data class for the expenditure code
- The use of the NUMCHEK and DATECHEK subprograms shown in this chapter
- The use of COPY for your symbolic map and for the linkage records that interface with the subprograms you use

Prepare the NUMCHEK and DATECHEK subprograms first, and compile and link them. Code your program, then compile and link it. Test your program to make sure that it works properly.

C. After completing exercises A and B, design and develop a subprogram to handle validation of the expenditure code, and to provide a 30-byte plain text description of each code value. Use the PLACCHEK subprogram as a guide, housing the expenditure code values and plain text explanation of each in a table. Use a linear SEARCH statement in the Procedure Division of this subprogram. Make sure you create an appropriate linkage record as the interface to this subprogram, including a one-byte status flag that can be interrogated by the CALLing program. Create a driver program to test your expenditure code module following the pattern of the driver we used to test NUMCHEK, shown in Figure 10.21. Test your expenditure validation module, obtaining test results similar to those shown in Figure 10.22. When your testing indicates that you have reason to trust the operation of your subprogram, modify your on-line Check Data Entry program to eliminate data class validation of the expenditure code and to use the subprogram instead. Then recompile your on-line program and test it thoroughly.

Note: conduct your separate subprogram testing by compiling the subprogram and your testing driver program with your normal non-CICS compile and link procedure. When you are ready to use the subprogram with your on-line Check Data Entry program, recompile your subprogram using your CICS compile and link job control language. You must follow this sequence of testing actions, because it is not productive to try to simulate the DFHEIBLK data to pass to the subprogram, as the subprogram will expect to receive once it is processed using your CICS compile and link job control language.

11

Programming On-Line Help

Terminal users often need access to information about what each PF key does within a specific transaction, or even more information about how to complete the entries on and use a screen. In this chapter we'll outline the broad categories of on-line help and show you how to implement two forms of on-line help in your CICS programs.

11.1 CATEGORIES OF ON-LINE HELP

Several different forms of **on-line help** can be provided to assist terminal operators in their use of CICS transactions. These different forms include:

- **Continuously displayed on-screen key definitions**, permanent legends that indicate PF key meanings
- **Keyboard maps**, indicating what various keys on the keyboard, such as PF and PA AID keys, cause to happen within the transaction
- **Static information screens** each explaining various things about a CICS transaction
- **Extended topic-specific** assistance (context sensitive help) accessible by PF key or with a code the terminal user enters
- **Full-scale interactive tutorials** intended to accomplish terminal operator training apart from "real work" that the operator accomplishes with the CICS transaction.

The first of these forms of on-line assistance—on-screen key definitions—is nothing more than screen literals. It's trivial, but also somewhat wasteful of screen geography. The second—keyboard maps—is also easy to provide, and does not even require BMS map coding. Beyond these two levels of help, you do have to make special arrangements to provide terminal operator assistance. We'll discuss each form of on-line help briefly, and we'll then demonstrate how you can readily implement keyboard maps and help screens.

11.2 CONTINUOUSLY DISPLAYED KEY DEFINITIONS

Figure 11.1 shows you the CALC1 screen you have seen many times already, from Chapter 7 onward. We have added two lines of legend at the bottom of this screen, to indicate the functions associated with various PF keys. You can see that the PF1, PF2, and PF3 keys have been assigned functions, while PF4 through PF12 perform no function (X) for this screen.

Continuously displayed key definitions such as you see in Figure 11.1 may seem like a good idea to new users, but they have several drawbacks. Continuously displayed key definitions:

- Consume room on the screen, reducing by two full lines the space available for data content
- Clutter the screen visually, making it a bit harder for the eye to see and catch the meaning of the bottom-of-screen prompt
- Do not provide much room for actual key definitions, perhaps 6 or 7 characters at the most. This can lead to cryptic definitions such as CLRSCR for "clear screen," which may intimidate new users even more than the lack of on-screen key definitions
- Are not needed once a terminal operator becomes familiar with PF key meanings for a transaction
- Consume additional time to transmit

```
===KEY MAP FOR THIS PROGRAM===

<ENTER> ACCEPTS ENTERED DATA
<CLEAR> EXITS THIS PROGRAM
  <PF1> SHOWS THIS KEY MAP
  <PF2> SHOWS A FULL HELP SCREEN
  <PF3> BLANKS OUT DATA FIELDS

===PRESS <ENTER> TO RESUME===
```

This keyboard map is summoned by pressing the **PF1** key and simply tells the terminal operator how to activate functions assigned to other attention identifier (AID) keys.

Figure 11.1 Adding continuously displayed key definitions to the CALC1 screen may be helpful, but it clutters the screen and is not very informative.

You will probably come across a small proportion of on-line systems that use continuously displayed key definitions. Some such systems, like TSO/ISPF itself, even provide a way for the terminal operator to shut off the definitions, freeing up more room on the screen for data display at the operator's option. But we need methods to provide more than a few characters of explanation for each program and PF key function. More advanced forms of on-line help are relatively easy to implement, and do not suffer from the disadvantages of continuously displayed key definitions.

11.3 KEYBOARD MAPS

Figure 11.2 shows you what a simple **keyboard map** for a version of the CALC1 program looks like. You can see that this is really just a small amount of text that informs the terminal operator of the functions of each of the AID keys that are valid for the transaction. For completeness, our keyboard map includes an entry for the PF1 key, although this is redundant. Why? Because the PF1 key is the key the operator presses to make the keyboard map visible! By common convention, most modern PC software places a help function at the PF1 key. Due to this practice, PF1 is the logical choice to associate with the initial level of on-line help in a CICS system.

Presenting a keyboard map is so simple that there is no reason to omit this in any CICS program. Once we consider the other levels of on-line help, we'll show you exactly how to code both the keyboard map and the logic to present it within a program.

```
===KEY MAP FOR THIS PROGRAM===

<ENTER> ACCEPTS ENTERED DATA
<CLEAR> EXITS THIS PROGRAM
  <PF1> SHOWS THIS KEY MAP
  <PF2> SHOWS A FULL HELP SCREEN
  <PF3> BLANKS OUT DATA FIELDS

===PRESS <ENTER> TO RESUME===
```

This keyboard map is summoned by pressing the **PF1** key and simply tells the terminal operator how to activate functions assigned to other attention identifier (AID) keys.

Figure 11.2 Keyboard map for the CALC1 program, indicating the AID keys regarded as valid, and their functions.

11.4 STATIC INFORMATION SCREENS

Figure 11.3 illustrates a **static information screen** we developed for the revised CALC1 program. This screen, unlike a simple keyboard map, is so dense with text that it requires coding a BMS map to house it. We housed this BMS map in a completely separate mapset from the original CALC1 screen.

```
==============================================================================
                      Help Screen for C360A001 Program
Purpose of Program
------------------
C360A001 accepts quantity and price values and validates them to make sure
they are numeric.  It then computes the extended price as the product of these
values, computes sales tax at the rate of 8%, and computes grand total price.
If you make a mistake entering either input, you will receive a specific
message indicating the incorrect entry.

Keys and the Functions They Perform
-----------------------------------
<PF1>    causes a concise key map to be displayed.  Data on the screen is lost.
<PF2>    causes this help screen to appear.  Data on the screen is lost.
<PF3>    erases data from entry and computed fields ("cleans" the screen)
<Enter>  accepts inputs for processing and initiates their validation
<Clear>  terminates use of this program

If you press function keys other than these you will receive a message
indicating that the key press was invalid.
==============================================================================
   Press the <Enter> key to exit from this help screen and resume processing
```

Figure 11.3 Static information (Help) screen for the revised CALC1 program.

Presenting the static help screen with program logic requires a separate paragraph dedicated to sending it to the terminal screen. It also requires a bit of special handling so that the program "knows," after sending it, that the next time it is awakened by the pressing of an AID key, the first order of business is to restore the "startup" CALC1 screen (as if it were the "first time" the program was being executed by the terminal). You'll see how we handle that with a variation on the coding of the RETURN command and the WS-COMMUNICATION-AREA we pass to the next pseudoconverse.

Developing the BMS map code for a static information screen by hand would be an absolutely revolting task to undertake, akin to writing a detailed memo by pasting together hundreds of letters cut from a newspaper! But using a screen painter makes the development of a static information screen easy. We used the GENMAP screen painter discussed in Chapter 4 to prepare the BMS map code for the information screen. The BMS code generated by GENMAP is shown in Figure 11.4. It requires no manual intervention at all before processing it into a physical map using the MAPJOB job control language. Since there are no enterable fields on the information screen, no symbolic map is required for it, and we send it (at lines 36800 through 37400 in program C360A00X) using the MAPONLY option of the SEND command.

11.5 PROVIDING EXTENDED TOPIC-SPECIFIC ASSISTANCE

Another description of **extended topic-specific assistance** is **context-sensitive help**. This level of on-line help can take the form of a series of static help screens, one or more for each field on a data entry screen. Not only does this level of help require quite a bit of documentation preparation, it also requires some thought as to how to package the screens. Since a mapset can house more than one map, it's appealing to house the several maps of help text in one mapset, giving each map a unique name.

Context-sensitive help also requires some form of sensing mechanism to detect what help is required. While you could force an operator to indicate this with a code, the handiest way for an operator to summon this form of help is by pressing a designated PF key *when the*

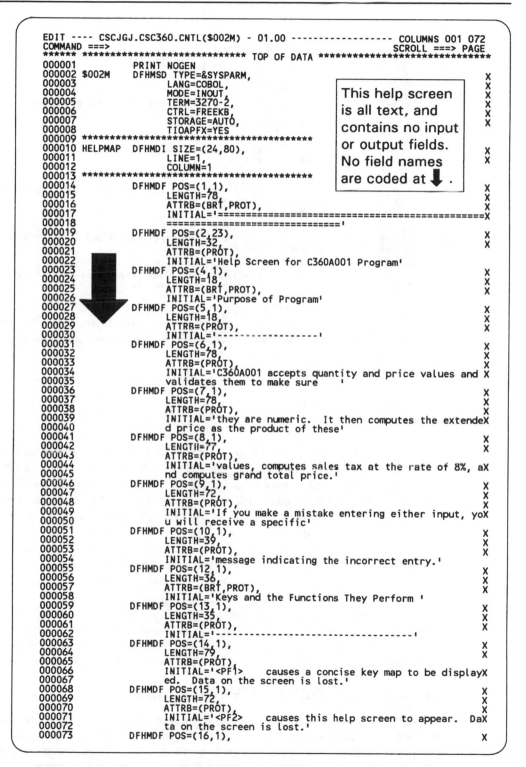

```
EDIT ---- CSCJGJ.CSC360.CNTL($002M) - 01.00 ----------------- COLUMNS 001 072
COMMAND ===>                                                  SCROLL ===> PAGE
****** ****************************** TOP OF DATA ******************************
                PRINT NOGEN
$002M           DFHMSD TYPE=&SYSPARM,                                          X
                       LANG=COBOL,                                             X
                       MODE=INOUT,                                             X
                       TERM=3270-2,                                            X
                       CTRL=FREEKB,                                            X
                       STORAGE=AUTO,                                           X
                       TIOAPFX=YES
*****************************************************
HELPMAP         DFHMDI SIZE=(24,80),                                           X
                       LINE=1,                                                 X
                       COLUMN=1
*****************************************************
                DFHMDF POS=(1,1),                                              X
                       LENGTH=78,                                              X
                       ATTRB=(BRT,PROT),                                       X
                       INITIAL='=========================================X
                       ================================='
                DFHMDF POS=(2,23),                                             X
                       LENGTH=32,                                              X
                       ATTRB=(PROT),                                           X
                       INITIAL='Help Screen for C360A001 Program'
                DFHMDF POS=(4,1),                                              X
                       LENGTH=18,                                              X
                       ATTRB=(BRT,PROT),                                       X
                       INITIAL='Purpose of Program'
                DFHMDF POS=(5,1),                                              X
                       LENGTH=18,                                              X
                       ATTRB=(PROT),                                           X
                       INITIAL='------------------'
                DFHMDF POS=(6,1),                                              X
                       LENGTH=78,                                              X
                       ATTRB=(PROT),                                           X
                       INITIAL='C360A001 accepts quantity and price values and X
                       validates them to make sure    '
                DFHMDF POS=(7,1),                                              X
                       LENGTH=78,                                              X
                       ATTRB=(PROT),                                           X
                       INITIAL='they are numeric.  It then computes the extendeX
                       d price as the product of these'
                DFHMDF POS=(8,1),                                              X
                       LENGTH=77,                                              X
                       ATTRB=(PROT),                                           X
                       INITIAL='values, computes sales tax at the rate of 8%, aX
                       nd computes grand total price.'
                DFHMDF POS=(9,1),                                              X
                       LENGTH=72,                                              X
                       ATTRB=(PROT),                                           X
                       INITIAL='If you make a mistake entering either input, yoX
                       u will receive a specific'
                DFHMDF POS=(10,1),                                             X
                       LENGTH=39,                                              X
                       ATTRB=(PROT),                                           X
                       INITIAL='message indicating the incorrect entry.'
                DFHMDF POS=(12,1),                                             X
                       LENGTH=36,                                              X
                       ATTRB=(BRT,PROT),                                       X
                       INITIAL='Keys and the Functions They Perform '
                DFHMDF POS=(13,1),                                             X
                       LENGTH=35,                                              X
                       ATTRB=(PROT),                                           X
                       INITIAL='-----------------------------------'
                DFHMDF POS=(14,1),                                             X
                       LENGTH=79,                                              X
                       ATTRB=(PROT),                                           X
                       INITIAL='<PF1>     causes a concise key map to be displayX
                       ed.  Data on the screen is lost.'
                DFHMDF POS=(15,1),                                             X
                       LENGTH=72,                                              X
                       ATTRB=(PROT),                                           X
                       INITIAL='<PF2>     causes this help screen to appear.  DaX
                       ta on the screen is lost.'
                DFHMDF POS=(16,1),                                             X
```

This help screen is all text, and contains no input or output fields. No field names are coded at ↓ .

Figure 11.4 BMS map source code for the static information screen sent by the revised CALC1 program.

```
                  LENGTH=73,                                            X
                  ATTRB=(PROT),                                         X
                  INITIAL='<PF3>    erases data from entry and computed fiX
                  elds ("cleans" the screen)'
         DFHMDF POS=(17,1),                                             X
                  LENGTH=69,                                            X
                  ATTRB=(PROT),                                         X
                  INITIAL='<Enter>  accepts inputs for processing and initX
                  iates their validation'
         DFHMDF POS=(18,1),                                             X
                  LENGTH=39,                                            X
                  ATTRB=(PROT),                                         X
                  INITIAL='<Clear>  terminates use of this program'
         DFHMDF POS=(20,1),
                  LENGTH=70,                                            X
                  ATTRB=(PROT),                                         X
                  INITIAL='If you press function keys other than these youX
                   will receive a message'
         DFHMDF POS=(21,1),                                             X
                  LENGTH=42,                                            X
                  ATTRB=(PROT),                                         X
                  INITIAL='indicating that the key press was invalid.'
         DFHMDF POS=(23,1),                                             X
                  LENGTH=78,                                            X
                  ATTRB=(BRT,PROT),                                     X
                  INITIAL='============================================X
                  ================================'
         DFHMDF POS=(24,4),                                             X
                  LENGTH=73,                                            X
                  ATTRB=(PROT),                                         X
                  INITIAL='Press the <Enter> key to exit from this help scX
                  reen and resume processing'
***********************************************************************
         DFHMSD TYPE=FINAL
         END
```

Figure 11.4 *(Continued)*

cursor is positioned in the field for which help is desired. You can, of course, determine where on the screen the cursor is located, using the EIBCPOSN field of the execute interface block. As indicated in Appendix A, EIBCPOSN returns as a value 0 through 1919, each value representing one of the 1,920 positions on the terminal screen where the cursor could be positioned. With appropriate logic you could figure out which field the cursor was positioned in based on its location, and then send the appropriate help screen for that field.

Apart from the logic needed to figure out which field the terminal operator is "pointing to" with the cursor, there is not much difference in programming one static information screen or several field-specific help screens. We leave to you as an exercise the implementation of multiple field-specific help screens based on this technique.

If you didn't want to hard code multiple help screens for field-specific help text, you could, with more complication, house the help text in an indexed file. With appropriate choice of the primary key of the lines of help text, you could detect the field in which the cursor is positioned, then start reading records sequentially from the appropriate point in the help text file to the screen.

11.6 FULL-SCALE INTERACTIVE TUTORIALS

Interactive tutorials are an appealing training mechanism. They can provide simulated experience with realistic situations, and represent a type of self-study. Using such a tutorial, a terminal operator is guided to make certain entries as a training exercise, and operator responses (either correct or incorrect) are evaluated and critiqued in screen windows or messages.

Interactive tutorials are potentially very complex and require a high degree of specialized knowledge in both teaching/learning methods and programming. Since the instructional content of interactive tutorials is so high, many implementations of them don't actually use the "real" on-line software involved at all. Instead, they simulate interaction with it to better channel and control what is presented, often by using copies of actual screens that have been stored as text files.

Interactive tutorials are more accurately regarded as computer-based-training (CBT) or computer-aided instruction (CAI), rather than as a form of on-line help built into a production system. A variety of specialized authoring systems exist to facilitate the development of interactive courseware. While the subject of interactive tutorials and their development is a fascinating one, preparing this form of courseware is outside the scope of our present discussion.

11.7 C360A00X: A PROGRAM WITH KEYBOARD MAP AND HELP SCREEN

Figure 11.5 shows you the complete source code for a program named C360A00X, a revision of the structured C360A001 program (CALC1) of Chapter 8. This program provides both a keyboard map and static help screen. The terminal operator obtains the keyboard map by pressing PF1, and the static help screen by pressing PF2. Pressing PF3 invokes a clean-the-screen function of the same type as you have already seen in Chapter 10. Clearly, this represents a major upgrade in functionality from the original structured CALC1 program.

We'll point out to you how we implemented the keyboard map and help screen in C360A00X. You'll see how simple adding this functionality to a structured program really is. As in earlier chapters, our discussion is tied to letter annotations we have placed on the program source code, in Figure 11.5.

a. Here you see the literal values for the mapset name and map name of the static information screen, which we named mapset $002M, map HELPMAP.

b. Our WS-FIRST-TIME-FLAG will receive the EIBCALEN value from the execute interface block after each reawakening of the program. We have made the WS-COMMUNICATION-AREA (at letter "c") two bytes now instead of one. Therefore, WS-FIRST-TIME-FLAG will normally be 0 when the program is first executed, and 2 each time it is reawakened. But if we arrange to send back just one byte to ourselves, after presenting either the keyboard map or the static help screen, we can do "first time" screen transmission processing then, too. You'll see that we do send back just one byte to ourselves in paragraphs 9300 (letter "g") and 9400 (letter "i") for this very reason, using the LENGTH clause of the RETURN command.

The **LENGTH clause** is optional, and if you do not code it, CICS uses the full length of the field the program sends back to itself. If you code LENGTH as a value smaller than the field length, you limit the number of characters actually conveyed by CICS back to the program. The value in the EIBCALEN field when the program is next awakened reflects the actual length of the data passed back to the program.

c. We make WS-COMMUNICATION-AREA two bytes now instead of one, so that we can distinguish between the real first time execution of the program, execution after presentation of a keyboard map or help screen, and execution after ordinary data entry. (See the discussion at "b" above, and at letters "g" and "i".)

```
EDIT ---- CSCJGJ.CSC360.COBOL(C360A00X) - 01.01 ------------- COLUMNS 007 078
COMMAND ===>                                                  SCROLL ===> PAGE
****** ***************************** TOP OF DATA ******************************
       ID DIVISION.
       PROGRAM-ID.      C360A00X.
       AUTHOR.          J JANOSSY.

      *-----------------------------------------------------------------
      *   VERSION C360A00X
      *   THIS IS THE REVISED CALC1 PROGRAM IN CICS VERSION 3.3.  IT
      *   INCLUDES ACCESS TO AN ON-LINE HELP SCREEN STORED AS A MAP.
      *   A KEY MAP PROVIDED BY PRESSING <PF1> REVEALS THAT THE FULL
      *   SCREEN OF HELP IS SELECTABLE BY PRESSING <PF2>.
      *
      *   THIS PROGRAM IS THE MOST CAPABLE EXAMPLE OF THE CALC1 PROGRAM
      *   WE DEMONSTRATE.  IT USES A FIRST-TIME FLAG OF LENGTH 0, 1, OR
      *   2 TO "RECOVER" FROM USE OF THE KEY MAP OR HELP SCREEN.
      *-----------------------------------------------------------------

       DATA DIVISION.
       WORKING-STORAGE SECTION.
       01  WS-TRANS-ID                 PIC X(4)   VALUE '$001'.

       01  WS-MAPSET-NAME              PIC X(8)   VALUE '$001M   '.
       01  WS-MAP-NAME                 PIC X(8)   VALUE 'CALCMAP '.
                                                                    (A)
       01  WS-MAPSET-NAME-2            PIC X(8)   VALUE '$002M   '.
       01  WS-MAP-NAME-2               PIC X(8)   VALUE 'HELPMAP '.

       01  WS-FIRST-TIME-FLAG          PIC S9(4) BINARY.
           88 FIRST-TIME                          VALUES 0, 1.    (B)

       01  WS-GOOD-BAD-FLAG            PIC X(1)   VALUE 'G'.
           88 DATA-GOOD                           VALUE 'G'.

       01  WS-RESPONSE-CODE            PIC S9(8) BINARY.
       01  WS-SALES-TAX-RATE           PIC V99    VALUE .08.        (C)
       01  WS-COMMUNICATION-AREA       PIC X(2).
       01  WS-END-MESSAGE              PIC X(60) VALUE
           'QUITTING AS REQUESTED -- USE  CESF LOGOFF  TO END CICS'.

       01  WS-ERROR-MESSAGES.
           05 PIC X(35) VALUE '** CICS ERROR -- CONTACT HELP DESK '.
           05 PIC X(35) VALUE '-- REPORT THIS INFORMATION **      '.
           05 PIC X(9)  VALUE SPACES.

           05 WS-ERROR-LINE1.
              10              PIC X(14)     VALUE '   EIBTRNID = '.
              10 WS-EIBTRNID  PIC X(4).
              10              PIC X(61)     VALUE SPACES.

           05 WS-ERROR-LINE2.
              10              PIC X(14)     VALUE '   EIBRSRCE = '.
              10 WS-EIBRSRCE  PIC X(8).
              10              PIC X(57)     VALUE SPACES.

           05 WS-ERROR-LINE3.
              10              PIC X(14)     VALUE '   EIBRESP  = '.
              10 WS-EIBRESP   PIC ZZZZZZZ9.
              10              PIC X(57)     VALUE SPACES.

           05 WS-ERROR-LINE4.
              10              PIC X(14)     VALUE '   EIBRESP2 = '.
              10 WS-EIBRESP2  PIC ZZZZZZZ9.
              10              PIC X(57)     VALUE SPACES.

           05 PIC X(79) VALUE ALL '*'.
```

Figure 11.5 Source code for the C360A00X (revised CALC1) program, which provides both keyboard map and static help screen.

D

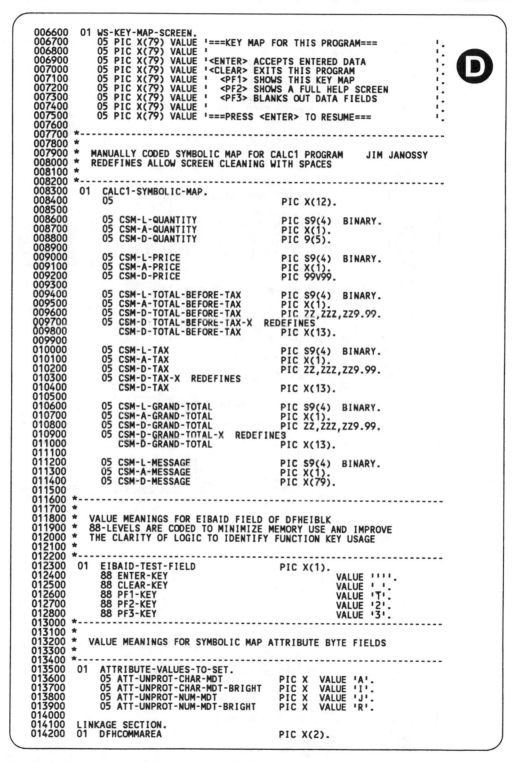

```
 01 WS-KEY-MAP-SCREEN.
     05 PIC X(79) VALUE '===KEY MAP FOR THIS PROGRAM===                   '.
     05 PIC X(79) VALUE '                                                 '.
     05 PIC X(79) VALUE '<ENTER> ACCEPTS ENTERED DATA                     '.
     05 PIC X(79) VALUE '<CLEAR> EXITS THIS PROGRAM                       '.
     05 PIC X(79) VALUE '   <PF1> SHOWS THIS KEY MAP                      '.
     05 PIC X(79) VALUE '   <PF2> SHOWS A FULL HELP SCREEN                '.
     05 PIC X(79) VALUE '   <PF3> BLANKS OUT DATA FIELDS                  '.
     05 PIC X(79) VALUE '                                                 '.
     05 PIC X(79) VALUE '===PRESS <ENTER> TO RESUME===                    '.

*-----------------------------------------------------------------
*
*  MANUALLY CODED SYMBOLIC MAP FOR CALC1 PROGRAM    JIM JANOSSY
*  REDEFINES ALLOW SCREEN CLEANING WITH SPACES
*
*-----------------------------------------------------------------
 01  CALC1-SYMBOLIC-MAP.
     05                               PIC X(12).

     05 CSM-L-QUANTITY                PIC S9(4)  BINARY.
     05 CSM-A-QUANTITY                PIC X(1).
     05 CSM-D-QUANTITY                PIC 9(5).

     05 CSM-L-PRICE                   PIC S9(4)  BINARY.
     05 CSM-A-PRICE                   PIC X(1).
     05 CSM-D-PRICE                   PIC 99V99.

     05 CSM-L-TOTAL-BEFORE-TAX        PIC S9(4)  BINARY.
     05 CSM-A-TOTAL-BEFORE-TAX        PIC X(1).
     05 CSM-D-TOTAL-BEFORE-TAX        PIC ZZ,ZZZ,ZZ9.99.
     05 CSM-D-TOTAL-BEFORE-TAX-X  REDEFINES
        CSM-D-TOTAL-BEFORE-TAX        PIC X(13).

     05 CSM-L-TAX                     PIC S9(4)  BINARY.
     05 CSM-A-TAX                     PIC X(1).
     05 CSM-D-TAX                     PIC ZZ,ZZZ,ZZ9.99.
     05 CSM-D-TAX-X  REDEFINES
        CSM-D-TAX                     PIC X(13).

     05 CSM-L-GRAND-TOTAL             PIC S9(4)  BINARY.
     05 CSM-A-GRAND-TOTAL             PIC X(1).
     05 CSM-D-GRAND-TOTAL             PIC ZZ,ZZZ,ZZ9.99.
     05 CSM-D-GRAND-TOTAL-X  REDEFINES
        CSM-D-GRAND-TOTAL             PIC X(13).

     05 CSM-L-MESSAGE                 PIC S9(4)  BINARY.
     05 CSM-A-MESSAGE                 PIC X(1).
     05 CSM-D-MESSAGE                 PIC X(79).

*-----------------------------------------------------------------
*
*  VALUE MEANINGS FOR EIBAID FIELD OF DFHEIBLK
*  88-LEVELS ARE CODED TO MINIMIZE MEMORY USE AND IMPROVE
*  THE CLARITY OF LOGIC TO IDENTIFY FUNCTION KEY USAGE
*
*-----------------------------------------------------------------
 01  EIBAID-TEST-FIELD                PIC X(1).
     88 ENTER-KEY                                 VALUE ''''.
     88 CLEAR-KEY                                 VALUE '_'.
     88 PF1-KEY                                   VALUE 'T'.
     88 PF2-KEY                                   VALUE '2'.
     88 PF3-KEY                                   VALUE '3'.
*-----------------------------------------------------------------
*
*  VALUE MEANINGS FOR SYMBOLIC MAP ATTRIBUTE BYTE FIELDS
*
*-----------------------------------------------------------------
 01  ATTRIBUTE-VALUES-TO-SET.
     05 ATT-UNPROT-CHAR-MDT           PIC X  VALUE 'A'.
     05 ATT-UNPROT-CHAR-MDT-BRIGHT    PIC X  VALUE 'I'.
     05 ATT-UNPROT-NUM-MDT            PIC X  VALUE 'J'.
     05 ATT-UNPROT-NUM-MDT-BRIGHT     PIC X  VALUE 'R'.

 LINKAGE SECTION.
 01  DFHCOMMAREA                      PIC X(2).
```

Figure 11.5 *(Continued)*

```
PROCEDURE DIVISION.
*-----------------------------------------------------------------
0000-MAINLINE.
    PERFORM 3333-ALWAYS-TEST.

    EVALUATE  TRUE

       WHEN  FIRST-TIME
          PERFORM 9000-FIRST-TIME

       WHEN  PF1-KEY
          PERFORM 9300-SHOW-KEY-MAP-SCREEN

       WHEN  PF2-KEY
          PERFORM 9400-SHOW-HELP-SCREEN

       WHEN  PF3-KEY
          PERFORM 9100-CLEAN-THE-SCREEN

       WHEN  ENTER-KEY
          PERFORM 0500-NORMAL-PROCESSING

       WHEN  OTHER
          PERFORM 9200-INVALID-KEY-MESSAGE

    END-EVALUATE.

    PERFORM 8000-RETURN-WITH-TRANS-ID.

*-----------------------------------------------------------------

0500-NORMAL-PROCESSING.
    PERFORM 1000-RECEIVE-MAP.

    PERFORM 5000-VALIDATE-FIELDS
    IF DATA-GOOD
       PERFORM 5500-COMPUTE-RESULTS
    END-IF.

    PERFORM 1200-SEND-MAP-DATAONLY.

*-----------------------------------------------------------------

1000-RECEIVE-MAP.
    EXEC CICS
       RECEIVE MAP        (WS-MAP-NAME)
               MAPSET     (WS-MAPSET-NAME)
               INTO       (CALC1-SYMBOLIC-MAP)
               RESP       (WS-RESPONSE-CODE)
    END-EXEC.

*================

    EVALUATE  WS-RESPONSE-CODE

*----------------

       WHEN  DFHRESP(NORMAL)
          CONTINUE

*----------------

       WHEN  DFHRESP(MAPFAIL)
          MOVE -1 TO CSM-L-QUANTITY
          MOVE 'NO DATA ENTERED; ENTER DATA OR <CLEAR> TO QUIT'
             TO CSM-D-MESSAGE
          PERFORM 1200-SEND-MAP-DATAONLY
          PERFORM 8000-RETURN-WITH-TRANS-ID

*----------------

       WHEN  OTHER
          PERFORM 9999-ABORT

    END-EVALUATE.
*================
```

Figure 11.5 *(Continued)*

```
 1200-SEND-MAP-DATAONLY.
     EXEC CICS
          SEND MAP       (WS-MAP-NAME)
               MAPSET    (WS-MAPSET-NAME)
               FROM      (CALC1-SYMBOLIC-MAP)
               DATAONLY
               CURSOR
     END-EXEC.

*-----------------------------------------------------------------

 3333-ALWAYS-TEST.
     MOVE EIBAID    TO  EIBAID-TEST-FIELD.
     IF CLEAR-KEY
        PERFORM 8900-QUIT.
     MOVE EIBCALEN  TO  WS-FIRST-TIME-FLAG.

*-----------------------------------------------------------------

 5000-VALIDATE-FIELDS.

     MOVE ATT-UNPROT-NUM-MDT TO  CSM-A-QUANTITY
                                 CSM-A-PRICE.

     IF CSM-D-PRICE NOT NUMERIC
        MOVE 'B' TO WS-GOOD-BAD-FLAG
        MOVE ATT-UNPROT-NUM-MDT-BRIGHT TO CSM-A-PRICE
        MOVE -1 TO CSM-L-PRICE
        MOVE 'PRICE MUST BE NUMERIC; CORRECT, PRESS <ENTER>'
           TO CSM-D-MESSAGE
     END-IF.

     IF CSM-D-QUANTITY NOT NUMERIC
        MOVE 'B' TO WS-GOOD-BAD-FLAG
        MOVE ATT-UNPROT-NUM-MDT-BRIGHT TO CSM-A-QUANTITY
        MOVE -1 TO CSM-L-QUANTITY
        MOVE 'QUANTITY MUST BE NUMERIC; CORRECT, PRESS <ENTER>'
           TO CSM-D-MESSAGE
     END-IF.

*-----------------------------------------------------------------

 5500-COMPUTE-RESULTS.
     COMPUTE CSM-D-TOTAL-BEFORE-TAX =
        CSM-D-QUANTITY * CSM-D-PRICE.
     COMPUTE CSM-D-TAX =
        CSM-D-QUANTITY * CSM-D-PRICE * WS-SALES-TAX-RATE.
     COMPUTE CSM-D-GRAND-TOTAL =
        CSM-D-QUANTITY * CSM-D-PRICE * WS-SALES-TAX-RATE +
        CSM-D-QUANTITY * CSM-D-PRICE.
     MOVE 'RESULTS COMPUTED, ENTER MORE DATA OR <CLEAR> TO QUIT'
        TO CSM-D-MESSAGE.
     MOVE -1 TO CSM-L-QUANTITY.

*-----------------------------------------------------------------

 8000-RETURN-WITH-TRANS-ID.
     EXEC CICS
        RETURN TRANSID   (WS-TRANS-ID)
               COMMAREA  (WS-COMMUNICATION-AREA)
     END-EXEC.

*-----------------------------------------------------------------

 8900-QUIT.
     EXEC CICS
          SEND TEXT FROM (WS-END-MESSAGE)
               ERASE
               FREEKB
     END-EXEC.

     EXEC CICS
          RETURN
     END-EXEC.

*-----------------------------------------------------------------
```

Figure 11.5 *(Continued)*

```
9000-FIRST-TIME.
    MOVE LOW-VALUES TO CALC1-SYMBOLIC-MAP.
    MOVE 'ENTER VALUES, PRESS <ENTER>, <CLEAR> TO QUIT'
       TO CSM-D-MESSAGE.
    MOVE -1 TO CSM-L-QUANTITY.

    EXEC CICS
         SEND MAPSET    (WS-MAPSET-NAME)
              MAP       (WS-MAP-NAME)
              FROM      (CALC1-SYMBOLIC-MAP)
              ERASE
              CURSOR
    END-EXEC.

*-----------------------------------------------------------------

9100-CLEAN-THE-SCREEN.
    MOVE LOW-VALUES TO CALC1-SYMBOLIC-MAP.
    MOVE SPACES TO  CSM-D-TOTAL-BEFORE-TAX-X
                    CSM-D-TAX-X
                    CSM-D-GRAND-TOTAL-X.

    MOVE 'ENTER VALUES, PRESS <ENTER>, <CLEAR> TO QUIT'
       TO CSM-D-MESSAGE.
    MOVE -1 TO CSM-L-QUANTITY.

    EXEC CICS
        SEND MAP       (WS-MAP-NAME)
             MAPSET    (WS-MAPSET-NAME)
             FROM      (CALC1-SYMBOLIC-MAP)
             DATAONLY
             ERASEAUP
             CURSOR
    END-EXEC.

*-----------------------------------------------------------------

9200-INVALID-KEY-MESSAGE.
    MOVE LOW-VALUES TO CALC1-SYMBOLIC-MAP.
    MOVE 'YOU PRESSED WRONG KEY! PRESS <ENTER>, <CLEAR> TO QUIT'
       TO CSM-D-MESSAGE.
    MOVE -1 TO CSM-L-QUANTITY.
    PERFORM 1200-SEND-MAP-DATAONLY.

*-----------------------------------------------------------------

9300-SHOW-KEY-MAP-SCREEN.
    EXEC CICS
       SEND TEXT FROM (WS-KEY-MAP-SCREEN)
            ERASE
            FREEKB
    END-EXEC.

* NOTE: PASSING COMMAREA OF LENGTH 1 INSTEAD OF LETTING THE
* LENGTH DEFAULT TO THE ACTUAL LENGTH OF 2 WILL CAUSE THE
* MAINLINE TO TREAT THE NEXT PROGRAM ACTIVATION AS "FIRST
* TIME" AND BRINGS BACK A FRESH WORKING SCREEN.

    EXEC CICS
       RETURN TRANSID   (WS-TRANS-ID)
              COMMAREA  (WS-COMMUNICATION-AREA)
              LENGTH    (1)
    END-EXEC.
```

Figure 11.5 *(Continued)*

```
036600
036700  9400-SHOW-HELP-SCREEN.
036800      EXEC CICS
036900           SEND MAPSET     (WS-MAPSET-NAME-2)
037000                MAP        (WS-MAP-NAME-2)
037100                MAPONLY
037200                ERASE
037300                CURSOR
037400      END-EXEC.
037500
037600 * NOTE: PASSING COMMAREA OF LENGTH 1 INSTEAD OF LETTING THE
037700 * LENGTH DEFAULT TO THE ACTUAL LENGTH OF 2 WILL CAUSE THE
037800 * MAINLINE TO TREAT THE NEXT PROGRAM ACTIVATION AS "FIRST
037900 * TIME" AND BRING BACK A FRESH WORKING SCREEN.
038000
038100      EXEC CICS
038200         RETURN TRANSID    (WS-TRANS-ID)
038300                COMMAREA   (WS-COMMUNICATION-AREA)
038400                LENGTH     (1)
038500      END-EXEC.
038600
038700 *-----------------------------------------------------------------
038800
038900  9999-ABORT.
039000      MOVE EIBTRNID    TO  WS-EIBTRNID.
039100      MOVE EIBRSRCE    TO  WS-EIBRSRCE.
039200      MOVE EIBRESP     TO  WS-EIBRESP.
039300      MOVE EIBRESP2    TO  WS-EIBRESP2.
039400
039500      EXEC CICS
039600         SEND TEXT FROM (WS-ERROR-MESSAGES)
039700              ERASE
039800              ALARM
039900              FREEKB
040000      END-EXEC.
040100
040200      EXEC CICS
040300           RETURN
040400      END-EXEC.
```

Figure 11.5 *(Continued)*

d. Here you see the text of the keyboard map. Notice that we coded each line as 79 bytes, so that each would appear on a new line when the entire group was sent to the terminal screen using the **SEND TEXT** command at line 34900. (When prefaced automatically with an attribute byte by the SEND TEXT command, the 79 bytes fills one screen line.) A more efficient way to code and send this keyboard map involves making each text line shorter, and coding "newline" control bytes, hex value X'15', after each line. Figure 11.6 shows you alternate coding for the keyboard map that presents the same information with less data transmission.

e. The mainline EVALUATE of the revised program now includes recognition of the PF1 and PF3 keys as valid, sending control to a "show keymap" and "show help screen" paragraphs. Note that the code after the mainline in this revised program has not changed further except for the addition of the 9300-SHOW-KEY-MAP-SCREEN and 9400-SHOW-HELP-SCREEN paragraphs. This reflects the flexibility inherent in functional modularization.

f. The 9300-SHOW-KEY-MAP-SCREEN paragraph sends the keymap to the terminal screen, then returns control to CICS.

g. After sending the keyboard map, we pass back just one byte of WS-COMMUNICATION-AREA, not its full length of two. This is how we'll "recover" from the

```
EDIT ---- CSCJGJ.CSC360.COBOL(C360A00Y) - 01.02 -------------- COLUMNS 007 078
COMMAND ===>                                                  SCROLL ===> PAGE
 01 WS-KEY-MAP-SCREEN.
    05 PIC X(39) VALUE '===KEY MAP FOR THIS PROGRAM===          '.
    05 PIC X(01) VALUE X'15'.
    05 PIC X(39) VALUE '                                        '.
    05 PIC X(01) VALUE X'15'.
    05 PIC X(39) VALUE '<ENTER> ACCEPTS ENTERED DATA            '.
    05 PIC X(01) VALUE X'15'.
    05 PIC X(39) VALUE '<CLEAR> EXITS THIS PROGRAM              '.
    05 PIC X(01) VALUE X'15'.
    05 PIC X(39) VALUE '  <PF1> SHOWS THIS KEY MAP              '.
    05 PIC X(01) VALUE X'15'.
    05 PIC X(39) VALUE '  <PF2> SHOWS A FULL HELP SCREEN        '.
    05 PIC X(01) VALUE X'15'.
    05 PIC X(39) VALUE '  <PF3> BLANKS OUT DATA FIELDS          '.
    05 PIC X(01) VALUE X'15'.
    05 PIC X(39) VALUE '                                        '.
    05 PIC X(01) VALUE X'15'.
    05 PIC X(39) VALUE '===PRESS <ENTER> TO RESUME===           '.
    05 PIC X(01) VALUE X'15'.
```

Figure 11.6 Revised coding for a keyboard map, using "Newline" X'15' bytes and shorter coded text lines to minimize data transmission.

presentation of the keyboard map, and make the program replace the actual data entry screen the next time it is reawakened.

h. The 9400-SHOW-HELP-SCREEN paragraph sends the static information help screen to the terminal, then returns control to CICS.

i. After sending the help screen, we pass back just one byte of WS-COMMUNICATION-AREA, not its full length of two. This is how we'll "recover" from the presentation of the help screen, and make the program replace the actual data entry screen the next time it is reawakened.

We think you'll agree that including keyboard map and a static information help screen functions in CICS programs is easy and quite manageable when the existing code is functionally structured. In the last several chapters of this book you'll see how more functions to accomplish input and output to files can also be added to structured CICS programs in a highly manageable, modular way.

11.8 FOR YOUR REVIEW

The following terms were introduced or reviewed in this chapter. If you understand this chapter, you should be comfortable with defining each of these terms in relationship to CICS:

Context-sensitive help
Continuously displayed key definitions
Extended topic-specific assistance
Interactive tutorials
Keyboard maps
LENGTH clause
On-line help
SEND TEXT command
Static information screens

11.9 REVIEW QUESTIONS

1. Identify and describe the five categories of on-line help that might be provided to a terminal user, indicating briefly for each category what programming effort is involved in supplying it to the terminal operator.
2. Discuss three of the major problems of continuously displayed key definitions.
3. Is BMS map code required in order to provide a keyboard map to the end user? Discuss how a keyboard map can be provided without map code.
4. Describe why the PF1 key is a logical choice for the function key that summons the first level of on-line help in CICS system.
5. Discuss why a separate set of BMS map code is usually required to provide even a single static information screen, and explain the most practical way to develop its code.
6. When a program provides a keyboard map as described in this chapter, or a static information screen, explain why you must expand the amount of information the program passes back to itself using the COMMAREA and WS-COMMUNICATION-AREA.
7. Describe the most convenient sensing mechanism to identify the topic for which a terminal wants context-specific help.
8. Describe what interactive tutorials are, and why specialized authoring systems are usually used to develop them.
9. Describe what the LENGTH clause of the CICS RETURN command does, explaining what happens (a) when you don't code it, and (b) when you code it with a value shorter than the actual length of the field the program passes back to itself.
10. Why is the length of each text line at lines 6700 through 7500 in the C360A00X program in Figure 11.5, coded as 79 bytes, when much less than this number of characters is actually coded in each line of the keyboard map? Describe an alternative way to achieve the same effect with less data transmission.

11.10 HANDS-ON EXERCISES

A. Install a clean-the-screen function similar to paragraph 9100-CLEAN-THE-SCREEN in program C360A00X (Figure 11.5) in one of the structured CICS programs you have already designed and implemented. Develop a keyboard map for your revised program. Include in this keyboard map the definition of the PF1 key as the key associated with display of the keyboard map, and information on any other PF keys recognized by the program. Add logic to your program to recognize the PF1 key and display the keyboard map when it is pressed, and to restore the screen to its original startup content when an AID key is next pressed. Thoroughly test your revised program.

B. Develop a static information screen for one of the structured CICS programs you have already designed and implemented. Implement the information screen using BMS map code and a valid map id in your installation. Add logic to your program to recognize the PF2 key and display the information screen when it is pressed, and to restore the screen to its original startup content when an AID key is next pressed. If your program also provides a keyboard map with the PF1 key, don't forget to add the PF2 key definition to the keyboard map! Thoroughly test your revised program.

C. If you have completed exercise B, extend the help screen support in your program to provide two static information screens, each accessible with a different PF key. Add the code for the second map to the same mapset housing your first help screen. Include logic in your program to recognize an additional PF key to cause display of the second help screen, and modify text of the first help screen and your keyboard map to mention it. Thoroughly test your revised program.

D. A more challenging assignment: Research the operation of the EIBCPOSN field of the execute interface block using Appendix A, and develop a way to provide field-specific on-line help in a structured CICS program you have already developed. Assign the field-specific help to the PF4 key. Choose a program that has only a few fields, and arrange logic to summon the field-specific assistance by detecting which field the cursor is positioned in. House the separate information screens as maps within a single mapset, similar to the way you would approach exercise C above. Debug and thoroughly test your program.

12

Using Machine-Generated Symbolic Maps

In the first eleven chapters of this book, we discussed how communication takes place between terminals and programs using CICS. We described the **data transmission record** that carries data to and from the terminal screen, and we showed you how this record is formed. In our programming examples, however, we have up to now demonstrated only our use of manually coded (or GENMAP generated) **symbolic maps**, representing COBOL descriptions of data transmission records. In this chapter, we convert one of our simpler programs to use the machine-generated symbolic map that you can produce from your BMS map source code. We'll show you how to create a machine-generated symbolic map, where to store it, what it looks like, how you use it, and the impact its use has on program coding and readability.

In many ways, machine-generated symbolic maps make CICS programs harder to work with, since they force the use of very short, cryptic data names for the fields of the data transmission record. If you will continue to use manually coded or screen painter-generated symbolic maps, you need not read this chapter with the same intensity as if you plan on using machine-generated symbolic maps. We do, however, use machine-generated symbolic maps in the file update examples that follow, so you need to at least briefly examine this chapter, even if you'll not apply it to your own work!

12.1 WHERE DO MACHINE-GENERATED SYMBOLIC MAPS ORIGINATE?

Machine-generated symbolic maps are produced from the same BMS map source code that you use to create a physical map for a screen. We showed you the BMS map code for our initial CALC1 screen in Chapter 4, Figure 4.4, and an annotated version of the same BMS map code in Chapter 5 in Figure 5.4. Refresh your memory of these two chapters in general, and these figures in particular, for the discussion that follows.

12.2 HOW BMS MAP CODE FIELD NAMES ARE USED

When you use your BMS map source code to produce the physical map for a screen, the field names you code on your input/output fields, highlighted in Figure 5.4, are important simply for their presence. The presence of a field name makes the field accessible to a program by making the field a part of the data transmission record. For the purpose of the physical map, the value of the actual field name itself is unimportant. The actual field name does not appear in the data transmission record, nor is the actual field name represented in the physical map.

When you use your BMS map source code to produce a machine-generated symbolic map, the actual values of the field names you code in your BMS map code do become important. If you compare the BMS map code field names in Figure 5.4 with the machine-generated symbolic map shown in Figure 5.8, you'll see that the symbolic map field names consist of the field names coded in the BMS map code, plus a letter such as L, F, A, I, or O.

You can use BMS map code field names of up to only seven characters. The field names you code must be unique (and hopefully meaningful!) within this constraint. BMS map field names must be formed using only letters and numbers. The first character of a field name must be a letter, and you cannot use punctuation of any type within a BMS field name.

12.3 PICIN AND PICOUT CODING

If you refer back to Chapter 4, Figure 4.10, you'll see an example of BMS map code for a field named CNAME (for "customer name") coded with the clause PICIN. If you look at Figure 4.11, you'll see extracted BMS map code for a field named TOTB4, with the coding PICOUT. We have coded these to document and describe the input or output format of the field.

When you use **manually coded symbolic maps**, you do not actually need to use the PICIN and PICOUT clauses in your hand-coded or screen painter-generated BMS map source code. In this case, the only thing you do with your BMS map code is process it into a physical map. A physical map does not contain any field formatting information from PICIN or PICOUT. Even including **NUM** in ATTRIB coding for a field does not involve or require any form of PICIN coding.

PICIN and PICOUT are present only for the assembler's use in producing machine-generated symbolic maps. These clauses "pass through" your intended PIC coding for each field to the machine-generated symbolic map. If you do not code a PICIN or a PICOUT for a field, the field's PIC will automatically be generated as PIC X(..), in other words, alphanumeric, with the length equal to the number of bytes you have indicated for the LENGTH in your BMS map source code.

```
EDIT ---- CSCJGJ.CSC360.CNTL(MAPJOB) - 01.08 ---------------- COLUMNS 001 072
COMMAND ===>                                                  SCROLL ===> PAGE
****** ****************************** TOP OF DATA ******************************
//CSCJGJA   JOB 1,                   ACCOUNTING INFORMATION
//   'BIN 7--JANOSSY',               PROGRAMMER NAME AND DELIVERY BIN
//   CLASS=A,                        INPUT QUEUE CLASS
//   MSGLEVEL=(1,1),                 HOW MUCH MVS SYSTEM PRINT DESIRED
//   MSGCLASS=X,                     PRINT DESTINATION X A L N OR O
//   TIME=(0,6),                     SAFETY LIMIT: RUN TIME UP TO 6 SECS
//   REGION=2M,                      ALLOW UP TO 2 MEGS VIRTUAL MEMORY
//   NOTIFY=CSCJGJ                   WHO TO TELL WHEN JOB IS DONE
//*-----------------------------------------------------------------------
//*  PREPARE PHYSICAL AND SYMBOLIC MAPS FROM BMS MAP CODE
//*  THIS JCL IS STORED AT CSCJGJ.CSC360.CNTL(MAPJOB)
//*-----------------------------------------------------------------------
//*
//   SET  SORCLIB='CSCJGJ.CSC360.CNTL',     SOURCE LIBRARY FOR MAP CODE
//          BNAME='EX7MAP',                 BMS MAP CODE MEMBER NAME
//*
//        LOADLIB='CCP.LOADLIB',            CICS LOAD LIBRARY
//          PNAME='$001M',                  PHYSICAL MAP MEMBER NAME
//*
//        COPYLIB='CSCJGJ.CSC360.COPYLIB',  COBOL LIBRARY FOR SYM MAPS
//          SNAME='A001S'                   SYMBOLIC MAP MEMBER NAME
```

Figure 12.1 You can create a machine-generated symbolic map using the MAPJOB job control language.

12.4 PRODUCING A MACHINE-GENERATED SYMBOLIC MAP

You create a machine-generated symbolic map by processing your BMS map source code with the IBM assembler, giving the assembler the execution parm value SYSPARM(DSECT). You can see the job control language to accomplish this in Chapter 5, Figure 5.10, within the JCL for the MAPJOB job stream. STEP030 of the MAPJOB job stream, at lines 74 through 87, processes BMS map source code into a symbolic map. The symbolic map is written to the //SYSPUNCH DD statement at line 87. You can see that our MAPJOB JCL writes this as a member of a library. The name of the library &COPYLIB and the name of the member within it &SNAME are assigned by the SET statements at the top of the MAPJOB job stream.

Figure 12.1 illustrates just the top part of the MAPJOB job stream. We purposely arranged this job stream using the MVS/ESA Version 4 SET and symbolic parameter feature so that you could assign the intended values to all symbolic parameters by just accessing the first screenful of JCL. You can see that we have assigned the name of the library to house the machine-generated symbolic map as CSCJGJ.CSC360.COPYLIB, and the member name for the symbolic map as A001S. You can house the machine-generated symbolic map in any partitioned data set housing 80-byte fixed-length records. The member name follows the same rules as any partitioned data set member name: up to eight bytes, consisting of letters and numbers only, with the first character being a letter. You cannot use any punctuation symbols within a member name.

12.5 CONTENT OF A MACHINE-GENERATED SYMBOLIC MAP

Figure 12.2 shows you the machine-generated symbolic map generated by the EX7MAP BMS map source code shown in Figures 4.4 and 5.4. You can see that this is really a rather poorly formatted COBOL description of the data transmission record illustrated graphically in Figure 5.5. In this description, CALCMAPI is the data transmission record defined for input (RECEIVE MAP), while its redefinition named CALCMAPO is the very same record described for outputting (SEND MAP) purposes. The name itself, CALCMAPI, comes from the name we coded in

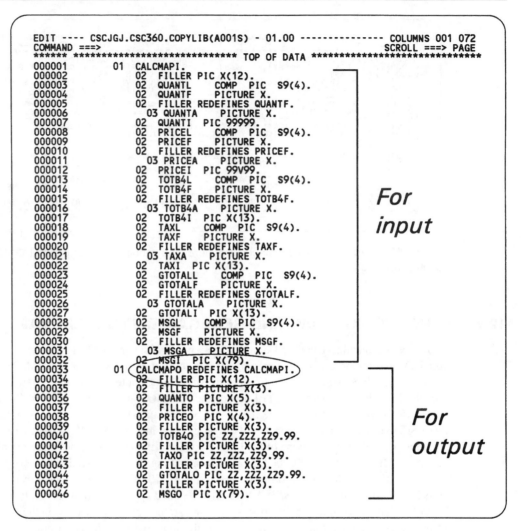

```
EDIT ---- CSCJGJ.CSC360.COPYLIB(A001S) - 01.00 --------------- COLUMNS 001 072
COMMAND ===>                                                   SCROLL ===> PAGE
****** ****************************** TOP OF DATA ******************************
          01  CALCMAPI.
              02  FILLER PIC X(12).
              02  QUANTL     COMP  PIC  S9(4).
              02  QUANTF     PICTURE X.
              02  FILLER REDEFINES QUANTF.
                03 QUANTA     PICTURE X.
              02  QUANTI  PIC 99999.
              02  PRICEL     COMP  PIC  S9(4).
              02  PRICEF     PICTURE X.
              02  FILLER REDEFINES PRICEF.
                03 PRICEA     PICTURE X.
              02  PRICEI  PIC 99V99.
              02  TOTB4L     COMP  PIC  S9(4).
              02  TOTB4F     PICTURE X.
              02  FILLER REDEFINES TOTB4F.
                03 TOTB4A     PICTURE X.
              02  TOTB4I  PIC X(13).
              02  TAXL    COMP  PIC  S9(4).
              02  TAXF     PICTURE X.
              02  FILLER REDEFINES TAXF.
                03 TAXA     PICTURE X.
              02  TAXI  PIC X(13).
              02  GTOTALL     COMP  PIC  S9(4).
              02  GTOTALF     PICTURE X.
              02  FILLER REDEFINES GTOTALF.
                03 GTOTALA     PICTURE X.
              02  GTOTALI  PIC X(13).
              02  MSGL    COMP  PIC  S9(4).
              02  MSGF    PICTURE X.
              02  FILLER REDEFINES MSGF.
                03 MSGA     PICTURE X.
              02  MSGI  PIC X(79).
          01  CALCMAPO REDEFINES CALCMAPI.
              02  FILLER PIC X(12).
              02  FILLER PICTURE X(3).
              02  QUANTO  PIC X(5).
              02  FILLER PICTURE X(3).
              02  PRICEO  PIC X(4).
              02  FILLER PICTURE X(3).
              02  TOTB4O PIC ZZ,ZZZ,ZZ9.99.
              02  FILLER PICTURE X(3).
              02  TAXO PIC ZZ,ZZZ,ZZ9.99.
              02  FILLER PICTURE X(3).
              02  GTOTALO PIC ZZ,ZZZ,ZZ9.99.
              02  FILLER PICTURE X(3).
              02  MSGO  PIC X(79).
```

For input (lines CALCMAPI through MSGI)

For output (lines CALCMAPO through MSGO)

Figure 12.2 A machine-generated symbolic map actually contains two definitions of the data transmission record.

the BMS map code for the map (not mapset) name. Let's examine the coding generated for the QUANTITY field ("QUANTx") to see what the parts of this description are intended for.

Input record:

QUANTL — The name of the keystroke "length" field. Lets us access the two-byte binary number that houses the number of key entries the terminal operator made in the QUANT field.

QUANTF
QUANTA — These names are synonymous, and both access the attribute byte for the QUANT field. It is odd that they are located in the "input" description, because you would use them to put a new value into the attribute byte for a field before you SEND the symbolic map to the terminal. (IBM's multiple-level coding for these synonyms, and the fact that two names are defined, is also odd, and contributes to the strange appearance of the machine-generated symbolic map.)

QUANTI The name of the "input" data field. This field is coded with the value you coded for **PICIN**.

Output record:

QUANTO The name of the same data field as defined as QUANTI, except the **PICOUT** picture has automatically been coded here.

You can see that the two-byte length and one-byte attribute byte are accounted for in the output record description as simply FILLER PIC X(3). These must be accounted for, in the correct positions, because both the CALCMAPI and the CALCMAPO redefinition really describe the same, single data transmission record.

It's important to understand that a data transmission record is just that—a record—and that CICS conveys it to the terminal just as an airline carries containerized freight. If you ship a freight container, the airline really doesn't know or care what you put into it (assuming the contents are not dangerous or explosive, and there are no international customs considerations). You load the container, the container fits into an airliner, and it is conveyed from airport to airport for you.

You access and load the data fields of the transmission record as your own business. The "airline," CICS in this case, ships your data transmission record contents to the terminal without knowing or caring about what you have put into each field. If you have used a formatted numeric picture to load the contents of a given screen field, the field appears numerically formatted. But CICS neither knows about nor cares about your use of formatted numeric pictures in symbolic map fields. How you form the values you want to have conveyed to the terminal screen and displayed is up to you. The same goes for how you interpret the data fields conveyed from the screen to your program.

With this in mind, you can see that a machine-generated symbolic map, while much different from a manually coded symbolic map, really does the same thing. It is nothing special, in the way of a COBOL record description, which is why we can choose to use a manually coded one instead. The only advantage of using the machine-generated symbolic map is that it can be gotten free of any real effort, and it always matches the data transmission record produced by a **physical map** (terminal screen image) generated from the same BMS map source code. This is why some installations prefer machine-generated symbolic maps, even though their field name limitations make CICS program coding less clear and more cryptic.

12.6 CALC1 USING A MACHINE-GENERATED SYMBOLIC MAP

Figure 12.3 shows you the VS COBOL II source code for the structured CALC1 program originally illustrated in Chapter 8. Compare this program to the original program listed in Figure 8.2. You will see that at line 6000 we have now used **COPY** to bring in the symbolic map, accessing the member A001S.

The changes in the CALC1 program made necessary by our use of the machine-generated symbolic map begin at line 14800 and continue throughout the program. We have marked most of the changes with arrows. You'll notice that it is easy to make mistakes in coding the field names because they are so short, and the only difference between the several names associated with a field is the last letter.

```
EDIT ---- CSCJGJ.CSC360.COBOL(C360A00M) - 01.01 ------------- COLUMNS 007 078
COMMAND ===>                                                   SCROLL ===> PAGE
****** ****************************** TOP OF DATA *****************************
       ID DIVISION.
       PROGRAM-ID.    C360A001.
       AUTHOR.        J JANOSSY.

      *-----------------------------------------------------------------
      *  VERSION C360A00M
      *  THIS IS THE REVISED CALC1 PROGRAM CHANGED TO USE A MACHINE-
      *  GENERATED SYMBOLIC MAP INSTEAD OF A MANUALLY CODED SYMBOLIC
      *  MAP.  COPY BRINGS THE SYMBOLIC MAP INTO THE PROGRAM
      *-----------------------------------------------------------------

       DATA DIVISION.
       WORKING-STORAGE SECTION.
       01  WS-TRANS-ID                PIC X(4)  VALUE '$001'.
       01  WS-MAPSET-NAME             PIC X(8)  VALUE '$001M   '.
       01  WS-MAP-NAME                PIC X(8)  VALUE 'CALCMAP '.

       01  WS-FIRST-TIME-FLAG         PIC S9(4) BINARY.
           88 FIRST-TIME                        VALUE 0.

       01  WS-GOOD-BAD-FLAG           PIC X(1)  VALUE 'G'.
           88 DATA-GOOD                         VALUE 'G'.

       01  WS-RESPONSE-CODE           PIC S9(8) BINARY.
       01  WS-SALES-TAX-RATE          PIC V99   VALUE .08.
       01  WS-COMMUNICATION-AREA      PIC X(1).
       01  WS-END-MESSAGE             PIC X(60) VALUE
           'QUITTING AS REQUESTED -- USE  CESF LOGOFF  TO END CICS'.

       01  WS-ERROR-MESSAGES.
           05 PIC X(35) VALUE '** CICS ERROR -- CONTACT HELP DESK '.
           05 PIC X(35) VALUE '-- REPORT THIS INFORMATION **      '.
           05 PIC X(9)  VALUE SPACES.

           05 WS-ERROR-LINE1.
              10              PIC X(14)      VALUE '    EIBTRNID = '.
              10 WS-EIBTRNID  PIC X(4).
              10              PIC X(61)      VALUE SPACES.

           05 WS-ERROR-LINE2.
              10              PIC X(14)      VALUE '    EIBRSRCE = '.
              10 WS-EIBRSRCE  PIC X(8).
              10              PIC X(57)      VALUE SPACES.

           05 WS-ERROR-LINE3.
              10              PIC X(14)      VALUE '    EIBRESP  = '.
              10 WS-EIBRESP   PIC ZZZZZZZ9.
              10              PIC X(57)      VALUE SPACES.

           05 WS-ERROR-LINE4.
              10              PIC X(14)      VALUE '    EIBRESP2 = '.
              10 WS-EIBRESP2  PIC ZZZZZZZ9.
              10              PIC X(57)      VALUE SPACES.

           05 PIC X(79) VALUE ALL '*'.

      *--------------------------------
      *  MACHINE-GENERATED SYMBOLIC MAP
      *--------------------------------
           COPY A001S.

      *--------------------------------
      *
      *  VALUE MEANINGS FOR EIBAID FIELD OF DFHEIBLK
      *  88-LEVELS ARE CODED TO MINIMIZE MEMORY USE AND IMPROVE
      *  THE CLARITY OF LOGIC TO IDENTIFY FUNCTION KEY USAGE
      *
      *-----------------------------------------------------------------
       01  EIBAID-TEST-FIELD                       PIC X(1).
           88 ENTER-KEY                                     VALUE ''''.
           88 CLEAR-KEY                                     VALUE '_'.
           88 PF1-KEY                                       VALUE '1'.
           88 PF2-KEY                                       VALUE '2'.
```

Symbolic map is copied into the program here (see Figure 12.2).

Figure 12.3 The CALC1 program using a machine-generated symbolic map instead of a manually coded symbolic map; note the effect on procedure division statements.

```
     88 PF3-KEY                                      VALUE '3'.

*-------------------------------------------------------------
*
*  VALUE MEANINGS FOR SYMBOLIC MAP ATTRIBUTE BYTE FIELDS
*
*-------------------------------------------------------------
 01  ATTRIBUTE-VALUES-TO-SET.
     05 ATT-UNPROT-CHAR-MDT             PIC X  VALUE 'A'.
     05 ATT-UNPROT-CHAR-MDT-BRIGHT      PIC X  VALUE 'I'.
     05 ATT-UNPROT-NUM-MDT              PIC X  VALUE 'J'.
     05 ATT-UNPROT-NUM-MDT-BRIGHT       PIC X  VALUE 'R'.

 LINKAGE SECTION.
 01  DFHCOMMAREA                        PIC X(1).

 PROCEDURE DIVISION.
*-------------------------------------------------------------

 0000-MAINLINE.
     PERFORM 3333-ALWAYS-TEST.

     EVALUATE  TRUE

        WHEN  FIRST-TIME
           PERFORM 9000-FIRST-TIME

        WHEN  PF3-KEY
           PERFORM 9100-CLEAN-THE-SCREEN

        WHEN  ENTER-KEY
           PERFORM 0500-NORMAL-PROCESSING

        WHEN  OTHER
           PERFORM 9200-INVALID-KEY-MESSAGE

     END-EVALUATE.

     PERFORM 8000-RETURN-WITH-TRANS-ID.

*-------------------------------------------------------------

 0500-NORMAL-PROCESSING.
     PERFORM 1000-RECEIVE-MAP.

     PERFORM 5000-VALIDATE-FIELDS
     IF DATA-GOOD
        PERFORM 5500-COMPUTE-RESULTS
     END-IF.

     PERFORM 1200-SEND-MAP-DATAONLY.

*-------------------------------------------------------------

 1000-RECEIVE-MAP.
     EXEC CICS
        RECEIVE MAP       (WS-MAP-NAME)
                MAPSET    (WS-MAPSET-NAME)
                INTO      (CALCMAPI)
                RESP      (WS-RESPONSE-CODE)
     END-EXEC.

*================

     EVALUATE  WS-RESPONSE-CODE

*----------------

       WHEN  DFHRESP(NORMAL)
          CONTINUE

*----------------

       WHEN  DFHRESP(MAPFAIL)
          MOVE -1 TO QUANTL
          MOVE 'NO DATA ENTERED; ENTER DATA OR <CLEAR> TO QUIT'
```

Figure 12.3 *(Continued)*

```
                TO MSGO
            PERFORM 1200-SEND-MAP-DATAONLY
            PERFORM 8000-RETURN-WITH-TRANS-ID

      *---------------


          WHEN  OTHER
            PERFORM 9999-ABORT

          END-EVALUATE.
      *================

      *-------------------------------------------------------------

       1200-SEND-MAP-DATAONLY.
           EXEC CICS
               SEND MAP        (WS-MAP-NAME)
                    MAPSET     (WS-MAPSET-NAME)
                    FROM       (CALCMAPI)
                    DATAONLY
                    CURSOR
           END-EXEC.

      *-------------------------------------------------------------

       3333-ALWAYS-TEST.
           MOVE EIBAID    TO  EIBAID-TEST-FIELD.
           IF CLEAR-KEY
              PERFORM 8900-QUIT.
           MOVE EIBCALEN  TO  WS-FIRST-TIME-FLAG.

      *-------------------------------------------------------------

       5000-VALIDATE-FIELDS.

           MOVE ATT-UNPROT-NUM-MDT TO  QUANTA
                                       PRICEA.

           IF PRICEI NOT NUMERIC
              MOVE 'B' TO WS-GOOD-BAD-FLAG
              MOVE ATT-UNPROT-NUM-MDT-BRIGHT TO PRICEA
              MOVE -1 TO PRICEL
              MOVE 'PRICE MUST BE NUMERIC; CORRECT, PRESS <ENTER>'
                 TO MSGO
           END-IF.

           IF QUANTI NOT NUMERIC
              MOVE 'B' TO WS-GOOD-BAD-FLAG
              MOVE ATT-UNPROT-NUM-MDT-BRIGHT TO QUANTA
              MOVE -1 TO QUANTL
              MOVE 'QUANTITY MUST BE NUMERIC; CORRECT, PRESS <ENTER>'
                 TO MSGO
           END-IF.

      *-------------------------------------------------------------

       5500-COMPUTE-RESULTS.
           COMPUTE TOTB4O  = QUANTI * PRICEI.
           COMPUTE TAXO    = PRICEI * WS-SALES-TAX-RATE.
           COMPUTE GTOTALO =
              QUANTI * PRICEI * WS-SALES-TAX-RATE +
              QUANTI * PRICEI.
           MOVE 'RESULTS COMPUTED, ENTER MORE DATA OR <CLEAR> TO QUIT'
              TO MSGO.
           MOVE -1 TO QUANTL.

      *-------------------------------------------------------------

       8000-RETURN-WITH-TRANS-ID.
           EXEC CICS
              RETURN TRANSID   (WS-TRANS-ID)
                     COMMAREA  (WS-COMMUNICATION-AREA)
           END-EXEC.

      *-------------------------------------------------------------

```

Figure 12.3 *(Continued)*

```
8900-QUIT.
    EXEC CICS
         SEND TEXT FROM (WS-END-MESSAGE)
              ERASE
              FREEKB
    END-EXEC.

    EXEC CICS
         RETURN
    END-EXEC.

*-------------------------------------------------------------

9000-FIRST-TIME.
    MOVE LOW-VALUES TO CALCMAPI.
    MOVE 'ENTER VALUES, PRESS <ENTER>, <CLEAR> TO QUIT'
       TO MSGO.
    MOVE -1 TO QUANTL.

    EXEC CICS
        SEND MAPSET     (WS-MAPSET-NAME)
             MAP        (WS-MAP-NAME)
             FROM       (CALCMAPI)
             ERASE
             CURSOR
    END-EXEC.

*-------------------------------------------------------------

9100-CLEAN-THE-SCREEN.
    MOVE LOW-VALUES TO CALCMAPI.
    MOVE SPACES TO  TOTB4I
                    TAXI
                    GTOTALI.

    MOVE 'ENTER VALUES, PRESS <ENTER>, <CLEAR> TO QUIT'
       TO MSGO.
    MOVE -1 TO QUANTL.

    EXEC CICS
        SEND MAP        (WS-MAP-NAME)
             MAPSET     (WS-MAPSET-NAME)
             FROM       (CALCMAPI)
             DATAONLY
             ERASEAUP
             CURSOR
    END-EXEC.

*-------------------------------------------------------------

9200-INVALID-KEY-MESSAGE.
    MOVE LOW-VALUES TO CALCMAPI.
    MOVE 'YOU PRESSED WRONG KEY! PRESS <ENTER>, <CLEAR> TO QUIT'
       TO MSGO.
    MOVE -1 TO QUANTL.
    PERFORM 1200-SEND-MAP-DATAONLY.

*-------------------------------------------------------------

9999-ABORT.
    MOVE EIBTRNID   TO  WS-EIBTRNID.
    MOVE EIBRSRCE   TO  WS-EIBRSRCE.
    MOVE EIBRESP    TO  WS-EIBRESP.
    MOVE EIBRESP2   TO  WS-EIBRESP2.

    EXEC CICS
       SEND TEXT FROM (WS-ERROR-MESSAGES)
            ERASE
            ALARM
            FREEKB
    END-EXEC.

    EXEC CICS
         RETURN
    END-EXEC.
```

Figure 12.3 *(Continued)*

```
EDIT ---- CSCJGJ.CSC360.CNTL(PGMJOB) - 01.25 ---------------- COLUMNS 001 072
COMMAND ===>                                                  SCROLL ===> PAGE
****** ****************************** TOP OF DATA ******************************
//CSCJGJA   JOB 1,                      ACCOUNTING INFORMATION
//   'BIN 7--JANOSSY',                  PROGRAMMER NAME AND DELIVERY BIN
//   CLASS=A,                           INPUT QUEUE CLASS
//   MSGLEVEL=(1,1),                    HOW MUCH MVS SYSTEM PRINT DESIRED
//   MSGCLASS=X,                        PRINT DESTINATION X A L N OR O
//   TIME=(0,6),                        SAFETY LIMIT: RUN TIME UP TO 6 SECS
//   REGION=2M,                         ALLOW UP TO 2 MEGS VIRTUAL MEMORY
//   NOTIFY=CSCJGJ                      WHO TO TELL WHEN JOB IS DONE
//*-----------------------------------------------------------------------
//*  TRANSLATE, COMPILE, AND LINK A CICS PROGRAM
//*  THIS IS A LOCALLY CUSTOMIZED VERSION OF STANDARD PROC DFHEITVL
//*  THIS JCL IS STORED AT CSCJGJ.CSC360.CNTL(PGMJOB)
//*-----------------------------------------------------------------------
//*
//   SET  SORCLIB='CSCJGJ.CSC360.COBOL',     SOURCE LIB WITH PROGRAM CODE
//        SORNAME='C360A00M',                SOURCE PROGRAM MEMBER NAME
//        COPYLIB='CSCJGJ.CSC360.COPYLIB',   YOUR COBOL COPY LIBRARY
//*
//        LOADLIB='CCP.LOADLIB',             CICS LOAD LIBRARY
//        LOADNAM='C360A001'                 LOAD MODULE MEMBER NAME
//*
```

Figure 12.4 The PGMJOB job control language lets you specify the name of the library housing the symbolic map.

12.7 SPECIFYING THE SYMBOLIC MAP LIBRARY FOR COMPILING

We use the job control language named for PGMJOB to translate and compile our programs. This JCL provides the name of the library housing COPY members at the //SYSLIB DD statement of the compiler. As you can see in Figure 12.4, the PGMJOB JCL provides a symbolic parameter for **copy library name**, so that you can assign the name of this library on the first screen of the JCL. Your local translate, compile, and link proc will most likely make it similarly easy for you to specify the name of the copy member library you use.

12.8 FOR YOUR REVIEW

The following terms were introduced or reviewed in this chapter. If you understand this chapter, you should be comfortable with defining each of these terms in relationship to CICS:

COPY
Copy library
Data transmission record
Machine-generated symbolic map
Manually coded symbolic map
NUM
Physical map
PICIN
PICOUT
Symbolic map

12.9 REVIEW QUESTIONS

1. Explain in your own words what a data transmission record is and how it is used by CICS.
2. Discuss the two ways you can obtain the COBOL description for the data transmission record for a given screen.

3. Identify the advantage of using a machine-generated symbolic map, such as the one illustrated in this chapter in connection with the revised CALC1 program.
4. Identify the major disadvantage of using a machine-generated symbolic map such as the one illustrated in this chapter in connection with the revised CALC1 program.
5. Explain what the origin of a given machine-generated symbolic map is.
6. Identify and describe the two points of significance about field names in BMS map source code in connection with machine-generated symbolic maps.
7. Explain where the values you put into a BMS map with the PICIN and PICOUT clauses appear in the symbolic map produced by the MAPJOB job control language.
8. If you specify NUM within the ATTRIB coding in the BMS map code for a given field, do you also have to code a PICIN clause with a numeric PICture? Explain why or why not.
9. Identify and discuss two reasons why the fields of a machine-generated symbolic map with suffix "F" and "A" are unusual.
10. Discuss why the data transmission record for a screen acts very much like a containerized freight airline in its operation.

12.10 HANDS-ON EXERCISES

A. Use job control language, such as MAPJOB, to prepare a machine-generated symbolic map from some BMS map source code you have already developed. Have the symbolic map written as a member into a partitioned data set. Then, use TSO or job control language to print a copy of the symbolic map and identify these things on it:

- The input coding for the data transmission record
- The output coding for the data transmission record
- The input PIC resulting from your use of the PICIN clause in a BMS map code field definition
- The output PIC resulting from your use of the PICOUT clause in a BMS map code field definition
- The input and output PICs for a field on which you did not code PICIN or PICOUT

B. After completing exercise A, make a copy of the program that drives the screen you used in exercise A. Convert the program to use the machine-generated symbolic map you developed in exercise A. Then translate, compile, and link your revised program using JCL similar to PGMJOB. After you achieve a clean compile, test your program to make sure that it works identically to the original version.

13

Indexed File Inquiry

One of the most important aspects of CICS/COBOL programming involves updating indexed files. **Updating** involves adding, deleting, and changing records in a file. Essential to all of these operations is **random access** to a file, which we begin to explore in this chapter with an **inquiry function** to a **VSAM Key Sequenced Data Set.** In Chapter 14 we'll increase the functionality of our basic inquiry program, to show you the VS COBOL II code that handles add, change, and delete actions.

13.1 AN EXAMPLE CICS SCREEN

Figure 13.1 illustrates the screen for Samuel's Worthless Finance Company, a firm that will loan money to people unfortunate enough to do business with it. Samuel's will loan up to five "charge" amounts and two cash advances to a customer, and exact finance charges for these loans.

The screen in Figure 13.1 will ultimately allow a terminal operator to add, delete, change, or simply view a record containing borrower information. To view a record, the terminal operator enters "V" as a choice of action at the top of the screen, enters an account number, and presses the Enter key.

```
                  -=SAMUEL'S WORTHLESS FINANCE COMPANY=-                    FILEMAP
                         ****** FILE UPDATE ******                            SMSAM

(A)dd, (D)elete, (C)hange, or (V)iew: a
Name:                                        Account Number:

------------------------------- CHARGE ITEMS -------------------------------
  Charge Amount 1:
  Charge Amount 2:
  Charge Amount 3:
  Charge Amount 4:
  Charge Amount 5:                           Total Charge Items:

------------------------------ CASH ADVANCES ------------------------------
Cash Adv Amount 1:
Cash Adv Amount 2:                          Total Cash Advances:
                                Finance Charge On Cash Advances:

                               =============================================

                                                  Total Debits:

ENTER A CHOICE ABOVE
```

Figure 13.1 Inquiry and update screen for Samuel's Worthless Finance Company.

Samuel's houses information about a customer in a record that contains this information:

Account number	8 digits
Charge amount 1	PIC 9(4)V99
Charge amount 2	PIC 9(4)V99
Charge amount 3	PIC 9(4)V99
Charge amount 4	PIC 9(4)V99
Charge amount 5	PIC 9(4)V99
Cash advance amount 1	PIC 9(4)V99
Total charge amounts	PIC 9(5)V99
Total advance amounts	PIC 9(5)V99
Finance charges	PIC 9(3)V99
Total debt	PIC 9(5)V99
Borrower name	PIC X(30)

Each record appears as illustrated in Figure 13.2 in graphic form, for a total length of 160 bytes. The "gaps" in the record are actually unused FILLER space. If you compare the **graphic record layout** with the screen shown in Figure 13.1, you can readily see the correspondence between the screen fields and the record fields.

13.2 CREATING THE BORROWER VSAM FILE

We created the file housing Samuel's borrower records before creating any CICS program to access it. We named the data set CCPV00.CSC.BASE1F. There are two ways to go about this; both are illustrated in Appendix D:

- Prepare a sequential file of records with appropriate information in each field. This is known as a **load file** and could be prepared by conversion from some existing information storage file, or by a test data generator. Sort the load file records using job

Primary Key														Alternate Key	
	Chargee Amounts					Advance Amounts									
ACCT-NUM	Amt-1	Amt-2	Amt-3	Amt-4	Amt-5	Adv-1	Adv-2	Total Charges	Total Advances	Finance Charge	Total Debt	Filler	ACCT-NAME	Filler
9(8)	9(4)V99	9(4)V99	9(4)V99	9(4)V99	9(4)V99	9(4)V99	9(4)V99	9(5)V99	9(5)V99	9(3)V99	9(5)V99	x(44)	x(30)	x(10)
1 8	9 14	15 20	21 26	27 32	33 38	39 44	45 50	51 57	58 64	65 69	70 76	77 120	121 150	151 160

Figure 13.2 Graphic record layout for the records in data set CCPV001F, which houses data for borrowers of Samuel's Worthless Finance Company.

control language and the sort utility, putting the records into ascending sequence of primary key, the account number. After sorting, use additional job control language and control statements for the **IDCAMS utility** to define a Key Sequenced Data Set to house the records, and copy (REPRO) the sequential records to this data set, and build any alternate indexes and data access paths. We illustrate this method in Appendix D for a master file of pleasure cruise passenger ticket information.

- Use job control language and the IDCAMS utility to define a VSAM data set, and use a COBOL program to read a file of test data, build appropriate load records "on the fly," and WRITE the records to the VSAM data set. After data set loading, use additional IDCAMS steps to build any alternate indexes and data access paths. We demonstrate this in Appendix D with the actual JCL, named JOBLOAD, IDCAMS control statements, and program, named COBLOAD, that we used to create the master file for Samuel's Worthless Finance Company.

Neither of these actions has anything to do with CICS. This work is done simply to created an appropriate VSAM Key Sequenced Data Set that could be accessed by both on-line CICS programs as well as purely batch non-CICS programs.

13.3 A BASIC CICS SHELL PROGRAM

Figure 13.3 is a basic **shell program** that uses the same modular design we illustrated in previous chapters. We call it a shell program because it provides the generic housing for a CICS program dealing with data sets. While the program contains a file-specific description, it does not, in its present form, contain file-specific logic. Examine this start of a program and you will see that "worker" paragraphs 115-ADD-ROUTINE, 125-DELETE-ROUTINE, 135-CHANGE-ROUTINE, and 145-VIEW-ROUTINE at letters "A", "B", "C", and "D" are all stubs. **Stubs** are program logic statements that receive control as would a "real" function, but simply give evidence of having received control, then return control to their invoker. If you exclude the stubs in this program, you wind up with almost the identical program structure we presented in Chapter 8 for a purely computational structured CICS program.

Figure 13.4 is a structure chart for our shell program, which we have named UPDATE1. We'll add logic to this basic program to flesh out the inner workings of each of the worker paragraphs in this and the next chapters.

13.4 FILE ACCESS IN CICS

If you examine the UPDATE1 program in Figure 13.3, you will notice that the borrower file is not described in it as it would be in a batch COBOL program. Although UPDATE1 will deal with the borrower file, there is no INPUT-OUTPUT SECTION in this program, and no SELECT or FD statements describing the file and records. The layout of the records in the borrower file is simply described in the WORKING-STORAGE SECTION of this program, at lines 3300 through 4800.

How will the UPDATE1 program ultimately "talk" to the VSAM file? We arranged for the CICS systems programmer to make an entry in the **File Control Table (FCT),** associating this file name with the CICS filename CCPV001F. The FCT entry created by the systems programmer informs CICS about the physical file name of the data set, in this case CCPV00.CSC.BASE1F, a name which will never appear in the program. All of our access to

```
EDIT ---- CSCJGJ.CSC360.COBOL(UPDATE1) - 01.01 --------------- COLUMNS 007 078
COMMAND ===>                                                  SCROLL ===> PAGE
****** ***************************** TOP OF DATA ******************************
       ID DIVISION.
       PROGRAM-ID.  UPDATE1.

      *================================================================
      *   THIS PROGRAM IS A SHELL THAT PROVIDES THE STARTING POINT FOR
      *   AN INTERACTIVE ADD, INQUIRY, CHANGE, AND DELETE PROGRAM.
      *   THIS SHELL DOES NOTHING; IT HAS CODING STUBS AT THE LOCATIONS
      *   WHERE ACTUAL ROUTINES TO ACCOMPLISH THESE FUNCTIONS WILL BE
      *   LOCATED.
      *
      *   COPYRIGHT 1994 STEVE SAMUELS AND JIM JANOSSY
      *================================================================

       ENVIRONMENT DIVISION.
       DATA DIVISION.
       WORKING-STORAGE SECTION.

       01  WS-TRANS-ID          PIC X(4)      VALUE 'SMSA'.
       01  WS-MAPSET-NAME       PIC X(8)      VALUE 'SMSAM   '.
       01  WS-MAP-NAME          PIC X(8)      VALUE 'FILEMAP '.
       01  WS-FILENAME          PIC X(8)      VALUE 'CCPW001F'.

       01  WS-FIRST-TIME-FLAG   PIC S9(8)     BINARY.
           88 FIRST-TIME                      VALUE 0.

       01  WS-RESPONSE-CODE                PIC S9(8) COMP.

       01  COMMUNICATION-AREA              PIC X(1).

       01  END-OF-SESSION-MESSAGE          PIC X(50)  VALUE
           'UPDATE1 ENDED, USE  CESF LOGOFF  TO END CICS'.

       01  ACCT-REC.
           05  ACCT-NUM         PIC 9(8).
           05  AMT-1            PIC 9(4)V99.
           05  AMT-2            PIC 9(4)V99.
           05  AMT-3            PIC 9(4)V99.
           05  AMT-4            PIC 9(4)V99.
           05  AMT-5            PIC 9(4)V99.
           05  ADV-1            PIC 9(4)V99.
           05  ADV-2            PIC 9(4)V99.
           05  TOT-CHG          PIC 9(5)V99.
           05  TOT-ADV          PIC 9(5)V99.
           05  FIN-CHG          PIC 9(3)V99.
           05  TOT-DEB          PIC 9(5)V99.
           05  GAP-1            PIC X(44).
           05  ACCT-NAME        PIC X(30).
           05  GAP-2            PIC X(10).


           COPY SMSAM.


       01  EIBAID-TEST-FIELD        PIC X(1).
           COPY KEYDEFS.

       LINKAGE SECTION.
       01  DFHCOMMAREA          PIC X(1).

```

Figure 13.3 Basic CICS "shell" program into which we will insert functional logic for view (Inquiry) and add, delete, and change.

```
      *===========================================================
       PROCEDURE DIVISION.
      *===========================================================
       000-MAINLINE.

           PERFORM 633-ALWAYS-TEST.

           EVALUATE TRUE

              WHEN EIBCALEN = ZERO
                  PERFORM 800-START-TERMINAL-SESSION

              WHEN ENTER-KEY
                  PERFORM 100-CHOOSE-ROUTINE

              WHEN OTHER
                  MOVE LOW-VALUES TO FILEMAPI
                  MOVE -1 TO CHOICEL
                  MOVE 'INVALID KEY PRESSED' TO ERRORI
                  PERFORM 700-SEND-ACCOUNT-SCREEN

            END-EVALUATE.

           EXEC CICS
              RETURN  TRANSID   (WS-TRANS-ID)
                      COMMAREA  (COMMUNICATION-AREA)
           END-EXEC.

      *-----------------------------------------------------------
      *  THE USER ENTERS DATA AND THE DATA IS RECEIVED BY THE PROGRAM.
      *  THE ADD, DELETE, CHANGE, OR VIEW ROUTINES ARE EXECUTED
      *  DEPENDING ON THE CHOICE A D C OR V.
      *-----------------------------------------------------------
       100-CHOOSE-ROUTINE.

           PERFORM 150-RECEIVE-ACCOUNT-SCREEN.

              EVALUATE CHOICEI

                 WHEN 'A'
                    PERFORM 115-ADD-ROUTINE

                 WHEN 'D'
                    PERFORM 125-DELETE-ROUTINE

                 WHEN 'C'
                    PERFORM 135-CHANGE-ROUTINE

                 WHEN 'V'
                    PERFORM 145-VIEW-ROUTINE

                 WHEN OTHER
                    MOVE 'INVALID CHOICE!  TRY AGAIN' TO ERRORI
                    MOVE -1 TO CHOICEL

              END-EVALUATE.

           PERFORM 700-SEND-ACCOUNT-SCREEN.

      *-----------------------------------------------------------
      *  THIS STUB IS INVOKED IF CHOICE "A" IS SELECTED
      *-----------------------------------------------------------
       115-ADD-ROUTINE.
           MOVE -1 TO CHOICEL.
           MOVE 'ADD FUNCTION NOT WORKING' TO ERRORI.
      *-----------------------------------------------------------
      *  THIS STUB IS INVOKED IF CHOICE "D" IS SELECTED
      *-----------------------------------------------------------
       125-DELETE-ROUTINE.
           MOVE -1 TO CHOICEL.
           MOVE 'DELETE FUNCTION NOT WORKING' TO ERRORI.
```

A

B

Figure 13.3 *(Continued)*

```
*-----------------------------------------------------------------
*  THIS STUB IS INVOKED IF CHOICE "C" IS SELECTED
*-----------------------------------------------------------------
 135-CHANGE-ROUTINE.
     MOVE -1 TO CHOICEL.
     MOVE 'CHANGE FUNCTION NOT WORKING' TO ERRORI.

*-----------------------------------------------------------------
*  THIS STUB IS INVOKED IF CHOICE "V" IS SELECTED
*-----------------------------------------------------------------
 145-VIEW-ROUTINE.
     MOVE -1 TO CHOICEL.
     MOVE 'VIEW FUNCTION NOT WORKING' TO ERRORI.

*-----------------------------------------------------------------
*  THIS ROUTINE SENDS DATA BACK TO CICS
*-----------------------------------------------------------------
 150-RECEIVE-ACCOUNT-SCREEN.
     EXEC CICS
          RECEIVE MAP      (WS-MAP-NAME)
                  MAPSET   (WS-MAPSET-NAME)
                  INTO     (FILEMAPI)
     END-EXEC.

*-----------------------------------------------------------------
*  THIS ROUTINE IS USED AT THE START OF EACH PSEUDOCONVERSE
*-----------------------------------------------------------------
 633-ALWAYS-TEST.
     MOVE EIBAID    TO  EIBAID-TEST-FIELD.
     IF CLEAR-KEY
        PERFORM 900-SEND-TERMINATION-MESSAGE
        EXEC CICS  RETURN  END-EXEC.

     MOVE EIBCALEN  TO  WS-FIRST-TIME-FLAG.

*-----------------------------------------------------------------
*  THIS ROUTINE SENDS DATA FROM CICS TO SCREEN
*-----------------------------------------------------------------
 700-SEND-ACCOUNT-SCREEN.
     EXEC CICS
          SEND  MAP       (WS-MAP-NAME)
                MAPSET    (WS-MAPSET-NAME)
                FROM      (FILEMAPI)
                DATAONLY
                CURSOR
     END-EXEC.

*-----------------------------------------------------------------
*  INVOKED ONLY IF EIBCALEN = 0, A FIRST-TIME ROUTINE
*-----------------------------------------------------------------
 800-START-TERMINAL-SESSION.
     MOVE LOW-VALUES TO FILEMAPI.
     MOVE -1 TO CHOICEL.
     EXEC CICS
          SEND  MAP       (WS-MAP-NAME)
                MAPSET    (WS-MAPSET-NAME)
                FROM      (FILEMAPI)
                ERASE
                CURSOR
     END-EXEC.

*-----------------------------------------------------------------
*  LAST SCREEN SENT WHEN PROGRAM ENDS NORMALLY
*-----------------------------------------------------------------
 900-SEND-TERMINATION-MESSAGE.
     EXEC CICS
          SEND   TEXT FROM(END-OF-SESSION-MESSAGE)
                 ERASE
                 FREEKB
     END-EXEC.
```

Figure 13.3 *(Continued)*

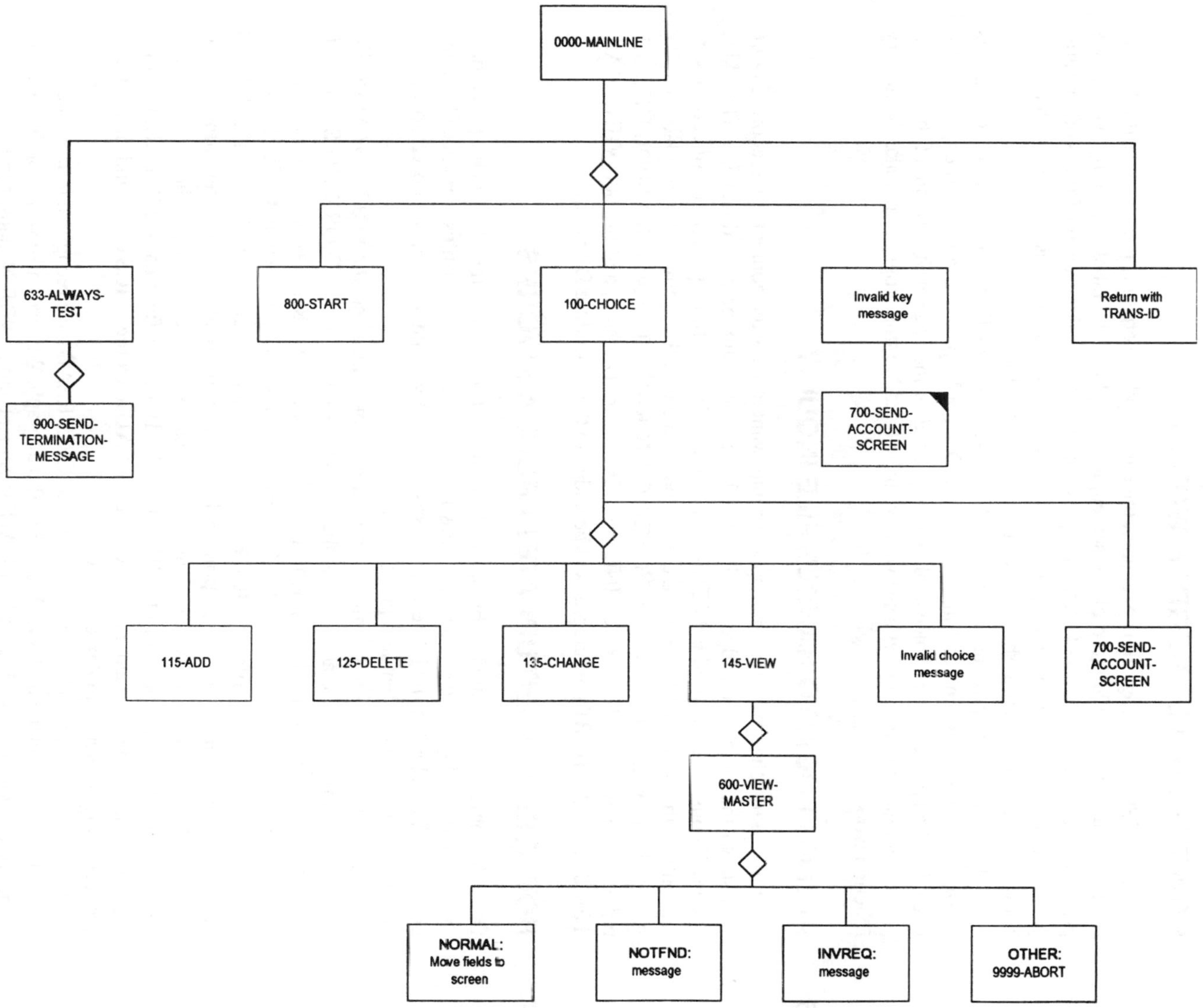
0000-MAINLINE
633-ALWAYS-TEST
900-SEND-TERMINATION-MESSAGE
800-START
100-CHOICE
Invalid key message
700-SEND-ACCOUNT-SCREEN
Return with TRANS-ID
115-ADD
125-DELETE
135-CHANGE
145-VIEW
Invalid choice message
700-SEND-ACCOUNT-SCREEN
600-VIEW-MASTER
NORMAL: Move fields to screen
NOTFND: message
INVREQ: message
OTHER: 9999-ABORT

Figure 13.4 Structure chart for the basic shell program, showing stub paragraphs for view, add, delete, and change functions.

the file will be done using the CICS **filename** established in the FCT, which in this case is CCPV001F.

13.5 HOW THE SHELL PROGRAM WORKS

When the UPDATE1 program is executed, the entire update screen is presented, with the cursor positioned at the middle top of the screen, to the right of the label indicating the various processing choices. Since the UPDATE1 program has stub logic at each of the worker paragraphs, no matter what valid choice the terminal operator enters, a message is presented at the bottom of the screen stating that the function is not operable.

The driver of this program is really the 100-CHOOSE-ROUTINE. The terminal operator is presented with various choices. Valid choices (A, D, C, or V) pass control to worker paragraphs, while invalid choices or no choice at all results in an error message at the bottom of the screen.

Not much fun in this! Let's see what we have to add to this program to make the inquiry function work.

13.6 ADDING LOGIC TO HANDLE FILE INQUIRY

Prior to making changes, a terminal operator may want to view the contents of a record. Figure 13.5 shows the logic we'll add to the UPDATE1 program to support record viewing. The added code will consist of one field in WORKING-STORAGE, and three paragraphs of code. (Note that although Figure 13.5 shows these added elements all together in one place, COPY ABRTMSGS will be inserted into WORKING-STORAGE. The 145-VIEW-ROUTINE will replace the stub 145-VIEW-ROUTINE in the Procedure Division, and the 600-VIEW-MASTER and 9999-ABORT paragraphs will be added to the Procedure Division.

13.7 HOW THE REVISED UPDATE1 PROGRAM WORKS

Once the logic we illustrated in Figure 13.5 has been inserted into the UPDATE1 program at the appropriate places, we can use it to view records in Samuel's Worthless Finance Company borrower file. The terminal operator makes choice "V" and is then supposed to enter a borrower's account number, and press Enter.

If the terminal operator enters a numeric account number, the 600-VIEW-MASTER paragraph is invoked. The account number entered is moved to the WORKING-STORAGE area containing the record description. A CICS random access **READ** command is executed. In the READ command the "INTO (ACCT-REC)" clause indicates where CICS is to put the record it obtains from the file. The **RIDFLD** ("read id field") clause (ACCT-NUM) tells CICS the name of the field containing the primary key value of the record we are attempting to view. The **RESP** clause returns a value signifying success or failure in finding the record, which CICS (at our direction) puts into the WORKING-STORAGE field named WS-RESPONSE-CODE. We have summarized the clauses of the READ and other CICS commands in the CICS programming reference in Appendix A.

Is a record obtained by the random access CICS READ? We recognize four possible outcomes for the read in the 600-VIEW-MASTER paragraph. We recognize which of the four outcomes has materialized with the EVALUATE statement and its WHEN clauses in Figure 13.5:

- If a record is found, DFHRESP(NORMAL) applies and we move the information read into WORKING-STORAGE to the screen fields which will be sent to the screen in 700-SEND-ACCOUNT-SCREEN.

```
       COPY ABRTMSGS.
```

```
*-----------------------------------------------------------------
*  THIS ROUTINE IS PERFORMED IF CHOICE "V" IS SELECTED.  IF THE
*  KEY IS NUMERIC AN ATTEMPT IS MADE TO READ A RECORD.  IF THE
*  READ IS SUCCESSFUL THE RECORD IS DISPLAYED ON THE SCREEN.
*-----------------------------------------------------------------
 145-VIEW-ROUTINE.

     IF ACTNUML > 0 AND ACTNUMI NUMERIC
        PERFORM 600-VIEW-MASTER
     ELSE
        MOVE 'ENTER A VALID NUMBER' TO ERRORI
        MOVE -1 TO ACTNUML.
```

```
*-----------------------------------------------------------------
*  THIS ROUTINE READS A RECORD FROM THE VSAM FILE, UNLESS NO
*  RECORED WITH THE KEY VALUE CAN BE FOUND
*-----------------------------------------------------------------
 600-VIEW-MASTER.

     MOVE ACTNUMI TO ACCT-NUM.
     EXEC CICS
          READ  DATASET  (WS-FILENAME)
                INTO     (ACCT-REC)
                RIDFLD   (ACCT-NUM)
                RESP     (WS-RESPONSE-CODE)
     END-EXEC.

     MOVE -1 TO CHOICEL.

     EVALUATE WS-RESPONSE-CODE

        WHEN DFHRESP(NORMAL)
           MOVE ACCT-NAME     TO ACTNAMEI
           MOVE AMT-1         TO AMT1I
           MOVE AMT-2         TO AMT2I
           MOVE AMT-3         TO AMT3I
           MOVE AMT-4         TO AMT4I
           MOVE AMT-5         TO AMT5I
           MOVE ADV-1         TO ADV1I
           MOVE ADV-2         TO ADV2I
           MOVE TOT-CHG       TO TOTCHGO
           MOVE TOT-ADV       TO TOTADVO
           MOVE FIN-CHG       TO FINCHGO
           MOVE TOT-DEB       TO TOTDEBO
           MOVE 'RECORD DISPLAYED' TO ERRORI
           MOVE -1 TO CHOICEL

        WHEN DFHRESP(NOTFND)
           MOVE SPACES TO ACTNAMEI
           MOVE 0 TO AMT1I AMT2I AMT3I AMT4I AMT5I
                     ADV1I ADV2I
                     TOTCHGO TOTADVO FINCHGO TOTDEBO
           MOVE 'RECORD NOT FOUND, NO VIEW POSSIBLE'
              TO ERRORI
           MOVE -1 TO CHOICEL

        WHEN DFHRESP(INVREQ)
           MOVE 'SOMEONE ELSE IS USING RECORD, TRY AGAIN LATER'
               TO ERRORI
           MOVE -1 TO CHOICEL

        WHEN OTHER
           PERFORM 9999-ABORT

     END-EVALUATE.
```

```
*-----------------------------------------------------------------
*  SCREEN SENT FOR ABORT CONDITION ONLY -- AS WHEN WE GET A RESP
*  WE COULD NOT DEAL WITH!
*-----------------------------------------------------------------
 9999-ABORT.
     MOVE EIBTRNID   TO  WS-EIBTRNID.
     MOVE EIBRSRCE   TO  WS-EIBRSRCE.
     MOVE EIBRESP    TO  WS-EIBRESP.
     MOVE EIBRESP2   TO  WS-EIBRESP2.

     EXEC CICS
         SEND  TEXT FROM (WS-ERROR-MESSAGES)
               ERASE
               ALARM
               FREEKB
     END-EXEC.

     EXEC CICS  RETURN  END-EXEC.
```

Figure 13.5 Code to be added to the basic shell program UPDATE1, to give it a file viewing capability.

- If a record cannot be found, DFHRESP(NOTFND) applies and we set up the appropriate "record not found" message which will be sent to the screen in 700-SEND-ACCOUNT-SCREEN.
- If someone else is already accessing the record (or another record in the same VSAM control interval), DFHRESP(INVREQ) will apply. Once again, we set up an appropriate message to be sent to the screen in 700-SEND-ACCOUNT-SCREEN.
- If none of the above outcomes materializes, the WHEN OTHER clause at the bottom of the EVALUATE receives control and invokes 9999-ABORT to terminate the program, presenting appropriate diagnostic values. At the bottom of Figure 13.5, you see MOVEs of fields from the execute interface block to reporting lines actually copied in with COPY ABRTMSGS. The declarations contained in copybook ABRTMSGS are shown in Chapter 10, Figure 10.10.

Except for the "OTHER" case, the program sends the screen and "dies," waiting to be awakened for another pseudoconverse by the pressing of the Enter key. If the terminal operator enters no account number (ACCNUML = 0) or a non-numeric account number, a message is displayed at the bottom of the screen asking for a valid account number. The cursor is placed at the account number area of the screen (we MOVE -1 TO CHOICEL) before sending the map. This cycle of operation continues until the operator presses the Clear key to end execution of the UPDATE1 program.

13.8 SYMBOLIC MAP FOR THE UPDATE1 PROGRAM

You'll note that at line 5100 in Figure 13.3, we COPY copybook item SMSAM into the UPDATE1 program. SMSAM is the machine-generated symbolic map for Samuel's Worthless Finance Company screen illustrated in Figure 13.1. The symbolic map code contained in SMSAM is listed in Figure 13.6. We didn't place this coding earlier in the chapter because, while you may want to refer to it as you examine the UPDATE1 source code, the symbolic map is not the main point of this chapter. You can see from the length of this symbolic map that machine-generated maps can really become voluminous and distracting.

13.9 BMS MAP SOURCE CODE FOR THE UPDATE1 PROGRAM

Figure 13.7 lists the BMS map code for the Samuel's Worthless Finance Company screen, as generated by the GENMAP screen painter. We used this to create both the physical map and the symbolic map used by the UPDATE1 program. We'll continue to use this screen in Chapters 14 and 15 as we include add, delete, and change capabilities into the UPDATE1 program.

13.10 MISCELLANEOUS FILE ACCESS INFORMATION

CICS/ESA Version 3.0 and later versions make obsolete some tasks formerly associated with file access. Now, when a CICS program accesses a file:

- There is no need to open the files ahead of time using the CEMT utility transaction. The file is automatically opened by CICS when it is first accessed by a program.
- There is no need for you to code HANDLE CONDITION statements. The RESP clause does an efficient job of detecting and handling information from CICS concerning file access success or failure. RESP makes it possible to distinguish between the potential outcomes of CICS command execution with the EVALUATE verb, sim-

```
EDIT ---- CCP.MACLIB(SMSAM) - 01.00 ------------------------- COLUMNS 001 072
COMMAND ===>                                                  SCROLL ===> PAGE
****** ***************************** TOP OF DATA ******************************
       01  FILEMAPI.
           02  FILLER PIC X(12).
           02  DATEL    COMP  PIC  S9(4).
           02  DATEF    PICTURE X.
           02  FILLER REDEFINES DATEF.
             03 DATEA    PICTURE X.
           02  DATEI  PIC X(8).
           02  TIMEL    COMP  PIC  S9(4).
           02  TIMEF    PICTURE X.
           02  FILLER REDEFINES TIMEF.
             03 TIMEA    PICTURE X.
           02  TIMEI  PIC X(8).
           02  CHOICEL    COMP  PIC  S9(4).
           02  CHOICEF    PICTURE X.
           02  FILLER REDEFINES CHOICEF.
             03 CHOICEA    PICTURE X.
           02  CHOICEI  PIC X.
           02  ACTNAMEL    COMP  PIC  S9(4).
           02  ACTNAMEF    PICTURE X.
           02  FILLER REDEFINES ACTNAMEF.
             03 ACTNAMEA    PICTURE X.
           02  ACTNAMEI  PIC X(30).
           02  ACTNUML    COMP  PIC  S9(4).
           02  ACTNUMF    PICTURE X.
           02  FILLER REDEFINES ACTNUMF.
             03 ACTNUMA    PICTURE X.
           02  ACTNUMI  PIC 9(8).
           02  AMT1L    COMP  PIC  S9(4).
           02  AMT1F    PICTURE X.
           02  FILLER REDEFINES AMT1F.
             03 AMT1A    PICTURE X.
           02  AMT1I  PIC 9(4)V99.
           02  AMT2L    COMP  PIC  S9(4).
           02  AMT2F    PICTURE X.
           02  FILLER REDEFINES AMT2F.
             03 AMT2A    PICTURE X.
           02  AMT2I  PIC 9(4)V99.
           02  AMT3L    COMP  PIC  S9(4).
           02  AMT3F    PICTURE X.
           02  FILLER REDEFINES AMT3F.
             03 AMT3A    PICTURE X.
           02  AMT3I  PIC 9(4)V99.
           02  AMT4L    COMP  PIC  S9(4).
           02  AMT4F    PICTURE X.
           02  FILLER REDEFINES AMT4F.
             03 AMT4A    PICTURE X.
           02  AMT4I  PIC 9(4)V99.
           02  AMT5L    COMP  PIC  S9(4).
           02  AMT5F    PICTURE X.
           02  FILLER REDEFINES AMT5F.
             03 AMT5A    PICTURE X.
           02  AMT5I  PIC 9(4)V99.
           02  TOTCHGL    COMP  PIC  S9(4).
           02  TOTCHGF    PICTURE X.
           02  FILLER REDEFINES TOTCHGF.
             03 TOTCHGA    PICTURE X.
           02  TOTCHGI  PIC X(9).
           02  ADV1L    COMP  PIC  S9(4).
           02  ADV1F    PICTURE X.
           02  FILLER REDEFINES ADV1F.
             03 ADV1A    PICTURE X.
           02  ADV1I  PIC 9(4)V99.
           02  ADV2L    COMP  PIC  S9(4).
           02  ADV2F    PICTURE X.
           02  FILLER REDEFINES ADV2F.
             03 ADV2A    PICTURE X.
           02  ADV2I  PIC 9(4)V99.
           02  TOTADVL    COMP  PIC  S9(4).
           02  TOTADVF    PICTURE X.
           02  FILLER REDEFINES TOTADVF.
             03 TOTADVA    PICTURE X.
           02  TOTADVI  PIC X(9).
           02  FINCHGL    COMP  PIC  S9(4).
```

We use this machine-generated symbolic map in the inquiry and update program examples. It's copied into the UPDATE1 program at line 5100.

Figure 13.6 Symbolic map code for Samuel's Worthless Finance Company screen.

```
         02  FINCHGF    PICTURE X.
         02  FILLER REDEFINES FINCHGF.
           03 FINCHGA    PICTURE X.
         02  FINCHGI  PIC X(6).
         02  TOTDEBL     COMP  PIC  S9(4).
         02  TOTDEBF     PICTURE X.
         02  FILLER REDEFINES TOTDEBF.
           03 TOTDEBA    PICTURE X.
         02  TOTDEBI  PIC X(10).
         02  MESSAGEL    COMP  PIC  S9(4).
         02  MESSAGEF    PICTURE X.
         02  FILLER REDEFINES MESSAGEF.
           03 MESSAGEA    PICTURE X.
         02  MESSAGEI  PIC X(78).
         02  ERRORL     COMP  PIC  S9(4).
         02  ERRORF     PICTURE X.
         02  FILLER REDEFINES ERRORF.
           03 ERRORA    PICTURE X.
         02  ERRORI  PIC X(75).
         02  DUMMYL     COMP  PIC  S9(4).
         02  DUMMYF     PICTURE X.
         02  FILLER REDEFINES DUMMYF.
           03 DUMMYA    PICTURE X.
         02  DUMMYI  PIC X(1).
     01  FILEMAPO REDEFINES FILEMAPI.
         02  FILLER PIC X(12).
         02  FILLER PICTURE X(3).
         02  DATEO  PIC X(8).
         02  FILLER PICTURE X(3).
         02  TIMEO  PIC X(8).
         02  FILLER PICTURE X(3).
         02  CHOICEO  PIC X(1).
         02  FILLER PICTURE X(3).
         02  ACTNAMEO  PIC X(30).
         02  FILLER PICTURE X(3).
         02  ACTNUMO  PIC X(8).
         02  FILLER PICTURE X(3).
         02  AMT1O  PIC X(6).
         02  FILLER PICTURE X(3).
         02  AMT2O  PIC X(6).
         02  FILLER PICTURE X(3).
         02  AMT3O  PIC X(6).
         02  FILLER PICTURE X(3).
         02  AMT4O  PIC X(6).
         02  FILLER PICTURE X(3).
         02  AMT5O  PIC X(6).
         02  FILLER PICTURE X(3).
         02  TOTCHGO PIC ZZ,ZZ9.99.
         02  FILLER PICTURE X(3).
         02  ADV1O  PIC X(6).
         02  FILLER PICTURE X(3).
         02  ADV2O  PIC X(6).
         02  FILLER PICTURE X(3).
         02  TOTADVO PIC ZZ,ZZ9.99.
         02  FILLER PICTURE X(3).
         02  FINCHGO PIC ZZ9.99.
         02  FILLER PICTURE X(3).
         02  TOTDEBO PIC $$$,$$9.99.
         02  FILLER PICTURE X(3).
         02  MESSAGEO  PIC X(78).
         02  FILLER PICTURE X(3).
         02  ERRORO  PIC X(75).
         02  FILLER PICTURE X(3).
         02  DUMMYO  PIC X(1).
```

Figure 13.6 *(Continued)*

```
EDIT ---- CSCSMS.CSC.ASM3(FILEMAP) - 01.99 ------------------- COLUMNS 001 072
COMMAND ===>                                                  SCROLL ===> PAGE
****** ***************************** TOP OF DATA ******************************
         PRINT NOGEN
SMSAM    DFHMSD TYPE=&SYSPARM,                                         X
               LANG=COBOL,                                             X
               MODE=INOUT,                                             X
               TERM=3270-2,                                            X
               CTRL=FREEKB,                                            X
               STORAGE=AUTO,                                           X
               TIOAPFX=YES
***********************************************************************
FILEMAP  DFHMDI SIZE=(24,80),                                          X
               LINE=1,                                                 X
               COLUMN=1
***********************************************************************
DATE     DFHMDF POS=(1,1),                                             X
               LENGTH=8,                                               X
               ATTRB=PROT
         DFHMDF POS=(1,20),                                            X
               LENGTH=38,                                              X
               ATTRB=PROT,
               INITIAL='-=SAMUEL''S WORTHLESS FINANCE COMPANY=-'
         DFHMDF POS=(1,72),                                            X
               LENGTH=7,                                               X
               ATTRB=(NORM,PROT),                                      X
               INITIAL='FILEMAP'
***********************************************************************
TIME     DFHMDF POS=(2,1),                                             X
               LENGTH=8,                                               X
               ATTRB=PROT
         DFHMDF POS=(2,27),                                            X
               LENGTH=25,                                              X
               ATTRB=PROT,                                             X
               INITIAL='****** FILE UPDATE ******'
         DFHMDF POS=(2,74),                                            X
               LENGTH=5,                                               X
               ATTRB=(NORM,PROT),                                      X
               INITIAL='SMSAM'
***********************************************************************
         DFHMDF POS=(4,1),                                             X
               LENGTH=37,                                              X
               ATTRB=(BRT,PROT),                                       X
               INITIAL='(A)dd, (D)elete, (C)hange, or (V)iew:'
CHOICE   DFHMDF POS=(4,39),                                            X
               LENGTH=1,                                               X
               ATTRB=(UNPROT,FSET),                                    X
               PICIN='X'
         DFHMDF POS=(4,41),                                            X
               LENGTH=1,                                               X
               ATTRB=ASKIP
***********************************************************************
         DFHMDF POS=(5,1),                                             X
               LENGTH=5,                                               X
               ATTRB=(BRT,PROT),                                       X
               INITIAL='Name:'
ACTNAME  DFHMDF POS=(5,8),                                             X
               LENGTH=30,                                              X
               ATTRB=(UNPROT,FSET),                                    X
               PICIN='X(30)'
         DFHMDF POS=(5,39),                                            X
               LENGTH=1,                                               X
               ATTRB=ASKIP
***********************************************************************
         DFHMDF POS=(5,44),                                            X
               LENGTH=15,
               ATTRB=(BRT,PROT),                                       X
               INITIAL='Account Number:'
ACTNUM   DFHMDF POS=(5,61),                                            X
               LENGTH=8,                                               X
               ATTRB=(UNPROT,NUM,FSET),                                X
               PICIN='9(8)'
         DFHMDF POS=(5,70),                                            X
               LENGTH=1,                                               X
               ATTRB=ASKIP
***********************************************************************
```

We generated this code using GENMAP

Figure 13.7 BMS map source code for Samuel's Worthless Finance Company screen.

```
         DFHMDF POS=(7,1),                                             X
               LENGTH=32,                                              X
               ATTRB=PROT,                                             X
               INITIAL='--------------------------------'
         DFHMDF POS=(7,34),                                            X
               LENGTH=12,                                              X
               ATTRB=PROT,                                             X
               INITIAL='CHARGE ITEMS'
         DFHMDF POS=(7,47),                                            X
               LENGTH=32,                                              X
               ATTRB=PROT,                                             X
               INITIAL='--------------------------------'
***********************************************************************
         DFHMDF POS=(8,3),                                             X
               LENGTH=16,                                              X
               ATTRB=(BRT,PROT),                                       X
               INITIAL='Charge Amount 1:'
AMT1     DFHMDF POS=(8,21),                                            X
               LENGTH=6,                                               X
               ATTRB=(UNPROT,NUM,FSET),                                X
               PICIN='9(4)V99'
         DFHMDF POS=(8,28),                                            X
               LENGTH=1,                                               X
               ATTRB=ASKIP
***********************************************************************
         DFHMDF POS=(9,3),                                             X
               LENGTH=16,                                              X
               ATTRB=(BRT,PROT),                                       X
               INITIAL='Charge Amount 2:'
AMT2     DFHMDF POS=(9,21),                                            X
               LENGTH=6,                                               X
               ATTRB=(UNPROT,NUM,FSET),                                X
               PICIN='9(4)V99'
         DFHMDF POS=(9,28),
               LENGTH=1,                                               X
               ATTRB=ASKIP
***********************************************************************
         DFHMDF POS=(10,3),                                            X
               LENGTH=16,                                              X
               ATTRB=(BRT,PROT),                                       X
               INITIAL='Charge Amount 3:'
AMT3     DFHMDF POS=(10,21),                                           X
               LENGTH=6,                                               X
               ATTRB=(UNPROT,NUM,FSET),                                X
               PICIN='9(4)V99'
         DFHMDF POS=(10,28),                                           X
               LENGTH=1,                                               X
               ATTRB=ASKIP
***********************************************************************
         DFHMDF POS=(11,3),                                            X
               LENGTH=16,                                              X
               ATTRB=(BRT,PROT),                                       X
               INITIAL='Charge Amount 4:'
AMT4     DFHMDF POS=(11,21),                                           X
               LENGTH=6,                                               X
               ATTRB=(UNPROT,NUM,FSET),
               PICIN='9(4)V99'
         DFHMDF POS=(11,28),                                           X
               LENGTH=1                                                X
               ATTRB=ASKIP
***********************************************************************
         DFHMDF POS=(12,3),                                            X
               LENGTH=16,                                              X
               ATTRB=(BRT,PROT),                                       X
               INITIAL='Charge Amount 5:'
AMT5     DFHMDF POS=(12,21),                                           X
               LENGTH=6,                                               X
               ATTRB=(UNPROT,NUM,FSET),                                X
               PICIN='9(4)V99'
         DFHMDF POS=(12,28),                                           X
               LENGTH=1                                                X
               ATTRB=ASKIP
***********************************************************************
         DFHMDF POS=(12,44),                                           X
               LENGTH=19,                                              X
               ATTRB=PROT,                                             X
```

Figure 13.7 *(Continued)*

```
                      INITIAL='Total Charge Items:'
       TOTCHG   DFHMDF POS=(12,65),
                      LENGTH=9,                                        X
                      ATTRB=(ASKIP),                                   X
                      PICOUT='ZZ,ZZ9.99'
       ***********************************************************************
                DFHMDF POS=(14,1),                                     X
                      LENGTH=31,                                       X
                      ATTRB=PROT,                                      X
                      INITIAL='-----------------------------'
                DFHMDF POS=(14,33),                                    X
                      LENGTH=13,                                       X
                      ATTRB=PROT,                                      X
                      INITIAL='CASH ADVANCES'
                DFHMDF POS=(14,47),                                    X
                      LENGTH=31,                                       X
                      ATTRB=PROT,                                      X
                      INITIAL='-----------------------------'
       ***********************************************************************
                DFHMDF POS=(15,1),                                     X
                      LENGTH=18,                                       X
                      ATTRB=(BRT,PROT),                                X
                      INITIAL='Cash Adv Amount 1:'
       ADV1     DFHMDF POS=(15,21),
                      LENGTH=6,                                        X
                      ATTRB=(UNPROT,NUM,FSET),                         X
                      PICIN='9(4)V99'
                DFHMDF POS=(15,28),                                    X
                      LENGTH=1,                                        X
                      ATTRB=ASKIP
       ***********************************************************************
                DFHMDF POS=(16,1),                                     X
                      LENGTH=18,                                       X
                      ATTRB=(BRT,PROT),                                X
                      INITIAL='Cash Adv Amount 2:'
       ADV2     DFHMDF POS=(16,21),                                    X
                      LENGTH=6,                                        X
                      ATTRB=(UNPROT,NUM,FSET),                         X
                      PICIN='9(4)V99'
                DFHMDF POS=(16,28),                                    X
                      LENGTH=1,                                        X
                      ATTRB=ASKIP
       ***********************************************************************
                DFHMDF POS=(16,43),                                    X
                      LENGTH=20,                                       X
                      ATTRB=PROT,
                      INITIAL='Total Cash Advances:'
       TOTADV   DFHMDF POS=(16,65),                                    X
                      LENGTH=9,                                        X
                      ATTRB=(ASKIP),                                   X
                      PICOUT='ZZ,ZZ9.99'
       ***********************************************************************
                DFHMDF POS=(17,31),                                    X
                      LENGTH=32,                                       X
                      ATTRB=PROT,                                      X
                      INITIAL='Finance Charge On Cash Advances:'
       FINCHG   DFHMDF POS=(17,68),                                    X
                      LENGTH=6,                                        X
                      ATTRB=(ASKIP),                                   X
                      PICOUT='ZZ9.99'
       ***********************************************************************
                DFHMDF POS=(19,30),                                    X
                      LENGTH=45,                                       X
                      ATTRB=PROT,                                      X
                      INITIAL='============================================='
       ***********************************************************************
                DFHMDF POS=(21,50),                                    X
                      LENGTH=13,
                      ATTRB=PROT,                                      X
                      INITIAL='Total Debits:'
       TOTDEB   DFHMDF POS=(21,64),                                    X
                      LENGTH=10,                                       X
                      ATTRB=(ASKIP),                                   X
                      PICOUT='$$$,$$9.99'
       ***********************************************************************
```

Figure 13.7 *(Continued)*

```
MESSAGE  DFHMDF POS=(23,1),                                               X
               LENGTH=78,                                                 X
               ATTRB=(BRT,PROT),                                          X
               INITIAL='ENTER A CHOICE ABOVE'
ERROR    DFHMDF POS=(24,1),                                               X
               LENGTH=75,                                                 X
               ATTRB=(BRT,PROT)
DUMMY    DFHMDF POS=(24,78),                                              X
               LENGTH=1,                                                  X
               ATTRB=(DRK,PROT),                                          X
               INITIAL=' '
*************************************************************************
         DFHMSD TYPE=FINAL
         END
```

Figure 13.7 *(Continued)*

plifying the recognition process and fostering easy-to-follow structured coding and a consistent error detection mechanism. RESP makes obsolete the convoluted and branching logic associated with HANDLE CONDITION. We do not consider HANDLE CONDITION coding in this book.

13.11 FOR YOUR REVIEW

The following terms were introduced or reviewed in this chapter. If you understand this chapter, you should be comfortable with defining each of these terms in relationship to CICS:

File control table (FCT)
Filename
Graphic record layout
IDCAMS utility
Inquiry function
Key sequenced data set
Load file
Random access
READ
RESP
RIDFLD
Shell program
Stubs
Updating function
VSAM

13.12 REVIEW QUESTIONS

1. Explain why random access files, such as relative or indexed files, are necessary to support updating and inquiry actions.
2. Briefly describe two ways to develop a VSAM Key Sequenced Data Set to be able to test an on-line inquiry program.
3. Discuss the difference between a load library and a load file, explaining what each one is and is used for.
4. Explain what a shell program is and why it is called this.
5. Describe what stubs are, and explain how we use them in CICS programming.
6. Discuss in detail how a CICS program accesses a file, and by what name it refers to the file.
7. Identify where, within a CICS program, you code the description of the records in a file to be read.

8. Explain the role of the File Control Table (FCT) and identify who usually makes entries in it.
9. Explain what the RIDFLD clause of the CICS READ command refers to, and how you use it.
10. You READ a file seeking a record with a particular primary key value, but no such record exists in the file. Explain how your program detects this fact, and what your program logic should do about it.

13.13 HANDS-ON EXERCISES

A. Upgrading MY FIRST CICS SCREEN

If you have completed exercise D in Chapter 7 and exercises C and D in Chapter 8, you have developed a map entitled MY FIRST CICS SCREEN, which contains name, rate of pay, hours worked, amount of pay, and "pay to" name fields. You will also have developed a program to drive this screen and validate entries made into its fields by the terminal operator. Now take these steps to enhance this program and give it file access capabilities:

- Revise the screen and logic to accommodate a nine-byte social security number field of PIC X(9); the validation for this field should help insure that only numeric contents enter it.
- Design a record to house the fields captured by the screen, designating social security number as the primary key and last name as alternate key. Develop the data content of at least six test data records in a sequential file, and use the examples in Appendix D to allocate and load a VSAM Key Sequenced Data Set with these records. Make the appropriate arrangements in your installation to establish the name of your data set in your CICS File Control Table and have a CICS filename associated with it.
- Using the inquiry example in this chapter, add logic to your program to allow it to inquire in your data set by primary key and present the contents of any record already in it. Since you will not yet include logic to write records to this data set, you can deactivate the existing data entry function in your program by commenting out the logic in your mainline that accesses it. (We'll activate those functions again when we include update capabilities in your program after Chapter 14.)
- Compile and test your revised program. Don't forget to use the CECI NEWCOPY function as described in Appendix B to make CICS aware of the new versions of your map and program.

Additional challenging comprehensive exercises

Each of the following "from scratch" hands-on exercises involves the development of BMS map source code and the preparation of physical and symbolic maps, and the preparation of a program to drive the mapset and accomplish appropriate data validation. Each exercise leads to your development and loading of a VSAM data set to house data records that the screen is used to retrieve and present (inquire against). The specific steps to accomplish each of these exercises is as follows:

1. Design a screen appropriate for the exercise, and prepare BMS map source code for it.
2. Prepare a physical map for the screen.
3. Use the CECI transaction and SEND MAP to view the map, as described in Appendix B.
4. Write a COBOL program including appropriate CICS command level statements that will enable the terminal operator to view the map, enter information and see the appropriate computed information. Data entry validations should insure that the content of any numeric field is really numeric; the transaction should never "bomb." Include other validations as appropriate and as suggested in each exercise.
5. Compile and link your program using appropriate JCL.
6. Execute the transaction in CICS. If problems exist, edit and recompile the program in TSO/ISPF. Go back to CICS and use the CECI transaction to make CICS aware of the new program copy. Try the transaction again. Repeat steps 5 and 6 until the transaction works satisfactorily.
7. Design a record to contain the data content of the screen, develop at least six test data records, and use the examples in Appendix D to create a VSAM Key Sequenced Data Set to store the records.
8. Insert appropriate logic in your program to access and display information from the Key Sequenced Data Set associated with the program.
9. Thoroughly test your program, entering record keys known to be in the file, and record keys known not to be in the file.

   We provide these scenarios to challenge you to apply your CICS skills. Each is an independent comprehensive inquiry requirement, and each will be expanded to include add, change, and delete capabilities as you consider the update function in Chapter 14.

B. Podunk University grade screen

The screen provides fields for title, appropriate labels and entry fields for student name, student social security number (SSN), semester or quarter as PIC X(3), (for example S95 would mean "Spring, 1995") and five letter grades A, B, C, D, or F (uppercase letters only!). The primary key of the record is the combined PIC X(12) field formed by SSN and semester or quarter code. For example, 123456789S95 is the primary key for student 123456789 for Spring, 1995. In other words, code the primary key field as a group field containing two elementary fields. The program will allow the terminal operator to enter one to five grades, hence, don't check for length=0 on the grade entries. You should require the entry of X in a grade field if no grade is present for it. The program computes:

Course grade points: An A counts for 4 points, a B counts for 3 points, a C for 2 points and a D counts for 1 point. A grade of F receives no grade points.

Total grade points = Sum of all course grade points

Grade point average = Total grade points / Number of courses

C. Podunk Bookstore order entry

This bookstore does a high volume of business with institutions ordering a large quantity of the same books for use in junior colleges. A given customer can order one book on a given screen. The screen provides fields for book title, appropriate labels and entry fields for customer name, customer number as PIC X(6), order date (YYMMDD), book name, book ISBN number (10 characters), quantity of the book in Podunk's warehouse, retail price, wholesale price, and quantity of book ordered. The primary key of the record is the combined field customer number, order date, and ISBN. In other words, code the primary key field as a group field containing three elementary fields. For example, primary key 5000001230940471573167 is for customer 500000, order date 123094, ISBN 0471573167. The program computes:

Net profit = (Retail price - Wholesale price * Quantity of book ordered)

Remaining quantity in warehouse = Quantity in warehouse - Quantity of book ordered

Remaining quantity value = Remaining quantity in warehouse * Wholesale price

The program will check for and reject a quantity of book ordered greater than quantity on hand, and check for and reject wholesale price greater than retail price.

D. Podunk Power Company electricity billing

The screen provides fields for customer number as PIC X(6), billing period as month and year, name, address, previous electricity meter reading (five digits), present electricity meter reading, and cost per kilowatt. The primary key of the record is customer number and billing period, for example, 1234560395 where 123456 is the customer number and 0395 is March, 1995. In other words, code the primary key field as a group field containing two elementary fields. The program computes:

Number of kilowatts of electricity used = Present meter reading - Previous meter reading

Electricity cost = Number of kilowatts used * Cost per kilowatt

City usage tax = Electricity cost * 8.5%

Total bill = Electricity cost + City usage tax

The program must take into account that electric meters "roll over" when going from 99999 to 00000; your logic has to properly compensate for this. For example, if the previous meter reading was 99999 and the present meter reading is 00003, the number of kilowatts used is not 00003 - 99999 = -99996! When a meter hits 00000, it really means 100,000. 100,003 - 99,999 = 4 kilowatts of electricity. The computation for number of kilowatts used demands a little decisionmaking logic, not just a simple subtraction in all cases.

E. Podunk University course registration

The screen provides fields for student name, student social security number, semester or quarter as PIC X(3), and up to five course numbers. Course numbers are PIC X(6) fields. The primary key of the record is the combined field SSN and semester/quarter code, for example, 123456789S95 for student 123456789 in Spring, 1995. In other words, code the primary key field as a group field containing two elementary fields. The program determines and displays:

Course name: Looked up in a table stored in a subprogram, as was done with state abbreviation by the PLACCHEK subprogram in Chapter 10. You will need to develop a table of 30 to 50 courses, names, and credit hours for each.
Course credit hours: Obtained by the lookup for course name

Course fee = $255 per credit hour * Course credit hours

Total credit hours = Sum of all course credit hours

Total course fees = Sum of all course fees

Total registration cost = Sum of total course fee + $35 registration charge

14

Indexed File Update

Adding records to a file, deleting records from a file, or reading, changing, and rewriting records to update them is a central task of on-line business data processing. In this chapter, we build on the UPDATE1 program you considered in Chapter 13. You will see how we add the logic to UPDATE1 to give it the capability to do record adds, changes, and deletes. You will also see a way to prevent the loss of data integrity when multiple terminal operators have access to the same file and may concurrently perform updates to it.

14.1 WHAT AN UPDATE PROGRAM DOES

Figure 14.1 shows you the screen for Samuel's Worthless Finance Company. We introduced this screen is Chapter 13, but accessed it with a program that responded only to the "view"

```
                    -=SAMUEL'S WORTHLESS FINANCE COMPANY=-               FILEMAP
                           ****** FILE UPDATE ******                       SMSAM

(A)dd, (D)elete, (C)hange, or (V)iew: A
Name:  pat t. kake                         Account Number:  87654321

------------------------------- CHARGE ITEMS ------------------------------
  Charge Amount 1:  2000
  Charge Amount 2:  5000
  Charge Amount 3:
  Charge Amount 4:
  Charge Amount 5:                         Total Charge Items:

------------------------------ CASH ADVANCES ------------------------------
Cash Adv Amount 1:  550
Cash Adv Amount 2:  350                   Total Cash Advances:
                              Finance Charge On Cash Advances:

                             ==============================================

                                                  Total Debits:

ENTER A CHOICE ABOVE
```

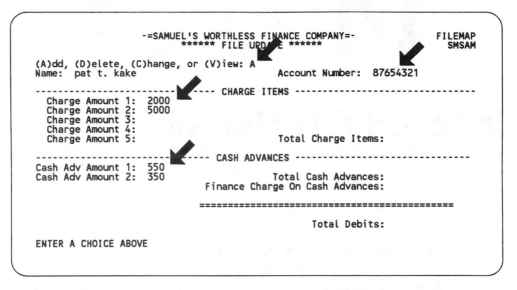

Figure 14.1 Samuel's Worthless Finance Company account screen as we begin to add a record to the borrower file.

choice of function. Here, you see the screen as we start an "add" operation. We have selected "A" at the middle top of the screen, entered an account number, and entered two charges and two cash advances. We have not yet pressed the Enter key.

In Figure 14.2, you see how our update program responds to entry of a new record. The fields at the right side of the screen have been computed and presented, and, as the prompt

```
                    -=SAMUEL'S WORTHLESS FINANCE COMPANY=-               FILEMAP
                           ****** FILE UPDATE ******                       SMSAM

(A)dd, (D)elete, (C)hange, or (V)iew: A
Name:  PAT T. KAKE                         Account Number:  87654321

------------------------------- CHARGE ITEMS ------------------------------
  Charge Amount 1:  002000
  Charge Amount 2:  005000
  Charge Amount 3:  000000
  Charge Amount 4:  000000
  Charge Amount 5:  000000                 Total Charge Items:        70.00

------------------------------ CASH ADVANCES ------------------------------
Cash Adv Amount 1:  000550
Cash Adv Amount 2:  000350                Total Cash Advances:         9.00
                              Finance Charge On Cash Advances:         0.11

                             ==============================================

                                                  Total Debits:      $79.11

ENTER A CHOICE ABOVE
RECORD ADDED
```

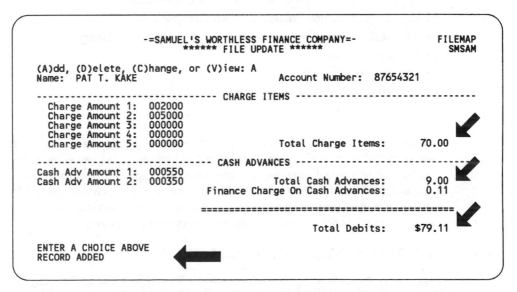

Figure 14.2 Account screen after new record has been added to the borrower file.

indicates, a new record has been added to the file. The computed fields are actually represented by fields within the record we have written to the borrower master file.

We can also change an existing record using an update program. In Figure 14.3, you see our entry of "c" at the top of the screen, and the use of the same account number to retrieve the record for Pat T. Kake. We have changed the data values at the left, but have not yet pressed the Enter key. In Figure 14.4, you see the completion of this change. The values at the right have

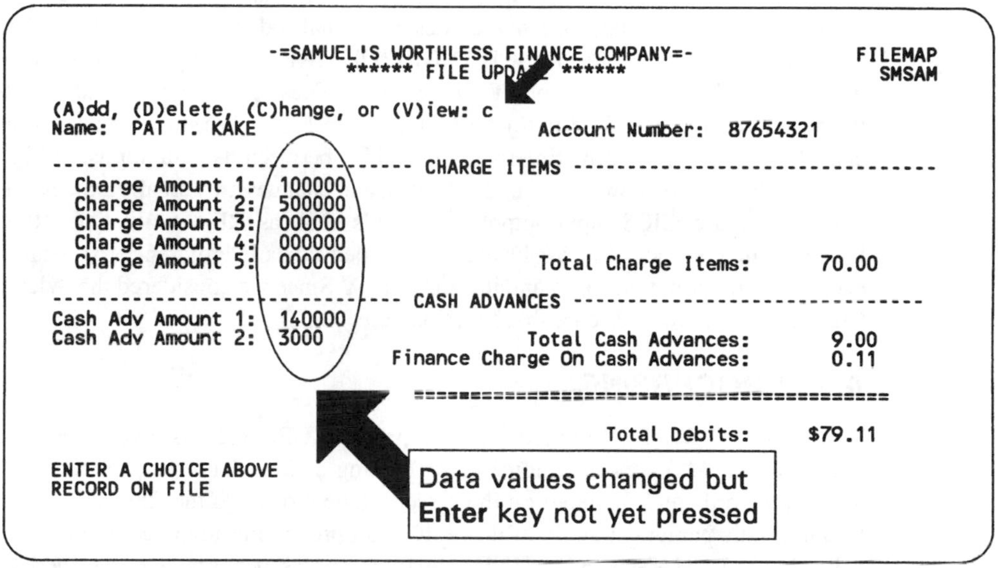
-=SAMUEL'S WORTHLESS FINANCE COMPANY=-
****** FILE UPDATE ******
FILEMAP
SMSAM
(A)dd, (D)elete, (C)hange, or (V)iew: c
Name: PAT T. KAKE
Account Number: 87654321
CHARGE ITEMS
Charge Amount 1: 100000
Charge Amount 2: 500000
Charge Amount 3: 000000
Charge Amount 4: 000000
Charge Amount 5: 000000
Total Charge Items: 70.00
CASH ADVANCES
Cash Adv Amount 1: 140000
Cash Adv Amount 2: 3000
Total Cash Advances: 9.00
Finance Charge On Cash Advances: 0.11
Total Debits: $79.11
ENTER A CHOICE ABOVE
RECORD ON FILE
Data values changed but
Enter key not yet pressed

Figure 14.3 Samuel's Worthless Finance Company account screen as we begin to change a record in the borrower file.

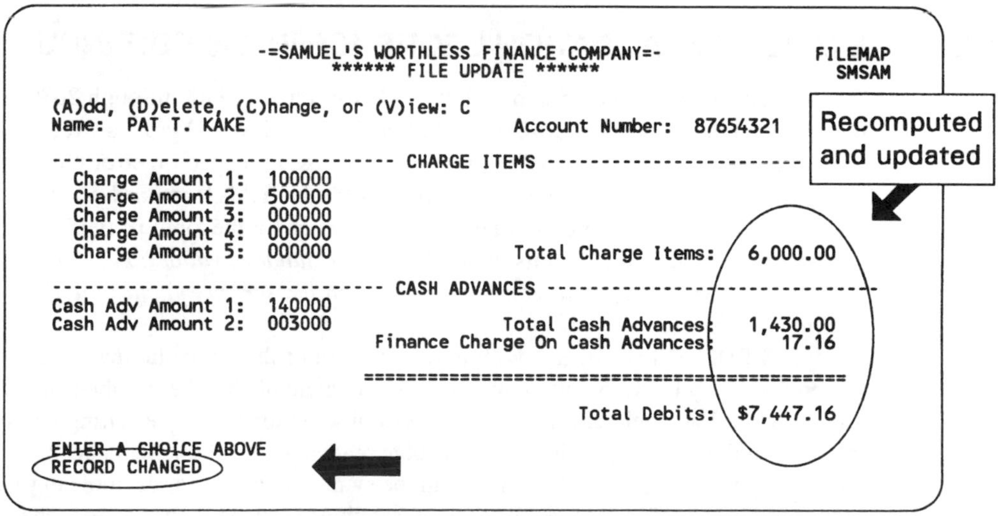
-=SAMUEL'S WORTHLESS FINANCE COMPANY=-
****** FILE UPDATE ******
FILEMAP
SMSAM
(A)dd, (D)elete, (C)hange, or (V)iew: C
Name: PAT T. KAKE
Account Number: 87654321
Recomputed
and updated
CHARGE ITEMS
Charge Amount 1: 100000
Charge Amount 2: 500000
Charge Amount 3: 000000
Charge Amount 4: 000000
Charge Amount 5: 000000
Total Charge Items: 6,000.00
CASH ADVANCES
Cash Adv Amount 1: 140000
Cash Adv Amount 2: 003000
Total Cash Advances: 1,430.00
Finance Charge On Cash Advances: 17.16
Total Debits: $7,447.16
ENTER A CHOICE ABOVE
RECORD CHANGED

Figure 14.4 Account screen after the record has been changed and rewritten to the borrower file.

been recomputed, and the program confirms with its prompt that the record has been changed and rewritten to the file.

14.2 CODING FOR AN UPDATE PROGRAM

Figure 14.5 provides you with complete source code for our CICS update program, which we have named UPDATE2. If you compare this to the UPDATE1 program in Chapter 13, Figure 13.3, and the code fragment in Figure 13.5, you'll see that UPDATE2 is really the same program. Now, however, the program includes functional code for the 115-ADD-ROUTINE, 125-DELETE-ROUTINE, and 135-CHANGE-ROUTINE paragraphs that were stubs in the inquiry-only UPDATE1 version of this program. These paragraphs are all illustrated on the third page of Figure 14.5, from lines 13200 through 17000. We show you a complete structure chart for this program, depicting the relationships between its paragraphs, in Figure 14.6.

Let's consider how record adds, deletes, and changes are actually processed. We'll point out how to use CICS input/output commands such as READ, WRITE, REWRITE, and DELETE in this discussion. We have also provided a detailed reference to the different parts of each CICS input/output command in Appendix A. Since we considered the "view" function in Chapter 13, we won't discuss that function here.

14.3 ADD PROCESSING

The 115-ADD-ROUTINE at letter "A" in program UPDATE2 is invoked when the terminal operator enters "A" for the choice of processing actions. This invokes an **add function** in which a record can be entered on the screen, to be written to the file, creating a new record. Examine this paragraph and you'll see that add processing involves three other paragraphs. Like the 135-CHANGE-ROUTINE, the first process performed for an add is 200-EDIT-INPUT, a validation routine. If the content of the fields entered on the screen is judged valid, we perform 1000-CALCULATE, followed by 300-WRITE-MASTER. Let's examine the workings of each of these three paragraphs in detail.

14.4 STANDARD VALIDATION SEQUENCE IN 200-EDIT-INPUT

The 200-EDIT-INPUT paragraph, at letter "D" from lines 19400 through 26800, implements the same validation sequence we presented in Chapter 10 with Marko's Credit Card Application program. Since the UPDATE2 program provides field-specific error messages, the order in which it validates fields is important. We validate the fields from the bottom of the screen to the top. This leaves in the prompt line the error message for the topmost field, which will be the topmost field containing -1 in its length field. *The standard validation sequence insures that the single error message that can be presented on the screen matches the field to which we position the cursor.*

200-EDIT-INPUT begins with reinitialization of the symbolic map and resetting of all screen data entry fields to normal intensity. The content of each field is then checked, one field after another. Each field check has the opportunity to move the byte setting that brightens the intensity of the field in question to its attribute byte in the symbolic map, position the cursor to the field by moving -1 to its length field in the symbolic map, and set Boolean flag INVALID-DATA to "true." When 200-EDIT-INPUT concludes, all fields have been checked, and the condition of INVALID-DATA (true or false) is tested by the logic that invoked 200-EDIT-INPUT to judge the overall goodness or badness of the screenful of data.

```
EDIT ---- CSCJGJ.CSC360.COBOL(UPDATE2) - 01.05 -------------- COLUMNS 007 078
COMMAND ===>                                                  SCROLL ===> PAGE
****** ***************************** TOP OF DATA ******************************
       ID DIVISION.
       PROGRAM-ID.  UPDATE2.

      *=================================================================
      *  THIS PROGRAM IS THE FIRST INVOKED BY THE 'SMSA' TRANSACTION.
      *  IT DISPLAYS A SCREEN FOR THE ON-LINE ACCOUNT FILE
      *  APPLICATION, WHICH PROMPTS THE USER FOR INPUT. IT THEN ADDS
      *  A RECORD TO A FILE, DELETES A RECORD FROM THE FILE, CHANGES
      *  A RECORD IN THE FILE, OR FETCHES A RECORD IN THE FILE FOR
      *  VIEWING, DEPENDING ON THE USER'S CHOICE.
      *
      *  COPYRIGHT 1994 STEVE SAMUELS AND JIM JANOSSY
      *=================================================================

       ENVIRONMENT DIVISION.
       DATA DIVISION.
       WORKING-STORAGE SECTION.

       01  WS-TRANS-ID          PIC X(4)      VALUE 'SMSA'.
       01  WS-MAPSET-NAME       PIC X(8)      VALUE 'SMSAM   '.
       01  WS-MAP-NAME          PIC X(8)      VALUE 'FILEMAP '.
       01  WS-FILENAME          PIC X(8)      VALUE 'CCPW001F'.

       01  WS-FIRST-TIME-FLAG   PIC S9(8)     BINARY.
           88 FIRST-TIME                      VALUE 0.

       01  WS-TOTCHG            PIC 9(5)V99   VALUE ZERO.
       01  WS-TOTADV            PIC 9(5)V99   VALUE ZERO.
       01  WS-FINCHG            PIC 9(3)V99   VALUE ZERO.
       01  WS-TOTDEB            PIC 9(5)V99   VALUE ZERO.

       01  PIC X(1)             VALUE 'V'.
           88 VALID-DATA        VALUE 'V'.
           88 INVALID-DATA      VALUE 'I'.

       01  WS-RESPONSE-CODE               PIC S9(8) COMP.

       01  COMMUNICATION-AREA             PIC X(1).

       01  END-OF-SESSION-MESSAGE         PIC X(50)  VALUE
           'UPDATE2 ENDED, USE  CESF LOGOFF  TO END CICS'.

       01  ACCT-REC.
           05  ACCT-NUM         PIC 9(8).
           05  AMT-1            PIC 9(4)V99.
           05  AMT-2            PIC 9(4)V99.
           05  AMT-3            PIC 9(4)V99.
           05  AMT-4            PIC 9(4)V99.
           05  AMT-5            PIC 9(4)V99.
           05  ADV-1            PIC 9(4)V99.
           05  ADV-2            PIC 9(4)V99.
           05  TOT-CHG          PIC 9(5)V99.
           05  TOT-ADV          PIC 9(5)V99.
           05  FIN-CHG          PIC 9(3)V99.
           05  TOT-DEB          PIC 9(5)V99.
           05  GAP-1            PIC X(44).
           05  ACCT-NAME        PIC X(30).
           05  GAP-2            PIC X(10).

           COPY SMSAM.

           COPY ABRTMSGS.

       01  EIBAID-TEST-FIELD    PIC X(1).
           COPY KEYDEFS.

       01  ATTRIBUTE-CONTROL-VALUE-GROUP.
           COPY ATTDEFS.
```

Compare the Procedure Division of this program to the visual table of contents in Figure 14.6 to gain a full understanding of basic add, change, delete, and inquiry programming.

Figure 14.5 Complete source code for the UPDATE2 program, which does add, change, delete, and view processing of the borrowers file for Samuel's Worthless Finance Company.

```

LINKAGE SECTION.
01  DFHCOMMAREA          PIC X(1).

*===============================================================
PROCEDURE DIVISION.
*===============================================================
000-MAINLINE.

    PERFORM 633-ALWAYS-TEST.

    EVALUATE TRUE

       WHEN FIRST-TIME
            PERFORM 800-START-TERMINAL-SESSION

       WHEN ENTER-KEY
            PERFORM 100-CHOOSE-ROUTINE

       WHEN OTHER
            MOVE LOW-VALUES TO FILEMAPI
            MOVE -1 TO CHOICEL
            MOVE 'INVALID KEY PRESSED' TO ERRORI
            PERFORM 700-SEND-ACCOUNT-SCREEN

     END-EVALUATE.

    EXEC CICS
       RETURN  TRANSID   (WS-TRANS-ID)
               COMMAREA  (COMMUNICATION-AREA)
    END-EXEC.

*---------------------------------------------------------------
*  THE USER ENTERS DATA AND THE DATA IS RECEIVED BY THE PROGRAM.
*  THE ADD, DELETE, CHANGE, OR VIEW ROUTINES ARE EXECUTED
*  DEPENDING ON THE CHOICE A D C OR V.
*---------------------------------------------------------------
 100-CHOOSE-ROUTINE.

    PERFORM 150-RECEIVE-ACCOUNT-SCREEN.

       EVALUATE CHOICEI

          WHEN 'A'
             PERFORM 115-ADD-ROUTINE

          WHEN 'D'
             PERFORM 125-DELETE-ROUTINE

          WHEN 'C'
             PERFORM 135-CHANGE-ROUTINE

          WHEN 'V'
             PERFORM 145-VIEW-ROUTINE

          WHEN OTHER
             MOVE 'INVALID CHOICE!  TRY AGAIN' TO ERRORI
             MOVE -1 TO CHOICEL

       END-EVALUATE.

    PERFORM 700-SEND-ACCOUNT-SCREEN.

```

Figure 14.5 *(Continued)*

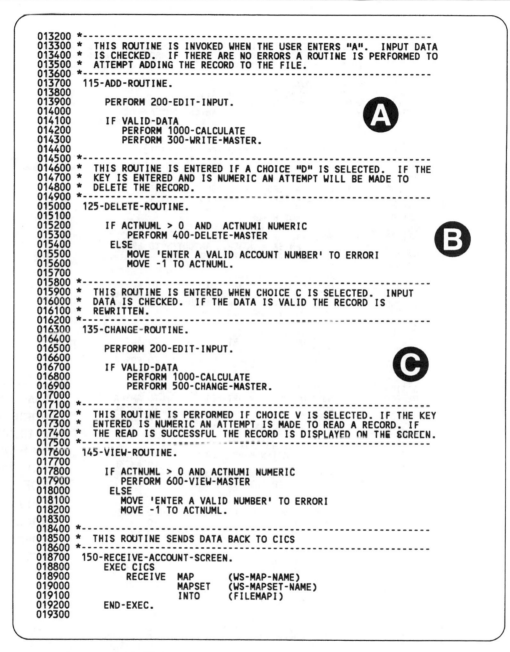

```
*------------------------------------------------------------------
*  THIS ROUTINE IS INVOKED WHEN THE USER ENTERS "A".  INPUT DATA
*  IS CHECKED.  IF THERE ARE NO ERRORS A ROUTINE IS PERFORMED TO
*  ATTEMPT ADDING THE RECORD TO THE FILE.
*------------------------------------------------------------------
 115-ADD-ROUTINE.

     PERFORM 200-EDIT-INPUT.

     IF VALID-DATA
        PERFORM 1000-CALCULATE
        PERFORM 300-WRITE-MASTER.

*------------------------------------------------------------------
*  THIS ROUTINE IS ENTERED IF A CHOICE "D" IS SELECTED.  IF THE
*  KEY IS ENTERED AND IS NUMERIC AN ATTEMPT WILL BE MADE TO
*  DELETE THE RECORD.
*------------------------------------------------------------------
 125-DELETE-ROUTINE.

     IF ACTNUML > 0  AND  ACTNUMI NUMERIC
         PERFORM 400-DELETE-MASTER
      ELSE
         MOVE 'ENTER A VALID ACCOUNT NUMBER' TO ERRORI
         MOVE -1 TO ACTNUML.

*------------------------------------------------------------------
*  THIS ROUTINE IS ENTERED WHEN CHOICE C IS SELECTED.  INPUT
*  DATA IS CHECKED.  IF THE DATA IS VALID THE RECORD IS
*  REWRITTEN.
*------------------------------------------------------------------
 135-CHANGE-ROUTINE.

     PERFORM 200-EDIT-INPUT.

     IF VALID-DATA
         PERFORM 1000-CALCULATE
         PERFORM 500-CHANGE-MASTER.

*------------------------------------------------------------------
*  THIS ROUTINE IS PERFORMED IF CHOICE V IS SELECTED. IF THE KEY
*  ENTERED IS NUMERIC AN ATTEMPT IS MADE TO READ A RECORD. IF
*  THE READ IS SUCCESSFUL THE RECORD IS DISPLAYED ON THE SCREEN.
*------------------------------------------------------------------
 145-VIEW-ROUTINE.

     IF ACTNUML > 0 AND ACTNUMI NUMERIC
        PERFORM 600-VIEW-MASTER
      ELSE
        MOVE 'ENTER A VALID NUMBER' TO ERRORI
        MOVE -1 TO ACTNUML.

*------------------------------------------------------------------
*  THIS ROUTINE SENDS DATA BACK TO CICS
*------------------------------------------------------------------
 150-RECEIVE-ACCOUNT-SCREEN.
     EXEC CICS
         RECEIVE  MAP      (WS-MAP-NAME)
                  MAPSET   (WS-MAPSET-NAME)
                  INTO     (FILEMAPI)
     END-EXEC.

```

Figure 14.5 *(Continued)*

```
      *-----------------------------------------------------------------
      *  THIS IS THE VALIDATION ROUTINE; IT SETS INVALID-DATA TO TRUE
      *  IF ANY FIELD(S) HAVE DATA CONTENT ERRORS.  FIELDS ARE TESTED
      *  IN BOTTOM TO TOP SEQUENCE IN THE STD VALIDATION SEQUENCE.
      *-----------------------------------------------------------------
       200-EDIT-INPUT.
           MOVE LOW-VALUES  TO ERRORI.
           MOVE UNPROT-NUM-MDT TO  AMT1A  AMT2A  AMT3A
                                   AMT4A  AMT5A
                                   ADV1A  ADV2A  ACTNUMA.

           IF AMT1L = ZERO   MOVE ZERO TO AMT1I.
           IF AMT2L = ZERO   MOVE ZERO TO AMT2I.
           IF AMT3L = ZERO   MOVE ZERO TO AMT3I.
           IF AMT4L = ZERO   MOVE ZERO TO AMT4I.
           IF AMT5L = ZERO   MOVE ZERO TO AMT5I.
           IF ADV1L = ZERO   MOVE ZERO TO ADV1I.
           IF ADV2L = ZERO   MOVE ZERO TO ADV2I.

           IF ADV2I NOT NUMERIC
              MOVE UNPROT-NUM-BRT-MDT          TO ADV2A
              MOVE -1                          TO ADV2L
              MOVE 'ENTER A NUMERIC AMOUNT'    TO ERRORI
              SET INVALID-DATA TO TRUE.

           IF ADV1I NOT NUMERIC
              MOVE UNPROT-NUM-BRT-MDT          TO ADV1A
              MOVE -1                          TO ADV1L
              MOVE 'ENTER A NUMERIC AMOUNT'    TO ERRORI
              SET INVALID-DATA TO TRUE.

           IF AMT5I NOT NUMERIC
              MOVE UNPROT-NUM-BRT-MDT          TO AMT5A
              MOVE -1                          TO AMT5L
              MOVE 'ENTER A NUMERIC AMOUNT'    TO ERRORI
              SET INVALID-DATA TO TRUE.

           IF AMT4I NOT NUMERIC
              MOVE UNPROT-NUM-BRT-MDT          TO AMT4A
              MOVE -1                          TO AMT4L
              MOVE 'ENTER A NUMERIC AMOUNT'    TO ERRORI
              SET INVALID-DATA TO TRUE.

      *    IF AMT3I NOT NUMERIC
      *       MOVE UNPROT-NUM-BRT-MDT          TO AMT3A
      *       MOVE -1                          TO AMT3L
      *       MOVE 'ENTER A NUMERIC AMOUNT'    TO ERRORI
      *       SET INVALID-DATA TO TRUE.

           IF AMT2I NOT NUMERIC
              MOVE UNPROT-NUM-BRT-MDT          TO AMT2A
              MOVE -1                          TO AMT2L
              MOVE 'ENTER A NUMERIC AMOUNT'    TO ERRORI
              SET INVALID-DATA TO TRUE.

           IF AMT1I NOT NUMERIC
              MOVE UNPROT-NUM-BRT-MDT          TO AMT1A
              MOVE -1                          TO AMT1L
              MOVE 'ENTER A NUMERIC AMOUNT'    TO ERRORI
              SET INVALID-DATA TO TRUE.

           IF  ACTNUML = ZERO
            OR ACTNUMI NOT NUMERIC
              MOVE UNPROT-NUM-BRT-MDT          TO ACTNUMA
              MOVE -1                          TO ACTNUML
              MOVE 'ENTER A NUMERIC ACCOUNT NUMBER' TO ERRORI
              SET INVALID-DATA TO TRUE.

           IF  ACTNAMEL = ZERO
            OR ACTNAMEI = SPACES
              MOVE -1                          TO ACTNAMEL
              MOVE UNPROT-BRT-MDT              TO ACTNAMEA
              MOVE 'YOU MUST ENTER A NAME'     TO ERRORI
              SET INVALID-DATA TO TRUE.
```

D

These lines commented out to force an ASRA abend for the CEDF debugging tutorial in Appendix C.

Figure 14.5 *(Continued)*

```
*-------------------------------------------------------------
*  THIS ROUTINE WRITES A NEW RECORD TO THE VSAM FILE UNLESS A
*  RECORD ALREADY EXISTS WITH THE KEY USED
*-------------------------------------------------------------
 300-WRITE-MASTER.
     MOVE ACTNAMEI     TO  ACCT-NAME.
     MOVE ACTNUMI      TO  ACCT-NUM.
     MOVE AMT1I        TO  AMT-1.
     MOVE AMT2I        TO  AMT-2.
     MOVE AMT3I        TO  AMT-3.
     MOVE AMT4I        TO  AMT-4.
     MOVE AMT5I        TO  AMT-5.
     MOVE ADV1I        TO  ADV-1.
     MOVE ADV2I        TO  ADV-2.
     MOVE WS-TOTCHG    TO  TOT-CHG.
     MOVE WS-TOTADV    TO  TOT-ADV.
     MOVE WS-FINCHG    TO  FIN-CHG.
     MOVE WS-TOTDEB    TO  TOT-DEB.
     MOVE SPACES       TO  GAP-1 GAP-2.

     EXEC CICS
         WRITE  DATASET   (WS-FILENAME)
                FROM      (ACCT-REC)
                RIDFLD    (ACCT-NUM)
                RESP      (WS-RESPONSE-CODE)
     END-EXEC.

     EVALUATE WS-RESPONSE-CODE

        WHEN DFHRESP(NORMAL)
           MOVE 'RECORD ADDED' TO ERRORI
           MOVE -1 TO CHOICEL

        WHEN DFHRESP(DUPREC)
           MOVE 'DUPLICATE RECORD, CANNOT ADD' TO ERRORI
           MOVE -1 TO CHOICEL

        WHEN OTHER
           PERFORM 9999-ABORT

     END-EVALUATE.

*-------------------------------------------------------------
*  THIS ROUTINE DELETES A RECORD FROM THE VSAM FILE UNLESS NO
*  RECORD WITH THE KEY VALUE CAN BE FOUND
*-------------------------------------------------------------
 400-DELETE-MASTER.
     MOVE ACTNUMI TO ACCT-NUM.

     EXEC CICS
         DELETE  DATASET   (WS-FILENAME)
                 RIDFLD    (ACCT-NUM)
                 RESP      (WS-RESPONSE-CODE)
     END-EXEC.

     EVALUATE WS-RESPONSE-CODE

        WHEN DFHRESP(NORMAL)
           MOVE 'RECORD DELETED' TO ERRORI
           MOVE -1 TO CHOICEL

        WHEN DFHRESP(NOTFND)
           MOVE 'RECORD NOT FOUND, NO DELETION' TO ERRORI
           MOVE -1 TO CHOICEL

        WHEN OTHER
           PERFORM 9999-ABORT

     END-EVALUATE.
```

Figure 14.5 *(Continued)*

```
      *----------------------------------------------------------------
      *  THIS ROUTINE CHANGES A RECORD UNLESS A RECORD WITH THE KEY
      *  CANNOT BE FOUND
      *----------------------------------------------------------------
       500-CHANGE-MASTER.
           MOVE ACTNUMI TO ACCT-NUM.

           EXEC CICS
                READ  DATASET    (WS-FILENAME)
                      INTO       (ACCT-REC)
                      RIDFLD     (ACCT-NUM)
                      UPDATE
                      RESP       (WS-RESPONSE-CODE)
           END-EXEC.

           EVALUATE WS-RESPONSE-CODE

              WHEN DFHRESP(NORMAL)
                 IF ACTNAMEI NOT = ACCT-NAME
                    MOVE 'NAME CHANGE FOR ACCOUNT NUMBER NOT ALLOWED'
                        TO ERRORI
                    MOVE -1 TO ACTNAMEL
                  ELSE
                    PERFORM 501-REWRITE
                 END-IF

              WHEN DFHRESP(NOTFND)
                 MOVE 'RECORD NOT FOUND, NO CHANGE POSSIBLE'
                    TO ERRORI
                 MOVE -1 TO CHOICEL

              WHEN DFHRESP(INVREQ)
                 MOVE 'SOMEONE ELSE IS USING RECORD, TRY AGAIN LATER'
                    TO ERRORI
                 MOVE -1 TO CHOICEL

              WHEN OTHER
                 PERFORM 9999-ABORT

           END-EVALUATE.

      *----------------------------------------------------------------
      *  INVOKED ONLY IF WE CAN PROCEED TO PUT THE CHANGED RECORD BACK
      *  INTO THE MASTER FILE
      *----------------------------------------------------------------
       501-REWRITE.
           MOVE AMT1I         TO AMT-1.
           MOVE AMT2I         TO AMT-2.
           MOVE AMT3I         TO AMT-3.
           MOVE AMT4I         TO AMT-4.
           MOVE AMT5I         TO AMT-5.
           MOVE ADV1I         TO ADV-1.
           MOVE ADV2I         TO ADV-2.
           MOVE WS-TOTCHG     TO TOT-CHG.
           MOVE WS-TOTADV     TO TOT-ADV.
           MOVE WS-FINCHG     TO FIN-CHG.
           MOVE WS-TOTDEB     TO TOT-DEB.

           EXEC CICS
                REWRITE  DATASET    (WS-FILENAME)
                         FROM       (ACCT-REC)
                         RESP       (WS-RESPONSE-CODE)
           END-EXEC.


           EVALUATE WS-RESPONSE-CODE

              WHEN DFHRESP(NORMAL)
                 MOVE 'RECORD CHANGED AND REWRITTEN' TO ERRORI
                 MOVE -1 TO CHOICEL

              WHEN OTHER
                 PERFORM 9999-ABORT

           END-EVALUATE.
```

Must READ with UPDATE to gain sufficient authority to REWRITE the record after changing it.

G

H

Figure 14.5 *(Continued)*

```

*-----------------------------------------------------------------
*  THIS ROUTINE READS A RECORD FROM THE VSAM FILE, UNLESS NO
*  RECORED WITH THE KEY VALUE CAN BE FOUND
*-----------------------------------------------------------------
 600-VIEW-MASTER.

     MOVE ACTNUMI TO ACCT-NUM.
     EXEC CICS
          READ  DATASET  (WS-FILENAME)
                INTO     (ACCT-REC)
                RIDFLD   (ACCT-NUM)
                RESP     (WS-RESPONSE-CODE)
     END-EXEC.

     MOVE -1 TO CHOICEL.

     EVALUATE WS-RESPONSE-CODE

        WHEN DFHRESP(NORMAL)
           MOVE ACCT-NAME    TO ACTNAMEI
           MOVE AMT-1        TO AMT1I
           MOVE AMT-2        TO AMT2I
           MOVE AMT-3        TO AMT3I
           MOVE AMT-4        TO AMT4I
           MOVE AMT-5        TO AMT5I
           MOVE ADV-1        TO ADV1I
           MOVE ADV-2        TO ADV2I
           MOVE TOT-CHG      TO TOTCHGO
           MOVE TOT-ADV      TO TOTADVO
           MOVE FIN-CHG      TO FINCHGO
           MOVE TOT-DEB      TO TOTDEBO
           MOVE 'RECORD DISPLAYED' TO ERRORI
           MOVE -1 TO CHOICEL

        WHEN DFHRESP(NOTFND)
           MOVE SPACES TO ACTNAMEI
           MOVE 0 TO AMT1I AMT2I AMT3I AMT4I AMT5I
                     ADV1I ADV2I
                     TOTCHGO TOTADVO FINCHGO TOTDEBO
           MOVE 'RECORD NOT FOUND, NO VIEW POSSIBLE'
             TO ERRORI
           MOVE -1 TO CHOICEL

        WHEN DFHRESP(INVREQ)
           MOVE 'SOMEONE ELSE IS USING RECORD, TRY AGAIN LATER'
              TO ERRORI
           MOVE -1 TO CHOICEL

        WHEN OTHER
           PERFORM 9999-ABORT

     END-EVALUATE.

*-----------------------------------------------------------------
*  THIS ROUTINE IS USED AT THE START OF EACH PSEUDOCONVERSE
*-----------------------------------------------------------------
 633-ALWAYS-TEST.
     MOVE EIBAID    TO  EIBAID-TEST-FIELD.
     IF CLEAR-KEY
        PERFORM 900-SEND-TERMINATION-MESSAGE
        EXEC CICS  RETURN  END-EXEC.

     MOVE EIBCALEN  TO  WS-FIRST-TIME-FLAG.

*-----------------------------------------------------------------
*  THIS ROUTINE SENDS DATA FROM CICS TO SCREEN
*-----------------------------------------------------------------
 700-SEND-ACCOUNT-SCREEN.
     EXEC CICS
         SEND  MAP       (WS-MAP-NAME)
               MAPSET    (WS-MAPSET-NAME)
               FROM      (FILEMAPI)
               DATAONLY
               CURSOR
     END-EXEC.
```

Figure 14.5 *(Continued)*

```
      *-------------------------------------------------------------
      *  INVOKED ONLY IF EIBCALEN = 0, A FIRST-TIME ROUTINE
      *-------------------------------------------------------------
       800-START-TERMINAL-SESSION.
           MOVE LOW-VALUES TO FILEMAPI.
           MOVE -1 TO CHOICEL.
           EXEC CICS
               SEND  MAP      (WS-MAP-NAME)
                     MAPSET   (WS-MAPSET-NAME)
                     FROM     (FILEMAPI)
                     ERASE
                     CURSOR
           END-EXEC.

      *-------------------------------------------------------------
      *  LAST SCREEN SENT WHEN PROGRAM ENDS NORMALLY
      *-------------------------------------------------------------
       900-SEND-TERMINATION-MESSAGE.
           EXEC CICS
               SEND   TEXT FROM(END-OF-SESSION-MESSAGE)
                      ERASE
                      FREEKB
           END-EXEC.

      *-------------------------------------------------------------
      *  DETERMINE THE PROGRAM-CALCULATED VALUES
      *-------------------------------------------------------------
       1000-CALCULATE.
           COMPUTE WS-TOTCHG = AMT1I + AMT2I + AMT3I + AMT4I + AMT5I
             ON SIZE ERROR
                MOVE 'E101, OVERFLOW ON WS-TOTCHG' TO WS-ERROR-LINE5
                PERFORM 9999-ABORT.

           COMPUTE WS-TOTADV = ADV1I + ADV2I
             ON SIZE ERROR
                MOVE 'E102, OVERFLOW ON WS-TOTADV' TO WS-ERROR-LINE5
                PERFORM 9999-ABORT.

           COMPUTE WS-FINCHG ROUNDED = WS-TOTADV * .012
             ON SIZE ERROR
                MOVE 'E103, OVERFLOW ON WS-FINCHG' TO WS-ERROR-LINE5
                PERFORM 9999-ABORT.

           COMPUTE WS-TOTDEB = WS-TOTCHG + WS-TOTDEB + WS-FINCHG
             ON SIZE ERROR
                MOVE 'E104, OVERFLOW ON WS-FINCHG' TO WS-ERROR-LINE5
                PERFORM 9999-ABORT.

           MOVE WS-TOTCHG  TO  TOTCHGO.
           MOVE WS-TOTADV  TO  TOTADVO
           MOVE WS-FINCHG  TO  FINCHGO.
           MOVE WS-TOTDEB  TO  TOTDEBO.

      *-------------------------------------------------------------
      *  SCREEN SENT FOR ABORT CONDITION ONLY -- AS WHEN WE GET A RESP
      *  WE COULD NOT DEAL WITH!
      *-------------------------------------------------------------
       9999-ABORT.
           MOVE EIBTRNID   TO  WS-EIBTRNID.
           MOVE EIBRSRCE   TO  WS-EIBRSRCE.
           MOVE EIBRESP    TO  WS-EIBRESP.
           MOVE EIBRESP2   TO  WS-EIBRESP2.

           EXEC CICS
               SEND  TEXT FROM (WS-ERROR-MESSAGES)
                     ERASE
                     ALARM
                     FREEKB
           END-EXEC.

           EXEC CICS  RETURN  END-EXEC.
```

Figure 14.5 *(Continued)*

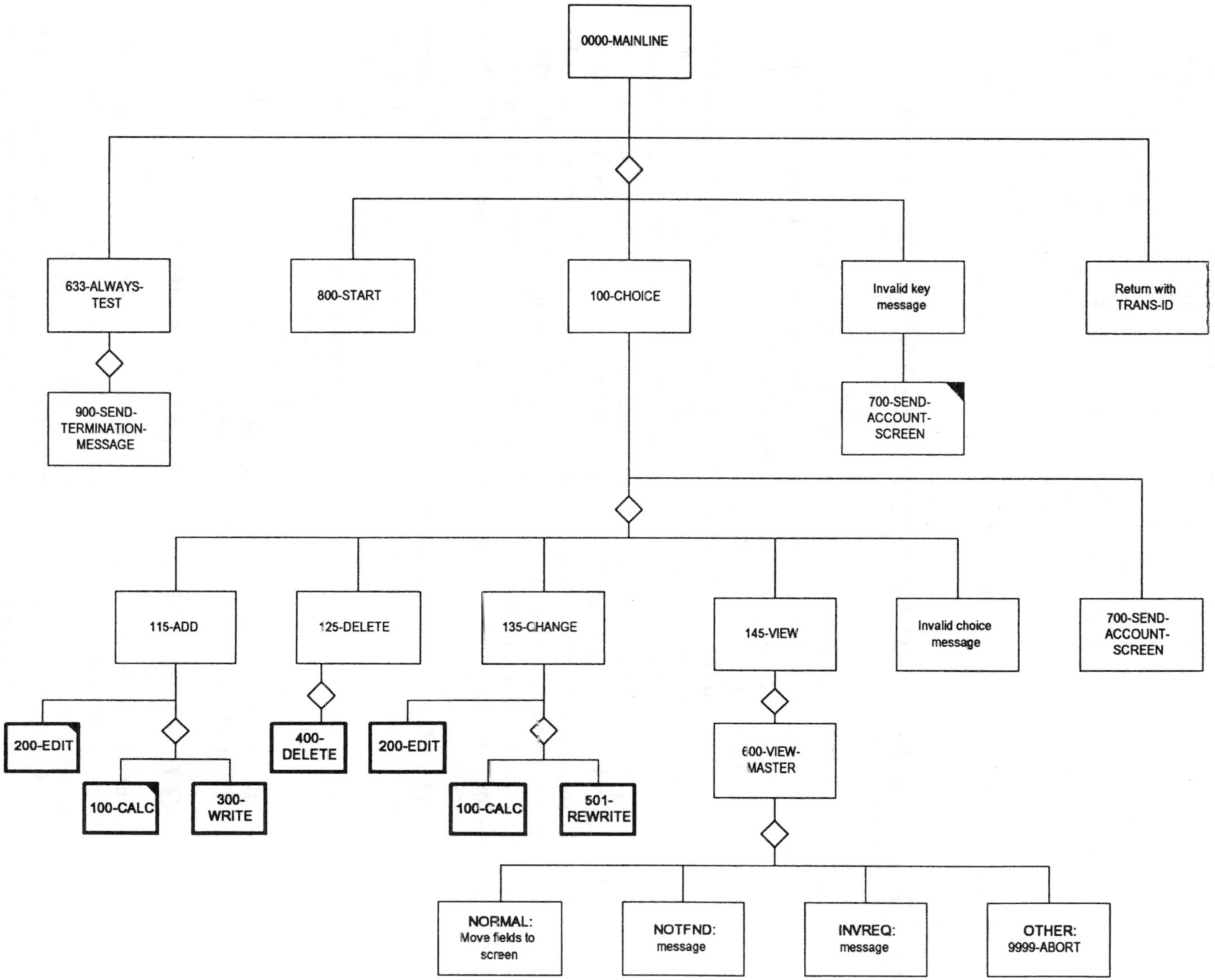
0000-MAINLINE
633-ALWAYS-TEST
800-START
100-CHOICE
Invalid key message
Return with TRANS-ID
900-SEND-TERMINATION-MESSAGE
700-SEND-ACCOUNT-SCREEN
115-ADD
125-DELETE
135-CHANGE
145-VIEW
Invalid choice message
700-SEND-ACCOUNT-SCREEN
200-EDIT
100-CALC
300-WRITE
400-DELETE
200-EDIT
100-CALC
501-REWRITE
600-VIEW-MASTER
NORMAL: Move fields to screen
NOTFND: message
INVREQ: message
OTHER: 9999-ABORT

Figure 14.6 Structure chart for the UPDATE2 program depicting the relationships between its paragraphs.

In 200-EDIT-INPUT, we test the length field of some of the entered data fields in the symbolic map as a part of validation actions. The length field lets us know if the terminal operator made any keystroke entries in the field. For example, if no name was entered in the account name field, the length attribute of this field, ACTNAMEL, is equal to 0. We also use this technique at the amount fields to put zero into any amount field in which the terminal operator has not made an entry, so that it does not remain initialized to LOW-VALUES.

Charge fields for which the operator has made no entry are set to zero. A record can be added by supplying only name and account number; it is possible that certain customers have no charges or cash advances. If non-numeric data (periods or minus signs) are entered in any of the numeric fields, INVALID-DATA becomes true and the cursor is placed in the first charge field that is not numeric. (Even the NUM attribute allows periods and hyphens to be entered into a field.)

14.5 CALCULATION ROUTINE 1000-CALCULATE AND THE ASRA ABEND

The 1000-CALCULATE paragraph, at letter "I" at lines 51500 through 54200, is common to both add and change transactions. It is invoked during processing for an add transaction only if all of the entered data has proven acceptable. This paragraph determines the totals that will be stored in the record and presented on the screen.

It's important to realize that if the validation logic in the 200-EDIT-INPUT paragraph is insufficient, and allows nonnumeric data to enter any of the amount or advance fields, the actions we take in the 1000-CALCULATE paragraph will cause an abend. Attempting to perform arithmetic on nonnumeric data will produce a data exception that will terminate the entire transaction. While this produces a 0C7 system completion code in a batch program, it results in an **ASRA abend code** in a CICS program, as listed in our abend code reference in Appendix E. You'll notice that we actually commented out lines 23700 through 24100 in the UPDATE2 program, within the data validation sequence, to force this type of problem for example purposes. We show you how to resolve abends using the CICS interactive debugger, CEDF, in Appendix C.

Strictly speaking, the total fields stored in the borrower record are extraneous. They need not be stored in the record, because they could always be computed from their constituent parts. Good database design would lead us to not store these computed values in the interest of conserving storage space, and, more importantly, in the interest of maintaining data integrity. If the value in a computed field in a record were to differ from the sum of the constituent fields, where would the error lie? In the Samuel's Worthless Finance Company example, we actually store these fields simply to make this example more interesting for demonstration purposes and to simplify batch sorting and reporting from this file.

14.6 WRITING TO AN INDEXED FILE USING CICS WRITE

We invoke the 300-WRITE-MASTER paragraph, at letter "E", during the add function to store validated input fields and fully computed calculated fields in a new record in the borrower file. This writing action is accomplished with the CICS WRITE command.

The **CICS WRITE** command at lines 28900 through 29400 is similar to **CICS READ** we used to support the view function, in that we use the same file and the same primary key field. Here, however, we dispatch a new record to the indexed file from a working storage record description rather than reading an existing record into this description.

The RESP clause of the WRITE command places a value into WS-RESPONSE-CODE indicating the outcome of the write that we attempted. We test the value of the response code using **DFHRESP** syntax, which is processed by the CICS translator and replaced with a value corresponding to the logical condition we actually coded. We see the test as a logical outcome; the translator worries about the actual numeric WS-RESPONSE-CODE values involved.

For example, if DFHRESP(NORMAL) is true, the record has been written. If DFHRESP(DUPREC) is true, the write failed; the primary key of the new record is already in use (it exists in the file already). Any other DFHRESP condition indicates a problem that we cannot anticipate and/or provide program logic to deal with. The "otherwise" case represented by the WHEN OTHER at lines 30600 and 30700 directs control to a standard "abort" paragraph that provides various Execute Interface Block fields for diagnostic purposes, and stops the program. As you can see, the response code value indicates the nature of the message we supply to the terminal operator in the prompt area, and what we do after the WRITE.

14.7 DELETE PROCESSING WITH CICS DELETE

Paragraph 125-DELETE-ROUTINE, at letter "B" at lines 14500 through 15700 in Figure 14.5, is invoked when the terminal operator enters a "D" as a choice. A **delete function**, deleting a specified record, involves no editing of fields, other than the account number, and no calculations. We check the account number only to avoid input/output actions when the value entered by the terminal operator is patently invalid. If the key entered is present and numeric, the CICS DELETE command coded in the 400-DELETE-MASTER paragraph at letter "F" at lines 31800 through 32200 is executed. Despite the appearance of this command, which might make it appear that it deletes an entire file, the **CICS DELETE** command removes just the record whose key is contained in the data name mentioned in the RIDFLD clause. As with all other CICS commands, the RESP clause places a value into the RESPONSE-CODE field, which we can test to determine the success or failure of the action. If DFHRESP(NORMAL) is true, the record has been deleted.

It's good software design practice to display the contents of a record that the terminal operator wants to delete, and request confirmation prior to proceeding with the delete. In this processing system for Samuel's Worthless Finance Company, the terminal operator uses the "view" function prior to attempting a delete to see the record to be eliminated. Viewing the record lets the terminal operator decide if the delete should proceed. To proceed with the delete, the operator simply changes the "C" function selection at the top of the screen to "D" and presses Enter again.

14.8 UPDATE PROCESSING WITH CICS READ/REWRITE

Update or **change function** processing is the most involved in our demonstration program because of the way the CICS READ command operates. Let's consider where the code that supports change processing is located in program UPDATE2, and how it works.

The 135-CHANGE-ROUTINE paragraph at letter "C" at lines 15800 through 16900 receives control when the terminal user chooses the "C" change function. If you compare this paragraph with 115-ADD-ROUTINE, you'll see that they are almost identical. In both cases, we perform 200-EDIT-INPUT to validate the contents of the transmitted data fields. Assuming that all fields are valid, the 1000-CALCULATE paragraph is executed to calculate the total fields and finance charges. If any of the input fields are invalid, neither 1000-CALCULATE nor 500-CHANGE-MASTER are executed.

If the terminal operator chooses to do a change transaction, and the input fields on the screen are checked and found to be valid, the 500-CHANGE-ROUTINE paragraph at letter "G" at lines 33900 through 37800 receives control. This paragraph is interesting because it contains two CICS commands, the READ with the UPDATE option and the REWRITE. We must READ with UPDATE before REWRITE to gain exclusive use of a record and the access authority that accompanies it. **READ with UPDATE** places a lock on the record (or, in the case of VSAM, the entire control interval in which the record is stored), so that no one else can access it during the time that our program remains active. (Similarly, our attempt to READ with UPDATE will not succeed if someone else already has the record "checked out" with READ with UPDATE.)

If our READ with UPDATE succeeds with DFHRESP(NORMAL) true, we perform 501-REWRITE at letter "H". This moves fields from the symbolic map fields to the record in WORKING-STORAGE, and the REWRITE command is executed. As the name implies, **REWRITE** puts a copy of the record back into the file, overlaying the old copy of the record. We check DFHRESP again after executing the REWRITE command in the 501-REWRITE paragraph. Here, the only response we can deal with in program logic is a successful REWRITE, with DFHRESP(NORMAL) true. Any failure to rewrite the record means that the diagnostic actions accomplished by the 9999-ABORT paragraph are necessary.

14.9 A PROBLEM INHERENT IN CONCURRENT ACCESS

We face a potential problem with the "change" function in our UPDATE2 program. This problem relates to **concurrent access**, the potential for more than one terminal operator to access the same record at the same time.

It's quite likely that you have not (until now) had to worry about multiple programs accessing the same file at the same time. Batch programs typically read entire files and make exclusive use of them during execution. But an on-line system is most often used by many people simultaneously, and any one person accesses only one or a few records at a time. Multiple users share access to the files supporting the on-line system.

Consider the on-line system by which a small business takes orders for products and keeps track of its inventory. Two or more personnel may be on the telephone entering new orders into the system at the same time that personnel in the warehouse are updating files to reflect stock removed from inventory. Someone elsewhere may be changing customer information while another person is also putting new customer records into the system. All of these people will be accessing the same files.

The problem that this can cause for Samuel's Worthless Finance Company is **lost updates**. Suppose a customer service employee named John begins an on-line change to the record for borrower 12345678 to add a charge received by mail. At the same time, another customer service employee named Wendy receives a call from the customer asking to add a cash advance. Wendy starts her on-line action after John but finishes it before he does; her copy of the record is rewritten with the new cash advance. When John finishes his update his copy of the record is rewritten. Is the cash advance posted by Wendy in the file? It's gone! Wendy updated the record, but John's rewrite replaced it with the old copy of the record he read first!

This situation may seems farfetched to you. But you have to consider concurrent access such as this when you program an interactive business application. Multiple-user business systems are vulnerable to events like this, which can damage **data integrity**, the correctness and/or completeness of data. Every interactive business system broader in scope than a single-user PC has to recognize and deal with this problem. Since CICS was designed to support huge numbers of terminal users concurrently accessing the same files or database, you must address the issue in any practical CICS update program.

14.10 METHODS TO DEAL WITH THE CONCURRENT UPDATE PROBLEM

A variety of methods exist to resolve the problem of data integrity and potential loss of update information in multiple-user interactive systems. These methods include:

- **Record locking** across a pseudoconverse, which READ for UPDATE cannot accomplish (the UPDATE lock is released when your program returns control to CICS)
- **Enqueuing** mechanisms, which force processes to proceed "single file" to completion, so one update is completely finished before another starts
- The use of a shared **scratch pad** to keep track of which records are currently in the process of update, and "agreement" among all programs that each program will check the scratchpad first to see if a record is in use before attempting to update it
- The use of a **record in use** flag within a record, set on by a program updating it (and rewritten before update), and "agreement" among all programs that each program will check the flag first to see if a record is in use, before attempting to update it
- **Prior/present record comparison** before rewrite, with cancellation of a transaction that would cause a lost update

These different approaches all have their strengths and costs, in terms of added complexity and/or resource usage. It's beyond our scope here to discuss all of these methods and the tradeoffs associated with their use. We discuss here the simplest (and quite reliable) way to preserve data integrity, which we demonstrate in an enhancement to the UPDATE2 program.

14.11 HOW PRIOR/PRESENT RECORD COMPARISON WORKS

In the prior/present record comparison method to prevent lost updates, we force a terminal operator to view a record before making an update. This is quite a natural action, since it brings to the screen the existing content of the record. The operator can then use the Tab key to move the cursor to the fields in which changes are to be made, and enter a new data value for any such field. The terminal operator then changes the function choice from "V" to "C" and presses the Enter key to cause the updated record to be rewritten to the file. This is exactly how the original version of the UPDATE2 program operates, from the terminal user's point of view. It is exactly how the enhanced UPDATE2 program will work also—when no one else has updated the record during the time that our update has been underway.

Figure 14.7 shows you a screen that will result from the enhanced UPDATE2 program when a terminal operator has, unknowingly, been updating a given record at the same time as someone else. When the terminal operator presses the Enter key to rewrite the changed record, he or she receives the response "ACTION CANCELLED, VIEW AND TRY AGAIN." Why does this happen, and how did we arrange for it to happen?

The "why" of Figure 14.7 is easy. Between the time that this terminal operator viewed the record for account number 22222222 and the time that the operator pressed the Enter key to rewrite the changed record, another terminal operator also viewed and rewrote the record. That other operator concluded his or her action before the operator responsible for the screen in

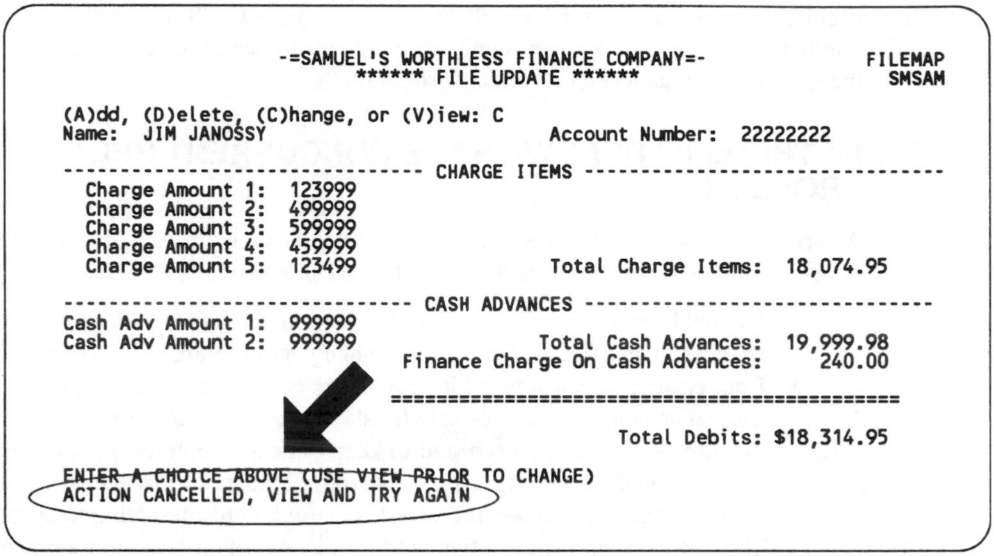
-=SAMUEL'S WORTHLESS FINANCE COMPANY=-
****** FILE UPDATE ******
FILEMAP
SMSAM
(A)dd, (D)elete, (C)hange, or (V)iew: C
Name: JIM JANOSSY
Account Number: 22222222
CHARGE ITEMS
Charge Amount 1: 123999
Charge Amount 2: 499999
Charge Amount 3: 599999
Charge Amount 4: 459999
Charge Amount 5: 123499
Total Charge Items: 18,074.95
CASH ADVANCES
Cash Adv Amount 1: 999999
Cash Adv Amount 2: 999999
Total Cash Advances: 19,999.98
Finance Charge On Cash Advances: 240.00
Total Debits: $18,314.95
ENTER A CHOICE ABOVE (USE VIEW PRIOR TO CHANGE)
ACTION CANCELLED, VIEW AND TRY AGAIN

Figure 14.7 This change transaction was cancelled because it would have caused a lost update; someone else had updated the record during the time that we were working on our update.

Figure 14.7. It was necessary to cancel our operator's transaction in order to prevent the loss of the update made by the other operator. Our operator will have to view the record again, and will get the updated copy as rewritten by the other operator, and can then proceed to update it.

The "how" of Figure 14.7 is conceptually simple, but a little more involved at the programming level. How did we detect that our operator's transaction had to be cancelled to prevent a lost update? This question really amounts to "How did we know that the record to be rewritten had been updated by someone else?" We can tell that it has been updated if it is different from the way it was when we read it. That is, if we compare the record as it was when we viewed it, and the record as it is when we READ with UPDATE just prior to rewriting it, we can tell if it was updated. If the records compared in this way are not identical, someone else had made an update while we were developing our update. This is how we know that our update transaction must be cancelled and attempted again.

You can see from this that we need to preserve a copy of the record as it was when we first read it. This preservation has to span *between pseudoconverses*. Our program "dies" when we complete a view action, and reawakens when we have updated fields on the screen and again press Enter. But a CICS program loses all of its WORKING-STORAGE when it returns control to CICS, even RETURN with TRANSID. To understand how we implement prior/present record comparison, you need to learn a bit more about the RETURN command, COMMAREA, and DFHCOMMAREA.

14.12 PRESERVING DATA BETWEEN PSEUDOCONVERSES

To preserve data between one pseudoconverse and the next, you have to "mail it to yourself." It's very much as if you suffered from a strange disease that, every night as you slept, made you forget everything you know about yourself. If you did nothing to make up for this strange occurrence, you would awake the next morning and not know who you were, where you lived, what you did for a living, and what you had done the day before. Suppose you could do nothing about the disease. You could still (at least partly) overcome the memory loss by mailing yourself a detailed letter the day before, to be handed to you when you woke up. Although you had forgotten everything about yourself, you could regain that knowledge by reading the letter from yourself handed to you, which told who you were and what you had done the day before.

A program "mails itself" any data it wishes using the CICS RETURN command with the TRANSID clause, by putting that data into the **COMMAREA** clause. As Figure 14.8 shows, whatever you name in COMMAREA is retained by CICS in its own memory, even though the program's WORKING-STORAGE is lost. When the program is again awakened, CICS puts a copy of the data retained in COMMAREA into the **DFHCOMMAREA** field in the program's LINKAGE SECTION, and the program can retrieve it from there.

Up to this point we have simply coded a one-byte field, named WS-COMMUNICATION-AREA, in WORKING-STORAGE, so that we could pass this back to ourselves. The purpose of this action was to insure that EIBCALEN—the length, in bytes, of the item passed back—was greater than zero after the first time the program had been invoked by a terminal. Up to now, we really have not cared about the actual data value passed back in WS-COMMUNICATION-AREA, just the fact that *something* was passed back.

Now, as you can see in Figure 14.8, we *do* care about the content of the item we pass back to ourselves. We code the pseudoconversational RETURN with TRANSID, naming the full record description, ACCT-REC, as the item to be preserved. We also code DFHCOMMAREA in the LINKAGE SECTION as PIC X(160), the length of this record, so that we can receive the full record back again the next time the program is reawakened. This is

```
 LINKAGE SECTION.
 01  DFHCOMMAREA          PIC X(160).

*===============================================================
 PROCEDURE DIVISION.
*===============================================================
 000-MAINLINE.

         PERFORM 633-ALWAYS-TEST.

         EVALUATE TRUE

            WHEN EIBCALEN = ZERO
                 PERFORM 800-START-TERMINAL-SESSION

            WHEN ENTER-KEY
                 PERFORM 100-CHOOSE-ROUTINE

            WHEN OTHER
                 MOVE LOW-VALUES TO FILEMAPI
                 MOVE -1 TO CHOICEL
                 MOVE 'INVALID KEY PRESSED' TO ERRORI
                 PERFORM 700-SEND-ACCOUNT-SCREEN

         END-EVALUATE.

         EXEC CICS
            RETURN  TRANSID   (WS-TRANS-ID)
                    COMMAREA  (ACCT-REC)
         END-EXEC.
```

CICS preserves data between pseudoconverses; what you put in COMMAREA in RETURN comes back to you in DFHCOMMAREA the next time the program is activated.

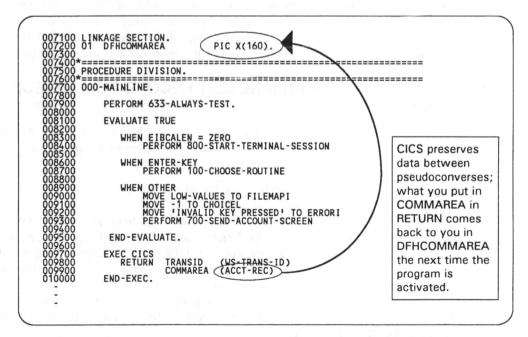

Figure 14.8 CICS will preserve whatever you put into the field named at COMMAREA in a RETURN with TRANSID, and provides it back to the program in the DFHCOMMAREA when the program is next awakened.

how we preserve the record as initially viewed, so that the program can compare it to the record as READ with UPDATE immediately before our changed record (in the symbolic map) is used to REWRITE the record.

14.13 LOGIC FOR PRIOR/PRESENT RECORD COMPARISON

Once we have arranged for the original record we have viewed to be preserved between pseudoconverses, as shown in Figure 14.8, it is a simple matter to actually compare the preserved record and the record we obtain with READ with UPDATE immediately before REWRITE. Figure 14.9 shows you how we have modified the 500-CHANGE-MASTER and 502-REWRITE paragraphs in the UPDATE2 program to do this. In fact, 502-REWRITE was previously named 501-REWRITE; we renumbered it because we had to insert a new paragraph, named 501-FURTHER-TESTS, to help accomplish the prior/present record comparison.

Paragraph 501-FURTHER-TESTS is invoked in Figure 14.9 if the READ with UPDATE succeeds. Here, we check first to see if the terminal operator has changed the name in the ACCT-NAME field, which this application prohibits. (This test is not part of the prior/present record comparison, it is specific to the way Samuel's Worthless Finance Company wanted its system to work.) But at line 38600, we make the following test and take cancellation actions if it is true:

```
IF ACCT-REC NOT = DFHCOMMAREA
   MOVE 'ACTION CANCELLED, VIEW AND TRY AGAIN' TO ...
   MOVE -1 TO ACTNAMEL
```

ACCT-REC currently contains the record just READ with UPDATE from the borrower file. DFHCOMMAREA contains the record as it was when we viewed it in the prior pseudoconverse. If these records differ, someone else has updated the record. In this case we cannot proceed to rewrite our update, because that other, prior, update would be lost.

14.14 NOTES ABOUT PRIOR/PRESENT RECORD COMPARISON USAGE

Prior/present record comparison is the simplest way to prevent lost updates. We suggest that you always provide for it as a minimum measure to preserve data integrity in CICS update programs. Here are some suggestions for its use:

- Include a message (label) on the screen reminding the terminal operator to view a record before attempting to update it.
- Don't forget to use your record layout, and not a field such as WS-COMMUNICATION-AREA, in the COMMAREA clause of your RETURN with TRANSID.
- Don't forget to code the length of your DFHCOMMAREA as the length of the record layout, or the program will always cancel every attempt at update (prior and present records will never compare as equal).
- Make sure the first action you code after a successful READ for UPDATE is the comparison between the record you just obtained and the original record viewed, in DFHCOMMAREA.

You may have already figured out that the prior/present comparison automatically enforces the "must view before update" rule indicated in the first point above. If the terminal operator has

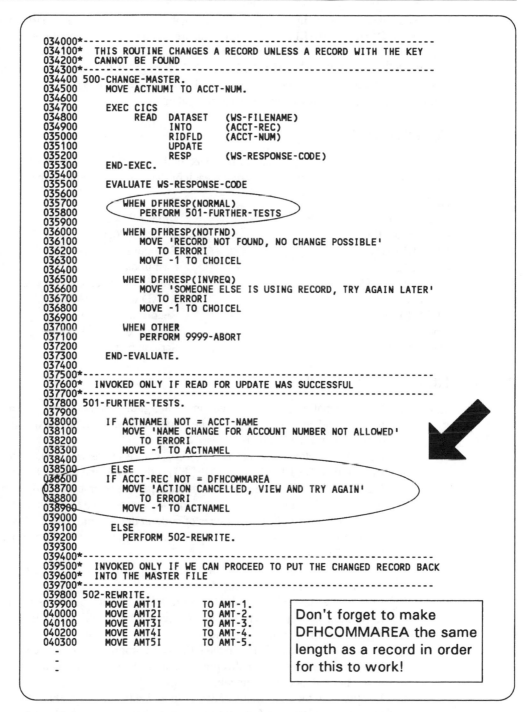

```
      *-----------------------------------------------------------------
      *  THIS ROUTINE CHANGES A RECORD UNLESS A RECORD WITH THE KEY
      *  CANNOT BE FOUND
      *-----------------------------------------------------------------
       500-CHANGE-MASTER.
           MOVE ACTNUMI TO ACCT-NUM.

           EXEC CICS
                READ  DATASET   (WS-FILENAME)
                      INTO      (ACCT-REC)
                      RIDFLD    (ACCT-NUM)
                      UPDATE
                      RESP      (WS-RESPONSE-CODE)
           END-EXEC.

           EVALUATE WS-RESPONSE-CODE

              WHEN DFHRESP(NORMAL)
                 PERFORM 501-FURTHER-TESTS

              WHEN DFHRESP(NOTFND)
                 MOVE 'RECORD NOT FOUND, NO CHANGE POSSIBLE'
                    TO ERRORI
                 MOVE -1 TO CHOICEL

              WHEN DFHRESP(INVREQ)
                 MOVE 'SOMEONE ELSE IS USING RECORD, TRY AGAIN LATER'
                    TO ERRORI
                 MOVE -1 TO CHOICEL

              WHEN OTHER
                 PERFORM 9999-ABORT

           END-EVALUATE.

      *-----------------------------------------------------------------
      *  INVOKED ONLY IF READ FOR UPDATE WAS SUCCESSFUL
      *-----------------------------------------------------------------
       501-FURTHER-TESTS.

           IF ACTNAMEI NOT = ACCT-NAME
              MOVE 'NAME CHANGE FOR ACCOUNT NUMBER NOT ALLOWED'
                 TO ERRORI
              MOVE -1 TO ACTNAMEL

            ELSE
           IF ACCT-REC NOT = DFHCOMMAREA
              MOVE 'ACTION CANCELLED, VIEW AND TRY AGAIN'
                 TO ERRORI
              MOVE -1 TO ACTNAMEL

            ELSE
              PERFORM 502-REWRITE.

      *-----------------------------------------------------------------
      *  INVOKED ONLY IF WE CAN PROCEED TO PUT THE CHANGED RECORD BACK
      *  INTO THE MASTER FILE
      *-----------------------------------------------------------------
       502-REWRITE.
           MOVE AMT1I          TO AMT-1.
           MOVE AMT2I          TO AMT-2.
           MOVE AMT3I          TO AMT-3.
           MOVE AMT4I          TO AMT-4.
           MOVE AMT5I          TO AMT-5.
      -
      -
      -
```

Don't forget to make DFHCOMMAREA the same length as a record in order for this to work!

Figure 14.9 Enhancements to program UPDATE2 to prevent lost updates with concurrent access; 500-CHANGE-MASTER and 502-REWRITE paragraphs are modified, and 501-FURTHER-TESTS has been added.

not viewed the record to be updated prior to starting the "C" change, the data passed back to the program in DFHCOMMAREA will never compare as equal to the record obtained with the READ with UPDATE. The terminal operator will then receive the "ACTION CANCELLED, VIEW RECORD AND TRY CHANGE AGAIN" message. If the terminal operator follows this prompt, the update may succeed the second time, and (hopefully) the operator will automatically become a bit smarter about using the system.

14.15 FOR YOUR REVIEW

The following terms were introduced or reviewed in this chapter. If you understand this chapter, you should be comfortable with defining each of these terms in relationship to CICS:

Add function
ASRA abend
Change function
CICS DELETE
CICS READ
CICS REWRITE
CICS WRITE
COMMAREA
Concurrent access
Data integrity
Delete function
DFHCOMMAREA
DFHRESP(..)
Enqueuing
Lost update
Prior/present record comparison
READ with UPDATE
Record in use flag
Record locking
Scratch pad

14.16 REVIEW QUESTIONS

1. Identify what program code economies are gained automatically when you support add and change functions in the same CICS program, and explain why these code economies are possible.
2. Describe in detail what purpose the RESP clause serves when you code it a CICS READ, WRITE, REWRITE, or DELETE command, and how you use it.
3. Describe what will happen if the terminal operator attempts to add a record using the UPDATE2 program, but a record already exists in the file with the key entered by the operator. Indicate what lines of code in the program handle this problem.
4. Explain what the standard data validation sequence is and why we use it in the UPDATE program.
5. Describe the circumstances under which a map is received by the program and the "length" field of an input field is zero.
6. Identify the specific data values that the NUM attribute prevents from being entered into an input screen field, and describe why we still check input in a NUM field to determine if it is numeric.
7. Lines 23700 through 24100 in the UPDATE2 program have been commented out. Identify the cases in which this program fails when you execute it, the cases where it will not fail, and the logic where failure will occur.
8. Identify why the total fields coded at lines 5200 through 5500 in the UPDATE2 program in Figure 14.5 would not usually be included in a record designed to support an interactive system.
9. Explain why we must read, a second time, a record that we are trying to REWRITE, and illustrate the coding involved in this second READ.

10. Describe what concurrent access is, and give an example of it related to business data processing.
11. Explain what a "lost update" problem is and how it can occur in a multiple-user interactive system.
12. Provide a concise definition for data integrity, and describe why this becomes of concern in CICS applications.
13. List five different ways we can deal with a potential problem inherent in concurrent access, and provide a brief description for each method.
14. Explain in detail how you can preserve data and pass it to a subsequent execution of the CICS program, and why this technique is of practical use in an update program.
15. Identify and describe the relationship between COMMAREA, DFHCOMMAREA, and EIBCALEN in a CICS update program.

14.17 HANDS-ON EXERCISES

Each of the exercises that follows is an extension of the exercise of the same letter in the Hands-On Exercises, section 13.13, in Chapter 13. In each case the exercise consists of installing add, change, and delete capabilities in the program you developed in the prior exercise.

A. Using the logic pattern shown in the UPDATE2 program for add, change, and delete functions, develop and include logic to support these functions in the program you developed in Chapter 13, exercise A (My First CICS Screen).
B. Using the logic pattern shown in the UPDATE2 program for add, change, and delete functions, develop and include logic to support these functions in the program you developed in Chapter 13, exercise B (Podunk University Grade Screen).
C. Using the logic pattern shown in the UPDATE2 program for add, change, and delete functions, develop and include logic to support these functions in the program you developed in Chapter 13, exercise C (Podunk Book Store Order Entry).
D. Using the logic pattern shown in the UPDATE2 program for add, change, and delete functions, develop and include logic to support these functions in the program you developed in Chapter 13, exercise D (Podunk Power Company Electricity Billing).
E. Using the logic pattern shown in the UPDATE2 program for add, change, and delete functions, develop and include logic to support these functions in the program you developed in Chapter 13, exercise E (Podunk University Course Registrations).

The following exercises deal with enhancements to the UPDATE2 program, or any of the above programs:

F. The UPDATE2 program lacks commonly expected numeric field de-editing capabilities, and presents charge and advance amounts without numeric formatting. Enhance UPDATE2 to provide numeric de-editing and numeric formatted display, using CALLs to the NUMCHEK subprogram as demonstrated in Chapter 10. Modify the map for the screen to accept the entry of these amounts into a character field, without NUM, and code the PICture of the input and output screen fields with appropriate leading zero suppression, comma insertion, and explicit decimal point.

G. Add a PF3 clean-the-screen function to the UPDATE2 program, so that adds can start with a fresh screen. Use the pattern introduced for this in Chapter 8 and further illustrated in Chapters 9, 10, and 11. (You will need REDEFINES of the numeric formatted output screen fields in your symbolic map to be able to move spaces to these fields in the clean-the-screen operation.)

15

Indexed File Browsing

Business system design must allow for occasions when we need to access information, but we do not know the primary key under which it is stored. Suppose, for example, you call your local electric company to learn your current account balance, but you don't happen to know your account number. A clerk will still be able to locate your account information based on your last name or address (assuming that indexed file design has specified one of these as an **alternate key**). With appropriate programming it's possible for the clerk to initiate a **browse** of records close to your name or address, and "thumb through" them much as you might thumb through the pages of a dictionary looking for a particular word. When your account information appears in a browsed record, the clerk learns your account number, and can then access to your information directly by primary key.

In this chapter, we'll show you the kind of screens produced by a browse program. We'll also present and discuss the complete source code for a browse program, and introduce the CICS STARTBR command. Browse access is not as efficient as direct access by primary key, but you need to know how to provide it!

15.1 WHAT AN ALTERNATE KEY BROWSE FUNCTION IS AND DOES

Generically speaking, a **browse function** is an orderly fishing expedition that lets us locate a record by something other than the primary key. While you can arrange a browse by primary key, a primary key browse is much less useful and common. Let's follow through with an example of a simple alternate key browse.

Figure 15.1 shows you the "browse" screen for Samuel's Worthless Finance Company. You will note that this screen is identical to the inquiry and update screens you saw in Chapters 13 and 14, except for the title at the top. Like the inquiry screen, the browse screen is intended only to display information. Unlike the inquiry, in which you know the primary key (account number) of the record to be displayed, browse inquiry is a "fishing expedition." You don't know the account number of the record you want to see. In fact, you may not even know the full name (alternate key) of the borrower you want to see, and so you must "jump in" and starting examining records, one by one, until you find the one you want.

Suppose we are looking for a record for a borrower named Holton, David. We don't know his account number, or even the correct spelling of his last name. Since we have stored names as "last name, first name" we could start a browse by entering "h" and, as the label

```
                      -=SAMUEL'S WORTHLESS FINANCE COMPANY=-                BRWSMAP
                             ****** FILE BROWSE ******                        SMSBM

Name:  h                                     Account Number:

-------------------------------- CHARGE ITEMS --------------------------------
  Charge Amount 1:
  Charge Amount 2:
  Charge Amount 3:
  Charge Amount 4:
  Charge Amount 5:                           Total Charge Items:

-------------------------------- CASH ADVANCES -------------------------------
Cash Adv Amount 1:
Cash Adv Amount 2:                          Total Cash Advances:
                              Finance Charge On Cash Advances:

                              ============================================

                                                 Total Debits:

PF1 = FORWARD, PF2 = BACKWARD,  PF3 = TOP, PF4 = BOTTOM  ..OR CLEAR KEY TO END
```

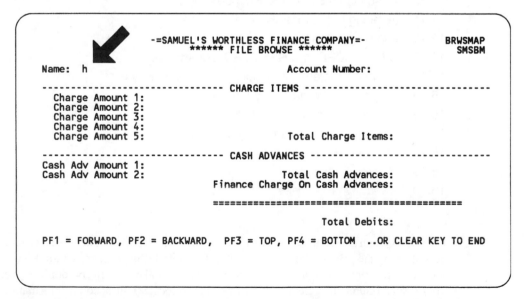

Figure 15.1 Our browse screen is like the inquiry screen, but you do not enter account number (primary key); instead, you begin viewing records in name sequence from the point at or beyond your full or partial name entry.

```
                    -=SAMUEL'S WORTHLESS FINANCE COMPANY=-                BRWSMAP
                           ****** FILE BROWSE ******                        SMSBM

Name: HATCHET, RAY                           Account Number:  00938920

-------------------------------- CHARGE ITEMS --------------------------------
  Charge Amount 1:  5,000.00
  Charge Amount 2:      0.00
  Charge Amount 3:      0.00
  Charge Amount 4:      0.00
  Charge Amount 5:      0.00               Total Charge Items:    5,000.00

-------------------------------- CASH ADVANCES -------------------------------
Cash Adv Amount 1:      0.00
Cash Adv Amount 2:      0.00                Total Cash Advances:       0.00
                                   Finance Charge On Cash Advances:       0.00

                                   ============================================

                                                 Total Debits:  $5,000.00

PF1 = FORWARD, PF2 = BACKWARD,  PF3 = TOP, PF4 = BOTTOM  ..OR CLEAR KEY TO END
```

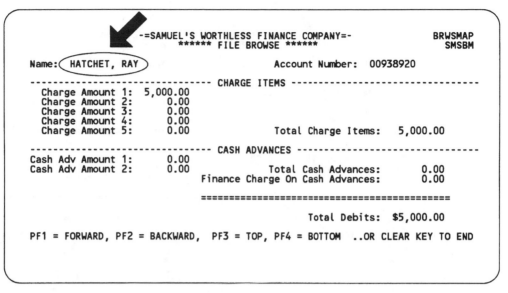

Figure 15.2 The browse shows us that the first record beginning with letter "h" is that of Ray Hatchet; press PF1 to continue moving forward record-by-record.

toward the bottom of the screen indicates, press the PF1 key to browse forward. We would expect to see the first record in the file that, were the records sorted in ascending sequence by name, started with the letter "h". In Figure 15.2, we see that this record is for Hatchet, Ray.

Each time we press PF1, the next record, sequentially by name, is presented by the browse screen. Doing this at the screen in Figure 15.2 produces the screen in Figure 15.3, which shows

```
                    -=SAMUEL'S WORTHLESS FINANCE COMPANY=-                BRWSMAP
                           ****** FILE BROWSE ******                        SMSBM

Name:  HILLTONE, JANE                        Account Number:  67820939

-------------------------------- CHARGE ITEMS --------------------------------
  Charge Amount 1:  3,000.00
  Charge Amount 2:  3,000.00
  Charge Amount 3:      0.00
  Charge Amount 4:      0.00
  Charge Amount 5:      0.00               Total Charge Items:    6,000.00

-------------------------------- CASH ADVANCES -------------------------------
Cash Adv Amount 1:  3,000.00
Cash Adv Amount 2:      0.00                Total Cash Advances:   3,000.00
                                   Finance Charge On Cash Advances:      36.00

                                   ============================================

                                                 Total Debits:  $9,036.00

PF1 = FORWARD, PF2 = BACKWARD,  PF3 = TOP, PF4 = BOTTOM  ..OR CLEAR KEY TO END
```

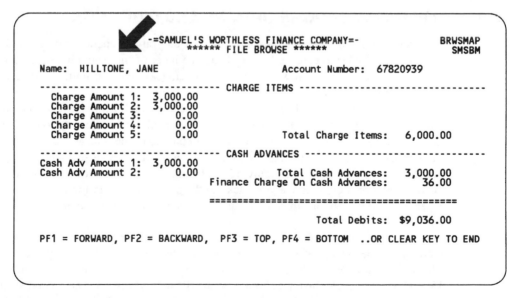

Figure 15.3 Pressing PF1 at the screen in Figure 15.2 produces this screen for the next record forward. Is a record for David Holton farther yet?

```
                    -=SAMUEL'S WORTHLESS FINANCE COMPANY=-              BRWSMAP
                         ****** FILE BROWSE ******                        SMSBM

Name:  HOLTON, DAVID                          Account Number:  88888888

-------------------------------- CHARGE ITEMS --------------------------------
  Charge Amount 1:        0.00
  Charge Amount 2:        0.00
  Charge Amount 3:        0.00
  Charge Amount 4:        0.00
  Charge Amount 5:        0.00                Total Charge Items:         0.00

-------------------------------- CASH ADVANCES -------------------------------
Cash Adv Amount 1:        0.00
Cash Adv Amount 2:        0.00               Total Cash Advances:         0.00
                                  Finance Charge On Cash Advances:         0.00

                                  ===========================================

                                                  Total Debits:          $0.00

PF1 = FORWARD, PF2 = BACKWARD,  PF3 = TOP, PF4 = BOTTOM  ..OR CLEAR KEY TO END
```

Figure 15.4 Pressing PF1 at the screen in Figure 15.3 produces this screen; we have browsed the file and located the record for David Holton.

the borrower record for Hilltone, Jane. Pressing PF1 again finally shows us the record for Holton, David, as you see in Figure 15.4. We can now see that Holton's account number is 88888888. If we wanted to update this record now, we would leave the browse function and invoke the update, gaining access to the record by primary key. (Access via alternate key does not permit update; you have to READ with UPDATE as we discussed in Chapter 14.)

15.2 DIFFERENT BROWSE OPTIONS AND DIRECTION

The example in Figures 15.1 through 15.4 showed you the operation of a simple **forward browse.** We needed to enter only as little as one letter of the beginning of the alternate key (name) in order to begin browsing forward, in name sequence, from the first record starting with that letter.

Browsing forward is the handiest browse mechanism. If a browse function provides only this, it is workable. A more capable browse also includes movement options beyond simply moving forward. Browsing backward, for example, could help us as we progress through a small range of records and perhaps go a bit too far, and want to reverse direction. If you pressed the PF2 key at the screen in Figure 15.4, showing the information for David Holton, our browse function would "move you back" to the screen shown in Figure 15.3. Pressing PF2 repeatedly would continue to, it would appear, read the file in reverse order, until you reached its beginning, or "top."

An especially capable browse function also provides a direct way to get to the bottom (end) or top (beginning) of a file. In our browse, pressing the PF3 key gets you to the top of the file, as shown in Figure 15.5, while pressing PF4 moves you to the end, as shown in Figure 15.6. Having gotten to the top or bottom of the file in this way, you can, of course, progress in forward sequence from the beginning, or in reverse sequence from the end, with the PF1 and PF2 keys.

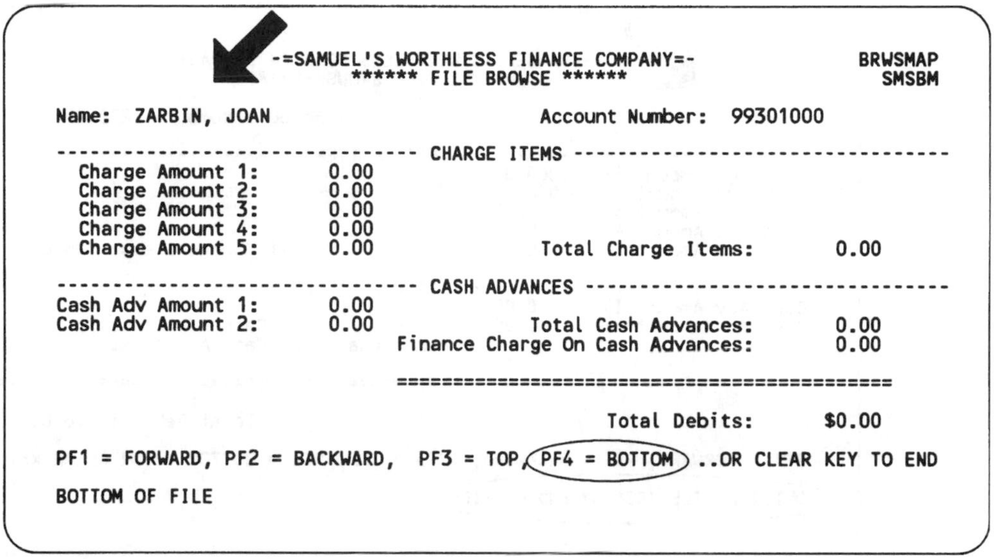
-=SAMUEL'S WORTHLESS FINANCE COMPANY=-
BRWSMAP
****** FILE BROWSE ******
SMSBM
Name: ZARBIN, JOAN
Account Number: 99301000
CHARGE ITEMS
Charge Amount 1: 0.00
Charge Amount 2: 0.00
Charge Amount 3: 0.00
Charge Amount 4: 0.00
Charge Amount 5: 0.00
Total Charge Items: 0.00
CASH ADVANCES
Cash Adv Amount 1: 0.00
Cash Adv Amount 2: 0.00
Total Cash Advances: 0.00
Finance Charge On Cash Advances: 0.00
Total Debits: $0.00
PF1 = FORWARD, PF2 = BACKWARD, PF3 = TOP, PF4 = BOTTOM ..OR CLEAR KEY TO END
BOTTOM OF FILE

Figure 15.5 Our browse lets you get to the last record (bottom) of the file (here, according to alternate key, Account Name) by pressing the PF4 key.

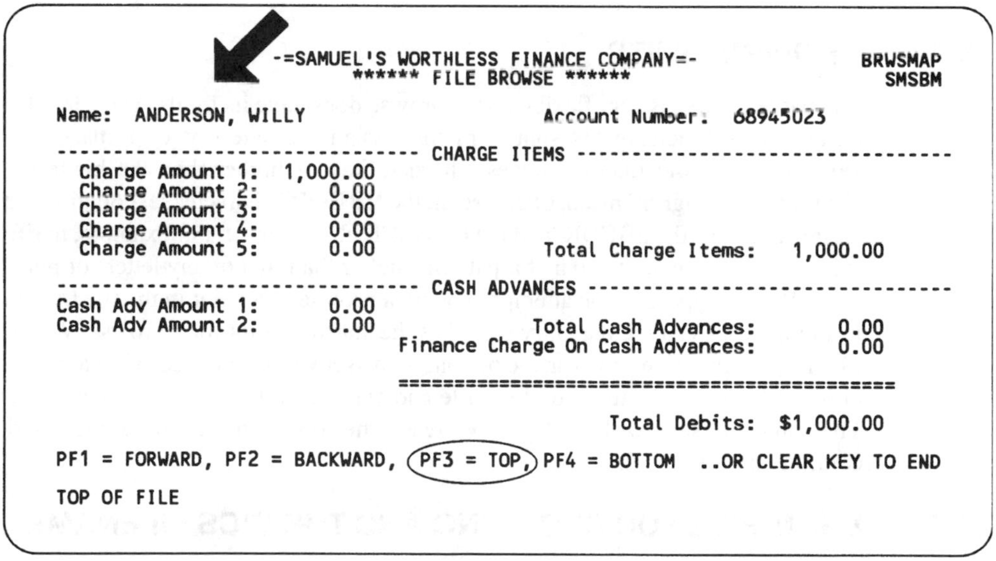
-=SAMUEL'S WORTHLESS FINANCE COMPANY=-
BRWSMAP
****** FILE BROWSE ******
SMSBM
Name: ANDERSON, WILLY
Account Number: 68945023
CHARGE ITEMS
Charge Amount 1: 1,000.00
Charge Amount 2: 0.00
Charge Amount 3: 0.00
Charge Amount 4: 0.00
Charge Amount 5: 0.00
Total Charge Items: 1,000.00
CASH ADVANCES
Cash Adv Amount 1: 0.00
Cash Adv Amount 2: 0.00
Total Cash Advances: 0.00
Finance Charge On Cash Advances: 0.00
Total Debits: $1,000.00
PF1 = FORWARD, PF2 = BACKWARD, PF3 = TOP, PF4 = BOTTOM ..OR CLEAR KEY TO END
TOP OF FILE

Figure 15.6 Our browse lets you get to the first record (top) of the file (here, according to alternate key, Account Name) by pressing the PF3 key.

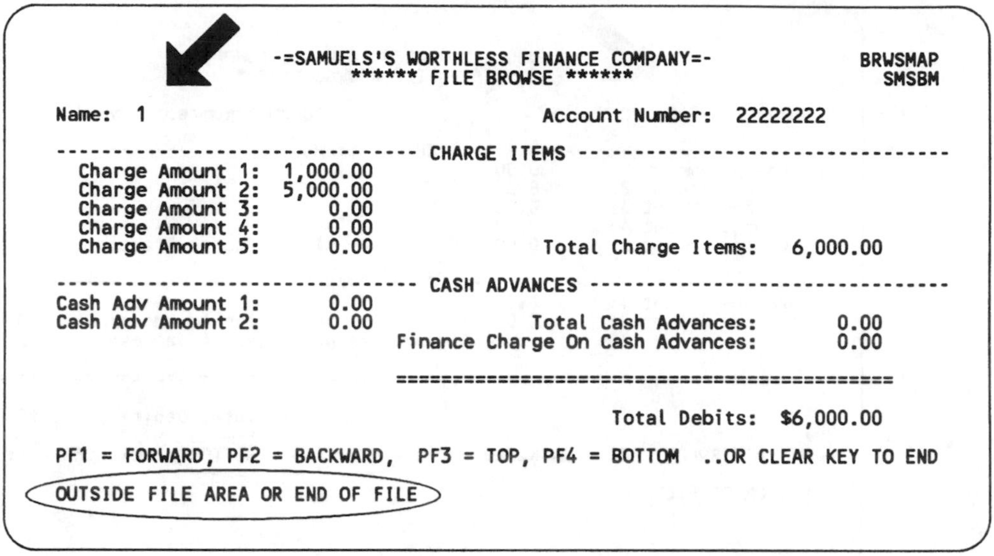

```
                  -=SAMUELS'S WORTHLESS FINANCE COMPANY=-                BRWSMAP
                         ****** FILE BROWSE ******                         SMSBM

Name:  1                                        Account Number:  22222222

-------------------------------- CHARGE ITEMS --------------------------------
  Charge Amount 1:  1,000.00
  Charge Amount 2:  5,000.00
  Charge Amount 3:      0.00
  Charge Amount 4:      0.00
  Charge Amount 5:      0.00                Total Charge Items:   6,000.00

-------------------------------- CASH ADVANCES -------------------------------
Cash Adv Amount 1:      0.00
Cash Adv Amount 2:      0.00                Total Cash Advances:       0.00
                              Finance Charge On Cash Advances:         0.00
                              ===========================================

                                                 Total Debits:  $6,000.00

PF1 = FORWARD, PF2 = BACKWARD,  PF3 = TOP, PF4 = BOTTOM  ..OR CLEAR KEY TO END
OUTSIDE FILE AREA OR END OF FILE
```

Figure 15.7 Since "1" is "higher" in EBCDIC collation sequence than any name (alternate key) in our VSAM file, we receive an "outside of file" message if we attempt to start a browse using "1".

15.3 BROWSE LIMITS

A capable browse is very flexible, but a browse does have its limits. You cannot browse something that isn't there, that is, something that has an alternate key (or primary key, in a primary key browse) lower than the lowest alternate key or higher than the highest alternate key. "Lower" and "higher" mean, of course, in the **EBCDIC** character set collation sequence, since mainframes use the EBCDIC and not the ASCII character set. For example, in EBCDIC, digits such as "1" are represented by bit patterns higher than that of any letters or punctuation.

What happens if you attempt to begin a browse at a point in the file that does not exist? In Figure 15.7 you see our entry of "1" as the starting point for a browse. When we press the PF1 key the message shown at the bottom of the screen is produced. The same message will be produced if we reach the end of the file and continue attempting to move forward with PF1. The same message will display if we reach the top of the file on a backward browse and continue pressing PF2.

15.4 VSAM FILE FOR BROWSING AND THE CICS FILENAME

In Chapter 13, section 13.2, we discussed the steps you need to take to develop records to be housed in an indexed file, that is, a VSAM Key Sequenced Data Set that will be accessed by CICS. Figure 13.2 illustrates the content of the borrower records in graphic form. You can see that account number, in positions 1 through 8, is designated as the **primary key,** while account name, in positions 121 through 150, is indicated as the **alternate key**. Designing a record like this, and documenting its layout in a diagram, is actually a part of the systems analysis process leading up to CICS program development. You typically think about providing an alternate key in a file design, when the business application appears to warrant the type of browse capability we discuss in this chapter.

Appendix D illustrates the job control language and IDCAMS control statements we used to create and load records into the VSAM borrowers file. Examine the COBLOAD and JCLLOAD illustrations in Figures D.8 and D.9 to see how the first "load" of borrower records are formed and how the alternate index is defined and built. Note in particular that an **alternate index path** must be established for access to the alternate index, in STEPE of the JCLLOAD job stream in Figure D.9. It is this path that the CICS systems administrator or systems programmer must relate to a CICS **filename** to allow us to access the borrower file in alternate key sequence. In our browse program, the CICS filename has been established as path name CCPW001P by our systems programmer. As a programmer, you don't make this association yourself; it must be made on your behalf and you are then made aware of the CICS filename assigned.

15.5 BROWSE PROGRAM LOGIC VISUAL TABLE OF CONTENTS

Now that you know what a browse function is and have seen several examples of browse operation, it's time for us to show you the logic that provides browse capabilities. Our browse program is named BROWSE4. Before we consider the source code for this program, let's approach its logical organization from a "top down" perspective using the **visual table of contents** (VTOC) shown in Figure 15.8. Don't be intimidated as you examine this chart. It has a lot of boxes on it, but it really is just a graphic illustration of the way the paragraphs of the browse program relate to one another. The chart also tells a bit about how the paragraphs operate.

Structured programming is based on three constructs: sequence, selection, and iteration. When you develop a structured program, you are actually choosing how to use each of these three building blocks of logic. A visual table of contents doesn't just show boxes for paragraphs of code, it shows how a programmer has chosen to use the structured programming constructs to implement a solution to a programming requirement.

As you examine Figure 15.8, realize that the small diamond symbol, as you see under the 000-MAINLINE box and in other places, indicates **selection.** Selection means "choice" or conditional execution. At the top of this chart, the direct lines between 000-MAINLINE and 633-ALWAYS and 700-SEND mean that these paragraphs are always executed, no question about that. The diamond between 000-MAINLINE and 800-START, 100-BEGIN, 260-SET-TOP, and 285-SET-BOTTOM means that a selection is made and only one of these four paragraphs is executed.

Although there is not usually much **iteration,** or "looping," in a CICS program, you do see a bit of it in Figure 15.9. The small circular arrow above 300-READ-NEXT at the bottom left of the chart indicates that this paragraph may be invoked more than one time. This, and the point above 400-READ-PREV, are the only places that looping is represented in this particular visual table of contents.

Perhaps obvious, but not to be left unstated, is the fact that the visual table of contents also tells you about how the last structured programming construct, **sequence,** is used in this program. The chart was drawn with the assumption that you would read the boxes from left to right, horizontally. For example, under 000-MAINLINE, box 633-ALWAYS is always executed, then a choice is made to execute either 800-START, 100-BEGIN, 260-SET-TOP, or 285-SET-BOTTOM. Finally, 700-SEND is always executed. Here is how you would read the bottom right side of the chart:

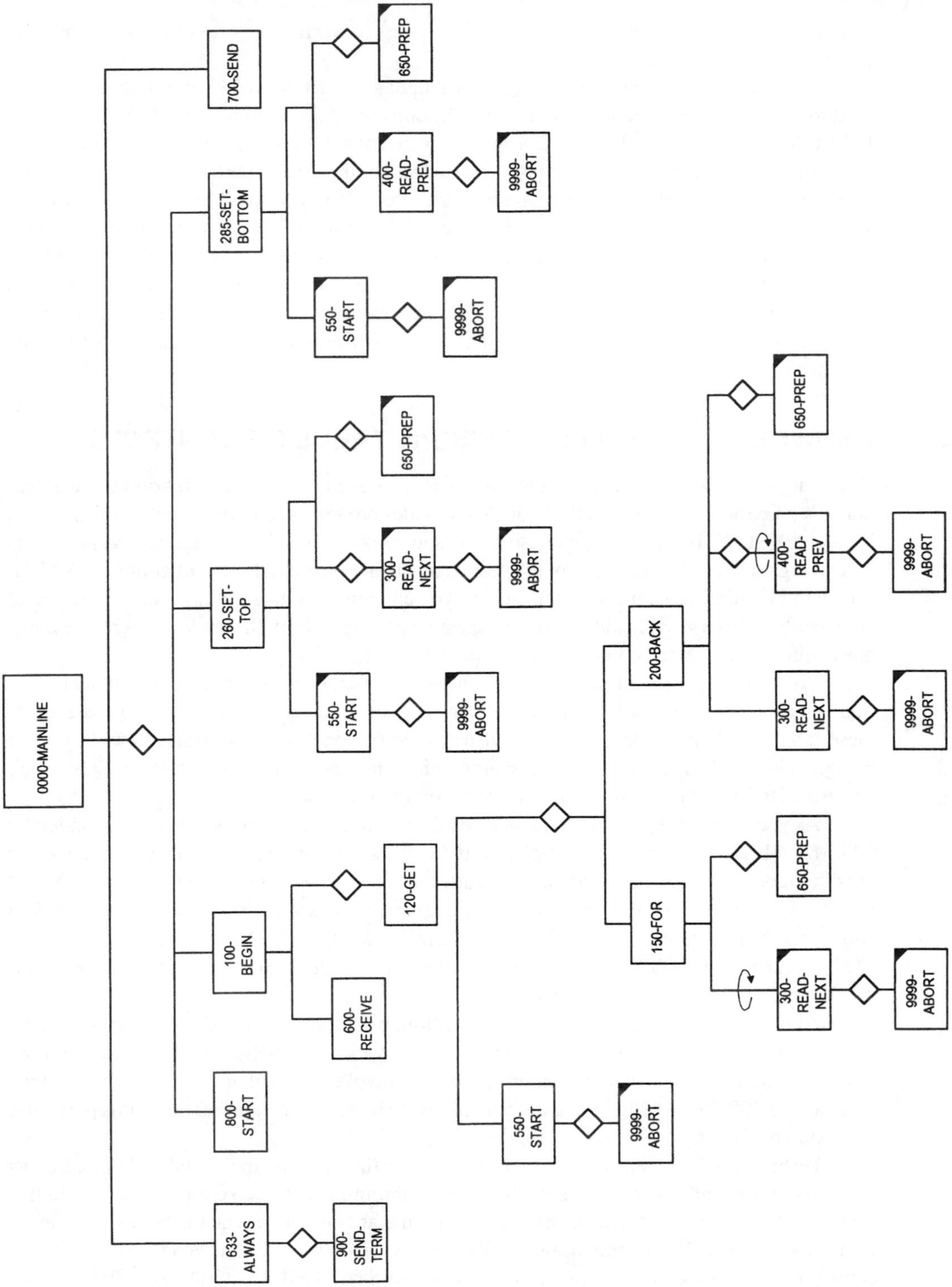
0000-MAINLINE
633-ALWAYS
900-SEND-TERM
800-START
100-BEGIN
600-RECEIVE
120-GET
550-START
9999-ABORT
150-FOR
300-READ-NEXT
9999-ABORT
650-PREP
200-BACK
300-READ-NEXT
9999-ABORT
400-READ-PREV
9999-ABORT
650-PREP
260-SET-TOP
550-START
9999-ABORT
300-READ-NEXT
9999-ABORT
650-PREP
285-SET-BOTTOM
550-START
9999-ABORT
400-READ-PREV
9999-ABORT
650-PREP
700-SEND

Figure 15.8 Visual table of contents for the BROWSE4 program, showing how its paragraphs relate to one another.

```
EDIT ---- CSCJGJ.CSC360.COBOL(BROWSE4) - 01.02 --------------- COLUMNS 007 078
COMMAND ===>                                                  SCROLL ===> PAGE
****** ***************************** TOP OF DATA ******************************
 ID DIVISION.
 PROGRAM-ID. BROWSE4.

*=================================================================
*  THIS PROGRAM IS INVOKED BY THE 'SMSB' TRANSACTION.  IT
*  ALLOWS THE TERMINAL OPERATOR TO BROWSE THROUGH THE BORROWER
*  FILE BY ALT KEY (NAME), SHOWS ONE BORROWER RECORD AT A TIME.
*
*  COPYRIGHT 1994 STEVE SAMUELS AND JIM JANOSSY
*=================================================================

 ENVIRONMENT DIVISION.
 DATA DIVISION.
 WORKING-STORAGE SECTION.
 01  WS-TRANS-ID                 PIC X(4)  VALUE '$001'.
 01  WS-MAPSET-NAME              PIC X(8)  VALUE 'SMSBM   '.
 01  WS-MAP-NAME                 PIC X(8)  VALUE 'BRWSMAP '.
 01  WS-DATASET                  PIC X(8)  VALUE 'CCPWO01P'.

 01  WS-FIRST-TIME-FLAG          PIC S9(4) BINARY.
     88 FIRST-TIME                         VALUE +0.

 01  PIC X(1)                    VALUE 'N'.
     88 NO-FILE-ERROR            VALUE 'N'.
     88 FILE-ERROR               VALUE 'F'.

 01  PIC X(1)                    VALUE 'F'.
     88 LETS-GO-FORWARD          VALUE 'F'.
     88 LETS-GO-BACKWARD         VALUE 'B'.

 01  WS-RESPONSE-CODE            PIC S9(8) BINARY.
 01  WS-READ-COUNT               PIC S9(4) BINARY.
 01  WS-WANTED-READS             PIC S9(4) BINARY.
 01  WS-COMMUNICATION-AREA       PIC X(30).

 01  WS-END-MESSAGE              PIC X(60) VALUE
     'QUITTING AS REQUESTED -- USE  CESF LOGOFF  TO END CICS'.

     COPY SMSBM.

     COPY ABRTMSGS.

 01  EIBAID-TEST-FIELD           PIC X(1).
     COPY KEYDEFS.

 01  ACCT-REC.
     05 ACT-NUM                  PIC X(8).
     05 AMT-1                    PIC 9(4)V99.
     05 AMT-2                    PIC 9(4)V99.
     05 AMT-3                    PIC 9(4)V99.
     05 AMT-4                    PIC 9(4)V99.
     05 AMT-5                    PIC 9(4)V99.
     05 ADV-1                    PIC 9(4)V99.
     05 ADV-2                    PIC 9(4)V99.
     05 TOT-CHG                  PIC 9(5)V99.
     05 TOT-ADV                  PIC 9(5)V99.
     05 FIN-CHG                  PIC 9(3)V99.
     05 TOT-DEB                  PIC 9(5)V99.
     05 GAP-1                    PIC X(44).
     05 ACCT-NAME                PIC X(30).
     05 GAP-2                    PIC X(10).

 LINKAGE SECTION.
 01  DFHCOMMAREA                 PIC X(30).
```

Compare this source code for a capable browse program with the visual table of contents in Figure 15.8 to gain an understanding of how browse logic works.

Figure 15.9 Source code for the BROWSE4 program.

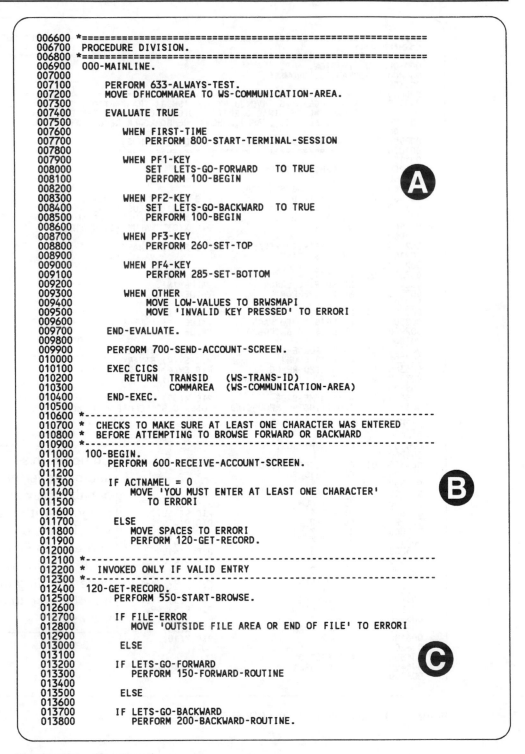

```
*===============================================================
 PROCEDURE DIVISION.
*===============================================================
 000-MAINLINE.

     PERFORM 633-ALWAYS-TEST.
     MOVE DFHCOMMAREA TO WS-COMMUNICATION-AREA.

     EVALUATE TRUE

        WHEN FIRST-TIME
            PERFORM 800-START-TERMINAL-SESSION

        WHEN PF1-KEY
            SET  LETS-GO-FORWARD   TO TRUE
            PERFORM 100-BEGIN                              A

        WHEN PF2-KEY
            SET  LETS-GO-BACKWARD  TO TRUE
            PERFORM 100-BEGIN

        WHEN PF3-KEY
            PERFORM 260-SET-TOP

        WHEN PF4-KEY
            PERFORM 285-SET-BOTTOM

        WHEN OTHER
            MOVE LOW-VALUES TO BRWSMAPI
            MOVE 'INVALID KEY PRESSED' TO ERRORI

     END-EVALUATE.

     PERFORM 700-SEND-ACCOUNT-SCREEN.

     EXEC CICS
        RETURN  TRANSID   (WS-TRANS-ID)
                COMMAREA  (WS-COMMUNICATION-AREA)
     END-EXEC.

*---------------------------------------------------------------
*  CHECKS TO MAKE SURE AT LEAST ONE CHARACTER WAS ENTERED
*  BEFORE ATTEMPTING TO BROWSE FORWARD OR BACKWARD
*---------------------------------------------------------------
 100-BEGIN.
     PERFORM 600-RECEIVE-ACCOUNT-SCREEN.

     IF ACTNAMEL = 0
        MOVE 'YOU MUST ENTER AT LEAST ONE CHARACTER'         B
           TO ERRORI

      ELSE
        MOVE SPACES TO ERRORI
        PERFORM 120-GET-RECORD.

*---------------------------------------------------------------
*  INVOKED ONLY IF VALID ENTRY
*---------------------------------------------------------------
 120-GET-RECORD.
     PERFORM 550-START-BROWSE.

     IF FILE-ERROR
        MOVE 'OUTSIDE FILE AREA OR END OF FILE' TO ERRORI

      ELSE
                                                             C
     IF LETS-GO-FORWARD
        PERFORM 150-FORWARD-ROUTINE

      ELSE

     IF LETS-GO-BACKWARD
        PERFORM 200-BACKWARD-ROUTINE.
```

Figure 15.9 *(Continued)*

```


*---------------------------------------------------------------------
*  IF FORWARD BROWSING IS ALREADY UNDERWAY, ACTNAMEI WILL
*  EQUAL DFHCOMMAREA SO WE CONTINUE BACKWARD BY:
*
*      READNEXT    GETS SAME RECORD
*      READNEXT    GETS NEXT RECORD TO BROWSE
*
*  IF ACTNAMEI DOES NOT EQUAL DFHCOMMAREA, IT MEANS TERMINAL
*  OPERATOR IS TRYING TO BEGIN A FORWARD BROWSE.  IN THIS
*  CASE WE HAVE TO GET TO THE RECORD THAT STARTS THE FORWARD
*  BROWSE USING ONLY READNEXT:
*
*      READNEXT    GETS FIRST RECORD TO START BROWSE
*
*  SUBSEQUENT PRESSING OF <PF2> WILL ENCOUNTER THE ACTNAMI =
*  DFHCOMMAREA CONDITION AND BROWSE FORWARD FROM THERE.
*---------------------------------------------------------------------
 150-FORWARD-ROUTINE.
     MOVE 0 TO WS-READ-COUNT.

     IF ACTNAMEI = DFHCOMMAREA
        MOVE 2 TO WS-WANTED-READS                                  D
      ELSE
        MOVE 1 TO WS-WANTED-READS.

     PERFORM 300-READ-NEXT
        UNTIL FILE-ERROR
           OR WS-READ-COUNT = WS-WANTED-READS.

     IF FILE-ERROR
        MOVE 'OUTSIDE FILE AREA OR END OF FILE' TO ERRORI
      ELSE
        MOVE ACCT-NAME TO WS-COMMUNICATION-AREA
        PERFORM 650-PREPARE-ACCOUNT-SCREEN.


*---------------------------------------------------------------------
*  IF BACKWARD BROWSING IS ALREADY UNDERWAY, ACTNAMEI WILL
*  EQUAL DFHCOMMAREA SO WE CONTINUE BACKWARD BY:
*
*      READNEXT    GETS SAME RECORD
*      READPREV    GETS SAME RECORD (STRANGE, BUT TRUE!)
*      READPREV    GETS RECORD ONE BACK, WHICH WE WANT
*
*  IF ACTNAMEI DOES NOT EQUAL DFHCOMMAREA, IT MEANS TERMINAL
*  OPERATOR IS TRYING TO BEGIN A BACKWARD BROWSE.  IN THIS
*  CASE WE HAVE TO GET TO THE RECORD THAT STARTS THE BACKWARD
*  BROWSE USING ONLY READNEXT:
*
*      READNEXT    GETS FIRST RECORD TO START BROWSE
*
*  SUBSEQUENT PRESSING OF <PF2> WILL ENCOUNTER THE ACTNAMI =
*  DFHCOMMAREA CONDITION AND BROWSE BACKWARD FROM THERE.
*---------------------------------------------------------------------
 200-BACKWARD-ROUTINE.

     PERFORM 300-READ-NEXT.
     IF FILE-ERROR
        MOVE 'OUTSIDE FILE AREA OR END OF FILE' TO ERRORI.

     IF ACTNAMEI = DFHCOMMAREA
        MOVE 0 TO WS-READ-COUNT
        PERFORM 400-READ-PREVIOUS                                  E
           UNTIL FILE-ERROR
              OR WS-READ-COUNT = 2.

     IF FILE-ERROR
        MOVE 'OUTSIDE FILE AREA OR END OF FILE' TO ERRORI
      ELSE
        MOVE ACCT-NAME TO WS-COMMUNICATION-AREA
        PERFORM 650-PREPARE-ACCOUNT-SCREEN.


```

Figure 15.9 *(Continued)*

```
*-----------------------------------------------------------------
*  FINDS THE FIRST RECORD IN THE FILE
*-----------------------------------------------------------------
260-SET-TOP.
    MOVE LOW-VALUES TO BRWSMAPI.

    PERFORM 550-START-BROWSE.

    IF NO-FILE-ERROR

       PERFORM 300-READ-NEXT
       IF NO-FILE-ERROR
          MOVE ACCT-NAME TO WS-COMMUNICATION-AREA
          PERFORM 650-PREPARE-ACCOUNT-SCREEN
          MOVE 'TOP OF FILE' TO ERRORI

        ELSE
          MOVE 'OUTSIDE FILE AREA OR END OF FILE' TO ERRORI

     ELSE
       MOVE 'OUTSIDE FILE AREA OR END OF FILE' TO ERRORI.

*-----------------------------------------------------------------
*  FINDS THE LAST RECORD IN THE FILE
*-----------------------------------------------------------------
285-SET-BOTTOM.
    MOVE LOW-VALUES   TO BRWSMAPI.
    MOVE HIGH-VALUES  TO ACTNAMEI.

    PERFORM 550-START-BROWSE.

    IF NO-FILE-ERROR

       PERFORM 400-READ-PREVIOUS
       IF NO-FILE-ERROR
          MOVE ACCT-NAME TO WS-COMMUNICATION-AREA
          PERFORM 650-PREPARE-ACCOUNT-SCREEN
          MOVE 'BOTTOM OF FILE' TO ERRORI

        ELSE
          MOVE 'OUTSIDE FILE AREA OR END OF FILE' TO ERRORI

     ELSE
       MOVE 'OUTSIDE FILE AREA OR END OF FILE' TO ERRORI.

*-----------------------------------------------------------------
*  FETCHES THE RECORD THAT WAS "POINTED TO" BY THE STARTBR
*  COMMAND.  AFTER FETCHING THAT RECORD THE DATA POINTER IS
*  MOVED TO THE NEXT RECORD ALONG THE KEY PATH.  IF THE READ
*  IS OUTSIDE THE FILE, AN ERROR CONDITION IS SET.
*-----------------------------------------------------------------
300-READ-NEXT.

    EXEC CICS
       READNEXT  DATASET  (WS-DATASET)
                 INTO     (ACCT-REC)
                 RIDFLD   (ACCT-NAME)
                 RESP     (WS-RESPONSE-CODE)
    END-EXEC.

    EVALUATE WS-RESPONSE-CODE

       WHEN DFHRESP(NORMAL)
          SET  NO-FILE-ERROR  TO TRUE
          ADD +1 TO WS-READ-COUNT

       WHEN DFHRESP(NOTFND)
          SET  FILE-ERROR     TO TRUE

       WHEN DFHRESP(ENDFILE)
          SET  FILE-ERROR     TO TRUE

       WHEN OTHER
          PERFORM 9999-ABORT

    END-EVALUATE.
```

Figure 15.9 *(Continued)*

```
*-----------------------------------------------------------------
*  MOVES THE DATA POINTER UP A RECORD FROM THE RECORD "POINTED
*  TO" BY THE STARTBR COMMAND.  THE RECORD NOW POINTED TO IS
*  FETCHED.  IF READPREV FAILS, AN ERROR CONDITION IS SET.
*-----------------------------------------------------------------
 400-READ-PREVIOUS.

     EXEC CICS
        READPREV   DATASET  (WS-DATASET)
                   INTO     (ACCT-REC)
                   RIDFLD   (ACCT-NAME)
                   RESP     (WS-RESPONSE-CODE)
     END-EXEC.

     EVALUATE WS-RESPONSE-CODE

        WHEN DFHRESP(NORMAL)
           SET  NO-FILE-ERROR  TO TRUE
           ADD +1 TO WS-READ-COUNT

        WHEN DFHRESP(NOTFND)
           SET  FILE-ERROR     TO TRUE

        WHEN DFHRESP(ENDFILE)
           SET  FILE-ERROR     TO TRUE

        WHEN OTHER
           PERFORM 9999-ABORT

     END-EVALUATE.

*-----------------------------------------------------------------
*  POSITIONS THE DATA POINTER TO THE RECORD WITH ALTERNATE KEY
*  NOT LESS THAN THE VALUE IN ACT-NAME.
*-----------------------------------------------------------------
 550-START-BROWSE.
     MOVE ACTNAMEI TO ACCT-NAME.

     EXEC CICS
        STARTBR   DATASET  (WS-DATASET)
                  RIDFLD   (ACCT-NAME)
                  RESP     (WS-RESPONSE-CODE)
     END-EXEC.

     EVALUATE WS-RESPONSE-CODE

        WHEN DFHRESP(NORMAL)
           SET  NO-FILE-ERROR  TO TRUE

        WHEN DFHRESP(NOTFND)
           SET  FILE-ERROR     TO TRUE

        WHEN OTHER
           PERFORM 9999-ABORT

     END-EVALUATE.

*-----------------------------------------------------------------
*  RECEIVES DATA FROM TERMINAL
*-----------------------------------------------------------------
 600-RECEIVE-ACCOUNT-SCREEN.
     EXEC CICS
         RECEIVE  MAP      (WS-MAP-NAME)
                  MAPSET   (WS-MAPSET-NAME)
                  INTO     (BRWSMAPI)
     END-EXEC.

*-----------------------------------------------------------------
*  THIS ROUTINE IS USED AT THE START OF EACH PSEUDOCONVERSE
*-----------------------------------------------------------------
 633-ALWAYS-TEST.
     MOVE EIBAID    TO  EIBAID-TEST-FIELD.
     IF CLEAR-KEY
        PERFORM 900-SEND-TERMINATION-MESSAGE
        EXEC CICS  RETURN  END-EXEC.
     MOVE EIBCALEN  TO  WS-FIRST-TIME-FLAG.
```

Figure 15.9 *(Continued)*

```
*-----------------------------------------------------------------
*  PUT DATA INTO THE SYMBOLIC MAP TO GET IT ON THE SCREEN
*-----------------------------------------------------------------
 650-PREPARE-ACCOUNT-SCREEN.
     MOVE ACCT-NAME   TO ACTNAMEI.
     MOVE ACT-NUM     TO ACTNUMI.
     MOVE AMT-1       TO AMT1O.
     MOVE AMT-2       TO AMT2O.
     MOVE AMT-3       TO AMT3O.
     MOVE AMT-4       TO AMT4O.
     MOVE AMT-5       TO AMT5O.
     MOVE ADV-1       TO ADV1O.
     MOVE ADV-2       TO ADV2O.
     MOVE TOT-CHG     TO TOTCHGO.
     MOVE TOT-ADV     TO TOTADVO.
     MOVE FIN-CHG     TO FINCHGO.
     MOVE TOT-DEB     TO TOTDEBO.
*-----------------------------------------------------------------
*  SENDS DATA FROM SCREEN TO TERMINAL
*-----------------------------------------------------------------
 700-SEND-ACCOUNT-SCREEN.
     MOVE -1 TO ACTNAMEL.
     EXEC CICS
          SEND    MAP        (WS-MAP-NAME)
                  MAPSET     (WS-MAPSET-NAME)
                  FROM       (BRWSMAPI)
                  DATAONLY
                  CURSOR
     END-EXEC.
*-----------------------------------------------------------------
*  INVOKED ONLY IF EIBCALEN = 0, FIRST TIME
*-----------------------------------------------------------------
 800-START-TERMINAL-SESSION.
     MOVE LOW-VALUES TO BRWSMAPI.
     MOVE -1 TO ACTNAMEL.
     EXEC CICS
          SEND    MAP        (WS-MAP-NAME)
                  MAPSET     (WS-MAPSET-NAME)
                  FROM       (BRWSMAPI)
                  ERASE
                  CURSOR
     END-EXEC.
*-----------------------------------------------------------------
*  INVOKED ONLY IF THE <CLEAR> KEY IS PRESSED
*-----------------------------------------------------------------
 900-SEND-TERMINATION-MESSAGE.
     EXEC CICS
          SEND    TEXT
                  FROM  (WS-END-MESSAGE)
                  ERASE
                  FREEKB
     END-EXEC.
*-----------------------------------------------------------------
*  SCREEN SENT FOR ABORT CONDITION ONLY -- AS WHEN WE GET A
*  RESP WE COULD NOT DEAL WITH!
*-----------------------------------------------------------------
 9999-ABORT.
     MOVE EIBTRNID   TO  WS-EIBTRNID.
     MOVE EIBRSRCE   TO  WS-EIBRSRCE.
     MOVE EIBRESP    TO  WS-EIBRESP.
     MOVE EIBRESP2   TO  WS-EIBRESP2.
     EXEC CICS
          SEND    TEXT
                  FROM  (WS-ERROR-MESSAGES)
                  ERASE
                  ALARM
                  FREEKB
     END-EXEC.
     EXEC CICS  RETURN  END-EXEC.
```

Figure 15.9 *(Continued)*

200-BACKWARD always executes 300-READ-NEXT first, which might invoke 9999-ABORT. Then 400-READ-PREV is executed one or more times, and it might invoke 9999-ABORT. Finally, 650-PREP might be executed.

As in the visual tables of contents you have seen in previous chapters, a shaded corner on a box represents that the box is a copy of another box. Only boxes with unshaded corners stand for actual code.

You see here our visual table of contents used to help explain the operation of our BROWSE4 program. As you gain more experience with structured CICS programming, you may find, as we do, that it is possible to plan program logic before actually writing it. You can plan your code using a visual table of contents or, as we showed in Chapter 8, Figure 8.3, with a table of contents turned sideways in the form of an **action diagram,** a form of graphic pseudocode.

15.6 BROWSE PROGRAM SOURCE CODE AND A LEARNING EXERCISE

Figure 15.9 lists the complete source code for our BROWSE4 program. We have arranged this using many of the techniques you have already seen in our inquiry and update programs, including the use of WORKING-STORAGE data names for the program's own transaction identifier, the mapset and map names, and the name of the data set (CICS filename) to be accessed. We have also developed the source code illustrations in such a way that paragraphs don't span page endings, making it as easy as possible for you to compare the actual program logic with the visual table of contents.

We propose a learning exercise at this point to help you see how the browse works. Make a paper copy of the source code listing in Figure 15.9, and physically cut apart each paragraph in the Procedure Division, cutting off the COBOL line numbers. Then arrange the paragraphs either in the form of a visual table of contents as you see in Figure 15.8, or in the form of an action diagram as in Chapter 8, Figure 8.3. Use a glue stick or tape to attach the paragraphs to a larger sheet of paper in either of these diagramming formats. Either of these representations of the actual program logic will help you see how this program works. (This is, incidentally, an excellent technique of program maintenance, to see how an existing program works before attempting to change it.)

We'll explain now the highlights of browse program operation, referring both to the visual table of contents in Figure 15.8 and the program source code in Figure 15.9. Neither the BMS map code or the symbolic map are central to considering BROWSE4 program logical operation, but we provide these items in Figures 15.10 and 15.11 so that you can refer to them as necessary.

15.7 HOW A TYPICAL BROWSE BEGINS

The 000-MAINLINE paragraph of the browse program, at letter "A" at lines 6900 through 10400 in Figure 15.9, decides what function the terminal operator has chosen, as the highest level of our visual table of contents in Figure 15.8 indicates. We'll first trace through the operation of a forward browse.

Let's assume that part of the VSAM file contains the following records with the following alternate keys:

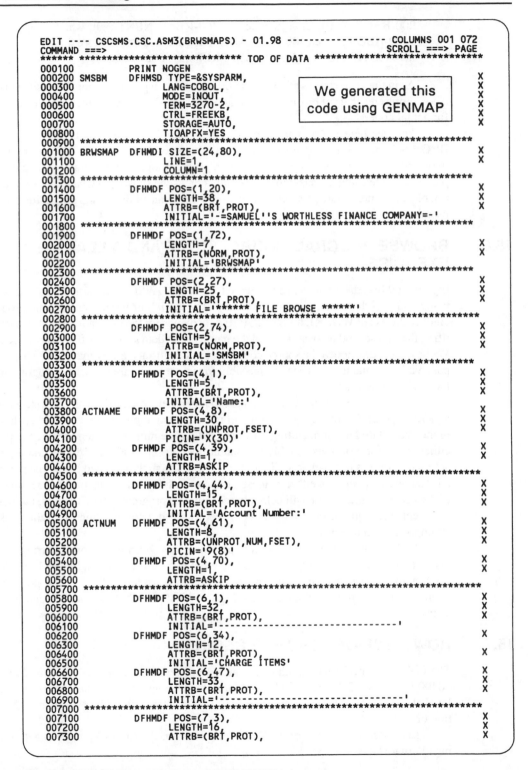

```
EDIT ---- CSCSMS.CSC.ASM3(BRWSMAPS) - 01.98 ------------------ COLUMNS 001 072
COMMAND ===>                                                   SCROLL ===> PAGE
****** ******************************** TOP OF DATA *******************************
                 PRINT NOGEN
        SMSBM    DFHMSD TYPE=&SYSPARM,                                           X
                       LANG=COBOL,                                               X
                       MODE=INOUT,                                               X
                       TERM=3270-2,                                              X
                       CTRL=FREEKB,                                              X
                       STORAGE=AUTO,                                             X
                       TIOAPFX=YES
***********************************************************************
        BRWSMAP  DFHMDI SIZE=(24,80),                                            X
                       LINE=1,                                                   X
                       COLUMN=1
***********************************************************************
                 DFHMDF POS=(1,20),                                              X
                       LENGTH=38,                                                X
                       ATTRB=(BRT,PROT),                                         X
                       INITIAL='-=SAMUEL''S WORTHLESS FINANCE COMPANY=-'
***********************************************************************
                 DFHMDF POS=(1,72),                                              X
                       LENGTH=7,                                                 X
                       ATTRB=(NORM,PROT),                                        X
                       INITIAL='BRWSMAP'
***********************************************************************
                 DFHMDF POS=(2,27),                                              X
                       LENGTH=25,                                                X
                       ATTRB=(BRT,PROT),                                         X
                       INITIAL='****** FILE BROWSE ******'
***********************************************************************
                 DFHMDF POS=(2,74),                                              X
                       LENGTH=5,                                                 X
                       ATTRB=(NORM,PROT),                                        X
                       INITIAL='SMSBM'
***********************************************************************
                 DFHMDF POS=(4,1),                                               X
                       LENGTH=5,                                                 X
                       ATTRB=(BRT,PROT),                                         X
                       INITIAL='Name:'
        ACTNAME  DFHMDF POS=(4,8),                                               X
                       LENGTH=30,                                                X
                       ATTRB=(UNPROT,FSET),                                      X
                       PICIN='X(30)'
                 DFHMDF POS=(4,39),                                              X
                       LENGTH=1,                                                 X
                       ATTRB=ASKIP
***********************************************************************
                 DFHMDF POS=(4,44),                                              X
                       LENGTH=15,                                                X
                       ATTRB=(BRT,PROT),                                         X
                       INITIAL='Account Number:'
        ACTNUM   DFHMDF POS=(4,61),                                              X
                       LENGTH=8,                                                 X
                       ATTRB=(UNPROT,NUM,FSET),                                  X
                       PICIN='9(8)'
                 DFHMDF POS=(4,70),                                              X
                       LENGTH=1,                                                 X
                       ATTRB=ASKIP
***********************************************************************
                 DFHMDF POS=(6,1),                                               X
                       LENGTH=32,                                                X
                       ATTRB=(BRT,PROT),                                         X
                       INITIAL='--------------------------------'
                 DFHMDF POS=(6,34),                                              X
                       LENGTH=12,                                                X
                       ATTRB=(BRT,PROT),                                         X
                       INITIAL='CHARGE ITEMS'
                 DFHMDF POS=(6,47),                                              X
                       LENGTH=33,                                                X
                       ATTRB=(BRT,PROT),                                         X
                       INITIAL='---------------------------------'
***********************************************************************
                 DFHMDF POS=(7,3),                                               X
                       LENGTH=16,                                                X
                       ATTRB=(BRT,PROT),
```

We generated this code using GENMAP

Figure 15.10 BMS map code for the BROWSE4 program.

```
                       INITIAL='Charge Amount 1:'
AMT1      DFHMDF POS=(7,21),                                        X
                 LENGTH=8,                                          X
                 ATTRB=(ASKIP),                                     X
                 PICOUT='Z,ZZ9.99'
*********************************************************************
          DFHMDF POS=(8,3),                                         X
                 LENGTH=16,                                         X
                 ATTRB=(BRT,PROT),                                  X
                 INITIAL='Charge Amount 2:'
AMT2      DFHMDF POS=(8,21),                                        X
                 LENGTH=8,
                 ATTRB=(ASKIP),                                     X
                 PICOUT='Z,ZZ9.99'
*********************************************************************
          DFHMDF POS=(9,3),                                         X
                 LENGTH=16,                                         X
                 ATTRB=(BRT,PROT),                                  X
                 INITIAL='Charge Amount 3:'
AMT3      DFHMDF POS=(9,21),                                        X
                 LENGTH=8,                                          X
                 ATTRB=(ASKIP),                                     X
                 PICOUT='Z,ZZ9.99'
*********************************************************************
          DFHMDF POS=(10,3),                                        X
                 LENGTH=16,                                         X
                 ATTRB=(BRT,PROT),                                  X
                 INITIAL='Charge Amount 4:'
AMT4      DFHMDF POS=(10,21),                                       X
                 LENGTH=8,                                          X
                 ATTRB=(ASKIP),                                     X
                 PICOUT='Z,ZZ9.99'
*********************************************************************
          DFHMDF POS=(11,3),
                 LENGTH=16,                                         X
                 ATTRB=(BRT,PROT),                                  X
                 INITIAL='Charge Amount 5:'
AMT5      DFHMDF POS=(11,21),                                       X
                 LENGTH=8,                                          X
                 ATTRB=(ASKIP),                                     X
                 PICOUT='Z,ZZ9.99'
*********************************************************************
          DFHMDF POS=(11,44),                                       X
                 LENGTH=19,                                         X
                 ATTRB=(BRT,PROT),                                  X
                 INITIAL='Total Charge Items:'
TOTCHG    DFHMDF POS=(11,65),                                       X
                 LENGTH=9,                                          X
                 ATTRB=(ASKIP),                                     X
                 PICOUT='ZZ,ZZ9.99'
*********************************************************************
          DFHMDF POS=(13,1),                                        X
                 LENGTH=32,                                         X
                 ATTRB=(BRT,PROT),                                  X
                 INITIAL='--------------------------------'
          DFHMDF POS=(13,34),
                 LENGTH=13,                                         X
                 ATTRB=(BRT,PROT),                                  X
                 INITIAL='CASH ADVANCES'
          DFHMDF POS=(13,48),                                       X
                 LENGTH=32,                                         X
                 ATTRB=(BRT,PROT),                                  X
                 INITIAL='--------------------------------'
*********************************************************************
          DFHMDF POS=(14,1),                                        X
                 LENGTH=18,                                         X
                 ATTRB=(BRT,PROT),                                  X
                 INITIAL='Cash Adv Amount 1:'
ADV1      DFHMDF POS=(14,21),                                       X
                 LENGTH=8,                                          X
                 ATTRB=(ASKIP),                                     X
                 PICOUT='Z,ZZ9.99'
*********************************************************************
          DFHMDF POS=(15,1),                                        X
                 LENGTH=18,                                         X
                 ATTRB=(BRT,PROT),                                  X
```

Figure 15.10 *(Continued)*

```
               INITIAL='Cash Adv Amount 2:'
ADV2     DFHMDF POS=(15,21),
               LENGTH=8,                                               X
               ATTRB=(ASKIP),                                          X
               PICOUT='Z,ZZ9.99'
***********************************************************************
         DFHMDF POS=(15,43),                                           X
               LENGTH=20,                                              X
               ATTRB=(BRT,PROT),                                       X
               INITIAL='Total Cash Advances:'
TOTADV   DFHMDF POS=(15,65),                                           X
               LENGTH=9,                                               X
               ATTRB=(ASKIP),                                          X
               PICOUT='ZZ,ZZ9.99'
***********************************************************************
         DFHMDF POS=(16,31),                                           X
               LENGTH=32,                                              X
               ATTRB=(BRT,PROT),                                       X
               INITIAL='Finance Charge On Cash Advances:'
FINCHG   DFHMDF POS=(16,68),                                           X
               LENGTH=6,                                               X
               ATTRB=(ASKIP),                                          X
               PICOUT='ZZ9.99'
***********************************************************************
         DFHMDF POS=(18,31),                                           X
               LENGTH=44,                                              X
               ATTRB=(BRT,PROT),                                       X
               INITIAL='============================================'
***********************************************************************
         DFHMDF POS=(20,50),                                           X
               LENGTH=13,                                              X
               ATTRB=(BRT,PROT),                                       X
               INITIAL='Total Debits:'
TOTDEB   DFHMDF POS=(20,64),                                           X
               LENGTH=10,                                              X
               ATTRB=(ASKIP),                                          X
               PICOUT='$$$,$$9.99'
***********************************************************************
         DFHMDF POS=(22,1),                                            X
               LENGTH=30,                                              X
               ATTRB=(BRT,PROT),                                       X
               INITIAL='PF1 = FORWARD, PF2 = BACKWARD,'
         DFHMDF POS=(22,33),                                           X
               LENGTH=23,                                              X
               ATTRB=(BRT,PROT),                                       X
               INITIAL='PF3 = TOP, PF4 = BOTTOM'
         DFHMDF POS=(22,57),                                           X
               LENGTH=22,                                              X
               ATTRB=(BRT,PROT),                                       X
               INITIAL=' ..OR CLEAR KEY TO END'
***********************************************************************
MESSAGE  DFHMDF POS=(23,1),                                            X
               LENGTH=78,                                              X
               ATTRB=(BRT,PROT)
ERROR    DFHMDF POS=(24,1),                                            X
               LENGTH=75,                                              X
               ATTRB=(BRT,PROT)
DUMMY    DFHMDF POS=(24,78),                                           X
               LENGTH=1,                                               X
               ATTRB=(DRK,PROT),                                       X
               INITIAL=' '
***********************************************************************
         DFHMSD TYPE=FINAL
         END
```

Figure 15.10 *(Continued)*

```
EDIT ---- CCP.MACLIB(SMSBM) - 01.00 -------------------------- COLUMNS 001 072
COMMAND ===>                                                   SCROLL ===> PAGE
****** ****************************** TOP OF DATA ******************************
           01  BRWSMAPI.
               02  FILLER PIC X(12).
               02  ACTNAMEL    COMP  PIC  S9(4).
               02  ACTNAMEF    PICTURE X.
               02  FILLER REDEFINES ACTNAMEF.
                 03 ACTNAMEA    PICTURE X.
               02  ACTNAMEI  PIC X(30).
               02  ACTNUML     COMP  PIC  S9(4).
               02  ACTNUMF     PICTURE X.
               02  FILLER REDEFINES ACTNUMF.
                 03 ACTNUMA    PICTURE X.
               02  ACTNUMI  PIC 9(8).
               02  AMT1L     COMP  PIC  S9(4).
               02  AMT1F     PICTURE X.
               02  FILLER REDEFINES AMT1F.
                 03 AMT1A     PICTURE X.
               02  AMT1I  PIC X(8).
               02  AMT2L     COMP  PIC  S9(4).
               02  AMT2F     PICTURE X.
               02  FILLER REDEFINES AMT2F.
                 03 AMT2A     PICTURE X.
               02  AMT2I  PIC X(8).
               02  AMT3L     COMP  PIC  S9(4).
               02  AMT3F     PICTURE X.
               02  FILLER REDEFINES AMT3F.
                 03 AMT3A     PICTURE X.
               02  AMT3I  PIC X(8).
               02  AMT4L     COMP  PIC  S9(4).
               02  AMT4F     PICTURE X.
               02  FILLER REDEFINES AMT4F.
                 03 AMT4A     PICTURE X.
               02  AMT4I  PIC X(8).
               02  AMT5L     COMP  PIC  S9(4).
               02  AMT5F     PICTURE X.
               02  FILLER REDEFINES AMT5F.
                 03 AMT5A     PICTURE X.
               02  AMT5I  PIC X(8).
               02  TOTCHGL     COMP  PIC  S9(4).
               02  TOTCHGF     PICTURE X.
               02  FILLER REDEFINES TOTCHGF.
                 03 TOTCHGA     PICTURE X.
               02  TOTCHGI  PIC X(9).
               02  ADV1L     COMP  PIC  S9(4).
               02  ADV1F     PICTURE X.
               02  FILLER REDEFINES ADV1F.
                 03 ADV1A     PICTURE X.
               02  ADV1I  PIC X(8).
               02  ADV2L     COMP  PIC  S9(4).
               02  ADV2F     PICTURE X.
               02  FILLER REDEFINES ADV2F.
                 03 ADV2A     PICTURE X.
               02  ADV2I  PIC X(8).
               02  TOTADVL     COMP  PIC  S9(4).
               02  TOTADVF     PICTURE X.
               02  FILLER REDEFINES TOTADVF.
                 03 TOTADVA     PICTURE X.
               02  TOTADVI  PIC X(9).
               02  FINCHGL     COMP  PIC  S9(4).
               02  FINCHGF     PICTURE X.
               02  FILLER REDEFINES FINCHGF.
                 03 FINCHGA     PICTURE X.
               02  FINCHGI  PIC X(6).
               02  TOTDEBL     COMP  PIC  S9(4).
               02  TOTDEBF     PICTURE X.
               02  FILLER REDEFINES TOTDEBF.
                 03 TOTDEBA     PICTURE X.
               02  TOTDEBI  PIC X(10).
               02  MESSAGEL     COMP  PIC  S9(4).
               02  MESSAGEF     PICTURE X.
               02  FILLER REDEFINES MESSAGEF.
                 03 MESSAGEA     PICTURE X.
               02  MESSAGEI  PIC X(78).
               02  ERRORL     COMP  PIC  S9(4).
```

Machine-generated symbolic maps do not seem to become any easier to deal with no matter how many of them you see. A cleaner version of a symbolic map for the browse program could have been generated by GENMAP (see Appendix F) or a similar screen painter.

Figure 15.11 Symbolic map for the BROWSE4 program.

```
           02  ERRORF    PICTURE X.
           02  FILLER REDEFINES ERRORF.
             03 ERRORA     PICTURE X.
           02  ERRORI  PIC X(75).
           02  DUMMYL      COMP  PIC  S9(4).
           02  DUMMYF      PICTURE X.
           02  FILLER REDEFINES DUMMYF.
             03 DUMMYA     PICTURE X.
           02  DUMMYI  PIC X(1).
       01  BRWSMAPO REDEFINES BRWSMAPI.
           02  FILLER PIC X(12).
           02  FILLER PICTURE X(3).
           02  ACTNAMEO  PIC X(30).
           02  FILLER PICTURE X(3).
           02  ACTNUMO  PIC X(8).
           02  FILLER PICTURE X(3).
           02  AMT1O PIC Z,ZZ9.99.
           02  FILLER PICTURE X(3).
           02  AMT2O PIC Z,ZZ9.99.
           02  FILLER PICTURE X(3).
           02  AMT3O PIC Z,ZZ9.99.
           02  FILLER PICTURE X(3).
           02  AMT4O PIC Z,ZZ9.99.
           02  FILLER PICTURE X(3).
           02  AMT5O PIC Z,ZZ9.99.
           02  FILLER PICTURE X(3).
           02  TOTCHGO PIC ZZ,ZZ9.99.
           02  FILLER PICTURE X(3).
           02  ADV1O PIC Z,ZZ9.99.
           02  FILLER PICTURE X(3).
           02  ADV2O PIC Z,ZZ9.99.
           02  FILLER PICTURE X(3).
           02  TOTADVO PIC ZZ,ZZ9.99.
           02  FILLER PICTURE X(3).
           02  FINCHGO PIC ZZ9.99.
           02  FILLER PICTURE X(3).
           02  TOTDEBO PIC $$$,$$9.99.
           02  FILLER PICTURE X(3).
           02  MESSAGEO  PIC X(78).
           02  FILLER PICTURE X(3).
           02  ERRORO  PIC X(75).
           02  FILLER PICTURE X(3).
           02  DUMMYO  PIC X(1).
```

Figure 15.11 *(Continued)*

HARPER, SHARON
HODIAK, JOHN
ICHABOD, MICHAEL
MALINSKI, CHERYL
MORGAN, AMY
NEWMAN, STEVE

Suppose the terminal operator brings up the browse screen, enters "JACKSON" at the name field, and presses the PF1 key. As a first action in a forward browse, the 100-BEGIN paragraph in Figure 15.9, at letter "B" at lines 10600 through 11900, receives control. This paragraph insures that the terminal operator has entered at least one character in the name field. If so, it passes control to the 120-GET-RECORD paragraph, at letter "C" at lines 12100 through 13800 in Figure 15.9, which invokes the 550-START-BROWSE paragraph at letter "J" in lines 32200 through 34600. In this paragraph, the name entered in the map is moved from the symbolic map field ACTNAMEI to the WORKING-STORAGE record description, ACCT-NAME.

Next, a CICS **STARTBR** command is executed to position the data pointer to a record containing a name equal to or greater than the name in ACCT-NAME. The **data pointer** is a value maintained by CICS, and points to the next record to be accessed by the **READNEXT** (sequential) read. In this instance, data pointer is positioned to point to the record containing "MALINSKI." *Note that this does not mean that a record has been retrieved yet!* The record containing the name MALINSKI would also have been pointed to if the terminal operator entered "MALINSKI, CHERYL" or just "MALINSKI", or even just "M". But if the name "MAZINSKI" was entered by mistake, the data pointer would point to the record containing "MORGAN", since it is the next after MAZINSKI.

DFHRESP is NORMAL as a result of the STARTBR in paragraph 550-START-BROWSE, because it positioned the data pointer successfully. But if the terminal operator had entered a value such as "ZZZZZ", which is greater than any name value above, the STARTBR would not have succeeded. Why? STARTBR would have failed, because it would have been impossible to find a record with alternate key equal to or greater than "ZZZZZ." In this case, DFHRESP would be NOTFND, a condition we intercept with the EVALUATE that follows the STARTBR command. Either way, control returns to paragraph 120-GET-RECORD, at letter "C" at line 12700.

If DFHRESP indicates a successful STARTBR we execute 150-FORWARD-ROUTINE at letter "D" at lines 14100 through 17400 in Figure 15.9. The name entered by the terminal operator was "JACKSON," and it reached the program in field name ACTNAMEI in the symbolic map. We did not give DFHCOMMAREA a value, and its content is not the same as ACTNAMEI. Therefore, the 300-READ-NEXT paragraph, at letter "H" at lines 25900 through 28900 in Figure 15.9, will only be executed once with the action of lines 16100 through 16800. In the 300-READ-NEXT paragraph, the FILE—the record—that the data pointer points to (MALINKSI, CHERYL) is read from the data set, and DFHRESP is NORMAL. Control passes back to the 150-FORWARD-ROUTINE. We move the WORKING-STORAGE record fields to the symbolic map in the 650-PREPARE-ACCOUNT-SCREEN paragraph at letter "L", and control passes back to the mainline. 700-SEND-ACCOUNT-SCREEN at letter "M" presents the data on the terminal screen.

The browse may seem to require quite a bit of processing. Compare the visual table of contents in Figure 15.8 to the source code in Figure 15.9 as you work through the code to develop an understanding of it. You'll see how the diamond shaped "selection" symbol adds information to the chart to help you see what logic is executed conditionally. With a bit more discussion, the method of browse operation will become clear to you.

15.8 HOW FORWARD BROWSE RESUMES AND CONTINUES

Beginning a browse involves a STARTBR to position the data pointer to the location in the data set where reading will begin. You then execute READNEXT to actually obtain the record. READNEXT updates the data pointer, making it point to the next record, to get set for the next READNEXT to obtain the next record. But here is where we face a problem. Our program returns control to CICS after presenting the record to the terminal operator, ending this pseudoconverse. The program dies and loses the data pointer and all of its WORKING-STORAGE fields. Just prior to losing all of these things, the contents and status of these variables are:

ACTNAMEI	MALINSKI, CHERYL
ACCT-NAME	MALINSKI, CHERYL
LETS-GO-FORWARD	TRUE
LETS-GO-BACKWARD	FALSE
DFHCOMMAREA	LOW-VALUES
WS-COMMUNICATION-AREA	MALINSKI, CHERYL
Data pointer	points to MORGAN, AMY

We need a way to preserve some of this information or we won't be able to, in the next pseudoconverse, progress forward from the first record obtained in the browse. What do we do?

Examine the 150-FORWARD-ROUTINE paragraph at lines 14100 through 17400 in Figure 15.9 and you will see that we have moved the ACCT-NAME—the name of the record last read from the data set—to WS-COMMUNICATION-AREA in line 17300. We did this because we pass WS-COMMUNICATION-AREA back to ourselves in the RETURN with TRANSID command:

```
EXEC CICS
   RETURN  TRANSID     (WS-TRANS-ID)
           COMMAREA    (WS-COMMUNICATION-AREA)
END-EXEC.
```

As you saw in Figure 14.8 in Chapter 14, whatever we cite in the COMMAREA clause is preserved by CICS and returns to our program, the next time it is reawakened, in the LINKAGE SECTION's DFHCOMMAREA field. In Chapter 14, we used this feature of CICS operation to pass a copy of a record back to ourselves to be able to detect if a concurrent update had occurred. Here, *we use this capability to preserve the alternate key of the record we last presented on the screen.*

When the program is next awakened by the terminal operator pressing the PF1 key, 000-MAINLINE is executed. One of the first actions we take is to move DFHCOMMAREA to WS-COMMUNICATION-AREA. Then these paragraphs execute:

100-BEGIN

600-RECEIVE-ACCOUNT-SCREEN

550-START-BROWSE

150-FORWARD-ROUTINE

300-READ-NEXT

300-READ-NEXT

650-PREPARE-SCREEN

700-SEND-ACCOUNT-SCREEN

After 600-RECEIVE-ACCOUNT-SCREEN at letter "K", the following is present in WORKING-STORAGE and the symbolic map fields:

ACTNAMEI	MALINSKI, CHERYL
ACCT-NAME	—
LETS-GO-FORWARD	TRUE

LETS-GO-BACKWARD	FALSE
DFHCOMMAREA	MALINSKI, CHERYL
WS-COMMUNICATION-AREA	MALINSKI, CHERYL
Data pointer	—

DFHCOMMAREA contains the value "MALINSKI, CHERYL" because we preserved this value. ACTNAMEI contains "MALINSKI, CHERYL," because it was transmitted back from the terminal to the program in the symbolic map. Therefore, ACTNAMEI=DFHCOMMAREA. The 550-BROWSE-ROUTINE sets the data pointer to the record with alternate key "MALINSKI, CHERYL." Then the 150-FORWARD-ROUTINE executes the 300-READ-NEXT paragraph twice. Why read twice? Because to browse forward, we need to actually obtain the record with alternate key "MALINKSI," then read again to get to the next record, containing alternate key values "MORGAN, AMY." After these actions we have the following in WORKING-STORAGE:

ACTNAMEI	MALINSKI, CHERYL
ACCT-NAME	*MORGAN, AMY*
LETS-GO-FORWARD	TRUE
LETS-GO-BACKWARD	FALSE
DFHCOMMAREA	MALINSKI, CHERYL
WS-COMMUNICATION-AREA	MALINSKI, CHERYL
Data pointer	points to NEWMAN, STEVE

When 650-PREPARE-ACCOUNT-SCREEN is executed, ACCT-NAME is placed in ACTNAMEI, and we also put it into WS-COMMUNICATION-AREA:

ACTNAMEI	MORGAN, AMY
ACCT-NAME	MORGAN, AMY
LETS-GO-FORWARD	TRUE
LETS-GO-BACKWARD	FALSE
DFHCOMMAREA	MALINSKI, CHERYL
WS-COMMUNICATION-AREA	*MORGAN, AMY*
Data pointer	points to NEWMAN, STEVE

The program again dies, having now presented the contents of the next record (MORGAN, AMY) on the screen for the terminal operator. The value "MORGAN, AMY" is preserved in COMMAREA when the program gives control back to CICS and dies, and will be given back to the program in DFHCOMMAREA when it is next awakened. The cycle repeats as long as the terminal operator continues pressing the PF1 key. When the end of file is reached, as a result of performing the 300-READ-NEXT paragraph at line 16600, FILE-ERROR becomes true. At lines 17000 through 17100, we move the message "OUTSIDE OF FILE AREA OR END OF FILE" to the prompt, and do not attempt to again preserve the alternate key value now in the symbolic map, or send new record data to the screen.

Walk through this code yourself, keeping track of what is in WORKING-STORAGE, what is moved, and what is preserved. You'll see how the forward browse starts and continues, based on the alternate key value we pass back to ourselves from one pseudoconverse to the next.

15.9 STARTING A BACKWARD BROWSE

The terminal operator initiates a **backward browse** in our BROWSE4 program by pressing the PF2 key. In a backward browse, records are presented as if the file is being read in reverse sequence, from the present location to the beginning of file. If you examine the 000-MAIN-LINE paragraph, you'll see that the only difference here between handling a forward browse and handling a backward browse is the setting of the LETS-GO-BACKWARD Boolean flag at either line 8000 or line 8400. After setting this flag to the appropriate value, both forward and backward browses perform the 100-BEGIN paragraph.

Unless the terminal operator has completely eliminated the contents of the name field on the screen, the 100-BEGIN paragraph passes control to 120-GET-RECORD at letter "C" at lines 12100 through 13800, which invokes 550-START-BROWSE. The net effect of this, for either a forward or backward browse, is to use STARTBR to position the data pointer to the same record last presented on the screen. For a backward browse, however, the 120-GET-RECORD paragraph performs 200-BACKWARD-ROUTINE, at letter "E", from line 13800 instead of 150-FORWARD-ROUTINE from line 13300.

The 200-BACKWARD-ROUTINE at letter "E" at lines 17700 through 21100 in Figure 15.9 is similar to the browse forward function. After executing READNEXT to actually obtain the record last presented on the screen, here is what 200-BACKWARD-ROUTINE does:

- If a change was made in the account name on the screen, that is, ACTNAMEI not = DFHCOMMAREA, we do not perform 400-READ-PREVIOUS at all; we just present the record.
- If no change in account name has been made on the screen, that is, ACTNAMEI= DFHCOMMAREA, we perform 400-READ-PREVIOUS at letter "I" twice and present the record.

In other words, this is what is executed to begin a backward browse:

```
100-BEGIN
600-RECEIVE-ACCOUNT-SCREEN
120-GET-RECORD
550-START-BROWSE
200-BACKWARD-ROUTINE
300-READ-NEXT                    <=== at line 19700
650-PREPARE-SCREEN
700-SEND-ACCOUNT-SCREEN
```

Beginning a backward browse means finding and presenting the record that satisfies the starting criteria, which is the one or more letters that the terminal operator entered on the screen. This will be the same record that we start with in the case of a forward browse!

15.10 RESUMING A BACKWARD BROWSE

Suppose the terminal operator has initiated backward browsing by pressing the PF2 key, then presses PF2 again to continue this browse. We detect this situation when a program reawakens. If no change in account name has been made on the screen, ACTNAMEI=DFHCOMMAREA. This means, of course, that the account name field transmitted back to the program from the terminal, and now in the symbolic map field (ACTNAMEI), is the same as the account name preserved for us in DFHCOMMAREA. Here is the processing action that occurs now:

```
100-BEGIN
600-RECEIVE-ACCOUNT-SCREEN
120-GET-RECORD
550-START-BROWSE
200-BACKWARD-ROUTINE
300-READ-NEXT                <=== at line 19700
400-READ-PREVIOUS            <=== at line 20300
400-READ-PREVIOUS            <=== at line 20300
650-PREPARE-SCREEN
700-SEND-ACCOUNT-SCREEN
```

This processing may seem strange. Understanding it is one of the hardest parts of CICS browse programming! The STARTBR in 550-START-BROWSE positions the data pointer for us, to the record last presented, and the READNEXT obtains this record, but also moves the data pointer ahead to point to the next record. **READPREV** repositions the data pointer first, then obtains the record pointed to, which is, once again, the record last presented on the screen. The second READPREV repositions the data pointer backward again one record, and obtains that record. This is the record one before the one last presented, and the one we want to present to the terminal user.

The key to understanding backward browse processing is the fact that READPREV works differently from READNEXT in how it manipulates the data pointer. READPREV repositions the data pointer, then obtains it, while READNEXT obtains the record pointed to now, then updates the data pointer.

15.11 JUMPING TO THE FIRST RECORD

Once you have grasped how forward and backward browses are implemented in a CICS program, it's relatively easy to consider two additional convenience features of a browse. We have included these two features, a "top" and "bottom" function, in our BROWSE4 program. By pressing PF3 the terminal operator can do a **jump to top,** shifting the data pointer to the beginning (top) of the file and seeing the first record, and preparing to browse forward. By pressing PF4, the operator can initiate a **jump to bottom** to see the last (highest alternate key value) record in the file, and prepare to browse backward from that point.

Examine the visual table of contents in Figure 15.8 and you will see that the "jump to top" function is handled by the 260-SET-TOP paragraph at lines 21400 through 23400, and "jump to bottom" is handled by the 285-SET-BOTTOM paragraph at letter "G" at lines 23600 through 25700. As the VTOC indicates, both the 260- and 285- paragraphs involve no new code. That is, all of the boxes hanging under these two paragraphs have shaded corners. The "top" and "bottom" functions just splice together code we already have.

The key to the operation of the "jump to top" function occurs at the first line in the 260-SET-TOP paragraph, at letter "F" at line 21800 in Figure 15.9, where we move LOW-VALUES to the entire symbolic map, BRWSMAPI. This of course fills the ACTNAMEI field with **LOW-VALUES,** the lowest possible bit pattern. When we perform the 550-START-BROWSE paragraph, it moves ACTNAMEI to ACCT-NAME at line 32700, then executes a CICS STARTBR command. This STARTBR positions the data pointer to the record with alternate key equal to or beyond the value in ACCT-NAME. Since ACCT-NAME contains LOW-VALUES, the lowest possible bit pattern, this STARTBR positions us to the first record (by alternate key) in the file. The subsequent actions, at line 22400, then 22700, and finally the perform 700-SEND-ACCOUNT-SCREEN at line 9900, simply finish up the presentation of this record.

15.12 JUMPING TO THE LAST RECORD

If you understand the "jump to top" function described above, little stands in the way of your understanding the "jump to bottom" function implemented in the 285-SET-BOTTOM paragraph. With minor differences this operates exactly the same way as the 260-SET-TOP paragraph.

The 285-SET-BOTTOM paragraph is located at lines 23600 through 25700 in Figure 15.9. Since we want to position the data pointer at the end of the file, we move **HIGH-VALUES**—the highest possible bit pattern—to ACTNAMEI in the symbolic map. When we then perform 550-START-BROWSE, the data pointer is positioned after the last record in the file. 400-READ-PREVIOUS at letter "I" then resets the data pointer back to the last record in the file and obtains it. The subsequent actions leading up to performing 700-SEND-ACCOUNT-SCREEN at line 9900 finish up the presentation of this record.

15.13 CICS ENDBR AND RESETBR COMMANDS

Our BROWSE4 program provides you with a complete working example you use as a model for your own browse programs. Two other CICS commands deal with browse processes, but neither of these demands your immediate attention.

You can use the **ENDBR** command to end a browse operation:

```
EXEC CICS
    ENDBR  DATASET  (filename)
           RESP     (WS-RESPONSE-CODE)
END-EXEC.
```

You don't normally have to code ENDBR, however, because CICS performs the same thing as ENDBR every time the program task ends. If you are attempting to do other things besides a browse in the same pseudoconverse (task), such as updating, you do need to code ENDBR before beginning the next operation. In such a circumstance, ENDBR releases CICS resources allocated to the browse, so they can be used to support other processes.

The **RESETBR** command is available to let you change the nature of the browse. For example, you might wish to change the default GTEQ option of the browse to EQUAL using RESETBR:

```
EXEC CICS
   RESETBR  DATASET  (filename)
            RIDFLD   (data-name)
            EQUAL
            RESP     (WS-RESPONSE-CODE)
END-EXEC.
```

GTEQ and EQUAL are mutually exclusive; if you don't specify either one when doing STARTBR, GTEQ applies. **GTEQ** allows positioning the file to a record with key equal to or greater than that specified in the RIDFLD data name. EQUAL allows STARTBR positioning to succeed only if an exact match exists between what you indicate as the starting position and a record in the file. (See Appendix A for more information on options of CICS commands.)

15.14 BROWSE PROBLEM WITH DUPLICATE ALTERNATE KEYS

The primary key of a VSAM Key Sequenced Data Set must be unique, that is, each record in the file must have a primary key value different from all the other records in the file. In contrast, the value in an alternate key field need not be unique. Since more than one record in the Key Sequenced Data Set can have the same alternate key value, we can say that the alternate key values have "duplicates." For example, while two borrowers each named John Smith will have different account numbers, they (obviously) have exactly the same name. We would call such a condition a **duplicate alternate key.** If this condition is to be supported, the alternate index is defined with the NONUNIQUEKEY attribute as illustrated in Figures D.3 and D.9 of Appendix D.

Our browse program does not provide for duplicate alternate key values. With its present coding of the READNEXT and READPREV CICS commands, the condition DFHRESP (DUPKEY), which is encountered if a duplicate alternate key is read, is not addressed and would fall into the "OTHER" category, triggering 9999-ABORT. DFHRESP takes the value 15 when a DUPKEY condition arises, and 9999-ABORT logic would make this visible.

If we choose to regard duplicate alternate keys as legitimate, we could add this additional WHEN condition following the test for DFHRESP(NORMAL):

```
WHEN DFHRESP(DUPKEY)
   SET NO-FILE-ERROR TO TRUE
   ADD +1 TO WS-READ-COUNT
```

This code recognizes DUPKEY as valid, and acts the same way in response to it as we do in response to the DFHRESP(NORMAL) condition. While this would prevent our browse from abending, it does not make the browse work acceptably. The browse will now get stuck once we move forward through records with duplicate names. Moving ahead requires repositioning on the first record that has the present key value (passed back to us in DFHCOMMAREA) and then reading the next one. Once you hit a series of records with duplicate alternate keys, this forward browse restart always gets the same record, which is the second occurrence of the alternate key!

How do we resolve this problem? The best way to resolve it is by making every alternate key unique. With a **unique alternate key,** no two records have the same alternate key value. This not only eliminates the browse problem, it simplifies the index structure for the VSAM file. As you will see, making the alternate index unique requires nothing fancy, just a bit of thought in designing the position of fields Key Sequenced Data Set record.

15.15 MAKING AN ALTERNATE KEY UNIQUE

It's unfortunate that many textbooks illustrate placement of the key field first in records in VSAM Key Sequenced Data Sets. Housing the primary key as the first field in a record makes it easier to view the key if you dump the records for analysis. But it does not represent optimal field placement when an alternate key is defined. Simply by positioning the primary key after the alternate key, you can make every alternate key unique by defining the alternate key to include the primary key.

For example, the layout of the borrower record in the form presented in our inquiry, update, and browse programs is not optimal. Since more than one person can have the same name, we will surely, sooner or later, have a duplication of the alternate key with this layout:

```
01  ACCT-REC.
    05 ACT-NUM      PIC X(8).        <=== primary key
    05 AMT-1        PIC 9(4)V99.
    05 AMT-2        PIC 9(4)V99.
    05 AMT-3        PIC 9(4)V99.
    05 AMT-4        PIC 9(4)V99.
    05 AMT-5        PIC 9(4)V99.
    05 ADV-1        PIC 9(4)V99.
    05 ADV-2        PIC 9(4)V99.
    05 TOT-CHG      PIC 9(5)V99.
    05 TOT-ADV      PIC 9(5)V99.
    05 FIN-CHG      PIC 9(3)V99.
    05 TOT-DEB      PIC 9(5)V99.
    05 GAP-1        PIC X(44).
    05 ACCT-NAME    PIC X(30).       <=== alternate key
    05 GAP-2        PIC X(10).
```

Here is a revised record layout, having exactly the same data content and record length, but with the primary and alternate key fields arranged to make the alternate key unique:

```
01  ACCT-REC.
    05 ACCT-NAME-ALT-KEY.                   <=== alternate key
       10 ACCT-NAME        PIC X(30).
       10 ACT-NUM          PIC X(8).   <=== primary key
    05 AMT-1               PIC 9(4)V99.
    05 AMT-2               PIC 9(4)V99.
    05 AMT-3               PIC 9(4)V99.
    05 AMT-4               PIC 9(4)V99.
    05 AMT-5               PIC 9(4)V99.
    05 ADV-1               PIC 9(4)V99.
    05 ADV-2               PIC 9(4)V99.
    05 TOT-CHG             PIC 9(5)V99.
    05 TOT-ADV             PIC 9(5)V99.
    05 FIN-CHG             PIC 9(3)V99.
    05 TOT-DEB             PIC 9(5)V99.
    05 GAP-1               PIC X(44).
    05 GAP-2               PIC X(10).
```

Notice that we have made the alternate key the first field, and the primary key the second field. In declaring the data structure (record), we provide a group name over both of these fields, and give it the data-name ACCT-NAME-ALT-KEY. The alternate key field defined to VSAM is actually 38 bytes long, not 30, and the presence of the primary key within it makes every alternate key values unique. We now define the alternate index of the Key Sequenced Data Set with the attribute UNIQUEKEY instead of NONUNIQUEKEY. Two people with identical names will now have unique alternate keys such as this:

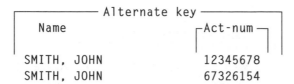

```
┌──────────── Alternate key ────────────┐
│  Name                  ┌Act-num ┐     │
│                        │        │     │
 SMITH, JOHN              12345678
 SMITH, JOHN              67326154
```

15.16 SUCCESSFUL BROWSE WITH DUPLICATE NAMES

Laying out the primary and alternate keys as describe above costs nothing in terms of file space, but resolves the problem of being able to browse forward and backward. But why doesn't placing the primary at the end of the alternate key, making the alternate longer and unique, impinge on our ability to browse?

Recall that you can start browsing by entering as little as one letter of the alternate key. If you enter more of the alternate key than this, you make the starting location of the browse more specific. If you wanted to start browsing at the first record for SMITH, JOHN listed above, you could enter all of the name field to begin the browse. It would make no difference to you that the primary key value is actually a part of the alternate key, beyond what you thought was the full extent of the alternate key.

For browsing purposes, you will find another beneficial by-product of housing the primary key at the end of the alternate key. When you browse by alternate key, you'll now see groups of records with the same alternate key "sorted" in primary key sequence. This makes a more orderly presentation of these groups of records, which might otherwise appear in an unpredictable sequence.

15.17 GOING BEYOND A SINGLE-RECORD BROWSE SCREEN

The browse screens we have presented here, shown in Figures 15.1 through 15.7, present the content of a single record only. This is adequate for many purposes and has the advantage of presenting all information for a given record during the browse. But it makes it a bit tedious to find records in a large file, in which many alternate keys such as name have the same or similar values.

Figure 15.12 shows you a **multi-record browse screen,** on which fields from many records are present at one time. This example browse screen shows 15 records at a time. Here, pressing PF1 moves ahead 15 records at a time.

While a multi-record browse does provide a convenience to terminal operators, programming this form of browse is more complex than implementing a **single-record browse screen.** We don't provide an example of a multi-record browse in this book, but we will give you some hints on the issues you have to confront to design and build this type of function:

- The symbolic map for a multi-record browse screen such as that shown in Figure 15.12 is best developed manually, so that you can code the repeating "detail line" with an OCCURS clause and treat this part of the screen as a table of 15 rows.
- Since you only have one line to present information from each record, you must design this line carefully. The alternate key field should be at the left side, for easy viewing, and the primary key should be next, to make it easy to find. The other fields to be presented in the detail line for each record should be those that will give the terminal operator the best chance to identify the correct record. Pretend that a customer will be on the telephone talking to the terminal operator at the time that the

```
                 -=SAMUEL'S WORTHLESS FINANCE COMPANY=-                 BRNUMAP
                 ****** MULTI-RECORD FILE BROWSE ******                  JGJBM6

NAME                           ACCOUNT   TOT CHARGE  TOT ADVANCE   TOT DEBITS

ANDERSON, WILLY                68945023    1,000.00         0.00     1,000.00
ANDREWS, JOHN                  37621021    2,500.00       300.00     2,816.52
ARTHUR, CAROL                  98362894      700.00         0.00       700.00
AVERY, ANNE                    87789931    3,500.00     1,000.00     4,598.13
BACALL, LUCY                   98836784    5,100.00       400.00     5,689.34
BALLARD, WALTER                76712257    4,000.00       350.00     4,598.70
BATTAGLIA, J.                  77655709    2,300.00       950.00     3,367.11
BONDAR, SERGE                  87612662      550.00       145.00       718.45
BOSWORTH, HAROLD               76212889    7,800.00     2,000.00    10,457.62
BRADLEY, ROBERT                00938920        0.00         0.00         0.00
BROWN, ALEX                    67820939    6,000.00     3,000.00     9,036.00
CANTWELL, GEORGE               88835188        0.00         0.00         0.00
CHADWICK, STEVE                12312054    1,000.00         0.00     1,000.00
COMSTOCK, CHARLES              64522222    6,000.00         0.00     6,000.00
CULHANE, NANCY                 99301000        0.00         0.00         0.00

PF1 = FORWARD, PF2 = BACKWARD,  PF3 = TOP, PF4 = BOTTOM  ..OR CLEAR KEY TO END

TOP OF FILE
```

Figure 15.12 How a multi-record browse screen for the borrower file might appear.

operator is using the multi-record browse. What type of questions could the operator ask the customer to help pinpoint the customer's record? Might this be address, or telephone number, or zip code, or birthdate? These are the types of fields to include in browse detail lines!

- Implementing a backward browse for multi-record browse screens is especially tricky. You need to position first on a record as we have done, with STARTBR and READNEXT, then READPREV twice to get the first (next backward) record. Realize that for a backward browse, this is the record at the *bottom* of the screen! As you READPREV to get records before this one, you have to load the repeating detail line in the symbolic map in reverse sequence, that is, upward from the bottom line.
- For multi-record forward browse, you pass the alternate key of the last record on the screen back to yourself using COMMAREA; for multi-record backward browse, you pass the alternate key of the first record on the screen back to yourself. If you want to provide some content overlap from one browse screen to the next, pass back the alternate on the second line of the screen for a backward browse, or the second line from the bottom for a forward browse.
- Remember to "blank out" unused detail lines when you reach the end of a file, so that information in those lines does not remain on the screen! This will involve moving spaces to these lines, not LOW-VALUES, since LOW-VALUES is not transmitted. When you reach the beginning of file for a backward browse, you will probably face a similar problem in having blank lines at the top of the screen. For a backward browse, consider including logic to shift the lines you have put record information into to the top of the screen, leaving the blank lines at the bottom. And don't forget to include a BOTTOM OF FILE or TOP OF FILE message on your screen in these situations!

- While a multi-record browse screen like that in Figure 15.12 resembles a report, refrain from designing any kind of column total or subtotal fields at the bottom of this screen. Totals and subtotals at column bottoms belong on paper reports, not on interactive screens, which serve a different purpose.

If you are really bitten by the CICS programming bug, try your hand at a multi-record browse. If you successfully implement one, consider taking another step and make it possible for the terminal operator to "point" to the line (record) for which he or she wants to see full information or perform an update. Refer to the information in Appendix A to develop logic to use the EIBCPOSN interface execute block field to determine the line the cursor is positioned on, and make it possible for the terminal operator to branch to an inquiry or update function by pressing a designated PF key. To fully implement this, you'll also need to consult Chapter 16, where we explain how to use the XCTL command to transfer control from one program to another.

15.18 FOR YOUR REVIEW

The following terms were introduced or reviewed in this chapter. If you understand this chapter, you should be comfortable with defining each of these terms in relationship to CICS:

Action diagram
Alternate index path
Alternate key
Backward browse
Browse function
Data pointer
Duplicate alternate key
EBCDIC character set
ENDBR
Filename
Forward browse
GTEQ
HIGH-VALUES
Iteration
Jump to bottom
Jump to top
LOW-VALUES
Multi-record browse screen
Primary key
READNEXT
READPREV
RESETBR
Selection
Sequence
Single-record browse screen
STARTBR
Structured programming
Unique alternate key
Visual table of contents

15.19 REVIEW QUESTIONS

1. Describe what a browse function is and explain what it allows the user of an interactive business system to accomplish.
2. Explain why a browse function is usually built upon an alternate key rather than on the primary key of an indexed file.
3. Describe how much or how little of an alternate key the terminal operator must supply in order to initiate a forward browse, and explain how this entry is used to position access to the file for the browse process.
4. Describe the general placement of letters and numbers in the EBCDIC collation sequence, and discuss the effect this has on the CICS browse process.
5. CICS filename is the name you code in the READNEXT command by which

forward browsing is conducted. Identify what the filename is and what it is associated with for an alternate key browse, and how this name is established.

6. Identify and briefly describe the "building blocks" of structured programming, and explain how a visual table of contents represents the use of each of these constructs.
7. Explain in detail what the data pointer is, and where it is maintained in a CICS program.
8. Explain in detail what the CICS STARTBR command does when you execute it, including its effect on the data pointer.
9. Explain in detail what the CICS READNEXT command does when you execute it, including its effect on the data pointer.
10. Identify and discuss two major ways that the operation of the READPREV command differs from that of the READNEXT command.
11. Discuss the relevance of COMMAREA/DFHCOMMAREA to the browsing process, and explain in detail how these have to be used to support a forward browse.
12. Summarize step-by-step the actions a program must take to begin a forward browse.
13. Summarize step-by-step the actions a program must take to continue a forward browse.
14. Summarize step-by-step the actions a program must take to begin a backward browse.
15. Summarize step-by-step the actions a program must take to continue a backward browse.
16. Describe how we arrange to have the pressing of a PF key cause the display of the first record in a file, so that browsing forward from that point can be done.
17. Describe what is contained in a field filled with LOW-VALUES, and what is contained in a field filled with HIGH-VALUES. If a field containing LOW-VALUES is moved to a field containing HIGH-VALUES, explain what is contained in the second field after the move.
18. Describe how we arrange to have the pressing of a PF key cause the display of the last record in a file, so that browsing backward from that point can be done.
19. Compare the effect of coding GTEQ in a STARTBR command to the effect of coding EQUAL in a STARTBR, clearly explaining which of these mutually exclusive options takes effect if you don't specify either one.
20. Describe what is meant by "duplicate alternate key" and "unique alternate key," and explain why duplicate alternate keys can interfere with an alternate key browse.
21. Explain in detail a method by which you can make any alternate key unique, which does *not* involve lengthening an indexed file record.
22. Suppose you follow the method you describe in your answer to question 22, to make an alternate key unique. Explain in detail why this change does not adversely affect the terminal operator's use of an alternate key browse.
23. Describe how a multi-record browse differs from a single-record browse, and identify at least three special programming concerns that you have to address if you program a multi-record browse screen.
24. Explain specifically why it's especially desirable to use a manually coded symbolic map if you are programming a multi-record browse screen.

15.20 HANDS-ON EXERCISES

Each of the exercises that follow is an extension of the exercise of the same letter at the end of Chapter 13. In each case, the exercise consists of installing an alternate key browse function in the program you developed in the prior exercise. (Note: In some cases you may have to revise your original record layout to form unique alternate keys, and modify your original VSAM Key Sequenced Data Set allocation and loading job stream.)

A. Using the logic pattern shown in the BROWSE4 program for alternate key browse, develop and include logic to support this function in the program you developed in Chapter 13, exercise A ("My First CICS Screen"). The alternate key is last name.

B. Using the logic pattern shown in the BROWSE4 program for alternate key browse, develop and include logic to support this function in the program you developed in Chapter 13, exercise B (Podunk University grade screen). The alternate key is student name.

C. Using the logic pattern shown in the BROWSE4 program for alternate key browse, develop and include logic to support this function in the program you developed in Chapter 13, exercise C (Podunk Book Store order entry). The alternate key is ISBN number.

D. Using the logic pattern shown in the BROWSE4 program for alternate key browse, develop and include logic to support this function in the program you developed in Chapter 13, exercise D (Podunk Power Company electricity billing). The alternate key is customer name.

E. Using the logic pattern shown in the BROWSE4 program for alternate key browse, develop and include logic to support this function in the program you developed in Chapter 13, exercise D (Podunk University course registrations). The alternate key is student name.

16

XCTL and LINK Commands and Menus

In Chapters 13, 14, and 15 you have seen examples of inquiry, add, change, delete, and browse programs that can serve as models for your own work with CICS. In earlier chapters, we accessed each of these functions directly by entering the transaction identifier of a program. In this chapter, we complete our suite of model CICS programs by showing you how a menu program can be arranged to simplify access to the various functions in an interactive application.

A menu program is a freestanding, separately developed and compiled CICS program. When a terminal operator activates the menu and selects a function using it, such as update, the menu program must transfer control to the update program. In this chapter, we'll show you how to use the XCTL command to transfer control from one program to another. We'll also demonstrate how a related, but now obsolescent command named LINK, can also be used to invoke one program from another.

After you complete reading and understanding this chapter, you will have developed sufficient mastery of CICS to actually use it to build a credible on-line application worthy of commercial use. CICS offers many capabilities beyond those you will have learned, but what you'll know will be more than sufficient to build workable interactive systems.

16.1 FUNCTIONS OF A MENU PROGRAM

A **menu program** presents a screen to a terminal operator, listing selections that can be made to accomplish various processing actions. Figure 16.1 shows you the appearance of the menu screen for Samuel's Worthless Finance Company. You can see that while this menu screen might ultimately provide access to ten different functions, only two are listed at the present time. This screen is sent to a terminal by our MENU3 program when the terminal operator enters the transaction identifier #003 ("#003" is a legitimate trans-id in our installation, and is associated with the program name C360B003).

The terminal operator selects a function from the menu screen in Figure 16.1 by entering the two-letter code for the function at the only enterable field on the menu screen. At the present time, you see "bb" in this field, indicating selection of the "Browse Borrower file" function. If the terminal operator enters a selection code that is not valid, the menu program responds with an error message indicating this fact, as shown in Figure 16.2.

A menu program might, in addition to providing convenient access to the functions supported by an interactive application, provide some security as well. We could include logic to

```
10/25/94      SAMUEL'S WORTHLESS FINANCE COMPANY ON-LINE SYSTEM          GENMENU
 5:08PM                                                                  #003M
                                                                         #003

                                  M E N U

                  Select from list, enter code ===>  bb


              UB  Update Borrower file by account number
              BB  Browse Borrower file by name
              --  (Reserved for future use)
              --  (Reserved for future use)
              --  (Reserved for future use)
              --  (Reserved for future use)
              --  (Reserved for future use)
              --  (Reserved for future use)
              --  (Reserved for future use)
              --  (Reserved for future use)

TYPE THE CODE FOR A CHOICE AND PRESS <ENTER>
```

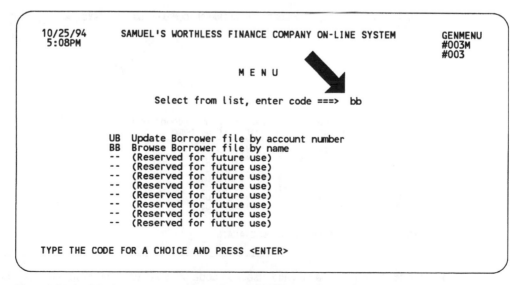

Figure 16.1 Menu screen presented by the MENU3 menu program.

request that the terminal operator enter some form of **operator identifier** and associated **password** before being allowed to access specific functions. We might also code the menu program so that it informed the terminal operator selectively about functions. For example, based on the operator's identity or the terminal identifier, the menu program could list only the functions that could be accessed, not all of the functions available in the interactive application. The menu program we demonstrate does not provide these enhanced capabilities, but it readily supports them, since the screen that it presents is dynamic and not fixed in content.

16.2 A GENERIC MENU SCREEN AND MENU LABELING

The menu screen you see in Figures 16.1 and 16.2 presents functional selections appropriate to our demonstration CICS system. But it's important for you to understand that as a model, this screen is not limited to our demonstration programs. Figure 16.3 shows you our design for the menu screen. As you can see, nearly everything on the screen is an input/output field. Each of the menu selection codes, and each of the menu selection labels, is simply a field into which the menu program puts text. In addition, the screen title at the top, the date and time at the upper left corner, and the program trans-id field at the upper right are all fields supplied by the menu program, as is the prompt line at the bottom. The menu screen is, in fact, generic and is suitable for most applications.

We could have "hard coded" a menu screen for the MENU3 program, as it might have been your first thought to do. We chose to develop a **generic menu** screen, mainly because it saves time in the long run, and makes it possible to insure a degree of consistency of appearance and operation across multiple applications. In addition, we can readily expand the number of functions accessible by the menu simply by changing the program that drives it. We'll show you how this process works in our example menu program, MENU3.

We named this menu screen GENMENU (as you can see labeled in the upper right corner). GENMENU is the actual map name for our code for this screen, shown in the BMS

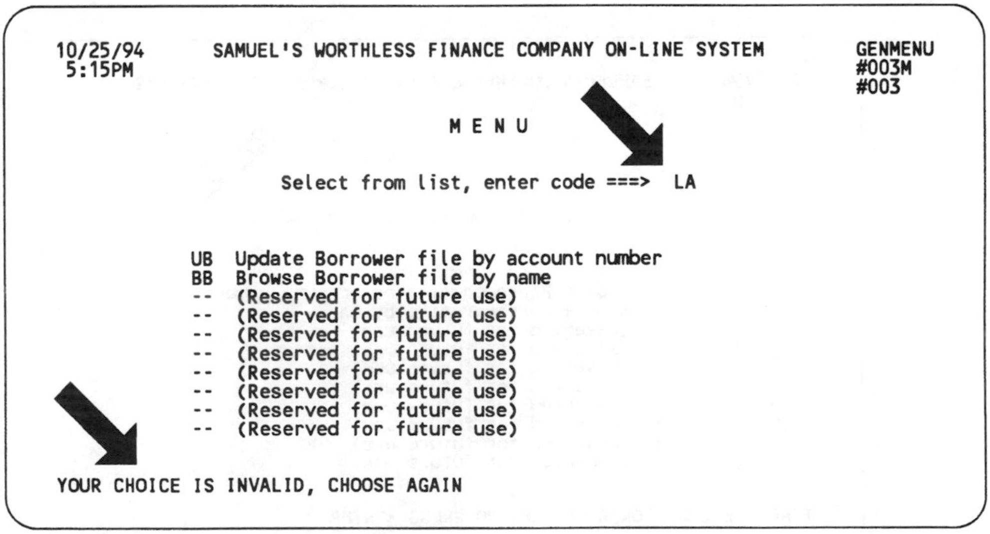

10/25/94
5:15PM
SAMUEL'S WORTHLESS FINANCE COMPANY ON-LINE SYSTEM
GENMENU
#003M
#003
M E N U
Select from list, enter code ===> LA
UB Update Borrower file by account number
BB Browse Borrower file by name
-- (Reserved for future use)
-- (Reserved for future use)
-- (Reserved for future use)
-- (Reserved for future use)
-- (Reserved for future use)
-- (Reserved for future use)
-- (Reserved for future use)
-- (Reserved for future use)
YOUR CHOICE IS INVALID, CHOOSE AGAIN

Figure 16.2 Entering an invalid selection code causes our menu program to produce this error message.

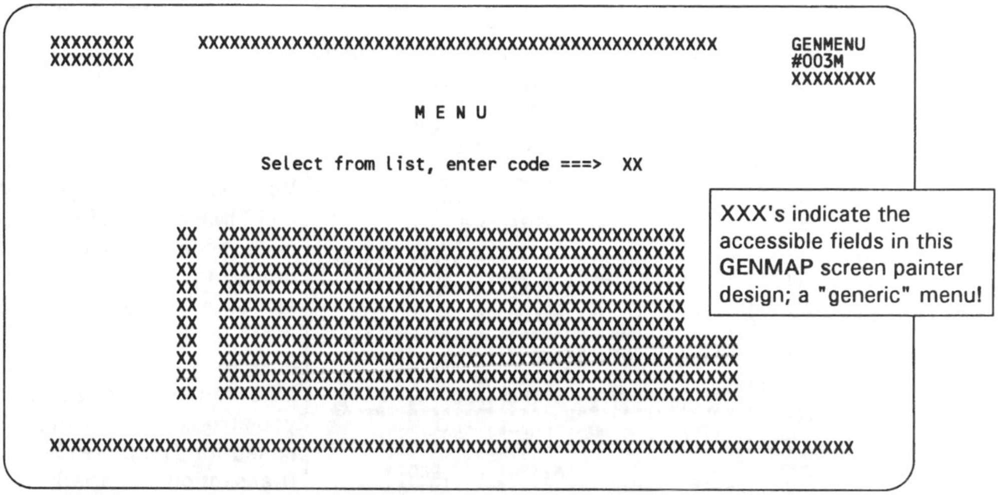
GENMENU
#003M
M E N U
Select from list, enter code ===> XX
XXX's indicate the accessible fields in this GENMAP screen painter design; a "generic" menu!

Figure 16.3 Design for the generic menu screen presented by the MENU3 program. The program supplies menu selection codes, selection labels, date, and time (prepared with the GENMAP screen painter).

map code in Figure 16.4. We stored this as mapset #003M. The third field at the upper right of the screen is the trans-id of the program, which is supplied by the menu program itself.

16.3 MENU3 PROGRAM SOURCE CODE: WORKING-STORAGE

Figure 16.5 provides the complete source code for the MENU3 program. We'll discuss this code in detail, using the same annotation technique we used in earlier chapters. Our discussion refers to the circled letters you see in Figure 16.5.

As you can see by examining Figure 16.5 at letter "a", we follow here the same pattern of WORKING-STORAGE coding we use in our other programs, beginning with data names for the trans-id, mapset name, and map name. We also provide a field named WS-PGM-FOR-XCTL, which we'll refer to as we discuss the functioning of the menu program.

You can readily see at letter "b" in Figure 16.5 that we store the menu selection text in a table. Each table row is 60 bytes in length, and contains a two-byte **selection code**, 50-byte **selection label**, and 8-byte program name. Only the selection code and selection label are placed into the menu screen; the program name is the name of the program that supports the function. By storing these values in one place, we make it especially easy to coordinate this information. This technique also allows us to add functionality to the application by simply changing the contents of this table. No other part of the menu program source code or map needs to be changed as we build and add more functions to the system.

Lines 7400 through 7900 of Figure 16.5, at letter "c", show you how the menu table setup is REDEFINEd so that we can access the menu selection codes, selection text, and program names by subscript or index. The field named "X" declared at line 8200, letter "d", will serve as a subscript, while M-IX is the name we declare for the index to the table. This is standard table-handling programming.

The remainder of WORKING-STORAGE is typical of the CICS programs you have already seen in previous chapters, except for the item we have named WS-DATE-TIME-

```
EDIT ---- CSCJGJ.CSC360.CNTL(GENMENU) - 01.00 ---------------- COLUMNS 001 072
COMMAND ===>                                                  SCROLL ===> PAGE
****** ***************************** TOP OF DATA ******************************
                PRINT NOGEN
MENU     DFHMSD TYPE=&SYSPARM,                                                X
               LANG=COBOL,                                                    X
               MODE=INOUT,                                                    X
               TERM=3270-2,                                                   X
               CTRL=FREEKB,                                                   X
               STORAGE=AUTO,                                                  X
               TIOAPFX=YES
***********************************
MENUMAP  DFHMDI SIZE=(24,80),                                                 X
               LINE=1,                                                        X
               COLUMN=1
***********************************
DATE     DFHMDF POS=(1,1),                                                    X
               LENGTH=8,                                                      X
               ATTRB=(PROT)
***********************************
TITLE    DFHMDF POS=(1,15),                                                   X
               LENGTH=50,                                                     X
               ATTRB=(BRT,PROT)
***********************************
         DFHMDF POS=(1,72),                                                   X
               LENGTH=7,                                                      X
               ATTRB=(PROT),                                                  X
               INITIAL='GENMENU'
TIME     DFHMDF POS=(2,1),                                                    X
               LENGTH=8,                                                      X
               ATTRB=(PROT)
***********************************
         DFHMDF POS=(2,72),                                                   X
               LENGTH=5,                                                      X
               ATTRB=(PROT),                                                  X
               INITIAL='#003M'
TRID     DFHMDF POS=(3,72),                                                   X
               LENGTH=8,                                                      X
               ATTRB=(PROT)
***********************************
         DFHMDF POS=(5,36),                                                   X
               LENGTH=7,                                                      X
               ATTRB=(BRT,PROT),                                              X
               INITIAL='M E N U'
         DFHMDF POS=(8,21),                                                   X
               LENGTH=33,                                                     X
               ATTRB=(BRT,PROT),                                              X
               INITIAL='Select from list, enter code ===>'
CHOICE   DFHMDF POS=(8,56),                                                   X
               LENGTH=2,                                                      X
               ATTRB=(UNPROT)
         DFHMDF POS=(8,59),                                                   X
               LENGTH=1,                                                      X
               ATTRB=ASKIP
***********************************************************************
S1CODE   DFHMDF POS=(12,13),                                                  X
               LENGTH=2,                                                      X
               ATTRB=(PROT)
***********************************************************************
S1TEXT   DFHMDF POS=(12,17),                                                  X
               LENGTH=50,                                                     X
               ATTRB=(PROT)
***********************************************************************
S2CODE   DFHMDF POS=(13,13),                                                  X
               LENGTH=2,                                                      X
               ATTRB=(PROT)
***********************************************************************
S2TEXT   DFHMDF POS=(13,17),                                                  X
               LENGTH=50,                                                     X
               ATTRB=(PROT)
***********************************************************************
```

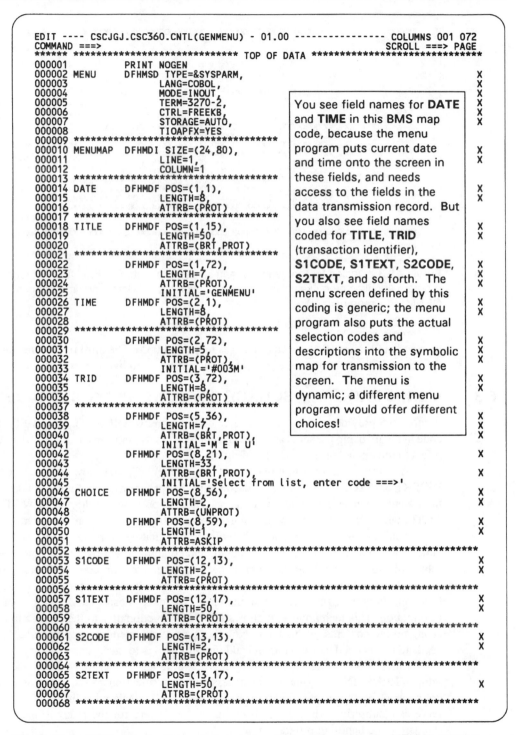

You see field names for **DATE** and **TIME** in this **BMS** map code, because the menu program puts current date and time onto the screen in these fields, and needs access to the fields in the data transmission record. But you also see field names coded for **TITLE**, **TRID** (transaction identifier), **S1CODE**, **S1TEXT**, **S2CODE**, **S2TEXT**, and so forth. The menu screen defined by this coding is generic; the menu program also puts the actual selection codes and descriptions into the symbolic map for transmission to the screen. The menu is dynamic; a different menu program would offer different choices!

Figure 16.4 BMS code for the generic menu screen presented by the MENU3 program.

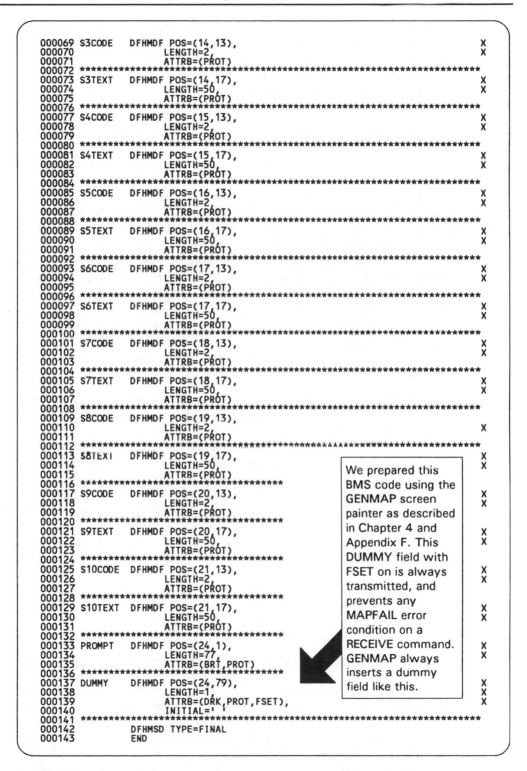

```
S3CODE   DFHMDF POS=(14,13),                                          X
               LENGTH=2,                                              X
               ATTRB=(PROT)
***********************************************************************
S3TEXT   DFHMDF POS=(14,17),                                          X
               LENGTH=50,                                             X
               ATTRB=(PROT)
***********************************************************************
S4CODE   DFHMDF POS=(15,13),                                          X
               LENGTH=2,                                              X
               ATTRB=(PROT)
***********************************************************************
S4TEXT   DFHMDF POS=(15,17),                                          X
               LENGTH=50,                                             X
               ATTRB=(PROT)
***********************************************************************
S5CODE   DFHMDF POS=(16,13),                                          X
               LENGTH=2,                                              X
               ATTRB=(PROT)
***********************************************************************
S5TEXT   DFHMDF POS=(16,17),                                          X
               LENGTH=50,                                             X
               ATTRB=(PROT)
***********************************************************************
S6CODE   DFHMDF POS=(17,13),                                          X
               LENGTH=2,                                              X
               ATTRB=(PROT)
***********************************************************************
S6TEXT   DFHMDF POS=(17,17),                                          X
               LENGTH=50,                                             X
               ATTRB=(PROT)
***********************************************************************
S7CODE   DFHMDF POS=(18,13),                                          X
               LENGTH=2,                                              X
               ATTRB=(PROT)
***********************************************************************
S7TEXT   DFHMDF POS=(18,17),                                          X
               LENGTH=50,                                             X
               ATTRB=(PROT)
***********************************************************************
S8CODE   DFHMDF POS=(19,13),
               LENGTH=2,                                              X
               ATTRB=(PROT)
***********************************************************************
S8TEXT   DFHMDF POS=(19,17),                                          X
               LENGTH=50,                                             X
               ATTRB=(PROT)
************************************
S9CODE   DFHMDF POS=(20,13),                                          X
               LENGTH=2,                                              X
               ATTRB=(PROT)
************************************
S9TEXT   DFHMDF POS=(20,17),                                          X
               LENGTH=50,                                             X
               ATTRB=(PROT)
************************************
S10CODE  DFHMDF POS=(21,13),                                          X
               LENGTH=2,                                              X
               ATTRB=(PROT)
************************************
S10TEXT  DFHMDF POS=(21,17),                                          X
               LENGTH=50,                                             X
               ATTRB=(PROT)
************************************
PROMPT   DFHMDF POS=(24,1),                                           X
               LENGTH=77,                                             X
               ATTRB=(BRT,PROT)
************************************
DUMMY    DFHMDF POS=(24,79),                                          X
               LENGTH=1,                                              X
               ATTRB=(DRK,PROT,FSET),                                 X
               INITIAL=' '
***********************************************************************
         DFHMSD TYPE=FINAL
         END
```

We prepared this BMS code using the GENMAP screen painter as described in Chapter 4 and Appendix F. This DUMMY field with FSET on is always transmitted, and prevents any MAPFAIL error condition on a RECEIVE command. GENMAP always inserts a dummy field like this.

Figure 16.4 *(Continued)*

AREA at letter "e". We'll use this area to receive the formatted current date and time from a module that we will LINK to as a part of processing, at lines 28800 through 29900, letter "o". The elementary items at letter "e" are not strictly required, since we'll access the date and time using the names DCA-DATE and DCA-TIME. We coded the elementary descriptions primarily to document the format of these fields.

16.4 MENU3 PROGRAM SOURCE CODE: SYMBOLIC MAP

Figure 16.6 shows you the symbolic map matching the GENMENU screen. From our earlier chapters, you know that the symbolic map describes the data transmission record that our BMS map code causes to be constructed as the interface between the terminal and a program driving the screen. We stored this description as member MENU3TAB, and it is copied into the WORKING-STORAGE of the MENU3 program at line 10500 in the source code shown, letter "f", in Figure 16.5.

We chose to use a **manually coded symbolic map** here because it lets us use an **OCCURS clause** to handle the 10 menu selection lines, as you can see at line 24 in Figure 16.6. There is nothing mysterious about this coding; it is simply a handier description of the menu screen data transmission record than the machine-generated symbolic map shown in Figure 16.7.

Some installations favor the use of the machine-generated symbolic map for screen communication, because it always matches the BMS map code. There are three reasons why we suggest that such a policy be tempered and an exception made (and a manually coded symbolic map be used) for a program such as MENU3:

- Using an OCCURS clause in the symbolic map makes it much easier and more reliable to code a menu program, and makes the program more flexible in accommodating added selections.
- The menu screen is generic and will not be subject to change as we add menu selections; there is little potential for the symbolic map to mismatch the screen due to program maintenance or enhancement.
- The manually coded symbolic map is, in this case, dramatically shorter and more concise. If you compare it to the machine-generated symbolic map in Figure 16.6, you'll see that the first 137 lines of the machine-generated symbolic map, dealing with input fields, is entirely useless, since the menu selection codes and labels are used for output only!

Even if you normally use machine-generated symbolic maps, consider using a manually coded symbolic map in any case where having the OCCURS clause in the symbolic map makes a difference, as in dynamic menus and multi-record browse screens.

16.5 MENU3 PROGRAM SOURCE CODE: PROCEDURE DIVISION

The Procedure Division for our MENU3 program begins at line 11500 in Figure 16.5. In order to help you see how the logic of the menu program works, we have mapped the operation of the Procedure Division in the visual table of contents in Figure 16.8. The shaded areas of Figure 16.8 depict the second or subsequent executions of the menu program, in which the terminal operator has made a valid selection from the menu and control is being transferred to another program with XCTL.

```
EDIT ---- CSCJGJ.CSC360.COBOL(MENU3) - 01.11 ---------------- COLUMNS 007 078
COMMAND ===>                                                 SCROLL ===> PAGE
****** ***************************** TOP OF DATA ******************************
       ID DIVISION.
       PROGRAM-ID.  MENU3.
      *============================================================
      *  THIS PROGRAM IS INVOKED BY THE #003 TRANSACTION.  IT
      *  DISPLAYS A MENU FOR SAMUEL'S WORTHLESS FINANCE COMPANY.
      *  SHOWS HOW TO SUPPLY MENU SELECTIONS VIA THE MENU PROGRAM
      *  RATHER THAN HARDCODED IN SCREEN MAP.  DEMONSTRATES HOW TO
      *  USE A "GENERIC" MENU SCREEN THAT SERVES FOR MOST MENU
      *  APPLICATIONS; PROGRAM CONTROLS WHAT IS SHOWN ON THE MENU.
      *  ALSO DEMONSTRATES THE CICS LINK COMMAND TO ACCESS ANOTHER
      *  PROGRAM (CSCJJJ8) TO FORMAT DATE AND TIME.
      *
      *  COPYRIGHT 1994 JIM JANOSSY AND STEVE SAMUELS
      *============================================================
       DATA DIVISION.
       WORKING-STORAGE SECTION.
       01  WS-TRANS-ID              PIC X(4)  VALUE '#003'.
       01  WS-MAPSET-NAME           PIC X(8)  VALUE '#003M   '.
       01  WS-MAP-NAME              PIC X(8)  VALUE 'MENUMAP '.
       01  WS-PGM-FOR-XCTL          PIC X(8).
      *------------------------------------------------------------
      *  CODE 10 MENU SELECTIONS HERE PROVIDING SELECTION CODE, TEXT
      *  THAT WILL APPEAR ON THE MENU, AND NAME OF PROGRAM THAT
      *  HANDLES THE FUNCTION.  YOU DON'T NEED TO CHANGE ANY OTHER
      *  PROGRAM CODE TO ADD OR CHANGE FUNCTIONAL PROGRAMS.
      *------------------------------------------------------------
       01  MENU-TABLE-SETUP.
           05 PIC X(2)  VALUE 'UB'.
           05 PIC X(50) VALUE 'Update Borrower file by account number'.
           05 PIC X(8)  VALUE 'C360B001'.
           05 PIC X(2)  VALUE 'BB'.
           05 PIC X(50) VALUE 'Browse Borrower file by name'.
           05 PIC X(8)  VALUE 'C360B002'.
           05 PIC X(2)  VALUE '--'.
           05 PIC X(50) VALUE '(Reserved for future use)'.
           05 PIC X(8)  VALUE 'XXXXXXXX'.
           05 PIC X(2)  VALUE '--'.
           05 PIC X(50) VALUE '(Reserved for future use)'.
           05 PIC X(8)  VALUE 'XXXXXXXX'.
           05 PIC X(2)  VALUE '--'.
           05 PIC X(50) VALUE '(Reserved for future use)'.
           05 PIC X(8)  VALUE 'XXXXXXXX'.
           05 PIC X(2)  VALUE '--'.
           05 PIC X(50) VALUE '(Reserved for future use)'.
           05 PIC X(8)  VALUE 'XXXXXXXX'.
           05 PIC X(2)  VALUE '--'.
           05 PIC X(50) VALUE '(Reserved for future use)'.
           05 PIC X(8)  VALUE 'XXXXXXXX'.
           05 PIC X(2)  VALUE '--'.
           05 PIC X(50) VALUE '(Reserved for future use)'.
           05 PIC X(8)  VALUE 'XXXXXXXX'.
           05 PIC X(2)  VALUE '--'.
           05 PIC X(50) VALUE '(Reserved for future use)'.
           05 PIC X(8)  VALUE 'XXXXXXXX'.
           05 PIC X(2)  VALUE '--'.
           05 PIC X(50) VALUE '(Reserved for future use)'.
           05 PIC X(8)  VALUE 'XXXXXXXX'.
```

A

B

Refer to the discussion of program coding that begins in Section 16.3 to learn the highlights associated with each letter.

Figure 16.5 Source code for the MENU3 program.

```
 01  MENU-TABLE  REDEFINES  MENU-TABLE-SETUP.
     05 MENU-TABLE-ROW  OCCURS 10 TIMES
                        INDEXED BY M-IX.
        10 MENU-CODE       PIC X(2).
        10 MENU-TEXT       PIC X(50).
        10 MENU-PGM        PIC X(8).

*-------------------------------------
 01  X                        PIC S9(4) BINARY.

 01  WS-FIRST-TIME-FLAG       PIC S9(4) BINARY.
     88 FIRST-TIME                      VALUE 0.

 01  WS-RESPONSE-CODE         PIC S9(8) BINARY.
 01  WS-COMMUNICATION-AREA    PIC X(1).
 01  WS-END-MESSAGE           PIC X(60) VALUE
     'QUITTING AS REQUESTED -- USE  CESF LOGOFF  TO END CICS'.

 01  WS-DATE-TIME-AREA.
     05 DCA-DATE.
        10 DCA-DATE-MO        PIC 99.
        10 DCA-SLASH-1        PIC X(1).
        10 DCA-DATE-DA        PIC 99.
        10 DCA-SLASH-2        PIC X(1).
        10 DCA-DATE-YR        PIC 99.
     05 DCA-TIME.
        10 DCA-TIME-HRS       PIC Z9.
        10 DCA-COLON          PIC X(1).
        10 DCA-TIME-MIN       PIC 99.
        10 DCA-TIME-AM-PM     PIC X(2).

     COPY MENU3TAB.

     COPY ABRTMSGS.

 01  EIBAID-TEST-FIELD        PIC X(1).
     COPY KEYDEFS.

 LINKAGE SECTION.
 01  DFHCOMMAREA              PIC X(1).

*================================================================
 PROCEDURE DIVISION.
*================================================================
 000-MAINLINE.

     PERFORM 633-ALWAYS-TEST.

     EVALUATE TRUE

       WHEN FIRST-TIME
          PERFORM 800-BUILD-AND-SEND-MENU

       WHEN ENTER-KEY
          PERFORM 100-HANDLE-CHOICE

       WHEN OTHER
          MOVE LOW-VALUES TO MENU-SYMBOLIC-MAP
          MOVE -1 TO MSM-CHOICE-L
          MOVE 'INVALID KEY PRESSED, USE <ENTER> KEY ONLY'
             TO MSM-PROMPT-D
          PERFORM 700-SEND-MENU-SCREEN

     END-EVALUATE.

     EXEC CICS
        RETURN  TRANSID   (WS-TRANS-ID)
                COMMAREA  (WS-COMMUNICATION-AREA)
     END-EXEC.

```

Figure 16.5 *(Continued)*

```
      *-----------------------------------------------------------------
      *  RECEIVE MAP
      *-----------------------------------------------------------------
       100-HANDLE-CHOICE.

           EXEC CICS
              RECEIVE   MAP      (WS-MAP-NAME)
                        MAPSET   (WS-MAPSET-NAME)
                        INTO     (MENU-SYMBOLIC-MAP)
                        RESP     (WS-RESPONSE-CODE)
           END-EXEC.

           EVALUATE WS-RESPONSE-CODE

             WHEN DFHRESP(NORMAL)
                PERFORM 150-ANALYZE

             WHEN DFHRESP(MAPFAIL)
                MOVE LOW-VALUES TO MENU-SYMBOLIC-MAP
                MOVE -1 TO MSM-CHOICE-L
                MOVE 'MAKE A CHOICE BEFORE PRESSING <ENTER>'
                   TO MSM-PROMPT-D
                PERFORM 700-SEND-MENU-SCREEN

             WHEN OTHER
                MOVE 'FAILED IN P100/RECEIVE MAP' TO WS-ERROR-LINE5
                PERFORM 999-ABORT

           END-EVALUATE.

      *-----------------------------------------------------------------
      *  ANALYZE SELECTION CODE
      *-----------------------------------------------------------------
       150-ANALYZE.

           SET M-IX TO 1.
           SEARCH MENU-TABLE-ROW

             AT END
                MOVE 'YOUR CHOICE IS INVALID, CHOOSE AGAIN'
                   TO MSM-PROMPT-D
                MOVE -1 TO MSM-CHOICE-L
                PERFORM 700-SEND-MENU-SCREEN

             WHEN MENU-CODE(M-IX) = MSM-CHOICE-D
                MOVE MENU-PGM(M-IX) TO WS-PGM-FOR-XCTL
                PERFORM 200-TRANSFER-CONTROL.

      *-----------------------------------------------------------------
      *  DO XCTL TO APPROPRIATE FUNCTIONAL PROGRAM
      *-----------------------------------------------------------------
       200-TRANSFER-CONTROL.

           EXEC CICS
               XCTL   PROGRAM    (WS-PGM-FOR-XCTL)
                      RESP       (WS-RESPONSE-CODE)
           END-EXEC.
      *
      *  NOTE: NO NEED TO TEST FOR DFHRESP(NORMAL) HERE BECAUSE IF
      *  DFHRESP IS NORMAL, WE ARE OUT OF HERE!  SUCCESSFUL XCTL
      *  MEANS CONTROL HAS BEEN TRANSFERRED TO ANOTHER PROGRAM.
      *
           EVALUATE WS-RESPONSE-CODE

             WHEN  DFHRESP(PGMIDERR)
                MOVE LOW-VALUES TO MENU-SYMBOLIC-MAP
                MOVE -1 TO MSM-CHOICE-L
                MOVE 'FUNCTION NOT AVAILABLE, NO PROGRAM FOR IT'
                   TO MSM-PROMPT-D
                PERFORM 700-SEND-MENU-SCREEN

             WHEN OTHER
                MOVE 'FAILED IN P200/XCTL' TO WS-ERROR-LINE5
                PERFORM 999-ABORT

           END-EVALUATE.
```

Figure 16.5 *(Continued)*

```
*---------------------------------------------------------------------
*  ALWAYS THE FIRST ROUTINE PERFORMED IN MAINLINE
*---------------------------------------------------------------------
 633-ALWAYS-TEST.
     MOVE EIBAID    TO  EIBAID-TEST-FIELD.
     MOVE EIBCALEN  TO  WS-FIRST-TIME-FLAG.

     IF CLEAR-KEY AND NOT FIRST-TIME
        PERFORM 900-SEND-TERMINATION-MESSAGE
        EXEC CICS   RETURN   END-EXEC.

*---------------------------------------------------------------------
*  SEND THE MENU SCREEN FOR ERROR PROMPTS ONLY
*---------------------------------------------------------------------
 700-SEND-MENU-SCREEN.

     PERFORM 875-GET-DATE-TIME.

     EXEC CICS
         SEND    MAP         (WS-MAP-NAME)
                 MAPSET      (WS-MAPSET-NAME)
                 FROM        (MENU-SYMBOLIC-MAP)
                 DATAONLY
                 CURSOR
     END-EXEC.

*---------------------------------------------------------------------
*  SEND MENU SCREEN FIRST TIME OR AFTER XCTL IN FROM A PROGRAM
*---------------------------------------------------------------------
 800-BUILD-AND-SEND-MENU.

     PERFORM 850-PREPARE-MENU-SCREEN.

     EXEC CICS
         SEND  MAP         (WS-MAP-NAME)
               MAPSET      (WS-MAPSET-NAME)
               FROM        (MENU-SYMBOLIC-MAP)
               ERASE
               CURSOR
     END-EXEC.

*---------------------------------------------------------------------
*  PUT MENU SELECTION CODES AND TEXT INTO THE SYMBOLIC MAP
*---------------------------------------------------------------------
 850-PREPARE-MENU-SCREEN.

     MOVE LOW-VALUES TO MENU-SYMBOLIC-MAP.
     MOVE -1 TO MSM-CHOICE-L.
     PERFORM 875-GET-DATE-TIME.
     MOVE 'SAMUEL''S WORTHLESS FINANCE COMPANY ON-LINE SYSTEM '
        TO MSM-SCREEN-TITLE-d
     MOVE WS-TRANS-ID TO MSM-TRANS-ID-D.

     PERFORM
        VARYING X FROM +1 BY +1
           UNTIL X > +10
               MOVE MENU-CODE(X) TO MSM-SELECTION-CODE-D(X)
               MOVE MENU-TEXT(X) TO MSM-SELECTION-TEXT-D(X)
     END-PERFORM.

     MOVE 'TYPE THE CODE FOR A CHOICE AND PRESS <ENTER>'
        TO MSM-PROMPT-D.

*---------------------------------------------------------------------
*  GET THE DATE AND TIME USING CICS LINK COMMAND
*---------------------------------------------------------------------
 875-GET-DATE-TIME.

     EXEC CICS
         LINK  PROGRAM   ('CSCJJJ8')
               COMMAREA  (WS-DATE-TIME-AREA)
     END-EXEC.

     MOVE DCA-DATE TO MSM-DATE-D.
     MOVE DCA-TIME TO MSM-TIME-D.
```

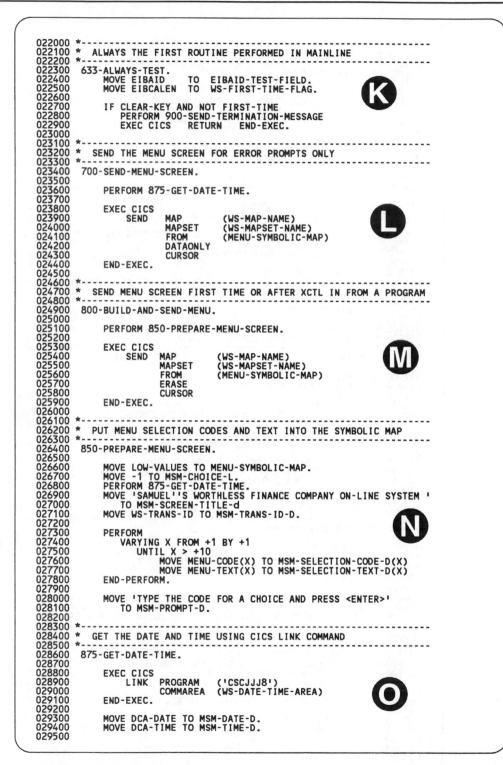

Figure 16.5 *(Continued)*

```
029600 *-----------------------------------------------------------------
029700 *  LAST SCREEN SENT WHEN PROGRAM ENDS NORMALLY
029800 *-----------------------------------------------------------------
029900  900-SEND-TERMINATION-MESSAGE.
030000
030100      EXEC CICS
030200         SEND     TEXT
030300                  FROM  (WS-END-MESSAGE)
030400                  ERASE
030500                  FREEKB
030600      END-EXEC.
030700
030800 *-----------------------------------------------------------------
030900 *  PERFORMED IN CASE OF CICS COMMAND FAILURE ONLY
031000 *-----------------------------------------------------------------
031100  999-ABORT.
031200
031300      MOVE EIBTRNID   TO  WS-EIBTRNID.
031400      MOVE EIBRSRCE   TO  WS-EIBRSRCE.
031500      MOVE EIBRESP    TO  WS-EIBRESP.
031600      MOVE EIBRESP2   TO  WS-EIBRESP2.
031700
031800      EXEC CICS
031900         SEND TEXT FROM (WS-ERROR-MESSAGES)
032000              ERASE
032100              ALARM
032200              FREEKB
032300      END-EXEC.
032400
032500      EXEC CICS   RETURN   END-EXEC.
```

Figure 16.5 *(Continued)*

The structured mainline of the MENU program, at letter "g", directs control to one of two "normal" courses of action, or to an error-handling routine for invalid PF key usage. All three courses of action result in the pseudoconversational RETURN of control to CICS at lines 13900 through 14200. You have seen this coding structure in all of our other programs; it's a consistently useful pattern.

Here are the three processing routes into which the mainline channels control:

- The FIRST-TIME "WHEN" clause in the MENU3 mainline at line 12400 is triggered by receipt of an EIBCALEN value of 0, as arranged for by the 633-ALWAYS-TEST paragraph, which also checks for receipt of a Clear key. As in other programs, FIRST-TIME causes the menu program to clear the terminal screen and send a map to "equip" the terminal screen for business.
- The ENTER-KEY "WHEN" clause invokes the main processing sequence of the menu program. We'll follow processing through a menu selection below.
- The OTHER "WHEN" clause simply sets up the prompt informing the terminal operator that he or she pressed an invalid AID key. Only Enter or Clear are regarded as valid AID keys by the menu program. You could expand this range of valid AID keys to include a general key map or help screens for the interactive application, as we showed in Chapter 11.

We'll discuss FIRST-TIME and ENTER-KEY processing in detail in the sections that follow.

```
EDIT ---- CSCJGJ.CSC360.COPYLIB(MENU3TAB) - 01.00 ----------- COLUMNS 001 072
COMMAND ===>                                                   SCROLL ===> PAGE
****** ***************************** TOP OF DATA ******************************
                  01  MENU-SYMBOLIC-MAP.
                      05  FILLER                                PIC X(12).
                *=================================================================
                      05  MSM-DATE-L                            PIC S9(4)    COMP.
                      05  MSM-DATE-A                            PIC X.
                      05  MSM-DATE-D                            PIC X(8).
                *-----------------------------------------------------------------
                      05  MSM-SCREEN-TITLE-L                    PIC S9(4)    COMP.
                      05  MSM-SCREEN-TITLE-A                    PIC X.
                      05  MSM-SCREEN-TITLE-D                    PIC X(50).
                *-----------------------------------------------------------------
                      05  MSM-TIME-L                            PIC S9(4)    COMP.
                      05  MSM-TIME-A                            PIC X.
                      05  MSM-TIME-D                            PIC X(8).
                *-----------------------------------------------------------------
                      05  MSM-TRANS-ID-L                        PIC S9(4)    COMP.
                      05  MSM-TRANS-ID-A                        PIC X.
                      05  MSM-TRANS-ID-D                        PIC X(8).
                *-----------------------------------------------------------------
                      05  MSM-CHOICE-L                          PIC S9(4)    COMP.
                      05  MSM-CHOICE-A                          PIC X.
                      05  MSM-CHOICE-D                          PIC X(2).
                *-----------------------------------------------------------------
                      05  MENU-SELECTION-GROUP   OCCURS 10 TIMES.
                          10  MSM-SELECTION-CODE-L              PIC S9(4)    COMP.
                          10  MSM-SELECTION-CODE-A              PIC X.
                          10  MSM-SELECTION-CODE-D              PIC X(2).

                          10  MSM-SELECTION-TEXT-L              PIC S9(4)    COMP.
                          10  MSM-SELECTION-TEXT-A              PIC X.
                          10  MSM-SELECTION-TEXT-D              PIC X(50).
                *-----------------------------------------------------------------
                      05  MSM-PROMPT-L                          PIC S9(4)    COMP.
                      05  MSM-PROMPT-A                          PIC X.
                      05  MSM-PROMPT-D                          PIC X(77).
                *-----------------------------------------------------------------
                      05  DUMMY-L                               PIC S9(4)    COMP.
                      05  DUMMY-A                               PIC X.
                      05  DUMMY-D                               PIC X.
```

Very handy coding!

Figure 16.6 Manually coded symbolic map for the GENMENU screen used by the MENU3 program.

16.6 FIRST-TIME PROCESSING IN THE MENU PROGRAM

The FIRST-TIME test is made possible by execution of the 633-ALWAYS-TEST paragraph, at lines 22000 through 22900, letter "k". 633-ALWAYS-TEST is a little different in the menu than in other programs, as we discuss in Section 16.13, because a menu program often receives control back from a menu selection due to Clear key usage. But its main function is as in other programs: It makes tests and data field arrangements vital to the EVALUATE in the mainline.

FIRST-TIME processing invokes the 800-BUILD-AND-SEND-MENU paragraph at lines 24600 through 25900, at letter "m" in Figure 16.5. This involves the execution of the 850-PREPARE-MENU-SCREEN paragraph, at letter "n", which demonstrates some of the power of housing menu selection codes and descriptive labels in MENU-TABLE. Notice that the inline PERFORM . . . VARYING at lines 27300 through 27800 accesses the rows in MENU-TABLE by subscript, and also accesses the selection code and text fields in the symbolic map by subscript. This loop "loads" the symbolic map for our "generic" menu with the specific

```
EDIT ---- CSCJGJ.CSC360.COPYLIB(B003S) - 01.00 --------------- COLUMNS 001 072
COMMAND ===>                                                   SCROLL ===> PAGE
****** ***************************** TOP OF DATA ******************************
000001        01  MENUMAPI.
000002            02  FILLER PIC X(12).
000003            02  DATEL     COMP  PIC  S9(4).
000004            02  DATEF     PICTURE X.
000005            02  FILLER REDEFINES DATEF.
000006              03 DATEA     PICTURE X.
000007            02  DATEI  PIC X(8).
000008            02  TITLEL     COMP  PIC  S9(4).
000009            02  TITLEF     PICTURE X.
000010            02  FILLER REDEFINES TITLEF.
000011              03 TITLEA     PICTURE X.
000012            02  TITLEI  PIC X(50).
000013            02  TIMEL     COMP  PIC  S9(4).
000014            02  TIMEF     PICTURE X.
000015            02  FILLER REDEFINES TIMEF.
000016              03 TIMEA     PICTURE X.
000017            02  TIMEI  PIC X(8).
000018            02  TRIDL     COMP  PIC  S9(4).
000019            02  TRIDF     PICTURE X.
000020            02  FILLER REDEFINES TRIDF.
000021              03 TRIDA     PICTURE X.
000022            02  TRIDI  PIC X(8).
000023            02  CHOICEL     COMP  PIC  S9(4).
000024            02  CHOICEF     PICTURE X.
000025            02  FILLER REDEFINES CHOICEF.
000026              03 CHOICEA     PICTURE X.
000027            02  CHOICEI  PIC X(2).
000028            02  S1CODEL     COMP  PIC  S9(4).
000029            02  S1CODEF     PICTURE X.
000030            02  FILLER REDEFINES S1CODEF.
000031              03 S1CODEA     PICTURE X.
000032            02  S1CODEI  PIC X(2).
000033            02  S1TEXTL     COMP  PIC  S9(4).
000034            02  S1TEXTF     PICTURE X.
000035            02  FILLER REDEFINES S1TEXTF.
000036              03 S1TEXTA     PICTURE X.
000037            02  S1TEXTI  PIC X(50).
000038            02  S2CODEL     COMP  PIC  S9(4).
000039            02  S2CODEF     PICTURE X.
000040            02  FILLER REDEFINES S2CODEF.
000041              03 S2CODEA     PICTURE X.
000042            02  S2CODEI  PIC X(2).
000043            02  S2TEXTL     COMP  PIC  S9(4).
000044            02  S2TEXTF     PICTURE X.
000045            02  FILLER REDEFINES S2TEXTF.
000046              03 S2TEXTA     PICTURE X.
000047            02  S2TEXTI  PIC X(50).
000048            02  S3CODEL     COMP  PIC  S9(4).
000049            02  S3CODEF     PICTURE X.
000050            02  FILLER REDEFINES S3CODEF.
000051              03 S3CODEA     PICTURE X.
000052            02  S3CODEI  PIC X(2).
000053            02  S3TEXTL     COMP  PIC  S9(4).
000054            02  S3TEXTF     PICTURE X.
000055            02  FILLER REDEFINES S3TEXTF.
000056              03 S3TEXTA     PICTURE X.
000057            02  S3TEXTI  PIC X(50).
   -
   -
   -
```

This machine-generated symbolic map is much less useful for the menu program than the compact, manually coded symbolic map shown in Figure 16.6, since it lacks an OCCURS clause for the menu selection codes and text. (We omit lines 58 through 117 from this figure because the coding is so repetitious.)

Figure 16.7 Machine-generated symbolic map for the GENMENU screen (not used in MENU3 program).

```
           02  S10CODEL     COMP  PIC  S9(4).
           02  S10CODEF     PICTURE X.
           02  FILLER REDEFINES S10CODEF.
             03 S10CODEA     PICTURE X.
           02  S10CODEI  PIC X(2).
           02  S10TEXTL     COMP  PIC  S9(4).
           02  S10TEXTF     PICTURE X.
           02  FILLER REDEFINES S10TEXTF.
             03 S10TEXTA     PICTURE X.
           02  S10TEXTI  PIC X(50).
           02  PROMPTL     COMP  PIC  S9(4).
           02  PROMPTF     PICTURE X.
           02  FILLER REDEFINES PROMPTF.
             03 PROMPTA     PICTURE X.
           02  PROMPTI  PIC X(77).
           02  DUMMYL    COMP  PIC  S9(4).
           02  DUMMYF    PICTURE X.
           02  FILLER REDEFINES DUMMYF.
             03 DUMMYA    PICTURE X.
           02  DUMMYI  PIC X(1).
       01  MENUMAPO REDEFINES MENUMAPI.
           02  FILLER PIC X(12).
           02  FILLER PICTURE X(3).
           02  DATEO  PIC X(8).
           02  FILLER PICTURE X(3).
           02  TITLEO  PIC X(50).
           02  FILLER PICTURE X(3).
           02  TIMEO  PIC X(8).
           02  FILLER PICTURE X(3).
           02  TRIDO  PIC X(8).
           02  FILLER PICTURE X(3).
           02  CHOICEO  PIC X(2).
           02  FILLER PICTURE X(3).
           02  S1CODEO  PIC X(2).
           02  FILLER PICTURE X(3).
           02  S1TEXTO  PIC X(50).
           02  FILLER PICTURE X(3).
           02  S2CODEO  PIC X(2).
           02  FILLER PICTURE X(3).
           02  S2TEXTO  PIC X(50).
           02  FILLER PICTURE X(3).
           02  S3CODEO  PIC X(2).
           02  FILLER PICTURE X(3).
           02  S3TEXTO  PIC X(50).
           02  FILLER PICTURE X(3).
           02  S4CODEO  PIC X(2).
           02  FILLER PICTURE X(3).
           02  S4TEXTO  PIC X(50).
           02  FILLER PICTURE X(3).
           02  S5CODEO  PIC X(2).
           02  FILLER PICTURE X(3).
           02  S5TEXTO  PIC X(50).
           02  FILLER PICTURE X(3).
           02  S6CODEO  PIC X(2).
           02  FILLER PICTURE X(3).
           02  S6TEXTO  PIC X(50).
           02  FILLER PICTURE X(3).
           02  S7CODEO  PIC X(2).
           02  FILLER PICTURE X(3).
           02  S7TEXTO  PIC X(50).
           02  FILLER PICTURE X(3).
           02  S8CODEO  PIC X(2).
           02  FILLER PICTURE X(3).
           02  S8TEXTO  PIC X(50).
           02  FILLER PICTURE X(3).
           02  S9CODEO  PIC X(2).
           02  FILLER PICTURE X(3).
           02  S9TEXTO  PIC X(50).
           02  FILLER PICTURE X(3).
           02  S10CODEO  PIC X(2).
           02  FILLER PICTURE X(3).
           02  S10TEXTO  PIC X(50).
           02  FILLER PICTURE X(3).
           02  PROMPTO  PIC X(77).
           02  FILLER PICTURE X(3).
           02  DUMMYO  PIC X(1).
```

Figure 16.7 *(Continued)*

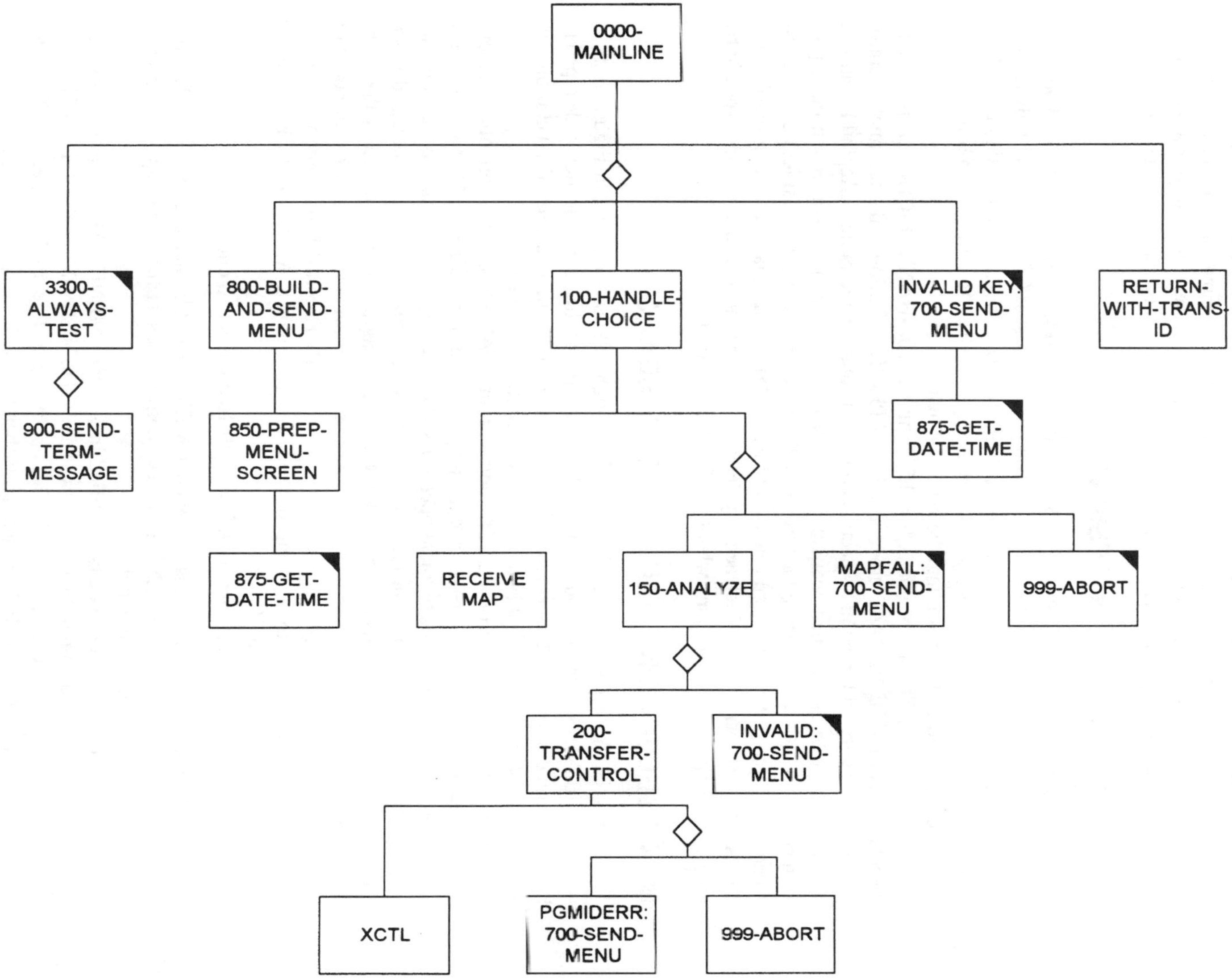
0000-MAINLINE
3300-ALWAYS-TEST
900-SEND-TERM-MESSAGE
800-BUILD-AND-SEND-MENU
850-PREP-MENU-SCREEN
875-GET-DATE-TIME
100-HANDLE-CHOICE
RECEIVE MAP
150-ANALYZE
MAPFAIL: 700-SEND-MENU
999-ABORT
200-TRANSFER-CONTROL
INVALID: 700-SEND-MENU
XCTL
PGMIDERR: 700-SEND-MENU
999-ABORT
INVALID KEY: 700-SEND-MENU
875-GET-DATE-TIME
RETURN-WITH-TRANS-ID

Figure 16.8 Visual table of contents of the MENU3 program.

functional choices to be presented. This loop coding does not require significant change, even if you expand the number of menu selection choices, the selection codes, or descriptive text.

Loading the menu with selection codes and text with a loop puts some of the power of the OCCURS clause to good use. As we discuss processing of a menu selection, you'll see that we also benefit from table processing power to identify the terminal operator's processing choice.

16.7 MENU SELECTION PROCESSING

When the terminal operator types in a menu selection and presses Enter, the MENU3 program mainline detects it at line 12700, at letter "g", and invokes the 100-HANDLE-CHOICE paragraph. 100-HANDLE-CHOICE is located at lines 14400 through 17100 in Figure 16.5, at letter "h". As you can see, this paragraph executes the RECEIVE command to bring the data entered by the terminal operator into the symbolic map.

The EVALUATE that begins at line 15500 in the 100-HANDLE-CHOICE paragraph detects normal RECEIVE MAP processing, a MAPFAIL condition if the terminal operator pressed Enter without typing in a selection code, or a catastrophic failure. Mapfail is handled with a message to the terminal operator, while other failure is handled—as in our other programs—by an "abort" paragraph that provides diagnostic reporting. Normal RECEIVE command execution is the norm. You can see at line 15800 that normal processing invokes the 150-ANALYZE paragraph, which actually determines if the menu selection code typed in by the terminal operator is valid, and what to do in response to it.

16.8 MENU SELECTION ANALYSIS USING SEARCH

The 150-ANALYZE paragraph at lines 17300 through 18900, letter "i", in Figure 16.5, is where the MENU3 program decides what to do in response to the menu selection code typed in by the terminal operator. This paragraph is perhaps the most unique in our MENU3 program, and also the paragraph that makes the program extremely flexible.

Rather than some form of IF/ELSE coding or an EVALUATE, which are often demonstrated in menu programs for menu selection interpretation, we use a **SEARCH** verb to identify the program to handle the terminal operator's choice of operation. This lets us eliminate the need to make any changes in logic as we expand the interactive application and place additional functions on the menu. The 150-ANALYZE paragraph is not affected by the quantity of menu selections the program puts on the screen, or by what the menu selection codes or corresponding functional program names are. The SEARCH coded here is entirely general purpose and does not need to be changed, because it responds to MENU-TABLE, whatever number of rows you code in it!

The SEARCH coded at lines 17900 through 18900 has two outcomes:

- The menu selection code is not found in MENU-TABLE, meaning that the code is not valid. In this case, AT END receives control and sets the screen up with an error message in the prompt field.
- The menu selection code is identified in a row of MENU-TABLE. In this case, the functional program name in that row is moved to WS-PGM-FOR-XCTL, a PIC X(8) field that will be used in the XCTL command in line 19700, letter "j". The 200-TRANSFER-CONTROL paragraph is then invoked.

In batch programs, we must code a SET statement as you see at line 17800 to insure complete search of the table the second and subsequent times SEARCH is executed. Strictly speaking, this

SET is not required in a pseudoconversational program, because the SEARCH will be executed only once per pseudoconverse. If the terminal operator enters an invalid menu selection code, SEARCH will have positioned the index at the end of the table. But the program then gives up control. The next time the program is invoked to continue the pseudoconversation (perhaps because the terminal operator has entered a different selection code), the program will start "fresh" and the index will by default be positioned at the beginning of the table.

Want to add a new function to the menu program? Just enter its selection code, descriptive label, and appropriate program name at an available row in MENU-TABLE-SETUP. The 150-ANALYZE paragraph will correctly process the selection, without any change to the SEARCH logic.

16.9 HOW THE MENU PASSES CONTROL TO ANOTHER PROGRAM

The 200-TRANSFER-CONTROL paragraph at lines 19100 through 21800, letter "j" in Figure 16.5, executes the **XCTL** command to invoke the program that processes the terminal operator's menu selection. XCTL will either succeed, in which case the menu program ends and is removed from memory, or fail and the menu program remains in memory. The only XCTL failure we can both recognize and deal with is **PGMIDERR** ("program id error"), detected in the EVALUATE at lines 20500 through 21800. PGMIDERR, as explained in reference Appendix E, indicates that the program to be transferred to cannot be found in the Program Control Table (PCT).That is, CICS doesn't "know about" such a program. In response, we can tell the terminal operator that the function to have been provided by the program is not available.

Why don't we code the WHEN clause for DFHRESP(NORMAL) first, as is customary in our EVALUATEs following a CICS command? If this question arises in your mind, you'll feel a bit foolish when we remind you of the answer. If the XCTL succeeds, the program being XCTLed to has assumed control, and the menu program is dead (removed from memory)! It would make no sense to code a test for normal outcome of XCTL, because the test would never have a chance to be satisfied.

16.10 THE XCTL COMMAND

Our menu program uses the XCTL command to pass control to the functional program, such as our update or browse programs, based on the menu selection made by the terminal operator. The XCTL command allows you to transfer control from one CICS program to another as a form of "GO TO". This command takes the form:

```
EXEC CICS
     XCTL  PROGRAM    ('program-name')
           COMMAREA   (data-name)
           RESP       (WS-RESPONSE-CODE)
END-EXEC.
```

Program-name is the actual name of the load module for a CICS program in the load library, not its transaction identifier. While you could code a literal value here, as implied in this example, we actually coded a data name in this location at line 19700 in the MENU3 program in Figure 16.5.

Coding the COMMAREA clause is optional. If you code it with XCTL, you ask CICS to convey the contents of the field specified as data name to the program that receives control.

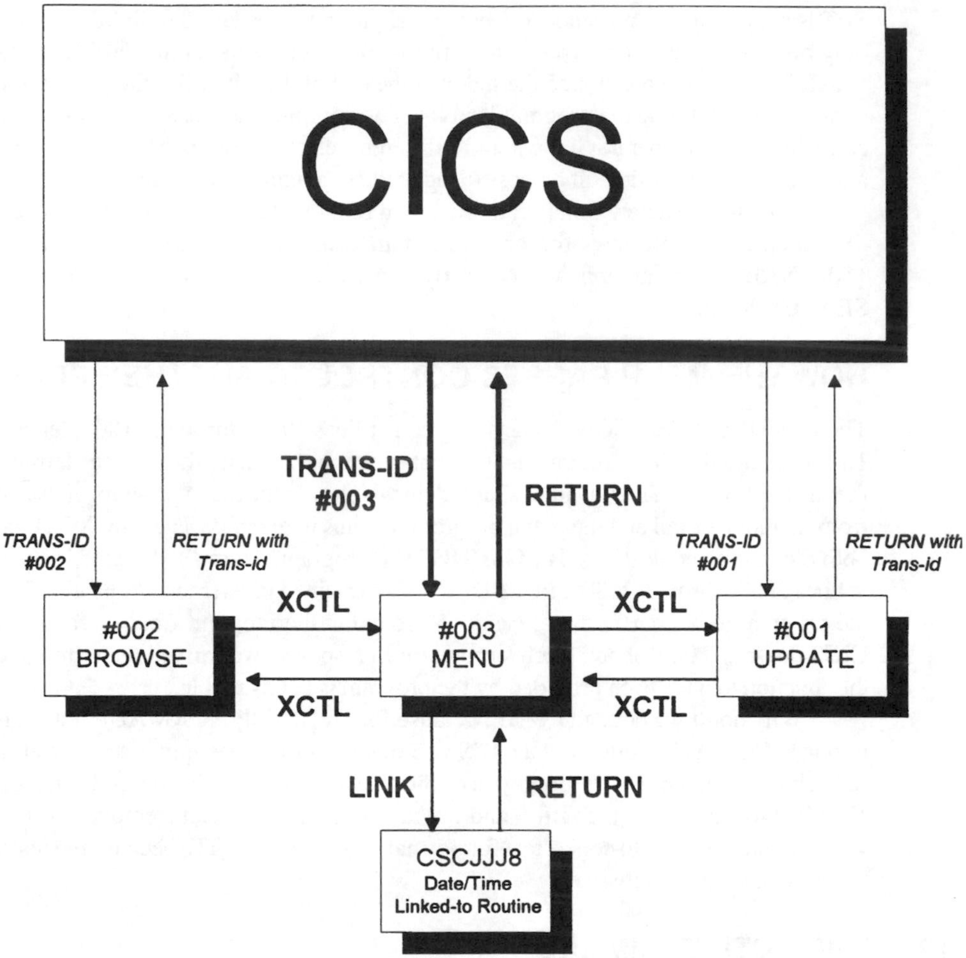
CICS
TRANS-ID
#003
RETURN
TRANS-ID
#002
RETURN with
Trans-id
TRANS-ID
#001
RETURN with
Trans-id
XCTL
XCTL
#002
BROWSE
#003
MENU
#001
UPDATE
XCTL
XCTL
LINK
RETURN
CSCJJJ8
Date/Time
Linked-to Routine

Figure 16.9 The XCTL command transfers control as a GO TO a program at the same level, while the LINK program is similar to a PERFORM or CALL and transfers control "down" a level.

The program will receive this data in its DFHCOMMAREA field in its LINKAGE SECTION. Note that the EIBCALEN field in the execute interface block of the program receiving control will not be zero when you pass data to the program using COMMAREA; EIBCALEN in the program receiving control will reflect the number of bytes of data passed. *Be careful! If you are using EIBCALEN=0 to detect first-time invocation within a program, using COMMAREA in your XCTL command will foul your first-time detection!*

We have illustrated the operation of the XCTL command in Figure 16.9, contrasting it to the LINK command which we will discuss in the next section. Here are some important points you need to know about XCTL:

- The program doing the XCTL is removed from memory when the XCTL succeeds, and it loses its WORKING-STORAGE. In this regard, XCTL is much like RETURN.
- The name of the program receiving control must be known to CICS in its Program

Control Table (PCT). If this name is not known, a PGMIDERR results when you execute XCTL.

- You share data with the XCTLed-to program with the COMMAREA option, citing the data name of a field in your WORKING-STORAGE section.
- The program receiving control does not "know" where it received control from, and CICS does not inform it of this either. If a functional program such as our update is to return control to the program that XCTLed to it, such as our menu, the name of the menu program has to be coded in the functional program at an XCTL statement sending control back to the menu. (The sending program could, however, pass its name to the program being XCTLed to, using COMMAREA in the XCTL command, if you adjust the first-time logic in the XCTLed-to program.)
- When and if the program receiving control with XCTL executes RETURN, it returns control to CICS, not the program that passed control to it. In an XCTLed-to program, **GOBACK** acts the same as CICS RETURN. (In contrast to what it may imply, GOBACK does not return control to the program that gave control to this program.)
- Due to the way it works, XCTL is ideal for passing control from a menu to a functional program, since it frees the memory formerly held by the menu program.

16.11 GETTING DATE AND TIME FROM CICS

The menu screen in Figures 16.1 and 16.2 presents the current date and time at the upper left corner, in the form of 10/25/94 and 5:08PM. While a program can obtain the date and time from CICS, these are not directly provided in the forms we need. The execute interface block provides the date in a field named **EIBDATE** with PIC S9(7) COMP-3 (packed decimal). The date is stored in Julian form YYDDD, where YY is the year and DDD is the number of the day within the year, starting with January 1 as day 1. The time is provided in the **EIBTIME** field, a PIC S9(7) COMP-3 field that contains the literal 0, then HHMMSS, where HH is the hour past midnight, MM is the minute in the hour, and SS is the current second.

You can see that the 700-SEND-MENU-SCREEN paragraph at lines 23100 through 24400, letter "l" in Figure 16.5, invokes another paragraph, 875-GET-DATE-TIME, to acquire the formatted date and time. 875-GET-DATE-TIME, at lines 28300 through 29400, letter "o", uses the LINK command to invoke a program named CSCJJJ8, sharing with it the 15 bytes of memory named WS-DATE-TIME-AREA. **LINK** acts much like a dynamic CALL, and invokes the LINKed-to program while having the linking program remain active in memory.

With slight changes in the CSCJJJ8 program, we could now accomplish the same thing as the LINK at lines 28800 through 29100 does using CALL instead, as we demonstrated in Chapter 10. Before VS COBOL II, it was not legitimate to use CALL in a CICS program, so LINK became popular. We demonstrate LINK here so you can recognize it, but we suggest you consider using CALL instead in new programs as a matter of execution efficiency.

16.12 THE LINK COMMAND

The LINK command allows one CICS program to invoke the service of another, without giving up its own memory. When you execute a LINK, you bring the LINKed-to program into memory, and you can communicate with it through a shared data area. LINK operates much like CALL, in that the data you want to share with the LINKed-to program can be located in your WORKING-STORAGE, and the LINKed-to program receives it in its DFHCOMMAREA field in its LINKAGE SECTION.

```
EXEC CICS
     LINK  PROGRAM    ('program-name')
           COMMAREA   (data-name)
           RESP       (WS-RESPONSE-CODE)
END-EXEC.
```

LINK has typically been used much like CALL, to invoke the services of a subprogram. Since CALL was not legitimate in COBOL/CICS programs until VS COBOL II, LINK was commonly used in its place. LINK resembles most of all a dynamic CALL, in that the program being LINKed to must be located and brought into memory at the time the LINK is executed. This extra input/output disk access is avoided with a hard-linked CALL as we demonstrated in Chapter 10, and you need not arrange for a Program Control Table (PCT) entry for a CALLed program. (A hard-linked CALL does, however, make the CICS load module larger. In addition, since a hard-linked CALL binds the CALLing and CALLed program at linkage edit time, changing the CALLed program makes it necessary to re-link any program that uses it.)

We illustrate the operation of the LINK command in Figure 16.9, lines 19600 through 19900, contrasting it to the XCTL command which we discussed in the previous section. Here are some important points you need to know about LINK:

- The program doing the LINK remains in memory when the LINK is processed, and continues to consume CICS resources. For this reason LINK is not a good way for a CICS menu program to pass control to a functional program such as an update or browse.
- The name of the program receiving control must be known to CICS in its Program Control Table (PCT). If this name is not known, a PGMIDERR results when you execute XCTL.
- You share data with the LINKed-to program with the COMMAREA option, citing the data name of a field in your WORKING-STORAGE section.
- The program receiving control does not "know" where it received control from, but CICS does keeps track of this. Control will return from the LINKed-to program to the program doing the LINK when the LINKed-to program completes execution.
- The LINKed-to program ends execution with CICS RETURN, and CICS gives control back to the program that did the LINK. If you prefer, you can code GOBACK instead of CICS RETURN. In a LINKed-to program, GOBACK acts the same as CICS RETURN.
- Due to the way it works, LINK is suitable for invoking small computational routines such as a date and time formatting program. But in modern CICS programming, CALL is better suited and more efficient than LINK for this purpose, and has the added advantage that the name of the CALLed program does not have to be known to CICS in the Program Control Table (PCT).

In modern CICS programming, consider using a CALL instead of a LINK in places where you need to invoke a service routine such as a date and time formatter.

16.13 CHANGE IN CLEAR KEY DETECTION IN THE MENU

Pressing the Clear key is a nearly universal way to end CICS program execution. Our update and browse programs regard the terminal operator's pressing of Clear as the indication that the

```
022000 *-----------------------------------------------------------------
022100 *  ALWAYS THE FIRST ROUTINE PERFORMED IN MAINLINE
022200 *-----------------------------------------------------------------
022300  633-ALWAYS-TEST.
022400      MOVE EIBAID     TO  EIBAID-TEST-FIELD.
022500      MOVE EIBCALEN   TO  WS-FIRST-TIME-FLAG.
022600
022700      IF CLEAR-KEY AND NOT FIRST-TIME
022800         PERFORM 900-SEND-TERMINATION-MESSAGE
022900         EXEC CICS   RETURN   END-EXEC.
023000
```

Prevents menu program from ending immediately when control transfers back from a program.

Figure 16.10 Revised "ALWAYS TEST" paragraph for the menu program, to avoid premature menu program termination.

operator wants to terminate program use. This continues to be the case when we make these functions accessible via the MENU3 program. The menu program itself regards the Clear key as the "time to quit" indication.

We face a slight problem in regard to detection of the Clear key by the menu program, however. When a program executes XCTL to transfer control back to the menu program, it does so because Clear was pressed. The execute interface block received by the program transferring control back to the menu contains the code for the Clear key in its EIBAID field. The menu program "inherits" this value in the EIBAID field, since Clear was the most recently pressed AID key.

If you examine the 000-MAINLINE paragraph of the MENU3 program in lines 11500 through 14200, letter "g" in Figure 16.5, you'll see that, as in all of our programs, a paragraph such as 633-ALWAYS-TEST is executed immediately upon the program receiving control. We test for receipt of the Clear key as the means by which the program was activated. As lines 22000 through 22900 in Figure 16.5, as well as Figure 16.10 indicate, we have modified this test slightly in the menu from the way it is handled in other programs. In order to avoid ending the menu program prematurely when a program transfers control back to it using XCTL, we change the 633-ALWAYS-TEST logic so that Clear is cause for program termination only if it is detected after the first time the menu program receives control. In other words, Clear does not cause menu program termination unless it is pressed in response to a menu screen.

It's important for you to understand why our modification of the 633-ALWAYS-TEST paragraph is necessary. We detect "first-time" execution of the menu program using the EIBCALEN field of the execute interface block, as we have done in all of our programs. EIBCALEN indicates the number of characters passed with COMMAREA to the program receiving control. EIBCALEN will be zero when you first invoke the menu program, but will be greater than zero if the menu program executes CICS RETURN with TRANSID and COMMAREA, since it passes one byte of data back to itself. But—and here is an important point—EIBCALEN will be zero after the menu program receives control from a terminated selection program only if the terminating program that does an XCTL back to the menu *does not* pass any data back to the menu program using COMMAREA. Our update and browse programs do not pass data back to the menu, and do not use COMMAREA in the XCTL command. This makes our modification of the 633-ALWAYS-TEST paragraph sufficient for menu program purposes.

16.14 CHANGES IN FUNCTIONAL PROGRAMS FOR MENU OPERATION

We separately execute and test our CICS programs before arranging for them to be invoked using the menu program. Therefore, these programs end execution by executing the CICS RETURN command without trans-id:

```
EXEC CICS
     RETURN
END-EXEC.
```

When we want to have the update or browse program selectable from the menu program, we have to change this termination logic in the programs. We change it so that these functional programs return control to the menu, not CICS, when they end. This change occurs in the 633-ALWAYS-TEST paragraph of the update and browse programs, and involves the use of the XCTL command:

```
EXEC CICS
     XCTL PROGRAM ('C360B003')
END-EXEC.
```

We do not bother to code RESP for this command, since there is no sufficient handling mechanism within a functional program if transfer of control back to the menu program fails. If the functional program cannot return control to the menu program, we allow CICS to handle the failure with an abend, which we will diagnose based on the CICS abend code.

This change, as well as a change to limit program invocation to menu selection, is shown in Figure 16.11.

```
EDIT ---- CSCJGJ.CSC360.COBOL(UPDATE3X) - 01.07 ------------- COLUMNS 001 072
COMMAND ===>                                                  SCROLL ===> PAGE

       *-----------------------------------------------------------------
       *  ALWAYS THE FIRST ROUTINE PERFORMED IN MAINLINE
       *-----------------------------------------------------------------
        633-ALWAYS-TEST.
            MOVE EIBAID    TO  EIBAID-TEST-FIELD.
            MOVE EIBCALEN  TO  WS-FIRST-TIME-FLAG.

            IF EIBTRNID = WS-TRANS-ID  AND  FIRST-TIME
               MOVE 'PROGRAM INVOKED INCORRECTLY' TO WS-ERROR-LINE5
               PERFORM 9999-ABORT.

            IF CLEAR-KEY
               EXEC CICS
                    XCTL  PROGRAM('C360B003')
               END-EXEC.
```

This test involving EIBTRNID prevents the terminal operator from executing the program directly by trans-id, once the program has been made accessible from a menu program.

Figure 16.11 Revised "ALWAYS TEST" paragraph in programs invoked from menu, so they return control to menu when terminated.

```
** CICS ERROR -- CONTACT HELP DESK -- REPORT THIS INFORMATION **
   EIBTRNID = #001
   EIBRSRCE =
   EIBRESP  =          0
   EIBRESP2 =          0
PROGRAM INVOKED INCORRECTLY
*****************************************************************************
```

> We tried to execute the update program directly by entering its trans-id, #001. Here you see how the logic in Figure 16.11 prevents the update program from being executed in this way. *With the change shown in Figure 16.11, the only way to execute the update program now is from the menu!*

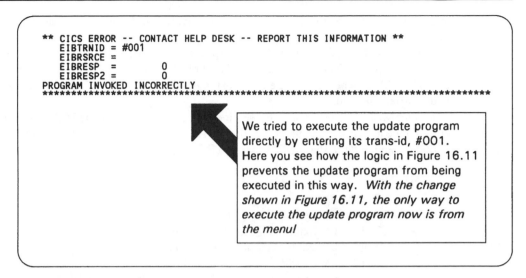

Figure 16.12 The revised update program ends immediately with this screen if the terminal operator attempts to invoke it by trans-id, outside of the menu program.

16.15 LIMITING A PROGRAM TO MENU EXECUTION ONLY

While we tested our update and browse programs separate from the menu as we presented them in this book, it is a good idea to prevent terminal operators from accessing programs directly. That is, you should force terminal operators to use the menu; they should not be able to invoke programs separately by trans-id.You can readily modify the 633-ALWAYS-TEST paragraph to accomplish this.

WS-TRANS-ID is the data name our examples consistently use for the field in which the program's own transaction identifier is stored. You can compare this to the **EIBTRNID** field in the execute interface block to see if the program was invoked using its trans-id, and if so, to cancel its execution. We have included such a test in the 633-ALWAYS-TEST paragraph of our revised update and browse program. Figure 16.11 shows you how to code this test, as well as the XCTL command by which a functional program such as the update or browse program returns control to the menu program, not CICS, when it is terminated.

Figure 16.12 shows you the screen that results if the terminal operator attempts to invoke a functional program such as our update program using the program's trans-id rather than the menu. It's important to remember to make the test for EIBTRNID=WS-TRANS-ID a compound test involving the FIRST-TIME condition. The first time a functional program is invoked (from the menu), the trans-id of the menu program, as the most recent trans-id invoked, is in the EIBTRNID field. Once pseudoconversation begins in the functional program, however, its own trans-id will legitimately be in the EIBTRNID field!

16.16 THE CSCJJJ8 DATE AND TIME FORMATTER PROGRAM

The menu screen you saw in Figures 16.1 and 16.2 presents the current date and time at the upper left corner, in the form of 10/25/94 and 5:08PM. While a program can obtain the date and time from CICS, these are not directly provided in these forms. Instead, the execute interface block provides the date in Julian form as we explained in section 16.11, in the EIBDATE field as a PIC S9(7) COMP-3 (packed decimal) field. Similarly, CICS provides the time in the EIBTIME field, also a PIC S9(7) COMP-3 field that contains the literal 0, then HHMMSS, where HH is the hour past midnight, MM is the minute in the hour, and SS is the current second.

Our MENU3 program uses the services of a small program named CSCJJJ8 to obtain the current date and time formatted as we desire. The menu executes the LINK command at lines 19600 through 19900, sharing WS-DATE-TIME-AREA with CSCJJJ8:

```
01  WS-DATE-TIME-AREA.
    05 DCA-DATE.
       10 DCA-DATE-MO       PIC 9(2).
       10 DCA-SLASH-1       PIC X(1).
       10 DCA-DATE-DA       PIC 9(2).
       10 DCA-SLASH-2       PIC X(1).
       10 DCA-DATE-YR       PIC 9(2).
    05 DCA-TIME.
       10 DCA-TIME-HRS      PIC Z9.
       10 DCA-COLON         PIC X(1).
       10 DCA-TIME-MIN      PIC 9(2).
       10 DCA-TIME-AM-PM    PIC X(2).
```

This is simply a 15-byte length of memory, that is, an 8-byte field for the date, and a 7-byte field for the time. The MENU3 program does not provide any information to the CSCJJJ8 program. Rather, as you can see in the source code of CSCJJJ8 in Figure 16.13, this LINKed-to program obtains the date and time for itself from CICS. CSCJJJ8 takes the actions necessary to format the date and time, converting the Julian date into Gregorian form, and the time from 24-hour clock to 12-hour AM/PM representation. CSCJJJ8 gives the shared memory back to the MENU3 program with this data ready for use on the screen.

Examine the source code for the CSCJJJ8 program in Figure 16.13. If you follow through with the straight-through code in this program, you quickly see how it converts 24-hour time format to 12-hour, AM/PM format in the EVALUATE in lines 10200 through 11800. You can also see how the table lookup in lines 13200 through 14200 converts the Julian date to Gregorian format. The conversion process relies on finding the row in MONTH-TABLE (lines 3100 through 5200) that equals or exceeds the value of the Julian day, subtracting this number of days from the Julian day, and correcting for a potential zero condition. Note that we coded MONTH-TABLE with two sets of values, representing the number of days before each month in both non-leap years and leap years.

CSCJJJ8 puts the computed date and time values into DFHCOMMAREA, which is really memory "owned" by the program that LINKed to it. CSCJJJ8 then ends execution with a CICS RETURN command. Because CSCJJJ8 was LINKed to, RETURN causes control to transfer "up" one level to the program that LINKed to CSCJJJ8, our MENU3 program, not to CICS, as illustrated in Figure 16.9. When this RETURN is executed, the CSCJJJ8 is removed from memory. If you prefer, you can code GOBACK instead of CICS RETURN; in a LINKed-to program, GOBACK acts just like RETURN.

```
EDIT ---- CSCJGJ.CSC360.COBOL(CSCJJJ8) - 01.00 --------------- COLUMNS 007 078
COMMAND ===>                                                  SCROLL ===> PAGE
****** ***************************** TOP OF DATA ******************************
 ID DIVISION.
 PROGRAM-ID. CSCJJJ8.
*===============================================================
*  SUBPROGRAM THAT YOU CAN LINK TO, TO GET FORMATTED DATE AND
*  TIME.  SHARE A 15 BYTE WS-COMMUNICATION-AREA WITH THIS
*  PROGRAM.  AFTER YOUR LINK COMMAND, THE DATE AND TIME WILL
*  BE IN YOUR WS-COMMUNICATION-AREA IN THIS FORMAT:
*
*  TIME    PIC X(7)   EXAMPLE:   12:34AM
*  DATE    PIC X(8)   EXAMPLE:   10/22/94
*
*  TIME WILL BE 12-HOUR CLOCK WITH AM OR PM AS SHOWN.  FIRST
*  HOUR OF DAY WILL BE 12:00AM NOT 00:00
*
*  DATE WILL HAVE LEADING ZERO SUPPRESSION FOR FIRST DIGIT,
*  FOR EXAMPLE, JULY 4, 1995 IS  7/04/95 NOT 07/04/95
*
*  SINCE THIS SUBPROGRAM GETS EIBDATE AND EIBTIME FOR ITSELF
*  YOU NEED NOT PROVIDE THESE INPUT VALUES TO IT.
*
*  COPYRIGHT 1994 JIM JANOSSY AND STEVE SAMUELS
*  BATCH TESTED 10/30/94 USING CSCJJJ8D DRIVER -JJ
*===============================================================

 DATA DIVISION.
 WORKING-STORAGE SECTION.
*---------------------------------------------------------------
*  THIS TABLE STORES NUMBER OF DAYS BEFORE EACH MONTH FOR BOTH
*  NON-LEAP AND LEAP YEARS:
*---------------------------------------------------------------
 01  MONTH-TABLE-SETUP.
     05 JAN        PIC X(8)  VALUE '000 000 '.
     05 FEB        PIC X(8)  VALUE '031 031 '.
     05 MAR        PIC X(8)  VALUE '059 060 '.
     05 APR        PIC X(8)  VALUE '090 091 '.
     05 MAY        PIC X(8)  VALUE '120 121 '.
     05 JUN        PIC X(8)  VALUE '151 152 '.
     05 JUL        PIC X(8)  VALUE '181 182 '.
     05 AUG        PIC X(8)  VALUE '212 213 '.
     05 SEP        PIC X(8)  VALUE '243 244 '.
     05 OCT        PIC X(8)  VALUE '273 274 '.
     05 NOV        PIC X(8)  VALUE '304 305 '.
     05 DEC        PIC X(8)  VALUE '334 335 '.
     05 ENDITEM    PIC X(8)  VALUE '999 999 '.

 01  MONTH-TABLE  REDEFINES  MONTH-TABLE-SETUP.
     05 MONTH-ROW   OCCURS 13 TIMES
                    INDEXED BY ROW-INDEX.
        15 MONTH-DATA   OCCURS 2 TIMES
                        INDEXED BY DATA-INDEX.
           18 MD-VALUE       PIC 9(3).
           18                PIC X(1).

 01  WS-VALUE                PIC 9(3).
 01  WS-REMAINDER            PIC 9(1).

 01  WS-RAW-DATE-TIME.
     05 WS-TIME                   PIC 9(7).
     05 WS-TIME-PARTS  REDEFINES WS-TIME.
        10                        PIC X(1).
        10 WS-HRS                 PIC 9(2).
        10 WS-MIN                 PIC 9(2).
        10                        PIC X(2).

     05 WS-DATE                   PIC 9(7).
     05 WS-DATE-PARTS  REDEFINES WS-DATE.
        10                        PIC X(2).
        10 WS-DP-YEAR             PIC 9(2).
        10 WS-DP-JULIAN-DAY       PIC 9(3).

```

This program functions much like a subprogram, but is accessed with the CICS **LINK** command. It uses this table to convert the Julian date provided by CICS in the EIBDATE field to a MM/DD/YY format Gregorian date. The two columns of values indicate the number of days before the start of each month in a non-leap year and in a leap year.

Figure 16.13 Source code of the CSCJJJ8 date and time formatter program LINKed-to by the MENU3 program.

```
 LINKAGE SECTION.
*----------------------------------------------------------------
*  THESE ARE THE FIELDS YOU MUST SHARE WITH CSCJJ8 IN COMMAREA:
*----------------------------------------------------------------
 01  DFHCOMMAREA.
     05 DCA-DATE.
        10 DCA-DATE-MO       PIC 9(2).
        10 DCA-SLASH-1       PIC X(1).
        10 DCA-DATE-DA       PIC 9(2).
        10 DCA-SLASH-2       PIC X(1).
        10 DCA-DATE-YR       PIC 9(2).
     05 DCA-TIME.
        10 DCA-TIME-HRS      PIC Z9.
        10 DCA-COLON         PIC X(1).
        10 DCA-TIME-MIN      PIC 9(2).
        10 DCA-TIME-AM-PM    PIC X(2).
```

This is the memory shared by a program with CSCJJJ8 when the program executes a **LINK** to CSCJJJ8. CSCJJJ8 obtains the date and time from CICS, reformats it, and puts it here for the LINKing program to receive.

```
*================================================================
 PROCEDURE DIVISION.
*================================================================
 0000-MAINLINE.
     EXEC CICS   ASKTIME   END-EXEC.
     MOVE EIBTIME TO WS-TIME.
     MOVE EIBDATE TO WS-DATE.
     MOVE ':'  TO  DCA-COLON.
     MOVE '/'  TO  DCA-SLASH-1  DCA-SLASH-2.
*----------------------------------------------------------------
*  FORMAT THE TIME TO AM/PM WITH FIRST HOUR OF DAY AS "12:"
*----------------------------------------------------------------
     MOVE WS-MIN  TO DCA-TIME-MIN.

     EVALUATE WS-HRS
        WHEN 0
           MOVE 12        TO DCA-TIME-HRS
           MOVE 'AM'      TO DCA-TIME-AM-PM

        WHEN 1 THRU 12
           MOVE WS-HRS    TO DCA-TIME-HRS
           MOVE 'AM'      TO DCA-TIME-AM-PM

        WHEN 13 THRU 24
           COMPUTE DCA-TIME-HRS = WS-HRS - 12
           MOVE 'PM'      TO DCA-TIME-AM-PM

        WHEN OTHER
           MOVE WS-HRS    TO DCA-TIME-HRS
           MOVE 'ER'      TO DCA-TIME-AM-PM
     END-EVALUATE.
```

Converts 24-hour time to 12-hour AM/PM time, and makes the first hour of the day 12:nn instead of 00:nn.

```
*----------------------------------------------------------------
*  CONVERT THE DATE FROM JULIAN YYDDD TO GREGORIAN MMDDYY.
*  USE TEST FOR LEAP YEAR: LEAP YEARS ARE EVENLY DIVISIBLE BY
*  4.  (THIS TEST IS ACCURATE THROUGH 2099.)  DATA-INDEX POINTS
*  TO EITHER THE ORDINARY YEAR SIDE OF TABLE OR LEAP YEAR SIDE.
*----------------------------------------------------------------
     DIVIDE 4 INTO WS-DP-YEAR
        GIVING WS-VALUE  REMAINDER WS-REMAINDER.
     IF WS-REMAINDER > 0
        SET DATA-INDEX TO 1
      ELSE
        SET DATA-INDEX TO 2.

     SET ROW-INDEX TO 1.
     SEARCH MONTH-ROW
        AT END
           MOVE WS-DATE TO DCA-DATE
        WHEN
           MD-VALUE(ROW-INDEX, DATA-INDEX) >= WS-DP-JULIAN-DAY
             SET ROW-INDEX DOWN BY 1
             SET DCA-DATE-MO TO ROW-INDEX
             COMPUTE DCA-DATE-DA =
               WS-DP-JULIAN-DAY - MD-VALUE(ROW-INDEX, DATA-INDEX)
             MOVE WS-DP-YEAR TO DCA-DATE-YR.

     IF DCA-DATE-DA = 0        MOVE 1 TO DCA-DATE-DA.
     IF DCA-DATE(1:1) = '0'    MOVE ' ' TO DCA-DATE(1:1).
     EXEC CICS   RETURN   END-EXEC.
```

Computes Gregorian date from Julian date.

Figure 16.13 *(Continued)*

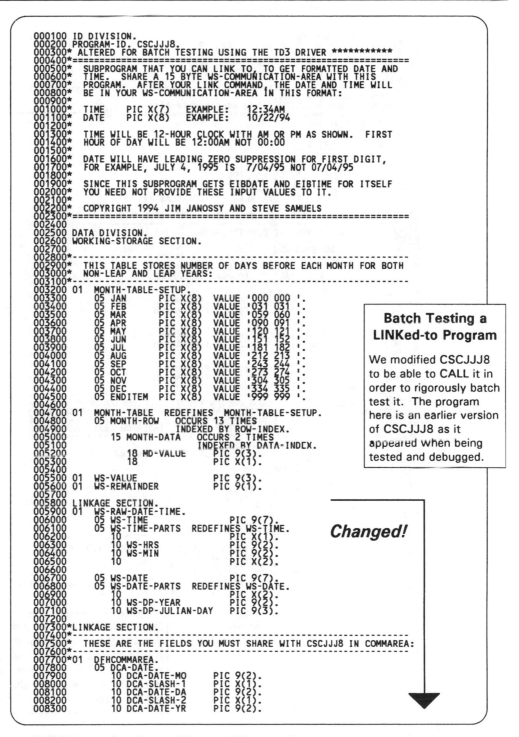

```
 ID DIVISION.
 PROGRAM-ID. CSCJJJ8.
* ALTERED FOR BATCH TESTING USING THE TD3 DRIVER ***********
*===============================================================
*  SUBPROGRAM THAT YOU CAN LINK TO, TO GET FORMATTED DATE AND
*  TIME.  SHARE A 15 BYTE WS-COMMUNICATION-AREA WITH THIS
*  PROGRAM.  AFTER YOUR LINK COMMAND, THE DATE AND TIME WILL
*  BE IN YOUR WS-COMMUNICATION-AREA IN THIS FORMAT:
*
*  TIME    PIC X(7)    EXAMPLE:   12:34AM
*  DATE    PIC X(8)    EXAMPLE:   10/22/94
*
*  TIME WILL BE 12-HOUR CLOCK WITH AM OR PM AS SHOWN.  FIRST
*  HOUR OF DAY WILL BE 12:00AM NOT 00:00
*
*  DATE WILL HAVE LEADING ZERO SUPPRESSION FOR FIRST DIGIT,
*  FOR EXAMPLE, JULY 4, 1995 IS  7/04/95 NOT 07/04/95
*
*  SINCE THIS SUBPROGRAM GETS EIBDATE AND EIBTIME FOR ITSELF
*  YOU NEED NOT PROVIDE THESE INPUT VALUES TO IT.
*
*  COPYRIGHT 1994 JIM JANOSSY AND STEVE SAMUELS
*===============================================================
 DATA DIVISION.
 WORKING-STORAGE SECTION.
*---------------------------------------------------------------
*  THIS TABLE STORES NUMBER OF DAYS BEFORE EACH MONTH FOR BOTH
*  NON-LEAP AND LEAP YEARS:
*---------------------------------------------------------------
 01  MONTH-TABLE-SETUP.
     05 JAN      PIC X(8)   VALUE '000 000 '.
     05 FEB      PIC X(8)   VALUE '031 031 '.
     05 MAR      PIC X(8)   VALUE '059 060 '.
     05 APR      PIC X(8)   VALUE '090 091 '.
     05 MAY      PIC X(8)   VALUE '120 121 '.
     05 JUN      PIC X(8)   VALUE '151 152 '.
     05 JUL      PIC X(8)   VALUE '181 182 '.
     05 AUG      PIC X(8)   VALUE '212 213 '.
     05 SEP      PIC X(8)   VALUE '243 244 '.
     05 OCT      PIC X(8)   VALUE '273 274 '.
     05 NOV      PIC X(8)   VALUE '304 305 '.
     05 DEC      PIC X(8)   VALUE '334 335 '.
     05 ENDITEM  PIC X(8)   VALUE '999 999 '.
 01  MONTH-TABLE  REDEFINES  MONTH-TABLE-SETUP.
     05 MONTH-ROW     OCCURS 13 TIMES
                      INDEXED BY ROW-INDEX.
        15 MONTH-DATA     OCCURS 2 TIMES
                          INDEXED BY DATA-INDEX.
           18 MD-VALUE        PIC 9(3).
           18                 PIC X(1).
 01  WS-VALUE                 PIC 9(3).
 01  WS-REMAINDER             PIC 9(1).
 LINKAGE SECTION.
 01  WS-RAW-DATE-TIME.
     05 WS-TIME                         PIC 9(7).
     05 WS-TIME-PARTS   REDEFINES WS-TIME.
        10                              PIC X(1).
        10 WS-HRS                       PIC 9(2).
        10 WS-MIN                       PIC 9(2).
        10                              PIC X(2).
     05 WS-DATE                         PIC 9(7).
     05 WS-DATE-PARTS   REDEFINES WS-DATE.
        10                              PIC X(2).
        10 WS-DP-YEAR                   PIC 9(2).
        10 WS-DP-JULIAN-DAY             PIC 9(3).
*LINKAGE SECTION.
*---------------------------------------------------------------
*  THESE ARE THE FIELDS YOU MUST SHARE WITH CSCJJJ8 IN COMMAREA:
*---------------------------------------------------------------
*01  DFHCOMMAREA.
     05 DCA-DATE.
        10 DCA-DATE-MO        PIC 9(2).
        10 DCA-SLASH-1        PIC X(1).
        10 DCA-DATE-DA        PIC 9(2).
        10 DCA-SLASH-2        PIC X(1).
        10 DCA-DATE-YR        PIC 9(2).
```

Changed!

> **Batch Testing a LINKed-to Program**
>
> We modified CSCJJJ8 to be able to CALL it in order to rigorously batch test it. The program here is an earlier version of CSCJJJ8 as it appeared when being tested and debugged.

Figure 16.14 CSCJJJ8 program as modified for batch testing and debugging using a driver program.

Changed!

```
008400      05 DCA-TIME.
008500         10 DCA-TIME-HRS     PIC Z9.
008600         10 DCA-COLON        PIC X(1).
008700         10 DCA-TIME-MIN     PIC 9(2).
008800         10 DCA-TIME-AM-PM   PIC X(2).
008900
009000*==========================================================
009100*PROCEDURE DIVISION.
009100 PROCEDURE DIVISION using ws-raw-date-time.
009200*=========================================
009300 0000-MAINLINE.
009400
009500*     EXEC CICS
009600*         ASKTIME
009700*     END-EXEC.
009800
009900*     MOVE EIBTIME TO WS-TIME.
010000*     MOVE EIBDATE TO WS-DATE.
010100      MOVE ':'  TO  DCA-COLON.
010200      MOVE '/'  TO  DCA-SLASH-1  DCA-SLASH-2.
010300*----------------------------------------------------------
010400*  FORMAT THE TIME TO AM/PM WITH FIRST HOUR OF DAY AS "12:"
010500*----------------------------------------------------------
010600      MOVE WS-MIN  TO DCA-TIME-MIN.
010700
010800      EVALUATE WS-HRS
010900         WHEN 0
011000            MOVE 12       TO DCA-TIME-HRS
011100            MOVE 'AM'     TO DCA-TIME-AM-PM
011200
011300         WHEN 1 THRU 12
011400            MOVE WS-HRS   TO DCA-TIME-HRS
011500            MOVE 'AM'     TO DCA-TIME-AM-PM
011600
011700         WHEN 13 THRU 24
011800            COMPUTE DCA-TIME-HRS = WS-HRS - 12
011900            MOVE 'PM'     TO DCA-TIME-AM-PM
012000
012100         WHEN OTHER
012200            MOVE WS-HRS   TO DCA-TIME-HRS
012300            MOVE 'ER'     TO DCA-TIME-AM-PM
012400      END-EVALUATE.
012500*---------------------------------------------------------
012600*  CONVERT THE DATE FROM JULIAN YYDDD TO GREGORIAN MMDDYY.
012700*  USE TEST FOR LEAP YEAR: LEAP YEARS ARE EVENLY DIVISIBLE BY
012800*  4.  (THIS TEST IS ACCURATE THROUGH 2099.)  DATA-INDEX POINTS
012900*  TO EITHER THE ORDINARY YEAR SIDE OF TABLE OR LEAP YEAR SIDE.
013000*----------------------------------------------------------
013100      DIVIDE 4 INTO WS-DP-YEAR
013200         GIVING WS-VALUE  REMAINDER WS-REMAINDER.
013300      IF WS-REMAINDER > 0
013400         SET DATA-INDEX TO 1
013500       ELSE
013600         SET DATA-INDEX TO 2.
013700
            SET ROW-INDEX TO 1.
013800      SEARCH MONTH-ROW
013900         AT END
014000            MOVE WS-DATE TO DCA-DATE
014100         WHEN
014200            MD-VALUE(ROW-INDEX, DATA-INDEX) > WS-DP-JULIAN-DAY
014300              SET ROW-INDEX DOWN BY 1
014400              SET DCA-DATE-MO TO ROW-INDEX
014500              COMPUTE DCA-DATE-DA =
014600                 WS-DP-JULIAN-DAY - MD-VALUE(ROW-INDEX, DATA-INDEX)
014700              MOVE WS-DP-YEAR TO DCA-DATE-YR.


014900      IF DCA-DATE(1:1) = '0'
               MOVE ' ' TO DCA-DATE(1:1).

015000*     EXEC CICS   RETURN   END-EXEC.
015100      GOBACK.
```

Program is messy since it is in the process of being debugged! we had to change the relational test at line 14200 to > = to correct the problem revealed by the batch testing output in Figure 16.17.

Figure 16.14 *(Continued)*

16.17 TESTING A LINKED-TO PROGRAM

We needed to test the CSCJJJ8 time and date formatter before including it in real systems and this book. Batch testing proved to be quick and very helpful, especially because this routine ordinarily gets its input from CICS as the current date and time. Trying to test the routine in use would mean that the test would take months! We completed testing and debugging of CSCJJJ8 in less than two hours, and removed several serious bugs. We could have done this on a mainframe, of course, but instead we found it handier to accomplish it using a PC-based COBOL compiler. (Even though the LINKed-to program will eventually be run under CICS, you can batch test it without any involvement with CICS. The PC COBOL compiler we used is actually an educational version supplied with a standard COBOL textbook. It was thoroughly sufficient to accomplish this testing!)

The process for batch testing a LINKed-to program is similar to that for CALLed programs, which we demonstrated in Chapter 10, but a bit more messy. Unlike the case with CALLed program testing, you have to modify the LINKed-to program in order to test it. We began the process by including the last part of the WORKING-STORAGE of CSCJJJ8 within the LINKAGE SECTION, so that fields used as input by the program could be supplied to it by a CALL from a driver program. Figure 16.14 shows you the modified CSCJJJ8 program as we worked with it in testing and debugging. We commented out the original LINKAGE SECTION heading and the 01 DFHCOMMAREA coding, and inserted a LINKAGE SECTION heading above the original input time and date fields. We also commented out any reference to CICS commands and execute interface block fields, at lines 9500 through 10000, and the RETURN command at line 15000. We then coded GOBACK at line 15100 to end the program when CALLed, and compiled the modified CSCJJJ8 as a batch program.

Next, we formed test data conforming to the layout of the WS-RAW-DATE-TIME fields in the modified CSCJJJ8 LINKAGE SECTION, shown in Figure 16.15. Since CSCJJJ8 uses only some of the digits within these, we coded only the digits actually used,

```
0000    94001
0059    94030
0800    94031
1100    94032
1200    94058
1201    94059
1259    94060
1301    94061
1402    94090
1503    94091
1604    94092
1705    94365
1907    92058
2008    92059
2109    92060
2210    92061
2300    92364
2359    92365
0001    92366
```

This is one set of test data we used to batch test the CSCJJJ8 LINKed-to program. Each line represents one test case (pair of inputs). The left value is the part of EIBTIME that CSCJJJ8 will use (hour and minute), and the right value is the part of the EIBDATE Julian date (YY and DDD) that CSCJJJ8 will use. We developed black box test case criteria using boundary value analysis, equivalence classes, and error guessing, and included test cases like 94365, 92365 and 92366 to test output value limits (1992 was a leap year, while 1994 was not). You can see the result of a test run using this input data in Figure 16.17. Appropriate batch testing the algorithms in a LINKed-to program requires slight program modification but is worth the investment because it allows rapid first-round comprehensive functional testing in isolation from CICS.

Figure 16.15 Simulated EIBTIME and EIBDATE data to batch test the CSCJJJ8 LINKed-to program.

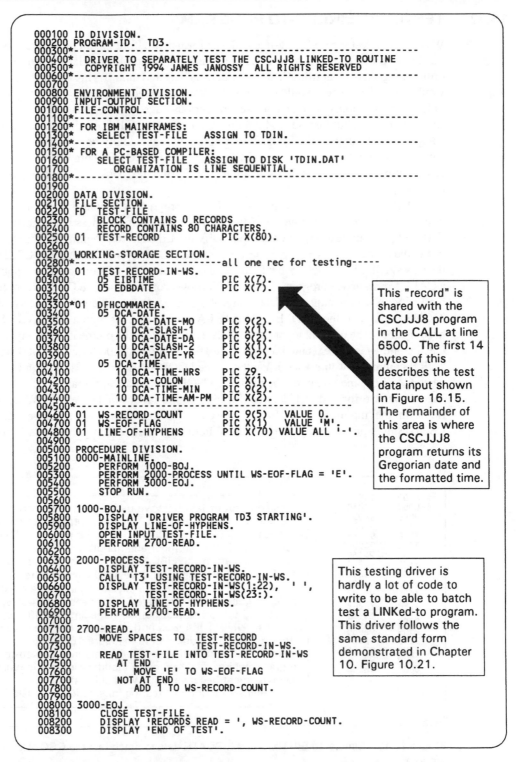

```
000100 ID DIVISION.
000200 PROGRAM-ID.  TD3.
000300*-----------------------------------------------------------------
000400*  DRIVER TO SEPARATELY TEST THE CSCJJJ8 LINKED-TO ROUTINE
000500*  COPYRIGHT 1994 JAMES JANOSSY  ALL RIGHTS RESERVED
000600*-----------------------------------------------------------------
000700
000800 ENVIRONMENT DIVISION.
000900 INPUT-OUTPUT SECTION.
001000 FILE-CONTROL.
001100*-----------------------------------------------------------------
001200*  FOR IBM MAINFRAMES:
001300*      SELECT TEST-FILE   ASSIGN TO TDIN.
001400*-----------------------------------------------------------------
001500*  FOR A PC-BASED COMPILER:
001600       SELECT TEST-FILE   ASSIGN TO DISK 'TDIN.DAT'
001700           ORGANIZATION IS LINE SEQUENTIAL.
001800*-----------------------------------------------------------------
001900
002000 DATA DIVISION.
002100 FILE SECTION.
002200 FD  TEST-FILE
002300     BLOCK CONTAINS 0 RECORDS
002400     RECORD CONTAINS 80 CHARACTERS.
002500 01  TEST-RECORD                PIC X(80).
002600
002700 WORKING-STORAGE SECTION.
002800*-----------------------------all one rec for testing-----
002900 01  TEST-RECORD-IN-WS.
003000     05 EIBTIME                 PIC X(7).
003100     05 EDBDATE                 PIC X(7).
003200
003300*01  DFHCOMMAREA.
003400     05 DCA-DATE.
003500        10 DCA-DATE-MO          PIC 9(2).
003600        10 DCA-SLASH-1          PIC X(1).
003700        10 DCA-DATE-DA          PIC 9(2).
003800        10 DCA-SLASH-2          PIC X(1).
003900        10 DCA-DATE-YR          PIC 9(2).
004000     05 DCA-TIME.
004100        10 DCA-TIME-HRS         PIC Z9.
004200        10 DCA-COLON            PIC X(1).
004300        10 DCA-TIME-MIN         PIC 9(2).
004400        10 DCA-TIME-AM-PM       PIC X(2).
004500*---------------------------------------------------------
004600 01  WS-RECORD-COUNT            PIC 9(5)    VALUE 0.
004700 01  WS-EOF-FLAG                PIC X(1)    VALUE 'M'.
004800 01  LINE-OF-HYPHENS            PIC X(70) VALUE ALL '-'.
004900
005000 PROCEDURE DIVISION.
005100 0000-MAINLINE.
005200     PERFORM 1000-BOJ.
005300     PERFORM 2000-PROCESS UNTIL WS-EOF-FLAG = 'E'.
005400     PERFORM 3000-EOJ.
005500     STOP RUN.
005600
005700 1000-BOJ.
005800     DISPLAY 'DRIVER PROGRAM TD3 STARTING'.
005900     DISPLAY LINE-OF-HYPHENS.
006000     OPEN INPUT TEST-FILE.
006100     PERFORM 2700-READ.
006200
006300 2000-PROCESS.
006400     DISPLAY TEST-RECORD-IN-WS.
006500     CALL 'T3' USING TEST-RECORD-IN-WS.
006600     DISPLAY TEST-RECORD-IN-WS(1:22),  ' ',
006700             TEST-RECORD-IN-WS(23:).
006800     DISPLAY LINE-OF-HYPHENS.
006900     PERFORM 2700-READ.
007000
007100 2700-READ.
007200     MOVE SPACES  TO  TEST-RECORD
007300                      TEST-RECORD-IN-WS.
007400     READ TEST-FILE INTO TEST-RECORD-IN-WS
007500        AT END
007600           MOVE 'E' TO WS-EOF-FLAG
007700        NOT AT END
007800           ADD 1 TO WS-RECORD-COUNT.
007900
008000 3000-EOJ.
008100     CLOSE TEST-FILE.
008200     DISPLAY 'RECORDS READ = ', WS-RECORD-COUNT.
008300     DISPLAY 'END OF TEST'.
```

This "record" is shared with the CSCJJJ8 program in the CALL at line 6500. The first 14 bytes of this describes the test data input shown in Figure 16.15. The remainder of this area is where the CSCJJJ8 program returns its Gregorian date and the formatted time.

This testing driver is hardly a lot of code to write to be able to batch test a LINKed-to program. This driver follows the same standard form demonstrated in Chapter 10. Figure 10.21.

Figure 16.16 Testing driver program TD3, used to test the CSCJJJ8 LINKed-to program before use with CICS.

making the test data easier to view. As you can see, we picked values at or near time and date boundaries such as beginning of day and hour, and month ends and beginnings for both leap and non-leap years.

As with testing a program intended to be CALLed in actual use, testing a program intended to be LINKed to requires constructing a test driver. The driver reads test data from a file, displays it, passes it to the program being tested using a CALL, then displays the result. Our driver for this purpose is named TD3, and is listed in Figure 16.16. It's very similar to the generic testing driver we demonstrated in Chapter 10.

Figure 16.17 shows you one of the four runs we made in testing CSCJJJ8 as we debugged

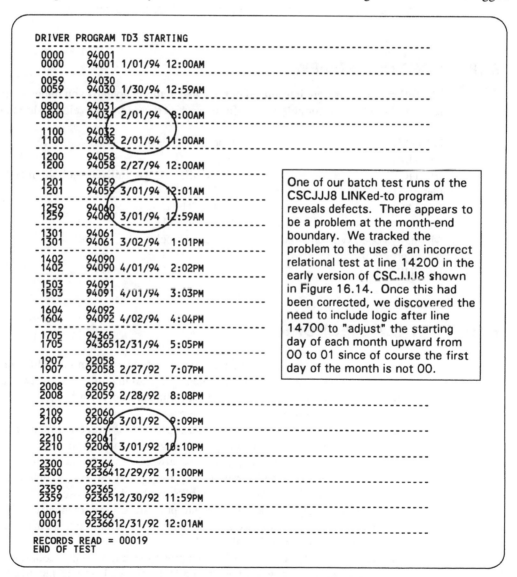

```
DRIVER PROGRAM TD3 STARTING
-----------------------------------------------------------------
0000    94001
0000    94001  1/01/94  12:00AM
-----------------------------------------------------------------
0059    94030
0059    94030  1/30/94  12:59AM
-----------------------------------------------------------------
0800    94031
0800    94031  2/01/94   8:00AM
-----------------------------------------------------------------
1100    94032
1100    94032  2/01/94  11:00AM
-----------------------------------------------------------------
1200    94058
1200    94058  2/27/94  12:00AM
-----------------------------------------
1201    94059
1201    94059  3/01/94  12:01AM
-----------------------------------------
1259    94060
1259    94060  3/01/94  12:59AM
-----------------------------------------
1301    94061
1301    94061  3/02/94   1:01PM
-----------------------------------------
1402    94090
1402    94090  4/01/94   2:02PM
-----------------------------------------
1503    94091
1503    94091  4/01/94   3:03PM
-----------------------------------------
1604    94092
1604    94092  4/02/94   4:04PM
-----------------------------------------
1705    94365
1705    9436512/31/94   5:05PM
-----------------------------------------
1907    92058
1907    92058  2/27/92   7:07PM
-----------------------------------------
2008    92059
2008    92059  2/28/92   8:08PM
-----------------------------------------------------------------
2109    92060
2109    92060  3/01/92   9:09PM
-----------------------------------------------------------------
2210    92061
2210    92061  3/01/92  10:10PM
-----------------------------------------------------------------
2300    92364
2300    9236412/29/92  11:00PM
-----------------------------------------------------------------
2359    92365
2359    9236512/30/92  11:59PM
-----------------------------------------------------------------
0001    92366
0001    9236612/31/92  12:01AM
-----------------------------------------------------------------
RECORDS READ = 00019
END OF TEST
```

One of our batch test runs of the CSCJJJ8 LINKed-to program reveals defects. There appears to be a problem at the month-end boundary. We tracked the problem to the use of an incorrect relational test at line 14200 in the early version of CSCJJJ8 shown in Figure 16.14. Once this had been corrected, we discovered the need to include logic after line 14700 to "adjust" the starting day of each month upward from 00 to 01 since of course the first day of the month is not 00.

Figure 16.17 Test results from an early batch test run of the CSCJJJ8 program, indicating the need for debugging and correction.

it. You can see here how we detected a problem in the table lookup logic WHEN clause. The output Gregorian dates at month end were incorrect, and required changing the ">" at line 14200 in CSCJJJ8 to a ">=" condition. We identified and resolved this and other problems using the batch testing method. After testing was complete, we removed the modifications to CSCJJJ8 necessary to conduct the test, and uncommented the CICS commands. We were then able to install a clean, algorithmically correct final version of CSCJJJ8 on our system.

We strongly suggest that you consider a similar testing strategy and procedure for any CICS modules you develop in your work. The small amount of time required to modify a LINKed-to program for batch testing, and the construction of a test driver, are amply repaid with the ability to test the routine thoroughly and comprehensively.

16.18 FOR YOUR REVIEW

The following terms were introduced or reviewed in this chapter. If you understand this chapter, you should be comfortable with defining each of these terms in relationship to CICS:

- EIBDATE
- EIBTIME
- EIBTRNID
- Generic menu
- GOBACK
- LINK
- Manually coded symbolic map
- Menu program
- OCCURS clause
- Operator identifier
- Password
- PERFORM . . . VARYING symbolic map loading
- PGMIDERR
- SEARCH
- Selection code
- Selection label (text)
- XCTL

16.19 REVIEW QUESTIONS

1. Explain concisely what the function of a menu program is, and identify some of the enhancements possible in a menu program in terms of security of access.
2. Describe what the XCTL and LINK commands do, identifying the major similarities and differences in their operation.
3. Identify and describe the differences between a hardcoded menu and a generic menu, explaining the advantages of the generic menu Approach.
4. Identify and describe the differences between a machine-generated symbolic map and a manually coded symbolic map for a generic menu, explaining the advantages of the manually coded symbolic map for this purpose.
5. Explain briefly how a generic menu program using a manually coded symbolic map loads the selection codes and labels to the symbolic map, and why this technique is particularly flexible.
6. Explain briefly how a generic menu program using selection codes, selection text, and processing program names in a table can analyze and identify the terminal operator's selection, in a way that is flexible and inherently expandable.

7. Explain what "PGMIDERR" means, how it arises in a CICS program, and the response a menu program can use to deal with it.
8. Describe the changes needed in FIRST-TIME execution detection logic required in a menu program that make this process different from the analogous process in a program such as an update or browse, and explain in detail why these changes are necessary.
9. Identify how a program such as an update or a browse needs to be modified when it is to be made selectable via a menu program, and explain what happens if the program is not changed in this way.
10. Explain why it is not necessary to check for "normal" execution of the XCTL command in the EVALUATE that follows this command.
11. Describe what would happen if a program selected from the MENU3 program were to attempt to pass data back to MENU3 using COMMAREA in its XCTL command.
12. Explain the effect of coding GOBACK instead of CICS RETURN at the logical end of a program that receives control with XCTL, and the effect of coding GOBACK instead of CICS RETURN at the logical end of a program that receives control with LINK.
13. Identify and describe the differences between using a CALL and using the LINK command to invoke a routine from a CICS program, and explain the advantages and disadvantages of each approach.
14. Describe how you can limit a program so that it can be invoked only from a menu, and not directly with its own transaction identifier, and why you might want to do this.
15. Describe the kinds of temporary changes you must make in a LINKed-to program to be able to batch test it using a driver program and file-stored test data.

16.20 HANDS-ON EXERCISES

A. Using the menu program in this chapter as a guide, build a menu program that allows selection and execution of at least three of the CICS programs you have already constructed, even if the programs are logically unrelated. In this initial menu, do not attempt to place the date and time on the screen.

B. After completing exercise A, install the logic to put date and time on your menu screen, using a LINK or CALL to a program similar to CSCJJJ8.

C. After completing exercise A, install a keymap and help screen for your menu-selectable programs in your menu program. Use the programs in Chapter 11 as a guide in enhancing your menu program with on-line help.

D. Build a menu to access five new CICS subprograms. Construct the five subprograms so that each one handles one arithmetic operation using two numbers and produces one answer. One menu selectable subprogram will add two numbers, another will subtract two numbers, the third subprogram will multiply two numbers, the fourth subprogram will divide two numbers, and the fifth subprogram will take the first number to the power indicated by the second number. Use the menu program shown in this chapter as a guide, and invoke each subprogram using CALL instead of XCTL.

```
11/01/94             JIM'S SPIFFY 26-ITEM GENERIC MENU SCREEN              GENMENU2
10:34AM                                                                    #004M
                                                                           #004
                                    M E N U
                         Select from list, enter code ===> _

    IB  Inquire into Borrower file          --  (Reserved for future use)
    UB  Update Borrower file                --  (Reserved for future use)
    BB  Browse Borrower file                --  (Reserved for future use)
                                            --  (Reserved for future use)
    IL  Inquire into Loan file              --  (Reserved for future use)
    UL  Update Loan file                    --  (Reserved for future use)
    BL  Browse Loan file                    --  (Reserved for future use)
                                            --  (Reserved for future use)
    RP  Review Projections                  --  (Reserved for future use)
    AC  Amortization Calculator             --  (Reserved for future use)
                                            --  (Reserved for future use)
    --  (Reserved for future use)           --  (Reserved for future use)
    --  (Reserved for future use)           --  (Reserved for future use)

TYPE THE CODE FOR A CHOICE AND PRESS <ENTER>
```

Figure 16.18 Menu with 26 selectable items in two columns, as discussed in Hands-On exercise E.

E. Modify the GENMENU map and the MENU3 program to construct a generic menu having 26 selection codes in two columns, as shown in Figure 16.18. Allow some of the 26 menu item lines to be blank so that selections can be logically grouped and the menu is visually pleasing. (Hint: this does not require any special programming!) Test this modified menu program by using it in place of the menu program you developed in exercises A or D.

APPENDIX

A

CICS Programming Reference

We have collected in this appendix several items you may find it handy to refer to as you learn about and begin to use CICS. You can see here the copybook members IBM supplies with CICS for AID key recognition, attribute bytes, and the execute interface block. We have also provided a unique reference, in alphabetical order, to the 12 most commonly used CICS commands, which are demonstrated in the programs in this book.

A.1 EXECUTE INTERFACE BLOCK CONTENTS

The execute interface block consists of 85 bytes of data comprising 31 fields provided to each program when it is activated by CICS. The CICS translator inserts the definition for the execute interface block into the LINKAGE SECTION of each program, creating the 01 item named DFHEIBLK. You can see a documented description of these fields in Figure A.1.

Execute interface block field				Contents
01 DFHEIBLK.				
	02 EIBTIME	PIC S9(7)	COMP-3.	Time in OHHMMSS format
	02 EIBDATE	PIC S9(7)	COMP-3.	Date in 00YYDDD format
	02 EIBTRNID	PIC X(4).		Trans id
	02 EIBTASKN	PIC S9(7)	COMP-3.	Task number
	02 EIBTRMID	PIC X(4).		Terminal identifier
	02 DFHEIGDI	PIC S9(4)	COMP.	(reserved for future use)
	02 EIBCPOSN	PIC S9(4)	COMP.	Cursor position
	02 EIBCALEN	PIC S9(4)	COMP.	Length of COMMAREA
	02 EIBAID	PIC X(1).		Code of AID key last pressed
	02 EIBFN	PIC X(2).		Function code
	02 EIBRCODE	PIC X(6).		Response code in hex
	02 EIBDS	PIC X(8).		Data set name
	02 EIBREQID	PIC X(8).		Request identifier
	02 EIBRSRCE	PIC X(8).		Resource name
	02 EIBSYNC	PIC X(1).		X'FF' means "syncpoint requested"
	02 EIBFREE	PIC X(1).		X'FF' means "free requested"
	02 EIBRECV	PIC X(1).		X'FF' means "received required"
	02 EIBSEND	PIC X(1).		(reserved for future use)
	02 EIBATT	PIC X(1).		X'FF' means "attach data requested"
	02 EIBEOC	PIC X(1).		X'FF' means "EOC received"
	02 EIBFMH	PIC X(1).		X'FF' means "FMHS received"
	02 EIBCOMPL	PIC X(1).		X'FF' means "data complete"
	02 EIBSIG	PIC X(1).		X'FF' means "signal received"
	02 EIBCONF	PIC X(1).		X'FF' means "confirm requested"
	02 EIBERR	PIC X(1).		X'FF' means "error received"
	02 EIBERRCD	PIC X(4).		Error (abend) code received
	02 EIBSYNRB	PIC X(1).		X'FF' means "sync rollback requested"
	02 EIBNODAT	PIC X(1).		X'FF' means "no applic. data received"
	02 EIBRESP	PIC S9(8)	COMP.	Response code in decimal
	02 EIBRESP2	PIC S9(8)	COMP.	More response details (some cases)
	02 EIBRLDBK	PIC X(1).		X'FF' means "rolled back"

Figure A.1 Fields in the execute interface block and their contents.

A.2 USING EXECUTE INTERFACE BLOCK FIELDS

You may find eight of the 31 fields in the execute interface block of use. We list these here with some idea of how they are relevant to your programming:

```
EIBTIME       PIC S9(7) COMP-3     Time in OHHMMSS format
```

Move this field to a PIC 9(7) and use the parts of the time as you wish:

```
———MOVE———>  01 WS-TIME        PIC 9(7).
             01 WS-TIME-X   REDEFINES WS-TIME.
                05 FILLER      PIC X(1).
                05 WS-HRS      PIC X(2). ———MOVE———>
                05 WS-MIN      PIC X(2). ———MOVE———>
                05 WS-SEC      PIC X(2). ———MOVE———>
```

```
EIBDATE       PIC S9(7) COMP-3     Date in 00YYDDD format
```

Move this field to a PIC 9(7) and use the parts of the date as you wish:

```
———MOVE———>  01 WS-DATE        PIC 9(7).
             01 WS-DATE-X   REDEFINES WS-DATE.
                05 FILLER      PIC X(2).
                05 WS-YEAR     PIC 9(2). ———MOVE———>
                05 WS-DAY      PIC 9(3). ———MOVE———>
```

You may want to give WS-JULIAN to a subprogram that converts a Julian date into the more common Gregorian date format for presentation on the screen.

```
EIBTRNID      PIC X(4)       Trans-id
```

This field indicates the transaction identifier used to invoke the current task. You can use this in a program intended to be invoked via a menu, comparing it to the trans-id of the program itself. If the comparison indicates an equal condition, it means that the program is being invoked directly, not through a menu program, and you can arrange logic to have the program issue a message and quit.

```
EIBTRMID      PIC X(4)       Terminal identifier
```

This is the unique identifier of the terminal that is invoking the program. This is of interest if you are attempting to shield certain programs from execution by specific terminals, or trying to limit program execution to certain specific terminals.

```
EIBCPOSN      PIC S9(4) COMP       Cursor position
```

The cursor position is expressed as a number from 0 through 1919. This can be of use to you in two ways:

1. **Determining which line the cursor is positioned on,** in a program that lets the terminal user point to a line to select something related to the next action. For example, you might let a user place the cursor on a record on a browse screen, and

press a designated PF key to branch to a detailed information screen for the record. To do this, define fields like the following, and take the actions shown:

```
01  WS-WORKFIELD      PIC S9(4)V999     COMP-3.
01  WS-ROW            PIC S9(4)         COMP.
------------------------------------------
    COMPUTE WS-WORKFIELD = (EIBCPOSN + 80) / 80.
    MOVE WS-WORKFIELD TO WS-ROW.
```

After these actions, WS-ROW will contain a number from 1 through 24, indicating the line on which the cursor is positioned. If you have set up your screen using a manually coded symbolic map that has your browse lines defined as a repeating row, and you have saved the key values of the records displayed on the screen in a table with corresponding row numbers, you can use WS-ROW to determine the key of the record that the user is pointing to. (Note: You will have had to preserve the contents of your key table since the last pseudoconverse using the COMMAREA clause of the RETURN command and receiving it in DFHCOMMAREA.)

2. **Determining the field pointed to by the terminal user to trigger context-specific help.** This requires you to carefully compose an EVALUATE statement containing the beginning and ending positions of each data field on the screen for which on-line help is available, so that you can identify the field the cursor is positioned on when the terminal operator presses a designated PF key requesting help. Such an EVALUATE might be similar to this:

```
EVALUATE EIBCPOSN
   WHEN 174 THRU 179  PERFORM SEND-HELP1
   WHEN 256 THRU 260  PERFORM SEND-HELP2
   WHEN 345 THRU 359  PERFORM SEND-HELP3
   WHEN 420 THRU 428  PERFORM SEND-HELP4
   WHEN 502 THRU 504  PERFORM SEND HELP5
   WHEN 590 THRU 599  PERFORM SEND-HELP6
   WHEN 650 THRU 662  PERFORM SEND-HELP7
   WHEN 738 THRU 751  PERFORM SEND-HELP8
   WHEN OTHER
      PERFORM SEND-INVALID-CURSOR-POS-MSG.
```

You can readily compute field starting and ending positions using these simple formulas:

```
start = ( (row -1) * 80 ) + (column -1)
end   = start + length - 1
```

For example, for POS=(1,10),LENGTH=5 you can compute the starting and ending positions as 9 and 13 like this:

```
start = ( ( 1 -1) * 80 ) + ( 10   -1)
      =         0          +  9
      = 9
end   = 9 + 5 - 1
      = 13
```

You must, obviously, update the values in this EVALUATE if you change the layout of the screen or add fields to it. (While the point of providing context-sensitive on-line help is to make the terminal user's life easier, no one ever said that providing context-sensitive on-line help was trivial!)

```
EIBCALEN    PIC S9(4) COMP    Length of COMMAREA
```

This field indicates the number of bytes of data the program previously requested CICS to retain and give back to it for the present pseudoconverse. This value is zero when a program is first invoked by a terminal. The programs in this book show you how to use EIBCALEN to detect the first time a program is invoked.

```
EIBAID      PIC X(1)          Code of AID key last pressed
```

You can use this to identify the PF key that the user pressed by examining the code received here. In Chapter 9 we show you how to use our KEYDEFS copybook member to evaluate the contents of the EIBAID field. You can, alternatively, use the DFHAID copybook member shown in this appendix to determine the meaning of the code in the EIBAID field.

```
EIBRESP     PIC S9(8) COMP    Response code in decimal
```

You can check the value in this field after executing a CICS command such as RECEIVE MAP or READ DATASET to determine if the command executed successfully. Beginning in Chapter 7 of this book, we show you how to streamline your coding to interrogate the response code value using the RESP option of CICS commands and a field named WS-RESPONSE-CODE in WORKING-STORAGE.

A.3 DFHAID AND KEYDEFS COPYBOOK MEMBERS (EIBAID)

You need to COPY into your CICS programs either the DFHAID copybook member shown in Figure A.2, or a more conveniently arranged member named KEYDEFS that we illustrated in Chapter 10 in Figure 10.11.

DFHAID is the plain-vanilla IBM copybook member to assist you in identifying the AID key that a terminal user pressed to activate the program. DFHAID defines 36 one-byte fields, each carrying the code for an AID key. KEYDEFS, on the other hand, in Figure 10.11, contains 88-level coding that may be associated with a one-byte field into which your logic MOVEs the EIBAID field.

A.4 DFHBMSCA AND ATTDEFS COPYBOOK MEMBERS (ATTRIBUTE BYTES)

You need to COPY into your CICS programs either the DFHBMSCA copybook member shown in Figure A.3, or a more conveniently arranged member named ATTDEFS that we illustrated in Chapter 10 in Figure 10.12. You need a member such as this to be able to assign appropriate values to attribute bytes to control the intensity and protection status of screen fields. DFHBMSCA is the old IBM copybook member for this purpose. ATTDEFS is a newer member we developed, which provides more recognizable data names for each of the commonly used attribute settings.

```
EDIT ---- CICS330.SDFHCOB(DFHAID) - 01.00 ------------------ COLUMNS 001 072
COMMAND ===>                                                  SCROLL ===> PAGE
****** ***************************** TOP OF DATA ******************************
==MSG> -CAUTION- DATA CONTAINS INVALID (NON-DISPLAY) CHARACTERS.  USE COMMAND
==MSG>          ===> FIND P'.'          TO POSITION CURSOR TO THESE CHARACTERS.
000001         01   DFHAID.
000002           02 DFHNULL    PIC  X  VALUE IS ' '.
000003           02 DFHENTER   PIC  X  VALUE IS ''''.
000004           02 DFHCLEAR   PIC  X  VALUE IS '_'.
000005           02 DFHCLRP    PIC  X  VALUE IS '┬'.
000006           02 DFHPEN     PIC  X  VALUE IS '='.
000007           02 DFHOPID    PIC  X  VALUE IS 'W'.
000008           02 DFHMSRE    PIC  X  VALUE IS 'X'.
000009           02 DFHSTRF    PIC  X  VALUE IS 'h'.
000010           02 DFHTRIG    PIC  X  VALUE IS '"'.
000011           02 DFHPA1     PIC  X  VALUE IS '%'.
000012           02 DFHPA2     PIC  X  VALUE IS '>'.
000013           02 DFHPA3     PIC  X  VALUE IS ','.
000014           02 DFHPF1     PIC  X  VALUE IS '1'.
000015           02 DFHPF2     PIC  X  VALUE IS '2'.
000016           02 DFHPF3     PIC  X  VALUE IS '3'.
000017           02 DFHPF4     PIC  X  VALUE IS '4'.
000018           02 DFHPF5     PIC  X  VALUE IS '5'.
000019           02 DFHPF6     PIC  X  VALUE IS '6'.
000020           02 DFHPF7     PIC  X  VALUE IS '7'.
000021           02 DFHPF8     PIC  X  VALUE IS '8'.
000022           02 DFHPF9     PIC  X  VALUE IS '9'.
000023           02 DFHPF10    PIC  X  VALUE IS ':'.
000024           02 DFHPF11    PIC  X  VALUE IS '#'.
000025           02 DFHPF12    PIC  X  VALUE IS '@'.
000026           02 DFHPF13    PIC  X  VALUE IS 'A'.
000027           02 DFHPF14    PIC  X  VALUE IS 'B'.
000028           02 DFHPF15    PIC  X  VALUE IS 'C'.
000029           02 DFHPF16    PIC  X  VALUE IS 'D'.
000030           02 DFHPF17    PIC  X  VALUE IS 'E'.
000031           02 DFHPF18    PIC  X  VALUE IS 'F'.
000032           02 DFHPF19    PIC  X  VALUE IS 'G'.
000033           02 DFHPF20    PIC  X  VALUE IS 'H'.
000034           02 DFHPF21    PIC  X  VALUE IS 'I'.
000035           02 DFHPF22    PIC  X  VALUE IS '\'.
000036           02 DFHPF23    PIC  X  VALUE IS '.'.
000037           02 DFHPF24    PIC  X  VALUE IS '<'.
```

You can identify which AID key was pressed to begin a pseudoconverse by comparing the contents of the EIBAID field in the execute interface block to these fields.

Figure A.2 DFHAID copybook member, useful for identifying the AID key indicated by the code in the EIBAID field (see also KEYDEFS copybook member in Figure 10.11).

Both DFHBMSCA and ATTDEFS must make use of some non-displayable values for certain attribute settings. DFHBMSCA, in particular, contains many such values, and may appear strange when viewed or printed in listings. Figure A.4 shows you the first few fields of DFHBMSCA with the TSO/ISPF edit screen set to “hex on” for character and hexadecimal display. You can see in hex that the fields that appear to contain a space in ordinary edit mode actually contain different non-displayable literal values.

A.5 NOTES ON CICS COMMAND REFERENCE

CICS 3.3 supports scores of commands. However, to be “fluent” and productive with CICS requires a working knowledge of only 12 commands. We have drawn information about these 12 most commonly used CICS commands from IBM’s CD-ROM reference materials, entitled *Online Library Omnibus Edition, MVS Collection,* SK2T-0710-04. In the consolidated reference that follows, we use the [ ] symbols to indicate optional clauses of commands, and the vertical bar | to indicate that a choice of a clause is permitted. In various places we use the term “data structure” as a synonym for “record.”

```
EDIT ---- CSCJGJ.CSC360.COPYLIB(DFHBMSCA) - 01.00 ----------- COLUMNS 001 072
COMMAND ===>                                                  SCROLL ===> PAGE
****** ***************************** TOP OF DATA ******************************
==MSG> -CAUTION- DATA CONTAINS INVALID (NON-DISPLAY) CHARACTERS.  USE COMMAND
==MSG>        ===> FIND P'.'        TO POSITION CURSOR TO THESE CHARACTERS.
             01      DFHBMSCA.
               02    DFHBMPEM  PICTURE X   VALUE  IS  ' '.
               02    DFHBMPNL  PICTURE X   VALUE  IS  ' '.
               02    DFHBMPFF  PICTURE X   VALUE  IS  ' '.
               02    DFHBMPCR  PICTURE X   VALUE  IS  ' '.
               02    DFHBMASK  PICTURE X   VALUE  IS  '0'.
               02    DFHBMUNP  PICTURE X   VALUE  IS  ' '.
               02    DFHBMUNN  PICTURE X   VALUE  IS  '&'.
               02    DFHBMPRO  PICTURE X   VALUE  IS  '-'.
               02    DFHBMBRY  PICTURE X   VALUE  IS  'H'.
               02    DFHBMDAR  PICTURE X   VALUE  IS  '<'.
               02    DFHBMFSE  PICTURE X   VALUE  IS  'A'.
               02    DFHBMPRF  PICTURE X   VALUE  IS  '/'.
               02    DFHBMASF  PICTURE X   VALUE  IS  '1'.
               02    DFHBMASB  PICTURE X   VALUE  IS  '8'.
               02    DFHBMEOF  PICTURE X   VALUE  IS  ' '.
               02    DFHBMCUR  PICTURE X   VALUE  IS  ' '.
               02    DFHBMEC   PICTURE X   VALUE  IS  'b'.
               02    DFHBMFLG  PICTURE X.
                   88   DFHERASE VALUES ARE ' ', 'b'.
                   88   DFHCURSR VALUES ARE ' ', 'b'.
               02    DFHBMDET  PICTURE X   VALUE  IS  ' '.
               02    DFHBMPSO  PICTURE X   VALUE  IS  ' '.
               02    DFHBMPSI  PICTURE X   VALUE  IS  ' '.
               02    DFHSA     PICTURE X   VALUE  IS  ' '.
               02    DFHCOLOR  PICTURE X   VALUE  IS  ' '.
               02    DFHPS     PICTURE X   VALUE  IS  ' '.
               02    DFHHLT    PICTURE X   VALUE  IS  ' '.
               02    DFH3270   PICTURE X   VALUE  IS  '{'.
               02    DFHVAL    PICTURE X   VALUE  IS  'A'.
               02    DFHOUTLN  PICTURE X   VALUE  IS  'B'.
               02    DFHBKTRN  PICTURE X   VALUE  IS  ' '.
               02    DFHALL    PICTURE X   VALUE  IS  ' '.
               02    DFHERROR  PICTURE X   VALUE  IS  ' '.
               02    DFHDFT    PICTURE X   VALUE  IS  ' '.
               02    DFHDFCOL  PICTURE X   VALUE  IS  ' '.
               02    DFHBLUE   PICTURE X   VALUE  IS  '1'.
               02    DFHRED    PICTURE X   VALUE  IS  '2'.
               02    DFHPINK   PICTURE X   VALUE  IS  '3'.
               02    DFHGREEN  PICTURE X   VALUE  IS  '4'.
               02    DFHTURQ   PICTURE X   VALUE  IS  '5'.
               02    DFHYELLO  PICTURE X   VALUE  IS  '6'.
               02    DFHNEUTR  PICTURE X   VALUE  IS  '7'.
               02    DFHBASE   PICTURE X   VALUE  IS  ' '.
               02    DFHDFHI   PICTURE X   VALUE  IS  ' '.
               02    DFHBLINK  PICTURE X   VALUE  IS  '1'.
               02    DFHREVRS  PICTURE X   VALUE  IS  '2'.
               02    DFHUNDLN  PICTURE X   VALUE  IS  '4'.
               02    DFHMFIL   PICTURE X   VALUE  IS  ' '.
               02    DFHMENT   PICTURE X   VALUE  IS  ' '.
               02    DFHMFE    PICTURE X   VALUE  IS  ' '.
               02    DFHUNNOD  PICTURE X   VALUE  IS  '('.
               02    DFHUNIMD  PICTURE X   VALUE  IS  'I'.
               02    DFHUNNUM  PICTURE X   VALUE  IS  'J'.
               02    DFHUNINT  PICTURE X   VALUE  IS  'R'.
               02    DFHUNNON  PICTURE X   VALUE  IS  ')'.
               02    DFHPROTI  PICTURE X   VALUE  IS  'Y'.
               02    DFHPROTN  PICTURE X   VALUE  IS  '%'.
               02    DFHMT     PICTURE X   VALUE  IS  ' '.
               02    DFHMFT    PICTURE X   VALUE  IS  ' '.
               02    DFHMET    PICTURE X   VALUE  IS  ' '.
               02    DFHMFET   PICTURE X   VALUE  IS  ' '.
               02    DFHDFFR   PICTURE X   VALUE  IS  ' '.
               02    DFHLEFT   PICTURE X   VALUE  IS  ' '.
               02    DFHOVER   PICTURE X   VALUE  IS  ' '.
               02    DFHRIGHT  PICTURE X   VALUE  IS  ' '.
               02    DFHUNDER  PICTURE X   VALUE  IS  ' '.
               02    DFHBOX    PICTURE X   VALUE  IS  ' '.
               02    DFHSOSI   PICTURE X   VALUE  IS  ' '.
               02    DFHTRANS  PICTURE X   VALUE  IS  '0'.
               02    DFHOPAQ   PICTURE X   VALUE  IS  ' '.
```

Several values the same? Not really. Use HEX ON to see what the different attribute byte values really are!

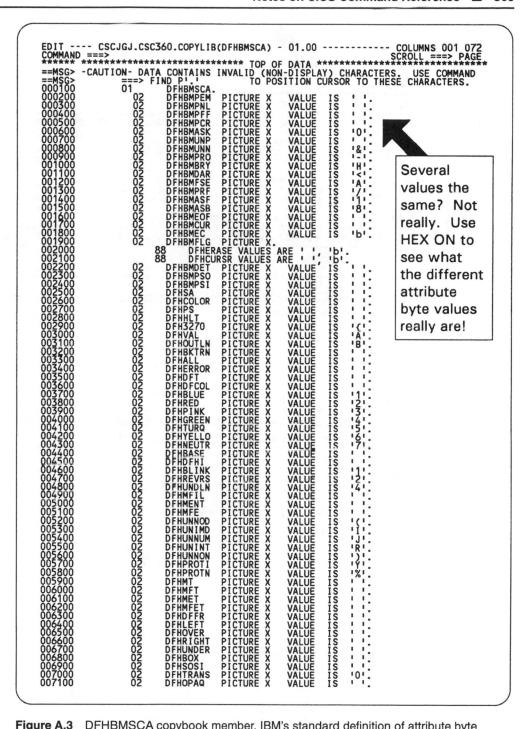

Figure A.3 DFHBMSCA copybook member, IBM's standard definition of attribute byte values (see also ATTDEFS copybook member in Figure 10.12).

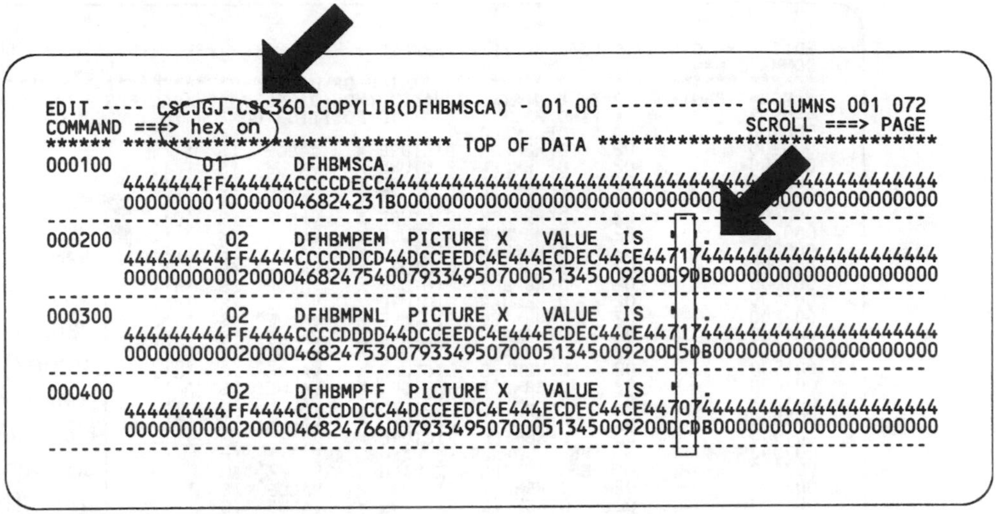
EDIT ---- CSCJGJ.CSC360.COPYLIB(DFHBMSCA) - 01.00 ----------- COLUMNS 001 072
COMMAND ===> hex on
SCROLL ===> PAGE
****** ***************************** TOP OF DATA ******************************
000100 01 DFHBMSCA.
000200 02 DFHBMPEM PICTURE X VALUE IS
44444444FF4444CCCCDDCD44DCCEEDC4E444ECDEC44CE4471744444444444444444444
0000000002000046824754007933495070005134500920009DB0000000000000000000
000300 02 DFHBMPNL PICTURE X VALUE IS
44444444FF4444CCCCDDDD44DCCEEDC4E444ECDEC44CE4471744444444444444444444
00000000020000468247530079334950700051345009200D5DB0000000000000000000
000400 02 DFHBMPFF PICTURE X VALUE IS
44444444FF4444CCCCDDCC44DCCEEDC4E444ECDEC44CE4470744444444444444444444
00000000020000468247660079334950700051345009200DCDB0000000000000000000

Figure A.4 DFHBMSCA viewed using hexadecimal data display to show the actual contents of various attribute byte settings.

A.6 DELETE

Purpose

Remove a record from a Key Sequenced Data Set or a Relative Record Data Set (not, as the command might appear to indicate, delete the entire data set!)

Coding Pattern

```
EXEC CICS
  DELETE     DATASET    ( filename)
             RIDFLD     ( field-name)
             [ RRN     | RBA ]
             RESP       ( WS-RESPONSE-CODE )
END-EXEC
```

Coding Sample

```
EXEC CICS
  DELETE     DATASET     ('CCPV001F')
             RIDFLD      (ACCT-NUM)
             RESP        (WS-RESPONSE-CODE)
END-EXEC
```

DATASET

Filename is the name of the dataset from which a record is to be removed, as defined in the File Control Table (FCT). Note that this is not the actual data set name, but a name assigned by the systems programmer who updates the CICS control tables. If you use a data name to house *filename,* the field must be defined to be eight characters long.

RIDFLD

Field-name is the name of the key field of the record to be deleted, which presumes that you are processing a VSAM Key Sequenced Data Set (KSDS). This field is located in WORKING-STORAGE and can be alphanumeric. Code this field as numeric and specify RRN, for "relative record number," if you are deleting a record from a VSAM Relative Record Data Set (RRDS), so that this is interpreted as the record number.

RRN

Code RRN if you are deleting a record from a Relative Record Data Set and wish to identify the record by its record number.

RBA

Code RBA if you are deleting a record from an Entry Sequenced Data Set and wish to identify the record by its relative byte address.

RESP

WS-RESPONSE-CODE is a PIC S(4) COMP field in WORKING-STORAGE to receive the response code issued by CICS, indicating if the command executed successfully.

Errors This Command Might Generate (see Appendix E)

DISABLED, FILENOTFOUND or DSIDERR, DUPKEY, ILLOGIC, INVREQ, IOERR, NOTAUTH, NOTFND, NOTOPEN, SYSIDERR

A.7 ENDBR

Purpose

Pronounced "end browse," this command formally ends browsing of a file, making it ready for random access READ and for READ/UPDATE. If you do not execute ENDBR, CICS does it automatically at the end of task execution.

Coding Pattern

```
EXEC CICS
     ENDBR   DATASET  ( filename)
             RESP     ( WS-RESPONSE-CODE)
END-EXEC
```

Coding Sample

```
EXEC CICS
     ENDBR   DATASET   ('CCPV001F')
             RESP      (WS-RESPONSE-CODE)
END-EXEC
```

DATASET

Filename is the name of the dataset that has been browsed, as defined in the File Control Table (FCT). Note that this is not the actual data set name, but a name assigned by the systems programmer who updates the CICS control tables. If you use a data name to house *filename,* the field must be defined to be eight characters long.

RESP

WS-RESPONSE-CODE is a PIC S(4) COMP field in WORKING-STORAGE to receive the response code issued by CICS, indicating if the command executed successfully.

Errors This Command Might Generate (see Appendix E)

DISABLED, FILENOTFOUND or DSIDERR, ILLOGIC, INVREQ, NOTAUTH, NOTOPEN, SYSIDERR

A.8 LINK

Purpose

Transfers control to another program, but has CICS retain in memory the program transferring control. The program from which control is transferred will receive control again when the linked-to program ends execution with RETURN with no trans-id. LINK provided a mechanism similar to CALL before CALL was fully supported. You can now use CALL instead, as illustrated in Chapter 10 of this book, and eliminate the need to establish in the Program Control Table (PCT) the name of the program being transferred to.

Coding Pattern

```
EXEC CICS
     LINK   PROGRAM    ( progname)
            COMMAREA   ( data-name)
            RESP       ( WS-RESPONSE-CODE)
END-EXEC
```

Coding Sample

```
EXEC CICS
     LINK   PROGRAM    ('CSCSMS9')
            COMMAREA   (COMM-DATE-AREA)
            RESP       (WS-RESPONSE-CODE)
END-EXEC
```

PROGRAM

Progname specifies the name of the program to be transferred to. This name must be defined in the Program Control Table (PCT). If you use a data name to house *progname,* the field must be defined to be eight characters long.

COMMAREA

Data-name specifies a data field or structure to be passed to the program that control is transferred to. The linked-to program accesses the passed data in its DFHCOMMAREA field.

RESP

WS-RESPONSE-CODE is a PIC S(4) COMP field in WORKING-STORAGE to receive the response code issued by CICS, indicating if the command executed successfully. If the LINK command did not complete successfully, the program attempting to transfer control remains active and should take error recovery or notification actions.

Errors This Command Might Generate (see Appendix E)

PGMIDERR, NOTAUTH

A.9 READ

Purpose

Obtain a record from a Key Sequenced Data Set, Relative Record Data Set, or Entry Sequenced Data Set directly using the record key, number, or relative byte address (RBA). (Unlike the case in batch COBOL, this READ does not accomplish sequential reading; for sequential reading, see the READNEXT command.)

Coding Pattern

```
EXEC CICS
    READ   DATASET    ( filename)
           INTO       ( data-name)
           RIDFLD     ( field-name)
           [ RRN      | RBA ]
           [ UPDATE ]
           RESP       ( WS-RESPONSE-CODE)
END-EXEC
```

Coding Sample

```
EXEC CICS
    READ   DATASET    ('CCPV001F')
           INTO       (ACCT-REC)
           RIDFLD     (ACCT-NUM)
           UPDATE
           RESP       (WS-RESPONSE-CODE)
END-EXEC
```

DATASET

Filename is the name of the dataset to be read from, as defined in the File Control Table (FCT). Note that this is not the actual data set name, but a name assigned by the systems programmer who updates the CICS control tables. If you use a data-name to house *filename* the field must be defined to be eight characters long.

INTO

Data-name is the 01 level name of the record description in WORKING-STORAGE where the record to be read is to be placed.

RIDFLD

Field-name is the name of the key field of the record to be read, which presumes that you are reading a VSAM Key Sequenced Data Set (KSDS). This field is located in WORKING-STORAGE and can be alphanumeric. Code this field as numeric and specify RRN, for "relative record number," if you are reading a record from a VSAM Relative Record Data Set (RRDS), so that this is interpreted as the record number. If you are reading a record from a VSAM Entry Sequenced Data Set (ESDS), code this field as numeric and code RBA, for "relative byte address."

RRN

Code RRN if you are reading a record from a Relative Record Data Set and wish to identify the record by its record number.

RBA

Code RBA if you are reading a record from an Entry Sequenced Data Set and wish to identify the record by its relative byte address.

UPDATE

Stipulates that you are intending to later REWRITE or DELETE the record, and "locks" it against access by others as long as your program is active. (The lock is removed when your program executes CICS RETURN, as it is not held between pseudoconverses.)

RESP

WS-RESPONSE-CODE is a PIC S(4) COMP field in WORKING-STORAGE to receive the response code issued by CICS, indicating if the command executed successfully.

Errors This Command Might Generate (see Appendix E)

DISABLED, FILENOTFOUND or DSIDERR, DUPKEY, ILLOGIC, INVREQ, IOERR, LENGERR, NOTAUTH, NOTFND, NOTOPEN, SYSIDERR

A.10 READNEXT

Purpose

Obtain the next record from a file sequentially. The first READNEXT executed after a STARTBR command will obtain the record that the STARTBR positioned on. Each subsequent READNEXT will obtain the record with the next highest key.

Coding Pattern

```
EXEC CICS
   READNEXT   DATASET    ( filename)
              INTO       ( data-name)
              RIDFLD     ( field-name)
              RESP       ( WS-RESPONSE-CODE )
END-EXEC
```

Coding Sample

```
EXEC CICS
   READNEXT   DATASET    ('CCPV001F')
              INTO       (ACCT-REC)
              RIDFLD     (ACCT-NUM)
              RESP       (WS-RESPONSE-CODE)
END-EXEC
```

DATASET

Filename is the name of the dataset to be read from, as defined in the File Control Table (FCT). Note that this is not the actual data set name, but a name assigned by the systems programmer who updates the CICS control tables. If you use a data-name to house *filename* the field must be defined to be eight characters long.

INTO

Data-name is the 01 level name of the record description in WORKING-STORAGE where the record to be read is to be placed.

RIDFLD

Field-name is the name of the key field of the record to be read, which presumes that you are reading a VSAM Key Sequenced Data Set (KSDS). This field is located in WORKING-STORAGE and can be alphanumeric.

RESP

WS-RESPONSE-CODE is a PIC S(4) COMP field in WORKING-STORAGE to receive the response code issued by CICS, indicating if the command executed successfully.

Errors This Command Might Generate (see Appendix E)

DISABLED, FILENOTFOUND or DSIDERR, DUPKEY, ENDFILE, ILLOGIC, INVREQ, IOERR, LENGERR, NOTAUTH, NOTFND, NOTOPEN, SYSIDERR

A.11 RECEIVE MAP

Purpose

Transfer information from a terminal to a CICS program using the Basic Mapping Support (BMS) subsystem.

Coding Pattern

```
EXEC CICS
    RECEIVE   MAP       ( mapname)
              MAPSET    ( mapsetname)
              INTO      ( data-name)
              RESP      ( WS-RESPONSE-CODE)
END-EXEC
```

Coding Sample

```
EXEC CICS
    RECEIVE   MAP       ('FILEMAP')
              MAPSET    ('SMSAM')
              INTO      (FILEMAPI)
              RESP      (WS-RESPONSE-CODE)
END-EXEC
```

MAP

Mapname is the name of the map to be received, as coded in the BMS map source code. If you use a data name to house *mapname,* the field must be defined to be eight characters long.

MAPSET

Mapsetname is the name of the mapset in which the map is located, as coded in the BMS map source code. This name must be defined in the Program Control Table (PCT). If you use a data name to house *mapsetname,* the field must be defined to be eight characters long.

INTO

The 01 level data name in WORKING-STORAGE of the symbolic map (data transmission record description) into which the data received from the terminal is to be placed.

RESP

WS-RESPONSE-CODE is a PIC S(4) COMP field in WORKING-STORAGE to receive the response code issued by CICS, indicating if the command executed successfully.

Errors This Command Might Generate (see Appendix E)

INVMPSZ, MAPFAIL, INVPARTN, PARTNFAIL

A.12 RETURN

Purpose

Gives control back to CICS, either with the intention of resuming program operation when the terminal operator presses an AID key, or without this intention.

Coding Pattern

```
EXEC CICS
    RETURN   TRANSID    ( name)
             COMMAREA   ( data-name)
             LENGTH     ( data-value)
END-EXEC
```

Coding Sample

```
EXEC CICS
    RETURN   TRANSID    ('#001')
             COMMAREA   (WS-COMM-AREA)
END-EXEC
```

TRANSID

Name is the name of the transaction to be activated when the terminal user next presses an AID key. The trans-id must be defined in the Program Control Table (PCT). The trans-id is most often that of the program itself, so that pseudoconversation can be resumed. If you execute RETURN without TRANSID and *name,* you end the pseudoconversation and CICS resumes full control, making it necessary to manually enter a new transaction identifier or CESF LOGOFF. If you use a data name to house *name,* the field must be defined to be four characters long.

COMMAREA

Data-name is the data name of the field or structure in WORKING-STORAGE that will be preserved by CICS and passed to the program when it is again activated. The program receives the retained data in its LINKAGE-SECTION in the DFHCOMMAREA field.

LENGTH

Data-value indicates the number of bytes to be preserved by CICS until the program again becomes active. You need not code this if you want to preserve the full length of the field referred to by *data-name* mentioned in the COMMAREA clause, since by default the full length will automatically be preserved. If you code LENGTH, *data-value* can be either the name of a PIC S9(4) COMP field or a numeric literal. The value conveyed with LENGTH cannot be larger than the size, in bytes, of the item at *data-name.*

Errors This Command Might Generate (see Appendix E)

INVREQ, NOTAUTH

A.13 REWRITE

Purpose

Replaces a record in a Key Sequenced Data Set, Relative Record Data Set, or Entry Sequenced Data Set, completing an update action.

Coding Pattern

```
EXEC CICS
   REWRITE   DATASET     ( filename)
             FROM        ( data-name)
             RESP        ( WS-RESPONSE-CODE)
END-EXEC
```

Coding Sample

```
EXEC CICS
   REWRITE  DATASET     ('CCPV001F')
            FROM        (ACCT-REC)
            RESP        (WS-RESPONSE-CODE)
END-EXEC
```

DATASET

Filename is the name of the dataset to be rewritten to, as defined in the File Control Table (FCT). Note that this is not the actual data set name, but a name assigned by the systems programmer who updates the CICS control tables. If you use a data name to house *filename* the field must be defined to be eight characters long.

FROM

Data-name is the 01 level name of the record description in WORKING-STORAGE where the record to be rewritten is located in the program.

RESP

WS-RESPONSE-CODE is a PIC S(4) COMP field in WORKING-STORAGE to receive the response code issued by CICS, indicating if the command executed successfully.

Note: You can REWRITE a record only after obtaining it, within the same pseudo-converse, with the READ DATASET command *with* the UPDATE option. Unless you do this READ *with* UPDATE immediately before attempting the REWRITE, you do not have sufficient authority to rewrite the record and your REWRITE will fail. READ with UPDATE locks the record for your use, preventing other tasks from accessing it while you update it. (Your READ with UPDATE will fail if another task is already updating the record.)

Errors This Command Might Generate (see Appendix E)

DISABLED, FILENOTFOUND or DSIDERR, DUPKEY, ILLOGIC, INVREQ, IOERR, LENGERR, NOSPACE, NOTAUTH, NOTFND, NOTOPEN, SYSIDERR

A.14 SEND MAP

Purpose

Sends a screen image to a terminal, either with both labels and data, or labels only, or data only. To send both labels and data, do not code MAPONLY or DATAONLY.

Coding Pattern

```
EXEC CICS
    SEND    MAP         ( mapname)
            MAPSET      ( mapsetname)
            FROM        ( data-name)
            [ MAPONLY| DATAONLY ]
            [  ERASE | ERASEAUP ]
            [ CURSOR [ data-value] ]
            RESP        ( WS-RESPONSE-CODE)
END-EXEC
```

Coding Sample

```
EXEC CICS
    SEND    MAP         ('FILEMAP')
            MAPSET      ('SMSAM')
            FROM        (FILEMAPI)
            ERASE
            CURSOR
            RESP        (WS-RESPONSE-CODE)
END-EXEC
```

MAP

Mapname is the name of the map to be sent, as coded in the BMS map source code. This name is from one to seven characters long and is *not* predefined in any CICS table. If you use a data name to house *mapname,* the field must be defined to be eight characters long.

MAPSET

Mapsetname is the mapset name as coded in the BMS map source code. This name *must* be predefined to CICS as an entry in the Program Control Table (PCT). If you use a data name to house *mapsetname,* the field must be defined to be eight characters long.

FROM

Data-name is the data name in WORKING-STORAGE of the symbolic map (data transmission record description) from which data will be sent to the screen. Specify this unless you also code the MAPONLY option.

MAPONLY

Causes only the physical map to be transmitted, that is, only screen labels to be transmitted. If you specify this, it makes no sense to code FROM, since the symbolic map is not sent.

DATAONLY

Causes only non LOW-VALUES data in the symbolic map to be transmitted, and the physical map is not accessed. You can't specify both MAPONLY and DATAONLY in the same SEND command.

ERASE

Indicates that you want the terminal screen to be completely blanked out before the new transmission reaches it.

ERASEAUP

Tells CICS to erase "all unprotected fields" rather than the entire screen, before the transmission is received.

CURSOR

Tells CICS to put the cursor into the first enterable (unprotected) field it encounters that contains a negative value in its "length" indicator. This is commonly used to position the cursor to the first enterable field on the screen, or to the first field with a data content error.

CURSOR(nn)

(nn) indicates the specific location for cursor placement as a value from 0 to 1919. 0 is the same as map coding of POS=(1,1), 80 is the same as POS=(2,1), and 1919 is the same as POS=(24,80). This is not commonly used for cursor positioning.

RESP

WS-RESPONSE-CODE is a PIC S(4) COMP field in WORKING-STORAGE to receive the response code issued by CICS, indicating if the command executed successfully.

Errors This Command Might Generate (see Appendix E)

INVMPSZ, INVREQ, OVERFLOW, TSIODERR

A.15 STARTBR

Purpose

Pronounced "start browse," this command positions CICS for sequential reading of records from a data set using the READNEXT command. STARTBR does not actually acquire a record itself. (Note: Additional optional clauses exist for STARTBR. We document here only those options useful to the type of programs illustrated in this book.)

Coding Pattern

```
EXEC CICS
   STARTBR   DATASET     ( filename)
             RIDFLD      ( field-name)
             [ EQUAL | GTEQ ]
             RESP        ( WS-RESPONSE-CODE)
END-EXEC
```

Coding Sample

```
EXEC CICS
   STARTBR    DATASET  ('CCPV001F')
              RIDFLD   (ACCT-NAME)
              RESP     (WS-RESPONSE-CODE)
END-EXEC
```

DATASET

Filename is the name of the dataset to be read from, as defined in the File Control Table (FCT). Note that this is not the actual data set name, but a name assigned by the systems programmer who updates the CICS control tables. If you use a data name to house *filename,* the field must be defined to be eight characters long.

RIDFLD

Field-name is the name of the key field of the record that sequential reading is to begin with. This field is located in WORKING-STORAGE and can be alphanumeric.

EQUAL

Indicates that the start browse is to be successful only if the entire length of the data value in RIDFLD is found in a key field of a record in the file. The condition is the default if you do not code EQUAL or GTEQ.

GTEQ

Pronounced "greater than or equal to," this allows the STARTBR command to succeed if an exact match is found between the RIDFLD value and a key field in a record in the file, or, if no exact match is found, if there is at least a record in the file with a key value higher than the RIDFLD value. This is the default.

RESP

WS-RESPONSE-CODE is a PIC S(4) COMP field in WORKING-STORAGE to receive the response code issued by CICS, indicating if the command executed successfully.

Errors This Command Might Generate (see Appendix E)

DISABLED, FILENOTFOUND or DSIDERR, ILLOGIC, INVREQ, IOERR, NOTAUTH, NOTFND, NOTOPEN, SYSIDERR

A.16 WRITE

Purpose

Insert a record into a Key Sequenced Data Set, Relative Record Data Set, or Entry Sequenced Data Set.

Coding Pattern

```
EXEC CICS
   WRITE   DATASET    ( filename)
           FROM       ( data-name)
           RIDFLD     ( field-name)
           [ RRN | RBA ]
           RESP       ( WS-RESPONSE-CODE)
END-EXEC
```

Coding Sample

```
EXEC CICS
   WRITE   DATASET    ('CCPV001F')
           FROM       (ACCT-REC)
           RIDFLD     (ACCT-NUM')
           RESP       (WS-RESPONSE-CODE)
END-EXEC
```

DATASET

Filename is the name of the dataset to be written to, as defined in the File Control Table (FCT). Note that this is not the actual data set name, but a name assigned by the systems programmer who updates the CICS control tables. If you use a data name to house *filename,* the field must be defined to be eight characters long.

FROM

Data-name is the 01 level name of the record description in WORKING-STORAGE where the record to be written is located in the program.

RIDFLD

Field-name is the name of the key field of the record to be written, which presumes that you are writing a VSAM Key Sequenced Data Set (KSDS). This field is located in WORKING-STORAGE and can be alphanumeric. Code this field as numeric and specify RRN, for "relative record number," if you are writing a record to a VSAM Relative Record Data Set (RRDS), so that this is interpreted as the record number. If you are writing a record to a VSAM Entry Sequenced Data Set (ESDS), code this field as numeric and code RBA, for "relative byte address."

RRN

Code RRN if you are writing a record to a Relative Record Data Set and wish to identify the record by its record number.

RBA

Code RBA if you are writing a record to an Entry Sequenced Data Set and wish to identify the record by its relative byte address.

RESP

WS-RESPONSE-CODE is a PIC S(4) COMP field in WORKING-STORAGE to receive the response code issued by CICS, indicating if the command executed successfully.

Errors This Command Might Generate (see Appendix E)

DISABLED, FILENOTFOUND or DSIDERR, DUPKEY, ILLOGIC, INVREQ, IOERR, LENGERR, NOSPACE, NOTAUTH, NOTOPEN, SYSIDERR

A.17 XCTL

Purpose

Transfers control to another program without having CICS retain any knowledge of the program giving up control. The program from which control is transferred is removed from memory.

Coding Pattern

```
EXEC CICS
   XCTL    PROGRAM    ( progname)
           COMMAREA   ( data-name)
           RESP       ( WS-RESPONSE-CODE )
END-EXEC
```

Coding Sample

```
EXEC CICS
   XCTL    PROGRAM    ('CSCSMSA')
           RESP       (WS-RESPONSE-CODE)
END-EXEC
```

PROGRAM

Progname specifies the name of the program to be transferred to. This name must be defined in the Program Control Table (PCT). If you use a data name to house *progname,* the field must be defined to be eight characters long.

COMMAREA

Data-name specifies a field or data structure to be passed to the program that control is transferred to. The program accesses the passed data in its DFHCOMMAREA field.

RESP

WS-RESPONSE-CODE is a PIC S(4) COMP field in WORKING-STORAGE to receive the response code issued by CICS, indicating if the command executed successfully. If the XCTL command did not complete successfully, the program attempting to transfer control remains active and should take error recovery or notification actions.

Note: If you XCTL from a menu program to a program handling a menu selection, don't code COMMAREA or you will foul the program's ability to detect a "first-time" condition using EIBCALEN = 0. EIBCALEN will reflect the length of the COMMAREA passed from one program to another when you use XCTL.

Errors This Command Might Generate (see Appendix E)

PGMIDERR, NOTAUTH

APPENDIX

B

Using CECI NEWCOPY and SEND MAP

CECI is a powerful, general purpose utility transaction supplied by IBM with CICS. This appendix shows you how to use the CECI transaction to force CICS to update its control tables concerning a new copy of a physical map or program load module, and to test new screen maps. First we'll explain why this action is necessary, then we'll demonstrate its use with the actual screens you will see when you do this.

B.1 WHY CECI NEWCOPY IS NECESSARY

The CICS load library houses the machine language (physical maps) for your screen images and the machine language (load modules) for your CICS programs. Both physical maps and program load modules result from your submission of job control language to process source code.

While you don't access the CICS load library using TSO edit, it is, like your source code libraries, a partitioned data set. In fact, library is a traditional IBM mainframe synonym for partitioned data set. (Under MVS/ESA Version 4 and Storage Management Subsystem, this is changing slightly, with the data set name type LIBRARY associated with a new form of partitioned data set, the partitioned data set extended, or PDSE.) As with any partitioned data set, the load library has a directory, which contains entries that point to the members housed within the library. Each physical map or program load module is a member of the CICS load library.

If you change the BMS source code for a map and reprocess it, you place a new copy of the physical map in the CICS load library. If you change the COBOL program source code for a

CICS program and again translate, compile, and link edit it, you place a new copy of the program load module in the CICS load library. In neither case is the original copy of the physical map or load module replaced, however. Instead, the new copy is put into unused data space in the library, and the directory entry is changed to point to the new member. The old member remains in place, but its location is no longer known to the partitioned data set directory.

Ordinary software and TSO/ISPF use the directory of a partitioned data set to access a member. This software will always acquire the most recent copy of a member because it follows the partitioned data set directory to find the member. But CICS is not ordinary software. It does not follow the partitioned data set directory to find a member, except for its very first access to a given member. Once the member has been accessed, CICS records its actual physical location of the program in the load library in the CICS control tables. Every time you access the physical map or program after the first time, CICS saves time by using its own control table to find the member in the load library, rather than looking in the load library directory.

You can see where CICS's actions can lead in the case of a new copy of a physical map or program load module. Left to its own devices, CICS will continue to access the original copy of a physical map or program load module even after you have put a new copy of it in the library. In order to make CICS aware of the new copy, so that it finds it using the load library directory, you have to take special action. This special action involves the use of the NEWCOPY function of the special CECI service transaction.

B.2 USING CECI NEWCOPY

CECI is a CICS service transaction, that is, a special, multipurpose transaction provided preprogrammed with CICS. All transactions that begin with the letter "C" are special CICS transactions provided to help manage and control it.

You use CECI after putting a new copy of a physical map or program load module into the CICS load library. To use CECI, you need to know the name of the physical map or program load module that you have replaced. You of course will know this since you specify it in the job control language you submit for processing to replace it! In the case of the example in this appendix, we will use a program named C360A001, which has been associated with transaction $001. The transaction identifier is not used in the CECI command, however.

To begin using CECI, log onto CICS and press the Clear key to clear the screen. Then enter the command:

```
CECI SET PROGRAM(C360A001) NEWCOPY
```

as shown in Figure B.1. Note that you place the program name for which you want to have CICS become aware of a new copy within the parentheses. Press the Enter key. In response to this command you will receive the screen shown in Figure B.2.

CECI checks your entry before executing it, and lists the options available with the command before proceeding. Figure B.2 shows you the screen that results from successful checking of the command. Press the Enter key again to confirm that you want to proceed, or press F1 for help in understanding more about CECI.

If your CECI NEWCOPY command executed successfully, you will receive the screen shown in Figure B.3. You will know that the command worked, and that CICS updated its control tables with the current location of the most recent copy of the map or program, if the "response" indicator at the bottom of the screen is followed by the word "normal." If "nor-

```
ceci set program(c360a001) newcopy
```

Start the CECI transaction this way beginning with a blank screen.

Figure B.1 Initiate the CECI transaction from a blank screen to tell CICS about a new copy of a map or program.

```
SET PROGRAM(C360A001) NEWCOPY
STATUS:  ABOUT TO EXECUTE COMMAND                          NAME=
 EXEC CICS  SET Program( 'C360A001' )
  < CEDFStatus() | CEDF | NOcedf >
  < COpy() | NEwcopy | PHasein >
  < EXecutionset() | DPlsubset | Fullapi >
  < SHAREStatus() | PRivate | SHARED >
  < STatus() | DIsabled | ENabled >
  < Version() >

PF 1 HELP 2 HEX 3 END 4 EIB 5 VAR 6 USER 7 SBH 8 SFH 9 MSG 10 SB 11 SF
```

Press the **Enter** key to confirm your command for execution. (The extra information on this confirmation screen just shows you the options available with the SET command.)

Figure B.2 CECI checks your command before executing it, and shows you the options available with the command, before processing it.

```
SET PROGRAM(C360A001) NEWCOPY
STATUS:  COMMAND EXECUTION COMPLETE                                     NAME=
 EXEC CICS  SET Program( 'C360A001' )
  < CEDFStatus() | CEDF | NOcedf >
  < COpy() | NEwcopy | PHasein >
  < EXecutionset() | DPlsubset | Fullapi >
  < SHAREStatus() | PRivate | SHARED >
  < STatus() | DIsabled | ENabled >
  < Version( +0000000162 ) >




 RESPONSE: NORMAL                  EIBRESP=+0000000000 EIBRESP2=+0000000000
PF 1 HELP 2 HEX 3 END 4 EIB 5 VAR 6 USER 7 SBH 8 SFH 9 MSG 10 SB 11 SF
```

NORMAL indicates that your command processed successfully.

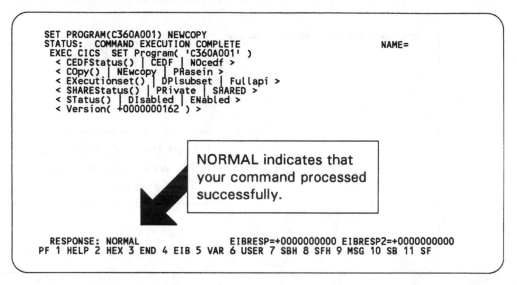

Figure B.3 After execution, CECI indicates that your command was successfully processed by putting the NORMAL message at the bottom of the screen.

mal" does not appear at this point, one of these errors has occurred. It is most likely you misspelled the program name, and CICS was not able to find such a map or program in the load library.

Once you have successfully executed NEWCOPY, press the PF3 key. You will receive the screen shown in Figure B.4. Then press the Clear key.

```
CECI SET PROGRAM(C360A001) NEWCOPY
 STATUS:  SESSION ENDED
```

Press the **PF3** key, then the **Clear** key, to quit CECI.

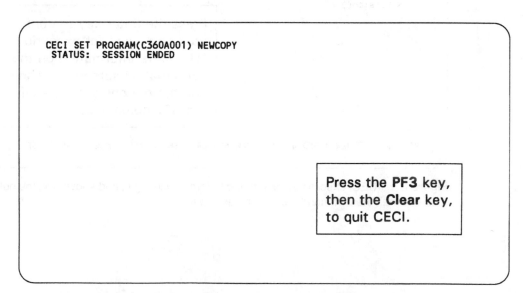

Figure B.4 To end execution of CECI, press the PF3 key, then the Clear key.

B.3 TRYING OUT CECI

Using CECI NEWCOPY is a necessary part of your work as a CICS programmer. Try it out for yourself in this way:

1. Using TSO/ISPF, create BMS source code for a map as described in Chapter 4.
2. Process your BMS code into a physical map using JCL similar to MAPJOB as shown in Chapter 5. You will need to have your CICS administration group (or instructor) issue you a defined CICS map name to accomplish this.
3. Create a program such as SHOWMAP in Chapter 6 to display your map on the screen.
4. Process your SHOWMAP program into a program load module using JCL similar to PGMJOB as shown in Chapter 6. You will need to have your CICS administration group (or instructor) issue you a defined CICS program name and corresponding trans-id to accomplish this.
5. Log onto CICS and execute your SHOWMAP program using its assigned trans-id.
6. Go back into TSO/ISPF and change your SHOWMAP program to move a different message to the map prompt field.
7. Repeat step 4, to put a new copy of the load module for your SHOWMAP program into the CICS load library.
8. Log onto CICS and execute your SHOWMAP program using its assigned trans-id. Does the original prompt or the new prompt message appear? You will see the original prompt, even though you replaced the program load module!
9. Execute the CECI NEWCOPY transaction as described in this appendix for the assigned CICS program name of your SHOWMAP program.
10. Log onto CICS and execute your SHOWMAP program using its assigned trans-id. Does the original prompt or the new prompt message appear? You should see the new prompt, since your successfully executed CECI NEWCOPY transaction forced CICS to learn the location of your replacement program load module using the load library directory.

If your new version of the program's prompt does not appear in step 10, you either made a syntax error in changing the source code of your SHOWMAP program, or you did not execute the CECI command properly. Check your program translate, compile, and link run (the PGMJOB reporting output) and try the CECI NEWCOPY transaction again.

B.4 USING CECI TO DISPLAY A MAP

You can make incidental use of CECI as an expedient to try out a physical map before completing a program that accesses it. This can be handy to see what a new screen will look like on a terminal, and to see that stopper fields have been coded properly.

To use CECI to display a map, begin on a blank screen and enter the CECI transaction with the SEND MAP command, as shown in Figure B.5. When you press the Enter key you will see a screen as illustrated in Figure B.6. CECI will confirm your command, checking its syntax, and showing a variety of options specific to the command. Press the Enter key again, and you will execute the command, producing a screen such as Figure B.7. (You may recognize Figure B.7 as the revised CALC1 screen we discuss in Chapter 9.)

A screen displayed by CECI as in Figure B.7 has no logic behind it, so you cannot expect it to be able to process data that you enter. You can, however, enter data into the unprotected

```
ceci send map(#002)
```

Use CECI with this command to test a new screen map before any program is ready to use it.

Figure B.5 Initiate the CECI transaction from a blank screen to display a map to check your field NUM and stopper field coding.

```
 SEND MAP(#002)
 STATUS:  ABOUT TO EXECUTE COMMAND                            NAME=
  EXEC CICS  SENd Map( '#002    ' )
   << FROm() > < Dataonly > | MAPOnly >
   < LEngth( +00004 ) >
   < MAPSet() >
   < FMhparm() >
   < Reqid() >
   < LDc() | < ACTpartn() > < Outpartn() > >
   < MSr() >
   < Cursor() >
   < Set() | PAging | Terminal < Wait > < LAst > >
   < PRint >
   < FREekb >
   < ALarm >
   < L40 | L64 | L80 | Honeom >
   < NLeom >
   < ERASE | ERASEAup >
   < ACCum >
+  < FRSet >

PF 1 HELP 2 HEX 3 END 4 EIB 5 VAR 6 USER 7 SBH 8 SFH 9 MSG 10 SB 11 SF
```

Press the **Enter** key to confirm your command for execution.

Figure B.6 CECI checks your SEND MAP command before executing it, and shows you the options available with the command, before processing it.

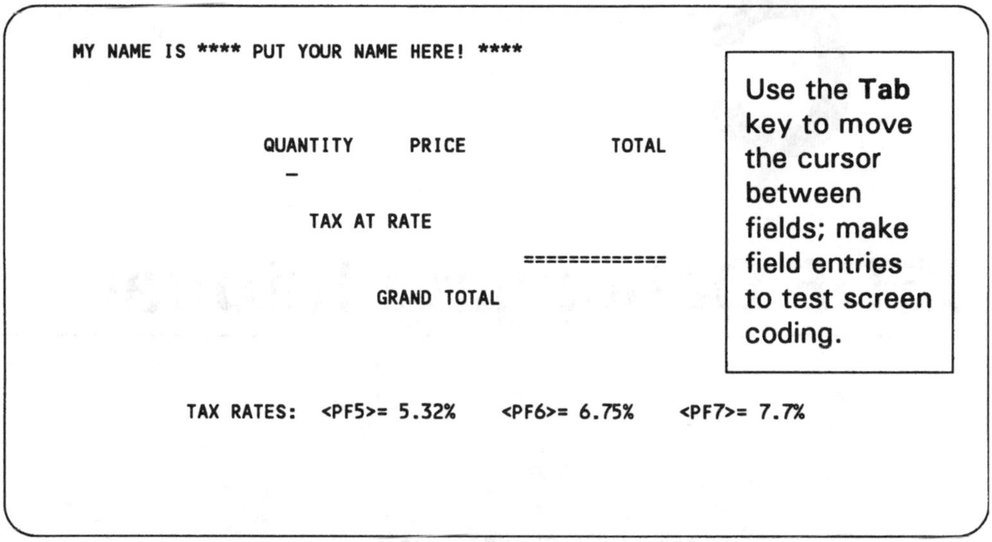
MY NAME IS **** PUT YOUR NAME HERE! ****
QUANTITY PRICE TOTAL
TAX AT RATE
=============
GRAND TOTAL
TAX RATES: <PF5>= 5.32% <PF6>= 6.75% <PF7>= 7.7%
Use the **Tab** key to move the cursor between fields; make field entries to test screen coding.

Figure B.7 A map displayed using CECI looks exactly the same as if sent to the screen by a program; use it to check out field NUM and stopper field coding.

fields of such a displayed screen, and NUM attribute by coding will work if coded for a field. One of the handiest uses of a CECI map display is to be able to check that NUM and stopper fields are coded properly. Use the Tab key to move to each enterable field, and enter data into each field, continuing to the end of the field. If your stopper fields are coded correctly, you should be able to enter only to the intended maximum length of each field.

To end display of a map with CECI, press the Enter key while you are viewing the screen; then press the PF3 key followed by the Clear key.

APPENDIX

C

CEDF Debugging Tutorial

While some installations purchase non-IBM debugging software to aid programmers in debugging CICS/COBOL programs, CICS provides a reasonably good debugging facility named Command Execution Diagnostic Facility, or CEDF. In this appendix, we show you how to use CEDF to investigate and resolve some types of problems in CICS code.

Aside from what it can do to help you resolve abends, CEDF is a good learning tool, since it lets you execute a CICS program step-by-step, seeing what is in the memory and execute interface block of the program. Just running a pseudoconversational program with CEDF can provide a concrete picture of how one pseudoconverse is handled as a task, and how multiple tasks begin and end to complete the processing of one transaction. We recommend that you do your execution of new programs under CEDF, to prevent a program with a serious problem from taking CICS itself down, or looping unintentionally and causing CICS to bog down for everyone else using it.

C.1 DEBUGGING CICS ABEND CODES

Appendix E shows you many different kinds of CICS abend codes. Of these many codes, a common one is ABM0, which you will receive when CICS encounters an illegal mapset name or map name. Another common abend code is ASRA, which is quite similar to an 0C7 data exception. We'll show you how to use CEDF in connection with abends of these two types.

C.2 DEBUGGING AN ABM0 FAILURE STEP BY STEP

In Figure C.1 you see how CICS reports an ABM0 failure. Let's assume that you executed the SMSA transaction (the update program of Chapter 14) and proceeded to "fill in" the screen, then pressed the Enter key. You received an ABM0 message at the bottom of the screen, and the record

```
                    -=SAMUEL'S WORTHLESS FINANCE COMPANY=-                FILEMAP
                            ****** FILE UPDATE ******                       SMSAM

(A)dd, (D)elete, (C)hange, or (V)iew: A
Name:  JOHNSON, SAM                         Account Number:  58203922

------------------------------- CHARGE ITEMS ------------------------------
  Charge Amount 1:  100000
  Charge Amount 2:  000000
  Charge Amount 3:  000000
  Charge Amount 4:  000000
  Charge Amount 5:  000000              Total Charge Items:

------------------------------ CASH ADVANCES -----------------------------
 Cash Ad Amount 1:  030000
 Cash Ad Amount 2:  000000               Total Cash Advances:
                                  Finance Charge On Cash Advances:

                                  ============================================

                                                   Total Debits:

DFHAC2206 15:20:44 DBDCCIC1 Transaction SMSA has failed with abend ABMO.
 Resource backout was successful.
```

Figure C.1 CICS reports an ABMO abend.

for SAMUEL JOHNSON was not added to the existing file. How can CEDF help you identify and resolve the problem? We'll show you how we would do it if we were in your shoes.

To use the CEDF debugging facility, you must enter CICS, clear the screen, and key in "cedf", then press the Enter key, as shown in Figure C.2. This puts the terminal into debugging mode, as indicated in Figure C.3. You can now clear the screen and re-execute the failed transaction, SMSA in this case.

```
cedf
```

Figure C.2 How to start CEDF.

```
THIS TERMINAL: EDF MODE ON
```

Figure C.3 CEDF confirms that it has been started for a terminal.

Figure C.4 shows you the CEDF "program initiation" screen, which details general information about the transaction taken from the execute interface block. The Julian date 94282, which means the 282nd day of 1994, and time, 15:21:28, that is, or 3:21 PM, are given, the transaction identifier (SMSA), task number (81), terminal identifier (M35D), and other related information. You also see that EIBCALEN contains 0: This is the first time the transaction has been executed by the terminal. EIBAID = X'7D' means that the last AID key pressed was the Enter key (You can look up these codes in the KEYDEFS member in Chapter 10, Figure

```
TRANSACTION: SMSA    PROGRAM: CSCSMSA     TASK NUMBER: 0000081   DISPLAY: 00
STATUS:  PROGRAM INITIATION

   EIBTIME       = 152128
   EIBDATE       = 94282
   EIBTRNID      = 'SMSA'
   EIBTASKN      = 81
   EIBTRMID      = 'M35D'

   EIBCPOSN      = 4
   EIBCALEN      = 0
   EIBAID        = X'7D'                                        AT X'0016D0DE'
   EIBFN         = X'0000'                                      AT X'0016D0DF'
   EIBRCODE      = X'000000000000'                              AT X'0016D0E1'
   EIBDS         = '........'
+  EIBREQID      = '........'

ENTER:  CONTINUE
PF1 : UNDEFINED            PF2 : SWITCH HEX/CHAR     PF3 : END EDF SESSION
PF4 : SUPPRESS DISPLAYS    PF5 : WORKING STORAGE     PF6 : USER DISPLAY
PF7 : SCROLL BACK          PF8 : SCROLL FORWARD      PF9 : STOP CONDITIONS
PF10: PREVIOUS DISPLAY     PF11: UNDEFINED           PF12: UNDEFINED
```

CEDF is indicating the start of a pseudoconverse (the program is being given control by CICS).

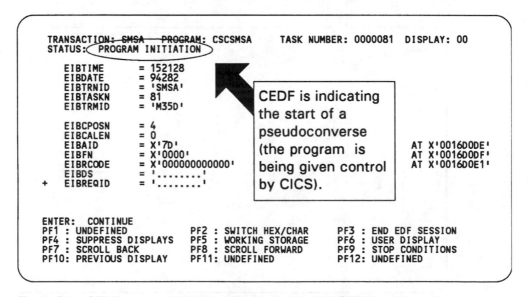

Figure C.4 CEDF program initiation screen, indicating that CEDF has begun to execute a program.

```
TRANSACTION: SMSA   PROGRAM: CSCSMSA   TASK NUMBER: 0000081   DISPLAY: 00
STATUS: ABOUT TO EXECUTE COMMAND
EXEC CICS SEND MAP
 MAP ('FILEMAP')
 FROM ('.......................................................................'...)
 LENGTH (354)
 MAPSET ('SMSAM   ')
 CURSOR (-1)
 TERMINAL
 ERASE

OFFSET:X'0007E4'     LINE:00487          EIBFN=X'0000'

ENTER:  CONTINUE
PF1 : UNDEFINED            PF2 : SWITCH HEX/CHAR     PF3 : UNDEFINED
PF4 : SUPPRESS DISPLAYS    PF5 : WORKING STORAGE     PF6 : USER DISPLAY
PF7 : SCROLL BACK          PF8 : SCROLL FORWARD      PF9 : STOP CONDITIONS
PF10: PREVIOUS DISPLAY     PF11: UNDEFINED           PF12: ABEND USER TASK
```

CEDF indicates what it is doing with the STATUS line. It leaps from CICS command execution to command execution.

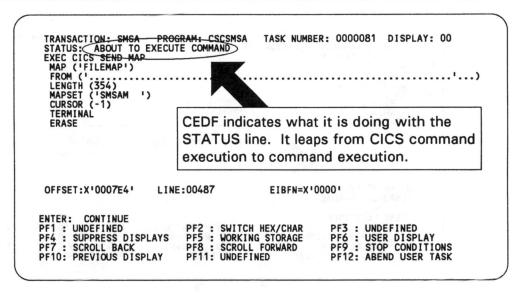

Figure C.5 CEDF prepares to execute the next CICS instruction.

10.11). The PF key information at the bottom of the CEDF screens indicates how to make CEDF display other data or take actions such as ending CEDF.

Every time you press the Enter key, CEDF will take the program to the next CICS instruction, showing you the "before" execution and "after" execution condition of the program. By pressing Enter at the screen in Figure C.4, we move to Figure C.5, showing that the next CICS instruction in the update program is SEND MAP. You see the clauses of the SEND MAP command, with actual values displayed, including the beginning of the content of the symbolic map. When you press the Enter key, the screen in Figure C.6 is presented. This is the result of

```
                 -=SAMUEL'S WORTHLESS FINANCE COMPANY=-                 FILEMAP
                        ****** FILE UPDATE ******                          SMSAM

(A)dd, (D)elete, (C)hange, or (V)iew: A
Name:   JOHNSON, SAM                         Account Number:   58392034

------------------------------- CHARGE ITEMS -------------------------------
  Charge Amount 1:   100000
  Charge Amount 2:   000000
  Charge Amount 3:   000000
  Charge Amount 4:   000000
  Charge Amount 5:   000000                  Total Charge Items:

------------------------------ CASH ADVANCES ------------------------------
Cash Adv Amount 1:   030000
Cash Adv Amount 2:   000000                 Total Cash Advances:
                                  Finance Charge On Cash Advances:

                                 ==========================================

                                                     Total Debits:

ENTER A CHOICE ABOVE
```

Figure C.6 Result of SEND MAP command execution by CEDF.

```
TRANSACTION: SMSA   PROGRAM: CSCSMSA    TASK NUMBER: 0000081   DISPLAY:  00
STATUS:  COMMAND EXECUTION COMPLETE
EXEC CICS SEND MAP
 MAP ('FILEMAP')
 FROM ('.............................................................'...)
 LENGTH (354)
 MAPSET ('SMSAM  ')
 CURSOR (-1)
 TERMINAL
 ERASE

OFFSET:X'0007E4'    LINE:00487          EIBFN=X'1804'
RESPONSE: NORMAL                        EIBRESP=0

ENTER:  CONTINUE
PF1 : UNDEFINED            PF2 : SWITCH HEX/CHAR      PF3 : END EDF SESSION
PF4 : SUPPRESS DISPLAYS    PF5 : WORKING STORAGE      PF6 : USER DISPLAY
PF7 : SCROLL BACK          PF8 : SCROLL FORWARD       PF9 : STOP CONDITIONS
PF10: PREVIOUS DISPLAY     PF11: UNDEFINED            PF12: ABEND USER TASK
```

Command executed successfully

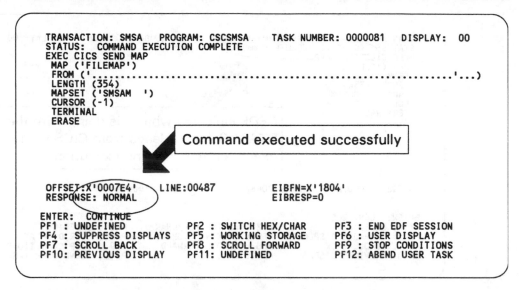

Figure C.7 Conclusion of SEND MAP execution by CEDF.

SEND MAP command execution. You can now enter the same information as was entered when the transaction abended, and press Enter, moving to Figure C.7. Here you see the conclusion of SEND MAP execution, reported as "normal." Press Enter again and you see CICS about to execute the next command, RETURN, in Figure C.8. Pressing Enter here allows the program to end execution, producing Figure C.9. We press Enter again, producing Figure C.10.

```
TRANSACTION: SMSA   PROGRAM: CSCSMSA    TASK NUMBER: 0000081   DISPLAY:  00
STATUS:  ABOUT TO EXECUTE COMMAND
EXEC CICS RETURN
 TRANSID ('SMSA')
 COMMAREA ('T')
 LENGTH (1)

OFFSET:X'0009BC'    LINE:00093          EIBFN=X'1804'

ENTER:  CONTINUE
PF1 : UNDEFINED            PF2 : SWITCH HEX/CHAR      PF3 : UNDEFINED
PF4 : SUPPRESS DISPLAYS    PF5 : WORKING STORAGE      PF6 : USER DISPLAY
PF7 : SCROLL BACK          PF8 : SCROLL FORWARD       PF9 : STOP CONDITIONS
PF10: PREVIOUS DISPLAY     PF11: UNDEFINED            PF12: ABEND USER TASK
```

Figure C.8 CEDF prepares to execute the RETURN instruction.

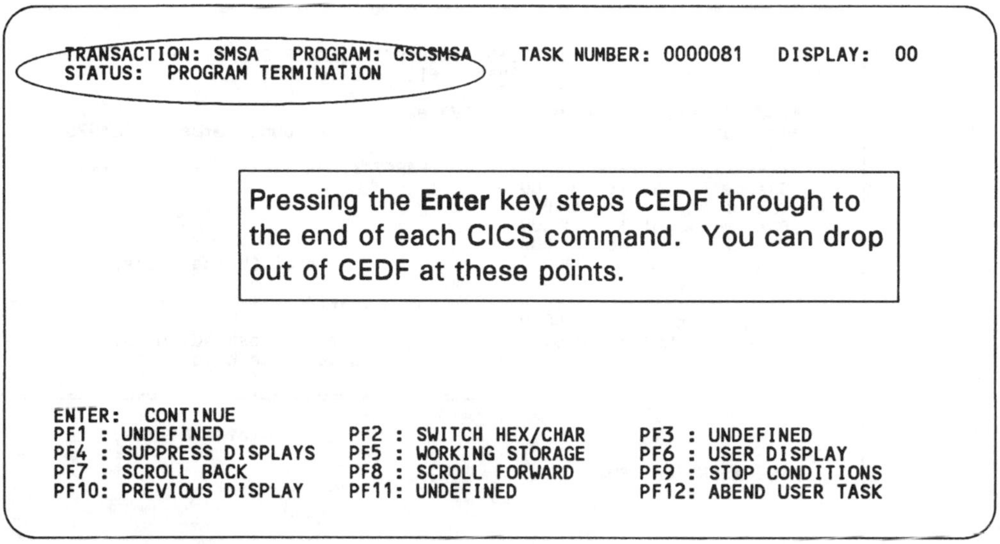
TRANSACTION: SMSA PROGRAM: CSCSMSA
TASK NUMBER: 0000081 DISPLAY: 00
STATUS: PROGRAM TERMINATION
Pressing the **Enter** key steps CEDF through to the end of each CICS command. You can drop out of CEDF at these points.
ENTER: CONTINUE
PF1 : UNDEFINED
PF2 : SWITCH HEX/CHAR
PF3 : UNDEFINED
PF4 : SUPPRESS DISPLAYS
PF5 : WORKING STORAGE
PF6 : USER DISPLAY
PF7 : SCROLL BACK
PF8 : SCROLL FORWARD
PF9 : STOP CONDITIONS
PF10: PREVIOUS DISPLAY
PF11: UNDEFINED
PF12: ABEND USER TASK

Figure C.9 CEDF is about to end program execution.

Figure C.10 presents an opportunity to end the involvement of CEDF with the operation of the transaction. Pressing Enter again allows CICS to terminate the task (unit of work to CICS) that the program represented. Before pressing Enter, however, we change the REPLY field from "NO" to "YES". This means that we want to continue overseeing program execution using CEDF. If we were to just press Enter, leaving "NO" at the REPLY field, we would drop out of CEDF and resume normal, "unmonitored" execution of the program.

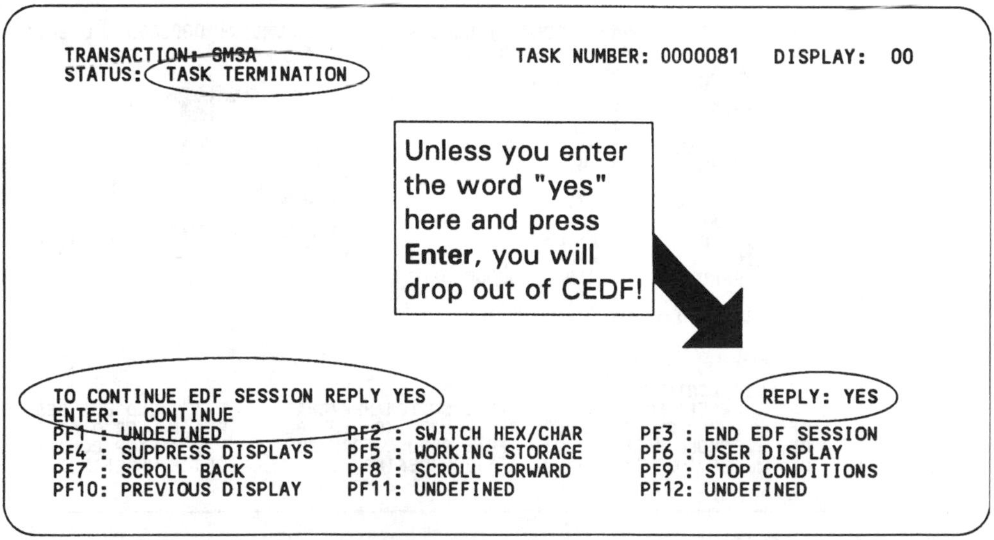
TRANSACTION: SMSA
TASK NUMBER: 0000081 DISPLAY: 00
STATUS: TASK TERMINATION
Unless you enter the word "yes" here and press **Enter**, you will drop out of CEDF!
TO CONTINUE EDF SESSION REPLY YES
REPLY: YES
ENTER: CONTINUE
PF1 : UNDEFINED
PF2 : SWITCH HEX/CHAR
PF3 : END EDF SESSION
PF4 : SUPPRESS DISPLAYS
PF5 : WORKING STORAGE
PF6 : USER DISPLAY
PF7 : SCROLL BACK
PF8 : SCROLL FORWARD
PF9 : STOP CONDITIONS
PF10: PREVIOUS DISPLAY
PF11: UNDEFINED
PF12: UNDEFINED

Figure C.10 Change the REPLY to YES or CEDF will "drop out" of debugging mode!

```
                  -=SAMUEL'S WORTHLESS FINANCE COMPANY=-                 FILEMAP
                             ****** FILE UPDATE ******                     SMSAM

(A)dd, (D)elete, (C)hange, or (V)iew: A
Name:  JOHNSON, SAM                           Account Number:  58392034

-------------------------------- CHARGE ITEMS -------------------------------
  Charge Amount 1:  100000
  Charge Amount 2:  000000
  Charge Amount 3:  000000
  Charge Amount 4:  000000
  Charge Amount 5:  000000                    Total Charge Items:

------------------------------- CASH ADVANCES ------------------------------
Cash Adv Amount 1:  030000
Cash Adv Amount 2:  000000                  Total Cash Advances:
                                  Finance Charge On Cash Advances:

                                 =============================================

                                                      Total Debits:

ENTER A CHOICE ABOVE
```

Figure C.11 The screen produced by the program being debugged is again displayed; enter data if you have not already done so.

At this point, the program screen (the update screen) shown in Figure C.11 appears again. Since we already entered information on this screen, we proceed by pressing Enter again. Had we not entered information at the screen in Figure C.6, we could enter it here, now.

Figure C.12 is produced by CEDF, indicating the program has been reawakened to start a new pseudoconverse. As you can see at the EIBCALEN field, we now receive a "1" here, the

```
TRANSACTION: SMSA   PROGRAM: CSCSMSA    TASK NUMBER: 0000095   DISPLAY:  00
STATUS:  PROGRAM INITIATION
   COMMAREA      = 'T'
   EIBTIME       = 152257
   EIBDATE       = 94282
   EIBTRNID      = 'SMSA'
   EIBTASKN      = 95
   EIBTRMID      = 'M35D'

   EIBCPOSN      = 279                  New task, new
   EIBCALEN      = 1                    task number
   EIBAID        = X'7D'                                    AT X'0016D0DE'
   EIBFN         = X'0000'                                  AT X'0016D0DF'
   EIBRCODE      = X'000000000000'                          AT X'0016D0E1'
   EIBDS         = '........'
+  EIBREQID      = '........'

ENTER:  CONTINUE
PF1 : UNDEFINED            PF2 : SWITCH HEX/CHAR     PF3 : END EDF SESSION
PF4 : SUPPRESS DISPLAYS    PF5 : WORKING STORAGE     PF6 : USER DISPLAY
PF7 : SCROLL BACK          PF8 : SCROLL FORWARD      PF9 : STOP CONDITIONS
PF10: PREVIOUS DISPLAY     PF11: UNDEFINED           PF12: UNDEFINED
```

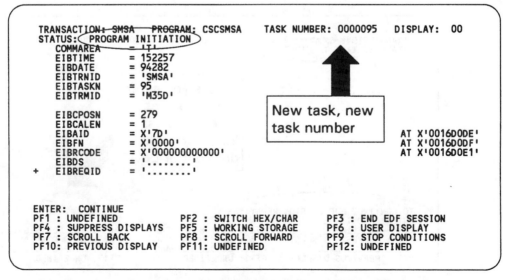

Figure C.12 CEDF reawakens the program and begins a new pseudoconverse as a new task.

```
TRANSACTION: SMSA   PROGRAM: CSCSMSA    TASK NUMBER: 0000095    DISPLAY:  00
STATUS:  ABOUT TO EXECUTE COMMAND
EXEC CICS RECEIVE MAP
 MAP ('FILEMOP')
 INTO ('.............................................................'...)
 MAPSET ('SMSAM  ')
 TERMINAL







OFFSET:X'000A22'    LINE:00237           EIBFN=X'0000'

ENTER:  CONTINUE
PF1 : UNDEFINED            PF2 : SWITCH HEX/CHAR      PF3 : UNDEFINED
PF4 : SUPPRESS DISPLAYS    PF5 : WORKING STORAGE      PF6 : USER DISPLAY
PF7 : SCROLL BACK          PF8 : SCROLL FORWARD       PF9 : STOP CONDITIONS
PF10: PREVIOUS DISPLAY     PF11: UNDEFINED            PF12: ABEND USER TASK
```

Figure C.13 CEDF prepares to execute the next CICS instruction.

length of the data we asked CICS to pass back to us when we executed the RETURN with trans-id that ended the previous pseudoconverse. Notice also that this reawakening of the program is now being handled as task 95.

Pressing Enter again produces the screen shown in Figure C.13, with CEDF about to execute the RECEIVE MAP instruction. Pressing Enter now produces the screen in Figure C.14, which shows an ABM0 abend at the bottom right of the screen. Now what do we do?

```
TRANSACTION: SMSA   PROGRAM: CSCSMSA    TASK NUMBER: 0000095    DISPLAY:  00
STATUS:  AN ABEND HAS OCCURRED
    COMMAREA      = 'T'
    EIBTIME       = 152257
    EIBDATE       = 94282
    EIBTRNID      = 'SMSA'
    EIBTASKN      = 95
    EIBTRMID      = 'M35D'

    EIBCPOSN      = 279
    EIBCALEN      = 1
    EIBAID        = X'7D'                                  AT X'0016D0DE'
    EIBFN         = X'0000'                                AT X'0016D0DF'
    EIBRCODE      = X'000000000000'                        AT X'0016D0E1'
    EIBDS         = '........'
+   EIBREQID      = '........'

ABEND :   ABM0

ENTER:  CONTINUE
PF1 : UNDEFINED            PF2 : SWITCH HEX/CHAR      PF3 : END EDF SESSION
PF4 : SUPPRESS DISPLAYS    PF5 : WORKING STORAGE      PF6 : USER DISPLAY
PF7 : SCROLL BACK          PF8 : SCROLL FORWARD       PF9 : STOP CONDITIONS
PF10: PREVIOUS DISPLAY     PF11: UNDEFINED            PF12: UNDEFINED
```

Press the **PF10** key to see the previous screen to investigate facts surrounding the abend.

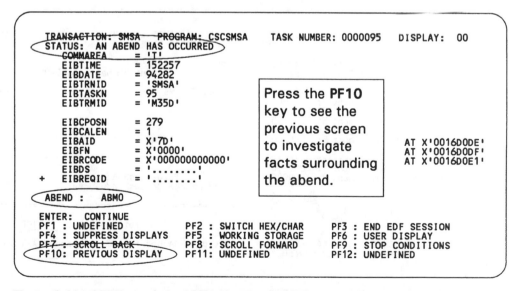

Figure C.14 CEDF reports an ABM0 abend; press PF10 to go back to the previous screen to see what mapname or mapsetname is incorrect to resolve the problem.

Now, unless we know what the abend code means, we must look it up in Appendix E. Having done this, we realize that ABM0 indicates a problem in map naming. We press PF10 to return to a previous screen, and look again at Figure C.13. We do this so that we can see the clauses of the SEND MAP command that abended. Either the mapname FILEMOP or the mapset name SMSAM is incorrect. Investigation shows that the mapname FILEMOP should actually be FILEMAP. It's now time to end CEDF execution and return to TSO to correct the program and retranslate/recompile it.

To end execution of CEDF at the screen shown in Figure C.13, we press Enter to move ahead to the screen in Figure C.14, then press PF3, as the bottom-of-screen legend indicates, to end the EDF (Execution Diagnostic Facility) session. After using TSO/ISPF to correct the program, we will use CECI (as shown in Appendix B) to make CICS aware of the new copy of the program, then use CEDF again to give it an initial test.

C.3 DEBUGGING AN ASRA FAILURE WITH A LIST LISTING

Debugging an abend such as ASRA is more involved than debugging an ABM0 failure, because you have to find the COBOL instruction, after CICS translation, of the statement that caused the data exception. CEDF will pinpoint this instruction for you. To force an ASRA abend for this tutorial, we commented out the lines that check for numeric data in the third charge amount on the update screen in Figure C.15. This stimulates our "forgetting" to include numeric testing for the data entered into this field. The ASRA message at the bottom of the panel appears after entering invalid data in this field, and pressing the Enter key.

We follow the same sequence of actions as shown in Figures C.2 and beyond to arrive at Figure C.16, which shows CEDF about to execute the program at its RECEIVE MAP instruction. We receive an ASRA abend, as shown in Figure C.17, and a brief interpretation of this abend at the lower right: DATA EXCEPTION. We look up this abend code in Appendix E and

```
                  -=SAMUEL'S WORTHLESS FINANCE COMPANY=-                  FILEMAP
                         ****** FILE UPDATE ******                          SMSAM

(A)dd, (D)elete, (C)hange, or (V)iew: A
Name:  JOHNSON, SAMUELS                         Account Number:  38592093

-------------------------------- CHARGE ITEMS -------------------------------
  Charge Amount 1:  010000
  Charge Amount 2:  000000
  Charge Amount 3:  .....0
  Charge Amount 4:  000000
  Charge Amount 5:  000000                      Total Charge Items:      100.00

-------------------------------- CASH ADVANCES ------------------------------
Cash Adv Amount 1:  000000
Cash Adv Amount 2:  000000                     Total Cash Advances:        0.00
                                      Finance Charge On Cash Advances:     0.00
                                      ===========================================
                                                     Total Debits:     $100.00
DFHAC2206 16:20:44 DBDCCIC1 Transaction SMSA has failed with abend ASRA.
 Resource backout was successful.
```

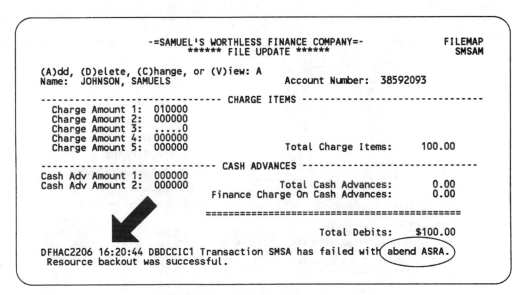

Figure C.15 A program abends with an ASRA abend code: data exception.

```
TRANSACTION: SMSA   PROGRAM: CSCSMSA     TASK NUMBER: 0000135    DISPLAY:  00
STATUS:  COMMAND EXECUTION COMPLETE
EXEC CICS RECEIVE MAP
 MAP ('FILEMAP')
 INTO ('....................................A...JOHNSON. SAMUEL         '...)
 MAPSET ('SMSAM  ')
 TERMINAL



OFFSET:X'000A1A'    LINE:00237             EIBFN=X'1802'
RESPONSE: NORMAL                           EIBRESP=0

ENTER:  CONTINUE
PF1 : UNDEFINED            PF2 : SWITCH HEX/CHAR     PF3 : END EDF SESSION
PF4 : SUPPRESS DISPLAYS    PF5 : WORKING STORAGE     PF6 : USER DISPLAY
PF7 : SCROLL BACK          PF8 : SCROLL FORWARD      PF9 : STOP CONDITIONS
PF10: PREVIOUS DISPLAY     PF11: UNDEFINED           PF12: ABEND USER TASK
```

Figure C.16 Re-executing the ASRA-failed program using CEDF, we arrive at the execution of this instruction.

it confirms that we face a data exception, the attempt to do arithmetic processing on non-numeric data. There's also a very important message near the bottom left of the CEDF screen, labeled OFFSET. OFFSET indicates where within the program's machine language the instruction that caused the abend is located. X'000BD0' means that the program counter was pointing to this relative address when the program "bombed."

```
TRANSACTION: SMSA   PROGRAM: CSCSMSA     TASK NUMBER: 0000135    DISPLAY:  00
STATUS:  AN ABEND HAS OCCURRED
   COMMAREA      = 'T'
   EIBTIME       = 162216
   EIBDATE       = 94282
   EIBTRNID      = 'SMSA'
   EIBTASKN      = 135
   EIBTRMID      = 'M35A'

   EIBCPOSN      = 279
   EIBCALEN      = 1
   EIBAID        = X'7D'                                   AT X'0016D0DE'
   EIBFN         = X'1802'  RECEIVE                        AT X'0016D0DF'
   EIBRCODE      = X'000000000000'                         AT X'0016D0E1'
   EIBDS         = '........'
 + EIBREQID      = '........'
OFFSET:X'000BD0'                        INTERRUPT: DATA EXCEPTION
ABEND :  ASRA                           PSW: X'078D2000 83F5BFFE 00060007'

ENTER:  CONTINUE
PF1 : UNDEFINED            PF2 : SWITCH HEX/CHAR     PF3 : END EDF SESSION
PF4 : SUPPRESS DISPLAYS    PF5 : WORKING STORAGE     PF6 : USER DISPLAY
PF7 : SCROLL BACK          PF8 : SCROLL FORWARD      PF9 : STOP CONDITIONS
PF10: PREVIOUS DISPLAY     PF11: UNDEFINED           PF12: REGISTERS AT ABEND
```

OFFSET tells you the location of the instruction that failed

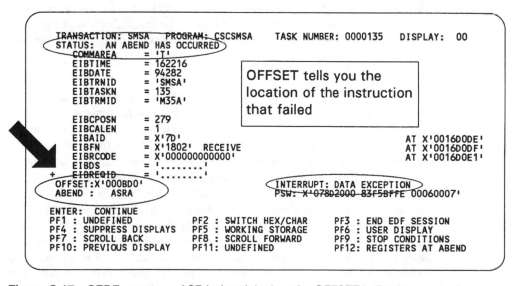

Figure C.17 CEDF reports an ASRA abend; look at the OFFSET indication to see the location of the instruction that failed.

```
SDSF OUTPUT DISPLAY CSCSMSD  JOB07891  DSID   103 LINE  CHARS 'BDO' FOUND
COMMAND INPUT ===>                                     SCROLL ===> PAGE
     000BD0  FA43 D26B D271          AP   619(5,13),625(4,13)   TS1=11
     000BD6  F245 D270 A180          PACK 624(5,13),384(6,10)   TS2=0
     000BDC  FA43 D26B D271          AP   619(5,13),625(4,13)   TS1=11
     000BE2  F235 D270 A189          PACK 624(4,13),393(6,10)   TS2=0
PP 5668-958 IBM VS COBOL II RELEASE 3.2 09/05/90               UPDATER   DATE
     000BE8  FA53 D26A D270          AP   618(6,13),624(4,13)   TS1=10
     000BEE  4710 B5F6               BC   1,1526(0,11)          GN=158(000C0A)
     000BF2  D501 D26A C026          CLC  618(2,13),38(12)      TS1=10
     000BF8  4720 B5F6               BC   2,1526(0,11)          GN=158(000C0A)
     000BFC  F363 A000 D26C          UNPK 0(7,10),620(4,13)     WS-TOTCHG
     000C02  96F0 A006               OI   6(10),X'F0'           WS-TOTCHG+6
     000C06  47F0 B5FC               BC   15,1532(0,11)         GN=159(000C10)
     000C0A                 GN=158   EQU  *
000822  MOVE
     000C0A  D208 A192 949B          MVC  402(9,10),1179(9)     (BLW=0)+402
     000C10                 GN=159   EQU  *
000823  COMPUTE
     000C10  F235 D270 A19E          PACK 624(4,13),414(6,10)   TS2=0
     000C16  F235 D278 A1A7          PACK 632(4,13),423(6,10)   TS2=8
     000C1C  FA33 D270 D278          AP   624(4,13),632(4,13)   TS2=0
     000C22  F363 A008 D270          UNPK 8(7,10),624(4,13)     WS-TOTADV
     000C28  96F0 A00E               OI   14(10),X'F0'          WS-TOTADV+6
```

Figure C.18 Viewing the assembler code output of a compile listing produced with the LIST option, and locating displacement hexadecimal 000BD0.

We now have to refer to a compile listing of the program that failed, to find what instruction is located at displacement X'000BD0'. The compile listing must be produced by running the compiler with the LIST option, which produces an assembler listing of the instructions. Since we had not compiled the program with this option originally, we have to recompile it with the option now. We'll show you how to do this at the end of this appendix.

We view the output of the compile done with the LIST option in Figure C.18, and find the relative address X'000BD0'. This is easy to find using the TSO/ISPF command:

```
COMMAND ===> find 000bd0
```

Realize, however, that each COBOL statement may generate many machine language statements. We're after the COBOL statement that caused generation of the instruction at 000BD0. Having found 000BD0, we press PF7 to view "up" in the listing, and look for the first verb listed above displacement 000BD0. In Figure C.19, we find that the COMPUTE statement, at line 820 in the program, is what generated the machine language instruction at 000BD0. Moving back up several hundred lines in the output, we can view this COMPUTE statement in the program itself, which appears as in Figure C.20.

Investigating the treatment of all of the fields involved in the COMPUTE statement in Figure C.20, we find that we did not check AMT3I for numeric data. We received the ASRA data exception when the COMPUTE instruction was executed because AMT3I contained non-numeric data. We can now end the use of CEDF, use TSO/ISPF to correct the program, and retranslate and recompile it. We can then use CECI, as described in Appendix B, to make CICS aware of the new copy of the program, and execute the transaction again using CEDF to give it an initial test.

```
SDSF OUTPUT DISPLAY CSCSMSD  JOB07891  DSID   103 LINE 1,756   COLUMNS 02- 81
COMMAND INPUT ===>                                             SCROLL ===> PAGE
000406  IF
   000BAC  95E8 A020                CLI  32(10),X'E8'          VALID-DATA-SW
   000BB0  58B0 C02C                L    11,44(0,12)           PBL=1
   000BB4  4770 B7F2                BC   7,2034(0,11)          GN=29(000E06)
000407  PERFORM
000820  COMPUTE
   000BB8  F2F5 D260 A165           PACK 608(16,13),357(6,10)  TS1=0
   000BBE  F235 D270 A16E           PACK 624(4,13),366(6,10)   TS2=0
   000BC4  FA33 D26C D270           AP   620(4,13),624(4,13)   TS1=12
   000BCA  F245 D270 A177           PACK 624(5,13),375(6,10)   TS2=0
   000BD0  FA43 D26B D271           AP   619(5,13),625(4,13)   TS1=11
   000BD6  F245 D270 A180           PACK 624(5,13),384(6,10)   TS2=0
   000BDC  FA43 D26B D271           AP   619(5,13),625(4,13)   TS1=11
   000BE2  F235 D270 A189           PACK 624(4,13),393(6,10)   TS2=0
PP 5668-958 IBM VS COBOL II RELEASE 3.2 09/05/90               UPDATER   DATE
   000BE8  FA53 D26A D270           AP   618(6,13),624(4,13)   TS1=10
   000BEE  4710 B5F6                BC   1,1526(0,11)          GN=158(000C0A)
   000BF2  D501 D26A C026           CLC  618(2,13),38(12)      TS1=10
   000BF8  4720 B5F6                BC   2,1526(0,11)          GN=158(000C0A)
   000BFC  F363 A000 D26C           UNPK 0(7,10),620(4,13)     WS-TOTCHG
   000C02  96F0 A006                OI   6(10),X'F0'           WS-TOTCHG+6
   000C06  47F0 B5FC                BC   15,1532(0,11)         GN=159(000C10)
```

Figure C.19 Moving "up" with PF7 to find the COBOL instruction in progress at the abend (COMPUTE).

```
SDSF OUTPUT DISPLAY CSCSMSD  JOB07891  DSID   103 LINE 898     COLUMNS 02- 81
COMMAND INPUT ===>                                             SCROLL ===> PAGE
 000818
 000819                  1000-CALCULATE.
 000820                      COMPUTE WS-TOTCHG = AMT1I + AMT2I + AMT3I + AMT4I +
 000821                         ON SIZE ERROR
 000822        1                   MOVE ZERO TO TOTCHGO.
 000823                      COMPUTE WS-TOTADV = ADV1I + ADV2I
 000824                         ON SIZE ERROR
 000825        1                   MOVE ZERO TO TOTADVO.
 000826                      COMPUTE WS-FINCHG ROUNDED = WS-TOTADV * .012
 000827                         ON SIZE ERROR
 000828        1                   MOVE ZERO TO FINCHGO.
 000829                      COMPUTE WS-TOTDEB = WS-TOTCHG + WS-TOTADV + WS-FINCH
 000830                         ON SIZE ERROR
 000831        1                    MOVE ZERO TO TOTDEBO.
 000832                      MOVE WS-TOTCHG TO TOTCHGO.
 000833                      MOVE WS-TOTADV TO TOTADVO
 000834                      MOVE WS-FINCHG TO FINCHGO.
 000835                      MOVE WS-TOTDEB TO TOTDEBO.
PP 5668-958 IBM VS COBOL II RELEASE 3.2 09/05/90                 UPDATER   DATE
AN "M" PRECEDING A DATA-NAME REFERENCE INDICATES THAT THE DATA-NAME IS MODIFIED

 DEFINED    CROSS-REFERENCE OF DATA NAMES   REFERENCES
```

Figure C.20 Viewing the offending COMPUTE statement in the source code portion of the compile listing.

```
EDIT ---- CSCJGJ.CSC360.CNTL(PGMJOB2) - 01.00 ---------------- COLUMNS 001 072
COMMAND ===>                                                  SCROLL ===> PAGE
****** ****************************** TOP OF DATA *****************************
//CSCJGJA   JOB 1,                     ACCOUNTING INFORMATION
//  'BIN 7--JANOSSY',                  PROGRAMMER NAME AND DELIVERY BIN
//  CLASS=A,                           INPUT QUEUE CLASS
//  MSGLEVEL=(1,1),                    HOW MUCH MVS SYSTEM PRINT DESIRED
//  MSGCLASS=X,                        PRINT DESTINATION X A L N OR O
//  TIME=(0,6),                        SAFETY LIMIT: RUN TIME UP TO 6 SECS
//  REGION=2M,                         ALLOW UP TO 2 MEGS VIRTUAL MEMORY
//  NOTIFY=CSCJGJ                      WHO TO TELL WHEN JOB IS DONE
//*-----------------------------------------------------------------------
//*  TRANSLATE, COMPILE, AND LINK A CICS PROGRAM WITH LIST, MAP <===
//*  THIS IS A LOCALLY CUSTOMIZED VERSION OF STANDARD PROC DFHEITVL
//*  THIS JCL IS STORED AT CSCJGJ.CSC360.CNTL(PGMJOB2)
//*-----------------------------------------------------------------------
//*
//  SET  SORCLIB='CSCJGJ.CSC360.COBOL',    SOURCE LIB WITH PROGRAM CODE
//       SORNAME='SHOWMAP',                SOURCE PROGRAM MEMBER NAME
//       COPYLIB='CSCJGJ.CSC360.COBOL',    YOUR COBOL COPY LIBRARY
//*
//       LOADLIB='CCP.LOADLIB',            CICS LOAD LIBRARY
//       LOADNAM='C360A001'                LOAD MODULE MEMBER NAME
//*
//**********************************************************************
//*
//*  TRANSLATE THE PROGRAM, REPLACING "EXEC CICS" WITH CALLS
//*
//**********************************************************************
//*
//STEP010  EXEC  PGM=DFHECP1$,                       TRANSLATOR
//  PARM='COBOL2',
//  REGION=2048K
//STEPLIB    DD  DSN=CICS330.SDFHLOAD,DISP=SHR      CICS 3.3 LIBRARY
//SYSIN      DD  DSN=&SORCLIB(&SORNAME),DISP=SHR    SOURCE CODE IN
//SYSPRINT   DD  SYSOUT=*                           SOURCE CODE LIST
//SYSPUNCH   DD  DSN=&&TEMP1,                       TRANSLATED CODE
//  DISP=(NEW,PASS,DELETE),
//  UNIT=VIO,
//  RECFM=FB,
//  LRECL=80,
//  BLKSIZE=3120,
//  SPACE=(CYL,(1,1),RLSE)
//*
//**********************************************************************
//*
//*  COMPILE THE TRANSLATED PROGRAM WITH VS COBOL II
//*
//**********************************************************************
//*
//     IF ( RC <= 4 ) THEN
//STEP020  EXEC  PGM=IGYCRCTL,
//  REGION=2048K,
//  PARM=('NOADV',                  PGM RESERVES CC BYTE COL 1
//       'NOCMPR2',                 DON'T EMULATE RELEASE 2
//       'NUMPROC(PFD)',            PREFERRED SIGN HANDLING
//       'FLAG(I,E)',               ALL MSGS; IMBED ERROR MSGS
//       'LIST',           <=== PRODUCE ASSEMBLER LISTING (DEBUGGING)
//       'LANGUAGE(UE)',            HEADING/MSGS UPPERCASE
//       'APOST',                   USE APOSTROPHE AS QUOTE
//       'FDUMP',                   GIVE FORMATTED ABEND DUMP
//       'LIB',                     COPY LIBRARY OK
//       'MAP',            <=== PRODUCE DATA MAPS, HEX OFFSETS
//       'OBJ',                     PRODUCE OBJECT CODE
//       'RES',                     MAKE CODE DYN RESIDENT
//       'NOOPT',                   NOOPT GIVES LINE# ON FDUMP
//       'XREF')                    PROVIDE IMBEDDED CROSS REF
```

Figure C.21 PGMJOB2 job control language, which compiles with the MAP and LIST options.

```
//STEPLIB     DD  DSN=SYS1.COB2COMP,DISP=SHR          VS COBOL II LIB
//SYSIN       DD  DSN=&&TEMP1,DISP=(OLD,DELETE)       TRANSLATED PGM IN
//SYSLIB      DD  DSN=CICS330.SDFHCOB,DISP=SHR        STD CICS COPY LIB
//            DD  DSN=CICS330.SDFHMAC,DISP=SHR        STD CICS COPY LIB
//            DD  DSN=&COPYLIB,DISP=SHR               YOUR COPY LIB
//SYSPRINT    DD  SYSOUT=*                            COMPILER LISTING
//SYSLIN      DD  DSN=&&OBJECT,                       OBJECT FILE
//  UNIT=VIO,
//  DISP=(NEW,PASS,DELETE),
//  RECFM=FB,
//  LRECL=80,
//  BLKSIZE=3120,
//  SPACE=(CYL,(1,1),RLSE)
//SYSUT1      DD  UNIT=VIO,SPACE=(CYL,(1,1))          COMPILER WORK FILE
//SYSUT2      DD  UNIT=VIO,SPACE=(CYL,(1,1))          COMPILER WORK FILE
//SYSUT3      DD  UNIT=VIO,SPACE=(CYL,(1,1))          COMPILER WORK FILE
//SYSUT4      DD  UNIT=VIO,SPACE=(CYL,(1,1))          COMPILER WORK FILE
//SYSUT5      DD  UNIT=VIO,SPACE=(CYL,(1,1))          COMPILER WORK FILE
//SYSUT6      DD  UNIT=VIO,SPACE=(CYL,(1,1))          COMPILER WORK FILE
//SYSUT7      DD  UNIT=VIO,SPACE=(CYL,(1,1))          COMPILER WORK FILE
//     ENDIF
//*
//*********************************************************************
//*
//*  LINK EDIT THE COMPILED PROGRAM
//*
//*********************************************************************
//*
//     IF ( RC <= 4 ) THEN
//STEP030  EXEC  PGM=IEWL,                            LINKAGE EDITOR PGM
//  REGION=2048K,
//  PARM='LIST,XREF'
//SYSLIN      DD  DSN=CICS330.SDFHCOB(DFHEILIC),DISP=SHR
//            DD  DSN=&&OBJECT,DISP=(OLD,DELETE)      OBJECT MODULE IN
//SYSLIB      DD  DSN=CICS330.SDFHLOAD,DISP=SHR       CICS 3.3 LIB
//            DD  DSN=SYS1.COB2CICS,DISP=SHR          COB2/CICS LIB
//            DD  DSN=SYS1.COB2LIB,DISP=SHR           VS COBOL II LIB
//            DD  DSN=&LOADLIB,DISP=SHR               LOAD MODULE LIB
//SYSLMOD     DD  DSN=&LOADLIB(&LOADNAM),DISP=SHR     NEW CICS PGM OUT
//SYSPRINT    DD  SYSOUT=*                            LINK EDIT REPORT
//SYSUT1      DD  UNIT=VIO,                           WORK FILE
//  DCB=BLKSIZE=1024,
//  SPACE=(CYL,(1,1))
//     ENDIF
//
```

Figure C.21 *(Continued)*

C.4 COMPILING WITH LIST TO GET AN ASSEMBLER LISTING

For certain types of CEDF debugging, you will need to compile or recompile a program with the LIST compiler option. This option adds potentially thousands of lines of print to a compile listing. These lines are largely useless except for debugging. We did not set this option on in our PGMJOB job control language in Chapter 6, Figure 6.3, because the assembler listing is not worth producing as a regular item. But we provide a second version of the PGMJOB JCL, named PGMJOB2. As you can see in Figure C.21, this alternative translate, compile, and link JCL does set on the LIST option, and also the MAP option, which can be of use in debugging.

To demonstrate the effect of the LIST and MAP options on a program's compile listing, we ran PGMJOB2, feeding in our tiny SHOWMAP program from Chapter 6, Figure 6.1. Compare the listing shown in Figure C.22, produced by PGMJCL2, with the listing produced by the PGMJCL, shown in Chapter 6, Figure 6.4. You'll notice that the MAP option adds embedded data field displacement information to the right of data fields within the program listing, and a "data map" with additional displacement information after the source code listing. The LIST

```
PP 5668-958 IBM VS COBOL II RELEASE 3.2 09/05/90              SHOWMAP   DATE 10/10/94  TIME 10:54:56   PAGE     2
  LINEID  PL SL  ----+-*A-1-B--+----2----+----3----+----4----+----5----+----6----+----7-|--+----8  MAP AND CROSS REFERENCE

  000001         000100 ID DIVISION.
  000002         000200 PROGRAM-ID. SHOWMAP.
  000003         000300
  000004         000400*-----------------------------------------------------------------
  000005         000500*  THIS SIMPLE CICS PROGRAM JUST PRESENTS A MAP AND THEN ENDS
  000006         000600*  EXECUTION.  CODING, COMPILING, AND ARRANGING TO EXECUTE IT
  000007         000700*  WILL GIVE YOU EXPERIENCE WITH THE MECHANICS OF CICS.
  000008         000800*-----------------------------------------------------------------
  000009         000900
  000010         001000 DATA DIVISION.
  000011         001100 WORKING-STORAGE SECTION.
  000012         001200*-----------------------------------------------------------------
  000013         001300*
  000014         001400*  MANUALLY CODED SYMBOLIC MAP FOR CALC1 PROGRAM    JIM JANOSSY
  000015         001500*
  000016         001600*-----------------------------------------------------------------
  000017         001700 01  CALC1-SYMBOLIC-MAP.                                              BLW=0000+000          0CL157
  000018         001800     05 FILLER                    PIC X(12).                          BLW=0000+000,0000000 12C
  000019         001900
  000020         002000     05 CSM-L-QUANTITY            PIC S9(4)  COMP.                    BLW=0000+00C,000000C 2C
  000021         002100     05 CSM-A-QUANTITY            PIC X(1).                           BLW=0000+00E,000000E 1C
  000022         002200     05 CSM-D-QUANTITY            PIC 9(5).                           BLW=0000+00F,000000F 5C
  000023         002300
  000024         002400     05 CSM-L-PRICE               PIC S9(4)  COMP.                    BLW=0000+014,0000014 2C
  000025         002500     05 CSM-A-PRICE               PIC X(1).                           BLW=0000+016,0000016 1C
  000026         002600     05 CSM-D-PRICE               PIC 99V99.                          BLW=0000+017,0000017 4C
  000027         002700
  000028         002800     05 CSM-L-TOTAL-BEFORE-TAX    PIC S9(4)  COMP.                    BLW=0000+01B,000001B 2C
  000029         002900     05 CSM-A-TOTAL-BEFORE-TAX    PIC X(1).                           BLW=0000+01D,000001D 1C
  000030         003000     05 CSM-D-TOTAL-BEFORE-TAX    PIC ZZ,ZZZ,ZZ9.99.                  BLW=0000+01E,000001E 13C
  000031         003100
  000032         003200     05 CSM-L-TAX                 PIC S9(4)  COMP.                    BLW=0000+02B,000002B 2C
  000033         003300     05 CSM-A-TAX                 PIC X(1).                           BLW=0000+02D,000002D 1C
  000034         003400     05 CSM-D-TAX                 PIC ZZ,ZZZ,ZZ9.99.                  BLW=0000+02E,000002E 13C
  000035         003500
  000036         003600     05 CSM-L-GRAND-TOTAL         PIC S9(4)  COMP.                    BLW=0000+03B,000003B 2C
  000037         003700     05 CSM-A-GRAND-TOTAL         PIC X(1).                           BLW=0000+03D,000003D 1C
    -
    -
    -
```

Added by the VS COBOL II compiler MAP option.

Figure C.22 Compile listing with embedded data map produced by the MAP option and the assembler code listing produced by the LIST option.

```
000121         004700 PROCEDURE DIVISION USING DFHEIBLK DFHCOMMAREA.                          87 119
000122         004800 1000-MAIN.
000123         004900
000124         005000     MOVE LOW-VALUES TO CALC1-SYMBOLIC-MAP.                              IMP 17
000125         005100     MOVE -1 TO CSM-L-QUANTITY.                                          20
000126         005200     MOVE 'HERE IS MY CALC1 MAP!  JIM JANOSSY' TO CSM-D-MESSAGE.         42
000127         005300
000128               *EXEC CICS
000129               *   SEND MAP    ('CALCMAP')
000130               *       MAPSET ('$001M')
000131               *       FROM   (CALC1-SYMBOLIC-MAP)
000132               *       ERASE
000133               *       CURSOR
000134               *END-EXEC.
000135         005400      MOVE '       S00054    ' TO DFHEIVO                             85
000136                     MOVE 'CALCMAP' TO DFHC0070                                     81
000137                     MOVE LENGTH OF CALC1-SYMBOLIC-MAP TO DFHB0020                  IMP 17 54
000138                     MOVE '$001M' TO DFHC0071                                       82
000139                     MOVE -1 TO DFHB0021                                            55
000140                    CALL 'DFHEI1' USING DFHEIVO  DFHC0070 CALC1-SYMBOLIC-MAP        EXT 85 81 17
000141                    DFHB0020 DFHC0071 DFHDUMMY DFHDUMMY DFHDUMMY DFHB0021.          54 82 84 84 84 55
000142         006100
000143               *EXEC CICS
000144               *       RETURN
000145               *END-EXEC.
000146         006200      MOVE '        00062   ' TO DFHEIVO                            85
000147                    CALL 'DFHEI1' USING DFHEIVO.                                    EXT 85
000148
   -
   -
   -
```

Embedded cross reference produced automatically by the VS COBOL II compiler.

```
          PP 5668-958 IBM VS COBOL II RELEASE 3.2 09/05/90          SHOWMAP   DATE 10/10/94  TIME 10:54:56   PAGE     9
DATA DIVISION MAP

DATA DEFINITION ATTRIBUTE CODES (RIGHTMOST COLUMN) HAVE THE FOLLOWING MEANINGS:
    D = OBJECT OF OCCURS DEPENDING    G = GLOBAL                        S = SPANNED FILE
```

Figure C.22 *(Continued)*

```
     E = EXTERNAL                      O = HAS OCCURS CLAUSE                  U = UNDEFINED FORMAT FILE
     F = FIXED LENGTH FILE             OG= GROUP HAS OWN LENGTH DEFINITION    V = VARIABLE LENGTH FILE
     FB= FIXED LENGTH BLOCKED FILE     R = REDEFINES                          VB= VARIABLE LENGTH BLOCKED FILE

SOURCE   HIERARCHY AND                                 BASE       HEX-DISPLACEMENT   ASMBLR DATA                 DATA DEF
LINEID   DATA NAME                                     LOCATOR    BLK   STRUCTURE    DEFINITION    DATA TYPE     ATTRIBUTES
     2  PROGRAM-ID SHOWMAP -----------------------------------------------------------------------------------------------*
    17   01 CALC1-SYMBOLIC-MAP. . . . . . . . . . . .  BLW=0000   000                DS 0CL157     GROUP
    18     02 FILLER. . . . . . . . . . . . . . . . .  BLW=0000   000   0 000 000    DS 12C        DISPLAY
    20     02 CSM-L-QUANTITY. . . . . . . . . . . . .  BLW=0000   00C   0 000 00C    DS 2C         BINARY
    21     02 CSM-A-QUANTITY. . . . . . . . . . . . .  BLW=0000   00E   0 000 00E    DS 1C         DISPLAY
    22     02 CSM-D-QUANTITY. . . . . . . . . . . . .  BLW=0000   00F   0 000 00F    DS 5C         DISP-NUM
    24     02 CSM-L-PRICE . . . . . . . . . . . . . .  BLW=0000   014   0 000 014    DS 2C         BINARY
    25     02 CSM-A-PRICE . . . . . . . . . . . . . .  BLW=0000   016   0 000 016    DS 1C         DISPLAY
    26     02 CSM-D-PRICE . . . . . . . . . . . . . .  BLW=0000   017   0 000 017    DS 4C         DISP-NUM
    28     02 CSM-L-TOTAL-BEFORE-TAX. . . . . . . . .  BLW=0000   01B   0 000 01B    DS 2C         BINARY
    29     02 CSM-A-TOTAL-BEFORE-TAX. . . . . . . . .  BLW=0000   01D   0 000 01D    DS 1C         DISPLAY
    30     02 CSM-D-TOTAL-BEFORE-TAX. . . . . . . . .  BLW=0000   01E   0 000 01E    DS 13C        NUM-EDIT
    32     02 CSM-L-TAX . . . . . . . . . . . . . . .  BLW=0000   02B   0 000 02B    DS 2C         BINARY
    33     02 CSM-A-TAX . . . . . . . . . . . . . . .  BLW=0000   02D   0 000 02D    DS 1C         DISPLAY
    34     02 CSM-D-TAX . . . . . . . . . . . . . . .  BLW=0000   02E   0 000 02E    DS 13C        NUM-EDIT
    36     02 CSM-L-GRAND-TOTAL . . . . . . . . . . .  BLW=0000   03B   0 000 03B    DS 2C         BINARY
    37     02 CSM-A-GRAND-TOTAL . . . . . . . . . . .  BLW=0000   03D   0 000 03D    DS 1C         DISPLAY
    38     02 CSM-D-GRAND-TOTAL . . . . . . . . . . .  BLW=0000   03E   0 000 03E    DS 13C        NUM-EDIT
    40     02 CSM-L-MESSAGE . . . . . . . . . . . . .  BLW=0000   04B   0 000 04B    DS 2C         BINARY
    41     02 CSM-A-MESSAGE . . . . . . . . . . . . .  BLW=0000   04D   0 000 04D    DS 1C         DISPLAY
    42     02 CSM-D-MESSAGE . . . . . . . . . . . . .  BLW=0000   04E   0 000 04E    DS 79C        DISPLAY
    44   01 DFHLDVER. . . . . . . . . . . . . . . . .  BLW=0000   0A0                DS 22C        DISPLAY
    45   01 DFHEIDO . . . . . . . . . . . . . . . . .  BLW=0000   0B8                DS 4P         PACKED-DEC
    46   01 DFHEIBO . . . . . . . . . . . . . . . . .  BLW=0000   0C0                DS 2C         BINARY
    47   01 DFHEICB . . . . . . . . . . . . . . . . .  BLW=0000   0C8                DS 8C         DISPLAY
    49   01 DFHB0040. . . . . . . . . . . . . . . . .  BLW=0000   0D0                DS 4C         BINARY
    50   01 DFHB0041. . . . . . . . . . . . . . . . .  BLW=0000   0D8                DS 4C         BINARY
    51   01 DFHB0042. . . . . . . . . . . . . . . . .  BLW=0000   0E0                DS 4C         BINARY
    52   01 DFHB0043. . . . . . . . . . . . . . . . .  BLW=0000   0E8                DS 4C         BINARY
    53   01 DFHB0044. . . . . . . . . . . . . . . . .  BLW=0000   0F0                DS 4C         BINARY
    54   01 DFHB0020. . . . . . . . . . . . . . . . .  BLW=0000   0F8                DS 2C         BINARY
    55   01 DFHB0021. . . . . . . . . . . . . . . . .  BLW=0000   100                DS 2C         BINARY
    56   01 DFHB0022. . . . . . . . . . . . . . . . .  BLW=0000   108                DS 2C         BINARY
    57   01 DFHB0023. . . . . . . . . . . . . . . . .  BLW=0000   110                DS 2C         BINARY
    58   01 DFHB0024. . . . . . . . . . . . . . . . .  BLW=0000   118                DS 2C         BINARY
    59   01 DFHB0025. . . . . . . . . . . . . . . . .  BLW=0000   120                DS 2C         BINARY
    60   01 DFHC0040. . . . . . . . . . . . . . . . .  BLW=0000   128                DS 4C         DISPLAY
```

Added by the VS COBOL II compiler MAP option.

Figure C.22 *(Continued)*

```
117      02 EIBRESP2. . . . . . . . . . . . . . . . . . . . . BLL=0001   050   0 000 050   DS 4C         BINARY
118      02 EIBRLDBK. . . . . . . . . . . . . . . . . . . . . BLL=0001   054   0 000 054   DS 1C         DISPLAY
119    01 DFHCOMMAREA . . . . . . . . . . . . . . . . . . . . BLL=0002   000               DS 1C         DISPLAY
```

```
      PP 5668-958 IBM VS COBOL II RELEASE 3.2 09/05/90                SHOWMAP   DATE 10/10/94  TIME 10:54:56   PAGE    11

000000                    SHOWMAP  DS    0H
                                   USING *,15
000000  47F0 F070                  B     112(,15)                     BYPASS CONSTANTS. BRANCH TO @STM
000004  23                         DC    AL1(35)                      SIGNATURE: LEN. PGM. I.D. CHARS.
000005  E2C8D6E6D4C1D740           DC    C'SHOWMAP '      @EPNAM:               PROGRAM NAME
00000D  40C3F240                   DC    C' C2 '                                COMPILER = COBOL II
000011  F14BF34BF240               DC    C'1.3.2 '                              VERSION/RELEASE/MOD.
000017  F1F061F1F061F9F4           DC    C'10/10/94 '                           DATE COMPILED
000020  F1F04BF5F44BF5F6           DC    C'10.54.56'                            TIME COMPILED
000028  00000054                   DC    A(*+44)          @APARM:               A(@PARMS)
00002C  61E8FC4C0000               DC    X'61E8FC4C0000'                        INFO. BYTES 1-6
000032  000010000008               DC    X'000010000008'                        INFO. BYTES 7-12
000038  000000000000               DC    X'000000000000'                        INFO. BYTES 13-18
00003E  0000008000                 DC    X'0000008000'                          INFO. BYTES 19-23
000043  00                         DC    X'00'                                  RESERVED
000044  0000005D                   DC    X'0000005D'                            # DATA DIV. STMTS.
000048  0000000B                   DC    X'0000000B'                            # PROC. DIV. STMTS.
00004C  0000                       DC    X'0000'                                INFO. BYTES 24-25
00004E  0000                       DC    2X'00'                                 RESERVED
000050  40404040                   DC    C'    '                                USER LEVEL INFO (LVLINFO)
000054  00000000                   DC    A(SHOWMAP)       @PARMS: 1) MAIN ENTRY POINT ADDRESS
000058  00000080                   DC    A(PGT)                   2) PGT ADDRESS
00005C  00003560                   DC    A(DAB)                   3) DAB ADDRESS
000060  00000005                   DC    A(*-91)                  4) A(@EPNAM)= E. P. NAME ADDRESS
000064  00000000                   DC    A(SHOWMAP)               5) CURRENT ENTRY POINT ADDRESS
000068  000001CA                   DC    A(START)         @BRVAL: PROCEDURE CODE ADDRESS
00006C  00000000                   DC    V(IGZEBST)               INITIALIZATION ROUTINE
000070  90EC D00C                  STM   14,12,12(13)     @STM:   SAVE CALLER'S REGISTERS
000074  5810 F028                  L     1,40(,15)                GET ADDR. OF PARMLIST FROM @APARM
000078  98EF F068                  LM    14,15,104(15)            LOAD ADDRESSES FROM @BRVAL
00007C  07FF                       BR    15                       DO ANY NECESSARY INITIALIZATION
```

Added by the VS COBOL II compiler LIST option

Figure C.22 *(Continued)*

```
PP 5668-958 IBM VS COBOL II RELEASE 3.2 09/05/90              SHOWMAP   DATE 10/10/94  TIME 10:54:56   PAGE    13

CONSTANT GLOBAL TABLE BEGINS AT LOCATION 000090 FOR 0000E9 BYTES
LITERAL POOL MAP FOR LITERALS IN THE CGT:

000098  (LIT+0)     00000001 00000000 009DFFFF C8C5D9C5 40C9E240 D4E840C3 C1D3C3F1 40D4C1D7  |............HERE IS MY CALC1 MAP|
0000B8  (LIT+32)    5A4040D1 C9D440D1 C1D5D6E2 E2E81804 F1000700 00000015 E2040000 20F0F0F0  |!  JIM JANOSSY..1.......S....000|
0000D8  (LIT+64)    F5F44040 40D3C440 E3C1C2D3 C540C4C6 C8C5C9E3 C1C240F3 F3F04B0E 08000007  |54   LD TABLE DFHEITAB 330......|
0000F8  (LIT+96)    00001000 F0F0F0F6 F2404040 E2C8D6E6 D4C1D740 E2E8E2D6 E4E34040 40404040  |....00062   SHOWMAP SYSOUT      |
000118  (LIT+128)   40404040 5BF0F0F1 D44040C3 C1D3C3D4 C1D70000 00000000 01340000 00010000  |    $001M  CALCMAP..............|
000138  (LIT+160)   01380000 00030000 00000000 00008000 00004080 00000000 25C00001 40000808  |................ ......... ...|
000158  (LIT+192)   00000800 74800000 000040C0 00014000 07080000 08007402 40000808 00000800  |......... ... ......... .......|
000178  (LIT+224)   74                                                                        |.                               |
   00017C                      GN=2     EQU  *
   00017C  D215 90A0 A04D               MVC  160(22,9),77(10)       DFHLDVER                PGMLIT AT +69
   000182  D203 90B8 C002               MVC  184(4,9),2(12)         DFHEIDO                 SYSLIT AT +2
   000188  D201 90C0 C000               MVC  192(2,9),0(12)         DFHEIBO                 SYSLIT AT +0
   00018E  D207 90C8 A084               MVC  200(8,9),132(10)       DFHEICB                 PGMLIT AT +124
   000194  D201 9320 C000               MVC  800(2,9),0(12)         DFHDUMMY                SYSLIT AT +0
   00019A  5820 D130                    L    2,304(0,13)            BL=1
   00019E  D203 2000 A00C               MVC  0(4,2),12(10)          SORT-CORE-SIZE          PGMLIT AT +4
   0001A4  D203 2008 A00C               MVC  8(4,2),12(10)          SORT-FILE-SIZE          PGMLIT AT +4
   0001AA  D203 2010 A00C               MVC  16(4,2),12(10)         SORT-MODE-SIZE          PGMLIT AT +4
   0001B0  D207 2018 A07C               MVC  24(8,2),124(10)        SORT-MESSAGE            PGMLIT AT +116
   0001B6  D203 2020 A00C               MVC  32(4,2),12(10)         TALLY                   PGMLIT AT +4
   0001BC  920E 2028                    MVI  40(2),X'0E'            SHIFT-OUT
   0001C0  920F 2030                    MVI  48(2),X'0F'            SHIFT-IN
   0001C4  5830 D17C                    L    3,380(0,13)            VN=1
   0001C8  07F3                         BCR  15,3
   0001CA                      START    EQU  *                      SHOWMAP
   0001CA  58A0 C008                    L    10,8(0,12)             CBL=1
   0001CE  5890 D134                    L    9,308(0,13)            BLW=0
   0001D2  5880 D13C                    L    8,316(0,13)            BLL=1
   0001D6  5870 D140                    L    7,320(0,13)            BLL=2
   0001DA  5820 1000                    L    2,0(0,1)
   0001DE  4120 2000                    LA   2,0(0,2)
   0001E2  5020 D13C                    ST   2,316(0,13)            BLL=1
   0001E6  1882                         LR   8,2
   0001E8  5820 1004                    L    2,4(0,1)
   0001EC  4120 2000                    LA   2,0(0,2)
   0001F0  5020 D140                    ST   2,320(0,13)            BLL=2
   0001F4  1872                         LR   7,2
   0001F6  D203 D0EC A008               MVC  236(4,13),8(10)        TGTFIXD+236
```

Address of each instruction

Assembler language program listing generated by the VS COBOL II compiler LIST option, useful for CEDF debugging purposes.

Figure C.22 *(Continued)*

```
    0001FC  9180 D184                 TM    388(13),X'80'       IPCB=1
    000200  58B0 C00C                 L     11,12(0,12)         PBL=1
    000204  4780 B0A0                 BC    8,160(0,11)         GN=5(00021C)
    000208  0520                      BALR  2,0
    00020A  5020 D14C                 ST    2,332(0,13)         TGT FDMP/TEST-INFO. AREA +0
    00020E  5820 D05C                 L     2,92(0,13)          TGTFIXD+92
    000212  58F0 21CC                 L     15,460(0,2)         V(IGZEMSG )
    000216  4110 A0CD                 LA    1,205(0,10)         PGMLIT AT +197
    00021A  05EF                      BALR  14,15
    00021C                 GN=5       EQU   *
    00021C  9680 D184                 OI    388(13),X'80'       IPCB=1
    000220  9140 D184                 TM    388(13),X'40'       IPCB=1
    000224  4710 B0C4                 BC    1,196(0,11)         GN=6(000240)
    000228  D203 D180 D17C            MVC   384(4,13),380(13)   PSV=1
    00022E  4120 B0BE                 LA    2,190(0,11)         GN=7(00023A)
    000232  5020 D17C                 ST    2,380(0,13)         VN=1
    000236  47F0 B000                 BC    15,0(0,11)          GN=2(00017C)
    00023A                 GN=7       EQU   *
    00023A  D203 D17C D180            MVC   380(4,13),384(13)   VN=1
    000240                 GN=6       EQU   *
    000240  9640 D184                 OI    388(13),X'40'       IPCB=1
000122  *
000122  *1000-MAIN
000124  MOVE
    000244  9200 9000                 MVI   0(9),X'00'          CALC1-SYMBOLIC-MAP
    000248  D29B 9001 9000            MVC   1(156,9),0(9)       CALC1-SYMBOLIC-MAP+1      CALC1-SYMBOLIC-MAP
000125  MOVE
    00024E  D201 900C A012            MVC   12(2,9),18(10)      CSM-L-QUANTITY            PGMLIT AT +10
000126  MOVE
    000254  D221 904E A014            MVC   78(34,9),20(10)     CSM-D-MESSAGE             PGMLIT AT +12
    00025A  9240 9070                 MVI   112(9),X'40'        CSM-D-MESSAGE+34
    00025E  D22B 9071 9070            MVC   113(44,9),112(9)    CSM-D-MESSAGE+35          CSM-D-MESSAGE+34
000135  MOVE
    000264  D216 9328 A036            MVC   808(23,9),54(10)    DFHEIVO                   PGMLIT AT +46
    00026A  9240 933F                 MVI   831(9),X'40'        DFHEIVO+23
    00026E  D22C 9340 933F            MVC   832(45,9),831(9)    DFHEIVO+24                DFHEIVO+23
000136  MOVE
    000274  D206 92C8 A093            MVC   712(7,9),147(10)    DFHC0070                  PGMLIT AT +139
000137  MOVE
    00027A  D201 90F8 A010            MVC   248(2,9),16(10)     DFHB0020                  PGMLIT AT +8
000138  MOVE
    000280  D206 92D0 A08C            MVC   720(7,9),140(10)    DFHC0071                  PGMLIT AT +132
000139  MOVE
```

Original lines of COBOL that caused the generation of specific assembler language instructions are shown interspersed between the lines of assembler.

Figure C.22 *(Continued)*

option places a lengthy assembler code at the end of the listing. It's the left side of a small portion of an assembler listing like this that you see in Figures C.18 through C.20.

Keep job control language such as PGMJOB2 in Figure C.21 in your tool box for use with CEDF debugging. You will occasionally have to use it. But don't consider printing out the voluminous output this JCL can generate! Instead, use the on-line capability of TSO/ISPF to view the listing, as we have shown here, and the "find" command to quickly work your way through it.

APPENDIX

D

VSAM Key Sequenced Data Set JCL and IDCAMS Example

Virtual Storage Access Method (VSAM) was introduced in 1973 as a replacement for IBM's Indexed Sequential Access Method (ISAM). VSAM is independent of the MVS/ESA operating system and exists on machines running DOS/VSE and VM. VSAM supports four forms of data set organization:

- **Sequential data sets,** known as Entry Sequenced Data Sets (ESDS)
- **Relative data sets,** known as Relative Record Data Sets (RRDS)
- **Indexed data sets,** known as Key Sequenced Data Sets (KSDS)
- **Linear space data sets,** the rough analog of RECFM=U "undefined" format data sets

VSAM is typically used to support CICS system operation, if no database such as IMS, IDMS, DB2, Oracle, or other product is used. In this appendix we show you the JCL and

---

(Note: This appendix is part of Appendix B in *Advanced MVS JCL Examples* by James Janossy, published in 1994 by John Wiley & Sons, Inc., and is reprinted here by permission of the publisher. Please consult that book if you require information about batch program access to the type of VSAM data set created by the example in this appendix, or MVS/ESA Version 4 JCL features.)

IDCAMS utility program control statements you need to use to create a typical VSAM data set. You can regard the JCL and control statements shown here as a model, and adapt them to suit your own purposes in defining, allocating, and loading any VSAM Key Sequence Data Set.

D.1 VSAM DATA SET ORGANIZATIONS

The internal organization of VSAM data sets is more complex than the sequential (PS) and partitioned (PO) data sets originally provided with OS. Records in a VSAM data set are stored in **control intervals** (roughly the equivalent of data blocks), which are themselves housed in larger physical groupings named **control areas.** While VSAM could supplant older data set organizations, it hasn't been used for that purpose and we still use sequential and partitioned data sets. The most common use of VSAM is to support indexed files (Key Sequenced Data Sets) for batch or interactive processing. As with any indexed sequential access method, you can obtain records from a VSAM Key Sequenced Data Set sequentially in ascending order of the primary or an alternate key, or you can obtain them directly by key.

D.2 IDCAMS AND CONTROL STATEMENTS

To create a VSAM data, you must establish information about it in the system catalog. The traditional way to do this is to execute the IDCAMS utility, giving it control statements that describe up to 60 parameters dictating the internal organization and placement of the data set on one or more disk volumes. It's possible, for example, to specify that the index for a data set reside on a different disk volume than the data, to speed access by reducing disk arm contention.

IDCAMS reads its control statement at its //SYSIN DD statement. Control statements begin with a keyword such as DELETE or DEFINE, which identifies a function that IDCAMS is to perform. Each function has several specifications and can span multiple lines of coding. Unlike JCL, you continue an IDCAMS control statement with a hyphen, not a comma.

These IDCAMS functions are accessed by control statements and are the most useful in creating and managing Key Sequenced Data Sets:

DELETE is analogous to IEFBR14 for eliminating all components of an existing VSAM data set

DEFINE establishes the names and characteristics of a new VSAM data set

SET LASTCC or **SET MAXCC** alters the COND CODE values left behind by IDCAMS (these values can be tested with IF control statements within the control statements input to IDCAMS)

REPRO copies data from one data set to another, and can be used to copy records from a sequential file to a VSAM data set to load it, or from a VSAM data set to a sequential backup

BLDINDEX creates an alternate index for an existing key sequenced data set

LISTCAT lists information about the data set, stored in the catalog, and makes it accessible for viewing

PRINT allows printing the contents of a VSAM or nonVSAM data set in hexadecimal, character, or dump format.

We have provided the examples in this appendix to give you a complete model for defining, loading, and analyzing the contents of a key sequenced data set in support of a CICS application. The annotations on the figures are intended to explain important points, and the places where you would have to make changes to use this model for your own data sets.

D.3 DATA TO LOAD AN INDEXED FILE

Figure D.1 shows you the beginning of a file of 80-byte records that we wish to house in an indexed file. Each of these records documents a voyage that has been booked on a pleasure cruise ship. Figure D.2 documents the layout of these records, including the length and starting position of each field in the records. (We would strongly suggest that you prepare a chart like this to document the location of primary and alternate key fields in any file to be loaded to VSAM.) You can see that the fields in the first record are:

Ticket number:	49321
Passenger last name:	ABAMA
Passenger first name:	AL
Sailing date (YYMMDD):	940507
Number of berths:	001
Deck code:	B
Sales agent:	UWANNAGO TRAVEL AGENCY
Ticket purchase date (YYMMDD):	931105

```
 BROWSE -- CSCJGJ.CSC.C204DATA(TICKETS) - 01.00 ----- LINE 00000000 COL 001 080
 COMMAND ===>                                                   SCROLL ===> PAGE
********************************* TOP OF DATA **********************************
49321ABAMA          AL             940507001B UWANNAGO TRAVEL AGENCY 931105
31574AH             GEORGE         940216001S1WORLD TRAVEL, INC.     940103
35112CABOOSE        LUCE           940331001B2ULTIMATE TRAVEL AGENCY 940121
43261CANNON         LUCE           940415001C FOX VALLEY TRAVEL      931004
31259DAY            HOLLY          940216001B HOLIDAY TOURS, INC.    930803
49257FOOEY          O.             940507004B1JACK SPRAT TRAVEL      930803
31779HEAD           M. T.          940216002C KOOK'S TOURS           940113
35189HOE            IDA            940331002S JACK SPRAT TRAVEL      930603
43483INA            CAROL          940415002S FOX VALLEY TRAVEL      940118
31257IPPI           MRS.           940216001B2JACK SPRAT TRAVEL      930817
49892JOE            CURLY          940507001C UWANNAGO TRAVEL AGENCY 940402
49514LITTLE         CHIC N.        940507014B1WORLD TRAVEL, INC.     940213
31260MALLOW         MARSHA         940216001B HOLIDAY TOURS, INC.    930805
49891MOE            LARRY          940507005C2HOLIDAY TOURS, INC.    940320
31256NILLY          WILLIE         940216002S1ULTIMATE TRAVEL AGENCY 930718
43507RITA           MARGA          940415002S WORLD TRAVEL, INC.     940401
43103SHANDELEER     CRYSTAL        940415002S JACK SPRAT TRAVEL      930827
31310SHAW           ARKAN          940216007S1HOLIDAY TOURS, INC.    930911
31778SLEEPING       R. U.          940216001B1UWANNAGO TRAVEL, INC.  940107
43480TOUR           D.             940415003C1HOLIDAY TOURS, INC.    940117
49322TUCKY          KEN            940507002C ULTIMATE TRAVEL AGENCY 931105
31307WARE           DELLA          940216004B1WORLD TRAVEL, INC.     930909
43484ZONA           HARRY          940415002C1UNRAVEL TRAVEL, INC.   940222
31668ZOORI          MOE            940216004S1FOX VALLEY TRAVEL      940103
  -
  -
  -
```

Figure D.1 Records documenting passage booked on a pleasure cruise ship.

```
                        1             2         3         4             5         6         7         8
             ----+----0----+----0----+----0----+----0---  -+---0----+----0----+--- -0----  +----0
             49321 ABAMA         AL             900507 001 B  UWANNAGO TRAVEL AGENCY 931105
             31574 AH            GEORGE         900216 001 S1 WORLD TRAVEL, INC.     940103
             35112 CABOOSE       LUCE           900331 001 B2 ULTIMATE TRAVEL AGENCY 940121
             43261 CANNON        LUCE           900415 001 C  FOX VALLEY TRAVEL      931004
             31259 DAY           HOLLY          900216 001 B  HOLIDAY TOURS, INC.    930803
             49257 FOOEY         O.             900507 004 B1 JACK SPRAT TRAVEL      930803
             31779 HEAD          M. T.          900216 002 C  KOOK'S TOURS           940113
             35189 HOE           IDA            900331 002 S  JACK SPRAT TRAVEL      930603
             43483 INA           CAROL          900415 002 S  FOX VALLEY TRAVEL      940118
             31257 IPPI          MRS.           900216 001 B2 JACK SPRAT TRAVEL      930817

Field length     5       14           15           6    3  2           23             6      6

Start position   1  6             20             35    41 44 46                     69     75
  End position      5          19             34    40  43 45                     68     74     80

Displacement     0  5             19             34    40 43 45                     68     74

Field      TICK-NUM  LAST-NAME    FIRST-NAME     SAIL  QTY DECK     SALES-AGENT        PURCH
```

Figure D.2 Record layout for pleasure cruise ship passenger records showing field positions and displacements.

These records exist in order of passenger name. To load them to an indexed file, the records will have to be sorted into ascending order of ticket number, the unique identifier that will be used as the primary key. (This example is further documented in *VS COBOL II Highlights and Techniques,* by James Janossy, published by John Wiley & Sons, Inc., 1992.) We therefore include a JCL sort in our job stream to define a Key Sequenced Data Set and load these records to it.

D.4 DEFINING AND LOADING A KEY SEQUENCED DATA SET

Figure D.3 shows you a two-step job stream that begins by sorting the ticket records into ascending sequence by the ticket number field, creating a temporary data set named &&TEMP1. In STEP020, we execute the IDCAMS utility to delete any existing copy of a data set named CSCJGJ.CSC.TICKKSDS, then define a data set of this name. Additional control statements copy the sorted ticket records to the newly defined data set, define and build an alternate index using the sales agent field as the alternate key, use LISTCAT to view the catalog information about the data set, and finally use PRINT to examine data set contents by primary key, alternate key, and the alternate index records themselves.

D.5 OUTPUT FROM THE DEFINE AND LOAD RUN

Figure D.4 shows you the full MVS/ESA system reporting for the define and load run, LISTCAT output that echoes back the data set characteristics stored in the catalog, and output of the print functions. We have edited the final PRINT output, showing the content of the alternate index records, so you can see how they are constructed to point to the primary keys of the records sharing a common (nonunique) alternate index value.

D.6 ACCESSING AN ALTERNATE INDEX WITH A COBOL PROGRAM

Figure D.5 lists the source code of the ALTEASY program, which prints records from the ticket KSDS in alternate key sequence. The annotation boxes on this 1985 COBOL (VS CO-

```
EDIT ---- CSCJGJ.ADV.CNTL(AB1KSDS) - 01.02 ------------------- COLUMNS 001 072
COMMAND ===>                                                   SCROLL ===> PAGE
****** ***************************** TOP OF DATA ******************************
//CSCJGJA   JOB 1,                           ACCOUNTING INFORMATION
//   'BIN 7--JANOSSY',                       PROGRAMMER NAME AND DELIVERY BIN
//   CLASS=A,                                INPUT QUEUE CLASS
//   MSGLEVEL=(1,1),                         HOW MUCH MVS SYSTEM PRINT DESIRED
//   MSGCLASS=X,                             PRINT DESTINATION X A L N OR O
//   TIME=(0,6),                             SAFETY LIMIT: RUN TIME UP TO 6 SECS
//   REGION=2M,                              ALLOW UP TO 2 MEGS VIRTUAL MEMORY
//*  TYPRUN=SCAN,                            UNCOMMENT THIS LINE TO DO SCAN ONLY
//   NOTIFY=CSCJGJ                           WHO TO TELL WHEN JOB IS DONE
//*
//* DEMONSTRATE HOW TO DEFINE AND LOAD A KEY SEQUENCE DATA SET
//* WITH AN ALTERNATE INDEX, AND TO DUMP INDEXES
//* THIS JCL IS STORED AT CSCJGJ.ADV.CNTL(AB1KSDS)
//*******************************************************************
//*                                                                 *
//*    SORT THE DATA TO BE LOADED IN TO KEY SEQUENCE                *
//*                                                                 *
//*******************************************************************
//STEP010  EXEC  PGM=SORT
//SYSOUT      DD  SYSOUT=*
//SORTIN      DD  DSN=CSCJGJ.CSC.C204DATA(TICKETS),
//   DISP=SHR
//SORTOUT     DD  DSN=&&TEMP1,
//   DISP=(NEW,PASS,DELETE),
//   UNIT=VIO,
//   RECFM=FB,
//   LRECL=80,
//   SPACE=(CYL,1)
//SORTWK01    DD  UNIT=VIO,SPACE=(CYL,1)
//SORTWK02    DD  UNIT=VIO,SPACE=(CYL,1)
//SORTWK03    DD  UNIT=VIO,SPACE=(CYL,1)
//SYSIN       DD  *
    SORT FIELDS=(1,5,CH,A)
//*
//*******************************************************************
//*                                                                 *
//*    DEFINE AND LOAD THE CUSTOMER KSDS                            *
//*                                                                 *
//*******************************************************************
//STEP020  EXEC  PGM=IDCAMS
//SYSPRINT    DD  SYSOUT=*
//MASTIN      DD  DSN=&&TEMP1,DISP=(OLD,DELETE)
//*
//WORKSRT1    DD  DSN=CSCJGJ.CSC.IDCUT1,
//   UNIT=SYSDA,
//   DISP=OLD,
//   AMP='AMORG',
//   VOL=SER=USER00
//*
//WORKSRT2    DD  DSN=CSCJGJ.CSC.IDCUT2,
//   UNIT=SYSDA,
//   DISP=OLD,
//   AMP='AMORG',
//   VOL=SER=USER00
//*
//SYSIN       DD  *
                                       /* HOUSEKEEPING DELETES  */

     DELETE        CSCJGJ.CSC.TICKKSDS -
                   CLUSTER

     DELETE        CSCJGJ.CSC.IDCUT1 -
                   CLUSTER

     DELETE        CSCJGJ.CSC.IDCUT2 -
                   CLUSTER

   SET LASTCC=0                        /* MAY NOT BE FOUND; GET */
   SET MAXCC=0                         /* RID OF COND CODE 8    */
```

Sort the records to be loaded to the indexed file into ascending order of primary key.

These work files are used by the BLDINDEX function as it creates the alternate index records.

Delete the file before defining and loading only for first-time loading!

This job stream defines and loads an indexed file with the ticket records shown in Figure D.1. The following page shows the control statements used to define the characteristics of the file.

Figure D.3 Job stream to define and load a VSAM Key Sequenced Data Set for the pleasure cruise ship passenger records.

Define base cluster

```

/* - - - - - - - - - - - - - CREATE BASE CLUSTER - - - - -*/

  DEFINE -
    CLUSTER    (   NAME(CSCJGJ.CSC.TICKKSDS) -
                   VOLUMES(USER01) -
                   RECORDSIZE(80 80) -
                   KEYS(5 0) -
                   TRACKS(1 1) -
                   SHAREOPTIONS(2 3) -
                   SPEED -
                   IMBED                             ) -
                   -
    DATA       (   NAME(CSCJGJ.CSC.TICKKSDS.DATA) -
                   CONTROLINTERVALSIZE(4096) -
                   FREESPACE(6 1)                    ) -
                   -
    INDEX      (   NAME(CSCJGJ.CSC.TICKKSDS.INDEX)     )

/* - - - - - - - - - - - - - IF CREATE OKAY, LOAD IT - - -*/
```

Load the file

```

IF LASTCC = 0 -
THEN -
  REPRO          INFILE(MASTIN) -
                 OUTDATASET(CSCJGJ.CSC.TICKKSDS)

/* - - - - - - - - - - - - - DEFINE THE ALTERNATE INDEX - */
```

Define and create the alternate index

```

   DEFINE -
     AIX       (   NAME(CSCJGJ.CSC.TICKKSDS.SALEAIX) -
                   RELATE(CSCJGJ.CSC.TICKKSDS) -
                   VOLUMES(USER02) -
                   RECORDSIZE(33 6600) -
                   KEYS(23 45) -
                   NONUNIQUEKEY -
                   TRACKS(1 1) -
                   SHAREOPTIONS(2 3) -
                   UNIQUE -
                   UPGRADE -
                   SPEED -
                   IMBED                                ) -
                   -
     DATA      (   NAME(CSCJGJ.CSC.TICKKSDS.SALEAIX.DATA) -
                   CONTROLINTERVALSIZE(4096) -
                   FREESPACE(2 1)                       ) -
                   -
     INDEX     (   NAME(CSCJGJ.CSC.TICKKSDS.SALEAIX.INDEX) )

   BLDINDEX      INDATASET(CSCJGJ.CSC.TICKKSDS) -
                 OUTDATASET(CSCJGJ.CSC.TICKKSDS.SALEAIX) -
                 WORKFILES(WORKSRT1 WORKSRT2) -
                 EXTERNALSORT

   DEFINE -
     PATH      (   NAME(CSCJGJ.CSC.TICKKSDS.SALEAIX.PATH) -
                   PATHENTRY(CSCJGJ.CSC.TICKKSDS.SALEAIX) )

/* - - - - - - - - - - - - - LIST CATALOG TO SEE INFO  - -*/
```

Show catalog info

```

  LISTCAT -
    ENTRIES      ( CSCJGJ.CSC.TICKKSDS -
                   CSCJGJ.CSC.TICKKSDS.SALEAIX ) -
                 ALL

/* - - - - - - - - - - -  PRINT IT IN PRIMARY KEY SEQ  - -*/
```

Show contents

```

  PRINT          INDATASET(CSCJGJ.CSC.TICKKSDS) -
                 COUNT(50) -
                 CHARACTER

/* - - - - - - - - - - -  NOW PRINT IT IN ALT KEY SEQ  - -*/

  PRINT          INDATASET(CSCJGJ.CSC.TICKKSDS.SALEAIX.PATH) -
                 COUNT(50) -
                 CHARACTER

/* - - - - - - - - - - -  THIS PRINTS THE AIX RECORDS  - -*/

  PRINT          INDATASET(CSCJGJ.CSC.TICKKSDS.SALEAIX) -
                 COUNT(50) -
                 CHARACTER
//
```

Figure D.3 *(Continued)*

```
                J E S 2   J O B   L O G  --  S Y S T E M   I B M 1  --  N O D E   N 1

17.09.53 JOB07869  IRR010I  USERID CSCJGJ   IS ASSIGNED TO THIS JOB.
17.09.54 JOB07869  ICH70001I CSCJGJ   LAST ACCESS AT 17:05:52 ON THURSDAY, MARCH 24, 1994
17.09.54 JOB07869  $HASP373 CSCJGJA  STARTED - INIT  1 - CLASS A - SYS IBM1
17.10.10 JOB07869  $HASP395 CSCJGJA  ENDED

------ JES2 JOB STATISTICS ------
  24 MAR 94 JOB EXECUTION DATE
        151 CARDS READ
        763 SYSOUT PRINT RECORDS
          0 SYSOUT PUNCH RECORDS
         41 SYSOUT SPOOL KBYTES
       0.27 MINUTES EXECUTION TIME

         1 //CSCJGJA   JOB 1,                    ACCOUNTING INFORMATION
           //  'BIN 7--JANOSSY',                 PROGRAMMER NAME AND DELIVERY BIN
           //  CLASS=A,                          INPUT QUEJE CLASS
           //  MSGLEVEL=(1,1),                   HOW MUCH MVS SYSTEM PRINT DESIRED
           //  MSGCLASS=X,                       PRINT DESTINATION X A L N OR O
           //  TIME=(0,6),                       SAFETY LIMIT: RUN TIME UP TO 6 SECS
           //  REGION=2M,                        ALLOW UP TO 2 MEGS VIRTUAL MEMORY
           //* TYPRUN=SCAN,                      UNCOMMENT THIS LINE TO DO SCAN ONLY
           //  NOTIFY=CSCJGJ                     WHO TO TELL WHEN JOB IS DONE
           //*
           //* DEMONSTRATE HOW TO DEFINE AND LOAD A KEY SEQUENCE DATA SET
           //* WITH AN ALTERNATE INDEX, AND TO DUMP INCEXES
           //* THIS JCL IS STORED AT CSCJGJ.ADV.CNTL(AE1KSDS)
           //*****************************************************************
           //*                                                               *
           //*   SORT THE DATA TO BE LOADED IN TO KEY SEQUENCE               *
           //*                                                               *
           //*****************************************************************
         2 //STEP010  EXEC  PGM=SORT
         3 //SYSOUT     DD  SYSOUT=*
         4 //SORTIN     DD  DSN=CSCJGJ.CSC.C204DATA(TICKETS),
           //  DISP=SHR
         5 //SORTOUT    DD  DSN=&&TEMP1,
           //  DISP=(NEW,PASS,DELETE),
           //  UNIT=VIO,
           //  RECFM=FB,
           //  LRECL=80,
           //  SPACE=(CYL,1)
```

This is the MVS/ESA system output that results from the submission of the AB1KSDS job stream in Figure D.3. We have included the complete output here, with annotations, to serve as a full example of VSAM Key Sequenced Data Set deletion, definition, loading, alternate index building, catalog information display, and data set content printing as accomplished with IDCAMS. At the very end of this listing you will find the third of three **PRINT** outputs, showing you the actual structure of the alternate index records as constructed by IDCAMS.

Figure D.4 MVS/ESA system and IDCAMS output for a Key Sequenced Data Set define and load run.

```
 6 //SORTWK01   DD  UNIT=VIO,SPACE=(CYL,1)
 7 //SORTWK02   DD  UNIT=VIO,SPACE=(CYL,1)
 8 //SORTWK03   DD  UNIT=VIO,SPACE=(CYL,1)
 9 //SYSIN      DD  *
   //*
   //*****************************************************************
   //*                                                               *
   //*   DEFINE AND LOAD THE CUSTOMER KSDS                           *
   //*                                                               *
   //*****************************************************************
10 //STEP020  EXEC  PGM=IDCAMS
11 //SYSPRINT   DD  SYSOUT=*
12 //MASTIN     DD  DSN=&&TEMP1,DISP=(OLD,DELETE)
   //*
13 //WORKSRT1   DD  DSN=CSCJGJ.CSC.IDCUT1,
   //   UNIT=SYSDA,
   //  DISP=OLD,
   //   AMP='AMORG',
   //   VOL=SER=USER00
   //*
14 //WORKSRT2   DD  DSN=CSCJGJ.CSC.IDCUT2,
   //   UNIT=SYSDA,
   //  DISP=OLD,
   //   AMP='AMORG',
   //   VOL=SER=USER00
   //*
15 //SYSIN      DD  *
```

The file at ddname **MASTIN** houses the sorted ticket records to be loaded to the Key Sequenced Data Set. **WORKSRT1** and **WORKSRT2** are sort work files used by the BLDINDEX function as it composes the alternate index. You may be able to eliminate explicit reference to these work files in your installation.

Figure D.4 *(Continued)*

```
ICH70001I CSCJGJ   LAST ACCESS AT 17:05:52 ON THURSDAY, MARCH 24, 1994

IEF236I ALLOC. FOR CSCJGJA STEP010
IEF237I JES2 ALLOCATED TO SYSOUT
IEF237I 111  ALLOCATED TO SORTIN
IEF237I VIO  ALLOCATED TO SORTOUT
IEF237I VIO  ALLOCATED TO SORTWK01
IEF237I VIO  ALLOCATED TO SORTWK02
IEF237I VIO  ALLOCATED TO SORTWK03
IEF237I JES2 ALLOCATED TO SYSIN
IEF237I 116  ALLOCATED TO SORTDK01
IEF237I 115  ALLOCATED TO SORTDK02
IEF237I 117  ALLOCATED TO SORTDK03
IEF142I CSCJGJA STEP010 - STEP WAS EXECUTED - COND CODE 0000
IEF285I   CSCJGJ.CSCJGJA.JOB07869.D0000103.?          SYSOUT
IEF285I   CSCJGJ.CSC.C204DATA                         KEPT
IEF285I   VOL SER NOS= USER00.
IEF285I   SYS94083.T170954.RA000.CSCJGJA.TEMP1        PASSED
IEF285I   SYS94083.T170954.RA000.CSCJGJA.R0002792     DELETED
IEF285I   SYS94083.T170954.RA000.CSCJGJA.R0002793     DELETED
IEF285I   SYS94083.T170954.RA000.CSCJGJA.R0002794     DELETED
IEF285I   CSCJGJ.CSCJGJA.JOB07869.D0000101.?          SYSIN
IEF285I   SYS94083.T170954.RA000.CSCJGJA.S01          DELETED
IEF285I   VOL SER NOS= USER02.
IEF285I   SYS94083.T170955.RA000.CSCJGJA.S02          DELETED
IEF285I   VOL SER NOS= USER01.
IEF285I   SYS94083.T170955.RA000.CSCJGJA.S03          DELETED
IEF285I   VOL SER NOS= USER03.
IEF373I STEP /STEP010 / START 94083.1709
IEF374I STEP /STEP010 / STOP  94083.1709 CPU   0MIN 00.52SEC SRB   0MIN 00.01SEC VIRT  1040K SYS   228K EXT   4096K SYS   9084K

IEF236I ALLOC. FOR CSCJGJA STEP020
IEF237I JES2 ALLOCATED TO SYSPRINT
IEF237I VIO  ALLOCATED TO MASTIN
IEF237I 111  ALLOCATED TO WORKSRT1
IEF237I 111  ALLOCATED TO WORKSRT2
IEF237I JES2 ALLOCATED TO SYSIN
IEF237I 115  ALLOCATED TO SYS00001
IEF237I 116  ALLOCATED TO SYS00001
IEF285I   CSCJGJ.CSC.TICKKSDS                         KEPT
IEF285I   VOL SER NOS= USER01,USER02.
IEF237I 115  ALLOCATED TO SYS00002
IEF237I 115  ALLOCATED TO SYS00004
```

The sort left behind **COND CODE 0000** as an indication that it operated successfully

MVS/ESA shows the VSAM Key Sequenced Data Set on ***two*** volumes, because I placed its data component on disk volume serial number USER01 and the index component on disk volume USER02.

Figure D.4 *(Continued)*

```
IEF285I   SYS94083.T171000.RA000.CSCJGJA.R0000002       KEPT
IEF285I   VOL SER NOS= USER01.
IEF285I   SYS94083.T171000.RA000.CSCJGJA.R0000004       KEPT
IEF285I   VOL SER NOS= USER01.
IEF237I 115  ALLOCATED TO SYS00006
IEF285I   CSCJGJ.CSC.TICKKSDS                           KEPT
IEF285I   VOL SER NOS= USER01.
IEF237I 116  ALLOCATED TO SYS00007
IEF237I 116  ALLOCATED TO SYS00009
IEF285I   SYS94083.T171002.RA000.CSCJGJA.R0000007       KEPT
IEF285I   VOL SER NOS= USER02.
IEF285I   SYS94083.T171002.RA000.CSCJGJA.R0000009       KEPT
IEF285I   VOL SER NOS= USER02.
IEF237I JES2 ALLOCATED TO SYSOUT
IEF237I 115  ALLOCATED TO SYS00011
IEF237I 116  ALLOCATED TO SYS00011
IEF237I 116  ALLOCATED TO SYS00012
IEF237I 117  ALLOCATED TO SORTWK01
IEF237I 117  ALLOCATED TO SORTWK02
IEF285I   SYS94083.T171004.RA000.CSCJGJA.R0000012       DELETED
IEF285I   VOL SER NOS= USER03.
IEF285I   SYS94083.T171005.RA000.CSCJGJA.R0000013       DELETED
IEF285I   VOL SER NOS= USER03.
IEF285I   CSCJGJ.CSC.TICKKSDS.SALEAIX                   KEPT
IEF285I   VOL SER NOS= USER02.
IEF285I   CSCJGJ.CSC.TICKKSDS                           KEPT
IEF285I   VOL SER NOS= USER01,USER02.
IEF237I 115  ALLOCATED TO SYS00015
IEF237I 116  ALLOCATED TO SYS00015
IEF285I   CSCJGJ.CSC.TICKKSDS                           KEPT
IEF285I   VOL SER NOS= USER01,USER02.
IEF237I 116  ALLOCATED TO SYS00016
IEF237I 115  ALLOCATED TO SYS00016
IEF285I   CSCJGJ.CSC.TICKKSDS.SALEAIX.PATH              KEPT
IEF285I   VOL SER NOS= USER02,USER01.
IEF237I 116  ALLOCATED TO SYS00017
IEF285I   CSCJGJ.CSC.TICKKSDS.SALEAIX                   KEPT
IEF285I   VOL SER NOS= USER02.
IEF142I CSCJGJA STEP020 - STEP WAS EXECUTED - COND CODE 0004
IEF285I   CSCJGJ.CSCJGJA.JOB07869.D0000104.?           SYSOUT
IEF285I   SYS94083.T170954.RA000.CSCJGJA.TEMP1          DELETED
IEF285I   CSCJGJ.CSC.IDCUT1                             KEPT
IEF285I   VOL SER NOS= USER00.
```

All of this MVS/ESA system reporting documents the allocation of devices to the many data sets accessed by IDCAMS as it follows my instructions to delete the existing CSCJGJ.CSC.TICKKSDS VSAM file (if it exists), define this data set catalog entry (cluster), populate its data component and build its index, and build its alternate index components. The listing of these allocation actions ends with the STEP WAS EXECUTED line, with **COND CODE 0004**.

IDCAMS accomplished all of the work I asked it to do, but left behind a "warning" indication with COND CODE 0004. You will see later in this system output the benign nature of this warning, and why in this case it poses no problem.

Figure D.4 *(Continued)*

```
IEF285I   CSCJGJ.CSC.IDCUT2                              KEPT
IEF285I   VOL SER NOS= USER00.
IEF285I   CSCJGJ.CSCJGJA.JOB07869.D0000102.?             SYSIN
IEF285I   CSCJGJ.CSCJGJA.JOB07869.D0000105.?             SYSOUT
IEF373I STEP /STEP020 / START 94083.1709
IEF374I STEP /STEP020 / STOP  94083.1710 CPU    0MIN 03.13SEC SRB    0MIN 00.07SEC VIRT  1436K SYS   248K EXT    4120K SYS    9120K
IEF375I  JOB /CSCJGJA / START 94083.1709
IEF376I  JOB /CSCJGJA / STOP  94083.1710 CPU    0MIN 03.65SEC SRB    0MIN 00.08SEC

ICE143I 0 BLOCKSET     SORT  TECHNIQUE SELECTED
ICE000I 1 --- CONTROL STATEMENTS/MESSAGES ---- 5740-SM1 REL 11.1 ---- 17.09.54 MAR 24, 1994 --

          SORT FIELDS=(1,5,CH,A)

ICE088I 1 CSCJGJA .STEP010 .        , INPUT LRECL = 80, BLKSIZE = 3840, TYPE = F
ICE093I 0 MAIN STORAGE = (MAX,4194304,4194304), NMAX = 20800
ICE156I 0 MAIN STORAGE ABOVE 16MB = (4142928,4142928)
ICE128I 0 OPTIONS: SIZE=4194304,MAXLIM=1048576,MINLIM=450560,EQUALS=N,LIST=Y,ERET=RC16 ,MSGDDN=SYSOUT
ICE129I 0 OPTIONS: VIO=N,RESDNT=ALL ,SMF=NO    ,WRKSEC=Y,OUTSEC=Y,VERIFY=N,CHALT=N,DYNALOC=N          ,ABCODE=MSG
ICE130I 0 OPTIONS: RESALL=4096,RESINV=0,SVC=109 ,CHECK=Y,WRKREL=Y,OUTREL=Y,CKPT=N,STIMER=Y,COBEXIT=COB1
ICE131I 0 OPTIONS: TMAXLIM=4194304,ARESALL=0,ARESINV=0,OVERRGN=65536,EXCPVR=NONE ,CINV=Y,CFW=Y
ICE132I 0 OPTIONS: VLSHRT=N,ZDPRINT=N,IEXIT=N,TEXIT=N,LISTX=N,EFS=NONE    ,EXITCK=S,PARMDDN=DFSPARM ,FSZEST=N
ICE133I 0 OPTIONS: HIPRMAX=OPTIMAL
ICE084I 0 EXCP ACCESS METHOD USED FOR SORTOUT
ICE084I 0 EXCP ACCESS METHOD USED FOR SORTIN
ICE090I 0 OUTPUT LRECL = 80, BLKSIZE = 22880, TYPE = F  (SDB)
ICE080I 0 IN MAIN STORAGE SORT
ICE055I 0 INSERT 0, DELETE 0
ICE054I 0 RECORDS - IN: 50, OUT: 50
ICE134I 0 NUMBER OF BYTES SORTED: 4000
ICE165I 0 TOTAL WORK DATA SET TRACKS ALLOCATED: 45 , TRACKS USED: 0
ICE180I 0 HIPERSPACE STORAGE USED = 0K BYTES
ICE052I 0 END OF DFSORT
```

These messages from the sort utility are output at its //SYSOUT DD statement. Notice that it reports on the number of records it received ("in") and the number of records it output ("out").

Figure D.4 *(Continued)*

```
IDCAMS  SYSTEM SERVICES                                    TIME: 17:09:57        03/24/94      PAGE   1
                              /* HOUSEKEEPING DELETES  */

   DELETE       CSCJGJ.CSC.TICKKSDS -
                CLUSTER

IDC0550I ENTRY (R) CSCJGJ.CSC.TICKKSDS.SALEAIX.PATH DELETED
IDC0550I ENTRY (D) CSCJGJ.CSC.TICKKSDS.SALEAIX.DATA DELETED
IDC0550I ENTRY (I) CSCJGJ.CSC.TICKKSDS.SALEAIX.INDEX DELETED
IDC0550I ENTRY (G) CSCJGJ.CSC.TICKKSDS.SALEAIX DELETED
IDC0550I ENTRY (D) CSCJGJ.CSC.TICKKSDS.DATA DELETED
IDC0550I ENTRY (I) CSCJGJ.CSC.TICKKSDS.INDEX DELETED
IDC0550I ENTRY (C) CSCJGJ.CSC.TICKKSDS DELETED
IDC0001I FUNCTION COMPLETED, HIGHEST CONDITION CODE WAS 0

   DELETE       CSCJGJ.CSC.IDCUT1 -
                CLUSTER

IDC3012I ENTRY CSCJGJ.CSC.IDCUT1 NOT FOUND
IDC3009I ** VSAM CATALOG RETURN CODE IS 8 - REASON CODE IS IGG0CLA3-42
IDC0551I ** ENTRY CSCJGJ.CSC.IDCUT1 NOT DELETED
IDC0001I FUNCTION COMPLETED, HIGHEST CONDITION CODE WAS 8

   DELETE       CSCJGJ.CSC.IDCUT2 -
                CLUSTER

IDC3012I ENTRY CSCJGJ.CSC.IDCUT2 NOT FOUND
IDC3009I ** VSAM CATALOG RETURN CODE IS 8 - REASON CODE IS IGG0CLA3-42
IDC0551I ** ENTRY CSCJGJ.CSC.IDCUT2 NOT DELETED
IDC0001I FUNCTION COMPLETED, HIGHEST CONDITION CODE WAS 8

  SET LASTCC=0                        /* MAY NOT BE FOUND; GET */
  SET MAXCC=0                         /* RID OF COND CODE 8    */

  /* - - - - - - - - - - - - - CREATE BASE CLUSTER - - - - -*/

   DEFINE -
     CLUSTER     (   NAME(CSCJGJ.CSC.TICKKSDS) -
                     VOLUMES(USER01) -
                     RECORDSIZE(80 80) -
                     KEYS(5 0) -
                     TRACKS(1 1) -
```

VSAM data set CSCJGJ.CSC.TICKKSDS already existed before this run, because I had run this job before. Here you see how IDCAMS reports the deletion of the components of the existing data set, starting with the alternate index path, then the alternate index, and finally the data, index, and base cluster itself. Every IDCAMS function such as **DELETE** returns a condition code value. The highest of these is reported as the COND CODE for the step at which IDCAMS is executed. The **DELETE**s for the sort work files, on the other hand, do not find these files present, and leave behind condition codes of 8. These condition codes could affect subsequent IDCAMS command processing unless I used **SET** to make the most recent (LASTCC) and highest (MAXCC) condition code values zero again.

Figure D.4 *(Continued)*

```
                   SHAREOPTIONS(2 3) -
                   SPEED -
                   IMBED                              ) -
                   -
   DATA       (    NAME(CSCJGJ.CSC.TICKKSDS.DATA) -
                   CONTROLINTERVALSIZE(4096) -
                   FREESPACE(6 1)                     ) -
                   -
   INDEX      (    NAME(CSCJGJ.CSC.TICKKSDS.INDEX)     )

IDC0508I DATA ALLOCATION STATUS FOR VOLUME USER01 IS 0
IDC0509I INDEX ALLOCATION STATUS FOR VOLUME USER01 IS 0
IDC0001I FUNCTION COMPLETED, HIGHEST CONDITION CODE WAS 0

 /* - - - - - - - - - - - - - IF CREATE OKAY, LOAD IT - - -*/

 IF LASTCC = 0 -
 THEN -
   REPRO          INFILE(MASTIN) -
                  OUTDATASET(CSCJGJ.CSC.TICKKSDS)

IDC0005I NUMBER OF RECORDS PROCESSED WAS 50
IDC0001I FUNCTION COMPLETED, HIGHEST CONDITION CODE WAS 0

 /* - - - - - - - - - - - - - DEFINE THE ALTERNATE INDEX - */

   DEFINE -
     AIX      (    NAME(CSCJGJ.CSC.TICKKSDS.SALEAIX) -
                   RELATE(CSCJGJ.CSC.TICKKSDS) -
                   VOLUMES(USER02) -
                   RECORDSIZE(33 6600) -
                   KEYS(23 45) -
                   NONUNIQUEKEY -
                   TRACKS(1 1) -
                   SHAREOPTIONS(2 3) -
                   UNIQUE -
                   UPGRADE -
                   SPEED -
                   IMBED                               ) -
                   -
    DATA      (    NAME(CSCJGJ.CSC.TICKKSDS.SALEAIX.DATA) -
                   CONTROLINTERVALSIZE(4096) -
                   FREESPACE(2 1)                      ) -
```

IDCAMS completed its base cluster **DEFINE** actions and reports here, with condition code 0, that all went well. The specifications I coded under CLUSTER, DATA, and INDEX have been recorded in the system catalog under the base cluster name. Next, you see that **REPRO** function worked and copied 50 records (the sorted ticket records that entered at ddname MASTIN) to the new VSAM Key Sequenced Data Set. Finally, you see the beginning of the echo of the **DEFINE** for the alternate index, which is in itself another Key Sequenced Data Set.

Figure D.4 *(Continued)*

```
                   -
      INDEX      (    NAME(CSCJGJ.CSC.TICKKSDS.SALEAIX.INDEX) )

IDC0508I DATA ALLOCATION STATUS FOR VOLUME USER02 IS 0
IDC0509I INDEX ALLOCATION STATUS FOR VOLUME USER02 IS 0
IDC0001I FUNCTION COMPLETED, HIGHEST CONDITION CODE WAS 0

    BLDINDEX     INDATASET(CSCJGJ.CSC.TICKKSDS) -
                 OUTDATASET(CSCJGJ.CSC.TICKKSDS.SALEAIX) -
                 WORKFILES(WORKSRT1 WORKSRT2) -
                 EXTERNALSORT

IDC0652I CSCJGJ.CSC.TICKKSDS.SALEAIX SUCCESSFULLY BUILT
IDC0001I FUNCTION COMPLETED, HIGHEST CONDITION CODE WAS 0

    DEFINE -
      PATH       (    NAME(CSCJGJ.CSC.TICKKSDS.SALEAIX.PATH) -
                      PATHENTRY(CSCJGJ.CSC.TICKKSDS.SALEAIX) )

IDC0001I FUNCTION COMPLETED, HIGHEST CONDITION CODE WAS 0

  /* - - - - - - - - - - - - - LIST CATALOG TO SEE INFO - - -*/

     LISTCAT -
       ENTRIES     ( CSCJGJ.CSC.TICKKSDS -
                     CSCJGJ.CSC.TICKKSDS.SALEAIX ) -
                   ALL

CLUSTER ------- CSCJGJ.CSC.TICKKSDS
    IN-CAT --- SYS1.USERCAT
    HISTORY
      DATASET-OWNER-----(NULL)       CREATION--------1994.083
      RELEASE----------------2       EXPIRATION------0000.000
    PROTECTION-PSWD-----(NULL)       RACF----------------(YES)
    ASSOCIATIONS
      DATA-----CSCJGJ.CSC.TICKKSDS.DATA
      INDEX----CSCJGJ.CSC.TICKKSDS.INDEX
      AIX------CSCJGJ.CSC.TICKKSDS.SALEAIX

  DATA ------- CSCJGJ.CSC.TICKKSDS.DATA
    IN-CAT --- SYS1.USERCAT
    HISTORY
      DATASET-OWNER-----(NULL)       CREATION--------1994.083
```

IDCAMS has completed constructing the alternate index with **BLDINDEX**, and then **DEFINEs** the path, as specified. Now, I have used the **LISTCAT** function to print the catalog-stored information about the base cluster and alternate index. **LISTCAT** will confirm what MVS/ESA knows about the new data set, and the statistics in the base cluster will indicate (on the next page) how many records are in the data set, how many have been updated, and how many have been read (retrieved). **LISTCAT**, in fact, indicates more than you usually want to know, so various options and methods exist to trim down how much of this you actually receive and perhaps print.

Figure D.4 *(Continued)*

```
    RELEASE----------------2      EXPIRATION------0000.000
  PROTECTION-PSWD-----(NULL)      RACF----------------(YES)
  ASSOCIATIONS
    CLUSTER--CSCJGJ.CSC.TICKKSDS
  ATTRIBUTES
    KEYLEN-----------------5      AVGLRECL--------------80      BUFSPACE-----------8704      CISIZE--------------4096
    RKP--------------------0      MAXLRECL--------------80      EXCPEXIT----------(NULL)     CI/CA-----------------10
    SHROPTNS(2,3)      SPEED      UNIQUE           NOERASE      INDEXED        NOWRITECHK    IMBED         NOREPLICAT
    UNORDERED        NOREUSE      NONSPANNED
  STATISTICS
    REC-TOTAL-------------50      SPLITS-CI--------------0      EXCPS------------------5
    REC-DELETED------------0      SPLITS-CA--------------0      EXTENTS----------------1
    REC-INSERTED-----------0      FREESPACE-%CI----------6      SYSTEM-TIMESTAMP:
    REC-UPDATED------------0      FREESPACE-%CA----------1          X'A906610510F9D800'
    REC-RETRIEVED---------50      FREESPC-BYTES------32768
  ALLOCATION
    SPACE-TYPE---------TRACK      HI-ALLOC-RBA-------40960
    SPACE-PRI--------------2      HI-USED-RBA--------40960
    SPACE-SEC--------------2
  VOLUME
    VOLSER------------USER01      PHYREC-SIZE---------4096      HI-ALLOC-RBA-------40960     EXTENT-NUMBER----------1
    DEVTYPE------X'30102004'      PHYRECS/TRK-----------10      HI-USED-RBA--------40960     EXTENT-TYPE--------X'40'
    VOLFLAG------------PRIME      TRACKS/CA--------------2
    EXTENTS:
    LOW-CCHH-----X'002B000D'      LOW-RBA----------------0      TRACKS-----------------2
    HIGH-CCHH----X'002B000E'      HIGH-RBA-----------40959

INDEX ------ CSCJGJ.CSC.TICKKSDS.INDEX
  IN-CAT --- SYS1.USERCAT
  HISTORY
    DATASET-OWNER-----(NULL)      CREATION--------1994.083
    RELEASE----------------2      EXPIRATION------0000.000
  PROTECTION-PSWD-----(NULL)      RACF----------------(YES)
  ASSOCIATIONS
    CLUSTER--CSCJGJ.CSC.TICKKSDS
  ATTRIBUTES
    KEYLEN-----------------5      AVGLRECL---------------0      BUFSPACE---------------0     CISIZE---------------512
    RKP--------------------0      MAXLRECL-------------505      EXCPEXIT----------(NULL)     CI/CA-----------------41
    SHROPTNS(2,3)   RECOVERY      UNIQUE           NOERASE      NOWRITECHK         IMBED     NOREPLICAT     UNORDERED
    NOREUSE
  STATISTICS
    REC-TOTAL--------------1      SPLITS-CI--------------0      EXCPS------------------5     INDEX:
    REC-DELETED------------0      SPLITS-CA--------------0      EXTENTS----------------2     LEVELS-----------------1
```

These statistics are about the base cluster data component.

These statistics are about the primary index.

Figure D.4 *(Continued)*

```
      REC-INSERTED-----------0    FREESPACE-%CI----------0    SYSTEM-TIMESTAMP:             ENTRIES/SECT-----------3
      REC-UPDATED------------0    FREESPACE-%CA----------0         X'A906610510F9D800'      SEQ-SET-RBA--------20992
      REC-RETRIEVED----------0    FREESPC-BYTES------20992                                  HI-LEVEL-RBA-------20992
    ALLOCATION
      SPACE-TYPE---------TRACK    HI-ALLOC-RBA-------21504
      SPACE-PRI--------------1    HI-USED-RBA--------21504
      SPACE-SEC--------------1
    VOLUME
      VOLSER------------USER01    PHYREC-SIZE----------512    HI-ALLOC-RBA-------20992    EXTENT-NUMBER----------1
      DEVTYPE-----X'30102004'     PHYRECS/TRK-----------41    HI-USED-RBA------------0    EXTENT-TYPE--------X'00'
      VOLFLAG------------PRIME    TRACKS/CA--------------1
      EXTENTS:
      LOW-CCHH-----X'00190007'    LOW-RBA----------------0    TRACKS-----------------1
      HIGH-CCHH----X'00190007'    HIGH-RBA-----------20991
    VOLUME
      VOLSER------------USER01    PHYREC-SIZE----------512    HI-ALLOC-RBA-------21504    EXTENT-NUMBER----------1
      DEVTYPE------X'30102004'    PHYRECS/TRK-----------41    HI-USED-RBA--------21504    EXTENT-TYPE--------X'80'
      VOLFLAG------------PRIME    TRACKS/CA--------------2
      EXTENTS:
      LOW-CCHH-----X'002B000D'    LOW-RBA------------20992    TRACKS-----------------2
      HIGH-CCHH----X'002B000E'    HIGH-RBA-----------21503

AIX ----------- CSCJGJ.CSC.TICKKSDS.SALEAIX
   IN-CAT --- SYS1.USERCAT
   HISTORY
     DATASET-OWNER-----(NULL)     CREATION--------1994.083
     RELEASE----------------2     EXPIRATION------0000.000
     SMS MANAGED-----------(NO)
   PROTECTION-PSWD-----(NULL)     RACF----------------(NO)
   ASSOCIATIONS
     DATA-----CSCJGJ.CSC.TICKKSDS.SALEAIX.DATA
     INDEX----CSCJGJ.CSC.TICKKSDS.SALEAIX.INDEX
     CLUSTER--CSCJGJ.CSC.TICKKSDS
     PATH-----CSCJGJ.CSC.TICKKSDS.SALEAIX.PATH
   ATTRIBUTES
     UPGRADE

   DATA ------- CSCJGJ.CSC.TICKKSDS.SALEAIX.DATA
     IN-CAT --- SYS1.USERCAT
     HISTORY
       DATASET-OWNER-----(NULL)     CREATION--------1994.083
         RELEASE----------------2   EXPIRATION------0000.000
     PROTECTION-PSWD-----(NULL)     RACF----------------(NO)
```

This information covers the alternate index, which is itself a Key Sequenced Data Set. Notice that IDCAMS and VSAM have already been updated to reflect the century in the date, so that problems surrounding the beginning of a new millennium in 2000 will be eliminated or at least minimized.

Figure D.4 *(Continued)*

```
  ASSOCIATIONS
    AIX------CSCJGJ.CSC.TICKKSDS.SALEAIX
  ATTRIBUTES
    KEYLEN----------------23     AVGLRECL--------------33     BUFSPACE------------8704     CISIZE--------------4096
    RKP--------------------5     MAXLRECL------------6600     EXCPEXIT----------(NULL)     CI/CA-----------------10
    AXRKP-----------------45
    SHROPTNS(2,3)      SPEED     UNIQUE           NOERASE     INDEXED       NOWRITECHK     IMBED           NOREPLICAT
    UNORDERED        NOREUSE     SPANNED       NONUNIQKEY
  STATISTICS
    REC-TOTAL-------------10     SPLITS-CI--------------0     EXCPS------------------2
    REC-DELETED------------0     SPLITS-CA--------------0     EXTENTS----------------1
    REC-INSERTED-----------0     FREESPACE-%CI----------2     SYSTEM-TIMESTAMP:
    REC-UPDATED------------0     FREESPACE-%CA----------1          X'A9066109490F4000'
    REC-RETRIEVED----------0     FREESPC-BYTES------36864
  ALLOCATION
    SPACE-TYPE---------TRACK     HI-ALLOC-RBA-------40960
    SPACE-PRI--------------2     HI-USED-RBA--------40960
    SPACE-SEC--------------2
  VOLUME
    VOLSER------------USER02     PHYREC-SIZE---------4096     HI-ALLOC-RBA-------40960     EXTENT-NUMBER----------1
    DEVTYPE------X'30102004'     PHYRECS/TRK-----------10     HI-USED-RBA--------40960     EXTENT-TYPE--------X'40'
    VOLFLAG------------PRIME     TRACKS/CA--------------2
    EXTENTS:
    LOW-CCHH-----X'00140007'     LOW-RBA----------------0     TRACKS-----------------2
    HIGH-CCHH----X'00140008'     HIGH-RBA-----------40959

INDEX ------ CSCJGJ.CSC.TICKKSDS.SALEAIX.INDEX
  IN-CAT --- SYS1.USERCAT
  HISTORY
    DATASET-OWNER-----(NULL)     CREATION--------1994.083
    RELEASE----------------2     EXPIRATION------0000.000
  PROTECTION-PSWD-----(NULL)     RACF----------------(NO)
  ASSOCIATIONS
    AIX------CSCJGJ.CSC.TICKKSDS.SALEAIX
  ATTRIBUTES
    KEYLEN----------------23     AVGLRECL---------------0     BUFSPACE---------------0     CISIZE---------------512
    RKP--------------------5     MAXLRECL-------------505     EXCPEXIT----------(NULL)     CI/CA-----------------41
    SHROPTNS(2,3)   RECOVERY     UNIQUE           NOERASE     NOWRITECHK         IMBED     NOREPLICAT     UNORDERED
    NOREUSE
  STATISTICS
    REC-TOTAL--------------1     SPLITS-CI--------------0     EXCPS------------------4     INDEX:
    REC-DELETED------------0     SPLITS-CA--------------0     EXTENTS----------------2     LEVELS-----------------1
    REC-INSERTED-----------0     FREESPACE-%CI----------0     SYSTEM-TIMESTAMP:            ENTRIES/SECT-----------3
```

These statistics are about the alternate index. There are 10 unique values in the sales agent field, so 10 alternate index records were created.

Figure D.4 *(Continued)*

```
    REC-UPDATED------------0     FREESPACE-%CA----------0          X'A9066109490F4000'     SEQ-SET-RBA--------20992
    REC-RETRIEVED----------0     FREESPC-BYTES------20992                                  HI-LEVEL-RBA-------20992
  ALLOCATION
    SPACE-TYPE---------TRACK     HI-ALLOC-RBA-------21504
    SPACE-PRI--------------1     HI-USED-RBA--------21504
    SPACE-SEC--------------1
  VOLUME
    VOLSER------------USER02     PHYREC-SIZE----------512     HI-ALLOC-RBA-------20992     EXTENT-NUMBER----------1
    DEVTYPE------X'30102004'     PHYRECS/TRK-----------41     HI-USED-RBA------------0     EXTENT-TYPE--------X'00'
    VOLFLAG------------PRIME     TRACKS/CA--------------1
    EXTENTS:
    LOW-CCHH-----X'0011000D'     LOW-RBA----------------0     TRACKS-----------------1
    HIGH-CCHH----X'0011000D'     HIGH-RBA-----------20991
  VOLUME
    VOLSER------------USER02     PHYREC-SIZE----------512     HI-ALLOC-RBA-------21504     EXTENT-NUMBER----------1
    DEVTYPE------X'30102004'     PHYRECS/TRK-----------41     HI-USED-RBA--------21504     EXTENT-TYPE--------X'80'
    VOLFLAG------------PRIME     TRACKS/CA--------------2
    EXTENTS:
    LOW-CCHH-----X'00140007'     LOW-RBA------------20992     TRACKS-----------------2
    HIGH-CCHH----X'00140008'     HIGH-RBA-----------21503

PATH ------- CSCJGJ.CSC.TICKKSDS.SALEAIX.PATH
  IN-CAT --- SYS1.USERCAT
  HISTORY
    DATASET-OWNER-----(NULL)     CREATION--------1994.083
    RELEASE----------------2     EXPIRATION------0000.000
  PROTECTION-PSWD-----(NULL)     RACF----------------(NO)
  ASSOCIATIONS
    AIX------CSCJGJ.CSC.TICKKSDS.SALEAIX
    DATA-----CSCJGJ.CSC.TICKKSDS.SALEAIX.DATA
    INDEX----CSCJGJ.CSC.TICKKSDS.SALEAIX.INDEX
    DATA-----CSCJGJ.CSC.TICKKSDS.DATA
    INDEX----CSCJGJ.CSC.TICKKSDS.INDEX

  ATTRIBUTES
    UPDATE
      THE NUMBER OF ENTRIES PROCESSED WAS:
                  AIX -------------------1
                  ALIAS -----------------0
                  CLUSTER ---------------1
                  DATA ------------------2
                  GDG -------------------0
                  INDEX -----------------2
```

Finally, at the end of the complete **LISTCAT**, path information is listed, including the associations of the path, which are all of the various components involved in using the path for data set access. The summary print shown at the bottom of this page, which continues to the top of the next page, indicates how many different components of various type the **LISTCAT** accessed.

Figure D.4 *(Continued)*

```
                  NONVSAM ---------------0
                  PAGESPACE -------------0
                  PATH ------------------1
                  SPACE -----------------0
                  USERCATALOG -----------0
                  TOTAL -----------------7
        THE NUMBER OF PROTECTED ENTRIES SUPPRESSED WAS 0
IDC0001I FUNCTION COMPLETED, HIGHEST CONDITION CODE WAS 0

  /* - - - - - - - - - -  PRINT IT IN PRIMARY KEY SEQ  - -*/
   PRINT       INDATASET(CSCJGJ.CSC.TICKKSDS) -
               COUNT(50) -
               CHARACTER

LISTING OF DATA SET -CSCJGJ.CSC.TICKKSDS

KEY OF RECORD - 31256
31256NILLY        WILLIE         940216002S1ULTIMATE TRAVEL AGENCY 930718

KEY OF RECORD - 31257
31257IPPI         MRS.           940216001B2JACK SPRAT TRAVEL      930817

KEY OF RECORD - 31258
31258MOOSE        MICKEY         940216004B2WORLD TRAVEL, INC.     930718

KEY OF RECORD - 31259
31259DAY          HOLLY          940216001B HOLIDAY TOURS, INC.    930803

KEY OF RECORD - 31260
31260MALLOW       MARSHA         940216001B HOLIDAY TOURS, INC.    930805

KEY OF RECORD - 31307
31307WARE         DELLA          940216004B1WORLD TRAVEL, INC.     930909

KEY OF RECORD - 31310
31310SHAW         ARKAN          940216007S1HOLIDAY TOURS, INC.    930911
 -
 -
 -

IDC0005I NUMBER OF RECORDS PROCESSED WAS 50
IDC0001I FUNCTION COMPLETED, HIGHEST CONDITION CODE WAS 0
```

The first **PRINT** I requested was by base cluster name. This will obtain the records in the data component in primary key sequence, regardless of how many records were added to the Key Sequenced Data Set in random access mode. (No such record additions were done in this job stream, but could have been done on-line.) All 50 records in the data set have been listed, but for publication purposes I edited some out.

Figure D.4 *(Continued)*

```
/* - - - - - - - - - - NOW PRINT IT IN ALT KEY SEQ - - -*/
  PRINT        INDATASET(CSCJGJ.CSC.TICKKSDS.SALEAIX.PATH) -
               COUNT(50) -
               CHARACTER
LISTING OF DATA SET -CSCJGJ.CSC.TICKKSDS.SALEAIX.PATH
KEY OF RECORD - FOX VALLEY TRAVEL
31375DUNNE         WILL B.         940216001B2FOX VALLEY TRAVEL       931015
KEY OF RECORD - FOX VALLEY TRAVEL
31668ZOORI         MOE             940216004S1FOX VALLEY TRAVEL       940103
KEY OF RECORD - FOX VALLEY TRAVEL
43261CANNON        LUCE            940415001C FOX VALLEY TRAVEL       931004
KEY OF RECORD - FOX VALLEY TRAVEL
43483INA           CAROL           940415002S FOX VALLEY TRAVEL       940118
KEY OF RECORD - FOX VALLEY TRAVEL
49662PIPER         PETER           940507005B FOX VALLEY TRAVEL       940301
KEY OF RECORD - HOLIDAY TOURS, INC.
31259DAY           HOLLY           940216001B HOLIDAY TOURS, INC.     930803
KEY OF RECORD - HOLIDAY TOURS, INC.
31260MALLOW        MARSHA          940216001B HOLIDAY TOURS, INC.     930805
 -
 -
 -
IDC0005I NUMBER OF RECORDS PROCESSED WAS 50
IDC0001I FUNCTION COMPLETED, HIGHEST CONDITION CODE WAS 0
```

The second **PRINT** I requested was by alternate index path name. This obtains the records in alternate key sequence. The system automatically reads the alternate index records in key sequence; the key of the alternate index records is a copy of the alternate key field value, in this case, the sales agent name. The alternate index records are used as "pointers" to obtain the data records themselves with random access behind the scenes. This form of access is inefficient and you should not consider it a substitute for sorting the data for high-volume access. It is useful, however, in specialized applications where part of an indexed file is "browsed" by alternate key.

Figure D.4 *(Continued)*

```
/* - - - - - - - - - - -  THIS PRINTS THE AIX RECORDS  - -*/
  PRINT        INDATASET(CSCJGJ.CSC.TICKKSDS.SALEAIX) -
               COUNT(50) -
               CHARACTER

LISTING OF DATA SET -CSCJGJ.CSC.TICKKSDS.SALEAIX

KEY OF RECORD - FOX VALLEY TRAVEL
.....FOX VALLEY TRAVEL      31375 31668 43261 43483 49662

KEY OF RECORD - HOLIDAY TOURS, INC.
.....HOLIDAY TOURS, INC.    31259 31260 31310 31450 31780 35190 43480 49467 49891

KEY OF RECORD - JACK SPRAT TRAVEL
.....JACK SPRAT TRAVEL      31257 31573 35189 43103 43501 49257 49872

KEY OF RECORD - KOOK'S TOURS
.....KOOK'S TOURS           31777 31779 35114 49473 49738

KEY OF RECORD - PODUNK TRAVEL AGENCY
.....PODUNK TRAVEL AGENCY   35115

KEY OF RECORD - ULTIMATE TRAVEL AGENCY
.....ULTIMATE TRAVEL AGENCY 31256 31447 31800 35112 43102 49322 49469

KEY OF RECORD - UNRAVEL TRAVEL, INC.
.....UNRAVEL TRAVEL, INC.   35257 43378 43484 49258 49480

KEY OF RECORD - UWANNAGO TRAVEL AGENCY
.....UWANNAGO TRAVEL AGENCY 49261 49321 49892

KEY OF RECORD - UWANNAGO TRAVEL, INC.
.....UWANNAGO TRAVEL, INC.  31778

KEY OF RECORD - WORLD TRAVEL, INC.
.....WORLD TRAVEL, INC.     31258 31307 31574 43101 43377 43507 49514

IDC11462I REQUESTED RANGE END BEYOND END OF DATA SET.
IDC0005I NUMBER OF RECORDS PROCESSED WAS 10
IDC0001I FUNCTION COMPLETED, HIGHEST CONDITION CODE WAS 4

IDC0002I IDCAMS PROCESSING COMPLETE. MAXIMUM CONDITION CODE WAS 4
```

In this third **PRINT**, I have indicated the name of the alternate index itself. IDCAMS lists the contents of the alternate index records. VSAM is elegant in its simplicity of support for alternate indexes. An alternate index is simply a Key Sequenced Data Set in which each record carries a key that is an alternate key in another data set. The "data" part of each of these records is really the primary key of the one or more data component records that carries the alternate key value. For "nonunique" alternate keys (COBOL "with duplicates"), more than one primary key exists in the alternate index record for each alternate key value. I have edited this to put a space between primary key fields. In unedited **PRINT** output the primary keys fields are printed with no space between them.

Figure D.4 *(Continued)*

```
EDIT ---- CSCJGJ.ADV.COBOL(ALTEASY) - 01.00 ----------------- COLUMNS 007 078
COMMAND ===>                                                  SCROLL ===> PAGE
****** ***************************** TOP OF DATA ******************************
000100  ID DIVISION.
000200  program-id.  alteasy.
000300
000400 *  Copyright 1994 James Janossy    All rights reserved
000500 *  Internet  janossy@cs.depaul.edu
000600 *  DePaul University Department of Computer Science
000700 *  243 S. Wabash, Room 450, Chicago, IL 60604
000800 *-------------------------------------------------------------
000900 *  This program reads a VSAM file sequentially by alternate
001000 *  key to demonstrate how START changes the key of reference
001100 *  and current record pointer (originated in RM/COBOL-85 and
001200 *  uploaded to the ES/9000 after testing).
001300
001400  ENVIRONMENT DIVISION.
001500  input-output section.
001600  file-control.
001700
001800 *--comment out the select statement that does not apply:
001900 *--select statement for RM/COBOL-85 on PC-------------------
002000 *
002100 *     select passenger-file       assign to 'tickksds.dat'
002200 *        organization             indexed
002300 *        access mode              sequential
002400 *        record key               pr-ticket-number
002500 *        alternate record key     pr-sales-agent  with duplicates
002600 *        file status              ws-status.
002700 *
002800 *--select statement for VS COBOL II & MVS/ESA---------------
002900 *
003000        select passenger-file       assign to tickets
003100           organization             indexed
003200           access mode              sequential
003300           record key               pr-ticket-number
003400           alternate record key     pr-sales-agent  with duplicates
003500           file status              ws-status.
003600
003700  DATA DIVISION.
003800  file section.
003900  fd  passenger-file
004000      record contains 80 characters.
004100  01  passenger-record.
004200      05 pr-ticket-number              pic x(5).
004300      05 pr-last-name                  pic x(14).
004400      05 pr-first-name                 pic x(15).
004500      05 pr-sailing-date               pic x(6).
004600      05 pr-qty-people                 pic 9(3).
004700      05 pr-deck-code                  pic x(2).
004800      05 pr-sales-agent                pic x(23).
004900      05 pr-purchase-date              pic x(6).
005000 *
005100  working-storage section.
005200  01  ws-status                        pic x(2).
005300  01  ws-records-read                  pic 9(5)   value 0.
005400 /
```

Needed for non-unique alternate key; without this clause duplicate alternate keys cause an error!

I developed this program to demonstrate how to use the START verb to change the key of reference and current record pointer to initiate sequential reading via alternate key. The program reads the VSAM Key Sequenced Data Set to which I have loaded the pleasure cruise ticket records shown in Figures D.1 and D.2. START shown at lines 9100 and 9200 involves the alternate key field, PR-SALES-AGENT. It positions the current record pointer to the first alternate index record that meets the requirement > = LOW-VALUES, which is the first record in the alternate index file. READ then obtains the first record according to the alternate index.

Figure D.5 Source code of the ALTEASY program.

```
PROCEDURE DIVISION.
*-----------------------------------------------------------------
*  In RM/COBOL-85 you need declaratives (even in dummy form) to
*  avoid abends even when non-zero File Status values are received
*  such as '10' at end-of-file on sequential reading.  This code
*  causes no harm on mainframe with VSAM.
*-----------------------------------------------------------------
declaratives.
0000-dummy    section.
    use after error procedure on passenger-file.
0000-real-dummy.  exit.
end declaratives.
*
0000-mainline-section   section.
0000-mainline.
    perform 1000-boj.
    perform 2000-process
       until ws-status(1:1) = '1'.
    perform 3000-eoj.
    stop run.
*
1000-boj.
    display '*** start of program alteasy'.
    open input passenger-file.
    if ws-status(1:1) = '0'
       or ws-status = '97'
          next sentence
     else
       display '*** Error opening indexed file, program ended'
       display '*** File status = ', ws-status
       stop run.
*-----------------------------------------------------------------
*  This START uses the alternate key field to position the file
*  access method to read sequentially on the alternate key:
*-----------------------------------------------------------------
    move low-values to pr-sales-agent.
    start passenger-file
       key >= pr-sales-agent.
    if ws-status(1:1) not = '0'
       display '*** Error on alt key start, program ended'
       display '*** File status = ', ws-status
       stop run.
    perform 2700-read.

2000-process.
    display   pr-ticket-number   ' '
              pr-last-name
              pr-first-name      ' '
              pr-sailing-date    ' '
              pr-qty-people      ' '
              pr-deck-code       ' '
              pr-sales-agent
              pr-purchase-date.
    perform 2700-read.

2700-read.
    read passenger-file.
*-----------------------------------------------------------------
*  For sequential reading (RM/COBOL-85 and IBM VSAM KSDS too):
*     File Status first-byte '0' means read was successful
*     File Status first-byte '1' means end of file
*     Any other file status value means access method failure
*-----------------------------------------------------------------
    if ws-status(1:1) = '0'
       add 1 to ws-records-read
     else
    if ws-status(1:1) = '1'
       next sentence
     else
       display '*** Error on read, program ended'
       display '*** File status = ', ws-status
       stop run.
*
3000-eoj.
    display '*** records read = ', ws-records-read.
    close passenger-file.
    if ws-status(1:1) not = '0'
       display '*** Error on file close, program ended'
       display '*** File status = ', ws-status
     else
    display '*** program ended normally'.
```

You have to check File Status after the OPEN. If you receive '0' in the first byte of File Status or '97' for the whole File Status value, the file opened properly.

START positions the current record pointer to the beginning of the alternate index. Subsequent READs follow the alternate index to read the data in the file.

Figure D.5 *(Continued)*

BOL II) program source code show you how to code the SELECT statement to access an alternate index and how to use the START verb to position the key of reference to the alternate key. Figure D.6 shows you the JCL required to run the ALTEASY program. Figure D.7 shows the output of the ALTEASY program, which confirms that sequential access to records via the alternate index has been arranged.

```
EDIT ---- CSCJGJ.ADV.CNTL(AB1JCL) - 01.00 ------------------- COLUMNS 001 072
COMMAND ===>                                                  SCROLL ===> PAGE
****** ***************************** TOP OF DATA ******************************
//CSCJGJA   JOB 1,                  ACCOUNTING INFORMATION
//  'BIN 7--JANOSSY',               PROGRAMMER NAME AND DELIVERY BIN
//  CLASS=A,                        INPUT QUEUE CLASS
//  MSGLEVEL=(1,1),                 HOW MUCH MVS SYSTEM PRINT DESIRED
//  MSGCLASS=X,                     PRINT DESTINATION X A L N OR O
//  TIME=(0,6),                     SAFETY LIMIT: RUN TIME UP TO 6 SECS
//  REGION=2M,                      ALLOW UP TO 2 MEGS VIRTUAL MEMORY
//* TYPRUN=SCAN,                    UNCOMMENT THIS LINE TO DO SCAN ONLY
//  NOTIFY=CSCJGJ                   WHO TO TELL WHEN JOB IS DONE
//*
//* DEMONSTRATE JCL TO EXECUTE A PROGRAM THAT ACCESSES A KSDS
//* SEQUENTIALLY BY ALTERNATE KEY
//* THIS JCL IS STORED AT CSCJGJ.ADV.CNTL(AB1JCL)
//*-----------------------------------------------------------------------
//STEP101  EXEC  PGM=ALTEASY
//STEPLIB    DD  DSN=CSCJGJ.ADV.LOADLIB,DISP=SHR
//           DD  DSN=SYS1.COB2LIB,DISP=SHR
//TICKETS    DD  DSN=CSCJGJ.CSC.TICKKSDS,DISP=SHR
//TICKETS1   DD  DSN=CSCJGJ.CSC.TICKKSDS.SALEAIX.PATH,DISP=SHR
//SYSOUT     DD  SYSOUT=*
//
```

This JCL shows you how to code the "extra" DD statement required when a program accesses a Key Sequenced Data Set by alternate key. The program contains just one SELECT statement, in this case coded as:

```
SELECT PASSENGER-FILE       ASSIGN TO TICKETS
   ORGANIZATION IS INDEXED
   ACCESS MODE  IS SEQUENTIAL
   RECORD KEY   IS PR-TICKET-NUMBER
   ALTERNATE RECORD KEY IS PR-SALES-AGENT
      WITH DUPLICATES
   FILE STATUS  IS WS-STATUS.
```

The JCL must include a DD statement for //TICKETS pointing to the base cluster name, *and a second DD statement* for //TICKETS1 pointing to the alternate index path. The VS COBOL II compiler "makes up" the second DD name by appending "1" to the original DD name, or replacing its last character with "1" if the original name is already eight characters long. A second ddname of TICKETS2 would be made up for a second alternate index, and so forth.

Figure D.6 Job control language required to access a VSAM data set sequentially via alternate key.

Alternate key sequence!

```
*** start of program listalt
31375 DUNNE       WILL B.        900216 001 B2 FOX VALLEY TRAVEL      891015
31668 ZOORI       MOE            900216 004 S1 FOX VALLEY TRAVEL      900103
43261 CANNON      LUCE           900415 001 C  FOX VALLEY TRAVEL      891004
43483 INA         CAROL          900415 002 S  FOX VALLEY TRAVEL      900118
49662 PIPER       PETER          900507 005 B  FOX VALLEY TRAVEL      900301
31259 DAY         B.             900216 001 B  HOLIDAY TOURS, INC.    890803
31260 MALLOW      MARSHA         900216 001 B  HOLIDAY TOURS, INC.    890805
31310 SHAW        ARKAN          900216 007 S1 HOLIDAY TOURS, INC.    890911
31450 FJORD       HENRI          900216 001 B2 HOLIDAY TOURS, INC.    891101
31780 CALLAHAN    SEYMOUR        900216 005 S  HOLIDAY TOURS, INC.    900114
35190 MONT        VERN           900331 002 C2 HOLIDAY TOURS, INC.    890618
43480 TOUR        D.             900415 003 C1 HOLIDAY TOURS, INC.    900117
49467 LURKI       TURKI          900507 015 B1 HOLIDAY TOURS, INC.    891224
49891 MOE         LARRY          900507 005 C2 HOLIDAY TOURS, INC.    900320
31257 IPPI        MRS.           900216 001 B2 JACK SPRAT TRAVEL      890817
31573 WALLBANGER  HARVEY         900216 002 B  JACK SPRAT TRAVEL      891214
35189 HOE         IDA            900331 002 S  JACK SPRAT TRAVEL      890603
43103 SHANDELEER  CRYSTAL        900415 002 S  JACK SPRAT TRAVEL      890827
43501 EASY        N. N.          900415 006 B  JACK SPRAT TRAVEL      900401
49257 FOOEY       O.             900507 004 B1 JACK SPRAT TRAVEL      890803
49872 FAWLTY      BASIL          900507 002 B2 JACK SPRAT TRAVEL      900319
31777 GUSH        BORGE          900216 019 C  KOOK'S TOURS           900107
31779 HEAD        M. T.          900216 002 C  KOOK'S TOURS           900113
35114 MAKEIT      WILLIE         900331 001 C  KOOK'S TOURS           891024
49473 RUMPOLE     HORACE         900507 002 S1 KOOK'S TOURS           891224
49738 LOWE        LERNER N.      900507 001 C1 KOOK'S TOURS           900319
35115 WOONT       NOEY           900331 003 S1 PODUNK TRAVEL AGENCY   900202
31256 NILLY       WILLIE         900216 002 S1 ULTIMATE TRAVEL AGENCY 890718
31447 TOTALLER    T.             900216 002 C1 ULTIMATE TRAVEL AGENCY 891017
31800 MCFARKLE    ARCHIE         900216 002 C  ULTIMATE TRAVEL AGENCY 900114
35112 CABOOSE     LUCE           900331 001 B2 ULTIMATE TRAVEL AGENCY 900121
43102 IFORNIA     CAL            900415 007 B2 ULTIMATE TRAVEL AGENCY 890807
49322 TUCKY       KEN            900507 002 C  ULTIMATE TRAVEL AGENCY 891105
49469 SULLIVAN    GILBERT N.     900507 001 C1 ULTIMATE TRAVEL AGENCY 891224
35257 MAGEE       MOSES          900331 001 B1 UNRAVEL TRAVEL, INC.   900217
43378 MALARKEY    SHARKEY        900415 006 C2 UNRAVEL TRAVEL, INC.   891123
43484 ZONA        HARRY          900415 002 C1 UNRAVEL TRAVEL, INC.   900222
49258 COOL        CALVIN         900507 001 C  UNRAVEL TRAVEL, INC.   890902
49480 HAMMERSTEIN RODGERS N.     900507 003 C  UNRAVEL TRAVEL, INC.   900209
49261 NALE        RUSTY          900507 001 B  UWANNAGO TRAVEL AGENCY 891014
49321 ABAMA       AL             900507 001 B  UWANNAGO TRAVEL AGENCY 891105
49892 JOE         CURLY          900507 001 C  UWANNAGO TRAVEL AGENCY 900402
31778 SLEEPING    R. U.          900216 001 B1 UWANNAGO TRAVEL, INC.  900107
31258 MOOSE       MICKEY         900216 004 B2 WORLD TRAVEL, INC.     890718
31307 WARE        DELLA          900216 004 B1 WORLD TRAVEL, INC.     890909
31574 AH          GEORGE         900216 001 S1 WORLD TRAVEL, INC.     900103
43101 DOE         JOHANN         900415 001 C2 WORLD TRAVEL, INC.     890413
43377 WHIZ        G.             900415 001 S  WORLD TRAVEL, INC.     891123
43507 RITA        MARGA          900415 002 S  WORLD TRAVEL, INC.     900401
49514 LITTLE      CHIC N.        900507 014 B1 WORLD TRAVEL, INC.     900213
*** records read = 00050
*** program ended normally
```

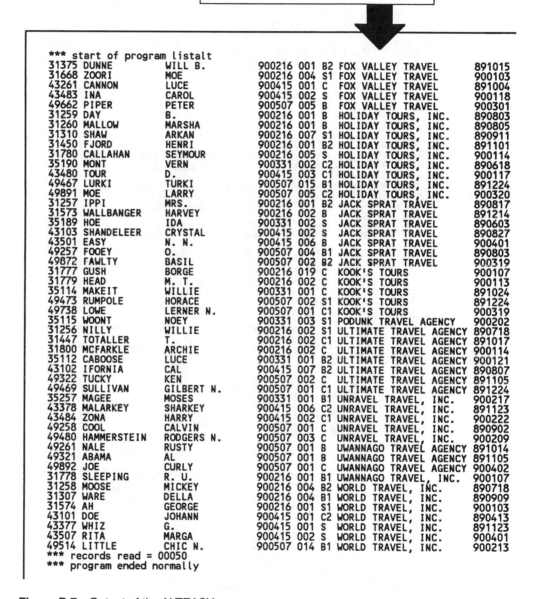

Figure D.7 Output of the ALTEASY program.

D.7 LOADING A VSAM KSDS USING A PROGRAM

You can, if you wish, use a program instead of the IDCAMS REPRO command to form the records to be loaded to a VSAM Key Sequenced Data Set. Figure D.8 illustrates the source code for a program named COBLOAD. This program reads 80-byte records presented to it

```
EDIT ---- CSCJGJ.CSC360.COBOL(COBLOAD) - 01.01 --------------- COLUMNS 007 078
COMMAND ===>                                                   SCROLL ===> PAGE
****** ***************************** TOP OF DATA ******************************
 ID DIVISION.
 PROGRAM-ID.  COBLOAD.
 AUTHOR.      STEVE SAMUELS.
*-----------------------------------------------------------------
*  CREATES SEQUENTIAL 160 BYTE RECORD TO LOAD TO A VSAM
*  FILE.  REVISED 10/12/94 TO DEAL WITH SIMPLER INPUT DATA FORMAT.
*-----------------------------------------------------------------

 ENVIRONMENT DIVISION.
 INPUT-OUTPUT SECTION.
 FILE-CONTROL.

*-----------------------------------------------------------------
* FOR TESTING USING A PC COMPILER:
*
*     SELECT INFILE          ASSIGN TO DISK  'SEQIN.DAT'
*        ORGANIZATION        IS LINE SEQUENTIAL.
*
*     SELECT MASTERFILE      ASSIGN TO DISK  'MASTOUT.DAT'
*        ORGANIZATION        IS LINE SEQUENTIAL
*        FILE STATUS         IS WS-FILE-STATUS.
*
*-----------------------------------------------------------------
* FOR USE ON IBM MAINFRAME TO WRITE TO VSAM FILE:

      SELECT INFILE          ASSIGN TO  SEQIN.

      SELECT MASTERFILE      ASSIGN TO  MASTOUT
         ORGANIZATION        IS INDEXED
         ACCESS MODE         IS SEQUENTIAL
         RECORD KEY          IS OUT-PRIMARY-KEY
         FILE STATUS         IS WS-FILE-STATUS.

*=================================================================
 DATA DIVISION.
*=================================================================
 FILE SECTION.

 FD  INFILE
     BLOCK CONTAINS 0 RECORDS
     RECORD CONTAINS 80 CHARACTERS.
 01  IN-REC.
     05 IN-PRIMARY-KEY                PIC X(8).
     05                               PIC X(1).
     05 IN-ALT-KEY                    PIC X(30).

*-----------------------------------------------------------------

*    FOLLOWING IS FORMAT FOR THE INDEXED-CICS RECORDS USED IN
*    THE CCP PROGRAM.  THE RECORD IS 160 BYTES IN LENGTH.
*    THE PRIMARY KEY IS 8 BYTES LONG AND IN POSITIONS 1-8
*    THE ALTERNATE KEY IS 30 BYTES LONG, NONUNIQUE, IN
*    POSITIONS 121-150.
*
*      YOU SHOULD USE THE DATASET NAMES THAT FOLLOW:
*             PRIMARY DATASET   =  CCP___1F
*           ALTERNATE DATASET   =  CCP___1P
*    WHERE "___" = YOUR ACCOUNT NUMBER (PP45 FOR EXAMPLE)

 FD  MASTERFILE
     RECORD CONTAINS 160 CHARACTERS.
 01  OUT-REC.
     05 OUT-PRIMARY-KEY               PIC X(8).
     05                               PIC X(112).
     05 OUT-ALT-KEY                   PIC X(30).
     05                               PIC X(10).

```

Figure D.8 Source code for the COBLOAD program.

```
*=================================================================
 WORKING-STORAGE SECTION.
*=================================================================

 01  WS-FILE-STATUS                PIC X(2).

 01  PIC X(1)          VALUE '0'.
     88 END-OF-FILE    VALUE '1'.

 01  WS-COUNT-IN                   PIC 9(5)  VALUE 0.
 01  WS-COUNT-OUT                  PIC 9(5)  VALUE 0.

*=================================================================
 PROCEDURE DIVISION.
*=================================================================

 1000-MAINLINE.
     PERFORM 1000-BEGIN.
     PERFORM 2000-PROCESS-A-RECORD
        UNTIL END-OF-FILE.
     PERFORM 3000-ENDER.
     STOP RUN.

*-----------------------------------------------------------------

 1000-BEGIN.
     DISPLAY 'COBLOAD PROGRAM STARTING'.
     OPEN  INPUT INFILE  OUTPUT MASTERFILE.
     MOVE ZEROS TO OUT-REC.
     PERFORM 2700-READ.

*-----------------------------------------------------------------

 2000-PROCESS-A-RECORD.
     DISPLAY IN-REC.
     MOVE IN-PRIMARY-KEY  TO  OUT-PRIMARY-KEY.
     MOVE IN-ALT-KEY      TO  OUT-ALT-KEY.
     WRITE OUT-REC
        INVALID KEY
           DISPLAY '** ERROR ON WRITE, FS = ', WS-FILE-STATUS,
                   '  INPUT RECORD = ', IN-REC
        NOT INVALID KEY
           ADD 1 TO WS-COUNT-OUT.
     PERFORM 2700-READ.

*-----------------------------------------------------------------

 2700-READ.
     READ INFILE
        AT END
           SET END-OF-FILE TO TRUE
        NOT AT END
           ADD 1 TO WS-COUNT-IN.

*-----------------------------------------------------------------

 3000-ENDER.
     CLOSE  INFILE  MASTERFILE.
     DISPLAY 'COBLOAD PROGRAM ENDED'.
     DISPLAY 'RECORDS READ     = ', WS-COUNT-IN.
     DISPLAY 'RECORDS WRITTEN = ', WS-COUNT-OUT.
     STOP RUN.
```

Figure D.8 *(Continued)*

```
EDIT ---- CSCJGJ.CSC360.CNTL(JCLLOAD) - 01.07 ---------------- COLUMNS 001 072
COMMAND ===>                                                   SCROLL ===> PAGE
****** ******************************* TOP OF DATA ****************************
//CSCJGJA   JOB 1,                     ACCOUNTING INFORMATION
//  'BIN 7--JANOSSY',                  PROGRAMMER NAME AND DELIVERY BIN
//  CLASS=A,                           INPUT QUEUE CLASS
//  MSGLEVEL=(1,1),                    HOW MUCH MVS SYSTEM PRINT DESIRED
//  MSGCLASS=X,                        PRINT DESTINATION X A L N OR O
//  TIME=(0,6),                        SAFETY LIMIT: RUN TIME UP TO 6 SECS
//  REGION=2M,                         ALLOW UP TO 2 MEGS VIRTUAL MEMORY
//  NOTIFY=CSCJGJ                      WHO TO TELL WHEN JOB IS DONE
//*-------------------------------------------------------------------
//*  JCL TO DEFINE AND LOAD BORROWER MASTER FILE FOR
//*  SAMUEL'S WORTHLESS FINANCE COMPANY
//*  THIS JCL IS STORED AT CSCJGJ.CSC360.COBOL(JCLLOAD)
//*-------------------------------------------------------------------
//*
//*  DELETE AND DEFINE THE VSAM KSDS
//*
//*-------------------------------------------------------------------
//STEPA    EXEC  PGM=IDCAMS
//SYSPRINT   DD  SYSOUT=*
//SYSIN      DD  *

    DELETE        CSCJGJ.CSC.BASE1F -
                  CLUSTER

  SET LASTCC=0
  SET MAXCC=0

    DEFINE -
      CLUSTER (   NAME(CSCJGJ.CSC.BASE1F) -
                  RECORDS (50 20) -
                  VOLUMES (USER01) -
                  RECORDSIZE (160 160) -
                  KEYS (8 0) -
                  SHAREOPTIONS (3 3) -
                  SPEED -
                  IMBED                            ) -
                  -
      DATA    (   NAME(CSCJGJ.CSC.BASE1F.DATA) -
                  CONTROLINTERVALSIZE (4096) -
                  FREESPACE (6 1)                  ) -
                  -
      INDEX   (   NAME(CSCJGJ.CSC.BASE1F.INDEX)    )

//*-------------------------------------------------------------------
//*
//*  COMPILE, LINK, AND RUN THE TEST DATA GENERATOR TO BUILD
//*  EACH 160-BYTE RECORD WITH PRIME AND ALT KEYS LISTED AT SEQIN
//*
//*-------------------------------------------------------------------
//      IF  ( NOT ABEND AND RC <= 4 )  THEN
//STEPB     EXEC  COB2J,
//      PDS='CSCJGJ.CSC360.COBOL',      <===SOURCE CODE LIBRARY
//  MEMBER='COBLOAD'                    <===PROGRAM NAME
//GO.MASTOUT  DD  DSN=CSCJGJ.CSC.BASE1F,DISP=SHR
//GO.SEQIN    DD  *
44444444 *THIS IS A 30-BYTE NAME FIELD!
55555555 DUMMYTWO  IDIOTB     B000000001
66666666 DUMMYTHREEIDIOTC     C000000002
77777777 DUMMYFOUR IDIOTD     D000000003
22222222 THIS ONE IS OUT OF SEQUENCE!!!
88888888 DUMMYFIVE IDIOTE     E000000004
//      ENDIF
```

Figure D.9 JCLLOAD job control language to define a VSAM data set and load it using a program.

```
//*-----------------------------------------------------------------
//*
//*  DEFINE THE ALTERNATE INDEX
//*
//*-----------------------------------------------------------------
//STEPC     EXEC  PGM=IDCAMS,COND=(4,LT)
//SYSPRINT    DD  SYSOUT=*
//SYSIN       DD  *

    DEFINE -
      AIX      (  NAME(CSCJGJ.CSC.AIX1F) -
                  RELATE(CSCJGJ.CSC.BASE1F) -
                  VOLUMES (USER01) -
                  RECORDSIZE (43 195) -
                  KEYS (30 120) -
                  NONUNIQUEKEY -
                  TRACKS (1 1) -
                  SHAREOPTIONS (3 3) -
                  UNIQUE -
                  UPGRADE -
                  SPEED -
                  IMBED                               ) -
                  -
      DATA     (  NAME(CSCJGJ.CSC.AIX1F.DATA) -
                  CONTROLINTERVALSIZE(512) -
                  FREESPACE (2 1)                     ) -
                  -
      INDEX    (  NAME(CSCJGJ.CSC.AIX1F.INDEX) -
                  CONTROLINTERVALSIZE(512)            )
//*-----------------------------------------------------------------
//*
//*  BUILD THE ALTERNATE INDEX
//*
//*-----------------------------------------------------------------
//STEPD     EXEC  PGM=IDCAMS,COND=(4,LT)
//SYSPRINT    DD  SYSOUT=*
//PRIMEI      DD  DSN=CSCJGJ.CSC.BASE1F,DISP=SHR
//ALTERI      DD  DSN=CSCJGJ.CSC.AIX1F,DISP=SHR
//SYSIN       DD  *
    BLDINDEX -
                  INFILE (PRIMEI) -
                  OUTFILE (ALTERI)
//*-----------------------------------------
//*
//*  DEFINE THE ALTERNATE INDEX PATH
//*
//*-----------------------------------------
//STEPE     EXEC  PGM=IDCAMS,COND=(4,LT)
//SYSPRINT    DD  SYSOUT=*
//SYSIN       DD  *
    DEFINE -
      PATH     (  NAME(CSCJGJ.CSC.AIX2F) -
                  PATHENTRY (CSCJGJ.CSC.AIX1F) -
                  UPDATE                              )
//*-----------------------------------------------------------------
//*
//*  VERIFY THE NEW DATA SET
//*
//*-----------------------------------------------------------------
//STEPF     EXEC  PGM=IDCAMS,COND=(4,LT)
//DD1         DD  DSN=CSCJGJ.CSC.BASE1F,DISP=OLD
//SYSPRINT    DD  SYSOUT=*
//SYSIN       DD  *
    VERIFY        FILE(DD1)
//*-----------------------------------------------------------------
//*
//*  PRINT THE NEW DATA SET
//*
//*-----------------------------------------------------------------
//STEPG     EXEC  PGM=IDCAMS,COND=(4,LT)
//SYSPRINT    DD  SYSOUT=*
//DD1         DD  DSN=CSCJGJ.CSC.BASE1F,DISP=SHR
//SYSIN       DD  *
    PRINT         INFILE(DD1) -
                  COUNT(50) -
                  DUMP
//
```

Alternate index is defined and created to support the alternate key browse illustrated in Chapter 15.

Figure D.9 *(Continued)*

```
 SDSF OUTPUT DISPLAY CSCJGJA  JOB01422  DSID   110 LINE 6       COLUMNS 02- 81
 COMMAND INPUT ===>                                            SCROLL ===> PAGE

 OUTPUT DATA SET SYS94285.T171530.RA000.CSCJGJA.GOSET IS ON VOLUME
 ** YOURPGM  DID NOT PREVIOUSLY EXIST BUT WAS ADDED AND HAS AMODE 31
 ** LOAD MODULE HAS RMODE ANY
 ** AUTHORIZATION CODE IS         0.

COBLOAD PROGRAM STARTING
44444444 *THIS IS A 30-BYTE NAME FIELD!
55555555 DUMMYTWO  IDIOTB    B000000001
66666666 DUMMYTHREEIDIOTC    C000000002
77777777 DUMMYFOUR IDIOTD    D000000003
22222222 THIS ONE IS OUT OF SEQUENCE!!!
** ERROR ON WRITE, FS = 21   INPUT RECORD = 22222222 THIS ONE IS OUT OF SEQUENCE
88888888 DUMMYFIVE IDIOTE    E000000004
COBLOAD PROGRAM ENDED
RECORDS READ    = 00006
RECORDS WRITTEN = 00005
```

Figure D.10 Output from the COBLOAD program as it loads a VSAM data set.

instream, and formats a longer record, here 160 bytes in length, from its input, moving the data input to the primary and alternate key fields of the intended output record. The resulting records are of the correct format and field placement to serve as initial data for an application. COBLOAD spares us having to work directly with records of larger than 80 bytes length. You can adjust COBLOAD to work with records of any length.

The job control language named JCLLOAD in Figure D.9 first executes IDCAMS to define a new VSAM Key Sequenced Data Set at STEPA, then executes a compile, link, and go of the COBLOAD program at STEPB. This results in the formation and loading of records to the KSDS. As you can see in STEPC of Figure D.9, the JCL again executes IDCAMS to define an alternate index for the new KSDS, and, at STEPD, to build the alternate index. The concluding steps of JCLLOAD define the alternate index access path, verify that the data set has been properly closed, and then print records from the new KSDS to confirm their contents. (You can eliminate the VERIFY at STEPF in most installations.) Figure D.10 shows the output of the COBLOAD step, which detects and reports on an out-of-sequence primary key condition while continuing to load properly sequenced records.

APPENDIX

E

CICS RESP Code / Abend Code Reference

In order to deal with CICS, you need to be able to determine the meaning of CICS response codes (RESP codes) and CICS abend codes. This reference documents the most common of both for you in one place. IBM provides a complete reference to CICS/ESA 3.3 error codes on disc 2 of its CD-ROM *Online Library Omnibus Edition, MVS Collection,* SK2T-0710-04.

E.1 CICS RESP CODES

CICS issues a numeric response code after processing each command you give it, placing this response code into the EIBRESP field in the execute interface block. By using the RESP option of a CICS command, you can have CICS copy this PIC S(8) BINARY value into a numeric field in WORKING-STORAGE, which you can then interrogate using an EVALUATE statement.

```
EXEC CICS
   RECEIVE MAP      (WS-MAP-NAME)
           MAPSET   (WS-MAPSET-NAME)
           INTO     (CALC1-SYMBOLIC-MAP)
           RESP     (WS-RESPONSE-CODE)
END-EXEC.
```

You code your EVALUATE statement in this form, anticipating potential causes of command failure:

```
EVALUATE WS-RESPONSE-CODE

   WHEN DFHRESP (NORMAL)
      CONTINUE
   WHEN DFHRESP (MAPFAIL)
      MOVE -1 TO CSM-L-QUANTITY
      MOVE 'NO DATA ENTERED; ENTER DATA, <CLEAR> TO QUIT'
         TO CSM-D-MESSAGE
      PERFORM 1200-SEND-MAP-DATAONLY
      PERFORM 8000-RETURN-WITH-TRANS-ID

   WHEN OTHER
      PERFORM 999-ABORT

END-EVALUATE.
```

The words that you code within parenthesis after DFHRESP must be one of the recognized words for an error condition. The RESP code list that follows serves two purposes. It shows you what conditions you can test for using DFHRESP, but our program examples also show you that. More importantly, this RESP code listing can help you diagnose problems in program operation. You can use this listing, which we prepared in RESP code order, to look up the meaning of a RESP code that triggers the display of the error reporting lines shown in Figure 8.6. In this listing, we have included the CICS "abend code" associated with each RESP code. You receive the CICS abend code for a given problem if the problem arises and you have not coded the RESP option in a CICS command.

RESP code	Abend code	DFHRESP (. .) word	Meaning of condition
00	——	NORMAL	DFHRESP (NORMAL) indicates no error
01	AEIA	ERROR	General error condition
02	AEIB	RDATT	—
03	AEIC	WRBRK	—
04	AEID	EOF	End of file indicator received
05	AEIE	EODS	End of data set
06	AEIF	EOC	—
07	AEIG	INBFMH	Request/response is management header
08	AEIH	ENDINPT	End of input indicator received
09	AEII	NONVAL	Nonvalid 3650 program name
10	AEIJ	NOSTART	3651 unit cannot initiate 3550 pgm
11	AEIK	TERMIDERR	Terminal ID is not in TCT
12	AEIL	FILENOTFOUND	Data set name is not in FCT (old DSIDERR)
13	AEIM	NOTFND	Desired record not found in data set
14	AEIN	DUPREC	Can't add duplicate prim or alt record key
15	AEIO	DUPKEY	Duplicate alt record key found in file

RESP code	Abend code	DFHRESP (. .) word	Meaning of condition
16	AEIP	INVREQ	Invalid CICS command request
17	AEIQ	IOERR	I/O error in CICS command execution
18	AEIR	NOSPACE	No disk space available for WRITE
19	AEIS	NOTOPEN	Data set is not open to CICS
20	AEIT	ENDFILE	End of file indicator received
21	AEIU	ILLOGIC	VSAM error, no other error code applies
22	AEIV	LENGERR	Length error on an I/O operation
23	AEIW	QZERO	Read TQ destination is empty
24	AEIX	SIGNAL	—
25	AEIY	QBUSY	—
26	AEIZ	ITEMERR	TS command item number out of range
27	AEI0	PGMIDERR	Program/map name not in PCT or disabled
28	AEI1	TRANSIDERR	Trans-id of START not in PCT
29	AEI2	ENDDATA	No more data for RETRIEVE task
30	AEI3	INVTSREQ	RETRIEVE dummy storage not supported
31	AEI4	EXPIRED	—
32	AEI5	RETPAGE	—
33	AEI6	RTEFAIL	—
34	AEI7	RTESOME	—
35	AEI8	TSIOERR	Temporary storage input/out error
36	AEI9	MAPFAIL	No data transmitted to RECEIVE MAP
37	AEYA	INVERRTERM	ROUTE terminal id is invalid
38	AEYB	INVMPSZ	Map width exceeds terminal screen width
39	AEYC	IGREQID	REQID prefix differs from previous prefix
40	AEYD	OVERFLOW	—
41	AEYE	INVLDC	LDC mnemonic not included in LDC list
42	AEYF	NOSTG	—
43	AEYG	JIDERR	Journal file is not in JCT
44	AEYH	QIDERR	Transient data destination is not in DCT
45	AEYI	NOJBUFSP	No journal buffer space
46	AEYJ	DSSTAT	Batch data interchange aborted/suspended
47	AEYK	SELNERR	Batch data interchange destination error
48	AEYL	FUNCERR	Batch data interchange execution error
49	AEYM	UNEXPIN	Unrecognized information received
50	AEYN	NOPASSBKRD	No passbook present for input
51	AEYO	NOPASSBKWR	No passbook present for output
52	AEYP	SEGIDERR	Segment id error, not in PCT
53	AEYQ	SYSIDERR	System id not in intersystem table

RESP code	Abend code	DFHRESP (. .) word	Meaning of condition
54	AEYR	ISCINVREQ	Unknown remote system error
55	AEYS	ENQBUSY	—
56	AEYT	ENVDEFERR	RETRIEVE with option not in START
57	AEYU	IGREQCD	Logic unit error on SEND/RECEIVE
58	AEYV	SESSIONERR	Name in session option not in TCTTE
59	AEYW	SYSBUSY	—
60	AEYX	SESSBUSY	—
61	AEYY	NOTALLOC	Command facility not owned
62	AEYZ	CBIDERR	Specific terminal options not found
63	AEY0	INVEXITREQ	Invalid user exit requested
64	AEY1	INVPARTNSET	SEND partition data set is invalid
65	AEY2	INVPARTN	Partition is not defined
66	AEY3	PARTNFAIL	Invalid partition supplied data
67	AEY4	—	—
68	AEY5	—	—
69	AEYX	USERIDERR	DFHEIP program internal logic error
70	AEY7	NOTAUTH	Resource security check failed
71	AEXV	VOLIDERR	Insufficient dynamic storage
72	AEXW	SUPPRESSED	Command not supported by DFHEIP program
75	AEXC	RESIDERR	—
80	AEXH	NOSPOOL	—
81	AEXI	TERMERR	—
82	AEXJ	ROLLEDBACK	—
83	AEXK	END	—
84	AEXL	DISABLED	—
85		ALLOCERR	—
86		STRELERR	—
87		OPENERR	—
88		SPOLBUSY	—
89		SPOLERR	—
90		NODEIDERR	—
91	AEXX	TASKIDERR	—
92	AEX0	TCIDERR	—
93	AEX1	DSNNOTFOUND	—
94	AEX2	LOADING	—
95	AEX3	MODELIDERR	—
96	AEX4	OUTDESCREER	—
97	AEX5	PARTNERIDERR	—
98	AEX6	PROFILEIDERR	—

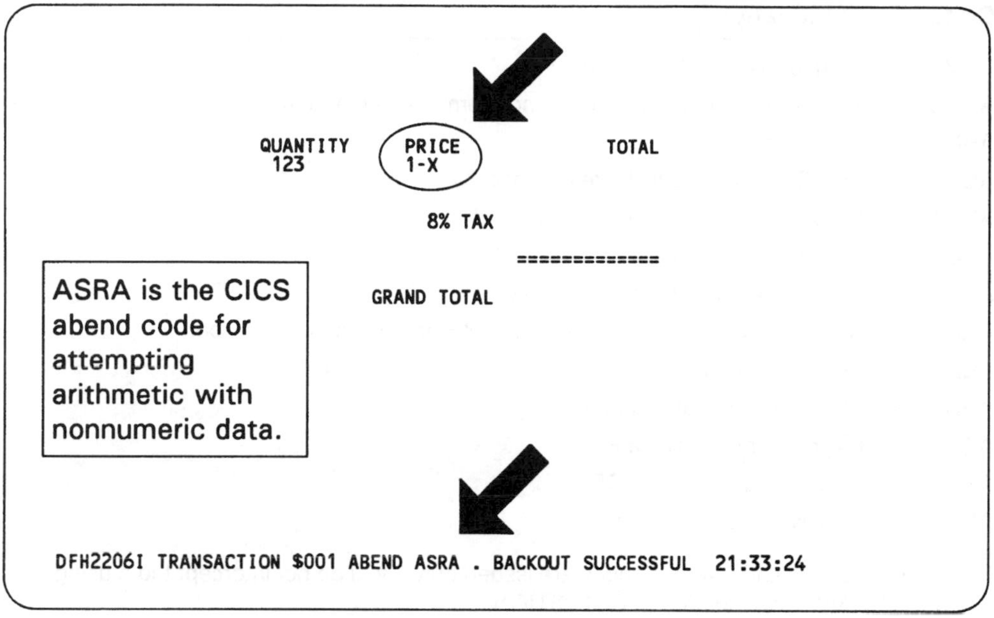
QUANTITY
123
PRICE
1-X
TOTAL
8% TAX
==============
GRAND TOTAL
ASRA is the CICS abend code for attempting arithmetic with nonnumeric data.
DFH2206I TRANSACTION $001 ABEND ASRA . BACKOUT SUCCESSFUL 21:33:24

FIGURE E.1 How CICS reports a program abend (abnormal ending).

E.2 CICS ABEND CODES

When CICS encounters a problem that your program has not anticipated, it issues a four-letter abend code and attempts to "back out" of the transaction gracefully. The abend code is presented within a brief message on the terminal screen, as shown in Figure E.1. The following pages list common CICS abend codes, with brief explanations. RESP codes associated with some of the abend codes are noted.

Code	Explanation
ABMB	Cursor position larger than current screen size
ABMD	Bad return code from send
ABMF	Send length too large
ABMG	BMS service not present
ABMI	Not input map
ABML	Invalid output
ABMM	Invalid map
ABMO	Not output map
ABMP	Undefined PA/PF key
ABMX	Invalid set attribute order in text
ABM0	Map could not be located
ABM1	BMS service requested from non-BMS-supported terminal

Code	Explanation
ABM2	No user data for BMS request
ABM3	BMS service requested from a non-terminal-oriented task
ABM4	Page error
AEC3	COBOL II failed to initialize a thread
AEC4	COBOL II failed to initialize a run-unit
AEC5	C/370 failed to initialize a thread
AEC6	C/370 failed to initialize a run-unit
AED1	Attempt to use EDF/DFHEDFBR/CEBR on unsupported device
AED2	EDF has terminated a task
AED3	EDF has terminated a task
AED4	Logic error in DFHEDFP
AED5	Internal logic error in EDF
AED6	Internal logic error in EDF

Note: The following CICS abend codes are issued only if you do not intercept them using DFHRESP(condition) or HANDLE CONDITION.

——	NORMAL	Resp code 0
AEIA	ERROR	Resp code 1
AEIB	RDATT	Resp code 2
AEIC	WRBRK	Resp code 3
AEID	EOF	Resp code 4
AEIE	EODS	Resp code 5
AEIF	EOC	Resp code 6
AEIG	INBFMH	Resp code 7
AEIH	ENDINPT	Resp code 8
AEII	NONVAL	Resp code 9
AEIJ	NOSTART	Resp code 10
AEIK	TERMIDERR	Resp code 11
AEIL	FILENOTFOUND	Resp code 12
AEIM	NOTFND	Resp code 13
AEIN	DUPREC	Resp code 14
AEIO	DUPKEY	Resp code 15
AEIP	INVREQ	Resp code 16
AEIQ	IOERR	Resp code 17
AEIR	NOSPACE	Resp code 18
AEIS	NOTOPEN	Resp code 19
AEIT	ENDFILE	Resp code 20
AEIU	ILLOGIC	Resp code 21
AEIV	LENGERR	Resp code 22

AEIW	QZERO	Resp code 23
AEIX	SIGNAL	Resp code 24
AEIY	QBUSY	Resp code 25
AEIZ	ITEMERR	Resp code 26
AEI0	PGMIDERR	Resp code 27
AEI1	TRANSIDERR	Resp code 28
AEI2	ENDDATA	Resp code 29
AEI3	INVTSREQ	Resp code 30
AEI4	EXPIRED	Resp code 31
AEI5	RETPAGE	Resp code 32
AEI6	RTEFAIL	Resp code 33
AEI7	RTESOME	Resp code 34
AEI8	TSIOERR	Resp code 35
AEI9	MAPFAIL	Resp code 36
AEYA	INVERRTERM	Resp code 37
AEYB	INVMPSZ	Resp code 38
AEYC	IGREQID	Resp code 39
AEYD	OVERFLOW	Resp code 40
AEYE	INVLDC	Resp code 41
AEYF	NOSTG	Resp code 42
AEYG	JIDERR	Resp code 43
AEYH	QIDERR	Resp code 44
AEYI	NOJBUFSP	Resp code 45
AEYJ	DSSTAT	Resp code 46
AEYK	SELNERR	Resp code 47
AEYL	FUNCERR	Resp code 48
AEYM	UNEXPIN	Resp code 49
AEYN	NOPASSBKRD	Resp code 50
AEYO	NOPASSBKWR	Resp code 51
AEYP	SEGIDERR	Resp code 52
AEYQ	SYSIDERR	Resp code 53
AEYR	ISCINVREQ	Resp code 54
AEYS	ENQBUSY	Resp code 55
AEYT	ENVDEFERR	Resp code 56
AEYU	IGREQCD	Resp code 57
AEYV	SESSIONERR	Resp code 58
AEYW	SYSBUSY	Resp code 59
—	SESSBUSY	Resp code 60
AEYX	USERIDERR	Resp code 69
AEYY	NOTALLOC	Resp code 61

AEYZ	CBIDERR	Resp code 62
AEY0	INVESITREQ	Resp code 63
AEY1	INVPARTNSET	Resp code 64
AEY2	INVPARTN	Resp code 65
AEY3	PARTNFAIL	Resp code 66
AEY6	Internal logic error in DFHUEM	
AEY7	NOTAUTH	Resp code 70
AEXV	VOLIDERR	Resp code 71
AEXW	SUPPRESSED	Resp code 72
AEXA	WRONGSTAT	Resp code 73
AEXB	NAMEERROR	Resp code 74
AEXC	RESIDERR	Resp code 75
AEXD	CCERROR	Resp code 76
AEXE	MAPERROR	Resp code 77
AEXF	ESCERROR	Resp code 78
AEXH	NOSPOOL	Resp code 80
AEXI	TERMERR	Resp code 81
AEXJ	ROLLEDBACK	Resp code 82
AEXK	END	Resp code 83
AEXL	DISABLED	Resp code 84
——	ALLOCERR	Resp code 85
——	STRELERR	Resp code 86
——	OPENERR	Resp code 87
——	SPOLBUSY	Resp code 88
——	SPOLERR	Resp code 89
——	NODEIDERR	Resp code 90
AEXX	TASKIDERR	Resp code 91
AEX0	TCIDERR	Resp code 92
AEX1	DSNNOTFOUND	Resp code 93
AEX2	LOADING	Resp code 94
AEX3	MODELIDERR	Resp code 95
AEX4	OUTDESCREER	Resp code 96
AEX5	PARTNERIDERR	Resp code 97
AEX6	PROFILEIDERR	Resp code 98

AICA	Runaway task
APCT	Requested program not found, disabled, or zero length
ASRA	Program interrupt (analogous to 0C7 in batch programs!)
ASRB	Operating system abend
ASRD	Illegal macro call or reference to CSA or TCA

APPENDIX

F

Obtaining JCL and Programs for Local Use

You can acquire the CICS program source code and job control language illustrated in this text for your own personal, noncommercial use. This software is supplied on a single high-density 3-1/2 inch PC-format diskette and costs $35 postpaid. Send your order to Caliber Data Training, Inc., at the following address, requesting diskette #114:

Caliber Data Training, Inc.
Suite 605
6160 N. Cicero Avenue
Chicago, Illinois 60646

Voice: (312) 794-1222
Fax: (312) 794-1225

The software diskette is free to college and university instructors using this text for noncommercial class purposes. To obtain a free copy, send a request on your educational institution's letterhead to the above address.

You can acquire a copy of the GENMAP screen painter and BMS map code generator described and illustrated in Chapter 4 for your own personal, noncommercial use. GENMAP is a software creation of Gary Weinstein of DePaul University. GENMAP is distributed on its own 3-1/2 inch diskette, separate from the program and JCL diskette described above. The cost of a copy of GENMAP is $35 postpaid. Send your order to Caliber Data Training, Inc., at the above address, requesting a copy of diskette #115. Sorry, free instructional copies of GENMAP are not provided.

Index